Formal Approaches to Computing and
Information Technology

Springer
London
Berlin
Heidelberg
New York
Barcelona
Budapest
Hong Kong
Milan
Paris
Santa Clara
Singapore
Tokyo

Also in this series:

Proof in VDM: a Practitioner's Guide
J.C. Bicarregui, J.S. Fitzgerald, P.A. Lindsay, R. Moore
and B. Ritchie
ISBN 3-540-19813-X

On the Refinement Calculus
C. Morgan and T. Vickers (eds.)
ISBN 3-540-19931-4

Systems, Models and Measures
A. Kaposi and M. Myers
ISBN 3-540-19753-2

Notations for Software Design
L.M.G. Feijs, H.B.M. Jonkers and C.A. Middelburg
ISBN 3-540-19902-0

K. Lano

Formal Object-Oriented Development

 Springer

Kevin Lano, BSc, MSc, PhD
Department of Computing
Imperial College of Science, Technology and Medicine
180 Queen's Gate
London SW7 2BZ, UK

Series Editor
S.A. Schuman, BSc, DEA, CEng
Department of Mathematical and Computing Sciences
University of Surrey, Guildford, Surrey GU2 5XH, UK

ISBN-13:978-3-540-19978-6   e-ISBN-13:978-1-4471-3073-4
DOI: 10.1007/978-1-4471-3073-4

British Library Cataloguing in Publication Data
Lano, Kevin
  Formal Object-oriented Development.
  (Formal Approaches to Computing & Information Technology Series)
  I. Title. II. Series
  005.11

Library of Congress Cataloging-in-Publication Data
Lano, K.
  Formal object-oriented development / Kevin Lano.
    p. cm. - - (Formal approaches to computing and information technology)
  ISBN-13:978-3-540-19978-6 (pbk. : acid-free paper)
  1. Object-oriented programming (Computer science) I. Title. II. Series.
  QA76.64.L363 1995   95-32281
  005.1'1 - - dc20

Typesetting: Camera ready by author

34/3830-543210 Printed on acid-free paper

Preface

This book gives an introduction to the formal object-oriented languages Z^{++} and VDM^{++}, and describes techniques for the use of formal methods in object-oriented development, and for the improvement of quality of software development.

It does not introduce a new method, or new notations (there are already an excess of such in the object-oriented field), but describes ways that object-oriented techniques can be used with a high degree of rigour (and, if necessary, formal proof).

It has been widely recognised that the practice of software engineering has not yet attained the level of rigour and reliance upon established mathematical techniques that other branches of engineering have achieved. Developing and maintaining software is still an area where "art" prevails over "craft", often to the detriment of software quality and cost. This becomes particularly problematic for software which is safety critical (for example, air traffic control applications) or financially critical (where the computations may form the basis for the economic survival of a company).

In these cases systematic and rigorous approaches to development and maintenance are essential. Structured diagrammatic and formal methods are two established techniques with proven ability to improve aspects of the software process. This book will consider how elements of these techniques can be used together or separately within object-oriented development in order to improve the rigour and traceability of development steps, the precision and verifiability of specifications, and the capability for reuse of developments.

The introduction of formal methods into development has often been regarded as a radical step into the unknown:

> *The software engineer's society, like other human societies, is regulated by its own "religion" and beliefs with a dominant dogma stipulating that* the truth is only in executable programs, *a ritual defined in terms of* phases of the software life cycle, *a clergy that is composed of* project leaders *and finally the congregation that is composed of* developers. *Introducing formal methods in such a society is like*

introducing new beliefs in a human society. The established order of things is shaken up and the new vision is preached. Therefore it is natural to see reticence and resistance from both developers and project leaders. [74].

In contrast, in this book we will try to emphasise a collaboration and integration between formal methods and existing practices – diagrammatic methods, measurement and testing.

A challenge for the widespread practical application of formal methods is *formal development*: the transformation of abstract specifications into procedural implementations, within a formal framework, and, ideally, a single language. For general acceptance in industrial software engineering such a formal method needs to be:

- effectively tool supported: by industrial quality tools, not research prototypes;
- linkable with effective techniques in current practice, such as diagrammatic methods;
- based on a well-defined and familiar mathematical foundation.

At present, there are only a few formal methods which approach these criteria, such as B Abstract Machine Notation [138], PVS [243] and RAISE [111]. VDM^{++}, described here, also has these properties.

Adopting a formal approach to development should provide a number of benefits:

- improved system correctness;
- improved communication between clients and developers, provided that it is possible to "execute" or animate the formal specification at an early development stage;
- reduced effort spent on error-correction in design and implementation, due to earlier detection of errors;
- improved maintainability and assessability, provided documented links exist between requirements, specification and implementation.

In adopting a formal development approach however, the need for other software quality criteria should not be disregarded, such as those enumerated by Meyer [225]:

1. modular decomposability;
2. modular composability;
3. modular understandability;
4. modular continuity.

This book takes the position that an object-oriented formal method is a strong basis for a formal development approach which also meets these additional criteria. Object-orientation and formal techniques are highly compatible in a number of ways:

- object-orientation encourages the creation of abstractions, and formal techniques provide the means to precisely describe such abstractions;
- object-orientation provides the structuring mechanisms and development disciplines needed to scale up formal techniques to large systems;
- formal techniques allow a precise meaning to be given to complex object-oriented mechanisms such as aggregation or statecharts.

The book will provide a number of development techniques, and an overall formal development architecture, together with examples illustrating these techniques, in the languages VDM^{++} and Z^{++} [188]. However, these techniques are applicable to other formal object-oriented languages, such as Object-Z [82]. Throughout, ways of incorporating formal techniques into existing development practices will be emphasised, through the integrated use of formal and diagrammatic methods, testing, animation and proof. Implementation in Eiffel, Ada and C++ will be described.

Chapters 1 and 2 introduce the notations used in the remainder of the book, and the development lifecycle. Each stage of the lifecycle is detailed in Chapters 3, 4 and 5, using examples from a variety of domains. Chapters 6, 7 and 8 address specialised issues such as proof, continuous real-time systems, and code generation. Chapter 9 gives larger case studies in the techniques, presenting examples of complete developments. Tutorial style exercises are given in Chapters 3 to 9. Version 5.2 of the VDM^{++} toolset has been used to check the VDM^{++} examples given. Extensions of VDM^{++} notation used by the book are identified.

Readers particularly interested in VDM^{++} should read Chapters 2, 3, 7, 8, 9 and Appendix B. A complete syntax description of VDM^{++} is contained in Appendix B. Readers interested in Z^{++} should read Chapters 2, 3, 4, 5, 6 and Appendix A. Appendix C gives solutions to the exercises. Finally, Appendix D gives information on task analysis.

A glossary of terms, and an extensive bibliography of the area are also provided.

Acknowledgements

The book has resulted from work in a number of research projects and industrial applications of formal methods and object-orientation. Howard Haughton, Penny Wheeler, Stephen Goldsack and the EROS working group on formal object-orientation contributed substantially to the ideas and methodology presented here, and Imperial College and the AFRODITE ESPRIT project provided assistance and support. Sophia Drossopoulou provided valuable comments on the text.

Foreword

One of the important ways in which science moves towards engineering and technology is in the development of so called engineering models. Such models incorporate basic theories from science and corresponding mathematical representations, but often via much more intuitive representations. These models can be manipulated in a manner which remains faithful to the underlying mathematics and science. These models thus represent an engineering view of the underlying science and mathematics which abstracts from the "deep" results by providing "interfaces" for manipulation which directly support the construction of artifacts rather than their foundational understanding.

Software Engineering (SE), and Computer Science (CS) in general, are no exceptions to this paradigm of technology transfer from foundations to engineering practice. Perhaps SE and CS are more leavened with less systematic and well founded practices than other engineering disciplines, but this may just be an inevitable consequence of the relative immaturity of the subject. It may also be a consequence of the fact that one aspect of the technology, i.e. hardware, experiences generational change every five years or so instead of the more relaxed pace of 25 years or longer experienced by most disciplines.

There is a clear place for the following work in this spectrum of transfer from foundations of SE to engineering practice. Object-orientation (OO) is itself a good example of it. One of the most important characteristics of objects is the concept of encapsulation. This is the support of componentry in this paradigm of software construction and its origins can be traced directly to the work on abstract data types in the seventies. The slogan of workers in the area was something like: "A data type is characterised completely by the operations available for the manipulation and examination of the underlying data structure." So OO is already heavily influenced by the results of this transfer to technology. Another important strand of work over the last 25 years in CS has been the development of formal (logic based) theories about the specification and (formal) design of systems. There are many approaches used, of which the algebraic techniques associated with data types, temporal logics associated with reactive systems and dynamic logics associated with programs are clear examples.

The present book by Kevin Lano takes another step in this direction by examining how techniques, from the latter two areas particularly, can be used to explain in a more systematic manner the technology of OO. Modelling techniques, design techniques and implementation techniques are all less well defined than a "true engineer" might hope and, it is clear for those of us sitting at the more foundational end of the spectrum, that some of the available theories could help in the systematisation of the technology. The book goes a long way towards substantiating this claim.

The foundational principles used have been developed over a reasonably long period of time and should have some stability. Their study should provide not just greater understanding of the emerging theories and techniques, but also, and more significantly for engineers, provide a frame of mind for practical problem solving which is more efficacious for the practising engineer.

Tom Maibaum, Professor of the Foundations of Software Engineering.
Head, Department of Computing,
Imperial College of Science Technology and Medicine.

Contents

1	**Introduction**	**1**
	1.1 Why is Mathematics Useful?	1
	1.2 Formal Methods in Software Development	3
	1.3 Formal Methods and Object-orientation	6
	1.4 Z^{++}	8
	1.5 VDM^{++}	11
	1.6 Adding Formality to Diagrammatic Methods	12
	1.7 Problems in Object-oriented Development	13
2	**The Software Development Process**	**15**
	2.1 Formal Object-oriented Development	15
	2.2 Example Development: Shapes and Points	19
	2.3 The Layered Development Paradigm	30
	2.4 Development Example in VDM^{++}	35
3	**From Analysis to Formal Specification**	**44**
	3.1 Formalisation of Object Models	45
	3.2 Aggregation	52
	3.3 Alternative Approaches	56
	3.4 Formalisation of Dynamic Models	58
	3.5 The Booch Method	73
	3.6 Specification Construction Principles	75
	3.7 Animation	79
4	**Specification Notations and Techniques**	**84**
	4.1 Attributes and Data Structures	85
	4.2 Operations	92
	4.3 Inheritance	111
	4.4 Subtyping	113
	4.5 Class Composition	120
	4.6 Object Identity	122

4.7	Dynamic Behaviour	126
4.8	Complex Data Types	132
4.9	VDM^{++}	134
5	**Design and Refinement**	**137**
5.1	Design Approaches	137
5.2	Refinement	146
5.3	Subtyping, Composition and Refinement	167
5.4	VDM^{++}	173
6	**Proof Methods and Techniques**	**176**
6.1	Safety Reasoning – Monitor and Gate	176
6.2	Liveness Reasoning – Dining Philosophers	180
6.3	Internal Consistency Proofs	182
6.4	Refinement and Subtyping Proofs	183
6.5	Object Identity	207
6.6	Reasoning About Concurrent Object Execution	212
6.7	Synchronisation Refinement Proofs	214
6.8	General Refinement Proof Techniques	218
7	**Concurrent and Real-time Behaviour**	**219**
7.1	Extended Harel Statecharts	219
7.2	Specifying Reactive System Properties	236
8	**Implementation and Code Generation**	**257**
8.1	Translation into Procedural Languages	257
8.2	Introducing Concurrency in Implementations	276
8.3	Implementation Case Study: Personnel System	278
8.4	Testing	281
9	**Case Studies**	**286**
9.1	Invoice System	286
9.2	Expedited Data Queue	297
9.3	Fire Control	299
9.4	Specification of Reactive Systems	303
9.5	Mine Pump Control	305
A	**Appendix: Z^{++}**	**332**
A.1	Mathematical Notation	332
A.2	Z Notation	336
A.3	Z^{++} Specification Notation	337
A.4	Z^{++}/RTL Logic	347

B Appendix: VDM^{++}   **365**
   B.1 VDM^{++} Mathematical Notation   365
   B.2 VDM^{++} Specification Notation   368
   B.3 The VDM^{++} Model of Concurrency   372
   B.4 The Semantics of Procedural Statements   374
   B.5 Tool Support   380
   B.6 Syntax Summary of VDM^{++} 383

C Exercise Answers   **388**

D Task Analysis   **415**

Chapter 1

Introduction

This chapter will address the question of why formal notations are useful in object-oriented development, both in terms of adherence to standards such as MOD 00-55 [234], and in terms of the general quality improvement obtainable from the use of well-defined notations. Cost benefits will be discussed, based on previous industrial experiences. Other developments in the area, such as the Fusion and Syntropy methods [58, 64], will also be described.

1.1 Why is Mathematics Useful?

Existing object-oriented development methods, such as OMT [261] or OOA [271], have been successfully used to develop object-oriented systems in a range of domains. Their benefits include an ability to capture requirements in notations which are intuitive and can be used to communicate descriptions of a system to people without expertise in software engineering or mathematics. In addition, the use of a number of separate but inter-related models (typically, a *static data* model, a *dynamic behaviour* model and a *process* model) provides a means for internal consistency and completeness checking.

As has been pointed out however, these notations, being primarily based on diagrams or natural language text, cannot express semantic details with the same precision as notations such as Z [276]. The imprecision of the notations also implies that some semantic ambiguities exist regarding interpretation of the diagrams. For example, OMT and the Booch method [29] take different interpretations as to whether events are queued or ignored in statecharts if they occur in a state for which there is no corresponding transition.

For safety-critical systems, that is, systems in which there is an implication for the possible loss of human life, environmental or severe economic damage, standards are increasingly requiring the use of "best practice" in software development [234, 151, 34, 62, 14]. For such systems there must be, in principle, a way of verifying development steps, ie, for formally proving that a section of code meets its specification. Such proof can only be carried out if the specification is given in a mathematically-based language. Examples of the application of formal methods in safety-critical domains include:

- train control systems, using the B Abstract Machine Notation (AMN) [32, 69, 52];
- nuclear power plant control systems, using VDM [143];
- medical systems, such as patient monitoring systems [23, 162].

In general, such applications have been successful, with [143] giving evidence that formal techniques can lead to lower costs than many other development approaches for critical systems, such as diverse software, because redevelopment and rework costs are reduced, even though analysis and specification costs are increased. In addition tool-supported formal methods provide a means to animate specifications and therefore to perform testing and validation at an early development stage.

Other forms of high-integrity systems include financially-critical systems, in which design errors can lead to major financial loss. In these cases a benefit of using formal languages is that such errors can be identified at the specification stage, because the precision of these languages encourages the elimination of ambiguity in specifications, and exposes any mistaken assumptions. They also allow tool-supported animation and internal consistency checks to be performed at the specification stage. As a result, the cost of rework and modification in response to errors is reduced compared to normal development. Some examples of the successful application of formal techniques in the commercial and general software domains include:

- formal specification and development of parts of the CICS system at IBM [61];
- the development of the Inmos T800 floating point unit [211];
- formal specification and test case generation for managed objects in communication systems at BT, using the ZEST formal object-oriented specification language [66].

Benefits have included a claimed 9% saving of costs in the case of the CICS system, which runs into several million pounds, and a one month reduction in the time to market in the case of the Inmos development.

For object-oriented software development, there are some additional benefits:

- in order to show that a class **D** is genuinely a subtype of a class **C**, in the sense that instances of **D** can always be used as if they were instances of **C**, we need a precise (mathematical) definition of subtyping and a language in which subtyping relations can be established;
- mathematical descriptions of classes which are at the boundary of a system, or which are being reused from a library, provide a concise, abstract yet complete description of the services provided by such classes and the semantics of their features. The alternatives are either insufficiently detailed (if only method signatures are given) or over-specific to a particular environment and excessively detailed (if complete source code is given);

- the task of implementing requirements can be separated into two easier tasks – precisely defining *what* is required for a system, free of any particular way of implementing these requirements; and defining *how* these formalised requirements can be coded;
- the precise meaning of diagrammatic notations can be defined. For example, the distinctions between the wide variety of forms of "aggregation" and association can be mathematically expressed much more clearly than in natural language or semi-formal notation (see Chapter 3).

1.2 Formal Methods in Software Development

Whether to introduce formal methods into software development, and how to do this, is an issue which depends on the state of current practice within the organisation (if this is not already systematised and disciplined then adding formal techniques will not usually be productive), the ways in which this current practice does not meet requirements (for example, regulatory requirements or requirements for more rapid development or reduced maintenance costs), and the expected training cost. Some reports which cover this issue are [113, 114, 133, 144]. In general a gradual approach, introducing the techniques in a controlled manner on selected projects, is advised, as is the precise measurement of changes in the cost profile and timing of projects as a result of the changed method, in order to evaluate its effects. For example, a project may decide to use formal languages just for the specification level, and to continue to pursue analysis using a structured method, and design using a pseudo-programming language. Or, as in the development described in Section 1.4, a formal language may be used for the logical design, but without formal refinement being undertaken. Once an initial pool of skills in the mathematical languages has been established, the range of use of formal methods in development can be expanded to meet particular project needs.

More research is however needed into the effects of introducing formal techniques (or any new techniques) into software projects: the initial cost of cultural change and disruption which follows the introduction of a new technique may outweigh its benefits for the earliest projects which adopt it, so distorting analysis of its advantages. At an educational level, more computer science courses need to cover (and emphasise) the process of software engineering, rather than simply teaching programming tricks in particular languages, and to at least introduce the concept of a formal specification. Since software maintenance or enhancement is also one of the main software engineering activities in practice, some education on the special features of these processes would also be useful.

Tool support is highly important for practical use of formal techniques, in reducing the cost of managing the large amount of documentation which formal specifications can produce, and in supporting consistency and completeness checks, such as type-checking. Animation tools are a particular advantage of adopting a precise description language at an early lifecycle stage, permitting validation of the descriptions against the users expectations and domain knowledge.

One approach which has been widely and successfully used is the integration of structured diagrammatic methods, such as SSADM, Yourdon or OMT, with formal methods [267, 107]. Integrating formal and diagrammatic methods has a number of advantages as a development approach: it can make use of the complementary strengths of these two techniques, and it can make use of existing software engineering expertise, rather than attempting to replace it. A recent survey on the use of formal methods in industry reported that 31% of the companies using formal methods were using them in conjunction with structured methods [13].

Figure 1.1 shows the various forms of integration that have been carried out in practice. These range from a highly focused use of formal techniques to verify a security critical or safety critical kernel of a system, to extensive combination at several life cycle stages. In the "degree of formality" scale we include the rigour of the correspondence between the formal and diagrammatic notations – ie, whether a precise translation can be carried out, or whether the mapping is intuitive.

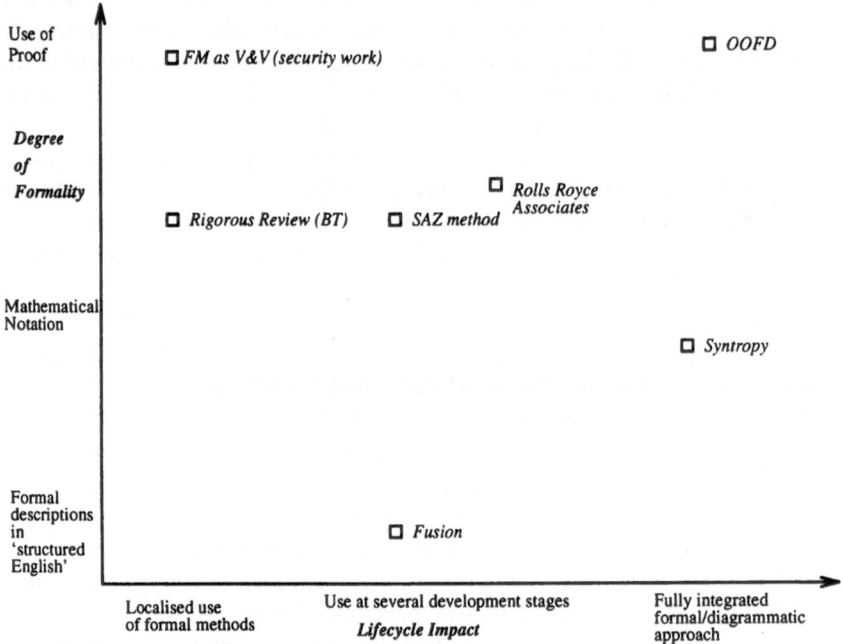

Figure 1.1: Forms of Method Integration

In the UK there has been a significant amount of work in the security field, whereby a "dual team" approach is used to support formal specification (and proof) of security-critical parts of an application, within an overall design defined using a structured method (SSADM) [79]. In this approach the team involved in the creation of diagrammatic models is separate from the team that is involved in the translation to a formal notation and in proof. This approach uses formal techniques to a greater extent than integration work in commercial fields, such as the rigorous review technique at BT [267]. Both of these approaches localise the use of formal methods to a single development stage, or in a tightly focused application subset. The benefits of this approach have been the relatively small disruption to an existing process, the increased error detection and verification capabilities of formal specification and proof, including the achievement of certification to the ITSEC standard [62] or equivalent, and the low training overhead.

In contrast, the Fusion and SAZ methods aim to support the combined use of formal specification and diagrammatic notations at several life-cycle stages. SAZ is a combination of Z and SSADM, developed at the University of York [248].

At a further level of integration, the method used at Rolls Royce and Associates to develop safety-critical submarine systems involves the use of structured methods (Yourdon) to give an architectural specification of a system, and formal notation (VDM) to specify the semantics of operations. The development process uses both notations at specification and design stages [143]. The benefits of this more complete integration include being able to formally specify large parts of an application, using the structuring facilities provided by the diagrammatic method. Similarly for Syntropy, formal notation can be added to the data model or used in place of this model, and can be used to define pre and postconditions on statecharts to describe the effect of events.

Finally, the methods described in this book could be used to give the integration approach labelled "OOFM". In particular, the Venus toolset for VDM^{++} and OMT supports such an extensive integration. The benefits at this level include being able to switch between formal or diagrammatic views of a system as required, in order to gain greater understanding of a system description, or to conduct specific forms of analysis. Some forms of transformation are more easily performed using the diagrammatic notations (for example, restructuring a complex data model by using a diagram editor) than formal textual equivalents, and a close integration would allow appropriate tools to be used at each stage. Consistency between formal and diagrammatic descriptions could also be automatically ensured. Integration in this manner could improve the assessability and maintainability of systems by ensuring traceability between the products of development stages, allowing proposed changes at the code level to be mapped into corresponding changes to requirements.

Sociological issues also arise in the application of formal techniques in computing [104]. Much of the theory of computing and software engineering has been oriented towards the view that writing computer programs is about automating mechanical procedures for well-defined problems. In contrast, the problem to be solved may sometimes only be fully identified after the system is implemented [35, 36]. The mathematical models of real world problems used in formal methods may also encourage an over-simplified view of the domain and application: it should be realised that any specific model is only one view of the problem, and alternative models could be better for a given purpose (for

example, a specification which is optimised for human comprehension may not
be ideal from the viewpoint of an automated proof tool).

The overly prescriptive way in which formal methods use in software engineering has sometimes been promoted also neglects practical complexities
in the software engineering and requirements capture processes. In Appendix
D we describe *task analysis*, which can be used in conjunction with formal
specification in order to support the design of software which is relevant to a
particular work practice and application context.

1.3   Formal Methods and Object-orientation

The field of combined formal and object-oriented techniques is a recent but
highly active area, which has been attracting increasing interest from major
US and European companies. There are two main parts of this field: the use of
object-oriented structuring to enhance formal notations and methods, and the
use of formal methods to analyse the semantics of object-oriented notations, or
to enhance these notations.

1.3.1   The Application of Object-orientation to Formal Methods

Formal methods have been researched and applied for over 25 years, having
their origin in the work of Dijkstra and Hoare on program verification, and
Scott, Stratchey and others on program semantics. The Z language was initially created by J. R. Abrial (his paper "Data Semantics" from 1974 could be
considered the birth of this language), and expanded and industrially applied
by many others in the 1980s onwards, with the Programming Research Group
at Oxford being the focus of much key work. The VDM language was initially
developed by the IBM research laboratories in Vienna, also in the early 80's,
and the University of Manchester group led by Cliff Jones became the focus of
research and tool development efforts, leading to the Mural toolkit [257].

Both Z and VDM are "model-based" formal specification languages, that is,
they use set theory and logic to build abstract models of required systems using
sets, sequences, functions, and so forth. "Algebraic" methods such as OBJ,
PLUSS and FOOPS [124, 123] use equational logic to provide more implicit
and abstract descriptions of systems. Algebraic descriptions are more easily
executable because of the restricted language used, but conversely may be
somewhat algorithmic and akin to functional programs in style (compare the
algebraic and model-based specifications of queues given in [159] for example).

The limitations of Z and VDM for specifying large systems in a modular
manner led to various investigations aimed at adding structuring mechanisms to
these languages. For example, [262] proposed adding a "chapter" mechanism to
decompose Z specifications into modules, and [150] identified a similar (object-
based but not object-oriented) approach using a combination of HOOD and Z.
Abrial and others at BP Research also developed an object-based extension of

Z, the B Abstract Machine Notation [138], which has had major applications in safety-critical transport systems [32]. The SmallVDM language [188, Chapter 10] combined an object-based structuring style derived from Smalltalk with VDM notation.

Researchers and practitioners were led in the direction of object-oriented mechanisms because these seemed to naturally complement model-based specification languages [65]. The first fully object-oriented extension of Z was the Object-Z language [47]. This featured the key aspects of object-oriented structuring:

- encapsulation of data and operations on that data into named modules (*classes*) which also define types;
- the possibility of creating subclasses of classes via *inheritance*, and the ability to use operations polymorphically between a subclass and its superclasses which contain a particular operation;
- the ability to use instances of a class (ie, *objects*) within another class – the concept of class *composition*. The class **C** containing instances of class **D** is termed a *client* of **D**, whilst **D** is termed a *supplier* of **C**.

It however initially restricted composition to be acyclic (class **A** could not contain an instance of class **B** if **B** contained an instance of **A**, or other cyclic situations). Object-orientation was found to provide advantages in terms of ease of education [278] and in terms of convergence with domain descriptions.

Other object-oriented extensions of Z were also developed in 1989–91, such as Z^{++} [164], MooZ [217], OOZE [5] and ZEST [65]. Of these, OOZE is distinctive as the only one to be based on an algebraic specification approach, using OBJ and FOOPS as its foundation but with a Z-like syntax. In the VDM world, the Fresco language was developed as a means of providing formal specification and verification support for Smalltalk development [293].

A number of applications of these languages were carried out, in the telecommunications and process control fields. The work of BT using ZEST is of particular note in this respect. The scope and power of the languages were extended as more challenging application areas were investigated. Thus concepts of object identity and cyclic composition structures were introduced in Z^{++} and Object-Z [175]. The VDM^{++} language represented a significantly more ambitious approach, based on ideas from VDM, Smalltalk and the DRAGOON Ada extension [11], it included Ada-style concurrency and synchronisation features, traces (as in CSP), and real-time aspects taken from the ideas of Hayes [141]. As with Fusion and ZEST, the involvement of a major company (in this case CAP Gemini) provided direct routes to significant industrial applications [91].

Real-time and concurrency aspects were incorporated into Z^{++} in a more declarative manner via the use of real-time logic [176].

A significant drawback with the use of object-oriented structuring is the degree to which this complicates reasoning about specifications. Until recently, there were no formal semantics for an object-oriented specification language. This has now been remedied, with an axiomatic semantics and reasoning system being provided for Object-Z [273] and Z^{++} [176], and a denotational semantics for MooZ [198]. The present book describes how such reasoning may be carried out even for complex reactive and real-time systems.

1.3.2   Application of Formal Methods to Object-orientation

Whilst this work on formal object-oriented languages was being carried out, other groups were investigating the converse process, of how formal specification can supplement object-oriented development, or help to clarify the semantics of object-oriented notations and concepts.

Examples of such work include formalisation of the OMG's core object model using Z [149], formalisation of the OOA notation using Z, and the Fusion [58] and Syntropy [64] methods. The work on OOA uncovered apparent weaknesses in its semantics, such as the lack of any relationship between the set of object identities of instances of a subtype to those of its supertypes.

Fusion grew out of work by Coleman, Dollin and others at Hewlett Packard Labs on formal enhancement of object-oriented notations such as statecharts [60]. It provides semi-formal notations (structured English) for operation pre-conditions, post-conditions and invariants, and uses the OMT object-model notation and Booch object interaction diagram notation, together with other notations, to provide a rigorous method for sequential systems. It is now used quite extensively within Hewlett Packard, across 15–20 divisions and in areas such as printer technology, network management software and test software. Other companies have taken up Fusion in the USA and Europe.

Syntropy is a more recent method in the same direction. It combines the statechart and object model notations of OMT with object interaction diagrams, and allows the use of Z notations on these diagrams to specify pre and post conditions, invariants and constraints. A partial formal semantics for the notation is also provided. Unlike Fusion, a treatment of concurrency is provided. Syntropy grew out of many years of industrial experience in consultancy, and has already been commissioned for use in financially critical applications in the UK.

1.4 Z^{++}

The Z^{++} language originated from a European ESPRIT project, REDO, where it was used to describe the abstracted specifications of legacy systems (massive COBOL data-processing applications) during a process of reverse engineering. The language has been extended since its initial definition in 1989 [164] by the inclusion of object reference semantics [175] and real-time logic [176]. Theoretical development has concentrated on obtaining an elegant definition of refinement with desirable properties [182]. An important concern has also been the integration of the language with existing diagrammatic methods, particularly OMT [261]. Systematic translations of OMT diagrammatic models into Z^{++} have been defined (Chapter 3 and [173]).

The language has been applied to a variety of domains, ranging from artificial intelligence [188] and reverse-engineering [189] to reactive systems [170]. The largest application of the language to date has been the specification and design of a static analysis tool [167], consisting of over 250 pages of annotated Z specifications corresponding to Z^{++} classes.

This development was an industrial application of the language, and involved the integrated use of formal and diagrammatic methods. The development process was as follows (Figure 1.2).

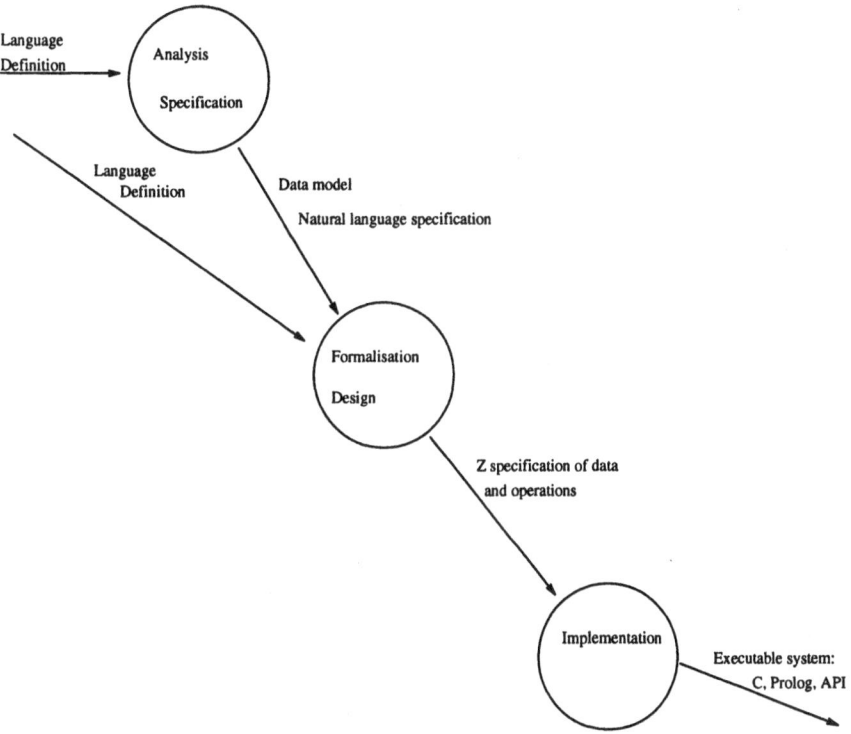

Figure 1.2: Development Process for Static Analysis Tool

It involved:

1. analysis of general third generation language features and the requirements for representing and analysing the particular dialects of COBOL, C and FORTRAN of interest. This stage produced a detailed diagrammatic specification of the language representation data models, and natural language descriptions of the population process. The scale of this specification was approximately 120 entities and 200 relationships and attributes; therefore the use of a diagram editor to iteratively construct the specification was essential – a formal specification could not have been effectively written without such prior analysis;

2. formalisation of the data model using Z^{++}, and a detailed description

of the population operations for each source language feature of OS/VS COBOL;

3. manual coding of the formal specification of the population operations in C, using the API (application programmers interface) to the IPSYS TBK database [156].

The development process involved feedback from later development stages: changes to the data model and to the textual specification of the population process were made as a result of mistakes and omissions discovered during formalisation. In addition, the formal specification was modified to increase its modularity and degree of convergence with the code description, as a result of the coding process.

Traceability of the system requirements through analysis to specification and code was considered important in order to assist future maintenance and modification of the system. (Since the system was being developed for a project aiming at maintenance improvement, the developers felt that they should at least attempt to abide by good practice themselves in this respect!).

Animation of the specifications before implementation was partly achieved by prototyping small extracts in Prolog. Formal specification notations were used at a stage which would correspond to a *logical design* in a conventional development, that is, a description of the required system which is independent of a particular implementation environment, but is detailed enough that particular physical designs can be directly generated from it.

This is in contrast to the conventional use of Z, which typically (for example, in the CICS development work at IBM) is at the initial functional specification stage.

Formal specification was recognised as useful in the development because:

- previous versions of the REDO toolset had combined the population and parsing process, attaching population actions to the **yacc** grammar rules used to parse source text. No specification of these processes had been produced, which resulted in a tool which was unmaintainable, unreliable and inflexible. Thus the importance of

  1. separating the parsing and population processes, and
  2. specifying the population actions in a implementation-independent manner

  was recognised;

- an initial attempt at specifying the population process was adopted for the JCL languages associated with the target COBOL dialect. This used a semi-formal entity and attribute notation. This specification, whilst an improvement on the previous approach, was found to be insufficiently precise to assist in the production of code, and it was ambiguous in expressing the scope of data used in population, and did not allow a modular specification of the population operations.

Formal specification was not used at the most abstract description level since:

- the data model already provided a completely precise description of the entities in the language representation scheme, including a specification of which relationships were inverse to others and of inheritance relationships between entities;
- the critical area of difficulty in developing the populator was exactly at the level of detailed (but implementation-independent) design. This required the specification, in a precise but clear manner, of exactly which information should be recorded in the database and how this information related to the original abstract syntax tree description produced by the parser;
- only one member of the development team was experienced in the use of Z, and producing a number of Z models, and establishing refinements between them, would have led to an unacceptable consumption of resources.

A deliberate attempt was therefore made to utilise Z as such a precise description language, or as a "mathematical pseudocode". This style of description then became used by the development team as a common language which they could use to describe particular database representations, in a more precise and concise manner than via instance diagrams, which had been previously used. The inheritance structure of the entities in the data model and population process was utilised in the development of the population operations, and allowed considerable code reuse between operations on supertypes and on subtypes.

The result of the application of formal specification was a significant shift in the relative cost of development stages. The original ratio of 5 : 2 in time spent coding versus time spent specifying became a ratio of 4 : 3, whilst the overall effort remained unchanged. The quality of the resulting product however was substantially improved.

Many subtle errors in the population specification were detected before a line of code was written, through intensive reviewing of the formal specification: these errors would not have been recognised in an informal specification, and their early detection saved considerable effort at the coding stage. The process of specification also identified some omissions and errors in the data models, which again could have had more severe consequences if left undetected until a later stage of development.

1.5 VDM++

VDM++ is an object-oriented extension of the VDM-SL language, which is now an ISO standard [72]. VDM++ has been developed by CAP Volmac in The Netherlands, and by other organisations within the AFRODITE ESPRIT project. It extends VDM by class declarations and types, and replaces VDM operation definitions by specification statements or hybrid method definitions involving method invocations, procedural code constructs, and specification statements. It also adds mechanisms for defining dynamic and concurrent behaviour, including real-time properties.

Substantial applications of the language were developed in the AFRODITE project, including:

- ship-load planning systems for bulk and chemical carriers;
- a minimum safe altitude warning system for an air traffic control network;
- data acquisition from particle accelerators;
- translation into a hardware description language.

Other applications have taken place in the field of reactive and real-time systems [91].

The results of the project include a toolset for VDM^{++}, including syntax and type-checking facilities, and code generation in C++. The toolset is integrated with a CASE tool for OMT, to allow translations of OMT into VDM^{++}, and graphical presentations of VDM^{++} specifications.

1.6   Adding Formality to Diagrammatic Methods

Two alternative ways of integrating diagrammatic and formal methods have been proposed and used in practice by groups and companies working in this area:

- *covert formality*, in which mathematical notation and an explicitly formal specification language may be avoided, but with a mathematical semantics being provided for structured English or diagrammatic specification forms;
- *overt formality*, involving translation processes from a diagrammatic notation into a formal notation, and sometimes in the reverse direction as well, and the use of development steps within the formal specification and design language.

The Fusion method of Hewlett-Packard [78] epitomises the former approach, whilst the VDM^{++} and Z^{++} methods described in this book adopt the latter. Fusion takes elements of the Booch and OMT methods, and extends these with operation specifications using (informal) pre and post conditions, and with concepts such as logical invariants.

Our contention is that, although the covert approach may be more immediately acceptable and usable within industrial software development, it does not provide the correct mechanisms for reasoning about or for formally refining models of a system. Mathematical notation cannot sensibly be avoided when proof begins to be used.

Centuries of development have led to present day set theoretic and logical notation, in order to produce a language which can express complex concepts in a concise and comprehensible manner. It is therefore beneficial to make use of this accumulated expertise when designing a specification language, and only create new notation where this is essential, as in the description of concepts of timing and synchronisation not covered in classical mathematics.

Complex mathematical notation is used in other engineering disciplines, combined with diagrammatic representations, and we believe that this approach is the best of the two in the long-term. However, in cases where only a small increase in rigour and formality is required, and where formal refinement and proof is not necessary, the first approach can be preferable.

1.7 Problems in Object-oriented Development

Some aspects of object-orientation have been considered harmful to the possibility of verifying or validating object-oriented software:

- the ambiguity of concepts such as *aggregation* and other aspects of diagrammatic object-oriented methods;
- polymorphism and dynamic binding, because these make it difficult to control which version of a method is actually to be executed at a particular invocation [249];
- inheritance, because this can be used to fragment the definition of a method across many classes, making its meaning difficult to determine [292];
- clientship, due to the use of aliasing and of interconnected networks of objects [148].

Formality can go some way to alleviating these problems:

- precise definitions can be given to particular forms of aggregation (considered in Chapter 3) and to concepts such as subtype migration (in Chapter 6). Mathematical notation can precisely express the intent of operations and semantic detail in data models which cannot be expressed in diagrams (for example, that one association is the transitive closure of another);
- a semantically meaningful definition of subtyping, along the lines of Liskov's ([200]):

  "A type hierarchy is composed of subtypes and supertypes. The intuitive idea of a subtype is one whose objects provide all the behaviour of another type (the supertype) plus something extra. What is wanted here is something like the following substitution property: If for every object o1 : S there is o2 : T such that for all programs P defined in terms of T, the behaviour of P is unchanged when o1 is substituted for o2, then S is a subtype of T."

  provides a means to infer results about subtype objects on the basis of theorems proved about a supertype.

  Thus, once we have proved that S is a subtype of T, we do not need to re-prove properties about programs P which rely on T, since by the intuitive definition these cannot be invalidated by instances of S. Dynamic binding therefore becomes less of an impediment to verification;

- inheritance can then be restricted to a purely syntactic role: code reuse and sharing, and module importation. As such, long chains of inheritance should not exist (flat hierarchies, as with C include files, could instead be used);
- aliasing is a major problem in preventing *modular* reasoning about a class. When class **A** depends on class **S** because it has an attribute **supplier** : **S** (in Z^{++} notation), then we have to take account of what other classes **B** also refer to **S** in their text, and which may therefore have instances **b** : **B** that can share instances of **S** with instances of **A**.

    There is no simple solution to this problem, which we address in part in Chapters 4 and 6. Instead, we will use specification languages which are expressive enough to assert properties about object identities and the set of existing objects in a system, in addition to inter-dependencies between objects. It is also possible to compose information about individual existing objects to produce information about the global state.

Conclusions

This chapter has described some ways in which formal techniques can be introduced into software development. The remainder of the book will give details of how the Z^{++} and VDM^{++} languages can be used to enhance the rigour and precision of object-oriented development.

Z^{++} is most appropriately used when highly abstract specifications of concurrent and real-time properties are required, or when an established use of Z exists in a company. VDM^{++} is most useful when tool support for analysis and specification is more important than support for proof, and when an established use of VDM-SL exists.

Chapter 2

The Software Development Process

This chapter will give an overview of the stages and steps typically performed in formal object-oriented development. It will introduce elements of the Z^{++} and VDM^{++} languages, and use these to illustrate the "layered development paradigm" which forms the basis of the development process given here. The roles of subtyping, inheritance and refinement will be identified and distinguished. Intuitive definitions of these concepts will be given. Detailed explanations of the concepts introduced in this chapter will be given in later chapters.

Section 2.1 describes the general development process, and Sections 2.2 and 2.4 give examples of the process in Z^{++} and VDM^{++} respectively. Section 2.3 describes the characteristics of the layered development paradigm used within the development process. For simplicity, we will use similar notation for the basic mathematical elements of VDM^{++} and Z^{++}, that is, sequences, sets and functions, etc. An introduction to this notation is given in Appendix A.

2.1 Formal Object-oriented Development

It has been claimed that the key differences between object-oriented development and conventional software development are that:

- more time, relatively, is spent in the early lifecycle stages of requirements capture and analysis;
- the specification of the system is oriented towards the definition of conceptually coherent and generalised classes based around the data manipulated by the system, instead of being purely focussed on the functions to be performed by the system.

For instance, see [225, 261, 30].

Another characteristic which may become increasingly noticeable as effective class libraries and reuse techniques become more available is the central role of reuse of existing classes and systems.

The introduction of formal techniques does not change the structure of the development lifecycle, but replaces specification and design notations based on natural language, diagrams or pseudocode with a precise, mathematically-based language, and replaces informal and unverifiable development steps with formalised and (in principle) verifiable *refinement* steps.

The general process of object-oriented development using formal techniques is as follows:

1. *requirements elicitation and analysis* of the problem, using a well-defined diagrammatic method such as OMT [261];
2. *formalisation* of diagrammatic notations in a formal specification language, using systematic processes for the translation of object classes in analysis models into specification classes;
3. *refinement* of specifications into implementation-oriented classes (in a sublanguage of the formal notation), making use of reusable specified components and the code of these components;
4. *implementation* of classes using classes which contain detailed algorithmic descriptions, which can be directly translated into classes or modules in particular programming languages.

This process is not linear, but will typically involve feedback from more advanced stages to earlier stages in order to resolve ambiguities, clarify these earlier documents in light of further understanding of the problem reached in later stages, and retrospectively correct errors. Diagrammatically the process could be envisaged as in Figure 2.1.

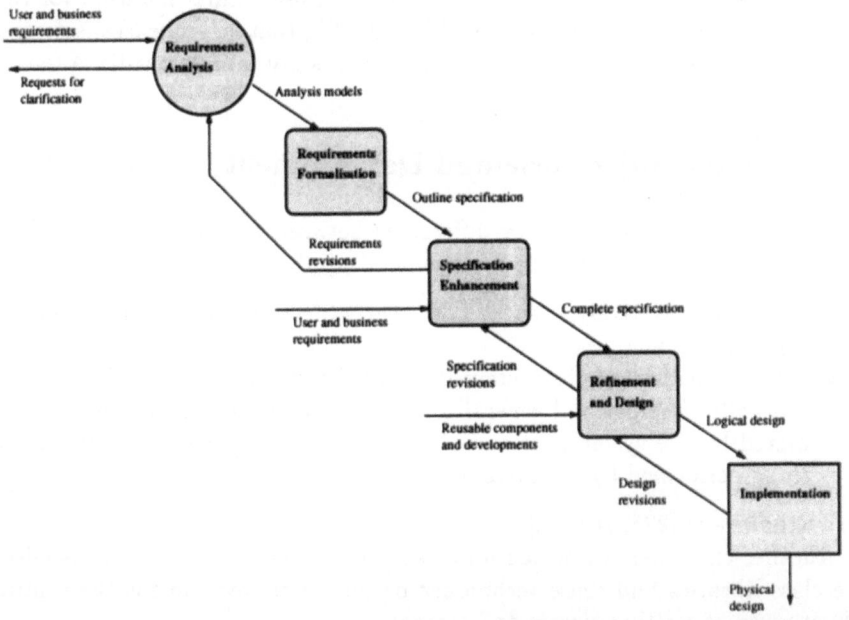

Figure 2.1: Formal Object-oriented Development Lifecycle

Naturally, revisions to the products of a particular lifecycle stage may necessitate revisions to the products of earlier stages, and may eventually require additional information from the client or application domain. The "spiral model" of Boehm could also be used to incorporate formal notations and refinement in a similar manner [27].

Formal techniques may be selectively used at each of these stages (ie, only at the specification level, or only at later design stages), depending on the needs of a particular project and the availability of skills. In addition, some parts of a development or enhancement activity may use formal techniques (ie, for critical parts of a system) whilst other parts will not. We will assume in the following that formal techniques will be used at each stage.

In more detail the development stages are:

1. *Requirements Analysis*:

    (a) elicitation of the user, business and domain requirements, making use of any information about existing systems which perform the required function within the client organisation, or on which it is to be based;

    (b) identification of the *boundary* of the software system, ie, which specification components are to be implemented or supplied via hardware and do not need to be refined to program code (however if the system is a simulator, these components may in addition be implemented as code);

    (c) development of a static data model describing the entities of relevance to the application, their attributes and inter-relationships, including inheritance structures and aggregations;

    (d) development of a dynamic behaviour model describing the life histories and responses to events of entities with a significant dynamic aspect;

    (e) development of an operation model describing the steps and object interactions involved in each system operation and the transfer of data between objects.

    Typically these models are compared with each other to check their mutex and internal consistency and are presented to the client to validate their correctness against requirements. Other details depend on the particular method chosen. In this book we will consider the OMT method of [261] and the Booch method of [30]. The Ward/Mellor real-time structured analysis method could also be used [222].

    This stage produces a set of mutually consistent **analysis models**;

2. *Requirements Formalisation*:

    (a) creation of object classes in a formal notation from the entities of the analysis models. Typically attributes of the entities identified by the requirements analysis will become attributes of the formal classes, as will associations or relationships in the analysis models (since, at present, there is no formal object-oriented language which includes a separate concept of association in the sense of OMT). Inheritance relationships will also have a direct formal expression as subtyping or inheritance assertions between formal classes;

(b) enhancement of the outline formal classes with outline operation descriptions derived from the static data and operation models and associated textual annotations. At a minimum, operations should be named and their signatures (set of input and output parameters together with types) should be identified;

(c) enhancement of formal classes with specifications of dynamic behaviour derived from the dynamic behaviour model.

It may not be necessary to formalise every aspect of the analysis models. For example, only one direction of data access provided by an association may actually be traversed in the implemented system or identified as required in the client requirements (an "enquiry access path" in the sense of SSADM 4 [97]). As a result, the formal specification can be simplified by omitting the formalisation of the superfluous direction.

In addition it is possible to defer making such design decisions by partially formalising analysis models, moving some elements of the diagrammatic descriptions into formal class descriptions, but retaining other elements as supplementary specification material. The prime example where this is useful is associations. Statecharts are sufficiently precise that they may also be retained in their entirety, with particular elements being expressed in mathematical notation when required for proof.

This stage produces an **outline specification** which formalises all structural elements of the analysis models;

3. *Specification Enhancement*:

   (a) formal expression of requirements which it was not possible to state in the analysis models except via natural language annotations;

   (b) internal consistency checking of the formal specification;

   (c) animation of the specification to validate it against requirements.

This stage produces a **formal specification** which should be complete in the sense that it provides sufficient information to verify further development steps. In particular, methods should be provided with a precise, if abstract, specification of their functionality;

4. *Refinement and Design*:

   (a) the development of more implementation-oriented versions of (some of) the specification classes, making use, where possible, of the specifications of existing components and prior developments which assist in fulfilling the specified functionality of the classes;

   (b) identification of refinement relations between refined classes and their more abstract sources;

   (c) in a fully formal development, proof of refinements.

Information from the domain and requirements may be used to select suitable refinements. However, essentially new functionality should not be introduced at stages subsequent to the complete formal specification.

It may be useful for quality improvement purposes to at least generate refinement proof obligations and to (semi-formally) carry out proofs of selected critical obligations.

This stage is completed when a level of description which is appropriate for generation of an executable system is reached. Typically this means that all operations have deterministic definitions expressed in terms of procedural code constructs, and that all mathematical datatypes such as sets and sequences have been eliminated;

5. *Implementation*:

    (a) generation of executable code in a specific implementation language, such as Ada or Eiffel;

    (b) testing of code modules and integrated system (unit and system testing) using developer-selected test cases, based on the requirements, and client-selected test cases.

This stage produces a validated **executable system**.

This series of steps is of course an idealised view. Real developments may deviate from this pattern; however, the final result of the development of a system which is of high integrity (in particular, if it is to be independently assessed) should include a documented series of stages of this form, together with evidence of verification and validation activities.

Maintenance is performed, ideally, by iterating modifications to the system upwards through such recorded development paths, with a stable and consistent state being produced at completion of the maintenance activities.

A development team may eventually contain a specific member whose role is to manage the addition and selection of components from a class library which contains the accumulated experience and requirements of other applications within the company. Such a library is a critical resource, and thus care is needed in performing modifications which might affect existing systems.

This "reuse manager" could also advise on opportunities to reuse existing components, and to identify when requirements for the current project have already been implemented in a previous development.

2.2 Example Development: Shapes and Points

A very simple example of the above process, which will serve to illustrate the combined use of formal and diagrammatic notations, is given in the following sections. This example will also introduce elements of the Z^{++} and VDM^{++} notations.

2.2.1 Requirements

The requirements of the system are:

- to allow the manipulation and display of general figures or shapes, which are specified as a set of points. Points may be added or removed from shapes;
- it should be possible to determine to which shape a point belongs. There may be many (conceptual) points at a given screen location;
- it should be possible to move a shape and a point: a point is moved by translating it by a specified horizontal and vertical displacement from its current position, whilst a shape is moved by moving all of the points it is described by.

2.2.2 Analysis

A conceptual analysis of the requirements would lead to a diagram such as that shown in Figure 2.2: this is in OMT Object Model notation, and describes a many-one relation or association between points and shapes, in which many points may be associated with a given shape (their owner). A rectangle denotes

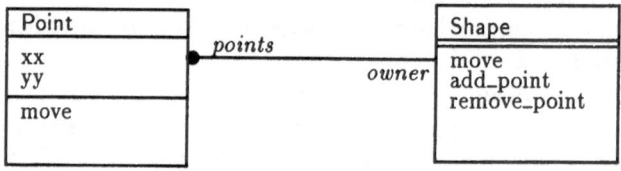

Figure 2.2: Object Model of Figure System

a class, whose name is that given at the top of the rectangle. In the second box within the rectangle are listed the attributes of the class, optionally with their types, and in the third box are listed the methods of the class, again, with optional types. Here we have not presented any types. Relationships between classes (termed *associations* in OMT) are indicated by lines, with cardinality indications given by circles at the ends of the lines (an absence of a circle indicates a cardinality of one, whilst a filled circle indicates a cardinality of 0 or more). The role that an entity plays in a relationship is named on the part of the relationship line nearest the entity.

Other OMT models include dynamic models, using statechart notation, discussed in Chapters 3 and 7, and operation models, using data flow diagrams. For this system the dynamic models are not significant. Examples of formalisation of dynamic and operation models are given in Chapters 3 and 7.

2.2.3 Formalisation

Formalisation of the object model proceeds by developing formal (Z^{++} or VDM^{++}) classes from the OMT classes, including the definition of suitable operations to meet the requirements, and filtering out elements of the model which are purely concerned with describing the domain, rather than expressing the requirements. In this case we cannot discard the two parts of the association **owner/points**, since both are apparently needed to satisfy the requirements. As part of the requirements formalisation stage we also need to add operations to maintain and manage this association: the details of how it is ensured that these operations are to be correctly used are given in Chapter 4.

Specification enhancement involves examining the natural language and diagrammatic descriptions of the operation functionalities produced during requirements analysis and expressing this functionality in mathematical notation.

The result of specification enhancement for the **Point** class is:

```
CLASS Point
OWNS
    owner :  Shape;
    xx :  ℝ;
    yy :  ℝ
OPERATIONS
    Init :  →;
    Set_owner :  Shape  →;
    Unset_owner :  →;
    Move :  ℝ ℝ  →
ACTIONS
          /*  When a point is created it is not a part of any shape :  */

    Init  ==>   xx' = 0 ∧ yy' = 0 ∧ owner' = nil_Shape;

          /*  Make the point part of the shape s? :  */

    Set_owner s?  ==>   owner' = s?;

          /*  Remove the point from its current shape :  */

    Unset_owner  ==>   owner' = nil_Shape;

    Move xin? yin?  ==>  xx' = xx + xin? ∧
                         yy' = yy + yin?
END CLASS
```

The structural aspects of this class (the attribute and method names and types) were derived automatically from the OMT model. The association is represented by "pointers" in each class, which are linked by an invariant (1):

$$\forall p : \overline{\text{Point}}; \ s : \overline{\text{Shape}} \bullet$$
$$p \in s.\text{points} \equiv s = p.\text{owner}$$

This asserts that the **owner** attribute of **Point** is an inverse to the **points** attribute of **Shape**.

In addition, the definitions of methods which simply modify or access attributes in standard ways can be mechanically generated. In contrast the **Move** operation was defined in the enhancement step.

The above class declaration defines a *type* **Point**, whose instances (declared via the notation **object : Point**) have three attributes: **owner** of the class type **Shape**, which identifies the shape to which the point belongs, and real-valued scalar quantities **xx** and **yy** which give the coordinates of the point instance.

There are types which are not classes (for instance, $\mathbb{R}$ or $\mathbb{N}$, or $\mathbb{Z}$ "given sets"), but every class does denote a type. Only instances of class types may have method invocations applied to them.

When the class name **Point** is used as a type in an attribute declaration, it actually denotes a structureless "given set" type @**Point** in Z terms – this set is the set of references for all possible objects of the class. The set of references which denote existing objects (points) is denoted by $\overline{\textbf{Point}}$. At all times it is a finite subset of the countably infinite set @**Point**. A method invocation **a.m**(e) is only well-defined if the target object reference **a** denotes an existing object whose class provides (or inherits, see Chapter 4) a definition of **m**.

If **State**$_C$ denotes the state schema of the class C (effectively the type of records whose fields are the attributes of C with their declared types), then a dereference map

$$*_C : @C \nrightarrow \textbf{State}_C$$

can be assumed to exist, which associates a *unique* object value to each object identity in $\overline{C}$, the set of existing instances of C. $\overline{C}$ is dom($*_C$). It is sometimes useful to have an explicit "nil" object reference **nil**$_C$: @C which can never be an element of $\overline{C}$. It is usually not necessary (or good practice) to explicitly refer to the dereference map $*_C$ or to $\overline{C}$ within a specification. They can however be implicitly referred to by uses of object creation or deletion operations. Further discussion of aliasing and object identity is given in Chapter 4.

In the usual way, different point instances may have different values for these attributes, and these attributes may be changed during the lifetime of the object by any *method* listed in the **OPERATIONS** clause of the class. This clause gives the signature of each method, as a pair **InputTypes** $\rightarrow$ **OutputTypes**, where **InputTypes** include one or more input parameter types, and **OutputTypes** one or more output parameter types. In this case there are four methods, each of which modifies the state of an instance of **Point**:

- **Init** – used to initialise the object. In this case it merely sets default values for the attributes: 0 for numeric attributes and an object reference with no associated existing object for object-valued attributes;
- **Set_owner** – defines the **owner** attribute. When a class name C is used as the type of a method parameter, it refers to $\overline{C}$ by default;
- **Unset_owner** – clears the **owner** attribute. This is needed in order to maintain the consistency of the two attributes (**owner** in **Point** and

> **points** in **Shape**) which together implement the association from the
> object model;
>
> - **Move** – moves the point by a certain horizontal translation **xin?** and
>   vertical translation **yin?**, but does not change the owner of the point.

The **Move** operation was the only method which required a non-trivial enhancement step, interpreting the text "**move** translates the point by a specified horizontal and vertical displacement from its current position" in the above manner.

As in Z, an attribute identifier decorated with a ′ denotes the value of this attribute at termination of the method or statement in whose definition it occurs. The undecorated identifier denotes the value of the attribute at initiation of execution of the method or statement.

Input parameters are (by convention) decorated by a ?, whilst output parameters are decorated by a !.

Unlike Z, the "frame" of an operation (the set of attributes which it changes) is specified implicitly: if **att′** does not occur in the definition of operation **op** then it can be assumed to not be changed by an execution of **op**[1].

An application of a method **M** of class **C** on an instance **object** of **C** is denoted by **object**.**M**(**parameters**). Such applications can occur in method definitions of a *client* class **D** of **C** in which **C** is used as a type, and where **object** is an expression which denotes an existing instance of class **C**.

For example, the **Move** method of **Point** could be invoked by a call of the form **p**.**Move**$(4, 5)$ in a class where **p** : **Point** is declared.

After specification enhancement the **Shape** class is:

```
CLASS Shape
OWNS
  points : F(Point)
OPERATIONS
  Init : →;
  Add_point : Point →;
  Remove_point : Point →;
  Move : R R →
ACTIONS
  Init ==> points′ = ∅;

  Add_point pp?  ==>  points′ = points ∪ { pp? };

  Remove_point pp?  ==>  points′ = points \ { pp? };

  Move xin? yin?  ==>
                        ⋀pp ∈ points  pp.Move(xin?, yin?)
END CLASS
```

The definition of **Move** was derived from the statement "the **move** operation on a shape translates every point in the shape by the given horizontal and verti-

---

[1] when op is used in a procedural, rather than logical context: see Chapter 4.

cal displacement". **Init, Add_point** and **Remove_point** are structural operations which correspond to the methods **Init, Set_owner** and **Unset_owner** of **Point** (that is, when executed together with them, they preserve the logical invariant (1) above).

This class contains an example of the combination of Z type constructors ($\mathbb{F}$) and class types (**Point**). For practical reasons the finite subset constructor $\mathbb{F}$ is considered a more suitable choice than $\mathbb{P}$ (arbitrary subsets), since any actual shape will be specified by only a finite number of points.

The operation **Init** here initialises the set of points contained in a shape to the empty set. The operation **Add_point** adds a new point to this set (it would be performed together with a suitable call of **Set_owner** by a user of the system, in order to maintain the invariant concerning the original association between shapes and points). The operation **Remove_point** deletes a point from the set, and would be performed with **Unset_owner**. Finally the **Move** operation translates every point in the shape by a given horizontal and vertical amount.

A convention which can be used to describe the application of an operation to a set of objects is the notation:

$$\bigwedge_{a \in \text{a\_set}} a.m(e)$$

where $\text{a\_set} \in \mathbb{P}(@C)$ for a class type **C**, and **m** is a method of **C**. This denotes the simultaneous application of **m**, with arguments **e**, to every instance of **C** in **a_set**. A formal definition is given in Appendix A.

This operation can therefore be refined by an actual parallel implementation, or by a sequentialisation in a loop. In this case the **Move** invocations on separate points will be independent of each other, so that concurrent execution is valid.

Finally, the class **System** which encapsulates the operations that a user expects to be able to apply can be specified by:

```
CLASS System
OWNS
  point_set :  F(Point);
  figures :  F(Shape)
OPERATIONS
  create_shape :  →  Shape;
  create_point :  →  Point;
  add_point_to_shape :  Point Shape  →;
  remove_point_from_shape :  Point Shape  →;
  move_shape :  Shape `R  R  →;
  move_point :  Point  R  R  →
INVARIANT
  ∀ p :  Point;   s :  Shape |
            p ∈ point_set ∧ s ∈ figures •
                       p ∈ s.points  ≡   s = p.owner
ACTIONS
  create_shape s!  ==>
     New_Shape[s!/shape!]  ∧
```

```
        s!.Init  ∧
        figures' = figures ∪ { s! };
create_point p!  ==>
        New_Point[p!/point!]  ∧
        p!.Init  ∧
        point_set' = point_set ∪ { p! };

add_point_to_shape p? s?  ==>
        PRE p? ∈ point_set ∧ s? ∈ figures ∧
            p?.owner = nil_Shape
        THEN
            s?.Add_point(p?)  ∧
            p?.Set_owner(s?)
        END ;
remove_point_from_shape p? s?  ==>
        PRE p? ∈ point_set ∧ s? ∈ figures ∧
            p? ∈ s?.points
        THEN
            s?.Remove_point(p?)  ∧
            p?.Unset_owner
        END ;
move_shape s? xin? yin?  ==>
        PRE s? ∈ figures
        THEN
            s?.Move(xin?, yin?)
        END ;
move_point p? xin? yin?  ==>
        PRE p? ∈ point_set
        THEN
            p?.Move(xin?, yin?)
        END
```

END CLASS

The operations of this class were derived directly from the original list of required operations for the application. $New_C[out!/c!]$ denotes renaming of the default output parameter $c! : \overline{C}$ of the creation operation New_C to out!.

This class is the first example we have given of a class with a non-trivial (ie, not **true**) invariant. This is a predicate which defines those values of the attributes of the class which are allowed at method initiation and termination times (and which can therefore be relied upon by external users at these times). The invariant does not need to be true at times within a method execution which are not initiation or termination times.

The invariant that **owner** is inverse to **points** is stated in this class, which is a client of both the **Shape** and **Point** classes, rather than in the individual classes, since it can only reasonably be maintained over the transitions of such a client which performs **Set_owner** / **Add_point** and **Unset_owner** / **Remove_point** operations in conjunction.

The internal consistency conditions for the above classes are for the most part immediately provable. For example the requirement that the state space of **Shape** is non-empty is

$$\exists \, \mathbf{P} : \mathbb{F}(\mathbf{Point}) \bullet \mathbf{true}$$

and there is an axiom that @**Point** is a countably infinite set, from which this requirement follows.

2.2.4   Refinement

A class **D** is a *refinement* of a class **C** if there is a data refinement relation **R** on their combined states (for simplicity we assume that the sets of feature identifiers in the two classes are disjoint) and a renaming ϕ of methods of **C** to those of **D**, such that ϕ is total and such that **R** satisfies the usual data refinement conditions between Z specifications (with some extensions, the full details are given in Chapter 5). The existence of such a refinement is asserted by the notation

$$\mathbf{C} \sqsubseteq^{\text{ref}}_{\phi, \mathbf{R}} \mathbf{D}$$

Intuitively, **R** defines how the abstract data of **C** are to be implemented by the more "concrete" (program-like) data of **D**, whilst ϕ does the same for the methods of **C**. ϕ is total since every external service (method) of **C** must have some implementation.

A number of approaches for selecting suitable refinements are possible. In this case we will adopt a "reuse-driven" approach – in which the developer examines a library of existing classes and developments and selects components which they believe will support the required functionality of the class(es) they wish to refine. Let **C** be a class in the system being developed which it is desired to refine. Then if **L** is a suitable library component, **C** will be refined to a class $\mathbf{C}_1$ which makes use of **L** by *composition* (ie, **L** is used as the type of an attribute or other data item in $\mathbf{C}_1$). An implementation $\mathbf{L}_1$ of **L**, together with executable code, will be presumed to already exist, removing the need to repeat development of the functionality given by **L**.

In this case the refinement of the **Shape** class uses a supposed library component for manipulating sets of objects, **Set_manager**, which is based upon a similar component provided in the B Toolkit for B AMN [138]. The refinements of **Shape** and **Point** are performed independently: it will be the case that both implementations are *refinement-preserving* in the sense of Section 2.3 since they will use only procedural code to define methods. Thus refinements of the individual components can be composed to form a refinement of the complete system.

The **Point** class is refined directly to **Point_1**:

```
CLASS Point_1
OWNS
  owner : Shape;
```

xx, yy : $\mathbb{R}$

OPERATIONS

  Init : $\rightarrow$;
  Set_owner : **Shape** $\rightarrow$;
  Unset_owner : $\rightarrow$;
  Move : $\mathbb{R} \ \mathbb{R} \ \rightarrow$

ACTIONS

  Init   ==>

          BEGIN
              xx := 0;
              yy := 0;
              Unset$_{Shape}$[owner$'$/shape$'$]
          END;

  Set_owner s?   ==>
              BEGIN **owner** := s?   END;

  Unset_owner   ==>
              BEGIN
                  Unset$_{Shape}$[owner$'$/shape$'$]
              END;

  Move xin? yin?   ==>
              BEGIN
                  xx := **xx** + **xin?**;
                  yy := **yy** + **yin?**
              END

END CLASS

A parallel execution of the assignments in **Init** and **Move** could be used, if such a construct was available in the chosen implementation language (in the present case, effectively the B0 language of B Abstract Machine Notation [138]). Note that the signature of operations cannot change in a refinement: a refinement merely provides an alternative description of the type specified by the abstract class, and must present the same external interface to clients as this class.

The operation Unset$_C$ is defined as follows:

Unset$_C$ ==>
          c$'$ = nil$_C$

It leaves $*_C$ and $\overline{C}$ unchanged but modifies c so that it becomes an object reference for which there is no corresponding object value. This is always possible because $\overline{C}$ is finite and @C is infinite.

The refinement relation here is the identity relation on the state (more precisely it equates corresponding attributes of the two classes). The renaming of methods is also the identity function.

The **Shape** class is then refined to use the **Set_manager** component (presumed to already possess an implementation in executable code). This component is *generic* since it has no specific dependence upon the type of elements

of the sets which it manipulates. The generic type parameter **X** is listed after
the class name, and may be used as a type within the text of the generic class.

```
CLASS Set_manager[X]
OWNS
  contents :  F(X);
  ordering :  seq(X);
  counter :  N
INVARIANT
  ran(ordering)  =  contents ∧
  #ordering  =  #contents ∧
  counter  ≤  #contents
OPERATIONS
  Init : →;
  Add_element :  X  →;
  Remove_element :  X  →;
  First :  →  X;
  Next :  →  X
RETURNS
  Finished : →
ACTIONS
  Init  ==>  contents'  =  ∅ ∧
             ordering'  =  ⟨ ⟩ ∧
             counter'  =  0;

  Add_element ee?  ==>
             contents'  =  contents ∪ { ee? } ∧
             ran(ordering')  =  contents' ∧
             #ordering'  =  #contents';

  Remove_element ee?  ==>
             contents'  =  contents \ { ee? } ∧
             ran(ordering')  =  contents' ∧
             #ordering'  =  #contents' ∧
             counter'  ≤  #contents';

  First ee!  ==>
           PRE #ordering  >  0
           THEN
           ee!  =  ordering(1) ∧
           counter'  =  1
           END;

  Next ee!  ==>
           (counter  <  #ordering ∧
                counter'  =  counter + 1  ∧
                ee!  =  ordering(counter'))  ∨
           (counter  ≥  #ordering ∧
                counter'  =  0 ∧
                ee!  ∈  contents);
```

Finished   ==>
     counter = 0 ∨
     counter ≥ #ordering

END CLASS

#st denotes the cardinality of a set st, whilst ran(sq) denotes the set of elements in a sequence sq, or, more generally, the range of a function. ∪ denotes set union, whilst \ denotes set subtraction. A summary of mathematical notation is given in Appendix A.

Notice that **Add_element** implicitly leaves **counter** unchanged. An operation listed in the RETURNS clause leaves all attributes unchanged – it is a pure enquiry access to the state. In Z and Z^{++} such an enquiry is written and used as a predicate – explicit boolean values as used in VDM and VDM^{++} do not appear.

Add_element and **Remove_element** may rearrange the internal ordering of the list elements. Thus during an iteration over the list, these operations should not be used.

In **Set_manager** the invariant asserts that **ordering** is a particular listing of the elements of **contents**, without repetitions. **counter** is an unspecified element of 0. .#**contents**. Both of these items are used to support the definition of the *iterator* operations **First**, **Next** and **Finished**, which provide a means to step through the elements of **contents** one by one in an exhaustive manner. The method **First** has a precondition, which expresses that it should only be executed if there is at least one element in the set. (If the operation is executed on an empty set, then no guarantee is made about its result except that the type of the resulting state and outputs will be correct.)

The refinement **Shape_1** of **Shape** is then:

CLASS Shape_1
OWNS
  p_set : Set_manager[Point]
OPERATIONS
  Init : →;
  Add_point : Point →;
  Remove_point : Point →;
  Move : ℝ ℝ →
ACTIONS
  Init ==> p_set.Init;

  Add_point pp? ==> p_set.Add_element(pp?);

  Remove_point pp? ==> p_set.Remove_element(pp?);

  Move xin? yin? ==>
     VAR local : Point
     IN
       p_set.First[local/ee!];

```
WHILE ¬ p_set.Finished
DO
  local.Move(xin?, yin?);
  p_set.Next[local/ee!]
END
END
```

```
END CLASS
```

The notation **First[local/ee!]** indicates that **local** is an actual output parameter of the operation. We could make explicit the fact that it is an output
parameter by the notation **local ⟵ First**, taken from B AMN.

The data refinement is that **points = p_set.contents**. The method renaming is again the identity. The main task of proving this refinement is in
identifying a suitable loop invariant for the procedural definition of **Move** and
establishing that the state on termination of the loop implies the poststate
predicate given in the abstract definition of **Move**.

A point we will return to in Chapter 5 is that a particular **Shape** instance
should have *exclusive ownership* of its associated **p_set** object for the refinement
to be formally correct.

Figure 2.3 shows the overall architecture of the system. This structure
would be the same even if we extended the functionality to include methods
to determine the part of a figure which overlaps the screen, or the centre of
gravity of a figure, etc.

The notation used here is explained in detail in Section **2**.3. Circles denote abstract specification classes, whilst squares denote implementation level
classes. Rounded squares will denote classes at intermediate stages of refinement. Library components are represented with dashed lines. This notation
follows that of [138] for B Abstract Machine Notation. The degree of dependence of a client upon a supplier class is represented by a lower case 'c' if the
client only uses the supplier class as a type, but does not invoke methods upon
objects of this type. A capitalised 'C' denotes full dependence and the use by
the client of method invocations on instances of the supplier.

A VDM++ version of this system is given in Section 2.4.

2.3   The Layered Development Paradigm

2.3.1   Refinements, Subtypes and Subclasses

Refinement (or reification in VDM terminology) subtyping and subclassing are
closely related concepts which have often been considered to be equivalent for
object-oriented formal languages. However, this book will distinguish them
on the basis of how they are used within a development, and will give precise
mathematical definitions of the concepts (in Chapters 4 and 5). *Reification* is
the process of replacing an abstract description of a subsystem or component
with a semantically equivalent description which is closer to an implementation

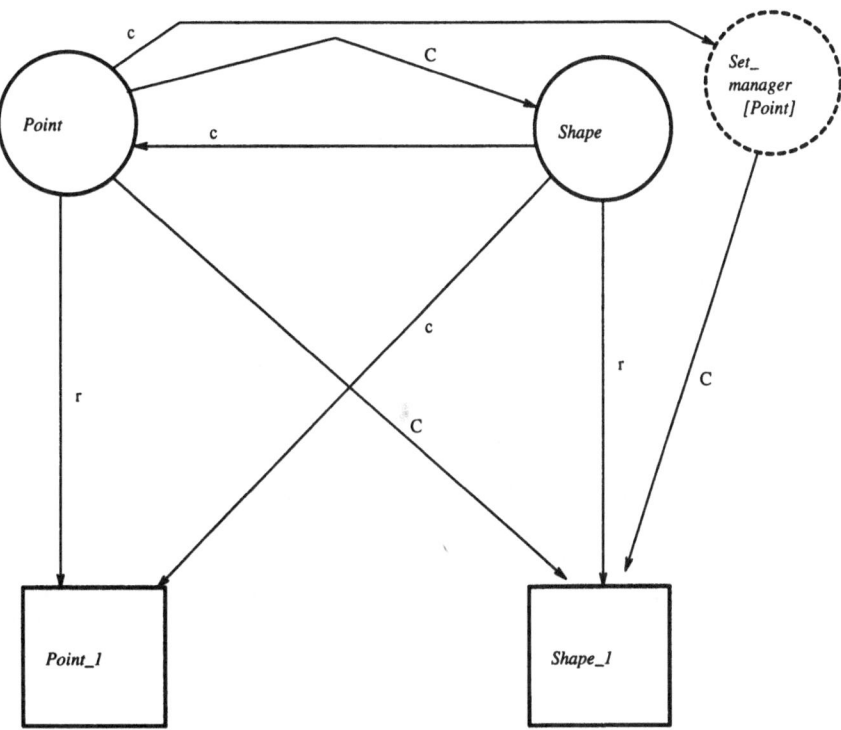

Figure 2.3: Structure of **Shapes** Development

in a programming language. *Subtyping* concerns however the ability of an element of a subtype to be substituted for an element of a supertype in any program involving the supertype. Subtyping provides the formal basis for the polymorphism supported by dynamic binding.

Reification and subtyping are also distinct since they relate to separate aspects of a class: a class is both a representative of a *type* and a template for an executable module. Typing is concerned with the logical properties of entities, whereas classes may describe finer distinctions, in particular, between logically equivalent but executionally distinct implementations of an abstract type. Such implementations can be regarded as being of the *same* type, in that they satisfy the same logical and external interface requirements, (or, due to the layered development discipline, can only be used via the same abstract interface) but will be different classes.

A particular case where the concepts are distinguished is where a subtype is a *specialisation* of a supertype, that is, its state is more constrained. Consider a VDM^{++} class with an attribute **colour** of an enumerated type:

```
class Elephant
types
  Colour = <grey> | <black> | <blue>
instance variables
  colour: Colour;
...
end Elephant
```

Then a descendent class **GreyElephant** in which the invariant **colour** $= <$ **grey** $>$ is stated is a subtype (provided there are no operations in **GreyElephant** or **Elephant** which change the **colour** attribute), but it does not represent progress towards implementation unless the original specification was an overgeneralisation of the problem.

In VDM^{++} the **instance variables** clause corresponds to the **OWNS** clause in Z^{++} and the **types** clause corresponds to the **TYPES** clause in Z^{++}, with however the details of these clauses following VDM syntax instead of Z syntax. The notation $<$ **item** $>$ is used to denote an element of an enumerated type.

In fact here it may be more natural to model **colour** as a constant, declared as:

```
values
  colour: Colour
```

Constraints on constants may also be placed in the invariant of a VDM^{++} class.

In Z^{++} the same example is also a case where subtyping is more general than refinement.

2.3.2   Development Architecture

An illustration of the formally-based software development architecture which will be used in the book is shown in Figure 2.4. The annotation 'i' on a line indicates that the source class is *inherited* by the destination class, an annotation 's' indicates that the destination is a subtype of the source, and an annotation 'r' indicates that the destination refines the source. 'c' indicates class composition of the source in the destination. Composition can be carried out by the source class being a supplier to the destination, or by the destination entity carrying out a "private inheritance" of the source: that is, inheriting it but not exporting any of its methods (ie, *delegation* in the sense of [261]).

The important point here is that software components are used or reused through their most abstract specification (eg, only the *specification* of the subsystem S3 is the source of a composition arrow, not its implementation I3). This is the essence of *information hiding*: users of the subsystem S3 should only rely on its public interface (specification), not on its internal implementation details. I4 is an implementation of S4 (a reification of it). I4 uses the actual interface of I3 and is guaranteed to get the behaviour specified in S3. Details of execution are hidden from S4 and I4, so that the subsystem described by S4 is insulated from changes in the implementation of S3.

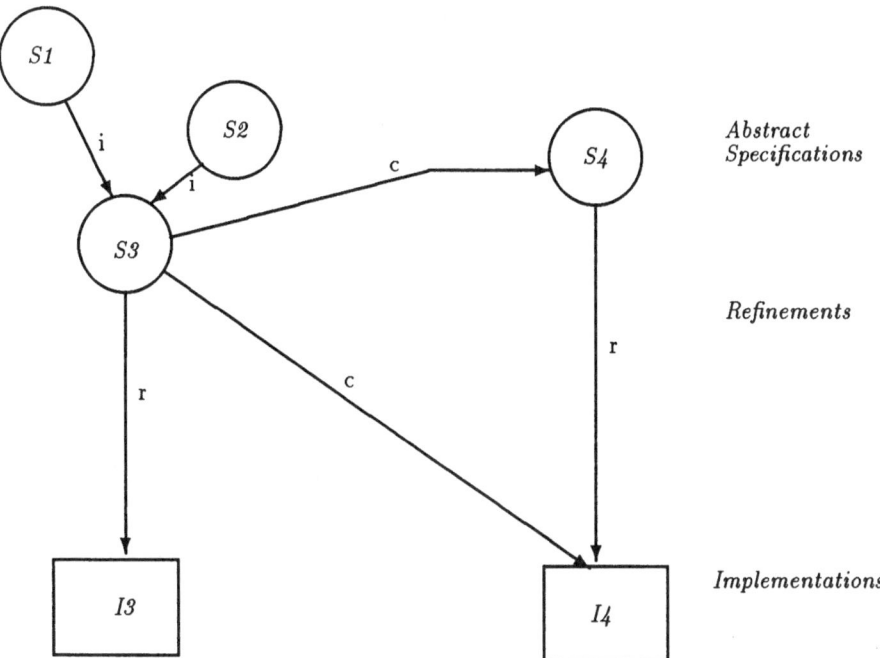

Figure 2.4: Typical Formal Development Architecture

Effectively a system development consists of a set of subsystems, subcomponents or *layers*, each of which will comprise an abstract specification and a single line of refinements down to an executable implementation.

A layer makes use of another layer, conceptually at a more basic level or lower granularity of functionality, via class composition. That is, one subsystem is implemented on the specification of another. The different refinement stages or levels within one layer represent alternative descriptions of the same subsystem. In the industrial applications of VDM[++] and Z[++] which have taken place, these levels correspond to a series of *models* of the required subsystem, increasing in semantic detail and procedural orientation as development proceeds. The abstract specification expresses the functionality that the subsystem is able to supply (and guarantees to supply) to any client. That is, it forms a *contract* statement. The more concrete refinements express how this functionality is to be implemented, and include decompositions of the abstract operations into (possibly) combinations of operations from previously developed subsystems, and the definition of particular algorithms for implementing the abstract functions. The specification of such a subsystem may itself be decomposed into separate parts via inheritance. The collection of modules comprising the specification and the single refinement path will be termed a *subsystem development* in the following. In VDM[++] the outermost specification layer is termed the *workspace* and manages the creation of instances of subordinate layers, and the ways in which external users can access the facilities of these layers.

Relationships between classes, such as subtyping or refinement, are generally asserted separately from the text of the classes themselves, thus enhancing the reusability of these classes[2].

The shapes and points development given in Section 2.2 is an illustration of such an architecture. The subsystems **Shape** and **Point** are both dependent upon each other, whilst the library subsystem **Set_manager** is subordinate to **Shape**.

2.3.3   Refinement Preservation: Decomposing Development

In a formal development the process of refinement replaces abstract data types and mathematically specified operations in the specification classes by data types and procedural statements which are closer to those of a typical third generation programming language. A specification of a method in the abstract specification is simply concerned with providing a concise and clear description of the state transition it achieves, whilst at the implementation level methods will be defined in terms of code, and the properties of these definitions will be used to prove the constraints expressed in the abstract specification.

It is useful for the implementation language to be quite restricted, for several reasons, including:

- a small language will be easy to map into a number of possible imperative programming languages, especially if it corresponds to a sublanguage of these languages;
- it will be easier to prove that the language *preserves refinement*.

The second condition is critical for *compositional implementation* to be possible. It is more precisely:

---

[2]In VDM[++] there is a proposal for a "design meta-language" which will describe such relationships.

- if a class **D** is a client of a class **C**, and **C**$_1$ refines **C**, then using **C**$_1$ in place of **C** in **D** to produce a class **D**$_1$ implies that **D**$_1$ refines **D**.

It could be said that **D** utilises **C** in a *refinement-preserving* manner, or that it is a *monotonic* context with respect to the refinement of **C**.

The property is important since it should be possible to implement **C** independently of the classes which are clients of it, and then use this implementation to produce an implementation for these clients. Similar properties would be desirable for private inheritance if this were to be used as a basis for composition.

2.4 Development Example in VDM++

Instead of a system of shapes and points, consider a closely related system dealing with files and directories.

2.4.1 Requirements

The requirements of the system are:

- to allow the manipulation of files and directories, which are specified as a set of files. Files may be added or removed from directories;
- it should be possible to determine to which directory a file belongs. There may be many files in the same filestore and partition;
- it should be possible to move a file and a directory, and to display the location of a file, defined as the filestore on which it resides.

A partition represents a particular area of memory. Memory is physically associated with particular filestore devices.

2.4.2 Analysis

This results in a diagram (Figure 2.5) which is similar to that produced for the case study of Section 2.2.

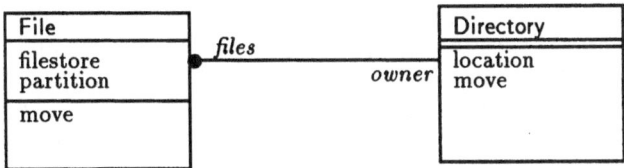

Figure 2.5: Object Model of Directory System

2.4.3 Formalisation

Formalisation proceeds by developing VDM^{++} classes from the OMT classes. Again, after specification enhancement, we obtain the following formal **File** class:

```
class File
instance variables
  owner: @Directory;
  filestore: nat;
  partition: nat;
init filestore, partition == filestore = 0 and partition = 0
methods
  set_owner(s: @Directory) ==
    [ ext wr owner
      post owner = s];

  move(fin, pin: nat) ==
    [ ext wr filestore, partition
      post filestore = fin  and
           partition = pin ]

end File
```

ASCII notation will be usually used for VDM^{++}, as this is the representation which is entered by a user of the VDM^{++} toolset. Mathematical notation will be used to discuss VDM^{++} specifications.

In VDM^{++} the distinction between the set @C of references to a class C and C itself is made explicit when the former is used as a type. **nat** corresponds to $\mathbb{N}$ in Z. The **init** clause specifies what initial states are allowed on object creation. It constrains a list of the attributes by a predicate, which here requires that **filestore** and **partition** are initially 0.

The operations are defined using *specification statements*. These have the syntax

> [ext wr **write frame**
>   rd **read frame**
> pre **precondition**
> post **postcondition**]

where the *write frame* is the set of attributes of the class and other variables in scope which the statement may modify, the *read frame* is the set of attributes whose values are only accessed by the operation, and the *precondition* must hold at initiation of the method if the *postcondition* is to hold at termination. In the postcondition, the value of an attribute **v** at initiation of the statement is expressed by $\overleftarrow{v}$ (if **v** is listed in the read frame, then **v** can be used in place of $\overleftarrow{v}$). ASCII notation for $\overleftarrow{v}$ is v~

The initial state of an object of a class at creation of this object is constrained by a predicate in the **init** clause of the class.

The **move** operation simply sets the new location of the file to be the filestore and partition given in the input parameters. The **Directory** class is then:

```
class Directory
instance variables
  files: set of @File;
init objectstate ==
  files = {}
methods
  add_file(pp: @File) ==
      [ext wr files
       post files = files~ union {pp}];

  remove_file(pp: @File) ==
      [ext wr files
       post
           files = files~ \ { pp }];

  location(pp: @File) value t: nat
      pre pp in set files ==
           (topology [ext wr t
                       post t = pp.filestore];
              return t);

  move(filestore_in, partition_in: nat) ==
      for all pp in set files do
           pp!move(filestore_in, partition_in)
```

end Directory

The notation **pp.filestore** in the definition of **location** denotes the value of the **filestore** attribute of **pp** – VDM++ currently only allows such references in a **topology** statement or the **aux reasoning** component of a class. It can be replaced by an explicit invocation of a enquiry operation of the supplier object.

The **move** operation here moves a directory by individually moving each of its files. The operation model which was used to define this operation is given in Figure 2.6, in a version of the object interaction graph notation of Booch.

move(f,p)

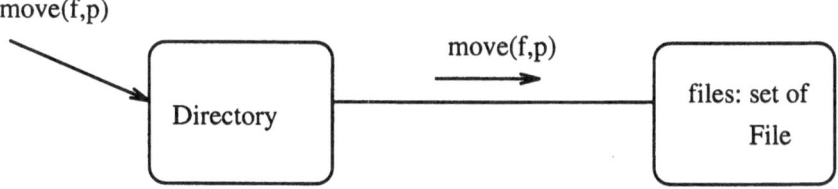

Figure 2.6: Operation Model of **move** on Directory

In the formal class it may appear to be specified in an overly procedural fashion, however the loop allows concurrent execution of its iterations if this

is semantically valid. Detailed syntax definitions for VDM^{++} are given in
Appendix B.

The type definition **set of @File** corresponds to $\mathbb{F}(\textbf{File})$ in Z^{++}. An operation may be given a completely non-deterministic definition within its typing
constraints by the clause **is not yet specified** in its body.

2.4.4   Refinement

The definition of reification in VDM^{++} is similar to that in Z^{++}, however
there is a key difference which is the requirement of *adequacy* that distinguishes
reification from subtyping in VDM^{++}. A discussion of this is given in Chapter
5. In addition, instead of a general refinement relation between the states of
the refined and unrefined classes, only a *retrieve* function is specified, which
maps any concrete state into a corresponding abstract state.

The **File** class is refined directly to **File_1**:

```
class File_1
-- refines File;
-- retrieve function: identity;
-- method renaming: identity;
instance variables
   owner: @Directory;
   filestore: nat;
   partition: nat;
init filestore, partition == filestore = 0 and partition = 0
methods

  set_owner(s: @Directory) ==
    owner := s;

  move(fin, pin: nat) ==
    (filestore := fin;
     partition := pin)

end File_1
```

Comments (lines beginning with a --) have been used to express refinement
relations. Ideally, a suitable tool should be able to interpret statements of
refinement, and formulate the proof obligations needed to establish that these
refinements hold.

Set_manager is defined as in Z^{++}. Because VDM^{++} does not allow generic
classes, it can only be defined as a textual template for (manually) generating
actual classes:

```
class Set_manager      -- of files
instance variables
  ordering: seq of @File;
  counter: nat;
init objectstate == ordering = []
```

```
                    and counter = 0;
inv objectstate ==
                    card(elems(ordering)) = len(ordering) and
                    counter <= len(ordering)
methods
  add_element(ee: @File) ==
      [ext wr ordering
       post
       if (ee not in set elems(ordering~))
       then
         ordering = ordering~ ^ [ee]    /* concatenation */
       else
         ordering = ordering~];

  remove_element(ee: @File) ==
      [ext wr ordering, counter
       post
            if (ee in set elems(ordering~))
            then
              elems(ordering) = elems(ordering~) \ {ee} and
              len(ordering) = len(ordering~) - 1  and
              counter <= len(ordering)
            else
              ordering = ordering~ and
              counter = counter~];

  first() value ee: @File
    pre len(ordering) > 0 ==
    ([ext rd ordering
         wr counter
      post ee = ordering(1) and
           counter = 1];
    return ee);

  next() value ee: @File ==
    ([ext rd ordering
         wr counter
      post if counter~ < len(ordering)
           then
             counter = counter~ + 1 and
             ee = ordering(counter)
           else
             counter = 0 and
             ee in set elems(ordering)];
     return ee);

  finished() value bb: bool ==
    ([ext rd ordering, counter
      post  bb = (counter = 0 or counter >= len(ordering))];
     return bb);
```

```
   in_set(ee: @File) value bool ==
       return (ee in set elems(ordering))

end Set_manager
```

Unlike Z^{++}, an explicit type **bool** (mathematical notation $\mathbb{B}$) is defined. Each method with an output parameter must include a return statement to define the resulting value. **len(ss)** denotes the length of a sequence **ss**, and **elems(ss)** the set of elements of **ss**.

   Directory_1 is:

```
class Directory_1
-- refines Directory;
-- retrieve function: files = elems(p_set.ordering);
-- method renaming: identity;
instance variables
  p_set: @Set_manager  -- of @File objects
-- init objectstate:
--         elems(p_set.ordering) = {};
methods
  add_file(pp: @File) ==
      p_set!add_element(pp);

  remove_file(pp: @File) ==
      p_set!remove_element(pp);

  location(pp: @File) value t: nat ==
      (dcl bb: bool := p_set!in_set(pp);
        if bb
        then
          t := pp!my_filestore()
        else
          t := 0;
        return t);

 move(fin,pin: nat) ==
      (dcl local: @File := p_set!first();
       dcl term: bool := p_set!finished();
       while not(term)
       do
         (local!move(fin,pin);
          local := p_set!next();
          term := p_set!finished()))

end Directory_1
```

where we have retrospectively added the method

```
  my_filestore() value nat ==
    return filestore
```

to **File**, as a result of analysing the requirements for **Directory_1**.

The `dcl` statement introduces a new local variable, with its type, and optionally initialises its value.

2.4.5 Implementation

Implementation of the above classes can be carried out in Eiffel [225], assuming the existence of a library generic class **LINKED_LIST[X]** which implements linked lists. A detailed process for this is given in Chapter 8. The code of the three subsystems of this development are given by:

```
class File_1
export
  filestore, set_owner, move
feature
  owner: Directory;
  filestore: INTEGER;
  partition: INTEGER;
-- initialisation to null, 0, 0 is implicit in Eiffel
  set_owner(s: Directory) is
    do
      owner := s
    ensure  owner = s
    end;

  move(fin, pin: INTEGER) is
    require
      fin >= 0; pin >= 0
    do
      filestore := fin;
      partition := pin
    ensure  filestore = fin; partition = pin
    end;

invariant
  filestore >= 0;
  partition >= 0
end -- class File


class Directory_1
export
  add_file, location, move
feature
  files: Set_manager[File];

  add_file(pp: File) is
    do
      files.add_element(pp)
```

```
      end;

  location(pp: File): INTEGER is
      do
        Result := pp.filestore
      ensure Result >= 0
      end;


  move(fin, pin: INTEGER) is
      require fin >= 0; pin >= 0
      local flocal: File;
            term: BOOLEAN
      do
        from
          flocal := files.first;
          term := files.finished;
        invariant
          true
        variant
          1
        until term
        loop
          flocal.move(fin,pin);
          flocal := files.next;
          term := files.finished
        end
      end
end -- class Directory_1
```

We have coded up the enquiry operation **location** in order to inspect the data being manipulated. Notice that **filestore** is made into an externally readable attribute of **File** by listing it in the **export** clause of **File_1**. This permits a simpler implementation of **location** than that given in the specification.

The library class is simply:

```
class Set_manager_1[T]
export
  add_element, first, next, finished
feature
  list: LINKED_LIST[T];

  add_element(ee: T) is
      do
        list.insert_right(ee)
      end;

  first: T is
      do
        Result := list.first
      end;
```

```
next: T is
  do
    list.forth;
    Result := list.value
  end;

finished: BOOLEAN is
  do
    Result := list.offright
  end;

end -- class Set_manager[T]
```

Conclusions

This chapter has introduced the main development and lifecycle concepts that will be used in the remainder of the book. The layered development approach is adapted from that proposed by Abrial for the B AMN language [3]. In subsequent chapters we will give more examples of this approach, and more details of techniques used and specialisations of the approach for particular domains.

Other books which cover object-oriented development with reference to formal techniques are due to Meyer, in the context of Eiffel [225], Ince, in the context of C++ [153], and the texts describing the Fusion [78] and Syntropy [64] methods. Booch [30] does suggest the use of pre-conditions, post-conditions and invariants, but does not provide any formal notation for these.

The important topic of design *patterns* is covered in [109, 54], and general object-oriented development techniques are also covered in [30, 64, 225, 261].

Chapter 3

From Analysis to Formal Specification

This chapter will describe a systematic process of formalisation of OMT analysis models: data, functional and dynamic, into Z^{++} and VDM^{++}. The main elements of the data and dynamic models of OMT will be covered in this chapter. The Booch method is also considered [30]. Chapter 7 will cover the OMT notation in greater depth, and also consider the OOA method [271]. The use of this translation process and of specification animation, in providing a common language between the specifier and the client, will be emphasised for its significance in reducing errors in requirements elicitation. It covers the stages of *requirements formalisation* and *specification enhancement* described in Chapter 2. Section 3.1 describes the formalisation of object models in Z^{++} and VDM^{++}, Section 3.2 describes how various forms of *aggregation* can be formally defined, Section 3.3 describes alternative approaches for operation formalisation, and for deferring the localisation of methods in classes. Section 3.4 describes the formalisation of dynamic models in the two languages, Section 3.5 considers translation from the notations of the Booch method, Section 3.6 describes general principles for creation of formal classes, and Section 3.7 describes the role of animation in specification enhancement.

There are several reasons why we may wish to use both structured and formal specifications in a development process, and to integrate these two approaches via (semi-) automatic translations. By translating structured models into formal specifications we aim to obtain a formal specification which has a close correspondence with the diagrammatic models, and which is therefore relatively easy to communicate with clients and to validate and assess. The quality of the resulting specifications is improved because a uniform and systematic approach has been used – instead of the sometimes excessively idiosyncratic ingenuity which some writers display in their formal specifications. Taking an extreme view, it could be said that formal specification without prior analysis simply re-introduces the hacker at an earlier lifecycle stage – where they may be more dangerous than at the code level.

In addition, some refinement steps (such as data transformations which correspond to relational data analysis [97]) can be performed on the diagrammatic notations in a simpler manner than on the formal specification. The translation step allows such choices in the timing of refinement steps to be made. It also supports proofs that intuitively correct transformations on structured notations do produce semantically equivalent models.

Formalisation of diagrammatic models forces a resolution of some ambiguities in the notation, for example, in statecharts, regarding whether events are queued or ignored if they arrive at a time when the target object is not in a state in which they can be accepted (in the formalisations given here, they are ignored).

The translation process is important in practical software development since it enables a combination of analysis and specification expertise to be applied to systems, with formal specifications being used to review and improve the informal specifications. It also supports the introduction of formal methods in an incremental way into current industrial practice, rather than these methods supplanting existing techniques, with a resulting loss of skills and cost of training.

3.1 Formalisation of Object Models

3.1.1 Z++

There are two main OMT models which form the input to the formalisation process. The first is the *Object Model* which describes the entities involved in the system, and their attributes, operations and the relationships between them (including inheritance or subtyping). A simple object model, describing railway stations which consist of sets of track sections, is shown in Figure 3.1.

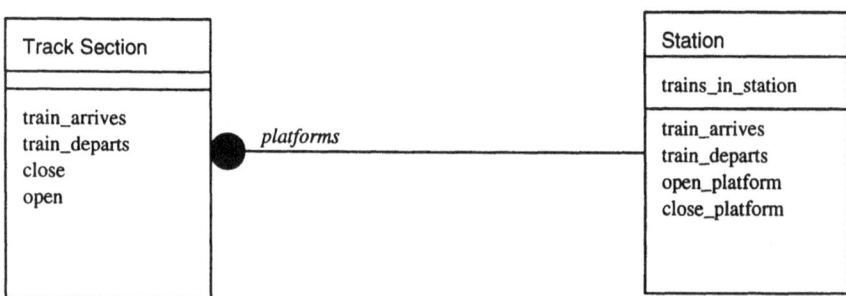

Figure 3.1: Object Model of Station

The textual requirements corresponding to this description are:

- a *track section* is a defined contiguous segment of track which can be occupied by at most one train at any time. In addition, it may be closed (eg, for engineering work) so that no trains may enter the section. A train will take a minimum of 60 seconds to clear a track section, and a closed track section will be closed for a minimum of 120 seconds;

- a *station* consists of a set of track sections, called *platforms*. There is an upper bound on the number of trains which may be in the station at any time, and this upper bound is at most the number of platforms. There are operations to allow the entry of a train to a specified platform of the station, to allow departure of a train, and to close and open a specified platform.

These models are used to build an initial outline specification, which will later be enhanced by consideration of the dynamic model, and by the addition of semantic detail which could not be expressed in the structured models.

The formalisation process for Z^{++} is as follows:

1. for each entity C in the object model, create a Z^{++} object class C;

2. each attribute of C becomes an attribute of C, with corresponding type. Initial values for attributes can be formalised as assignments within the initialisation operation **Init** of C;

3. each association r between entities C and D is examined to determine if both directions of the association are required in the final system. The required directions are then formalised as attributes r_1 of C, of type D (in the case of a many-one or one-one association from C to D), or of type $\mathbb{F}(D)$ or seq(D) (in the case of an unordered or ordered many-many or one-many association from C to D, respectively). Similarly for the inverse map r_2 from D to C, if this is required;

4. operations to manage associations – to add or remove links or to add or remove elements from multi-valued links – are added to each class in which a direction of the association is expressed by an attribute;

5. if D inherits from C, then the clause **EXTENDS** C is placed in the header of D. Conformant subtypes are expressed via suitable $\sqsubseteq$ assertions;

6. Operations are translated into outline specifications of operations, with however all signatures being completed;

7. formalisation of all assertions on an object model can be attempted, using the **INVARIANT** and **HISTORY** components of a class.

In the case of the Station system, we have the initial formal classes **TrackSection** and **Station**:

```
CLASS TrackSection
OPERATIONS
   init :  →;
   train_arrives :  →;
   train_departs :  →;
   open :  →;
   close :  →
END CLASS
```

By default, methods of this class are executed in mutual exclusion of each other and themselves. Further discussion of this point is given in Chapter 4.

```
CLASS Station
OWNS
    platforms :  seq(TrackSection);
    max_trains :  N;
    trains_in_station :  N
INVARIANT
    #platforms  =  #ran(platforms) ∧
    trains_in_station  ≤  max_trains   ∧
    max_trains  ≤  #platforms
OPERATIONS
    init :  →  ;
    train_arrives :  N  →;
    train_departs :  N  →;
    open_platform :  N  →;
    close_platform :  N  →  ;
    add_platform :  TrackSection  →;
    remove_platform :  TrackSection  →;
    set_max_trains :  N  →
ACTIONS
    init  ==>
            platforms'  =  〈 〉  ∧
            max_trains'  =  0 ∧ trains_in_station'  =  0;
    add_platform ts?  ==>
            platforms'  =  platforms  ⌒ 〈 ts? 〉;
    remove_platform ts?  ==>
            ran(platforms')  =  ran(platforms) \ { ts? } ∧
            trains_in_station'  ≤  max_trains'  ∧
            max_trains'  ≤  #platforms';
    set_max_trains mt?  ==>
            PRE mt?  ≤  #platforms ∧ trains_in_station  ≤  mt?
            THEN
              max_trains'  =  mt?
            END
HISTORY
    ∀ ts :  TrackSection •  #active(add_platform(ts)) +
                                #active(remove_platform(ts))  ≤  1
END CLASS
```

$⌒$ denotes sequence concatenation, whilst # is used for the size of sets and sequences. The history constraint formalises the assertion "no platform can be added and removed simultaneously". It states that no more than one invocation of the forms **add_platform(ts)** and **remove_platform(ts)** can ever be executing at any time, where the platform reference **ts** is the same for these invocations. As in Z, inputs to an operation are indicated by a ? decoration, whilst outputs have a ! decoration.

The **remove_platform** operation allows the ordering of the set of platforms to change completely as a result of removing one platform. A more refined and less non-deterministic version which preserves the ordering could also be specified.

Specification enhancement of this class will lead to further constraints upon its behaviour which prevent **close_platform** being performed on a platform which is occupied by a train, for example, and which therefore bring it into closer alignment with the real world situation being handled.

Identification of the detailed semantics of the non-structural operations is a step completed within the specification enhancement stage.

The **platforms** association has been formalised as a sequence, rather than as a set. This is an example where requirements revision has occurred as a result of initial formalisation – the recognition that the attribute should properly be ordered to reflect the domain properties leads to the (retrospective) addition of an {**ordered**} annotation on the TrackSection side of the association.

Internal consistency checking of this class could be performed even at this early stage. It would identify the necessity of the precondition on **set_max_trains** in order to preserve the invariant if this operation was to be applied. Similarly, it would identify that $Inv'_{Station}$ does not need to be explicitly stated in the definition of **add_platform**, as this operation cannot violate the invariant.

3.1.2   VDM^{++}

The formalisation process for VDM^{++} is very similar. It consists of defining VDM^{++} classes **C** for each entity C in the object model, with attributes as specified in the object model (with VDM^{++} types being used). Associations from C become attributes in **C** of type @**D**, $\mathbb{F}$(@**D**) or seq(@**D**) where D is the entity at the other end of the association. Again it may not be necessary to formalise both directions of every association. Operations are created to manage the required directions of the association. For instance, for a single-valued association r from D to C, an operation

```
set_r1(cc: @C) ==
    [ext wr r1
     post r1 = cc]
```

would be defined, where **r1** is the formalisation of the direction of r from D to C as an attribute of **D**. For a many-valued association there would be operations to add and remove an element of the association destination type from the corresponding attribute (compare with the shapes and points example of Chapter 2).

Inheritance is represented by **is subclass of** clauses.

A more complex example of an object model, involving inheritance and composed associations, is given by the following model of a system designed to organise personnel data.

The requirements for the system are:

1. to allow the management of facts about the age and employment status of a set of people;

2. for every person in the system a record should be kept of their address and age. It should be possible to add and remove people from the system;
3. for every working person a record should be kept of their current jobs, together with the salary and employer for each job;
4. an operation to return the total salary of a working person should be provided, and an operation to determine if a person is under the legal full-time employment age and is working.

We infer from these requirements that every working person is a person, ie, that there is a semantic subtyping relationship between these entities.

An OMT object model of the domain covered by the requirements is given in Figure 3.2. The significant step here is the decomposition of the many-many relationship between **WorkingPerson** and **Employer** into two many-one relationships. This representation is essential here, since the attribute **salary** is attached to the elements of this many-many association, rather than being part of the source or destination entity. A modelling approach using an attributed association could also have been used, but the resulting formalisation would have been the same.

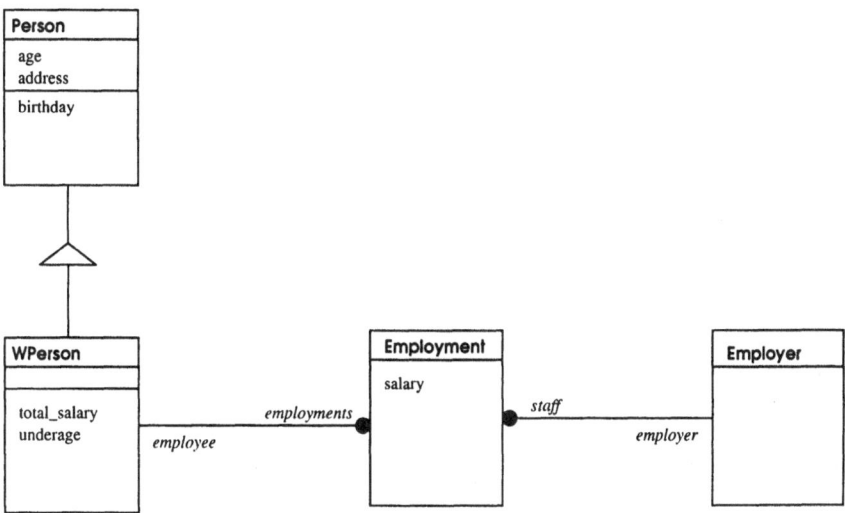

Figure 3.2: Object Model of Person System

This transformation has been carried out within the graphical notation, rather than within the formal specification. Alternative approaches are discussed in Section 3.3 and in Chapter 4.

Following the above procedure for converting OMT object models into VDM^{++}, we would obtain a set of four main classes, with mutual dependencies between **WorkingPerson**, **Employer** and **Employment**. Since the requirements do not mention any access from an employer to its set of associated staff however, this part of the analysis model does not need to be formalised.

We therefore have the following initial specification of **Person**:

```
class Person is subclass of PersonDefs
instance variables
  age: Age;
  address: String;
init objectstate ==
  age = 0 and address = []
methods
  change_address(nad: String) ==
      [ext wr address
        post address = nad];

  birthday()
    -- pre age < 200 ==
      is not yet specified;

  current_age() value a: Age ==
      ([ext rd age
        post a = age];
        return a)


end Person
```

Only some of the possible attribute access and modification operations have
been formalised – in this example an access operation for **address** and a modification operation for **age** would also be appropriate given the original requirements.

    The class

```
class PersonDefs
types
  Age = nat
  inv age == age <= 200;
  String = seq of char
functions
  Sigma: (seq of nat) -> nat
  Sigma(s) == if (s = [])
              then 0
              else hd(s) + Sigma(tl(s))
end PersonDefs
```

encapsulates types and functions which will be shared between several classes
in the specification.

    A **WorkingPerson** is a subtype of **Person**:

```
class WorkingPerson is subclass of Person
instance variables
  employments: seq of @Employment;
init objectstate == employments = []
methods
  total_salary() value r: nat
      is not yet specified;
```

```
underage() value b: bool
    is not yet specified
```

end WorkingPerson

The methods of this class are those of **Person** together with **total_salary** and **underage**. There are also operations to add and remove an employment which should be defined for **WorkingPerson**. **Employment** is the class:

```
class Employment
instance variables
  employee: @WorkingPerson;
  employer: @Employer;
  salary: nat;
init objectstate == salary = 0
methods

  set_employee(ee: @WorkingPerson) ==
    [ext wr employee
     post employee = ee];

  set_employer(ee: @Employer) ==
    [ext wr employer
     post employer = ee];

  set_salary(nsal: nat) ==
    [ext wr salary
     post salary = nsal];

  salary_value() value v: nat ==
    ([ext rd salary
      post v = salary];
      return v)
```

end Employment

An additional operation **change_salary** might be defined, encoding specific rules about how a salary should change (ie, that it, ideally, never decreases).

Finally, **Employer** is:

```
class Employer is subclass of PersonDefs
instance variables
  staff: set of @Employment;
  name: String;
init objectstate ==  staff = {} and name = []
methods
  add_job(ee: @Employment) ==
    [ext wr staff
     post staff = staff~ union {ee}]
```

end Employer

As discussed above, the variable **staff** and its associated operations could be dropped.

The structure of this specification is shown in Figure 3.3. This illustrates the close connection between the object model and the specification architectures produced from it. Note that although, in a mathematical sense **PersonDefs** is a supertype of **Person**, **WorkingPerson** and **Employer**, it is only being used as a shared set of definitions, rather than the description of an entity, and so we label these dependencies by **i**. The relationship between **Person** and **WorkingPerson** is however a genuine subtyping.

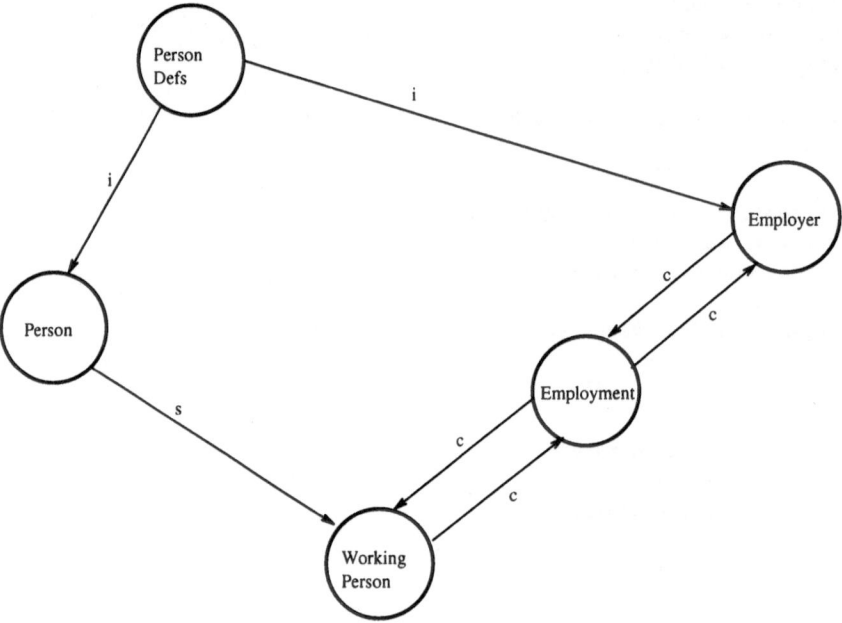

Figure 3.3: Specification Architecture of **Person** System

3.2   Aggregation

As an illustration of the use of mathematical formalisation of diagrammatic notations, consider the concept of *aggregation*. This has a variety of meanings in object-oriented methods, and even within particular methods it is often not precisely defined (Syntropy and Fusion being the exceptions). Thus an analyst or designer cannot rely on the person who reads their diagrams and textual models having the same interpretation of what an "aggregate" means as themselves.

The best way to approach this issue may be to categorise different forms of association (binary, for simplicity) in terms of lifetime dependencies and the possibility of sharing. Method propagation properties follow from these choices, to an extent.

Consider an aggregation as consisting of a set-valued link **agg** from a class **Container** to a class **Component**. We only consider links between existing objects. In other words:

$$\forall \text{ct} : @\textbf{Container}; \ \text{cp} : @\textbf{Component} \bullet$$
$$\text{cp} \in \text{ct.agg} \ \Rightarrow \ \text{cp} \in \overline{\textbf{Component}} \wedge \text{ct} \in \overline{\textbf{Container}}$$

"If **cp** is a component of **ct** via **agg**, then both **ct** and **cp** are existing objects".

For each **ct** $\in \overline{\textbf{Container}}$ we are only interested in those **cp** which are or have been at some time in the life of **ct** an element of **ct.agg**. This is the set **Member_at_some_time** defined by

$$\textbf{Member\_at\_some\_time} \ ==$$
$$\bigcup\{t : \textbf{TIME} \mid \text{ct} \in \overline{\textbf{Container}}\circledast t \bullet (\text{ct.att})\circledast t\}$$

exp$\circledast$**t** denotes the value of expression **exp** at time **t**. Chapter 4 discusses the properties of this operator. $\bigcup$ is "distributed union" and takes the union of all the sets in the collection given as its argument.

Then the three categories which are relevant to whether an association is an "aggregation" are:

1. **binding**: whether the component can exist without being part of this aggregate:

   $$\text{cp} \in \text{ct.agg} \ \equiv \ \text{cp} \in \overline{\textbf{Component}}$$

   If the equivalence holds then removing the link **agg** between **cp** and **ct** implies deleting **cp** (it is *bound* to the aggregate). Additionally, for **cp** $\in$ **Member_at_some_time**,

   $$\text{cp} \in \overline{\textbf{Component}} \ \Rightarrow \ \text{ct} \in \overline{\textbf{Container}}$$

   follows from the equivalence, so that the lifetime of the component is contained in that of the container. Otherwise the lifetime of **cp** can strictly exceed that of this instance of **agg** (*unbound*);

2. **replaceability**: whether the container can exist without having this particular value in the aggregation **agg**:

   $$\text{cp} \in \text{ct.agg} \ \equiv \ \text{ct} \in \overline{\textbf{Container}}$$

   If the equivalence holds then the value of **ct.agg** must remain unchanged for its lifetime. For **cp** $\in$ **Member_at_some_time** we have

   $$\text{ct} \in \overline{\textbf{Container}} \ \Rightarrow \ \text{cp} \in \overline{\textbf{Component}}$$

   so that the container cannot outlive any element which has been, at some time, one of its components;

3. **sharing**: whether two or more containers can share a common part:

$$\exists\, ct_1, ct_2 : \overline{\textbf{Container}} \mid ct_1 \neq ct_2 \bullet$$
$$cp \in ct_1.\textbf{agg} \cap ct_2.\textbf{agg}$$

Encapsulation (whether the **cp** can only be accessed by **ct**) is a further dimension that might be considered.

Table 3.1 lists the possible values for these categories, and their intuitive meaning. The second case is somewhat strange because it means that all con-

Unbound	*Replaceable*	*Shareable*	*Meaning*
×	×	×	is always part of one
×	×	√	is always part of
×	√	×	is part of one
×	√	√	part of
√	×	×	constant exclusive association
√	×	√	constant association
√	√	×	exclusive association
√	√	√	general association

Table 3.1: Categories of Aggregation

tainers which share a common component at any time in their lives must in fact have coincident lifetimes.

Figure 3.4 illustrates the general cases of the first four kinds of association listed above.

Some examples of these forms are:

- *"always part of one"*: cylinders (the machined holes, not the pistons that go into these holes) of a car engine. These cannot be shared between engines, replaced or removed from the engine. This type of strong aggregation occurs when we can identify a separate part of a whole entity, and when without this part the whole would cease to remain an entity of the same kind (an "engine without cylinders" is just a lump of metal). This is expressed by indexed inheritance in VDM^{++};
- *"is part of one"*: the relationship **is_division_of** between a division of a company and a company. This is unshareable, replaceable and bound: a division must be a part of a company (it has no separate existence), but the divisions of a company can change over time. Divisions cannot be shared between two companies;
- *"exclusive association"*: the relationship **is_wheel_of** between a wheel and a car, or **plays_for** between a player and a football team – wheels cannot be shared between different cars, but they can be removed from a car without either the car or the wheel ceasing to exist. Similarly for players of a team.

If **agg** is bound and unreplaceable, then operations of creation and deletion on **ct** must propagate to the elements of **ct.agg**. If it is in addition unshareable, then copy operations should also propagate.

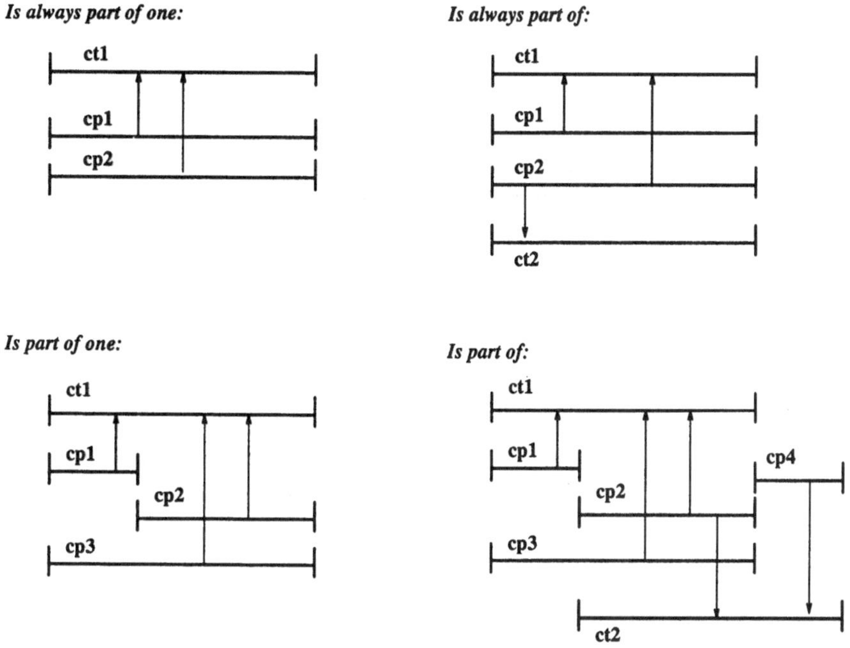

Is always part of one:

Is always part of:

ct1

cp1

cp2

ct1

cp1

cp2

ct2

Is part of one:

Is part of:

ct1

cp1

cp2

cp3

ct1

cp1

cp2

cp3

cp4

ct2

Figure 3.4: Aggregation Examples

We can express the "is always part of one" and "constant (shareable) association" aggregation forms directly in VDM^{++} and Z^{++}. For instance, if we have an aggregate of the form of Figure 3.5, then in VDM^{++} the class **Engine** would have a declaration:

class **Engine**
    is subclass of **Cylinder**$[1, \ldots, n]$

for a suitable (fixed) value of **n**. This means that there are **n** distinct copies of the features of **Cylinder** in **Engine**. Features **feat** of the **i**-th cylinder are referred to as **Cylinder**[i]'feat in **Engine**.

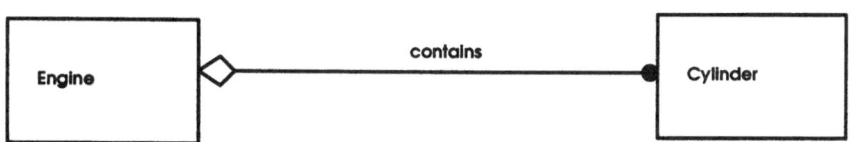

Figure 3.5: Engine as an Aggregate of Cylinders

As a result, components of an aggregation have a lifetime which coincides with the aggregation, and they cannot be shared.

In contrast, in Z^{++}, components of an aggregation are typically interpreted as constant object-valued attributes. The interpretation here would be:

CLASS **Engine**

FUNCTIONS
| contains : $\mathbb{F}(\overline{\text{Cylinder}})$

(using Z axiomatic definition notation). **contains** is a constant whose value is a finite set of (existing) object references. Thus the lifetime of the aggregation is contained in that of each of its components, but these components can, in principle, be shared, and continue to exist after their aggregate ceases to exist. Their participation in the aggregate is however coincident with its lifetime.

3.3 Alternative Approaches

Rather than formalising the operations of a system on a class-by-class basis at the analysis stage, it is also possible to defer allocation of methods to classes until the complete specification stage. This is useful in the case that the operations of the system involve the participation of several different objects, and where it is not clear what parts of the operation should be achieved within particular classes.

In the initial formalisation only the data aspects of classes would be formalised, and the operations of the overall system expressed in terms of the sets $\overline{\text{A}}$ of existing instances of each class, the attributes of classes, and the associations between classes (formalised as relations rather than as buried pointers). Thus for the personnel system described above, we could simply express the associations of the data model as:

$$\text{employments} : \overline{\text{WorkingPerson}} \rightarrow \text{seq}(@\text{Employment})$$
$$\text{employee} : \overline{\text{Employment}} \rightarrow @\text{WorkingPerson}$$
$$\text{employer} : \overline{\text{Employment}} \rightarrow @\text{Employer}$$
$$\text{staff} : \overline{\text{Employer}} \rightarrow \mathbb{F}(@\text{Employment})$$

with invariants:

$$\forall \text{wp} : \overline{\text{WorkingPerson}}; \text{emp} : \overline{\text{Employment}} \bullet$$
$$\text{emp} \in \text{ran}(\text{employments}(\text{wp})) \equiv \text{wp} = \text{employee}(\text{emp})$$
$$\forall \text{emp} : \overline{\text{Employment}}; \text{boss} : \overline{\text{Employer}} \bullet$$
$$\text{emp} \in \text{staff}(\text{boss}) \equiv \text{boss} = \text{employer}(\text{emp})$$

In other words, an association role is interpreted as a mapping from *existing* objects $\overline{\text{C}}$ of the class C at the end of the association opposite to the role name, to a possible instance of the class associated with the role. (Or to a sequence of set of such instances, depending on the cardinality or other annotation on the association.)

The class representing the overall operations of the system (termed the **Workspace** in VDM^{++} or **System** in Z^{++}) could then be specified abstractly by, for example:

create_person age_in? addr? pid! ==>

$$\exists \text{ oid}: \text{ @Person } \setminus \overline{\text{Person}} \bullet$$
$$\overline{\text{Person}}' = \overline{\text{Person}} \cup \{ \text{ oid } \} \wedge$$
$$\text{oid}'.\text{address} = \text{addr}? \wedge$$
$$\text{oid}'.\text{age} = \text{age\_in}? \wedge$$
$$\text{pid}! = \text{oid};$$

add_employment wp? emp? ==>
  PRE emp? $\notin$ dom(employee) $\wedge$
    wp? $\in$ dom(employments)
  THEN
    employee$'$ = employee $\oplus$ { emp? $\mapsto$ wp? } $\wedge$
    employments$'$ = employments $\oplus$
                   { wp? $\mapsto$ employments(wp?) $\frown$ $\langle$ emp? $\rangle$ } }
  END

In words, **create_person** selects an unused object identity from the type @**Person** and returns this identity, adding it to the set of used identities $\overline{\text{Person}}$. The address and age of the new person are set appropriately.

    add_employment adds a new (not previously assigned) employment to an existing working person. Syntropy notation could be used to support clearer specification of composed relationships and attributes in this style, together with abbreviations such as $\{a_1, \ldots, a_n\}.\text{att}$ ("apply an attribute to a set of objects") for $\{a_1.\text{att}, \ldots, a_n.\text{att}\}$.

    In refinement, the abstract specification of the operations can be replaced by a combination of method calls on supplier objects (and new classes may need to be created in order to support such methods). Both Syntropy and Fusion use this approach, in part.

    An example of this approach is given in Chapter 4 and 5 for the dining philosopher system.

    The approach has advantages in terms of abstraction, however it implies a translation between two quite different perspectives on system design:

- **the relational database view:**
  - integrity of data is the responsibility of the overall system;
  - membership of relationships is globally known;
- **the object-oriented/distributed systems view:**
  - objects control their own integrity;
  - objects know what other objects they are connected to.

This translation becomes difficult when the abstract model makes reference to long chains of relationships between objects (eg, $\text{age} \, {}^\circ_9 \, \text{employee} \, {}^\circ_9 \, \text{staff}$ from **Employer** to **Age**, if we view attributes also as functions from their owning entity type to their declared type, and **staff** as being of type $\overline{\text{Employer}} \leftrightarrow$ @**Employment**). Such long chains should be eliminated during design and the system partitioned into several "local clusters" of groups of classes which refer to each other, but make few references to classes outside their cluster.

Exercise (3.1): Show that **add_employment** maintains the invariant which links the **employments** and **employee** parts of the association between Employment and WorkingPerson. Is the precondition necessary?

3.4   Formalisation of Dynamic Models

3.4.1   Z^{++}

In real-time or reactive systems the dynamic model, based upon Harel statecharts, is the most significant analysis model. A basic statechart consists of a set of named states and directed transitions between them (Figure 3.6). It specifies a transformation process which accepts input events (which trigger certain changes of state in the statechart, indicated by transitions whose name **t** is the same as the event) and generates output events **actions** as a result of executing transitions or entering or leaving states. There may be transitions which do not correspond to input events, but are *internal* or *automatic*. In this book we will name such transitions by τ_1, τ_2, etc. Transitions may be guarded by conditions **E** which prevent the transition from occurring if **E** does not hold. A *condition-triggered* transition is a guarded anonymous transition – it is assumed to occur as soon as its condition becomes true, subject to any timing constraints present.

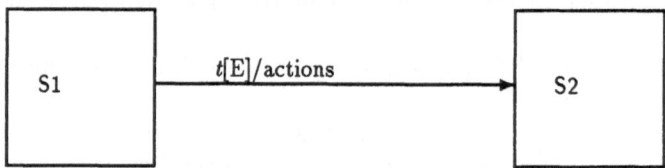

Figure 3.6: Statechart Transition from S1 to S2

We will also consider extensions of statecharts to include time bounds on transitions (see Figure 3.8 below). A timing indication $[\mathbf{l}, \mathbf{u}]$ on a transition **t** asserts that **t** cannot execute until at least **l** time units have elapsed since it most recently became enabled (ie, any guard condition **E** became true and its source state was entered), and must execute within at least **u** time units of the most recent time that it became enabled.

RTL notation will be used to express such models in the most general case – a definition of this notation can be found in Chapter 4 and Appendix A. The formalisation process for dynamic models is:

1. condition triggered transitions and anonymous (automatic) transitions are formalised as operations which are internally invoked, whilst event-triggered transitions are formalised as operations which are invokable from other objects;

2. states are formalised as elements of an enumerated set, and an attribute of this type is defined to record the current state. Methods formalising a transition modify this variable appropriately;

3. time bounds $[l, u]$ on transition t are expressed via the formula $\forall i : \mathbb{N}_1 \bullet \mathbf{fires}(t, i) \Rightarrow l \leq \mathbf{delay}(t, i) \leq u$.

   $\mathbf{delay}(m, i)$ abbreviates $\uparrow(m, i) - \rightarrow(m, i)$, the time that the i-th invocation instance of m waits for initiation of execution after its enabling or request time.

   $\mathbf{fires}(m, i)$ abbreviates $(\mathbf{self} \in \overline{C}) \odot \uparrow(m, i)$, and states that the i-th invocation does actually initiate executing at some time in the history of the object;

4. if the internal transition t has source state $S1$ and destination state $S2$ (assumed distinct) and guard condition **cond**, then:

$$(\mathbf{enabled}(t) \equiv (\mathbf{state} = S1) \wedge \mathbf{cond}) \quad \wedge$$
$$\forall i : \mathbb{N}_1 \bullet \exists j, k1, k2 : \mathbb{N}_1 \bullet$$
$$\clubsuit((\mathbf{state} = S1) \wedge \mathbf{cond} := \mathbf{true}, j) = \rightarrow(t, i) \ \wedge$$
$$((\mathbf{state} = S1) \wedge \mathbf{cond}) \odot \uparrow(t, i) \ \wedge$$
$$\downarrow(t, i) = \clubsuit((\mathbf{state} = S1) := \mathbf{false}, k1) \ \wedge$$
$$\downarrow(t, i) = \clubsuit((\mathbf{state} = S2) := \mathbf{true}, k2)$$

In words the quantified part of this formula asserts that t is (internally) requested exactly when it becomes enabled, ie, when the object is in the source state $S1$ of t and any guard condition is true. The formula involving the $\odot$ "holds at" predicate asserts that the guard condition is true at initiation of execution of t. The state change from $S1$ to $S2$ occurs at termination of t. If $S1 = S2$ then the last two conjuncts are omitted. If t is durative (in particular if $S1 \neq S2$) then the linear temporal logic properties

$$\Box(\underline{t} \Rightarrow \bigcirc(\mathbf{state} = S2))$$

defining the effect of the transition and

$$\Box(\underline{t} \Rightarrow \mathbf{state} = S1)$$

defining the permission for its execution can be used instead of the above more complex but more general statements.

If t has other sources and destinations then these can be generalised to use disjunctions of the form $\mathbf{state} = s_1 \vee \ldots \vee \mathbf{state} = s_r$ in place of the above equalities;

5. if t has an associated action **act** on supplier object **a**, then:

$$\forall i : \mathbb{N}_1 \bullet \exists k3 : \mathbb{N}_1 \bullet \uparrow(t, i) = \leftarrow((\mathbf{act}, a), k3)$$

That is, every time t initiates execution, a request for **a** to execute **act** is made. (We could alternatively specify that the request is only launched at termination of t, ie, in the target state.)

In an implementation the definition of t would involve an initial invocation **a.act**;

6. event triggered transitions are formalised in the same way, however they have:

$$\mathbf{enabled(t(p))} \equiv \mathbf{(state = S1)} \ \wedge$$
$$\forall \mathbf{i} : \mathbb{N}_1 \bullet \exists \mathbf{j} : \mathbb{N}_1 \bullet$$
$$\mathbf{(state = S1)} \odot \clubsuit \mathbf{(event(p), j)} \ \wedge$$
$$\clubsuit \mathbf{(event(p), j)} = \rightarrow \mathbf{(t(p), i)} \ \wedge$$
$$\mathbf{(state = S1)} \odot \uparrow \mathbf{(t(p), i)}$$

in place of the fourth definition above.

Each class corresponding to a statechart is mutex and self-mutex. In addition there are liveness constraints asserting that any non-terminal state must eventually be exited, and constraints asserting that states can only become true as a result of a transition into them. If there are no self-transitions on **S1** then the reachability or obligation assertion $\Box(\mathbf{state = S1} \Rightarrow \underline{t_1} \vee \ldots \vee \underline{t_n})$ states that **S1** can only be exited via transitions $\mathbf{t_1}, \ldots, \mathbf{t_n}$.

As an example, consider the statechart of track section objects shown in Figure 3.7.

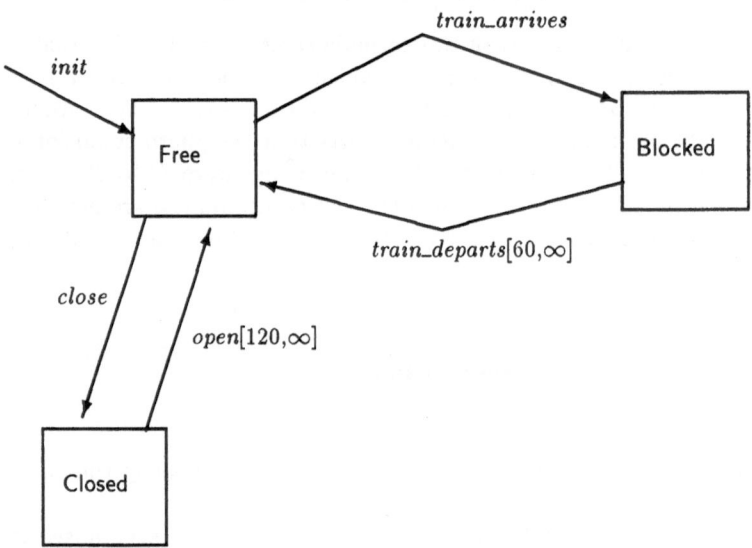

Figure 3.7: Statechart of TrackSection

Using this model, the initial formalisation of **TrackSection** is elaborated to produce:

CLASS **TrackSection**
TYPES
        / * **The state of the system is defined as an**
          enumerated type : */
   TState ::= **closed | free | blocked**

```
OWNS
  tstate :  TState
OPERATIONS
  init :  →;
  train_arrives :  →;
  train_departs :  →;
  open :  →;
  close :  →
ACTIONS
  init  ==>
          tstate'  =  free;

  train_arrives   ==>
          tstate'  =  blocked;

  train_departs   ==>
          tstate'  =  free;

  open   ==>
          tstate'  =  free;

  close   ==>
          tstate'  =  closed
HISTORY
```

/ * Mutual exclusion properties : */

mutex({ init, train_arrives, train_departs, open, close }) ∧
self_mutex({ init, train_arrives, train_departs, open, close }) ∧

/ * Permission predicates : */

□(train_arrives ⇒ tstate = free) ∧
□(train_departs ⇒ tstate = blocked) ∧
□(open ⇒ tstate = closed) ∧
□(close ⇒ tstate = free) ∧

/ * Definition of the transition effect : */

□(init ⇒ ○(tstate = free)) ∧
□(train_arrives ⇒ ○(tstate = blocked)) ∧
□(train_departs ⇒ ○(tstate = free)) ∧
□(open ⇒ ○(tstate = free)) ∧
□(close ⇒ ○(tstate = closed)) ∧

/ * Reachability properties : */

□(tstate = free ⇒ train_arrives ∨ close) ∧
□(tstate = blocked ⇒ train_departs) ∧
□(tstate = closed ⇒ open) ∧

/ ∗ State residence constraints : ∗/

$\forall$ i: N_1 • fires(train_departs, i) $\Rightarrow$ 60 $\leq$ delay(train_departs, i) $\wedge$
$\forall$ i: N_1 • fires(open, i) $\Rightarrow$ 120 $\leq$ delay(open, i)
END CLASS

There are additional logical properties which can be derived from the state-chart, however the above level of description is sufficient for most purposes and has the advantage of not explicitly referring to individual event times. The "definition of transition effect" predicates are redundant with the ACTIONS definitions of the methods, however they can be asserted in order to improve the clarity of the specification.

It is not easy to produce a dynamic model for a Station because this involves a structured value (a set or sequence) of another entity. Thus there are special cases concerned with the bound **trains_in_station** which complicate the description. In such cases it is often preferable to directly formalise the class concerned without creating an analysis model.

Specification enhancement of the **Station** class then produces the following:

CLASS **Station**
OWNS
    platforms : seq(**TrackSection**);
    max_trains : N;
    trains_in_station : N
INVARIANT
    #platforms = # ran(platforms) $\wedge$
    trains_in_station $\leq$ max_trains $\wedge$
    max_trains $\leq$ #platforms
OPERATIONS
    init : $\rightarrow$;
  ∗delta_trains : $\rightarrow$;
    train_arrives : N $\rightarrow$;
    train_departs : N $\rightarrow$;
    open_platform : N $\rightarrow$;
    close_platform : N $\rightarrow$;
    add_platform : **TrackSection** $\rightarrow$;
    remove_platform : **TrackSection** $\rightarrow$;
    set_max_trains : N $\rightarrow$
ACTIONS
    init   ==>
        platforms$'$ = $\langle\ \rangle$ $\wedge$
        max_trains$'$ = 0 $\wedge$ trains_in_station$'$ = 0;

  ∗delta_trains   ==>
        trains_in_station$'$ $\in$ 0 .. max_trains;

    train_arrives plat?   ==>
            PRE plat? $\in$ 1 .. #platforms
            THEN

                delta_trains ∧
                platforms(plat?).train_arrives
            END;

    train_departs plat? ==>
            PRE plat? ∈ 1 .. #platforms
            THEN
              delta_trains ∧
              platforms(plat?).train_departs
            END;

    open_platform plat? ==>
            PRE plat? ∈ 1 .. #platforms
            THEN
              delta_trains ∧
              platforms(plat?).open
            END;

    close_platform plat? ==>
            PRE plat? ∈ 1 .. #platforms
            THEN
              delta_trains ∧
              platforms(plat?).close
            END;

    add_platform ts? ==>
          platforms′ = platforms ⌢ ⟨ ts? ⟩;

    remove_platform ts? ==>
          platforms′ = squash(platforms ▷ { ts? }) ∧
          trains_in_station′ ≤ max_trains′ ∧
          max_trains′ ≤ #platforms′;

    set_max_trains mt? ==>
            PRE mt? ≤ #platforms ∧ trains_in_station ≤ mt?
            THEN
              max_trains′ = mt?
            END

HISTORY
  self_mutex({ remove_platform, add_platform }) ∧

  trains_in_station = #act(train_arrives) − #fin(train_departs) ∧

  ∀ i : ℕ₁; ts : **TrackSection** •
          (trains_in_station ≤ max_trains)⊙↑(train_arrives, i) ∧
          (ts.tstate = free)⊙↑(add_platform(ts), i) ∧
          (ts.tstate = closed)⊙↑(remove_platform(ts), i)

END CLASS

The use of logical conjunction in a method definition simply specifies that all the conjoined properties should be established by the operation. If method calls are part of a conjunction then the predicates defining the methods being called are implicitly conjoined to the other requirements (such calls are only a convenient way of specifying a state change, they do not indicate that the listed method should actually be invoked in an implementation of the specification). Here, **delta_trains** is a common factor of those operations which may execute concurrently with a change in the number of trains in the station. The "looseness" provided by this conjunct enables the specification to allow concurrent execution of methods which affect the same variable (**trains_in_station**): the precise definition of how this variable changes over time is given in the history clause.

squash converts a function with a finite $\mathbb{N}$-valued domain into a corresponding sequence with the same ordering. For example, $\text{squash}(\{2 \mapsto a, 5 \mapsto b, 6 \mapsto c\}) = \langle a, b, c \rangle$.

$r \rhd S$ is r with all pairs (a, b) with $b \in S$ removed (range anti-restriction). This version of **remove_platform** is a refinement of the more abstract specification given above, since it preserves the order of the **platforms** list after removing an element.

The history constraint given here implies that of the previous version of the class, since no track section can be simultaneously in a **free** and **closed** state. Thus since neither **add_platform(ts)** or **remove_platform(ts)** affect **ts.tstate**, if the first can execute then the second will be prevented from executing until it terminates. This ensures mutual exclusion of **add_platform(ts)** and **remove_platform(ts)**. Self-exclusion is ensured by the first conjunct of the history constraint.

The invariant **trains_in_station** $\leq$ **max_trains** is ensured by the history constraint

$$\Box^\tau(\text{trains\_in\_station} = \#\text{act}(\text{train\_arrives}) - \#\text{fin}(\text{train\_departs}))$$

together with the guard on **train_arrives**. This is a very simple form of "load management", which involves a look-ahead in time to consider the possible resource implications of allowing an operation (here **train_arrives**) to commence execution, and prevents such an execution if an unacceptable loading could result.

Once an initiation of execution of **train_arrives** which results in

$$\#\text{act}(\text{train\_arrives}) - \#\text{fin}(\text{train\_departs}) = \text{max\_trains}$$

occurs, there can be no further such initiation until there is at least one termination of **train_departs**. Thus at all times the invariant is maintained.

Chapter 7 contains more detail on the treatment of statechart structuring mechanisms such as AND composition and nesting, and on entry and exit actions.

3.4.2 VDM^{++}

In VDM^{++} dynamic behaviour of objects of a class **C** is specified in the `sync` or `thread` clauses. In the `sync` clause, which describes the behaviour of *passive* objects, either an explicit history of an object can be given, as a *trace* expression involving operations on sequences of method names, or a set of *permission* statements of the form:

per **Method** $\Rightarrow$ **Cond**

are given, restricting the conditions under which methods can be invoked. This statement asserts that **Method** cannot initiate execution unless **Cond** holds: it has the same semantics as permission guards in Z^{++}. Such permission guards are often used within classes that describe *shared* objects, in order to enable such objects to maintain control over their internal consistency in an environment where they may have multiple clients.

Threads describe the behaviour of active objects, and can involve general statements, including a `select` statement construct allowing execution paths to be chosen on the basis of which messages are received first by the object, similar to related constructs of Ada or OCCAM. In addition a declarative form of thread which specifies that a particular action should be periodically executed can be expressed by a *periodic thread* of the form

```
thread
  periodic(interval)(action)
```

This asserts that (where possible) execution of **action** is initiated at the times t_0, $t_0 + \textbf{interval}$, $t_0 + 2 * \textbf{interval}$, etc, where t_0 is the time that the current object was started. It guarantees that the **i**-th execution of **action** takes place entirely within the interval from $t_0 + \textbf{interval} * \textbf{i}$ to $t_0 + \textbf{interval} * (\textbf{i} + 1)$.

As an example, in the **Person** class of Section 3.1.2 it would be required that the **birthday** method is executed once every year. This requirement would be formalised by a thread of the form:

```
thread
  periodic(31536000)(birthday)
```

Multiple periodic threads can be specified, although care is needed not to produce inconsistencies since the use of a thread implies that the class is mutex and self-mutex. Numeric expressions can be used to increase clarity:

```
thread
  periodic(365*24*60*60)(birthday)
```

may be preferred to the previous version, for example. In this book we will assume that the time unit is the second, although alternative units can be set.

An example procedural thread is:

```
thread
  while true do
    sel
      x >= 10  answer m1 -> a!m(x-10),
      x <= 10  answer m2 -> a!m(x),
      x = 10    ->  self!m3()
```

An object whose behaviour is specified by this thread waits for the first request of m1 or m2 to be received, unless $x = 10$, when it may directly proceed to execute the m3 method on itself, provided there are no outstanding requests for m1 (considered first) or m2. If $x > 10$ then it must wait for a request for m1, and will then execute $a!m(x-10)$ on the supplier object a. If $x < 10$ then it must wait for a request for m2, and will then execute $a!m(x)$ on the supplier object a. Having completed the execution of the statement associated with the select clause, the thread of control will return to the loop and this behaviour will be repeated until the object is destroyed.

Let statecharts be described by pairs (S, T) of sets S of states and T of transitions. The formalisation steps for dynamic models are then:

1. for an entity C with statechart (S, T) extend the VDM++ class C with methods for each transition t in T, parameterised with formal parameters taken from those of t, with types added;

2. create an enumerated type SE with elements for each state of S, and a variable svar : SE representing the current state of an object from the class C;

3. each method m representing a transition with source s_1 and destination s_2 has the outline specification

```
m(p: PType)  ==  [ext wr svar
                  post  svar = <s_2>];
```

The input parameter p will be utilised either in the history specification (or thread) of enhanced versions of the class, or in refinements of the definition of m.

m has the permission statement

```
per m  =>  cond(m, s_1) and svar = <s_1>;
```

where cond(m, s_1) is the condition (if any) guarding this transition in the chart. If m has several possible sources and destinations, then the guard is the disjunction

$$(\text{svar} = <s_1> \wedge \text{cond}(m, s_1)) \vee \ldots \vee$$
$$(\text{svar} = <s_n> \wedge \text{cond}(m, s_n))$$

of all the possible source states $s_1, \ldots, s_n$ and enabling conditions $\text{cond}(m, s_1), \ldots, \text{cond}(m, s_n)$. The method postcondition is a conditional statement selecting the appropriate poststate on the basis of the prestate;

4. the initial state **ini** is represented by the initialisation

```
init svar ==  svar = <ini>;
```

5. the chart is represented by a thread specification:

```
while true do
   sel (svar = <s_1> and cond(m,s_1)) answer m ->
                                      action(m,s_1),
   ...;
```

where **action(m, s_1)** expresses any remote transition invocations associated with transition **m** from s_1, on the appropriate supplier objects: if the chart for **C** invokes operations on supplier chart instances $g_1 : D_1, \ldots,$ $g_m : D_m$, then these suppliers need to be declared as instance variables $g_i : @D_i$. Automatic transitions are invoked (on **self**) in the statement part of a select clause, and do not appear in the answer statement part of a select clause;

6. where several transitions lead away from the same state, the user must provide a priority order for the transitions. The select statement then lists the corresponding select clauses in this order.

The separation between the method definition for a transition, and the actions generated by this transition, is in order that callers of the method perceive it as being almost "instantaneous" (which is the statechart model of such transitions). Thus its definition should be the minimum possible: defining the change of state, and the transfer of any input parameters to suitable internal object data. The caller is then released to execute concurrently with the generated actions, which take place *in the state resulting from the transition*.

The thread described above is an infinite loop which always ensures that transitions are available to initiate execution if they are enabled. In addition it allows "timeouts" – execution of internal transitions provided that no higher priority external transition is not requested.

The above approach omits consideration of time-dependency in enabling conditions, or time bounds on transitions (or state residence). The general form of a timed transition is given in Figure 3.8.

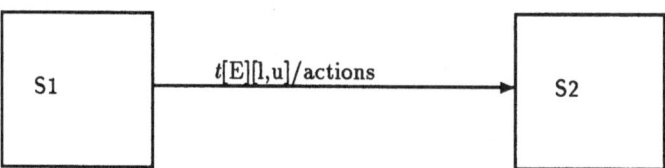

Figure 3.8: General Form of Timed Transition

In VDM[++] there is a global time-valued variable **now**, which gives the current time (assumed to be a non-negative real number). We can use a local time-valued variable **lastentered** to record the last time that a state was entered (ie, the last time that a transition terminated).

Constraints [l, u] on the delay of a method **m** from the time that its enabling condition holds until it fires become expressed as inequalities:

```
(now  <=  lastentered + u)  and  (lastentered + l  <=  now)
```

in the condition of the select clause controlling the firing of the method. This prevents execution of **m** until at least l time units from the time that the source state of the transition was entered. Again, there may be several (**source, destination**) cases to be accounted for in this specification, and each may have a timing constraint.

The equality **lastentered = now** is added to the postcondition of every method specification of a state-changing transition. Constraints on the duration of activities can be expressed using the value of **now** $-\overline{\text{now}}$. $\overline{\text{now}}$ denotes the time at initiation of the method in whose definition it occurs. An example is given below.

Monitor and Gate

The following is a standard example of a real-time and reactive system problem [242]. It involves two components: a track monitor which determines the location of a train on the track with respect to a level crossing, and the gate controller for the level crossing. Timing aspects are critical in this problem, and there is a safety obligation (that the gate is always closed when a train is passing the crossing) which can only be proved by detailed examination of timing constraints. Thus, if we wish to prove the system safe at an early development stage, we need to use a language which allows the expression of such properties.

The system is required to monitor a section of railway track, and to ensure that the gate of the associated level crossing is always down at all time points near to the time at which the train crosses the track of the crossing. A "safe period" of at least 100 seconds is required.

Since this system is a combination of software and hardware elements, these requirements are primarily constraints on the available hardware and its responsiveness, as much as on the software controlling this hardware. Once specific hardware elements have been chosen, the problem becomes one of specifying these elements in a formal language so that safety proofs can be undertaken.

OMT statecharts of the system, divided into a **Monitor** class and a **Gate** class are given in Figures 3.9 and 3.10.

The τ transitions are purely internal to a particular statechart, and represent spontaneous actions which are performed some interval after their source state is entered. In the case of the τ_4 transition, this execution can be interrupted at any point before the transition fires, and overridden by a transition **lower** to the **MoveDown** state. Such transitions really model the duration of residence of their source states.

The formalisation of **Gate** is:

```
class Gate
types
  GateState = <up> | <movedown> | <down> | <moveup>
```

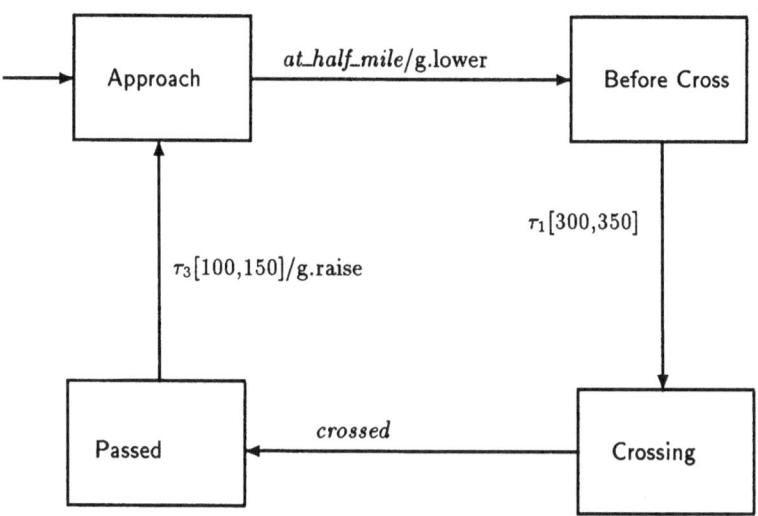

Figure 3.9: Statechart of Monitor

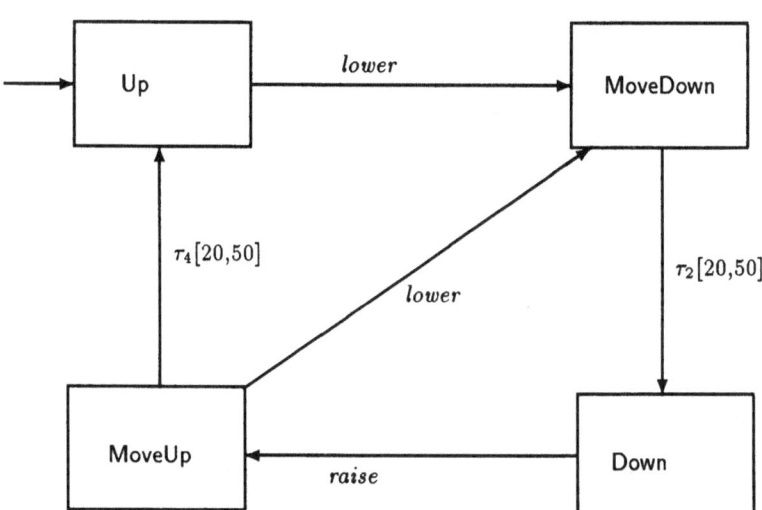

Figure 3.10: Statechart of Gate

```
instance variables
  gstate: GateState;
  lastentered: real;
init objectstate ==  gstate = <up> and
                     lastentered = now
methods
  lower()  ==
    [ext wr gstate, lastentered
     post gstate = <movedown> and
          lastentered = now];

  tau2() ==
    [ext wr gstate, lastentered
     post gstate = <down> and
          lastentered = now];

  raise() ==
    [ext wr gstate, lastentered
     post gstate = <moveup> and
          lastentered = now];

  tau4() ==
    [ext wr gstate, lastentered
     post
        gstate = <up> and
        lastentered = now]

sync
  per  lower  => (gstate = <up> or gstate = <moveup>);
  per  tau2   => gstate = <movedown>;
  per  raise  => gstate = <down>;
  per  tau4   => gstate = <moveup>

thread
  while true do
      sel (gstate = <up>) answer lower,
          (gstate = <movedown>  and
             now <= lastentered + 50  and
             lastentered + 20 <= now)  ->  self!tau2(),
          (gstate = <down>) answer raise,
          (gstate = <moveup>) answer lower,
          (gstate = <moveup> and
             now <= lastentered + 50  and
             lastentered + 20 <= now)  -> . self!tau4()

end Gate
```

The permission statements are redundant here, because the presence of **answer m** statements in a thread indicates that **m** can *only* be executed when the execution of the object thread is at such an answer statement, ie, when the relevant condition in the select clause is true. **tau2** and **tau4** do not have answer statements because they are purely internal to the object and cannot be invoked by external clients but only by the **self** object. This is an example of a discipline of concurrent specification which is described in Appendix B.

The absence of any time constraints on **lower** and **raise** imply that these transitions are driven by external events which may occur at any time. In contrast, the **movedown** and **moveup** states must be exited within a particular minimum and maximum time after they were entered.

The **Monitor** class is:

```
class Monitor
types
  MonitorState = <approach> | <beforecross> | <crossing> | <passed>
instance variables
  g: @Gate;
  mstate: MonitorState;
  lastentered: real;
init mstate, lastentered ==  mstate = <approach> and
                             lastentered = now
methods
  at_half_mile() ==
    [ext wr mstate, lastentered
      post mstate = <beforecross> and
        lastentered = now];

  tau1() ==
    [ext wr mstate, lastentered
      post mstate = <crossing> and
        lastentered = now];

  crossed() ==
    [ext wr mstate, lastentered
      post mstate = <passed> and
        lastentered = now];

  tau3() ==
    [ext wr mstate, lastentered
      post mstate = <approach> and
        lastentered = now]

sync
  per at_half_mile =>   mstate = <approach>;
  per tau1 =>   mstate = <beforecross>;
  per crossed =>   mstate = <crossing>;
  per tau3 =>  mstate = <passed>

thread
  while true do
      sel (mstate = <approach>) answer at_half_mile ->  g!lower(),
        (mstate = <beforecross> and
```

```
          now <= lastentered + 350 and
          lastentered + 300 <= now)  -> self!tau1(),
   (mstate = <crossing>  and
      now = lastentered) answer crossed,
   (mstate = <passed> and
      now <= lastentered + 150 and
      lastentered + 100 <= now)    ->
                                    (self!tau3();
                                     g!raise())
```

end Monitor

In this specification the invocation of an action of the **Gate** is expressed directly as a method call, specified to occur after the internal state transition of the **Monitor**[1]. **Monitor** is a client of **Gate** because it sends messages (commands) to the gate.

Finally, we can produce different configurations of the system, such as two monitors controlling a single gate, by appropriate choice of workspace specification. For example, we could have:

```
class Workspace
instance variables
  mon1, mon2: @Monitor;
  gate1: @Gate
methods

  initialise() ==
    (mon1 := Monitor!new;
    mon2 := Monitor!new;
    gate1 := Gate!new;
    topology [ext wr mon1, mon2
              post mon1.g = gate1 and mon2.g = gate1];
    gate1!start;
    mon1!start;
    mon2!start)
```

end Workspace

The monitors **mon**1 and **mon**2 are assumed to represent distinct objects – this is ensured by the semantics of **new**, in that it always returns a previously unutilised object identity.

A **topology** statement defines how the objects of a system are linked together. It has the syntax of a specification statement, except that attributes of a supplier object may be accessed via the notation **object.attribute**.

A **start** invocation initiates the execution of the thread of the target object – control then returns immediately to the callers flow of control. The gate is started before the monitors because the latter can invoke operations on the

---

[1] There are alternative interpretations of the ordering of transitions, transition actions and exit/entry actions – for instance see [64].

gate. We must ensure that the gate always exists when such invocations are made.

A **Workspace** corresponds to a **System** class in Z^{++}: it lists all the global operations which an external user can apply to the system (here, just an operation to initiate the system).

Reasoning about the temporal properties of the system, to prove its safety constraint, can be undertaken using the **now** variable and the individual state variables. An example of this will be given in Chapter 6.

3.5 The Booch Method

3.5.1 Class Diagrams

Booch class diagrams can be interpreted as a set of outline Z^{++} or VDM^{++} class specifications as for OMT. The formal language allows informally expressed constraints (such as "the devices managed by a particular environmental controller are not managed by any other controller") to be precisely expressed. If the class concerned is:

CLASS **Environmental_Controller**
OWNS
  lights : $\mathbb{F}$ **Light**;
  heater : **Heater**
  ⋮
END CLASS

then the appropriate global constraint is:

$$\forall e_1, e_2 : \overline{\textbf{Environmental\_Controller}} \mid e_1 \neq e_2 \bullet$$
$$e_1.\textbf{heater} \neq e_2.\textbf{heater} \ \wedge$$
$$e_1.\textbf{lights} \cap e_2.\textbf{lights} = \varnothing$$

"For every two distinct environmental controllers e_1 and e_2, their associated heaters are also distinct, and they have no lights in common."

Similarly constraints that there can be at most **n** instances of a class **C** in existence at any time are expressed via formulae

$$\#\overline{\textbf{C}} \leq \textbf{n}$$

3.5.2 Object Diagrams

An important notation in the Booch method are object diagrams, which represent how objects are connected and how they take part in communication with other objects. These diagrams assist in the definition of methods, particularly in identifying what requests for method executions each method makes upon suppliers of the class, and in identifying higher-level constraints on the ordering and sequencing of methods. Figure 3.11 gives a simple example of an object diagram which shows a method invocation m_1 which leads to two successive calls m_2 and m_3 which form a *callback* in that the initiator object **a** is itself the target of one of the method invocations that it has generated. Outlines of

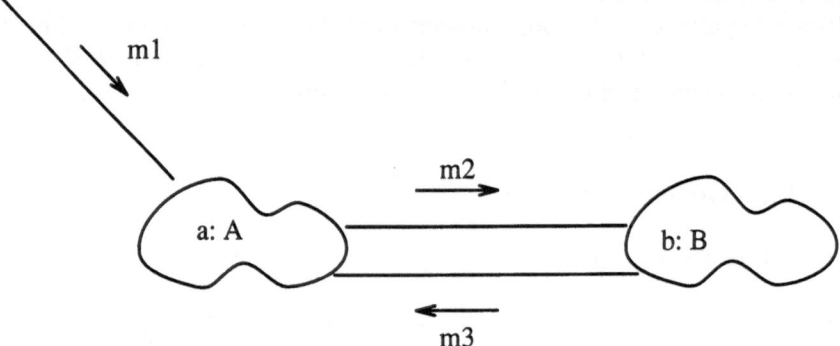

Figure 3.11: Example Object Diagram

the relevant formal classes could be as follows:

```
CLASS A
OWNS
  b: B
OPERATIONS
  m₁ : →;
  m₃ : →
HISTORY
  #fin(m₁)  =  #req(m₂, b)
END CLASS


CLASS B
OWNS
  a: A
OPERATIONS
  m₂ : →
HISTORY
  #fin(m₂)  =  #req(m₃, a)
END CLASS
```

Here the callback problem has been removed by requiring that the three method calls are sequentialised and non-overlapping: each invocation of m_1 must terminate in **a** before the invocation of m_2 that it triggers is launched, and similarly for **B**. This corresponds to a similar use of **threads** and select statements in VDM++ to remove overlapping method executions that result from callbacks (Chapter 7).

The particular method calling semantics adopted between objects (balking, timeout, asynchronous or synchronous) can be formally expressed in extended

RTL. For example, *balking* semantics asserts that a method call must be responded to immediately by its target object:

$$\forall\, \mathbf{i} : \mathbb{N}_1 \bullet \mathbf{fires}(\mathbf{m}, \mathbf{i}) \Rightarrow \mathbf{delay}(\mathbf{m}, \mathbf{i}) = 0$$

So either the invocation is not responded to at all or it is responded to immediately. Timeouts are a generalisation of this:

$$\forall\, \mathbf{i} : \mathbb{N}_1 \bullet \mathbf{fires}(\mathbf{m}, \mathbf{i}) \Rightarrow \mathbf{delay}(\mathbf{m}, \mathbf{i}) \leq \mathbf{timeout}$$

Scenarios will identify what are the required inter-connections between objects and classes, that is, which classes need to be clients of others. They also identify the signatures of methods and dependency relations between methods. The formal notations can again be used to define the precise semantics of a method, including its state transition behaviour, timing characteristics, preconditions and guard conditions.

Scenarios can be directly animated using an animation tool for event sequences in object-oriented specification, once a complete formalised specification for the required events has been produced.

3.6 Specification Construction Principles

In general diagrammatic models will be used as guidance for the construction of formal specifications, although the precise translation approach described above may not be used in its entirety. General principles for constructing an object-oriented formal specification are:

- identify the classes, based on the entities of the analysis models;
- identify the (required) relationships between classes, which will be represented by clientship, or by mathematical relations between class types;
- identify the attributes of classes – this may involve the identification of further inheritance relationships that were not apparent in the analysis models;
- locate operations in classes;
- construct operations by examining their textual requirements description and stated preconditions, partitioning their definitions into normal and error case operations if necessary.

It may be preferable to defer localising operations in particular classes until a later stage of development, and instead to initially write them as global operations as described in Section 3.3 and as in the Fusion method [58]. Formal specification of such "system level" operations can be carried out however, and later decomposed into method invocations and definitions at a design stage.

Real requirements are often extremely informal, incomplete or inconsistent. Written by domain experts, they will assume much knowledge which the specifier may have no access to. The specifier will often have to infer the existence of suitable data items or operations which have been implicitly assumed to exist by the user, without explicit description. An iterative process of requirements elicitation then ensues, with a gradual progression towards sufficient understanding (ideally!) being achieved. Requirements engineering techniques such as *task analysis* can be of assistance in identifying what are the real processes and steps used in the domain and required system, rather than simply those which have been textually described [157].

Exercise (3.2): construct analysis models and outline Z^{++} classes for the following set of requirements. Identify the preconditions of the operations and any class invariants that should hold.

- the system concerns the identification of radar tracks from a series of plots;
- the system takes as input plots, which arrive at (essentially random) time intervals. A plot contains a record of its arrival time, the range (distance) of the object causing the plot, and the bearing (direction) of the object causing the plot;
- a track is a sequence of plots arranged in increasing time order. Associated with a track is a status which can either be *confirmed* (a definite single object has been determined to be associated with this particular sequence of plots), *deleted* (if the track is no longer to be considered for extension by new plots) or *potential*, if no decision has yet been reached about its credibility;
- there are quality criteria which will determine which track(s) are the best candidates for extension by a new plot, and which tracks should be confirmed. If no existing track meets the quality criteria for addition of a new plot, then a new track containing just this plot is created;
- the following operations should be supported: add a new plot to the system; create a new track; confirm a track; delete a track.

The key aspects of this problem are identifying the classes and attributes, and locating the operations in classes. In addition there is an operation implied by the above requirements which is not explicitly listed.

3.6.1 Creating Method Specifications

A method such as OMT will produce method specifications from process descriptions on a functional model (akin to a data flow diagram in traditional structured methods such as SA/SD [303]). Booch, Fusion and Syntropy use an alternative form of operation specification consisting of a graph of objects involved in an operation, together with the messages passed between them. In order to create a formal method specification from a textual and diagrammatic process description, the data used by this process must be related to the formal state description of the object class for which it is a method. Then the transformations upon this data (expressed through natural language) must be given a specific interpretation as mathematical transformations on state and output data.

For example, assume we have a banking system with classes **Customer** and **Booth**, and an operation *Select_customer* which (once there is a free booth) selects the customer which has been waiting the longest, and assigns them to a free booth. We can arrive at a definition of the effect of this operation by drawing object instance diagrams of the state at commencement of the operation (the *prestate*) and at termination of the operation (the *poststate*). This can be a form of task analysis if it is performed by or in close co-operation with a user. In this case the transformation is almost trivial (Figure 3.12), but in more complex cases such diagrams can be very important in getting the formalisation correct.

Operation prestate:

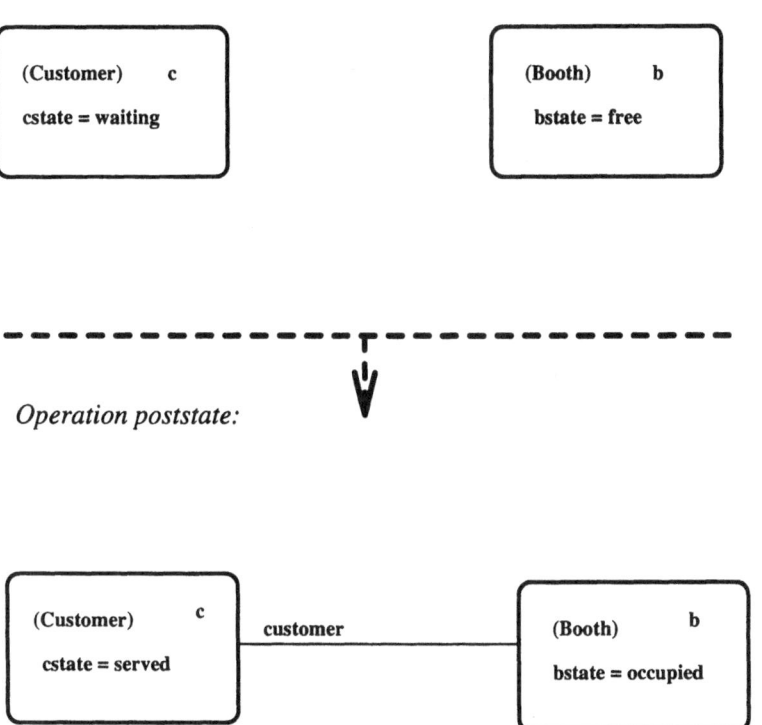

Operation poststate:

Figure 3.12: Pre and Post-states of *Select_customer* Operation

The operation can then be formalised abstractly as follows:

- Precondition: $\exists b : \textbf{booths} \bullet b.\textbf{bstate} = \textbf{free} \ \wedge \ \exists c : \textbf{customers} \bullet c.\textbf{cstate} = \textbf{waiting}$;

- Action:

      ANY c : **Customer**; b : **Booth**
      WHERE
          c $\in$ **customers** $\wedge$ b $\in$ **booths** $\wedge$
          b.bstate = **free** $\wedge$ c.cstate = **waiting** $\wedge$
          c.waiting_time =
              max({ cc : **Customer** | cc $\in$ **customers** $\wedge$
                                      cc.cstate = **waiting** •
                                          cc.waiting_time })
      THEN
          b'.bstate = **occupied** $\wedge$
          b'.customer = c $\wedge$
          c'.cstate = **served**
      END

under the assumption that we have outline formalised classes:

```
CLASS Customer
TYPES
   CState ::= waiting | served
OWNS
  cstate : CState;
  waiting_time : TIME
  ...
HISTORY
  waiting_time = residence(waiting)
END CLASS
```

```
CLASS Booth
TYPES
   BState ::= free | occupied
OWNS
  bstate : BState;
  customer : Customer
  ...
END CLASS
```

residence(state) gives the time that **state** has been occupied by the current object from the last time the state was entered continuously to the present. It is defined in Chapter 6.

The above operation is not located in any particular class, and its specification makes no assumption about the methods supported by **Customer** and **Booth**. After further analysis of the required system operations, we could arrive at the following method specifications in **Customer** and **Booth**:

```
CLASS Customer
  ...
OPERATIONS
  start_served : →;
  ...
```

```
ACTIONS
  start_served  ==>
       PRE cstate  =  waiting
       THEN
                cstate'  =  served
       END;
  ...
HISTORY
  waiting_time  =  residence(waiting)
END CLASS

CLASS Booth
  ...
OPERATIONS
  start_serving :  Customer  →;
  ...
ACTIONS
  start_serving c?  ==>
       PRE bstate  =  free
       THEN
                bstate'  =  occupied  ∧
                customer'  =  c?
       END
  ...
END CLASS
```

As a result, we can write the THEN clause of the action of the system operation as:

```
THEN
    b.start_serving(c)  ∧
    c.start_served
END
```

The system class (which encapsulates the overall required operations of an application) has the form:

```
CLASS System
OWNS
  customers :  F(Customer);
  booths :  F(Booth)
OPERATIONS
  select_customer :  →;
  ...
END CLASS
```

3.7 Animation

Animation of an abstract specification is a key means of validating an initial formalisation of a situation, and suggesting ways in which it should be enhanced. If tool support is available then animations can be presented in real time to the client, and immediate feedback gained on the correctness of the formalisation. The B AMN language [3], and the statechart formalism, both have such tools and animation facilities. Animation consists of identifying a set of *scenarios*, where a scenario is a sequence of events which may occur in the domain of the system, together with an initial system state. This sequence of events is then tested against the specification, starting from this initial state, to see whether the specification meets the user requirements in this scenario. Scenarios may represent both desired behaviour which the specification should allow, and undesired behaviour, which it should forbid. The latter type of scenario may, in the case of safety critical systems, arise from *hazard analysis* or other forms of safety analysis of the system requirements [234]. Animation is a form of testing which has a good ability to detect specification errors at an early stage, thus avoiding costs of reworks at later development stages.

Of course, it should be emphasised in such simulations that the interface of the animation tool need bear no relation to the eventual interface of the system being developed. Moreover, as with testing, it is an incomplete means of analysis for non-trivial systems.

As an example of an animation, consider the enhanced train control system of Section 3.4.1. Some scenarios which correspond to undesired situations that the specification of **Station** should forbid are:

- a train arrives at a platform whilst another is already present at that platform;
- a train arrival commences even though it will result in a violation of the constraint on the maximum number of trains present in the station;
- two train arrivals at the same platform overlap, with no intervening train departure from this platform.

These scenarios, informally expressed, must now be translated into particular histories of an instance of **Station**. In each case we will consider the starting state

$$\#\textbf{platforms} = 5 \qquad \textbf{max\_trains} = 3 \qquad \textbf{trains\_in\_station} = 2$$

with platforms 1 and 4 occupied. Scenario 1 is then the single event

↑**train_arrives**(1)

occurring when **platforms**(1).**tstate** = **blocked**.

As it stands, the specification of **Station** does not forbid this scenario. To see this, it should be realised that a call to a method of a supplier class in a client, at the abstract specification level, has no implication that the corresponding events of the supplier will occur – it simply is a means by which the relation between the pre and poststate of the client can be expressed in terms of existing relations provided by the supplier. If this relation can be achieved without an explicit invocation of the supplier method, then an implementation of the client method need not contain such an invocation. In this case the required post-condition of **train_arrives**(1) is that

platforms(1).**tstate** = **blocked**. But this is *already true* in the pre-state of this invocation! Thus no invocation of **platforms**(1).**train_arrives** is needed, and the synchronisation constraints of **TrackSection** cannot prevent the erroneous acceptance of the **train_arrives**(1) event by the station.

We identify that the problem is a neglect of the rule 5 of Section 3.4.1 for **train_arrives**. We should always require that this operation, when performed on a **Station** instance, invokes the corresponding operation on the appropriate **TrackSection** instance:

$$\forall i : \mathbb{N}_1; \ p : \mathbb{N}_1 \bullet \exists j : \mathbb{N}_1 \bullet \uparrow(\textbf{train\_arrives}(p), i) = \\ \uparrow((\textbf{train\_arrives}, \textbf{platforms}(p)), j)$$

(If **platforms** were a constant we could use $j = i$ here, because we could reason that **train_arrives** on a particular platform could only be invoked by the station that owns the platform via the **train_arrives** operation on this station.)

Similar assertions are added for the **train_departs** and other operations which involve requests for **TrackSection** operations. Thus we revise the specification to include these constraints. As with testing it may be necessary to re-run previous scenarios to check that these are still handled correctly by the revised specification. The present scenario is treated correctly by the revised specification since the permission guard **tstate** = **free** of **train_arrives** for a platform must now hold at each $\uparrow(\textbf{train\_arrives}(p), i)$ time in order for **train_arrives**(p) to execute – and this condition will not hold in the given scenario.

For scenario 2 we look at the following sequence of event times:

$$\uparrow(\textbf{train\_arrives}(3), i) < \uparrow(\textbf{train\_arrives}(2), j)$$

where no other events intervene (in particular, we are not assuming that the **train_arrives**(3) invocation terminates before the time $\uparrow(\textbf{train\_arrives}(2), j)$ that (**train_arrives**(2), j) initiates).

This scenario is successfully handled by the specification because at $\uparrow(\textbf{train\_arrives}(3), i)$ we have **trains_in_station** = 3 as a result of the assertion **trains_in_station** = #**act**(**train_arrives**) − #**fin**(**train_departs**) and the initial state (there is now one more activation of **train_arrives** and no more terminations of **train_departs** in the history of the **Station** object concerned). If the second event was to occur, then **trains_in_station** = 4 would hold at $\uparrow(\textbf{train\_arrives}(2), j)$ – which contradicts the permission guard for this method. Thus the class successfully forbids this scenario.

The third scenario is also forbidden by the (revised) specification. To see why, consider Figure 3.13, where $p3 = \textbf{platforms}(3)$. It is clear that $t2 \leq t3$ since **train_arrives** is self-mutex in **TrackSection**. But then the permission guard of **train_arrives** does not hold at the second $\uparrow((\textbf{train\_arrives}, p3), i)$ time unless an execution of (**train_departs**, p3) occurs in the interval $[t2, t3]$, which is not the case in this scenario. Thus the specification is valid in this case.

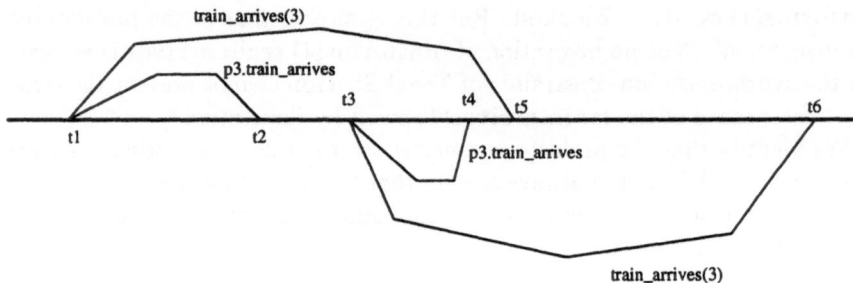

Figure 3.13: Hazardous Scenario – Multiple Arrivals at Same Platform

An animation tool which checks events has been written in SB-Prolog [174]. This tool provides operations to select a class, create an object of the current class, and to extend the history of this object. The following checks should be carried out for a new event **E** and time **t** (only some of these are currently implemented):

- check **E** is in the language of the class;
- check that **E** has not previously been accepted in this animation run;
- if **E** is $\uparrow(\mathbf{m}, \mathbf{i})$, that all permission guards for **m** are true, and that any formula involving **E**, **#act(m)**, **#waiting(m)** or **#active(m)** in the history constraint remains true, and any **delay(m, i)** requirements are true.
  There must have been a preceding $\rightarrow(\mathbf{m}, \mathbf{i})$.
  A state/inputs outside the precondition is flagged;
- if **E** is $\downarrow(\mathbf{m}, \mathbf{i})$, that all formulae involving **E**, **#fin(m)** or **#active(m)** remain true, and that **duration(m, i)** is as specified, and that all **duration(m, i)** requirements are satisfied.
  There must have been a preceding $\uparrow(\mathbf{m}, \mathbf{i})$;
- if **E** is $\rightarrow(\mathbf{m}, \mathbf{i})$, that all formulae involving **E**, **#req(m)** or **#waiting(m)** remain true, and that **i** is the previous value of **#req(m)** plus 1;
- at $\downarrow(\mathbf{m}, \mathbf{i})$ a possible new state is calculated from the state at $\uparrow(\mathbf{m}, \mathbf{i})$ and the inputs.
  The invariant should also be checked at this latter time.
  The write and read frame of methods should be given. This allows reasoning about interrupting executions – since if **n** starts during the execution of **m**, but **m** does not write any variables that **n** reads, then the pre-state of **m** can be used as that of **n**. At the implementation level **m** might also be decomposable into a series of read-only methods, followed by write methods. Co-executing methods can begin safely in the read-only part.

Exercise (3.3): Using the definition of **mutex** in Chapter 4, show why two methods $\mathbf{m_1}$ and $\mathbf{m_2}$ which are mutex can have overlaps in execution at a point, ie: why $\downarrow(\mathbf{m_1}, \mathbf{i}) = \uparrow(\mathbf{m_2}, \mathbf{j})$ can occur.

Conclusions

This chapter has described the basic elements of the requirements formalisation
step, using OMT and Z^{++} or VDM^{++}. Clearly other possible approaches for
formalisation, appropriate to particular environments, could be taken, but in
each case this approach should be systematic, documented and uniform across
a development. Such a process assists in creating specifications which have a
"natural" structure, correlated with that of the requirements documents, and
hence more accessible to a client. The precision of the translation means that
diagrammatic notations, particularly statecharts, could be incorporated into
the formal classes, with additional mathematical elements being written for
those properties which cannot be expressed in statecharts.

The VENUS toolset developed by Verilog, IFAD and CAP allows some
configuration in its translation between OMT object models and VDM^{++} class
descriptions. Associations are translated into embedded pointers in the classes
at either end of the association, although the user can specify that one or
other direction should not be formalised. Aggregation is interpreted as indexed
inheritance. By means of special-purpose notes, the user can write detailed
mathematical specifications within the OMT CASE tool.

There have been a number of other approaches to the integration of formal
and structured methods. These include the *rigorous review technique* used
by BT [12] and the SAZ method of York University [248]. There is a division
between those approaches which attempt to conceal the mathematical elements
of the method, either through the use of structured English as in [78], or through
the use of specialist staff separated from the main developers [79], and those
approaches in which the formal elements are central to the development process.
Our viewpoint is that the complexity of design requires a precise notation for
its basis, and that learning to use this notation is not a greater investment
of effort than learning a new programming language, or structured method.
Formal proof, if required, can be carried out by specialists, but all developers
should be familiar with the notation. Indeed, simple mathematical notation has
many benefits over unformalised natural language as a means of communication
of designs and specifications within a development team, as evidenced by the
application of Z^{++} to the development of static analysis tools described in [167]
and Chapter 1.

Animation has been recognised as an important issue in formal specification
for a number of years. The Prolog language has been used extensively for Z, for
example in [75], although only a small subset of the language can be effectively
animated in this way. An approach to animation of VDM is given in [31].

Chapter 4

Specification Notations and Techniques

This chapter will introduce a number of specification styles and techniques which can be used to develop specifications produced by the process described in the preceding chapter. It will also describe in more detail the Z^{++} and VDM^{++} specification languages, the formal requirements for subtyping in these languages and how these can be syntactically ensured.

The aim is to support the creation of "good" specifications. The idea of a "good" specification is not a precise concept, nevertheless guidelines have been produced, in the case of Z at least [129, 18]. For example, we should avoid complex mathematical expression of concepts unless this is really necessary – it is preferable to express an idea in a simpler mathematics, even if this may result in a less concise description. Whilst the ingenuity of a very concise means of expression might be satisfying to the specifier, the eventual reader of the specification might not be so pleased at being presented with a code-breaking exercise in order to understand it!

For similar reasons, specifications should be supplied with sufficient explanatory text – in the Z world it is often considered that the amount of this should equal the amount of formal specification text. This explanatory text should aim to link the formal specification elements to their meanings in the domain. The terms used in the formal specification should also not stray too far from the domain terminology. In the present methodology, the use of a close correspondence between analysis models and formal specifications should help to ensure these properties. If necessary, explicit reference can be made in the explanatory text to the analysis models. Guidelines for object-oriented specification can be found in [226, 225] and will largely be adopted in this book.

This chapter covers the stage of *specification enhancement* described in Chapter 2. Section 4.1 describes the role of the static data components of a class in formal specification. Section 4.2 describes the role of operations, and Sections 4.3 and 4.4 describe the roles of the inheritance and subtyping mechanisms. Section 4.5 describes class composition, and Section 4.6 gives examples of the way object identities are used in specifications. Section 4.7 describes a language for expressing real-time constraints which can be used with Z^{++} and VDM^{++}.

4.1 Attributes and Data Structures

The TYPES, FUNCTIONS, OWNS and INVARIANT components of a Z^{++} class formally describe the data of an entity or subsystem. In VDM^{++} these are the types, functions, values, instance variables and inv components – the only significant difference being that definitions of constant values are separated from the definition of auxiliary functions in VDM^{++}: both are described by *axiomatic definitions* in Z and Z^{++}.

4.1.1 Complex Attributes or Complex Classes?

The TYPES clause of a Z^{++} class contains a list of type definitions in the syntax of Z given set, enumerated set, schema type, free type or type abbreviation definitions. Unlike Z, class names can be used as types in these definitions. It is not usually necessary to define schema types in this clause. The type identifiers defined here must be unique within a class, and are available for use by all descendents of a class. They may be referred to in the qualified form **ClassName.TypeName**, by any descendent of classes **ClassName** which declare **TypeName**. If **TypeName** is unambiguous in the descendent class then it may be used on without qualification. In VDM^{++} name qualification of this kind is denoted by **ClassName'TypeName** and follows the same rules. There is no mechanism for hiding a local type from descendents.

Local types provide a means to define subtypes of the basic datatypes ($\mathbb{N}$, $\mathbb{Z}$, **String**, etc) which express the actual range of values which an attribute of an entity may take. Thus, in a system representing train speeds in miles per hour, a subrange type (in Z notation)

$$\textbf{SPEED} == 0..500$$

and declaration

$$\textbf{speed} : \textbf{SPEED}$$

would convey more meaning to a reader of the specification than the declaration

$$\textbf{speed} : \mathbb{N}$$

Such local types provide a means of detecting errors by type-checking, in the usual way: this facility is much the same as that provided by strongly-typed languages such as Pascal, although structural rather than named type equivalence is used in Z and VDM.

In a specification language however there is also the possibility of creating intricate mathematical structures, such as sequences of sequences of sets. It is our view that, at the abstract specification level at least, such structures are best avoided, and instead expressed via supplier/clientship relationships between suitable classes, derived directly from an analysis data model. Such structures are certainly sufficiently expressive, and lead to specification classes in which the most complex data structures involve only a single $\mathbb{F}$, $\rightarrow$, $\twoheadrightarrow$, seq or $\mathbb{P}$ operator (or other type constructor).

For example, assume we have a problem concerning the automatic monitoring of patient data in an intensive care unit [138]. The data structures here are maps from patient identifiers to sequences (representing time order) of time-stamped data readings. There may be a map for each attribute (if readings of one attribute are taken asynchronously with others) or a single map whose range includes all attribute values at each time.

In conventional Z we would probably arrive at a data specification such as the following:

Reading
timestamp : $\mathbb{N}$
attribute$_1$: $\mathbf{T_1}$;
$\dots$
attribute$_n$: $\mathbf{T_n}$

Reading is a schema used as a type – it encapsulates each measured patient attribute, and a timestamp identifying when the attribute readings were taken.

[PatientId]

PatientId is a *given* (unstructured) type representing the identifiers which will be used to distinguish patients.

PatientData
patient_readings : **PatientId** $\rightarrow$ seq(**Reading**)
$\dots$

           [other data management features]

$\forall$ pid : dom **patient_readings** $\bullet$
   $\forall$ **i, j** : $1 \dots$ #**patient_readings(pid)** | i < j $\bullet$
      patient_readings(pid)(i).timestamp <
      patient_readings(pid)(j).timestamp

PatientData encapsulates all information concerning patients and their readings up to a particular time. The sequences of readings for each patient are specified to be in strictly increasing time order.

The problems with this type of representation are that:

- it is a long way from an implementation in an object-oriented language;
- it leads to complex predicates involving several levels of data access (3 in the predicate of the **PatientData** schema);

- refinement relations must consider the entire data structure, and are correspondingly complex.

On the plus side, these structures are relatively free from implementation bias (that is, they can be refined in many different ways and do not force one particular implementation approach or language to be used), and they are presented in a short space of text, thus allowing more direct comprehension than if a number of separate classes were used.

The alternative approach is to construct an analysis data model of the system, and to formalise these data structures in classes directly from the analysis model. In this case we would have entities Patient, Reading and ICU (intensive care unit), with an ordered one-many association between patients and readings. As a result, we would have outline classes:

CLASS **Reading**
OWNS
   timestamp : $\mathbb{N}$;
   attribute$_1$: T_1;
   . . .
   attribute$_n$: T_n
. . .
END CLASS

CLASS **Patient**
TYPES
   ReadingSequence == seq(Reading)
OWNS
   reading_sequence : ReadingSequence;
   . . .
INVARIANT
   $\forall$ i, j : 1..#reading_sequence | i < j •
         reading_sequence(i).timestamp <
               reading_sequence(j).timestamp
END CLASS

The type **ReadingSequence** has been explicitly defined as it may prove to be a useful type in descendent or subtype classes.

CLASS **ICU**
OWNS
   patients : $\mathbb{F}$(Patient);
   . . .
END CLASS

In this specification the data types are close to those of an object-oriented language: instead of functions whose ranges are sequences of records, the most complex type involved is a sequence of object identities. There is also no need to distinguish patients and patient identities: the identities are provided automatically by the semantics of the language.

Although this book will mainly consider an approach in which the second specification is preferred over the first, we will consider the alternative development approach in Section 4.8 below.

4.1.2   Constant Data

The FUNCTIONS clause in a Z^{++} class contains a list of axiomatic and generic constant definitions in the sense of Z [276]. As in other clauses, class names can be used as types. This clause provides a means to define local functions and constants. The visibility of these items is as for local types. Additional predicates on existing constants may also be listed in this clause, as in Z.

The effect of a constant definition is to fix, for the lifetime of an object of the class, the value of the defined feature. Different objects of the class may however have different values, if this is allowed by the declaration.

As an example, consider the station system described in Chapter 3. A simplification of this problem would involve the additional sentence "The number of platforms is fixed" in the second paragraph of the requirements. As a result we could instead consider that there is an *aggregation* rather than an association between track sections and stations (Figure 4.1).

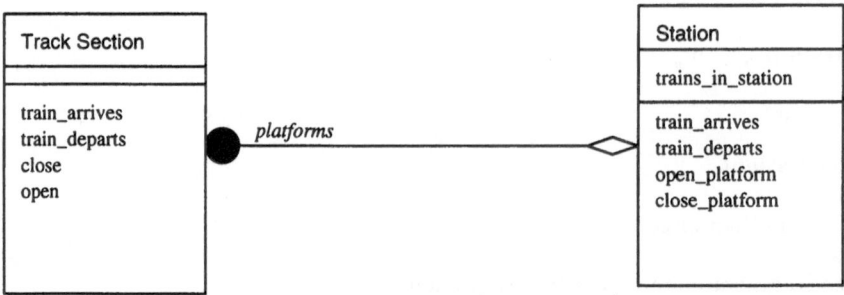

Figure 4.1: Revised Object Model of Station

Starting from these revised requirements, the declaration of **Station** is now:

CLASS Station
FUNCTIONS

$$
\begin{array}{|l}
\text{platforms} : \text{seq}(\overline{\text{TrackSection}}) \\
\text{pnumb} : \mathbb{N} \\
\hline
\#\text{platforms} = \#\,\text{ran}(\text{platforms}) \\
\text{pnumb} = \#\text{platforms}
\end{array}
$$

Typing declarations are listed above the line in an axiomatic definition, whilst logical constraints are given below the line. Here we have emphasised that **platforms** is a sequence of *existing* objects: this is the usual practice for constants.

OWNS
    max_trains : $\mathbb{N}$;
    trains_in_station : $\mathbb{N}$
INVARIANT
    trains_in_station $\leq$ max_trains $\wedge$
    max_trains $\leq$ pnumb

```
OPERATIONS
    init :  →  ;
    train_arrives :  ℕ  →;
    train_departs :  ℕ  →;
    open_platform :  ℕ  →;
    close_platform :  ℕ  →  ;
    set_max_trains :  ℕ  →
ACTIONS
    init  ==>
            ⋀_{p ∈ platforms}  p.init ∧
            max_trains' = 0 ∧ trains_in_station' = 0;

    set_max_trains mt?  ==>
            PRE mt? ≤ pnumb ∧ trains_in_station ≤ mt?
            THEN
              max_trains' = mt?
            END
```

END CLASS

with corresponding modifications at later development stages.

platforms is declared as a constant since one interpretation of an aggregation association is that the objects at the destination end of an instance of this association cannot be changed over the lifetime of the object at the source. Thus no operations to modify such links are required. However it is quite reasonable to apply methods to such constant object references, since methods do not change the value of the object identity (reference) – this style of specification is quite frequently adopted in Object-Z [188].

It is not specified which particular sequence of platforms is contained in the station, so that different instances of **Station** may have different sets of platforms – at a global system level it would probably be reasonable to specify that a track section can occur in at most one station.

A further example in which non-determinism is possible in the value that a constant has in a particular object is the following class:

```
CLASS TrafficLight
FUNCTIONS
    | in_amber :  ℕ_1
OWNS
    ...
```

END CLASS

where **in_amber** represents the time that the traffic light stays in the amber state. This must be at least 1, but is otherwise not constrained. Thus two different objects $tl_1, tl_2 :$ **TrafficLight** may have tl_1.**in_amber** $\neq tl_2$.**in_amber**. This definition allows the class to be specialised for particular purposes:

```
CLASS TrafficLight25s
EXTENDS  TrafficLight
FUNCTIONS
```

TrafficLight.in_amber = 25
```
END CLASS
```

represents traffic lights in which the time in the amber state is exactly 25 seconds. Since the identifier **in_amber** is unambiguous in this class, the constraint could be written more simply as **in_amber** = 25. This constant thus acts like a scalar parameter of the **TrafficLight** class, and inheritance is being used to instantiate it.

As will be seen in Section 4.4, this second class is actually a subtype of the first.

4.1.3   Data Invariants

The OWNS list of a Z^{++} class identifies the time-varying attributes of objects of the class, using the syntax of a Z state schema declaration, except that schema inclusion cannot be used (it is subsumed by inheritance, discussed in Section 4.3 below), and that classes can be used as types. The INVARIANT clause contains a predicate calculus constraint over these attributes and attributes from supplier and supertype classes.

The usual care should be taken to express invariants in a clear manner. For example, to say that a sequence-valued attribute **sq** has no duplicate elements, we could either use the formula **(i)**:

$$\forall i,j : \text{dom}(sq) \mid i \neq j \bullet sq(i) \neq sq(j)$$

or **(ii)**:

$$\# \text{ran}(sq) = \#sq$$

The first is more direct, and uses simpler mathematics, so would normally be preferred. However **(ii)** is not excessively cryptic, whilst **(i)** involves two negations and a quantification, so itself requires some inspection to ensure that it means what we expect it to mean. **(ii)** is slightly preferable for this reason.

In addition, specifications whose meaning is highly dependent upon the particular formalism of Z or VDM should be avoided. For example, in Z we could write

$$\textbf{graph}^+ \cap \textbf{id}(\textbf{NODE}) = \varnothing$$

where **graph** is a relation between nodes: **graph** : **NODE** $\leftrightarrow$ **NODE**, to state that there are no cycles in **graph** (r^+ for a relation **r** denotes the non-reflexive transitive closure of **r**, and **id(NODE)** is the identity relation on **NODE**).

This formula depends upon the fact that in Z relations and functions are simply sets of pairs – this formula would not be syntactically well-formed in RSL [111], VDM^{++} or in other specification languages which use a less specific representation of functions and relations.

Instead the formula could more generally be stated as

$$\forall \, a : \textbf{NODE} \bullet a \notin \textbf{graph}^{+}(\!\mid \{a\} \mid\!)$$

"for every node, it is not the case that it is reachable from itself by iterating **graph**".

It is sometimes considered that a "fear of quantifiers" exists for people new to formal methods, and that more functional alternatives to quantified formulae should be used. Thus for instance, we could write

$$\{p : \textbf{Philosophers} \mid p \in \textbf{philosophers} \land p.\textbf{pstate} \neq \textbf{eating}\} \neq \varnothing$$

instead of:

$$\exists \, p : \textbf{Philosophers} \mid p \in \textbf{philosophers} \bullet p.\textbf{pstate} \neq \textbf{eating}$$

$\forall$ can usually be eliminated in the same way.

Issues specific to the use of supplier and supertype object attributes in a class invariant are considered in Sections 4.3 and 4.5 below.

4.1.4 Object Creation and Initialisation

So far we have not considered how objects are to be brought into existence, that is, how elements of $\overline{C}$ for a class C can be created. An operation $\textbf{New}_C$ is provided for this purpose, and it has the specification:

```
NewC  c!   ==>
    ANY cval :  StateC;   c :  @C
    WHERE
        c ∉ C̄ ∧ c ≠ nilC
    THEN
        *'C  =  *C  ⊕  { c  ↦  cval }  ∧
        c!  =  c
    END
```

(in addition an appropriate representative of c! is added to each identified supertype of C in the specification).

This operation can be invoked in any method definition. Either the Z-style syntax $\textbf{New}_C[\textbf{out}!/\textbf{c}!]$ can be used to return **out!** as the new object identity, or the B AMN syntax **out!** $\longleftarrow$ **New**$_C$ can be used. It is provable that $\Box^{\tau}(@C \neq \overline{C})$, ie, at all times there are available "unused" object identities. Thus the above operation is always feasible.

At creation an object satisfies the invariant of the class. However if a more specialised starting state is required then an initialisation operation named **init** (in any case combination) should be defined to set up the appropriate state. As in C++, it is possible to define distinct initialisation operations with different signatures for the same class.

For example, in the **TrackSection** class of Chapter 3, we know from the dynamic model that the initial state of a track section should be **Free**, which we express as the operation init ==>   tstate' = free

in the formal model. **init** is by convention a predicate on $\mathbf{State}'_C$ (it makes little sense to refer to attributes of $\mathbf{State}_C$ in this operation since these will be arbitrary within the constraints of this type).

Usually **init** is required to be performed at the moment of object creation (this is asserted by an RTL axiom given in Appendix A). In this case its declaration and definition will be preceded by a *. However, as Meyer [225] points out, such a convention would lead to problems in general, especially with structures involving recursive object ownership. Thus unless **init** is declared as internal, it will be callable under client control (for an example, see the **Station** class given in Section 4.1.2), and does not necessarily occur at object creation.

init may take input parameters in the latter case, but will usually not have output parameters. It must be listed in the OPERATIONS clause.

VDM^{++} uses an initialisation predicate, rather than an initialisation operation. This predicate is assumed to hold at creation of an object, and it cannot invoke initialisations of other objects (via the **C!new**() operation of VDM^{++}), so that the problems of unbounded initialisation do not arise.

4.1.5   Generic Parameters

A Z^{++} class may be parameterised with a list of identifiers, denoting types:

CLASS C[$\mathbf{X}_1$, ..., $\mathbf{X}_n$]
...
END CLASS

These identifiers may be used as types within the body of **C**. The resulting construct is a *generic class* and may be used to construct other generic classes by composition, inheritance and subtyping, as usual. However it is not itself a class, and must be instantiated by a list $\mathbf{T}_1$, ..., $\mathbf{T}_n$ of actual types in order to be used as a class (this instantiation is denoted by $\mathbf{C}[\mathbf{T}_1, \ldots, \mathbf{T}_n]$). Library components are often specified as generic classes, in order to enhance their generality and reusability.

VDM^{++} does not support generic parameterisation of classes.

4.2   Operations

4.2.1   Method Declaration and Definition

The OPERATIONS clause of a Z^{++} class lists the signatures of the external and internal operations (methods) of the class. These signatures are presented as:

operation_identifier : IN $\rightarrow$ OUT

where **IN** and **OUT** are lists of types, possibly including class types[1].

The **RETURNS** clause has the same form, but the methods listed in this clause are assumed to only be predicates over the undecorated state of the class, and to not modify the class state. Method names must be unique within a class.

Since classes are designed to encapsulate complex data structures, it is usually not necessary to use complex type constructions in these lists. In addition, the signature of a method cannot be changed in refinements of a class, so that the signature types must correspond to types available in the eventual programming language of the executable version of the system, which implies that these types should usually be *basic*, that is, scalar types ($\mathbb{N}, \mathbb{Z}, \mathbb{R}$ or enumerated types or subranges of these types), strings, given set types or class types[2]. When modifications or access to a complex data structure contained in a class is required, this is then carried out in an element-by-element manner.

For example, in the **Shapes** development of Chapter 2, the class **Shape** contains methods of the following form:

Add_point : **Point** →;
Remove_point : **Point** →;
...
Add_point pp? ==> points′ = points ∪ { pp? };

Remove_point pp? ==> points′ = points \ { pp? };
...

which modify the **points** : $\mathbb{F}(\textbf{Point})$ attribute one element at a time. It was this characteristic which enabled direct use of the **Set_manager** library class.

The definition of a method is listed in the **ACTIONS** clause. Identifiers x? for input parameters are listed before identifiers y! for output parameters after the method identifier:

method_identifier x? y! ==> Definition

If a method listed in the **OPERATIONS** clause has no corresponding **ACTIONS** definition, then it is assumed to be the completely non-deterministic state transition on the class attributes and outputs: only the types of these items after the method execution may be assumed. (As a result, such methods will be marked as potentially inconsistent if a non-trivial class invariant is specified.) In VDM^{++} such undefined methods can be marked as intended to be defined in each subclass of the current class (that is, *deferred* or *virtual* definitions):

m(x: X)
        is subclass responsibility;

Alternatively they can be marked as intended to be defined at a later development stage of the class:

---

[1] By default, a class name **C** in a parameter type list denotes $\overline{\textbf{C}}$, the set of existing objects of **C**.

[2] Methods which are purely internal to a given class and are not intended to be externally called, do not need to obey this discipline if they are used only to clarify a specification but not to provide an implementation.

```
m(x: X)
        is not yet specified;
```

In Z^{++} a method may be marked as being callable only by the **self** object by prefixing its definition and declaration by a *. These methods are useful to express the specification of *active* objects, whose behaviour is internally determined on the basis of the current time or attribute values. As an extended example, see the traffic light specification of Chapter 7.

A method is defined using a combination of Z predicates, schema operators, B AMN *generalised substitution* forms, and method invocations. Different forms of construct are used at different development levels. At the most abstract level a method definition may use the following constructs:

- Z predicates, schema conjunction, disjunction, relational composition $\,\S\,$, and the iterated conjunction operator $\bigwedge$, where methods from the same class or from ancestors are used as predicates. $\Xi\mathbf{State}_C$ and $\Delta\mathbf{State}_C$ can be used to specify that all attributes of the class remain unchanged by an operation, or are all potentially modified by an operation. $\Xi(\mathbf{list})$ and $\Delta(\mathbf{list})$ have corresponding meanings for sublists **list** of the attributes of the class – however for these forms the class invariant is not included in the pre and post states;
- abstract B AMN constructs:
  - ANY **v** : **T** WHERE **P** THEN **Def** END;
  - PRE **P** THEN **Def** END;
  - CHOICE $\mathbf{S}_1$ OR $\mathbf{S}_2$ END;
  - SKIP – equivalent to $\Xi\mathbf{State}_C$;
  - IF **E** THEN $\mathbf{S}_1$ ELSE $\mathbf{S}_2$ END.
- direct reference to attributes of supplier objects, via the notation **object.attribute** or **object'.attribute** to refer to the values of these attributes before and after the operation.

However, method specifications using direct update of supplier attributes should be transformed into ones using calls to supplier object methods before production of the complete specification. They are included because they can be of use in devising suitable methods in the supplier classes, during a process of top-down design (cf. Chapter 5). In complete specifications the other forms given above can be used, and low-level procedural constructs (WHILE, VAR, sequencing, assignment) should not be used.

At the most abstract level, methods and method definitions are considered purely as predicates which express the transformation between the state **v** of the class instance at commencement of execution of the method, and the state **v'** at termination of execution of the method. A precondition **Pre** on a method m simply expresses the fact that only if the initial state satisfies **Pre** is there an obligation to satisfy the main definition **Def** of **m**. This is distinct from the notion of a *permission* predicate, which expresses that m *cannot* execute if a condition **G** is false. In RTL permission guards are asserted by formulae of the form $\forall \mathbf{i} : \mathbb{N}_1 \bullet \mathbf{G} \odot \uparrow(\mathbf{m}, \mathbf{i})$ – "at each execution initiation time $\uparrow(\mathbf{m}, \mathbf{i})$ of **m**, **G** must hold". Whilst weakening a precondition will lead to a refinement (since the method will have a more constrained result over a wider input domain), weakening a permission guard will usually not (since a weaker logical theory will result, and fewer synchronisation properties will be satisfied by the class).

The following conventions are used to simplify the statement of method definitions:

- the *write frame* of a method **m** – those attributes of the class which are modified by it – is interpreted as the set of attributes whose post-decorated form **att'** occurs in the definition of **m**. This also applies to supplier objects – only those supplier attributes **att** explicitly mentioned in the form **object'.att** are assumed to potentially change;
- the invariant of the class is not implicitly conjoined to the post-state of the method definition unless $\Xi\mathbf{State_C}$ or $\Delta\mathbf{State_C}$ are used. Instead, as in B AMN, the explicit definition of the method must establish the invariant for the post-state. This is checked during proof of internal consistency;
- when a method is used as a predicate, that is, as an argument of a mathematical operator $\wedge$, $\vee$, $\Rightarrow$, $\,_9^o$, etc, then only its explicit text is used, *not* the implicit frame predicate $\Xi(\mathbf{list})$ where **list** is the complement of the write frame.

These conventions may seem complex, however they do lead to much shorter method specifications, unobscured by explicit Ξ or Δ schemas. Naturally, a fully explicit approach could also be taken. For example, if we have a class **C**:

```
CLASS C
OWNS
  p :  F(N);
  q, r :  N
INVARIANT
  q ≤ #p
OPERATIONS
  add :  N  →
ACTIONS
  add x?   ==>
      p' = p ∪ { x? }
END CLASS
```

Then when **add** is invoked in a procedural context, the effect is the same as the explicit definition

```
add x?   ==>
    Ξ(q, r) ∧
    p' = p ∪ { x? }
```

that adds the identities $\mathbf{q'} = \mathbf{q}$ and $\mathbf{r'} = \mathbf{r}$ to the effect of the method.

Exercise (4.1): Give complete Z^{++} method specifications of the following operations:

1. an operation **inc** which adds the value of an integer input parameter **vv**? to an integer state variable **xx**, leaving the other state variable **yy** unchanged;
2. as for the previous exercise, but with **xx** being of type $\mathbb{N}$;
3. an operation **add** which adds an input value **vv**? : $\mathbb{N}$ to a state variable **ss** : seq($\mathbb{N}$) if **vv**? is not already in the range of **ss**, and leaves **ss** unchanged otherwise (**vv**? may be appended to the end or beginning of the sequence, or in some other way made a member of the sequence);
4. an operation **len** which returns the length of a state variable **ss** : seq($\mathbb{N}$).

The most abstract means of specifying a VDM^{++} method is via *specification statements*, which have the general form

```
[ext wr write frame
     rd read frame
 pre precondition
 post postcondition]
```

In the **postcondition** the value of an attribute **att** at initiation of execution of the specification statement is denoted by $\overleftarrow{\textbf{att}}$. Such statements describe the properties that the state resulting from the method should satisfy, and identify which attributes are modified or accessed by the method. Thus the method specification

```
search(xx :  ITEM)
    pre xx ∈ elems(contents)  ==
        [ext wr pointer
             rd contents
         post contents(pointer)  =  xx]
```

asserts that only **pointer** is changed by the method, and that at its termination it satisfies the equation given. In words "if **xx** occurs in the sequence **contents**, then set **pointer** to be the index of such an occurrence". Notice that if a variable **var** appears in the **rd** clause, then **var** may be used in place of $\overleftarrow{\textbf{var}}$ in the postcondition.

Input parameters automatically have **rd** modality, output parameters **wr** modality.

4.2.2   Using and Combining Methods

Methods can be used in one of two ways in Z^{++}:

- as predicates, when their invocations occur in the argument of a logical operator;

- as procedural operations, when their invocations occur in the argument of a code constructor ; , BEGIN END, VAR, WHILE, etc, including immediately within other method definitions.

When a method **m** from class **S** is used in a client class **C** on an object a : **S**, the syntax **a.m** is used. Input arguments are associated with formal parameters in the order listed in **m**'s definition. Actual output parameters **out** are listed in the same order as the corresponding formal parameters in an invocation of the form

$$\text{out} \longleftarrow \text{a.m}$$

However a method from class **C** can be used to define another method within class **C** without identifying **self** as the target object of the call. Thus the forms **m(e)** and **out** $\longleftarrow$ **m** can be used in this case. These forms are the only way in which an internal method can be invoked.

Methods, when used as predicates, can be combined using any of the Z predicate composition mechanisms (although use of $\Rightarrow$ and $\neg$ is not advised). In addition, relational composition ${}_{9}^{9}$ is defined by

$$\mathbf{S}_1 \, {}_{9}^{9} \, \mathbf{S}_2 \; == \; \exists \mathbf{v}'' : \mathbf{T} \bullet \mathbf{S}_1[\mathbf{v}''/\mathbf{v}'] \wedge \mathbf{S}_2[\mathbf{v}''/\mathbf{v}]$$

as usual, where **v** : **T** is the attribute list of **C**, and both **S**$_1$ and **S**$_2$ are predicates over **v** and **v**'.

An example of the use of method composition mechanisms is the following specification of the *dining philosophers* problem: we will examine the synchronisation and real-time properties of this system in Chapter 6.

The task in this problem is to design a controller for a system consisting of a group of resource users (philosophers) and resources (forks). The following are the requirements of the system:

1. each user requires exclusive access to exactly two resources **left fork** and **right fork** for the entire duration of an activity **Eating**;
2. each resource is shared between exactly two users;
3. each user has exactly two adjacent users: **left neighbour** and **right neighbour**, neither of which are equal to itself;
4. these adjacent users are the ones with which the resources of a user are shared, that is, **left fork** is the **right fork** of the **left neighbour**, and **right fork** is the **left fork** of the **right neighbour**;
5. a user is in exactly one of the following states at each time: **Thinking**, with no requirements for access to its resources; **Hungry**, waiting for access to its resources, or **Eating**, to which it can only progress once its resources become available. Each user should spend at most 600 seconds in the **Eating** state. A user will move from the **Thinking** to the **Hungry** state at some time point, bounded by 100 (minimum) and 300 (maximum) seconds from the time it last entered the **Thinking** state;

6. while a user is eating it may cease to be hungry (but still continue to eat). At any time after 60 seconds from when it starts to eat, the user may decide to release its resources and return to the thinking state. However, if either of the neighbours of the user are waiting to eat after 180 seconds have elapsed from the user starting to eat, then it is forced to abandon its resources;

7. once a user ceases to eat, it releases its resources.

The data model of the system is as shown in Figure 4.2. Requirements 1 to 4 are partially expressed on this diagram (the full requirements are expressed in the formal models).

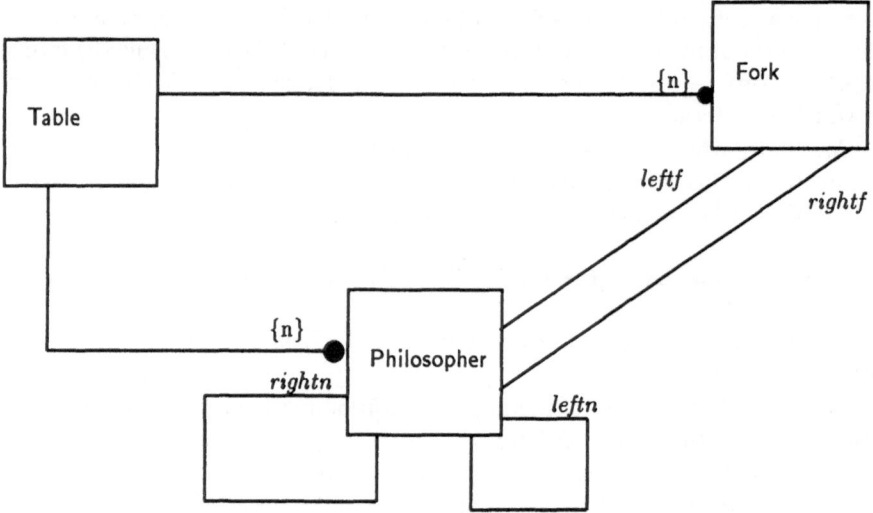

Figure 4.2: Outline Object Model of Philosopher System

Operations on the system will include adding a philosopher and a fork (simultaneously) and removing a philosopher and fork.

The initial formal model of a fork is simply:

```
CLASS Fork
TYPES
  FState ::= up | down
OWNS
  fstate : FState
OPERATIONS
  init : →;
  pick_up : →;
  release : →
ACTIONS
  init  ==>  fstate' = down;

  pick_up  ==>  fstate' = up;
```

```
release   ==>   fstate' = down
HISTORY
  mutex({ pick_up, init, release }) ∧
  self_mutex({ pick_up, init, release }) ∧
  □(pick_up ⇒ fstate = down) ∧
  □(release ⇒ fstate = up) ∧
  □(pick_up ⇒ ○release) ∧
  □(release ⇒ ○pick_up)
```

/∗ plus other statechart formalisation elements ∗/
END CLASS

There are no timing constraints for forks: they are simply passive objects whose histories are determined externally.

The dynamic model of a philosopher is shown in Figure 4.3. In this figure,

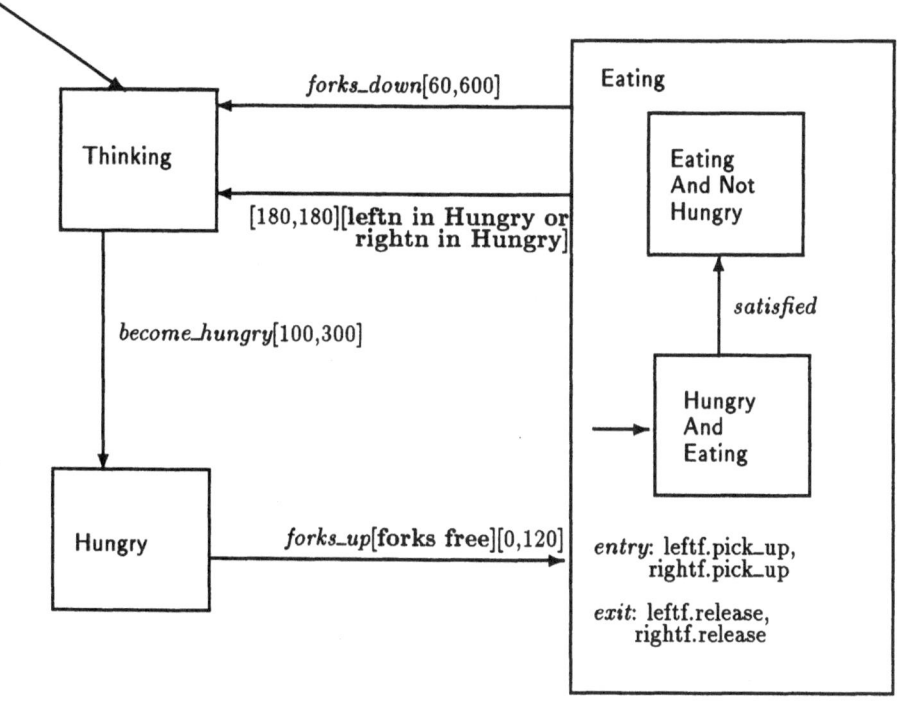

Figure 4.3: Statechart of Philosopher

forks free abbreviates the condition that **leftf not in Up and rightf not in Up.**

The formalisation of a philosopher is therefore:

CLASS **Philosopher**
TYPES

```
    PState  ::=  thinking | hungry | eating
    EState  ::=  eating_not_hungry | eating_and_hungry
OWNS
    pstate : PState;
    estate : EState;
    leftf, rightf : Fork;
    leftn, rightn : Philosopher
INVARIANT
    leftf ≠ rightf
OPERATIONS
      init : →;
  *  become_hungry : →;
  *  forks_up : →;
  *  satisfied : →;
  *  forks_down : →;
  *  τ₁ : →
            /*  become_hungry,  forks_up,  satisfied,
                forks_down  are effectively internal in that they
                are never externally invoked.                          */
ACTIONS
      init  ==>  pstate' = thinking ;

  *  become_hungry  ==>
            pstate' = hungry;

  *  forks_up  ==>
            pstate' = eating  ∧
            estate' = eating_and_hungry;

  *  satisfied  ==>
            estate' = eating_not_hungry;

  *  forks_down  ==>
            pstate' = thinking;

  *  τ₁  ==>
            pstate' = thinking

HISTORY
    /* Considered in Chapter 6 */
END CLASS
```

The invariant expresses requirement 1 (requirement 4 is expressed in the **Table** class).

The first, highly abstract, version of the class which defines a table is then:

```
CLASS Table
OWNS
    forks : F(Fork);
    philosophers : F(Philosopher)
INVARIANT
```

$\forall$ p : philosophers •
    p.leftn $\in$ philosophers $\wedge$
    p.rightn $\in$ philosophers $\wedge$
    p.leftf $=$ p.leftn.rightf $\wedge$
    p.rightf $=$ p.rightn.leftf $\wedge$
    p.leftn $\neq$ p $\wedge$
    p.rightn $\neq$ p $\wedge$
    p.leftf $\in$ forks $\quad\wedge$
    p.rightf $\in$ forks $\wedge$
$\forall$ p, q : philosophers •
    p.leftf $=$ q.leftf $\Rightarrow$ p $=$ q $\quad\wedge$
$\forall$ f : forks • $\exists$ p, q : philosophers •
    p.leftf $=$ f $\wedge$ q.rightf $=$ f $\quad\wedge$
#philosophers $=$ #forks

OPERATIONS
  init : $\rightarrow$;
  initialise : $\rightarrow$;
  add_fork_philo : Fork Philosopher $\rightarrow$;
  remove_philo : Philosopher $\rightarrow$

RETURNS
  choose_philo : $\rightarrow$ Philosopher

ACTIONS
    init $==>$ philosophers$'$ $=$ $\varnothing$ $\wedge$ forks$'$ $=$ $\varnothing$;

    initialise $==>$
        $\exists$ p1, p2 : Philosopher; f1, f2 : Fork $|$
                p1 $\neq$ p2 $\wedge$ f1 $\neq$ f2 •
        philosophers$'$ $=$ { p1, p2 } $\wedge$
        forks$'$ $=$ { f1, f2 } $\wedge$
        $\overline{\text{Philosopher}}'$ $=$ $\overline{\text{Philosopher}}$ $\cup$ { p1, p2 } $\wedge$
        p1 $\notin$ $\overline{\text{Philosopher}}$ $\wedge$
        p2 $\notin$ $\overline{\text{Philosopher}}$ $\wedge$
        $\overline{\text{Fork}}'$ $=$ $\overline{\text{Fork}}$ $\cup$ { f1, f2 } $\wedge$
        f1 $\notin$ $\overline{\text{Fork}}$ $\wedge$
        f2 $\notin$ $\overline{\text{Fork}}$ $\wedge$
        p1$'$.leftn $=$ p2 $\wedge$
        p2$'$.rightn $=$ p1 $\wedge$
        p1$'$.rightn $=$ p2 $\wedge$
        p2$'$.leftn $=$ p1 $\wedge$
        p1$'$.leftf $=$ f1 $\wedge$
        p2$'$.rightf $=$ f1 $\wedge$
        p1$'$.rightf $=$ f2 $\wedge$
        p2$'$.leftf $=$ f2;

The **initialise** operation creates the smallest non-empty configuration of philosophers and forks which satisfies the invariant. At this stage a completely abstract approach has been taken, even avoiding the use of the **New** operations, in order to define explicitly the effect of the operation. The semantics of the language implies that *Fork and *Philosopher are only changed on the elements **f1**, **f2** and **p1**, **p2** respectively by this operation, although this too could be explicitly stated.

This level of abstraction avoids commitment to the definition or use of particular methods, instead only the required state changes are described, and the decomposition of these changes into method calls is a later design step.

The object instance diagram from which this operation was formalised is shown in Figure 4.4. The **(new)** annotation on the objects indicates that they are created by this operation, and that therefore their attributes satisfy the values given by the initialisations of the respective classes.

Initialisation poststate:

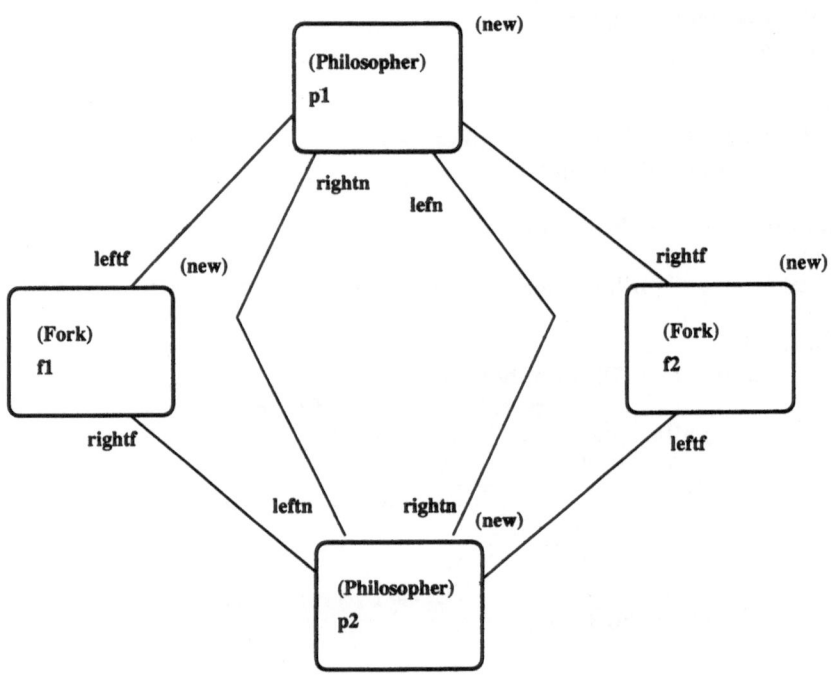

Figure 4.4: Initial Configuration of Table

An alternative for **initialise** would be to use the ANY construct:

```
initialise  ==>
      ANY p1, p2 : Philosopher;  f1, f2 : Fork
      WHERE p1 ≠ p2  ∧  f1 ≠ f2
      THEN
          philosophers' = { p1, p2 }  ∧
          ...
      END
```

Note that a complex invariant has led to a complex initialisation operation. Further operations use a similar style of specification:

choose_philo p!   ==>
    PRE
      ∃ p1, p2 : Philosopher | p1 ∈ philosophers ∧
                          p2 ∈ philosophers ∧
                          p1.pstate ≠ eating ∧
                          p2.pstate ≠ eating ∧
                          p2 = p1.rightn
    THEN
      p! ∈ philosophers ∧
      p!.pstate ≠ eating ∧
      p!.rightn.pstate ≠ eating
    END ;

/ * choose_philo selects a philosopher which is not eating and
    whose right neighbour is also not eating * /

add_fork_philo f? p?   ==>
    PRE
      f?.fstate = down ∧ p?.pstate ≠ eating ∧
      ∃ p1, p2 : Philosopher | p1 ∈ philosophers ∧
                          p2 ∈ philosophers ∧
                          p1.pstate ≠ eating ∧
                          p2.pstate ≠ eating ∧
                          p2 = p1.rightn ∧
      f? ∉ forks ∧ p? ∉ philosophers
    THEN
      ∃ p1, p2 : Philosopher; fork : Fork •
          p1 ⟵ choose_philo ∧
          p2 = p1.rightn ∧
          fork = p1.rightf ∧
          forks' = forks ∪ { f? } ∧
          philosophers' = philosophers ∪ { p? } ∧
          p?'.rightf = fork ∧
          p?'.leftf = f? ∧
          p?'.rightn = p2 ∧
          p?'.leftn = p1 ∧
          p1'.rightf = f? ∧
          p1'.rightn = p? ∧
          p2'.leftn = p?
    END ;

/ * add_fork_philo inserts the new philosopher p?
    as the right neighbour of a randomly selected non-eating
    philosopher p1. f? is inserted as p?'s left fork and
    other relationships are adjusted appropriately.   * /

Note that the operation does not explicitly change the value of **p1.leftf** or
p1.leftn. It is therefore assumed that these values are not changed by the
method when it is used as an operation.

The precondition of **choose_philo** has been duplicated in the precondition of **add_fork_philo** in order to ensure that **choose_philo** is always called within its precondition. This is an obligation of internal consistency.

The object instance diagram for **add_fork_philosopher** is shown in Figure 4.5. The informality of such diagrams can be seen to be a major drawback in their use for complex configuration changes – they should only be used for guidance and explanation purposes only.

add_fork_philo prestate:

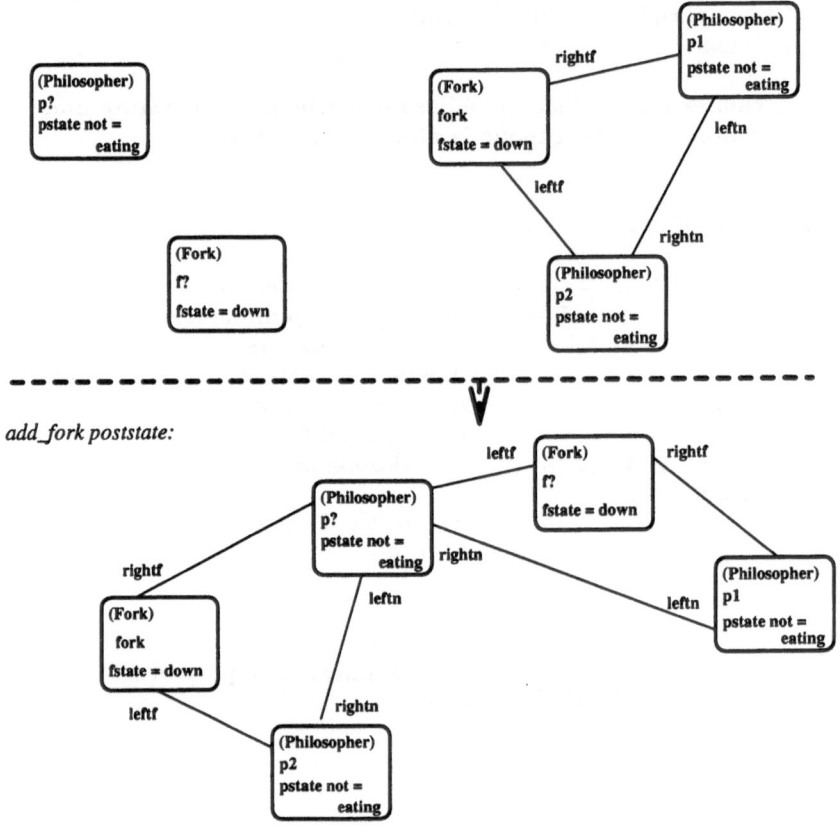

add_fork poststate:

Figure 4.5: Effect of **add_fork_philosopher**

The above specification of **Table** can be improved by recognising various auxiliary operations which are of use in factoring the main, external, operations presented above.

These auxiliary operations are:

OPERATIONS
* **Make_left_neighbour** : Philosopher Philosopher →;
* **Make_right_neighbour** : Philosopher Philosopher →;
* **Make_philosopher** : Philosopher Philosopher Philosopher
  Fork Fork →;

. . .

ACTIONS

    * Make_left_neighbour p? pleft? ==>
          p?'.leftn = pleft? ∧
          pleft?'.rightn = p?;

    * Make_right_neighbour p? pright? ==>
          Make_left_neighbour(pright?,p?);

    * Make_philosopher p? pleft? pright? fleft? fright? ==>
          Make_left_neighbour(p?,pleft?) ∧
          Make_right_neighbour(p?,pright?) ∧
          p?'.leftf = fleft? ∧
          p?'.rightf = fright? ;

These operations are then used, as predicates, as follows:

    initialise ==>
        ∃ p1, p2 : Philosopher; f1, f2 : Fork |
                p1 ≠ p2 ∧ f1 ≠ f2 •
        philosophers' = { p1, p2 } ∧
        forks' = { f1, f2 } ∧
        $\overline{\text{Philosopher}}'$ = $\overline{\text{Philosopher}}$ ∪ { p1, p2 } ∧
        p1 ∉ $\overline{\text{Philosopher}}$ ∧
        p2 ∉ $\overline{\text{Philosopher}}$ ∧
        $\overline{\text{Fork}}'$ = $\overline{\text{Fork}}$ ∪ { f1, f2 } ∧
        f1 ∉ $\overline{\text{Fork}}$ ∧
        f2 ∉ $\overline{\text{Fork}}$ ∧
        Make_philosopher(p1,p2,p2,f1,f2) ∧
        p2'.leftf = f2 ∧
        p2'.rightf = f1;

   . . .

    add_fork_philo f? p? ==>
        PRE
          f?.fstate = down ∧ p?.pstate ≠ eating ∧
          ∃ p1, p2 : Philosopher | p1 ∈ philosophers ∧
                          p2 ∈ philosophers ∧
                          p1.pstate ≠ eating ∧
                          p2.pstate ≠ eating ∧
                          p2 = p1.rightn ∧
          f? ∉ forks ∧ p? ∉ philosophers
        THEN
          ∃ p1, p2 : Philosopher; fork : Fork •
             p1 ⟵ choose_philo ∧
             p2 = p1.rightn ∧
             fork = p1.rightf ∧
             forks' = forks ∪ { f? } ∧
             philosophers' = philosophers ∪ { p? } ∧
             Make_philosopher(p?,p1,p2,f?,fork) ∧

$$p1'.rightf = f?$$
END;

It can then be recognised that suitable operations of the **Philosopher** class can be defined to implement the attribute assignments required by the **Table** class operations. These operations simply set the values of particular attributes of a **Philosopher**:

    set_leftn : **Philosopher** →;
    set_rightn : **Philosopher** →;
    set_leftf : **Fork** →;
    set_rightf : **Fork** →;
ACTIONS
    set_leftn ln?   ==>
            leftn' = ln?;

    / ∗ similarly for   set_rightn,   etc ∗ /

In addition the specification of the $\overline{\mathbf{S}}'$ values for the supplier classes **Fork** and **Philosopher** can be achieved by using calls to **News**. Thus we can write:

    initialise   ==>
        ∃ p1, p2 : Philosopher; f1, f2 : Fork •
            (philosophers' = { p1, p2 } ∧
             forks' = { f1, f2 }) ⍮
            ((p1 ⟵ New_Philosopher ⍮
              p2 ⟵ New_Philosopher) ∧
             (f1 ⟵ New_Fork ⍮
              f2 ⟵ New_Fork)) ⍮
            Make_philosopher(p1, p2, p2, f1, f2) ⍮
            p2.set_rightf(f1) ⍮
            p2.set_leftf(f2);

Note that $p1 \neq p2$ and $f1 \neq f2$ follow from the remainder of the definition. Similarly:

  ∗ Make_left_neighbour p? pleft?   ==>
            p?.set_leftn(pleft?) ⍮
            pleft?.set_rightn(p?);

  ∗ Make_right_neighbour p? pright? ==>
            Make_left_neighbour(pright?, p?);

  ∗ Make_philosopher p? pleft? pright? fleft? fright?   ==>
            Make_left_neighbour(p?, pleft?) ⍮
            Make_right_neighbour(p?, pright?) ⍮
            p?.set_leftf(fleft?) ⍮
            p?.set_rightf(fright?)

and so forth. This class is now in a form suitable for a complete specification of the dining philosophers system, and for a refinement to code, which will be described in Chapter 5.

Exercise (4.2):

1. how can error cases be treated in Z^{++} using the $\vee$ operator on internal methods? Specify a method **inc** : $\mathbb{Z} \to$ **REPORT** where **REPORT** ::= **ok** | **underflow** | **overflow** which increments an instance variable **xx** : 1 . . 20 by an input value, giving appropriate error reports if the increment cannot be achieved because of underflow or overflow in the value of **xx**. Why is the use of internal methods an improvement over the corresponding Z specification style?

In VDM^{++} method definitions can use any of the procedural statement forms of VDM-SL: sequential composition, **if then else**, **while**, **for** loops (both deterministic and non-deterministic), **let**, **def**, **dcl**, and assignment, in combination with specification statements and method invocations. A special **return** statement enables values to be returned to the caller of a method, and terminates the control flow block in which it occurs. Thus we could write, for example:

```
insert(x :  N)  ==
    if x  >  node_value
    then
      self!check_insert_right(x)
    else
      if x  <  node_value
      then
        self!check_insert_left(x);

check_insert_right(x :  N)  ==
    if void(right_subtree)
    then
      (dcl nn :  @Tree  :=  Tree!new;
                      --  Create a new tree node
        topology [post nn.node_value  =  x];
                      --  Set its value to x
          right_subtree  :=  nn)
      else
        right_subtree!insert(x)
```

for an insertion operation of a binary tree, and

```
leaf() value b :  B  ==
    ([ext rd left_subtree, right_subtree
      post b  =  void(left_subtree)  ∧  void(right_subtree)];
     return b)
```

for an enquiry operation.

At the abstract specification level **while** and **dcl** should be avoided in favour of **for** and **def**, and method calls on supplier objects represented more abstractly by specification statements. Thus in the **check_insert_right** operation we have used direct update to the supplier object **nn** attribute **node_value**, rather than invoking **nn!set_value(x)** where this method could be defined by:

set_value(x : $\mathbb{N}$) ==
        node_value := x;

A fundamental difference between the VDM^{++} and Z^{++} approaches concerns the way in which methods can be used as abstract declarative specifications of functionality, and combined using logical, rather than procedural operators. For example, consider a class

CLASS **StackSeq**
OWNS
  stacks : seq(**NatStack**)
OPERATIONS
  subtract : $\mathbb{N}\ \mathbb{N}\ \mathbb{N}\ \rightarrow$
ACTIONS
  subtract i? j? k?   ==>
        $\exists$ a, b : $\mathbb{N}$ •
          a $\longleftarrow$ s(i?).pop $\wedge$
          b $\longleftarrow$ s(j?).pop $\wedge$
          s(k?).push(a $-$ b)
END CLASS

where **NatStack** has operations **pop** and **push** which affect a sequence **contents** : seq($\mathbb{N}$). This operation can be expanded out into:

  subtract i? j? k?   ==>
        $\exists$ a, b : $\mathbb{N}$ •
            s'(i?).contents = tail(s(i?).contents) $\wedge$
            s'(j?).contents = tail(s(j?).contents) $\wedge$
            a = (s(i?).contents)(1) $\wedge$
            b = (s(j?).contents)(1) $\wedge$
            s'(k?).contents = $\langle$ a $-$ b $\rangle$ $^\frown$ s(k?).contents

If we have other information (such as that s has no duplicates, and that no other method can modify it during an execution of **subtract**) then we can additionally assert that $\{i?,j?,k?\} \lhd s$ = $\{i?,j?,k?\} \lhd s'$.

No such declarative combination of methods is possible in VDM^{++}: a specific sequential order must be chosen for the two **pop** and the **push** invocations, even though the two **pop** operations could be concurrently executed (if s had no duplicates).

4.2.3   Internal Consistency

The following rules give the formal requirements for internal consistency of a Z^{++} specification class **C**. Let the invariant of a class **C** be denoted by **Inv$_C$**, its data declaration by **Dec$_C$**, and for each method **m** of **C**, the input declaration by **In$_m$**, the output **Out$_m$**, and the precondition predicate and method definition by **Pre$_{m,C}$** and **Def$_{m,C}$** respectively.

Def$_{m,C}$ is a predicate expressing the effect of the method – it may contain implicit frame schemas Ξ(**list**) for lists of attributes, as described above. Any procedural method definition can be equivalently expressed as a predicate on the pre and post states $\mathbf{v}$ and $\mathbf{v}'$ of the class, so this definition is fully general.

The internal consistency obligations are then:

$$(\mathbf{i}) : \vdash \exists \, \mathbf{Dec_C} \bullet \mathbf{Inv_C}$$

That is, there is an element in the state space. This corresponds to the criterion of non-triviality of a specification in the *established strategy* for Z [18].

For each operation $\mathbf{m}$:

$$(\mathbf{ii}) : \vdash \forall \, \mathbf{Dec_C} \bullet \mathbf{Inv_C} \wedge \mathbf{Pre_{m,C}} \Rightarrow$$
$$\exists \, \mathbf{Dec'_C}; \; \mathbf{Out_m} \bullet \mathbf{Inv'_C} \wedge \mathbf{Def_{m,C}}$$

That is, the explicit precondition of the method implies its implicit precondition. This is termed the *feasibility* condition for $\mathbf{m}$ (in VDM, the *satisfiability* obligation of [159]);

$$(\mathbf{iii}) : \vdash \forall \, \mathbf{Dec_C}; \; \mathbf{Dec'_C}; \; \mathbf{In_m}; \; \mathbf{Out_m} \bullet \mathbf{Inv_C} \wedge \mathbf{Pre_{m,C}} \wedge$$
$$\mathbf{Def_{m,C}} \Rightarrow \mathbf{Inv'_C}$$

This asserts that $\mathbf{m}$, when executed within its precondition, guarantees to produce a state satisfying the invariant of the class.

If an initialisation operation **init** with definition ψ is specified, we must have:

$$(\mathbf{iv}) : \vdash \forall \, \mathbf{In_{init}} \bullet \exists \, \mathbf{Dec'_C}; \; \mathbf{Out_{init}} \bullet \mathbf{Inv'_C} \wedge \psi$$

If procedural code is used to define a method, then weakest preconditions need to be used to generate the internal consistency of operations. Specifically, if $[\,]_=$ is the weakest precondition operator (as defined in Appendix A), then the predicate $\neg \, [\mathbf{Code_{m,C}}]_= \neg \, (\mathbf{v} = \mathbf{v}')$ expresses the state transitions which may result from executing a code definition $\mathbf{Code_{m,C}}$ of method $\mathbf{m}$, where $\mathbf{v}$ is the tuple of attributes of $\mathbf{C}$.

Proofs of internal consistency can help to identify those points where a specification is incomplete (for example, because an operation specification is not strong enough to establish the class invariant for the post-state) and how it can be made complete. Even generating the proof obligations, without proof, can achieve this.

A class for which conditions (**i**) or (**iv**) fail is infeasible – there can be no executable system implementing the class. An operation failing (**ii**) is likewise not implementable by conventional procedural code. An operation failing (**iii**) may only be incomplete, rather than genuinely erroneous.

To resolve obligation (**ii**) we may need to redo some development steps and strengthen the precondition of the operation. To resolve obligation (**iii**) we may need to strengthen the definition of the operation so that it establishes the invariant for the post-state, or strengthen the precondition to forbid any input values/prestates which may lead to inconsistency.

Similar requirements for internal consistency hold for VDM^{++}, with the addition that the initialisation must imply the invariant.

As an example, consider the **birthday** method from the **Person** class of Chapter 3. If we defined it by

birthday() ==
　　age := age + 1

then this would violate obligations (**ii**) and (**iii**) above, since **age** has the type $0 \ldots 200$, and therefore **birthday** would produce a state outside the class invariant if it is applied when **age** $= 200$ before the operation.

To render it válid, we need to write:

birthday()
　　pre age < 200 ==
　　　　age := age + 1

A specification is complete when all of its classes are internally consistent, when all updates to supplier classes are expressed via calls to methods of these classes, and when all requirements have been formalised.

Exercise (4.3):

1. give the internal consistency proof obligations for the following class, and discharge the obligations:

   CLASS **Seq₁[X]**
   OWNS
   　　sq : seq(**X**)
   OPERATIONS
   　　add_element : **X** →;
   　　init : →;
   　　del : **X** →
   RETURNS
   　　is_in : **X** →
   ACTIONS
   　　add_element x? ==>
   　　　　sq' = sq ⌢ ⟨ x? ⟩;
   　　init ==>
   　　　　sq' = ⟨ ⟩;
   　　del x? ==>
   　　　　sq' = squash(sq ▷ { x? });
   　　is_in x? ==>
   　　　　x? ∈ ran(sq)
   END CLASS

   The standard Z definition of **squash** : $(\mathbb{N} \nrightarrow \mathbf{X}) \rightarrow \text{seq}(\mathbf{X})$ can be assumed;

2. Give the internal consistency proof obligations for the class **C** below. How can **C** (and **S**) be modified so that **C**'s operation is always feasible? [Hint: consider adding an enquiry operation to **S**].

```
CLASS C
OWNS
   d1, d2 : S
OPERATIONS
   push_2 : ℕ →
ACTIONS
   push_2 xx? ==>
          d1.push(xx?) ∧ d2.push(xx?)
END CLASS


CLASS S
FUNCTIONS
   | maxlen : ℕ₁
OWNS
   ss : seq(ℕ)
OPERATIONS
   push : ℕ →
ACTIONS
   push xx? ==>
          PRE #ss < maxlen
          THEN
               ss′ = ss ⌢ ⟨ xx? ⟩
          END
END CLASS
```

4.3 Inheritance

A class D *directly inherits* a class C if C is listed in D's EXTENDS list. D is termed an *immediate descendent* of C, and C is termed an *immediate ancestor* of D. A class D (indirectly) *inherits* C if it directly inherits C or some immediate ancestor of D inherits C. D is also termed a *descendent* of C, and C an *ancestor* of D[3].

Inheritance is a purely syntactic facility which enables the state of a class to be decomposed into several sub-states and groups of associated operations. A typical use of inheritance is module importation, that is, to include a set of shared definitions into a number of classes within a development. An example of this is given by the **Person** specification of Chapter 3. More generally, if a class **A** defines a method with an input type **T**, then **T** must be visible to **A**, either because **T** is a standard Z type, a class type or a type defined in a class which is (eventually) inherited by **A**. Any class **B** which invokes **m** on an instance of **A** (and which is therefore a client of **A**) must also have access to **T**. In this situation **T** could be defined in a class **TClass** which is then inherited by **A** and **B** and by any other class which needs access to **T**.

When **C** is inherited by **D** all attributes, constants, types and operations of **C** become corresponding items of **D**. If an identifier **iden** names two items

---

[3] In other words, inheritance is the non-reflexive transitive closure of direct inheritance.

inherited from distinct classes in **D**, then it must be qualified with the name of the appropriate class: C_1.**iden** or C_2.**iden**. In VDM^{++} the notation **C'item** is used to qualify a feature **item** to distinguish it from features of the same name defined in other classes.

The invariant of **C** is conjoined to the predicate written in the INVARIANT clause of **D** to form **Inv$_D$**. A useful rule to observe is that any operation of **D** which updates the attributes inherited from **C** should only do so via the operations of **C**. This rule of "no new operations" will ensure that the extended class preserves the invariant of **C** if **C** is internally consistent. It is also part of the formal requirement for subtyping of [201].

A method **m** of **C**, when used as an operation, is interpreted as the identity transformation on the (new) state of **D** (just as if its definition had been textually copied into **D**). **D** may redefine the identifier **m** to specialise its behaviour and add a description of how it modifies or accesses the new attributes of **D**. Such an extended method is distinguished from the original definition by prefixing it with **D**'s name: **D.m** (or in **D** itself or its clients, just **m**), whilst the original can be referred to as **C.m**[4].

As an example, consider a general class of push-able entities:

```
CLASS Pushable[X]
OPERATIONS
    push :  X  →
END CLASS
```

This can be specialised to add a degree of semantic detail:

```
CLASS Pushable_S[X] EXTENDS Pushable[X]
OWNS
   contents :  𝔽(X)
ACTIONS
   push x?  ==>
        x?  ∈  contents'
END CLASS
```

and used as the basis of both **queue** and **stack** specifications:

```
CLASS Stack[X] EXTENDS Pushable_S[X]
OWNS
   stack :  seq(X)
INVARIANT
   contents  =  ran(stack)
OPERATIONS
   pop :  →  X
ACTIONS
   push x?  ==>
        stack'  =  stack  ⌢  ⟨ x? ⟩  ∧
        contents'  =  ran(stack');
```

---

[4]C.m is only *internally* available for objects of **D** if **m** is explicitly redefined in **D** (ie, if **m** is listed in either the OPERATIONS or ACTIONS clauses of **D**).

```
pop y!  ==>
     PRE contents ≠ ∅
     THEN
            y!  =  last(stack) ∧
            stack'  =  front(stack) ∧
            contents'  =  ran(stack')
     END
END CLASS
```

Subtyping relationships could actually be specified here, since each class satisfies the specification of its ancestors.

The specification of **Queue[X]** is similar. Note that multiple inheritance could be used, if we had defined a class **Popable_S[X]** which defined a general **pop** method.

Inherited methods can be used as predicates and as operations within the inheritor, thus allowing explicit code reuse. For example, an implicit and non-deterministic specification of **push** for **Stack[X]** could have been written:

```
push x?  ==>
     Pushable_S[X].push ∧
     contents'  =  ran(stack')
```

This allows any new value of **stack'** such that **x?** ∈ ran(**stack'**).

In order to exploit polymorphism between **C** and **D**, **D** must however be asserted to be a subtype of **C**, and each method **m** of **D** will then be given an interpretation method $\phi(\mathbf{m})$ of **D** which will be used if a call **a.m(e)** is encountered in a context where **a** : **C** is declared but actually **a** ∈ $\overline{\mathbf{D}}$.

If a subtyping is based on an inheritance, then it will often be the case that $\phi(\mathbf{C.m}) = \mathbf{D.m}$.

In VDM^{++} the clause **is subclass of** after the class name indicates the previously declared classes that are being inherited in the class. A more restricted form, known as *controlled inheritance*, permits a class to be "privately inherited" in the sense of C++: all its external methods become internally usable in the inheriting class, but do not become exported as external methods by this class.

The theory of each ancestor class **C** of a class **D** can be assumed in **D**, with suitable qualification of feature names **f** declared in **C** to **C.f**.

4.4 Subtyping

4.4.1 Formal Definition

Subtyping is the key mechanism for expressing hierarchies of entities ordered by inclusion (for example "every working person is a person", and so forth). In logical terms, the subtyping relationship **C** $\sqsubseteq_{\phi,\mathbf{R}}$ **D** defined here will imply that every model (instance) of **D** will also provide a corresponding model of **C**.

The Z^{++} definition of this concept follows, the VDM^{++} definition is similar.

Class **C** is a *supertype* of a class **D**, which is then termed a *subtype* of **C**, if there is a total map $\phi :$ **methods**(**C**) $\rightarrow$ **methods**(**D**) (which takes external methods of **C** to external methods of **D**, and internal methods to internal methods) and a data refinement relation **R** on c; d such that the theory $\Gamma_{\mathbf{D}}$ of **D** extends the translation of the theory $\Gamma_{\mathbf{C}}$ of **C** under ϕ and **R**:

> For every $\varphi \in \mathcal{L}_{\mathbf{C}}$, $\Gamma_{\mathbf{C}} \vdash \varphi$ implies that $\Gamma_{\mathbf{D}} \vdash \Box^{\tau}(\mathbf{R}(\mathbf{u}, \mathbf{v})) \Rightarrow \phi(\varphi)$
> where **v** is the tuple of attributes of **D**, **u** of **C**.

$\phi(\varphi)$ for a formula or expression φ denotes the formula obtained by substituting $\phi(\mathbf{m})$ for **m** in each sub-expression of φ, for each method name **m** of **C**.

Interpretations of type and constant identifiers of **C** in **D** are also defined in general as part of the subtyping relation.

The theory of a Z^{++} class is defined in Appendix A. In practice we will work with a set of sufficient but not necessary conditions for this. These are the usual conditions that initialisations and invariants may be strengthened, preconditions weakened, and postconditions strengthened, all modulo the refinement relation **R**:

1. $\vdash \forall \mathbf{Dec_D}; \mathbf{Dec_C} \bullet \mathbf{Inv_D} \wedge \mathbf{R} \Rightarrow \mathbf{Inv_C}$;
2. $\vdash \forall \mathbf{Dec_C}; \mathbf{Dec_D}; \mathbf{In_m} \bullet \mathbf{Inv_D} \wedge \mathbf{Pre_{m,C}} \wedge \mathbf{R} \Rightarrow \mathbf{Pre_{n,D}}$;
3. $\vdash \forall \mathbf{Dec_C}; \mathbf{Dec_D}; \mathbf{Dec'_D}; \mathbf{In_m} \bullet \mathbf{Inv_D} \wedge \mathbf{Pre_{m,C}} \wedge$
   $\qquad\qquad \mathbf{R} \wedge \mathbf{Def_{n,D}} \Rightarrow \exists \mathbf{Dec'_C} \bullet \mathbf{Inv'_C} \wedge \mathbf{R'} \wedge \mathbf{Def_{m,C}}$;
4. $\mathbf{H_D} \vdash \Box^{\tau} \mathbf{R} \Rightarrow \phi(\mathbf{H_C})$.

n denotes $\phi(\mathbf{m})$.

Intuitively, these conditions mean that for every instance **d** of **D** there is a corresponding possible instance **c** of **C** which behaves in the same way to an external observer – the "is-a" criterion. Thus every element of the state space of **D** must be (must correspond via **R** to) an element of the state space of **C**, and every possible "execution" of an operation $\phi(\mathbf{m})$ of **D** must be a possible execution of the original method **m** of **C**, again, via **R**. In addition the specified dynamic behaviour $\mathbf{H_C}$ of objects of **C** must be satisfied by objects of **D**.

In terms of Liskov's informal criteria for subtyping (given in Chapter 1), every object o1 of the subtype **D** has a corresponding model (object) o2 of **C** with the same logical properties – this is the "reduct" of o1 via the interpretation of **C** in **D**. If this were not the case then the theory of **D** would not establish that of **C**, ie, there would be a model of **D** which did not satisfy the translated axioms of **C**.

A simplified version of this definition can be stated when **R** is functional, that is, for every element **v** of the state space of **D** there is a unique element **u** of the state space of **C** such that $\mathbf{R}(\mathbf{u}, \mathbf{v})$ holds. In this case, we can write **R** as a function

$$\mathbf{R} : \mathbf{T}_1 \times \ldots \times \mathbf{T_n} \rightarrow \mathbf{S}_1 \times \ldots \times \mathbf{S_m}$$

where $\mathbf{T}_1 \times \ldots \times \mathbf{T_n}$ is the cartesian product of the attribute types of **D**, and $\mathbf{S}_1 \times \ldots \times \mathbf{S_m}$ of **C**, and the definition of subtyping can be stated as:

For every $\varphi \in \mathcal{L}_{\mathbf{C}}$, $\Gamma_{\mathbf{C}} \vdash \varphi$ implies that $\Gamma_{\mathbf{D}} \vdash \phi(\varphi[\mathbf{R}(\mathbf{v})/\mathbf{u}])$ where $\mathbf{v}$ is the tuple of attributes of $\mathbf{D}$, $\mathbf{u}$ of $\mathbf{C}$.

Subtyping is distinguished from refinement in that it leads to a definition of a *new* type, the subtype, whose development path to code could, in principle, be entirely distinct from that of its supertype (ways in which they can be linked are discussed in Chapter 5). In contrast, a refinement $\mathbf{D}$ of $\mathbf{C}$ is essentially just an alternative description of the *same* type, since instances of $\mathbf{D}$ cannot be used except via the abstract interface of $\mathbf{D}$, which is given by that of $\mathbf{C}$.

A simple example of a subtyping is given by the classes

```
CLASS TrafficLight
FUNCTIONS
 | in_amber :  N₁
OWNS

  . . .

END CLASS
```

and

```
CLASS TrafficLight25s
EXTENDS   TrafficLight
FUNCTIONS
  in_amber  =  25
END CLASS
```

of Section 4.1.2 above.

It is clear that the interpretation **TrafficLight25s.in_amber** of **TrafficLight.in_amber** satisfies its axioms (in this case just the typing constraint), therefore, the resulting class is a subtype.

Our definition of class subtyping differs from that of Liskov and Wing [201], in that we do allow new methods to be introduced in the subtype which are not simply a procedural combination of existing methods on the supertype state. Instead, we are providing a more powerful language to specify history properties, and therefore supertype classes can explicitly declare what history properties can be expected of themselves (and all subtypes). An analogue of Liskov's constraint however holds if a locality axiom is included in the theory of a class. Details are in Chapter 6.

Subtypes are an extremely useful mechanism for supporting system extension and reuse. A typical situation is where a *virtual* class is used (that is, a class which has no actual instances, but which acts as a common supertype of other classes with actual instances). For example a generic **GraphicalFigure** class could provide only operations of **location** to identify its distinguished point, and **move** to move it by a given vertical and horizontal translation. Each subclass, such as **Circle**, **Parallelogram**, etc, could give a specific definition to these operations, and provide more specialised operations appropriate to their structure.

The formal specification of such a virtual class will (should) act as a contract stating to any client of the class what behaviour can be expected from any instance of any of the subtypes of the class. In particular, the system can be extended by the addition of new subtypes of this class, without requiring any further modification, provided that these subtypes obey the specification of the abstract class. This is an example of the *open-closed principle* of [225].

Other forms of virtual class include abstract data structures such as tables or stacks, which might each have a number of alternative specialisations concerned with particular types of access and operations. These specialisations will then have corresponding implementation routes to code (for example, a table adapted to repeated scans through its elements would not use a bit-map representation in its implementation, although this would be the implementation of other versions of a table class). The abstract virtual class itself would not be implemented except vicariously. This is a point we will return to in Chapter 5.

In developing a hierarchy of subtypes an iterative process is often used, where attributes and methods are first attached to specialised classes in the hierarchy and are then later realised to be more general, and can be moved up the hierarchy. Additionally, new intermediate subclasses of original root classes may be defined, which describe the commonalities of particular groups of subtypes of the root classes. Multiple inheritance may be introduced (sparingly) to factor classes into two or more subconcepts. This process mainly takes place in the analysis stage in our development model (where graphical tools can be used to rapidly modify class hierarchies), but may also take place as a result of new subtleties discovered during formalisation. Additionally, the creation of new classes during design may also lead to similar activity regarding these classes, particularly if a reuse-centered approach is adopted.

Subtyping does not necessarily arise from an inheritance. In particular, if we do "inheritance for convenience" in order to import a certain set of features from one class into another, but discard or redefine some of these features, then a semantic subtyping will not be provable. Consider a case where we inherit a **Stack** class into a **Queue** class in order to obtain data and operation signatures, but where the **push** method is (necessarily) redefined:

```
CLASS Queue
  EXTENDS Stack
ACTIONS
  push x?   ==>
     contents' =  contents ⌢ ⟨ x? ⟩


  ...
```

where in **Stack** this method is instead defined as:

```
  push x?   ==>
     contents' = ⟨ x? ⟩ ⌢ contents
```

Here the axioms of **Queue.push** will contradict those of **Stack.push**, rather than extending them. Thus we cannot use **Queue.push** to interpret **push** (and since **Stack.push** is *internal* in **Queue**, it cannot be used to interpret the external method **push** of **Stack**).

A more subtle example of an inheritance which is not a subtyping is given by the following pair of classes. Let a **Polynomial** be a figure with a fixed number **nsides** of sides and vertices:

```
CLASS Polynomial
OWNS
  nsides :  N ;
  edges :  seq(Edge)
INVARIANT
  #edges  =  nsides
OPERATIONS
  rotate :  Angle  →;
  shift :  Vector  →;
  ...
END CLASS
```

ExtendablePoly inherits from **Polynomial** and adds a single operation **add_edge** which increments the number of edges of the polynomial, rearranging the shape appropriately:

```
CLASS ExtendablePoly EXTENDS Polynomial
OPERATIONS
  add_edge :  Edge  →
ACTIONS
  add_edge ee?  ==>
          ... nsides' = nsides + 1  ...
END CLASS
```

The **ExtendablePoly** class is not a subtype of **Polynomial** because in **Polynomial** the formula

$$\Box(\text{nsides} = (\text{nsides} \circledast \clubsuit(\text{self} \in \overline{\textbf{Polynomial}} := \textbf{true}, 1)))$$

holds – that is, at all method initiation times of methods of **Polynomial**, the number of edges is the same as it was at object creation. This holds by induction, since no method of the class changes this quantity, and therefore, by encapsulation, no change can ever be made to this quantity during the lifetime of the object. However the interpretation of this formula is certainly not true in **ExtendablePoly**, since it would say that at each initiation time of **rotate**, **shift**, etc, **nsides** is unchanged from its initial value.

Intuitively we can also see that a program which expected an object **ob** : **Polynomial** to satisfy its specification could observe state changes to **ob** which were not explicable on the basis of this specification, if **ob** was shared with another client who applied the **add_edge** operation.

It is also possible to create inconsistent classes via subtyping and inheritance. A simple example would be the use of contradictory invariants in the ancestor and descendent classes, resulting in the latter being equivalent to the class **false** which is a subtype of every class with the same set of methods. Such classes are therefore useless as starting points for development to code: any refinement of them will also be equivalent to **false**.

VDM^{++} supports the same concept of subtyping as Z^{++}, with the restriction that the data refinement relations **R** are always functional.

4.4.2   Specialisation and Generalisation

An important use of subtyping is to support the expression of concepts required in a particular system as specialisations of more general concepts. Thus in the **Person** specification of Chapter 3, the application is actually concerned with the subtype **WorkingPerson** of **Person**, which is **Person** together with a new attribute:

```
class WorkingPerson is subclass of Person
instance variables
  employments: seq of @Employment;
init objectstate == employments = []
methods
  total_salary() value r: nat
     is not yet specified;

  underage() value b: bool
     is not yet specified

end WorkingPerson
```

Expressing this class as a subtype of **Person** makes the specification easier to comprehend, and may make the development more easily reusable. If we knew even more detail about the domain, for example, that every person we will deal with has exactly one employment, then we could further specialise this class to fit in with the problem:

```
class StandardWorkingPerson is subclass of WorkingPerson
inv employments == len(employments) = 1
end StandardWorkingPerson
```

In this case it would be simpler to change the internal data representation:

```
class StandardWorkingPerson is subclass of WorkingPerson
instance variables
  employment: @Employment;
inv employment == len(employments) = 1  and  employment = employments(1)
end StandardWorkingPerson
```

The concept of subtyping in VDM^{++} is similar to that of Z^{++}. In particular, if **D** is expressed as an immediate descendent of **C** by the class header

```
class  D  is subclass of  C
. . . .
```

and **D** only introduces a set of new attributes not logically linked to existing attributes, and a set of operations which only modify these new attributes, then **D** is a subtype of **C**.

Preconditions can be made more restrictive in specialisation subtypes, but only as a consequence of more restricted state in these subtypes. Thus, there is an identity subtype relation between the two classes in Figure 4.6, but no useful subtype relation between the two classes of Figure 4.7.

```
CLASS A
OWNS
  x : ℕ
OPERATIONS                         CLASS B
  new_x : ℕ →                        EXTENDS A
ACTIONS                            INVARIANT
  new_x n? ==>                       x ≤ 10
       PRE n? ≤ x                  END CLASS
       THEN
            x' = n?
       END
END CLASS
```

Figure 4.6: Specialisation Subtyping with Strengthened Precondition

```
                                   CLASS D
CLASS C                              EXTENDS C
OWNS                               INVARIANT
  eseq : seq(ℕ)                      #eseq ≤ 10
OPERATIONS                         ACTIONS
  add_e : ℕ →                        add_e x? ==>
ACTIONS                                 PRE #eseq < 10
  add_e x? ==>                          THEN
     eseq' = eseq ⌢ ⟨ x? ⟩                  C.add_e(x?)
END CLASS                               END
                                   END CLASS
```

Figure 4.7: Incorrect Specialisation Subtyping

In the first example, even though the precondition of **new_x** has been strengthened (by an implicit new conjunct **n?** ≤ 10), **B** is a subtype of **A**. In the second example however a genuine strengthening of the precondition has been performed. **C** should instead be re-specified in such a way (with a new data item representing an unspecified queue bound) that it serves as a supertype of each class representing a particular bounded length queue.

Exercise (4.4): Write such a general class.

4.5   Class Composition

Class composition refers to the use of one class as a type of an attribute, constant, method parameter or local variable in another. The used class is termed the *supplier*, the using class the *client*. Classes may be their own clients, and there may be mutually recursive clientship relationships between classes. Composition is a means by which the requirements of a system can be decomposed into requirements for the main (sub)system and a set of simpler requirements for subsystems which the main subsystem will then utilise via composition (compare with *delegation* [261]).

Thus in the dining philosophers example, **Table** makes use of **Fork** and **Philosopher** by composition, and **Philosopher** also makes use of **Fork** by composition. We could distinguish between *strong* and *weak* composition, where in the latter no use is made of the operations of the supplier in the client. Notationally these are distinguished as in Chapter 2.

It is possible to refer to the attributes of a supplier class in the client, however care should be taken in order not to create an infeasible specification or one which is overly complex and difficult to implement[5].

A case where such reference becomes necessary is where a group of classes are being defined which are designed to be used in a closely interacting manner. Such a group may be considered to form a "module" in their own right, and hence linking their states does not violate coupling and cohesion constraints.

As an example of the use of invariants to constrain suppliers to a class, consider a window system in which a **Screen** contains a set of **Window** instances, which may be ordered on the basis of concealment:

$$\forall \, a, b : \overline{\text{Window}} \bullet$$
$$a <_w b \equiv b \text{ partially\_conceals } a$$

where this definition depends on the sequences of operations applied within a particular **Window** object, in addition to the coordinates and extent of **a** and **b**.

It may be useful to explicitly record this ordering in a data structure at a later design stage, for example, so that an operation which transforms all

---

[5] A discussion on the validity of reference to supplier attributes is given in Appendix A.

windows can be applied to the most visible ones (maximal in the above partial order) first, so as to give an impression of speed. Thus we could have a class:

CLASS **Screen**
FUNCTIONS

$$
\begin{array}{|l|}
\hline
\text{\rule{0pt}{1em}}\ \_ <_{\mathbf{w}}\ \_ : \overline{\text{Window}} \leftrightarrow \overline{\text{Window}} \\
\hline
\ \ \cdots \\
\hline
\end{array}
$$

(A *generic constant* definition in Z notation)

OWNS
  windows : seq(**Window**)
INVARIANT
  #windows = # ran(windows) ∧
  ∀ i, j : 1 .. #windows |
                 windows(i) $<_{\mathbf{w}}$ windows(j) •
                            j < i

...
END CLASS

Clearly this invariant cannot be stated in the **Window** class since it depends on the global context, the set of all other existing windows managed by a particular **Screen** instance. On the other hand, it is only possible for a **Screen** instance to maintain this invariant if it has exclusive control over the windows it owns, ie, no operations of these instances can be applied except via this screen instance. (Otherwise, $<_{\mathbf{w}}$ might change without an operation of **Screen** being responsible, thus potentially violating the invariant.)

If instead there was a requirement which applied uniformly to each owned window instance, then this should be placed into the **Window** class. For example, assume that the type of **Screen** being specified only allows windows to have at most 5 associated descendents:

CLASS **Screen**
FUNCTIONS
...
OWNS
  windows : seq(**Window**)
INVARIANT
  #windows = # ran(windows) ∧
  ∀ i : 1 .. #windows • windows(i).numb_descendents ≤ 5 ∧
  ...
END CLASS

This would be more clearly specified if the invariant

numb_descendents ≤ 5

were added to a subtype **WindowDL5** of **Window** and this subtype used in **Screen**. This is the correct level to state the invariant since it can be maintained within **WindowDL5**, and refers only to attributes of this class.

In general invariant predicates should be stated as locally as possible. Where, as in the first case above, an invariant of a client class inevitably involves access to attributes of suppliers, it becomes the responsibility of the client to maintain this invariant, not that of the supplier objects.

As a further example, consider the **Philosopher** class shown in Section 4.2.2 above. It would be unwise to place the constraints

leftn.rightf = **leftf** $\wedge$
rightn.leftf = **rightf**

in the invariant of **Philosopher**, since these requirements cannot be guaranteed by the current philosopher and may hinder reuse since they code into this class information about one particular configuration in which it may be used: a more liberal domicile might allow philosophers to entirely own their own forks, for example. The invariant **leftf** $\neq$ **rightf** should be stated in **Philosopher** since it concerns only attributes of this class.

If a more general situation was needed, then this class should be defined as a subtype of a class which omits this constraint.

In VDM^{++} a supplier object is declared using the notation

obj : **@SupplierClass**

to emphasise that a *reference* to an object is being introduced, rather than an object value itself. In this book we interpret such a declaration as denoting a possibly void object reference (ie, one for which **void(obj)** may be true).

When a class **S** is used as a supplier in class **C**, the *relativisation* of the theory Γ_S can be assumed in **C**. This is explained in Appendix A.

4.6   Object Identity

Every instance of a class has an associated object identity, which is assumed to be an element of the countably infinite sets @**C** of tokens. As usual, this identity is set at object creation and cannot be modified by any operation. Data items declared to be of a class type actually hold such tokens as their values, and it is possible for attributes and variables to hold different tokens (different objects) at different times, as well as for different data items to hold the same token at the same time (*aliasing*).

Elements of the object reference sets @**C** can be compared for equality and inequality, passed as parameters to method calls and functions, be used as the target of method calls, and tested for existence via **void(obj)**.

Operations for modifying the sets $\overline{C}$ of existing references and the dereference maps $*_C$ include **New$_C$**, already introduced, and **Unset$_C$** and **Forget$_C$**, which are defined as follows:

Unset$_C$ ==>
$\quad\quad c' = nil_C$

This operation simply sets the value of c to a "void" reference, that is, one with no associated object.

$$\textbf{Forget}_C \ \ c? \ \ \Longrightarrow$$
$$*'_C \ = \ \{ \ c? \ \} \ \triangleleft \ *_C$$

This operation corresponds to the **Forget** operation of Eiffel [225] and deletes the link c? ⟼ **cval** between c? and its object value **cval**. Neither **Forget** or **New** modify the object to which they are applied, but rather the object identity sets $\overline{C}$ and the $*_C$ maps.

The identity of an object may be referred to within a class by the expression **self** – every effort should be made to avoid such reference however. The reason for this is that such references break a hierarchical approach to the definition of methods [158], and complicate reasoning.

Object identity becomes a significant issue when situations arise in which objects may be shared between other objects (including cycles of mutual references). Such situations may invalidate specifications and apparent refinement and subtyping relationships. For example, we might wish to replace a substate of a class by a supplier object (see Chapter 5 for more details of this kind of step, termed *annealing*):

```
CLASS Abstract
OWNS
  a : AType;
  b : BType;
  c : CType
INVARIANT
  ψ(a) ∧ φ(b, c)
OPERATIONS
  . . .
END CLASS

CLASS B
OWNS
  b : BType;
  c : CType
INVARIANT
  φ(b, c)
OPERATIONS
  . . .
END CLASS

CLASS Concrete
OWNS
  a : AType;
  bobj : B
INVARIANT
  ψ(a)
OPERATIONS
  . . .
END CLASS
```

It might be supposed that the class **Concrete** could be written in such a way that it is a refinement of **Abstract**, using the data refinement relation $b_{\mathbf{Abstract}} = \mathbf{bobj.b_B}$ and $c_{\mathbf{Abstract}} = \mathbf{bobj.c_B}$. However this will not be the case unless it can be guaranteed that **bobj** is *private* to particular instances of **Concrete**, that is, that only one object can access the value of this variable. If this were not the case, then the **frame** axiom of **Abstract** (discussed in Chapter 6) would not hold in **Concrete**. That is, it would be possible for the implementations $\mathbf{bobj.b_B}$ and $\mathbf{bobj.c_B}$ of $b_{\mathbf{Abstract}}$ and $c_{\mathbf{Abstract}}$ to change even over intervals in which none of the operations of **Abstract** (interpreted in **Concrete**) were executing.

Private ownership can be guaranteed by syntactic means, by creating private objects within the owning object, and by not allowing the attribute containing the private object reference to be accessed by clients, to be passed out of the owner object via operations, accessed by subtypes, or modified by operations.

The use of object references instead of actual objects as the values of a class type allows the clientship relationship to contain cycles. Indeed a class may depend upon itself as a supplier, for example, if an association such as manager/managed_by from an entity WorkingPerson to itself was formalised.

Recursive clientship is an extremely powerful technique, which allows very complex data structures to be specified via networks of interconnected objects. For example, a general directed graph can be formalised as:

CLASS **DG[X]**
OWNS
  successors : seq($\overline{\mathbf{DG[X]}}$);
  node : **X**
OPERATIONS
  add_successor : **DG[X]** →;
  remove_successor : **DG[X]** →
RETURNS
  access : $\mathbb{N}$ → **DG[X]**
ACTIONS
  . . .
END CLASS

where the methods have the obvious definitions. (**Exercise (4.5)**: complete the definition of these methods.)

An instance diagram of this class could look as in Figure 4.8 (showing only the instances of the **successors** association).

This diagram corresponds to the attribute values

    dg1.successors = $\langle \mathbf{dg2}, \mathbf{dg3}, \mathbf{dg4} \rangle$
    dg2.successors = $\langle \rangle$
    dg3.successors = $\langle \mathbf{dg6} \rangle$
    dg4.successors = $\langle \mathbf{dg6}, \mathbf{dg5}, \mathbf{dg1} \rangle$
    dg5.successors = $\langle \mathbf{dg6} \rangle$
    dg6.successors = $\langle \mathbf{dg2} \rangle$

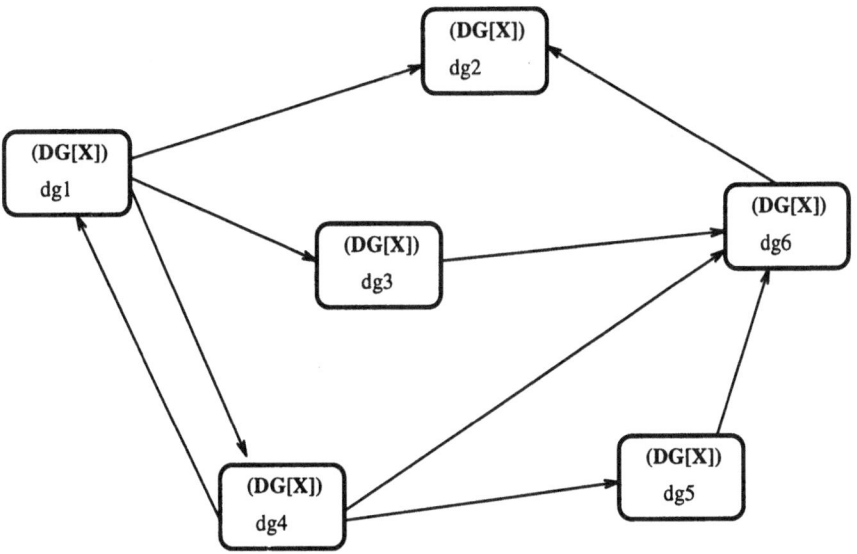

Figure 4.8: Instance Diagram of Graph

Exercise: how can it be stated that a graph involves no cycles?

Solution: define a function

> eventual_successors : $\overline{\text{DG[X]}} \rightarrow \mathbb{P}(\overline{\text{DG[X]}})$
> ___
> $\forall$ dg : $\overline{\text{DG[X]}}$ •
> eventual_successors(dg) =
>   ran(dg.successors) $\cup$
> $\bigcup$\{s : $\overline{\text{DG[X]}}$ | s $\in$ ran dg.successors • eventual_successors(s)\}

within **DG[X]**, then add the conjunct

> self $\notin$ eventual_successors(self)

to the invariant, to produce a subtype **DAG[X]**.

It may be preferable to omit use of **self**, whose use can be sometimes very difficult to understand. Instead, a higher level system could be defined:

CLASS **Graphs**
FUNCTIONS

> eventual_successors : $\overline{\text{DG[X]}} \rightarrow \mathbb{P}(\overline{\text{DG[X]}})$
> ___
> $\dots$

OWNS
  graph_nodes : $\mathbb{F} \ \overline{\text{DG[X]}}$

INVARIANT
    ∀ dg : graph_nodes • dg ∉ eventual_successors(dg)
END CLASS

This class also has the ability to prevent violation of this invariant by the graph operations, which the extended **DG[X]** class could not. However it is further from the form which would be implemented in an object-oriented programming language.

Exercise (4.6): complete the definitions of the operations of the classes of the radar track-former example from Exercise 3.1. [Hint: sequential composition, whilst not completely abstract, is a suitable technique here]. Assume that all classes are mutex at present.

4.7   Dynamic Behaviour

The HISTORY clause of a Z^{++} class contains an extended RTL (Real Time Logic) predicate which constrains the behaviour of objects of the class, considered as (possibly continuous and infinite) series of states segmented by occurrences of events. This predicate holds at all times (ie, it is implicitly enclosed by a $\Box^{\tau}$ modality operator).

RTL is based on a language of *events*, which include the event of creation of an object, and requests, execution initiations and execution terminations of invocation instances of methods of the class. The times of such events can be explicitly referred to, thus allowing a precise and moderately abstract expression of real-time properties.

We have extended basic RTL (which involves only action initiation and termination events) by including a concept of *invocation instance*, which links together termination, initiation and request times associated with the same call of a method. In addition we have added *request* events →**m** representing the arrival of a request for **m** at the current object. Further additions are temporal operators $\Box$ "at all future times" and ◇ "at some future time", and ⊙ "holds at". Also, counters #**req(m)**, #**act(m)** and #**fin(m)** for method events are included, which allow more direct expression of some synchronisation constraints than in basic RTL. The result is a highly expressive language which combines qualitative and quantitative time assertions.

Some examples of RTL specification are:

- a periodic obligation that **m** initiates every **t** seconds (and in the order of its requests) is expressed as

$$\forall i : \mathbb{N}_1 \bullet \uparrow(\mathbf{m(x)}, i+1) = \uparrow(\mathbf{m(x)}, i) + t$$

- to state that requests for **m** are honoured in the order of their reception by an object, the formula $\text{FCFS}_\mathbf{m}$:

$$\forall i, j : \mathbb{N}_1 \mid \rightarrow(\mathbf{m}, i) < \rightarrow(\mathbf{m}, j) \bullet \uparrow(\mathbf{m}, i) \leq \uparrow(\mathbf{m}, j)$$

can be used.

$\uparrow(\mathbf{m}(\mathbf{x}), \mathbf{i})$ denotes the time that the i-th request for invocation of $\mathbf{m}(\mathbf{x})$ received by the current object begins to execute, whilst $\clubsuit(\uparrow\mathbf{m}(\mathbf{x}), \mathbf{i})$ denotes the i-th time of the form $\uparrow(\mathbf{m}(\mathbf{x}), \mathbf{j})$. These may be different if invocations are not initiated in the order that they are received by an object. For example, consider Figure 4.9. In this situation the following equalities hold:

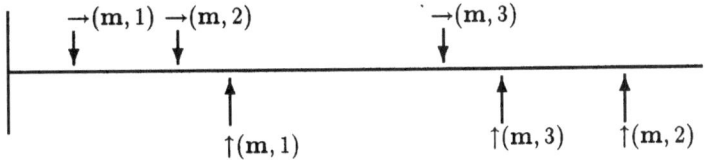

Figure 4.9: Event Times and Invocation Instances

$$\uparrow(\mathbf{m}, 1) = \clubsuit(\uparrow\mathbf{m}, 1) \quad \text{and} \quad \uparrow(\mathbf{m}, 2) = \clubsuit(\uparrow\mathbf{m}, 3)$$

since the 2nd invocation instance of $\mathbf{m}$ is delayed until after the 3rd has commenced execution. This is a counter-example to the $\text{FCFS}_\mathbf{m}$ predicate above.

A protocol such as "shortest job first" is stated as:

$$\forall \mathbf{i}, \mathbf{j} : \mathbb{N}_1 \mid \rightarrow(\mathbf{m}, \mathbf{i}) \leq \uparrow(\mathbf{m}, \mathbf{j}) \bullet$$
$$\mathbf{f}((\mathbf{m}, \mathbf{i}).\mathbf{x}) < \mathbf{f}((\mathbf{m}, \mathbf{j}).\mathbf{x}) \Rightarrow \uparrow(\mathbf{m}, \mathbf{i}) \leq \uparrow(\mathbf{m}, \mathbf{j})$$

That is, if $(\mathbf{m}, \mathbf{j})$ has not already started execution by the time $(\mathbf{m}, \mathbf{i})$ arrives, then $(\mathbf{m}, \mathbf{i})$ will be started first if it has a smaller value of some priority assigning function $\mathbf{f}$ on parameter(s) $\mathbf{x}$.

Full details of the RTL language and axiom system are given in Appendix A. Here we will only summarise the notation.

4.7.1 Events

For each method $\mathbf{m}$ of class $\mathbf{C}$ there is an associated set of events:

- $\uparrow\mathbf{m}(\mathbf{e})$, $\downarrow\mathbf{m}(\mathbf{e})$, $\rightarrow\mathbf{m}(\mathbf{e})$ for $\mathbf{e} \in \text{IN}$, denoting the initiation, termination and the arrival of a request at the object class of an invocation instance of $\mathbf{m}(\mathbf{e})$ respectively.

In addition, there are events of the form:

- $\theta := \mathbf{true}$, $\theta := \mathbf{false}$ for a predicate θ without modal operators or occurrences of **now**, which denote the events of this predicate becoming true or false, respectively.

These events, together with events of the form $\leftarrow(\mathbf{n}(\mathbf{x}1), \mathbf{a})$ for $\mathbf{a} : \mathbf{S}$ a supplier object to $\mathbf{C}$, and $\mathbf{n}$ a method of $\mathbf{S}$ (the sending of a request for $\mathbf{a}$ to execute $\mathbf{n}(\mathbf{x}1)$), are collectively referred to as $\mathbf{BasicEvent_C}$. The complete set of events of $\mathbf{C}$ also include the following:

- $\uparrow(\mathbf{n(x1)}, \mathbf{a})$, $\downarrow(\mathbf{n(x1)}, \mathbf{a})$, $\rightarrow(\mathbf{n(x1)}, \mathbf{a})$ where **a** and **n** are as above – method initiation, termination and request events on suppliers of the current class;
- $\leftarrow(\mathbf{n(x1)}, \mathbf{a}, \mathbf{b})$ where both **a** and **b** are supplier objects to **C**, $\mathbf{a} : \mathbf{S}$, and **n** is a method of **S** – the sending of a request from **b** to **a**.

The first set of events is denoted by **BasicEvent$_\mathbf{S}$(a)**. The complete collection of events of **C** is denoted by **Event$_\mathbf{C}$**.

4.7.2   Terms

For a given class **C**, the following terms can occur in the formulae of its RTL language:

1. variables $\mathbf{v_i}$: $\mathbf{i} \in \mathbb{N}$ – only variables can be quantified over;
2. attributes of the class, its ancestors and supertypes;
3. $\mathbf{f(e_1, \ldots, e_n)}$ for an **n**-ary function symbol **f** and terms $e_1, \ldots, e_n$, and other Z expressions in terms and schema texts;
4. ♣e where e is an *event occurrence* $(\mathbf{E}, \mathbf{i})$, where **E** is in **Event$_\mathbf{C}$** – the time at which e occurs, for $\mathbf{i} : \mathbb{N}_1$;
5. $\mathbf{Op(m(e), i)}$ where $\mathbf{m} \in \underline{\mathbf{methods}}(\mathbf{C})$, e in the input type of **m**, $\mathbf{i} : \mathbb{N}_1$ and $\mathbf{Op} \in \{\uparrow, \downarrow, \rightarrow\}$, and $\leftarrow((\mathbf{m(e)}, \mathbf{a}), \mathbf{i})$ for a supplier object $\mathbf{a} : \mathbf{D}$ and method **m** of **D**;
6. **self**, **now**;
7. e⊛t and ◯e where e is a term, t a time-valued term – the value of e at time t and at the next method initiation time, respectively;
8. $\mathbf{\#act(m(e))}$, $\mathbf{\#fin(m(e))}$, $\mathbf{\#req(m(e))}$, $\mathbf{\#req(m)}$, $\mathbf{\#fin(m)}$, $\mathbf{\#act(m)}$ for $\mathbf{m} \in \underline{\mathbf{methods}}(\mathbf{C})$;
9. method invocation parameters $(\mathbf{m}, \mathbf{i}).\mathbf{x}$ – corresponding to attributes of invocation records in [215].

$\mathbf{\#act(m(e))}$ counts the number of initiations of execution of $\mathbf{m(e)}$ up to the present time, $\mathbf{\#req(m(e))}$ the number of requests for execution of $\mathbf{m(e)}$ received by the current object up to the present time, and $\mathbf{\#fin(m(e))}$ the number of terminations of execution of $\mathbf{m(e)}$ up to the present time.

Time-valued terms are arithmetic combinations of terms of the form 4 or 5 and $\mathbb{N}$-valued terms. The domain **TIME** of time-valued terms is required to be a total order, that is, satisfying the axioms of a partial order together with a designated element 0 with $0 \le t$ for each element t of **TIME**, and with $t < t' \lor t = t' \lor t > t'$ for every pair of elements t, t' of **TIME**. The time domain satisfies the axioms of the set of non-negative elements of a totally ordered topological ring, with addition operation + and unit 0, and multiplication operation ∗ with unit 1. Thus $\mathbb{N} \subseteq \mathbf{TIME}$ can be assumed.

Relativised versions $\mathbf{\#act(m(e), a)}$, etc of event counters for suppliers $\mathbf{a} : \mathbf{D}$ to **C** are also included.

4.7.3 Formulae

For any class **C** the following are the formulae in its RTL language.

1. $P(e_1, \ldots, e_n)$ for an **n**-ary predicate symbol **P** and terms e_1, ..., e_n;
2. $\phi \wedge \psi$, $\phi \vee \psi$, $\phi \Rightarrow \psi$, $\neg \phi$ for formulae ϕ and ψ;
3. $\phi \odot t$ for formulae ϕ and time-valued terms **t** – "ϕ holds at time **t**";
4. $\forall\,\mathbf{SD} \bullet \phi$, $\exists\,\mathbf{SD} \bullet \phi$ for declarations **SD** and formulae ϕ;
5. $\Box^\tau \theta$, $\Box \theta$ and $\bigcirc \theta$ for formulae θ;
6. $\diamond^\tau \theta$, $\diamond \theta$ for formulae θ;
7. **enabled(m)** and **enabled(m(e))** for methods **m**, and expressions **e** in the input type of **m**.

Relativised forms of the latter predicates may also be used, ie, $\mathbf{enabled(m, a)}$ for suppliers **a** of **C**.

$\Box \phi$ denotes that ϕ holds at each initiation time of a method from the class. As in the formalism of [100] it is possible to relate the different interpretations of this operator in each class, in the case of subtypes or refinements (see Chapter 6). $\Box^\tau \phi$ denotes that ϕ holds at all future times – it is not relative to **C**. $\diamond$ and $\diamond^\tau$ are the corresponding "eventually" operators.

Details of the axioms of the system, and examples of reasoning, are given in Chapters 6 and 7. The following section gives some standard abbreviations.

4.7.4 Abbreviations

#active(m) abbreviates $\mathbf{\#act(m)} - \mathbf{\#fin(m)}$, the number of currently executing instances of **m**.

#waiting(m) abbreviates $\mathbf{\#req(m)} - \mathbf{\#act(m)}$, the number of instances of **m** awaiting execution.

$\mathbf{delay(m, i)}$ abbreviates $\uparrow(\mathbf{m, i}) - \rightarrow(\mathbf{m, i})$.

$\mathbf{duration(m, i)}$ abbreviates $\downarrow(\mathbf{m, i}) - \uparrow(\mathbf{m, i})$.

$\mathbf{mutex(\{m_1, \ldots, m_n\})}$ abbreviates the assertion

$$\mathbf{\#active(m_1)} = \sum_{i=1}^{n} \mathbf{\#active(m_i)} \quad \vee \ldots \vee$$

$$\mathbf{\#active(m_n)} = \sum_{i=1}^{n} \mathbf{\#active(m_i)}$$

$\mathbf{self\_mutex(\{m_1, \ldots, m_n\})}$ abbreviates the assertion

$$\mathbf{\#active(m_1)} \leq 1 \wedge \ldots \wedge \mathbf{\#active(m_n)} \leq 1$$

The conjunction of these formulae is equivalent to $\sum_{i=1}^{n} \mathbf{\#active(m_i)} \leq 1$.

$\underline{\mathbf{m}}$ abbreviates $\mathbf{\#active(m)} > 0$.

A *durative method* **m** is a method which satisfies $\mathbf{durative(m)}$: $\forall i : \mathbb{N}_1 \bullet \downarrow(\mathbf{m, i}) > \uparrow(\mathbf{m, i})$. A *durative class* is a class all of whose methods are durative. For such a class, the property $\forall i : \mathbb{N}_1 \bullet \underline{\mathbf{m}} \odot \uparrow(\mathbf{m, i})$ holds for each method **m**.

4.7.5   Writing RTL Specifications

By default, a Z^{++} class without a HISTORY clause is mutex and self-mutex. The same default applies to VDM^{++} classes without a **sync** clause, or with a **sync** clause specified using traces only.

The assertions **mutex($\underline{methods}$(C))** and **self_mutex($\underline{methods}$(C))** can be abbreviated by **Mutex$_C$** and **SelfMutex$_C$** respectively. **Durative$_C$** similarly abbreviates **durative(m_1)** $\wedge \ldots \wedge$ **durative(m_n)** for $\underline{methods}$(C) $=$ $\{m_1, \ldots, m_n\}$.

If a class C is formalised from a statechart then it will be mutex and self-mutex, and each transition is usually assumed to be durative (with a small, unspecified duration), and so its history constraint can be expressed in the format given for the **TrackSection** class in Chapter 3:

HISTORY

/ * **Mutual exclusion properties** : */

Mutex$_C$ $\wedge$ **SelfMutex$_C$** $\wedge$

/ * **Permission predicates** : */

$\square(\underline{m_1} \Rightarrow \text{cond}_1) \wedge \ldots \wedge$

/ * **Definition of the transition effect** : */

$\square(\underline{m_1} \Rightarrow \bigcirc\phi_1) \wedge \ldots \wedge$

/ * **Reachability properties** : */

$\square(\text{state} = s_1 \Rightarrow \underline{m_{1,1}} \vee \ldots \vee \underline{m_{1,r1}}) \wedge \ldots \wedge$

/ * **Delay and duration constraints** : */

$\forall \; i: \; \mathbb{N}_1; \; e: \; \text{IN}_m \; \bullet \; \text{duration}(m(e),i) \leq f(e) \wedge \ldots$

END CLASS

Other kinds of property, such as prioritisation of methods (particularly interrupts), fairness properties, and scheduling schemes such as "shortest job first" can all be specified using this language. Examples will be given in the following chapters.

The elements of a class have different roles in the specification of the static and dynamic behaviour of objects of the class. These are:

1. the INVARIANT places constraints on the attributes of the class which relate their values at all "quiescent" times in its history (that is, at time points where there is no active method of the class, and at method initiation times). It uses only conventional predicate calculus, not RTL formulae;

2. the **ACTIONS** specification defines the relationship between pre and post states. At the abstract specification level it does not specify temporal properties or the properties of states at times which are not the initiation or termination times of the method.

   At more refined stages it describes how the method execution is decomposed into executions of statements, including calls on other methods;

3. permission predicates $\forall i : \mathbb{N}_1 \bullet (\text{self} \in \overline{C} \Rightarrow \varphi) \circledcirc \uparrow(m, i)$ prevent execution of m outside of states satisfying φ (abbreviated by $\Box(\underline{m} \Rightarrow (\text{self} \in \overline{C} \Rightarrow \varphi))$ in a mutex and durative class);

4. mutex and self-mutex assertions constrain the objects of the class to execute their methods in a partially or fully mutually exclusive manner;

5. general RTL formulae provide an ability to constrain the duration of methods, to place bounds on delays in activating methods (eg, for asserting deadlines and priorities for interrupts), and to control the relative times which an object spends undertaking various activities.

An example of these distinct specification elements within the specification of an entity with dynamic behaviour is an abstract specification of a lift system:

```
CLASS   AbstractLift
TYPES
   Floor  ==  1 .. maxfloor
OWNS
   floor : Floor
OPERATIONS
   descend  :  →;
   call  :  Floor  →
ACTIONS
   descend   ==>
                     (floor  >  1   ∧   floor′  <  floor)  ∨
                     (floor  =  1   ∧   floor′  =  floor);
   call ff?   ==>
HISTORY
   ∀  i:  ℕ₁  •
     (∃  j,  f :  ℕ₁  |  f  <  floor⊛↑(descend, i)  •
               ↑(descend, i)   <    ↑(call(f),j)
                                 ≤   ↓(descend, i)  ∧
               floor⊛↓(descend, i)  =  f   ∧
               ↓(descend, i)  =   ↑(call(f),j)  +  1)  ∨
     ((¬  ∃  j,  f :  ℕ₁  |   f  <  floor⊛↑(descend, i)  •
               ↑(descend, i)   <    ↑(call(f),j)
                                 ≤   ↓(descend, i))   ∧
               floor⊛↓(descend, i)  =  1)
END CLASS
```

This specification states that if a descending lift is not interrupted by a call on its way down, then it stops at the bottom floor, otherwise, it stops at some such calling floor. The ACTIONS specification states a general functional property of the **descend** method: that it always strictly reduces the current floor if that is possible, whilst the details of dynamic behaviour are stated in the HISTORY clause. Similarly the ACTIONS specification of **call** states that it is the identity function on the state.

In this book we will use history constraints in the **aux reasoning** clause of VDM^{++} classes, in order to provide a declarative means of specifying dynamic and real-time behaviour.

4.8   Complex Data Types

One approach to the formalisation of complex data models is to interpret entity types as unstructured types (given sets in Z, token types in VDM) and associations as relations between these types. This approach has the advantage that it assumes nothing about the entity types other than what is explicitly specified on the diagram, and it is not biased towards an implementation involving pointer attributes.

Thus, for example, if we have two entity types A and B, with a many-one association r from A to B, we could write the following Z^{++} specification:

```
CLASS System
TYPES
   [AId,  BId]
OWNS
  aobjs :  F(AId);
  bobjs :  F(BId);
  r :  AId  ⇸  BId
INVARIANT
  dom(r)  =  aobjs  ∧  ran(r)  ⊆  bobjs
OPERATIONS
  ... operations to modify the variables ...
END CLASS
```

In fact only an attribute representing r is strictly necessary. $\mathbf{X} \nrightarrow \mathbf{Y}$ denotes the set of *finite* partial functions from $\mathbf{X}$ to $\mathbf{Y}$.

This is in contrast to the model which would arise as a result of the translation process described in Chapter 3. This would yield two classes **A** and **B** with **A** possessing an attribute **r** : **B**. Again, a **System_1** class would be specified, but instead of **r** it would just contain variables **aset** : $\mathbb{F}(\mathbf{A})$ and **bset** : $\mathbb{F}(\mathbf{B})$ that record the existing objects managed by the system – indeed only the former is strictly needed.

We cannot directly show that **System_1** refines **System** because we have no way to relate **AId** to **@A** and similarly for **B**. Instead we consider an extension of **System_1** to use classes

```
CLASS AClass
OWNS
  aid :  AId;
  rval :  BClass
OPERATIONS
```

```
...
END CLASS
```

and

```
CLASS BClass
OWNS
  bid : BId
OPERATIONS
  ...
END CLASS
```

The refinement relation is then

$$\text{aobjs} = \{a : \text{aset} \bullet a.\text{aid}\}$$
$$\text{bobjs} = \{a : \text{aset} \bullet a.\text{rval.bid}\}$$
$$r = \{a : \text{aset} \bullet a.\text{id} \mapsto a.\text{rval.bid}\}$$

In order that r is a function, we need the following invariant in **System_1**:

$$\forall a, a' : \text{aset} \mid a.\text{aid} = a'.\text{aid} \bullet a.\text{rval} = a'.\text{rval}$$

since otherwise there could be an element in the domain of the r defined above which has two possible **BId** values under r. A simple way of ensuring this invariant is to require that the **aid** and **bid** values uniquely identify the corresponding objects:

$$\forall a, a' : \text{aset} \mid a.\text{aid} = a'.\text{aid} \bullet a = a'$$

and similarly for **BClass**.

The view of the association in **System** is a "global" view, which explicitly represents the complete set of pairs in the relation as a single attribute. In contrast **System_1** takes a "local" view in which the elements of the relation are encapsulated within the objects of its domain. This is termed *annealing a map* in VDM^{++}.

It would also be possible to refine **System** to provide a table-like implementation of r, which is not so easy to achieve from **System_1**, so this approach has some advantages, although it may introduce unnecessary refinement steps.

As a further example, consider the specification of an intensive care unit given in Section 4.1.1. We could write a class which simply encapsulated the Z specification of this system, rather than decomposing the system specification into a number of classes:

```
CLASS ICU
TYPES
```

```
┌─ Reading ──────────────────────────────────────────
│ timestamp : N
│ attribute₁ : T₁;
│ ...
│ attributeₙ : Tₙ
└────────────────────────────────────────────────────
```

[PatientId]

OWNS
  patient_readings : PatientId $\rightarrow$ seq(**Reading**)
INVARIANT
  ∀ pid : dom **patient_readings** •
      ∀ i, j : 1 .. #patient_readings(pid) | i < j •
         patient_readings(pid)(i).timestamp   <
             patient_readings(pid)(j).timestamp
OPERATIONS
  . . .
END CLASS

This is more abstract than the Z^{++} specification previously presented, and allows a more conventional Z style development to be pursued until a late design stage, at which point suitable library classes managing the different layers of structure contained in the data of this class would need to be accessed by composition.

4.9   VDM^{++}

Many of the essential aspects of Z^{++} are shared by VDM^{++}, with the following differences:

- VDM^{++} does not allow direct write access to attributes of a supplier in a client method (nor any access to such attributes at all in a client class outside of **topology** statements and the **aux reasoning** parts);
- VDM^{++} does not support generic parameters, although the effect of these can be partly achieved by inheriting classes which provide specific definitions of a type given entirely abstractly in the "generic" class;
- abstract specifications are written using the specification statement constructs introduced in Chapter 2 – there are no logical operators such as the ∧ or ∨ of Z which can be used to construct method definitions;
- an additional form of inheritance, called *indexed inheritance* is provided, and supports an alternative means of representing aggregation;
- instead of RTL specifications, VDM^{++} uses three distinct notations to specify dynamic behaviour: permission guards, explicit trace expressions, and procedural and declarative threads. These notations are explained in Appendix B, and examples are given in the remainder of the book;
- active objects (that is, which have a **thread** specification) must additionally be activated by a **start** invocation in order to fully initialise them. **start** must be invoked on an existing object, so that the usual way of using this is:

```
(dcl obj: @ActiveClass := ActiveClass!new;
     topology [ post ....];
          -- establish connections between objects
```

```
obj!start)
        -- start the thread of obj
```

Unlike a standard method call **start** is asynchronous.

Conclusions

This chapter has described some of the ways that the Z^{++} and VDM^{++} languages can be used to specify systems in a formal object-oriented manner. We have introduced the concepts of inheritance, subtyping and composition, and described how they are used within a specification. In the following chapter more details of the refinement process will be given, and of the role of these mechanisms within that process.

The frame problem has been an aspect of object-oriented specification which has caused excessive complexity in some approaches (perhaps including our own). The dilemma is that we want to consider an operation as being both "open" in its frame (so it can be used as part of another operation, or executed in parallel with another operation of the same class) and "closed" (so that clients can be assured that only the attributes they expect to be changed by its execution are). In addition, we want to avoid specifying what happens to other objects in the system within a method definition that belongs to a single object. The solution chosen for Z^{++} is to allow a dual interpretation of a method definition text for these two purposes. In addition, for concurrent execution, we use weak versions of the functional specifications of the methods, whilst formulating a precise description of what happens in the HISTORY clause, in terms of events. The use of axioms such as the **frame** and **global frame** axioms supports inference about global state changes (or absence of changes) from local changes. Chapter 6 contains an example of the latter type of reasoning.

For VDM^{++} the problem has been addressed by not providing any operation combinator such as Z's ∧ or B AMN's ||.

The distinction between $\overline{C}$ and @C is also a notational complication which many object-oriented languages try to avoid. Unfortunately, if we want an abstract equivalent of creating a "new" object, this distinction needs to be made. It is also useful when defining self-recursive types such as trees, where void object references are needed to prevent infinite structures arising. We have specified some conventions to help avoid having to make the distinction except where absolutely necessary (ie, class names **A** used as attribute and local variable types denote @**A** by default, whilst used as method parameter types they denote $\overline{\mathbf{A}}$). VDM^{++} uses optional types [@**A**] or the **void** predicate to make this distinction.

Internal consistency includes the requirement that each method must preserve the invariant. For abstract specification classes this convention may require duplication of the invariant in the postcondition of each method (as $\mathbf{Inv'_C}$ in Z^{++}), which complicates the class definition. An alternative would be to implicitly include $\mathbf{Inv'_C}$ in the method definitions of abstract specification classes, but to then require that the definitions of methods in refinements of such classes can be proved to establish the invariant on termination. In contrast, this convention may be more natural in VDM^{++}, where procedural or hybrid specifications of methods can be used at the abstract specification level.

Specification techniques for Z are given in [18], whilst the tutorial [93] gives more detail on the use of VDM^{++} in specification.

Extensive research on the meaning and definitions of subtyping in object systems has taken place. Useful starting points are the papers [201] and [209].

Chapter 5

Design and Refinement

This chapter will provide a formal definition of refinement in VDM^{++} and Z^{++}, and will also provide a number of refinement techniques, such as "annealing" (replacing a group of attributes by a supplier object). The relationship between implementation structures and specification structures will be described. It will consider the *refinement and design* and *implementation* stages of Chapter 2.

Section 5.1 considers alternative design approaches and system development architectures which can be used. Section 5.2 gives a formal definition of refinement and describes refinement techniques for the languages, while Section 5.3 examines the interaction between refinement and the object-oriented structuring mechanisms. Finally, Section 5.4 considers the special aspects of refinement in VDM^{++}.

5.1 Design Approaches

Design is the process of creating a development architecture in which formal specification components are refined towards code-like implementations, and suitable decompositions of these components are devised in terms of components which are simpler to implement, or which are already implemented in some library of existing developments.

In the formal context this involves the use of a concept of refinement or *reification*, whereby a proposed refinement of a class can be expressed in mathematical terms, and verified against its specification in order to establish that it satisfies the functional requirements stated in this specification (and, that it introduces no essentially new functional requirements). A formal definition of refinement, and some refinement techniques, are given in Section 5.2. In this section we will consider general design techniques.

5.1.1 Implementation and Refinement Classes

At development stages beyond the complete specification, alternative language subsets are used in classes of the formal language. In Z^{++} a *refinement class*, which may be used at development stages between the complete specification and final implementation, but not at these stages, can include all the constructs of the language, except direct update reference to attributes of a supplier in a client method. The corresponding subset in VDM^{++} is the entire language (although in this book we allow direct enquiry access to supplier attributes at the abstract specification level, this is not allowed at the refinement level, or at any development level in standard VDM^{++}).

In Z^{++} an *implementation class* is a class which is directly translatable into a procedural object-oriented language. In such classes no abstract mathematical types are allowed, but only the following forms:

- enumerated sets;
- class (reference) types;
- other *basic* types – numeric and subrange types and string and character types;
- array types of the form $a..b \rightarrow T$ where T is one of the above types, and $a, b \in \mathbb{Z}$ – this form of type is only available if the procedural language concerned has a definition of arrays which satisfies the formal semantics of this mathematical definition. Otherwise, specialised library classes should be used to implement such a type.

Record types are implemented via class types. Methods may only be defined using the procedural constructs assignment, WHILE, VAR, method invocation, IF THEN ELSE, and sequencing. We could also include ||| (independent concurrent execution) if the target language supported this (for example, PAR in OCCAM). Similar constraints hold for VDM^{++}, with the statement constructs being restricted to `dcl`, `while`, `if then else`, assignment, method calls, `return`, sequencing, and related constructs such as case statements. Threads can additionally use `sel` and `answer` statements.

In Section 5.2.2 we will identify how each of the components of an abstract specification class are replaced by elements of corresponding refinement and implementation classes.

5.1.2 Development Structures

There are two general ways in which a set of specification components can be implemented in terms of a set of implementation components. These concern the relationship between the structuring used at the specification level and that used at the implementation level.

- *create separate decomposition.* In this approach (Figure 5.1) no use is made of the specification-level components as the origin of class composition, inheritance or subtyping dependencies in the implementation of the specification. Instead, the specification is progressed via possibly many intermediate data refinements until a level of detail is reached which allows the utilisation of previously developed components or library developments to implement the system. A typical example where such a process is used is in the implementation of a numerical function, where an original abstract recursive definition is carried into a loop implemented using library components which provide arithmetic operations upon scalar variables. This approach can also be used when the data items in the abstract specification correspond exactly to the specification of a library component (for example, the **Set_manager** class of Chapter 2 contains operations which are precisely those required to implement the **points** attribute of the **Shape** class).

The ability to define distinct decompositions of the specification and implementation of a system is an advantage of a development approach and language. For example, at a specification level, we may need to decompose the system description on the basis of domain concepts (*modular understandability* in the sense of [225]), whereas at the implementation level, we may decompose on the basis of what library or already developed components may exist (*modular decomposability*).

A particular case of this approach can be termed the "monolithic" approach (Figure 5.2), in which there is no implementation decomposition in terms of user-defined classes: all required library components are suppliers to a single implementation in which they serve to define a complex data structure in this implementation – typically each "layer" of structure in this data type will be provided by a specific library class. This would correspond to the approach discussed in Chapter 4 where all the structure of a complex data item is contained in a single class. This approach can lead to severe difficulties when formal proof is attempted;

- *continuity of structure*. In this case structure at the implementation level follows that at the specification level. Thus if an abstract specification class **C** was a client of a class **S**, then the implementation C_1 of **C** would also be a client of **S**. Similarly if **C** was a subtype of **D**, then C_1 could be defined as a subtype of **D** or of an implementation D_1 of **D**.

The general structure of this type of development is given in Figure 5.3.

Some of the comparative advantages and disadvantages of these approaches are:

- the monolithic approach can lead to more complex proof obligations, since:
  - partitioning an implementation into several developments means that operations of an implementation C_1 of a class **C** can invoke operations of a supplier class **S** (a specification-level class), rather than using the code (in S_1) which implements these operations. The specification-level definitions will almost always be simpler and more concise than the corresponding code;

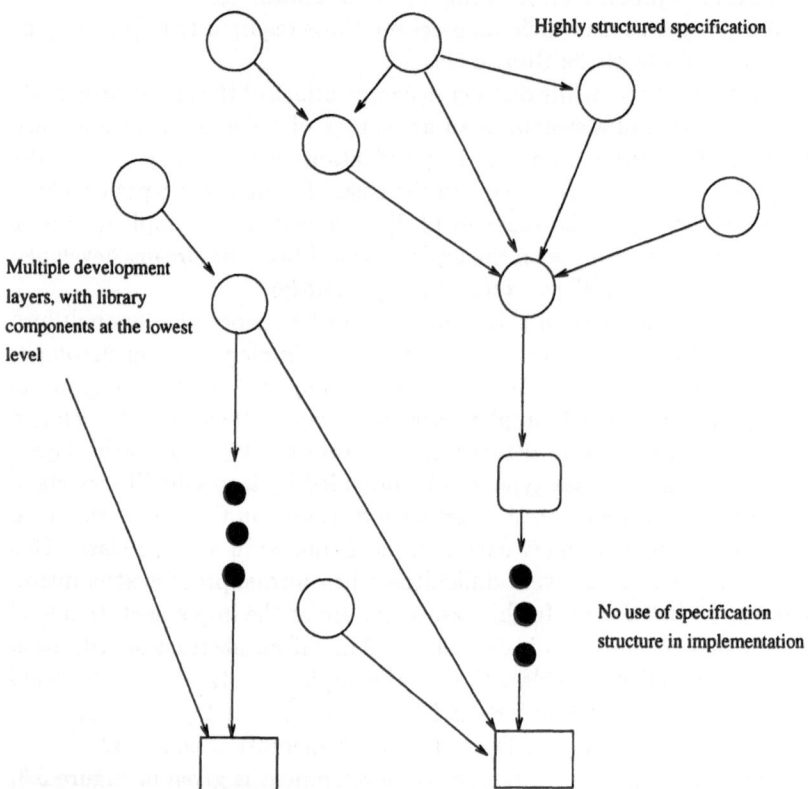

Figure 5.1: Independent Structuring of Specification and Implementation

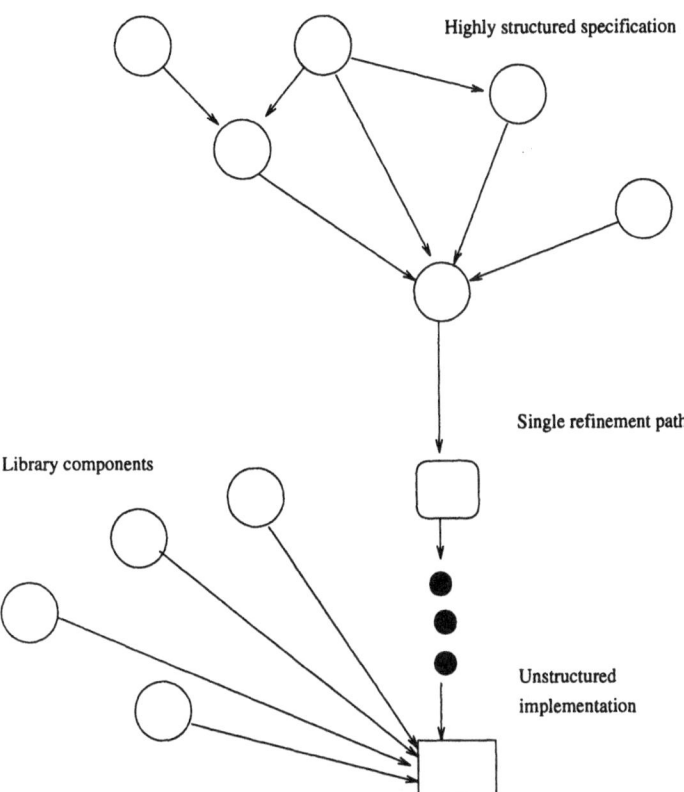

Figure 5.2: Monolithic Development

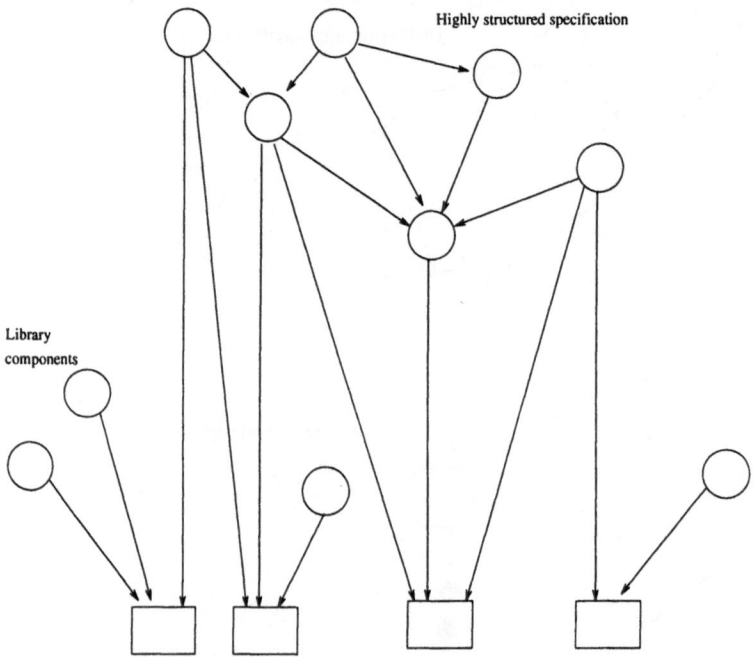

Figure 5.3: Continuity of Structure Approach

- implementation invariants can be simpler in a decomposed approach, since they need refer only to that part of the structure of the implementation data which is managed by the specific single development, and can defer to lower level developments the management of finer structure;

- there will be fewer attributes in the individual implementation components than in the single monolithic implementation.

A partitioned approach will also allow some proof obligations to be generated earlier than with the monolithic approach, since only parts of the implementation of the development need to be created at any one time;

- the advantages of the monolithic approach are:

  - it may make it easier to comprehend the entire system and the interrelationships between the layers of data involved, rather than these layers being separated into distinct developments;

  - it may improve the efficiency of the resulting code, since the cost of invoking methods between development layers is not present.

An example of the independent structuring approach is given by the *Hamming* development of Chapter 6: in this case the specification consists of two classes, with the refinement step requiring the specification or selection of four new subsystems, **Mult2**, **Mult3**, **Mult5** and **Sorter**, each of which is constructed by subtyping. This is also an example of monolithic development.

An example of the continuity of structure approach is the *Person* development of Chapters 3, 4, 6 and 8.

Exercise (5.1): Provide a refinement of the following class in which there is no reference to the abstract function **fact** in the executable code of the refinement.

```
CLASS Factorial
FUNCTIONS
```

$$\text{fact} : \mathbb{N} \to \mathbb{N}$$
$$\text{fact}(0) = 1 \ \wedge$$
$$\forall i : \mathbb{N} \bullet$$
$$\text{fact}(i+1) = (i+1) * \text{fact}(i)$$

```
OPERATIONS
  factorial : N  →  N
ACTIONS
  factorial i? f!  ==>
            f!  =  fact(i?)
END CLASS
```

5.1.3   Top-down Design

Top-down design is a process involving the development of the outermost or
highest level subsystems first, analysing the requirements which they place on
subsystems which they can make use of, and then specifying and developing
these subsystems. Suitable subsystems may:

- be contained in a library of existing developments, in which case only
  selection (and possibly adaption) of these components is necessary;
- already have specifications within the complete specification of the system, in which case only selection and development is needed – this includes the continuity of structure approach;
- or a new subsystem needs to be specified and developed to meet the
  requirements. At the lowest level of a system this may require the explicit
  writing of new library components with executable code – this leads to
  the independent structuring approach.

The process then continues until no new subsystems need to be developed.

In order to support later reuse it is important to ensure that any new
component which may be placed in a global, company, project or team library
should be of a reasonable level of generality, which may require the creation of
a supertype hierarchy of the actual subsystem specification which is needed in
this specific development.

The type of top-down design which will be used in this book is top-down
design with a degree of "lookahead" to guide development in the direction of
reusable classes which the developer is aware of and that they believe may
help to meet the requirements of the new system. As an example, recall the
shapes/points development of Chapter 2, in which the subsystem
Set_manager[Point] was selected from a library in order to implement the
requirements of the **Shape** class.

5.1.4   Bottom-up Design

Bottom-up design starts from the most elementary classes present in a specification, implements these, using some of the processes from the previous section, and then uses these classes to construct implementations of classes from
"higher" subsystems in the development. This approach leads towards a continuity of structure approach, since it encourages use, wherever possible, of
subsystems already present within a development in order to support the implementation of other subsystems in the development.

5.1.5   Decomposing Refinement by Subtyping

It is possible to simplify the task of refinement by decomposing a large class **C**
into a collection of auxilliary classes which together make up a definition of **C**,

but which can be refined independently of it.

Two cases of particular interest are, firstly, the use of inheritance at the specification level to share a set of static data components (types, functions and constants) between a number of specification classes. In this case inheritance is not being used to create a subtype relation or to support polymorphism, and it is not necessarily the case that the shared class will itself need to be implemented, except in a trivial way. In particular, the class may define a recursive function which is then implemented in code as a loop. In the system implementation there is therefore no application of the abstract function, and hence, no requirement for the shared class containing the function to be implemented. (See exercise 5.1 above.)

Secondly, if there is a virtual class A with a list of exclusive subtypes A_1, ..., A_n, it is not necessary to implement the declared features of A itself, but simply to implement each of the subtypes. This is because every instance of A is actually of exactly one of these strict subtypes. In the executable system implementing this development, only a virtual class A is needed in the programming language being used, together with the subtyping declarations corresponding to those given in the specification.

5.1.6 Introducing Auxilliary Operations

A useful extension of the conventional concepts of refinement and subtyping is to allow the introduction of new sub-operations into a refinement or subtype in order to facilitate the implementation of the required operations. For example, a developer could make a design decision to implement an operation m of C as a composition m_1; m_2 in a refinement D of C, where m_1 and m_2 are operations *introduced in* D. Such a decomposition could be chosen because it is known that m_1 and m_2 will be easier to develop separately than m. However m_1 and m_2 may change the state of C (modulo the refinement relation) in ways inexpressible as a procedural combination of existing operations of C. An example where this is useful is given in Chapter 6, involving abstract queues.

Introduction of such operations is however harmless provided that no other subsystem can invoke them. Thus they should be made private to the class. Such hiding would be guaranteed in the case of refinements if the restriction that only abstract specification classes (classes which are not refinements of other classes) can be suppliers was enforced. In Eiffel also, private routines are allowed within a class: these routines do not need to preserve the class invariant in an environment in which there cannot be interruption of a composition of such operations.

A number of problems would be introduced if this condition were violated and auxiliary operations created as part of the process of design of a component C were available to other components of a development. During enhancement or adaption of the system for example, C may be redesigned so that these operations were no longer needed. If other subparts of the system however depended upon them, then they would still need to be implemented in the development path of **C**, even though they might be quite inefficient or contradictory in approach with the new development of **C**.

5.2 Refinement

5.2.1 Formal Definition

In Z^{++} a class **D** is a refinement of a class **C** via a data refinement relation **R** and a renaming ϕ of methods, if **D** is a subtype of **C** via ϕ and **R**, and ϕ is *surjective* (it maps the set of external methods of **C** *onto* the set of external methods of **D**). That is, no new functional requirements are introduced in **D**. However, new, purely internal operations can be introduced in **D**.

This definition is reasonable since it should not be the case that a developer introduces new requirements during the development process which are not present in the complete specification. Of course, in real developments new requirements are introduced all the time, all the way down to the final steps of implementation – but ideally such new requirements should then be reflected back into revised analysis and complete specification models, as discussed in Chapter 2. At a minimum, the haphazard nature of the addition of such requirements should not be apparent to an external assessor who only has the final documents produced from the development to examine – this is "faking a rational design process" in the sense of Parnas [244].

The notation $\mathbf{C} \sqsubseteq^{\mathrm{ref}}_{\phi, \mathbf{R}} \mathbf{D}$ will be used to distinguish refinements from subtypings, where necessary. The key element of both refinement and subtyping is the criterion of theory extension, that is:

> For every $\varphi \in \mathcal{L}_{\mathbf{C}}$, $\Gamma_{\mathbf{C}} \vdash \varphi$ implies that $\Gamma_{\mathbf{D}} \vdash \Box^r \mathbf{R}(\mathbf{u}, \mathbf{v}) \Rightarrow \phi(\varphi)$
> where $\mathbf{v}$ is the tuple of attributes of **D**, $\mathbf{u}$ of **C**.

for the respective class theories $\Gamma_{\mathbf{C}}$ and $\Gamma_{\mathbf{D}}$. Ideally, axioms of **C** should be derivable from the corresponding axioms of **D**, ie:

$$\vdash \varphi_{\mathbf{D}} \wedge \Box^r \mathbf{R} \Rightarrow \phi(\varphi_{\mathbf{C}})$$

where $\varphi_{\mathbf{D}}$ and $\varphi_{\mathbf{C}}$ are the corresponding axioms of the two classes.

Refinement is reflexive and transitive, and implies subtyping. A special case is when **R** is functional, when the refinement obligation can be simplified to

> For every $\varphi \in \mathcal{L}_{\mathbf{C}}$, $\Gamma_{\mathbf{C}} \vdash \varphi$ implies that $\Gamma_{\mathbf{D}} \vdash \phi(\varphi[\mathbf{R}(\mathbf{v})/\mathbf{u}])$ where $\mathbf{v}$ is the tuple of attributes of **D**, $\mathbf{u}$ of **C**.

Notice that the second $\vdash$ is now carried out entirely within the language of **D**, rather than in the combined language of **C** and **D**.

In VDM^{++} refinement relations are always functional, and in addition to the above constraints on ϕ, a refinement in VDM^{++} must satisfy the *adequacy* condition (see Section 5.4).

In the following subsections we will introduce some refinement techniques for the static and dynamic components of specification classes.

5.2.2 Refinement Techniques

Refinement involves a process of invention, which relies to an extent on ingenuity to achieve design goals such as efficiency or a high level of reuse, but which is always guided by:

- the intended implementation mechanisms (for example, particular data structures or concepts);
- knowledge of existing models of such systems which are used in the domain (for example, particular procedures and conceptual frameworks for defining air traffic control systems). It is often useful to make use of such elaborated models, since this enables existing expertise to be reused and validation to be continued into the design phase. Task analysis can be used here [157];
- language constraints which state which constructs are suitable to use as refinements of others.

Refinement contains two main elements: the transformation of abstract data types into more directly implementable types, and the transformation of operations into procedural forms. These two aspects can be performed in either order, or simultaneously. From the viewpoint of proof it is beneficial to defer procedural refinement as long as possible, in order to avoid introducing the complexities arising from branching control flow and intermediate states within an operation. However it is sometimes advantageous to delay data refinement until after elaboration of an abstract algorithm in order to enhance the clarity of description of this algorithm. The final step of data refinement is then performed by utilising (via clientship or private inheritance) library classes encapsulating particular data structures and operations on them.

Refinement of Data
The following are some initial guidelines for eliminating abstract mathematical types from a specification, mainly through the use of library classes. Consider the case where we wish to refine a class C to a class C_1.

- where an attribute **att** has a type of a form $\mathbb{F}(\mathbf{D})$ or seq$(\mathbf{D})$ representing a many-valued association with **D** a class type, and does not involve specialised constraints, it can often be refined using an instance s of a library component **Set_manager[D]** or **Sequence_manager[D]** which encapsulates standard operations on sets and sequences respectively. The data refinement will include a conjunct **att = s.contents**. Typically only a few operations from these classes will be needed to implement the operations of C in C_1, and they will be used in a quite direct manner;
- for other attributes of this form, but for which complex invariants over the elements of the sequence or set are needed (eg, that the sequence is sorted on a particular supplier attribute or group of attributes) the same library classes may be used, however their operations may be utilised via complex algorithms which involve navigation across or iteration over

these structures. For example, an insertion into a sorted list could require two such iterations. If available, more specialised library components encapsulating data structures optimised for particular sets of operations (such as various types of tree) would be more efficient and result in a simpler definition of methods in **C_1**. Failing this, the developer may have to invent their own algorithms and data structures and generalise them for inclusion in a library;

- attributes of type $a \ldots b \rightarrow \mathbf{T}$, for integer values **a, b**, can be refined by attributes of type $a \ldots b \rightarrow \mathbf{T'}$, where **T'** implements **T**, provided that the eventual implementation language supports direct definition of array types. In Eiffel such types could be translated into particular instantiations of the generic **ARRAY** class;

- attributes of a general map type $\mathbf{T} \nrightarrow \mathbf{S}$ can be replaced by an instance of a **Map_manager[T, S]** class which encapsulates a range of operations on such maps;

- we may "anneal" individual attributes or groups of attributes into classes which encapsulate these attributes and characteristic operations upon them, if we recognise that such a grouping is conceptually appropriate, or can assist in further development. For instance, attributes **att** of the type $\mathbf{T} \nrightarrow \mathbf{S}$ can be replaced by attributes **satt** : $\mathbb{F}(\mathbf{Maplet[T, S]})$ where **Maplet[T, S]** encapsulates pairs **datt** : **T**; **ratt** : **S** of elements of the original map. Other examples are given in Section 5.2.3 below.

As an example of these rules, consider the **Philosophers** specification of Chapter 4. We can replace the set-based specification of the **Table** class with a suitable sequence:

CLASS **Table_2**
FUNCTIONS

$$place : \mathbb{Z} \times \mathbb{N} \rightarrow \mathbb{N}$$

$$\forall z : \mathbb{Z};\ n : \mathbb{N} \bullet$$
$$(\exists k : \mathbb{Z} \bullet z = k * n) \Rightarrow$$
$$place(z, n) = n\ \wedge$$
$$\neg (\exists k : \mathbb{Z} \bullet z = k * n) \Rightarrow$$
$$place(z, n) = z\ mod\ n$$

OWNS
  forks : seq(**Fork**);
  philosophers : seq(**Philosopher**);
  seats : $\mathbb{N}$
INVARIANT
  seats = #philosophers = # ran philosophers $\wedge$
  seats = #forks = # ran forks $\wedge$
  $\forall$ i : 1 .. seats; p : **Philosopher** | p = philosophers(i) $\bullet$
      p.leftn = philosophers(place(i − 1, seats)) $\wedge$
      p.rightn = philosophers(place(i + 1, seats)) $\wedge$

$$p.leftn \ne p \land$$
$$p.rightn \ne p \land$$
$$p.leftf = forks(i) \land$$
$$p.rightf = forks(place(i + 1, seats)) \land$$
$$p.leftf = p.leftn.rightf \land$$
$$p.rightf = p.rightn.leftf$$

The refinement relation in this case is that

$$philosophers_1 = ran(philosophers_2)$$
$$forks_1 = ran(forks_2)$$

where v_i is the attribute of this name in Table_i.
   The formulae

$$\forall \; p, \; q : \; ran(philosophers) \; \bullet$$
$$\qquad p.leftf = q.leftf \; \Rightarrow \; p = q \; \land$$
$$\forall \; f : \; ran(forks) \; \bullet \; \exists \; p, \; q : \; ran(philosophers) \; \bullet$$
$$\qquad p.leftf = f \land q.rightf = f \; \land$$
$$\#philosophers = \#forks$$

follow from the remainder of the invariant of Table_2 since

$$philosophers(i).leftf = philosophers(j).leftf \; \Rightarrow$$
$$\qquad forks(i) = forks(j) \; \Rightarrow$$
$$\qquad i = j$$

and

$$philosophers(i).leftf = forks(i) \; \land$$
$$philosophers(place(i - 1, seats)).rightf = forks(i)$$

for each $i, j : 1 .. seats$.
   In turn, these sequences can be replaced by corresponding instances of the
Sequence_manager class:

CLASS **Table_3**
FUNCTIONS

$$place : \mathbb{Z} \times \mathbb{N} \to \mathbb{N}$$

$$\forall z : \mathbb{Z}; \; n : \mathbb{N} \bullet$$
$$\quad (\exists k : \mathbb{Z} \bullet z = k * n) \; \Rightarrow$$
$$\qquad place(z, n) = n \; \land$$
$$\quad \neg \, (\exists k : \mathbb{Z} \bullet z = k * n) \; \Rightarrow$$
$$\qquad place(z, n) = z \bmod n$$

OWNS
   f_seq : **Sequence_manager**[Fork];
   p_seq : **Sequence_manager**[Philosopher];
   seats : $\mathbb{N}$
INVARIANT
   $seats = \#p\_seq.contents = \# ran(p\_seq.contents) \; \land$
   ...

The refinement relation in this case is that

$$philosophers_2 = p\_seq.contents$$
$$forks_2 = f\_seq.contents$$

Exercise (5.2): Prove correct the standard refinement of a set-based class by a sequence based class (Figure 5.4). The refinement relation is $s = ran(sq)$

```
CLASS Set[X]                       CLASS Seq[X]
OWNS                               OWNS
  s  :  F(X)                         sq  :  seq(X)
OPERATIONS                         OPERATIONS
  add_element  :  X  →;              add_element  :  X  →;
  init  :  →;                        init  :  →;
  del  :  X  →                       del  :  X  →
RETURNS                            RETURNS
  is_in  :  X  →                     is_in  :  X  →
ACTIONS                            ACTIONS
  add_element x?  ==>                 add_element x?  ==>
    s' = s ∪ { x? };                   sq' = sq ⌢ ⟨ x? ⟩;
  init ==>                            init ==>
    s' = ∅;                            sq' = ⟨ ⟩;
  del x?  ==>                         del x?  ==>
    s' = s \ { x? };                   sq' = squash(sq ⊳ { x? });
  is_in x?  ==>                       is_in x?  ==>
    x? ∈ s                             x? ∈ ran(sq)
END CLASS                          END CLASS
```

Figure 5.4: Refinement of Set by Sequence

(a proof of refinement of one generic class by another is actually a family of refinement proofs, one for each class that may be substituted as a parameter).

Refinement of Operations
The following general forms of translation are used to replace abstract and logical method definition constructs in Z^{++} with procedurally oriented ones.

- ∧ and || in a specification class are replaced by ; (sequencing) or by ||| (parallel composition). That is, a particular order for the updates specified in the abstract operation is selected, or, if ||| is available in the implementation language, and the arguments of the abstract operator are specifying updates on disjoint sets of variables, simultaneous execution of the updates is used. The transformation of || to ||| can always be directly carried out if the latter operation is available. As examples, the method definition predicate

  $$a' = a + 1 \wedge b' = b * a'$$

  can be refined to

$$\mathbf{a} := \mathbf{a} + 1;$$
$$\mathbf{b} := \mathbf{b} * \mathbf{a}$$

whilst

$$\mathbf{a}' = \mathbf{a} + \mathbf{b} \ \wedge \ \mathbf{b}' = \mathbf{a} * \mathbf{b}$$

is refined to

$$\mathbf{a} := \mathbf{a} + \mathbf{b};$$
$$\mathbf{b} := (\mathbf{a} - \mathbf{b}) * \mathbf{b}$$

or

$$\mathbf{a} := \mathbf{a} + \mathbf{b} \ ||| \ \mathbf{b} := \mathbf{a} * \mathbf{b}$$

(or a new local variable can be introduced in the latter case)[1];

- $\mathbin{\mathaccent0{,}9}$ is replaced by ; . This is a valid refinement step in general, since it reduces non-determinism;
- PRE is eliminated either by defining an explicit action in the case that the precondition fails, ie, replacing

> PRE **P**
> THEN **Def**
> END

by

> IF **P**
> THEN **D_1**
> ELSE **ErrorAction**
> END

where **D_1** refines **Def**, or by calling operations of supplier objects whose specifications contain preconditions which are equivalent to **P**;
- an evaluation of a recursively specified function becomes a WHILE loop, as do iterated conjunction $\bigwedge$ and predicates involving an implicit or explicit existential or universal quantifier;
- method calls are often left unchanged;
- atomic updates $\mathbf{att}' = \mathbf{e}$ become assignments $\mathbf{att} := \mathbf{e}$.

An example of the application of these rules is the refinement of the operation

---

[1] Notice that if we have bounded data types, $(a+b)-b \neq a$ can occur because of overflow: a fully formal development needs to start with such bounded data types, rather than N or Z.

```
choose_philo  p!  ==>
     PRE
        ∃ p1, p2 : Philosopher | p1 ∈ philosophers ∧
                                 p2 ∈ philosophers ∧
                                 p1.pstate ≠ eating  ∧
                                 p2.pstate ≠ eating  ∧
                                 p2 = p1.rightn
     THEN
        p! ∈ philosophers ∧
        p!.pstate ≠ eating ∧
        p!.rightn.pstate ≠ eating
     END ;
```

of the **Table** specification of Chapter 4 with a version which uses the sequence based state given in the previous section:

```
choose_philo  p!  ==>
     PRE
        ∃ p1, p2 : Philosopher | p1 ∈ ran(philosophers) ∧
                                 p2 ∈ ran(philosophers) ∧
                                 p1.pstate ≠ eating  ∧
                                 p2.pstate ≠ eating  ∧
                                 p2 = p1.rightn
     THEN
        p! ∈ ran(philosophers) ∧
        p!.pstate ≠ eating ∧
        p!.rightn.pstate ≠ eating
     END ;
```

then refined by replacing the precondition with a conditional:

```
choose_philo  p!  ==>
     IF
        ∃ p1, p2 : Philosopher | p1 ∈ ran(philosophers) ∧
                                 p2 ∈ ran(philosophers) ∧
                                 p1.pstate ≠ eating  ∧
                                 p2.pstate ≠ eating  ∧
                                 p2 = p1.rightn
     THEN
        p! ∈ ran(philosophers) ∧
        p!.pstate ≠ eating ∧
        p!.rightn.pstate ≠ eating
     ELSE
        Unset_Philosopher[p!/c']
     END ;
```

and finally by an iteration using **Sequence_manager[Philosopher]**:

```
choose_philo p!  ==>
        VAR i, found : ℕ;  philo, nextphilo : Philosopher
        IN
        i := 1;
```

```
found  :=  0;
p_seq.First[philo/ee!];
p_seq.Next[nextphilo/ee!];
 WHILE i ≤ seats ∧ found = 0
 DO
    IF philo.pstate ≠ eating ∧
       nextphilo.pstate ≠ eating
    THEN
       found := 1
    ELSE
       i := i + 1;
       philo := nextphilo;
       p_seq.Next[nextphilo/ee!]
    END
 END;
 IF found = 1
 THEN
    p! := philo
 ELSE
    Unset_Philosopher[p!/c']
 END
END
END
```

The **Next** operation for **Sequence_manager** cycles around the sequence **contents** it encapsulates.

Notice that a history constraint of **Table** should include mutual exclusion between the **add_fork_philosopher** and **remove_philo** operations and any operations on the component forks or philosophers.

Direct access to the **pstate** attribute may need to be replaced by a suitable enquiry operation, in some implementation languages (but not, for example, in Eiffel). A loop has arisen because the original operation involved an implicit existential quantifier or search in its definition ("find **p!** such that ...").

The refinement of operations may also require the use of new supplier objects, local to the operation or to the object, in order to implement an algorithm. There are two main cases:

- new objects are used to hold persistent data which is required from one invocation of an operation to the next – if this data is sufficiently complex (such as a sequence) it should not be held in a simple attribute of the class, but instead encapsulated in a supplier object;
- where objects are introduced to support parallel computation – parts of the processing required by the operation are then distributed into different objects.

An example of the first case is the Hamming development of Chapter 6. An example of the second case can be given by the following numerical computation: find the sum of squares of the natural numbers between two given natural numbers.

An abstract (VDM^{++}) specification could be:

```
class Sum_squares0
functions
   ssquares :  ℕ × ℕ → ℕ
   ssquares(a, b)  ==  if a > b
                       then 0
                       else a * a + ssquares(a + 1, b)
instance variables
   begin, finish :  ℕ;
init objectstate ==
   begin = 0 ∧ finish = 0
methods
   set_up(a,  b :  ℕ)  ==
           [ext wr begin, finish
             post begin = a   ∧   finish = b];

   sum_squares() value r :  ℕ  ==
           ([ext wr r
                 rd begin, finish
              post r = ssquares(begin, finish)];
            return r)
end Sum_squares0
```

A refinement using distributed computation is:

```
class Sum_squares
instance variables
   begin, finish, result :  ℕ;
init objectstate ==
   begin = 0 ∧ finish = 0 ∧ result = 0
methods
   set_up(a,  b :  ℕ)  ==
           (begin := a;  finish := b);

   sum_squares() value r :  ℕ  ==
           (r := result;
            return r)

thread
  ( sel answer set_up;
    if begin < finish
    then
        (dcl ss1 :  @Sum_squares  :=  Sum_squares!new;
         dcl ss2 :  @Sum_squares  :=  Sum_squares!new;
         dcl k :  ℕ  :=  (finish − begin)/2;
           ss1!start;
           ss2!start;
           ss1!set_up(begin, begin + k);
           ss2!set_up(begin + k + 1, finish);
           k := ss1!sum_squares();
           result := ss2!sum_squares();
           result := result + k;
```

```
            sel answer sum_squares)
    else
        (result  :=  begin * begin;
         sel answer sum_squares) )
end Sum_squares
```

Integer division is assumed to round down here. **answer m** statements cannot occur outside of a select statement, in the version 5.2 of the VDM++ tools used in this book.

Opportunities for concurrent execution occur in that the two threads of ss1 and ss2 can proceed independently of each other and are only synchronised by their caller at the beginning and end of their executions. In this case however the overhead of creating and calling objects would probably outweigh any benefit arising from this parallelisation.

5.2.3   Annealing

Annealing is the process of introducing new supplier objects into a class definition during development. Typically this is carried out by replacing attributes in an object state by new supplier objects.

As an example, consider the following abstract class describing an aircraft flight:

```
CLASS Flight
OWNS
  flightlegs :  seq(String × N × String × N);
  airline :  Airline
INVARIANT
  ∀ i :  1 .. #flightlegs − 1 •
          fourth(flightlegs(i))  <  second(flightlegs(i + 1))
    / *   A leg must depart after the preceding leg arrives  * /
OPERATIONS
  change_leg_dest :  N₁ String  →;
    ...
ACTIONS
  change_leg_dest i? legdest?  ==>
      PRE i?  ≤  #flightlegs
      THEN
          #flightlegs′  =  #flightlegs  ∧
          third(flightlegs′(i?))  =  legdest?  ∧
          first(flightlegs′(i?))  =  first(flightlegs(i?))  ∧
          second(flightlegs′(i?))  =  second(flightlegs(i?))  ∧
          fourth(flightlegs′(i?))  =  fourth(flightlegs(i?))  ∧
          ∀ j :  1 .. #flightlegs | j  ≠  i?  •
                          flightlegs′(j)  =  flightlegs(j)
      END

END CLASS
```

An alternative and perhaps simpler way of writing the last conjunct is

$$(\{i?\} \lhd \textbf{flightlegs}') = (\{i?\} \lhd \textbf{flightlegs})$$

"apart from on the element i?, **flightlegs'** is the same as **flightlegs**".

The complexity of the operation specification arises directly from the choice we have made to "expose" all the structure of the sequence of flight legs. **first**, **second**, etc are pre-defined generic functions which return the corresponding elements of a general cartesian product.

This structure can instead be embedded in one or more object classes:

```
CLASS Flight_1
OWNS
  flightlegs :  seq(FlightLeg);
  airline :  Airline
INVARIANT
  ∀ i :  1 .. #flightlegs − 1  •
          flightlegs(i).arrival_time  <  flightlegs(i + 1).depart_time
OPERATIONS
  change_leg_dest :  N₁ String  →;
  ...
ACTIONS
  change_leg_dest i? legdest?  ==>
        PRE i?  ≤  #flightlegs
        THEN
            flightlegs(i?).set_dest(legdest?)
        END

END CLASS
```

Notice that the global frame axiom (cf: Appendix A) ensures that no other object in the structure **flightlegs** is modified by the above method definition, and our conventions about the write frame of operations ensures that **flightlegs** itself is not modified (since the identifier **flightlegs'** does not appear in the method definition).

The new supplier class is:

```
CLASS FlightLeg
OWNS
  depart :  String;
  depart_time :  N;
  arrival :  String;
  arrival_time :  N
OPERATIONS
  set_dest :  String  →
ACTIONS
  set_dest ss?  ==>
        arrival'  =  ss?

END CLASS
```

The refinement relation is that

flightlegs₀(i) $=$

      (**flightlegs₁(i).depart, flightlegs₁(i).depart_time,**

       flightlegs₁(i).arrival, flightlegs₁(i).arrival_time)

for **i** : dom(**flightlegs₀**), where **flightlegs₀** is the variable of **Flight**, and **flightlegs₁** the variable of **Flight_1**.

There are three main issues which need to be resolved when carrying out such a transformation from **C** to **C_1**:

1. that the client **C_1** has exclusive access to the new supplier objects;
2. that the supplier objects are not void;
3. that any invariant which refers to the internal structure of the new supplier objects is maintained by **C_1**.

The first constraint ensures that no change to object attributes of the new suppliers can occur whilst methods of **C** are not executing. This is necessary, since we have as an axiom that **abs**⊛**t** = **abs**⊛**t′** for any abstract attribute **abs** of **C**, where no method of **C** executes between times **t** and **t′**. Thus if **abs** is implemented by an object attribute **supp.conc** (or an expression involving such attributes), certainly **C_1** must ensure that **supp.conc**⊛**s** = **supp.conc**⊛**s′** where **s** = $\phi(\mathbf{t})$, etc.

Exclusivity may be relaxed if this condition can be ensured in other ways. However in most cases it is a reasonable requirement, since we are replacing (private) attributes and data of a class by corresponding (private) data in suppliers of its refinement.

The second constraint is necessary in order that every state of the concrete class has a corresponding abstract state. In the present situation this can be guaranteed by defining **flightlegs′** = ⟨⟩ as the initialisation in both classes, and requiring that new objects added to the **flightlegs₁** sequence are non-void.

The third constraint is related to the first, but may require additional work to ensure if the invariant of **C** linked data items which in **C_1** are expressed by data in distinct objects. Suitable enquiries of the supplier object states may be needed to detect possible violations of the invariant. In the above classes if the method **change_leg_dest** could have violated the invariant of **Flight** (which links successive elements of the **flightlegs** attribute), the corresponding operation of **Flight_1** would need to have placed a suitable enquiry on the state of **flightlegs₁** in its precondition.

Further examples of annealing in this book are the **Person** specification of Chapters 4, 6 and 8, where a **Sequence_manager** class is introduced to handle the sequence structure in **WorkingPerson**, and the similar approach for the **Philosopher** specification given above.

5.2.4 Annealing Relations

A further application of annealing is in transforming an abstract model of relationships into a more concrete implementation, which may make use of

pre-existing library components. Thus we might have the following abstract
representation of a relation **rel** between two sets of data **AData** and **BData**:

```
class Rel
  is subclass of RTypes
instance variables
  rel: set of (AData*BData);
init objectstate ==
  rel = {}
methods
  add_rel(a: AData, b: BData) ==
      [ext wr rel
       post  rel = rel~ union { mk_(a,b) }]

end Rel
```

where:

```
class RTypes
types
  AData = token;
  BData = token
end RTypes
```

defines the details of these types.

    Rel may be annealed into a class where the many-many relation **rel** is repre-
sented instead by two many-valued attributes of classes separately representing
AData and **BData**:

```
class AClass
  is subclass of RTypes
instance variables
  a: AData;
  rel_b: set of @BClass;
init rel_b == rel_b = {}
methods
  set_data(anew: AData) ==
      [ext wr a
       post a = anew];

  add_rel_b(b: @BClass) ==
      [ext wr rel_b
       post rel_b = rel_b~ union { b }]

end AClass


class BClass
  is subclass of RTypes
instance variables
  b: BData;
  rel_a: set of @AClass;
```

```
init rel_a == rel_a = {}
methods
  set_data(bnew: BData) ==
      [ext wr b
       post b = bnew];

  add_rel_a(a: @AClass) ==
      [ext wr rel_a
       post rel_a = rel_a~ union { a }]

end BClass
```

These follow a standard specification for managing sets of objects, and can be produced by inheritance from the instantiation of a template class such as **Set_manager**.

The refinement is then:

```
class Rel_1
  is subclass of RTypes
instance variables
  amap: map AData to @AClass;
  bmap: map BData to @BClass;
-- inv objectstate ==
--   (forall ad: AData & ad in set dom(amap) => amap(ad).a = ad)   and
--   (forall bd: BData & bd in set dom(bmap) => bmap(bd).b = bd)

-- retrieve function:
--   rel = { mk_(a.a,b.b) | a in set ran(amap) and
--                          b in set ran(bmap) and
--                          b in set a.rel_b }
--
init objectstate ==
  amap = { |-> }  and  bmap = { |-> }
methods
  add_rel(a: AData, b: BData) ==
      (dcl aobj: @AClass;
       dcl bobj: @BClass;

       if a in set dom(amap)
       then
         if b in set dom(bmap)
         then
             (aobj := amap(a);
              bobj := bmap(b))
         else
             (dcl bobj: @BClass := BClass!new;
              bobj!set_data(b);
              bmap := bmap ++ { b |-> bobj };
              aobj := amap(a))
       else
         if b in set dom(bmap)
```

```
      then
          (dcl aobj: @AClass := AClass!new;
              aobj!set_data(a);
              amap := amap ++ { a |-> aobj };
              bobj := bmap(b))
      else
          (dcl aobj: @AClass := AClass!new;
           dcl bobj: @BClass := BClass!new;

              aobj!set_data(a);
              bobj!set_data(b);
              amap := amap ++ { a |-> aobj };
              bmap := bmap ++ { b |-> bobj });

    aobj!add_rel_b(bobj);
    bobj!add_rel_a(aobj))
```

end Rel_1

Here ++ is the map override operator. **amap** and **bmap** record respectively the associations between data items and objects which the system knows about.

The complex case consideration is needed to minimise the number of objects which are created to represent data items.

5.2.5   Finite Differencing

A technique which can be used to increase the implementation orientation of a class is to replace a computed function by a local attribute. This only helps if a relatively simple definition of the changes in value to this function resulting from the other state transformation effects of methods of the class can be given.

As a simple example, consider a class encapsulating a sequence with standard operations on this, and an enquiry operation to return its length:

CLASS **Seq_example[X]**
OWNS
  contents : seq **X**
OPERATIONS
  init : $\rightarrow$;
  postappend_element : **X** $\rightarrow$;
  cut : $\mathbb{N}$ $\rightarrow$;
  ...
RETURNS
  len : $\rightarrow$ $\mathbb{N}$
ACTIONS
  init ==>
        contents$'$ = $\langle\ \rangle$;
  postappend_element x? ==>
        contents$'$ = contents $\frown$ $\langle$ x? $\rangle$;
  cut n? ==>

$$\text{contents}' = (1 \; .. \; \text{n?}) \lhd \text{contents};$$
len n! ==>
$$\text{n!} = \#\text{contents}$$
END CLASS

A refinement via finite differencing would be:

CLASS **Seq_example_1[X]**
OWNS
  contents : seq **X**;
  rlen : ℕ
OPERATIONS
  init : →;
  postappend_element : **X** →;
  cut : ℕ →;
  ...
RETURNS
  len : → ℕ
ACTIONS
  init ==>
$$\text{contents}' = \langle \; \rangle \; \land$$
$$\text{rlen}' = 0;$$

  postappend_element x? ==>
$$\text{contents}' = \text{contents} \frown \langle \; \text{x?} \; \rangle \; \land$$
$$\text{rlen}' = \text{rlen} + 1;$$

  cut n? ==>
$$\text{contents}' = (1 \; .. \; \text{n?}) \lhd \text{contents} \; \land$$
$$\text{rlen}' = \min(\text{rlen,n?});$$

  len n! ==>
$$\text{n!} = \text{rlen}$$
END CLASS

The refinement relation here is that **rlen** = #**contents**. This optimisation step would be less beneficial if we had an operation which changed the length of **contents** in some complex manner difficult to express in terms of its previous length.

5.2.6 Refinement Using Semaphores

A general approach for the refinement of classes with non-trivial synchronisation constraints is to utilise classes, such as semaphores, which provide specific synchronisation facilities. That is, a class **C** with synchronisation requirements expressed in its HISTORY clause will be refined by a class **C_1** which has a supplier class **S** whose properties can be used to prove the requirements of **C**. **C_1** itself may not need to contain any synchronisation mechanisms.

An example of an abstract synchronisation class is the following binary semaphore:

```
CLASS Semaphore
OPERATIONS
   signal :  →;
   release :  →
HISTORY
   #fin(signal)  ≥  #act(release)   ∧
   #fin(release)  + 1  ≥  #act(signal)
END CLASS
```

This class would be included in a class library of primitive synchronisation facilities.

As usual, the history constraint is implicitly quantified by a $\Box^\tau$ operator. It constrains objects of the class to execute **signal** and **release** in a strictly alternating fashion, with **signal** leading. If it were known that all methods of **Semaphore** were durative then this could be equivalently stated in RTL as

$$\underline{\text{signal}}\odot\clubsuit(\#\text{act}(\text{signal}) + \#\text{act}(\text{release}) = 0 \; := \; \text{false}, 1) \; \wedge$$
$$\Box(\underline{\text{signal}} \Rightarrow \bigcirc\underline{\text{release}}) \wedge \Box(\underline{\text{release}} \Rightarrow \bigcirc\underline{\text{signal}})$$

That is, **signal** is the first method (out of the two) to execute, and every execution of **signal** is followed next by one of **release**, and every execution of **release** is followed next by one of **signal**.

self_mutex({**signal, release**}) follows from the remainder of the class specification, since:

$$\#\text{active}(\text{signal}) + \#\text{active}(\text{release}) =$$
$$\#\text{act}(\text{signal}) - \#\text{fin}(\text{signal}) + \#\text{act}(\text{release}) - \#\text{fin}(\text{release}) =$$
$$(\#\text{act}(\text{signal}) - \#\text{fin}(\text{release})) + (\#\text{act}(\text{release}) - \#\text{fin}(\text{signal}))$$
$$\leq 1$$

Similarly **mutex**({**signal, release**}) follows from the remainder of the class specification.

Some examples of how this class can be used to establish required synchronisation properties follow.

5.2.7 Implementing Self and Mutual Exclusion

Consider the case where it is required that a particular method **m** is self-mutex:

```
CLASS C
OWNS
   ...
OPERATIONS
   m :  X  →  Y;
   ...
ACTIONS
   m x? y!   ==>   Def_m ;
   ...
```

```
HISTORY
  self_mutex({ m })
END CLASS
```

Then **C** can be implemented by using an instance of **Semaphore**, as follows:

```
CLASS C_1
OWNS
  s :  Semaphore;
  ...
OPERATIONS
  m :  X  →  Y;
  ...
ACTIONS
  m  x?  y!   ==>
              BEGIN
                s.signal;
                Code;
                s.release
              END;
  ...
END CLASS
```

where **Code** implements the state transitions defined in $\mathbf{Def_m}$.

Informally **C_1** refines **C** since (if **s** is only used by the method **m** and by a unique instance of **C**)

$$\forall \mathbf{i} : \mathbb{N}_1 \bullet \uparrow(\mathbf{m}, \mathbf{i}) = \uparrow((\mathbf{signal}, \mathbf{s}), \mathbf{i}) \ \wedge \\ \downarrow(\mathbf{m}, \mathbf{i}) = \downarrow((\mathbf{release}, \mathbf{s}), \mathbf{i})$$

and it is impossible for there to be two successive initiations of **signal** on **s** without an intervening **release**, so that there can be at most one invocation of **m** currently executing at any time.

Formally:

$$\#\mathbf{active}(\mathbf{m}) \ = \ \#\mathbf{act}(\mathbf{m}) - \#\mathbf{fin}(\mathbf{m}) \\ = \#\mathbf{act}(\mathbf{signal}, \mathbf{s}) - \#\mathbf{fin}(\mathbf{release}, \mathbf{s}) \ \leq \ 1$$

from the history constraint of **Semaphore**.

An extension of this approach allows the implementation of

$$\mathbf{self\_mutex}(\underline{\mathbf{methods}}(\mathbf{C})) \wedge \mathbf{mutex}(\underline{\mathbf{methods}}(\mathbf{C}))$$

Let **C_1** have the form:

```
CLASS C_1
OWNS
  s :  Semaphore;
  ...
OPERATIONS
  m₁ :  X₁  →  Y₁;
```

. . .
$m_n :$ X_n $\rightarrow$ Y_n
ACTIONS
  m_1 x_1? y_1!   ==>
            BEGIN
              s.signal;
              $Code_1$;
              s.release
            END ;

  ...
  m_n x_n? y_n!   ==>
            BEGIN
              s.signal;
              $Code_n$;
              s.release
            END

END CLASS

Then

$$\sum_{i=1}^{n} \#\text{active}(m_i) \; = \; \#\text{act}(\text{signal}, s) - \#\text{fin}(\text{release}, s) \; \leq \; 1$$

because

$$\sum_{i=1}^{n} \#\text{act}(m_i) \; = \; \#\text{act}(\text{signal}, s)$$
$$\sum_{i=1}^{n} \#\text{fin}(m_i) \; = \; \#\text{fin}(\text{release}, s)$$

More complex synchronisation behaviour can also be implemented using one
or more semaphores.   To obtain **self_mutex(methods(C))** without
mutex(methods(C)), **C_1** must use **n** distinct semaphore instances s_1, ...,
s_n, and the code of m_i must be bracketed by calls s_i.**signal** and s_i.**release** as
above.

5.2.8   Enforcing Interval Relations

A weaker concept of semaphore is one for which **release** can always occur,
but for which a **signal** can only occur after an immediately preceding **release**.
This could be specified as:

CLASS BasicSemaphore
OPERATIONS
  signal : $\rightarrow$;
  release : $\rightarrow$
HISTORY
  mutex({ signal, release }) $\wedge$

   self_mutex({ signal, release }) $\wedge$
   durative(signal) $\wedge$ durative(release) $\wedge$
   $\Box\neg$ ($\underline{\text{signal}}$ $\wedge$ $\bigcirc\underline{\text{signal}}$)
END CLASS

The final formula states that there cannot be two successive executions of
signal.
   This is sufficient to establish a relation between two execution intervals such
as "m_2 must finish before m_1 can start":

CLASS **Murphy**
OPERATIONS
   $m_1 :$ X_1 $\rightarrow$ Y_1;
   $m_2 :$ X_2 $\rightarrow$ Y_2
HISTORY
   $\forall$ i: $\mathbb{N}_1$ | i > 1 $\bullet$
         $\exists$ j: $\mathbb{N}_1$ $\bullet$ $\uparrow(m_1,i) \geq \downarrow(m_2,j)$
END CLASS

This can be implemented using the class:

CLASS **Murphy_1**
OWNS
   s1 : **BasicSemaphore**
ACTIONS
   m_1 x_1? y_1!   ==>
         BEGIN
            s1.signal;
            Code$_1$
         END;

   m_2 x_2? y_2!   ==>
         BEGIN
            Code$_2$;
            s1.release
         END

END CLASS

   The reason for the name of this class is that we want to use this idea to
"enhance" the **Station** specification of Chapter 3 with the requirement that a
train can only arrive on platform 3 after or at the same time as its connecting
train leaves from platform 4: a situation familiar to all commuters.
   This can be achieved by writing:

   train_arrives plat?   ==>
         PRE plat? $\in$ 1 .. #platforms
         THEN
            IF plat? = 3 $\wedge$ platforms(4).tstate = blocked
            THEN
                  s.signal
                        / * *The train must wait for its connecting train*

*on platform 4 to leave before it can arrive * /*

```
        END;
            trains_in_station  :∈  0 .. max_trains;
            platforms(plat?).train_arrives
        END;

train_departs plat?   ==>
        PRE plat? ∈ 1 .. #platforms
        THEN
            trains_in_station  :∈  0 .. max_trains;
            platforms(plat?).train_departs;
            IF plat? = 4
            THEN
                    s.release
            END
        END
```

in a refinement of **Station**. (The notation **var** :∈ set abbreviates ANY **var₀** : **T**
WHERE **var₀** ∈ set THEN **var** := **var₀** END, where set : $\mathbb{P}(\mathbf{T})$.)

This works because, if **s** is exclusively owned by a station object, then
each time $\downarrow(\mathbf{train\_arrives}(3), \mathbf{i})$ at which **platforms(4).tstate = blocked** is
equal to some $\downarrow((\mathbf{signal}, \mathbf{s}), \mathbf{i_0}) + \mathbf{d_0}$ for some small time interval $\mathbf{d_0}$. But at
$\uparrow((\mathbf{signal}, \mathbf{s}), \mathbf{i_0})$ there must be an immediately preceding termination
$\downarrow((\mathbf{release}, \mathbf{s}), \mathbf{j})$ of an **release** invocation (or this **signal** is the first in the
history). Thus there must have been a **train_departs**(4) invocation with
$\downarrow(\mathbf{train\_departs}(4), \mathbf{j}) = \downarrow((\mathbf{release}, \mathbf{s}), \mathbf{j})$, as required.

Similarly, using the original **Semaphore**, the requirement that every execution interval of $\mathbf{m_2}$ must be contained in one of $\mathbf{m_1}$ is implemented by:

```
ACTIONS
  m₁ x₁? y₁!   ==>
        BEGIN
            s1.signal;
            Code₁;
            s2.release
        END;

  m₂ x₂? y₂!   ==>
        BEGIN
            s1.release;
            Code₂;
            s2.signal
        END

END CLASS
```

The benefit of this approach is that the synchronisation requirements of a
wide variety of classes can be delegated to simple requirements of a single class.
However, semaphores are a low-level and rather error-prone synchronisation
mechanism, and more sophisticated approaches are discussed in Chapter 8.

Other interval relations and their interpretation in RTL are given in Appendix A.

5.3 Subtyping, Composition and Refinement

This section will consider the interaction between the three main development concepts of subtyping, composition and refinement, and how subtyping and composition structures may be used to decompose the task of refinement.

Because refinement is a form of subtyping, it is possible to apply polymorphism for methods between an abstract class and its refinements. This is most often used when there are several distinct alternative refinement paths for an abstract concept, which represent particular optimisations of the abstraction for specialised purposes.

As an example, consider various forms of **Table**, where the most abstract **Table[X, Y]** class simply models a table as a map **contents : X $\twoheadrightarrow$ Y** as in Chapter 6, with operations **defined**, **access** and **enter** to test membership, obtain a table entry, and update the table, respectively. More detailed models, which are both refinements in the sense of being steps towards implementation, and subtypes, in the sense of specialising the abstract table concept, could be **TableAsLinkedList**, **TableAsBST** (binary search tree), **TableAsBBST** (balanced binary search tree), and so forth. Thus we could have a development diagram as in Figure 5.5. Each of the classes within the dashed line represent models (using mathematical data types and abstract operation specifications) of particular ways of storing and manipulating tables. Complex algorithms may be used to describe their methods, or only the desired effect of these methods may be defined. Each of these classes can be used as a supplier to other classes, such as **Client** in the diagram.

For instance, **Client** could be:

```
CLASS Client
TYPES
  RESULT ::= present | absent
OWNS
  table :  Table[N,String]
OPERATIONS
  set_table :  Table[N,String]  →;
  test :  →  RESULT
ACTIONS
  set_table tab?  ==>
      table′  =  tab?;

  test res!  ==>
      BEGIN
          table.init ⅋
          table.enter(1,"test1") ⅋
          table.enter(2,"test2") ⅋
          (res!  =  present  ≡  table.defined(3))
```

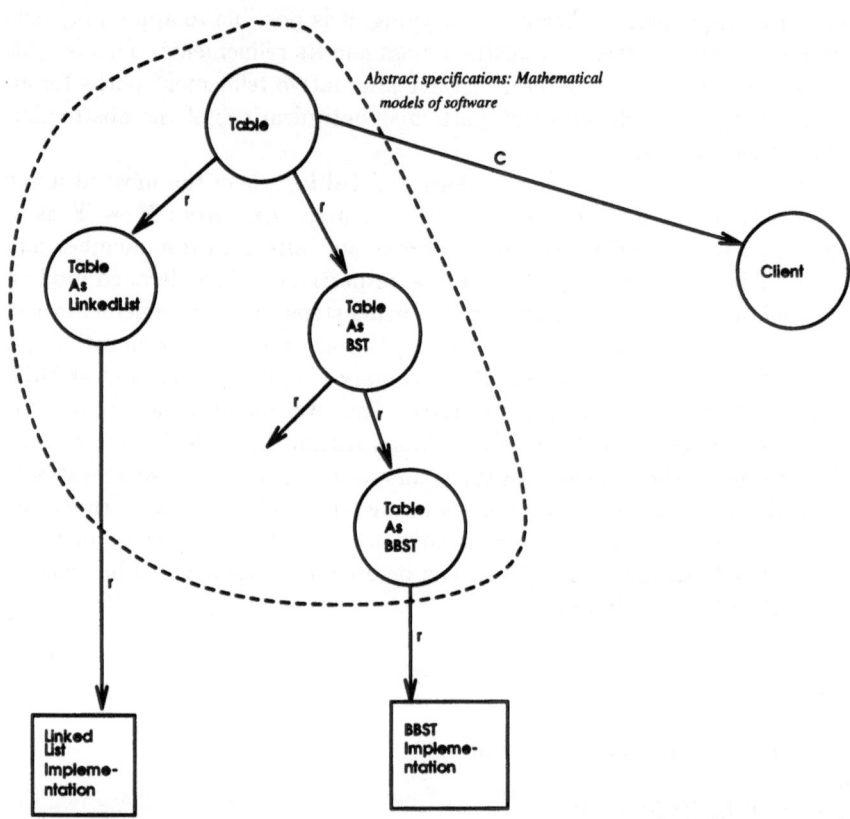

Figure 5.5: Refinements of **Table**

END
END CLASS

This class will work satisfactorily with any kind of table. As with subtyping, the particular meaning of the **enter** and **defined** methods will depend upon the actual type of **table** supplied by the **set_table** method.

However a more specialised class may require stronger properties of its table in order to satisfy requirements of efficiency or capacity, and so it would be a client of some refinement of table (which may itself have alternative refinements).

5.3.1   Using Subtypes in Refinements

A situation of some interest is when a subtype T_1 of an implementation S_1 of a class S can be used to implement a corresponding subtype T of S. This promotes code reuse – saving the duplication of work in implementing similar specification elements in two distinct refinement paths.

The two versions of a semaphore specification given in Section 5.2.6 provide an example of this technique.

An implementation of **Semaphore** can be given in terms of updates on a variable:

CLASS **Semaphore_1**
OWNS
   x : $\mathbb{N}$
OPERATIONS
   signal : $\rightarrow$;
   release : $\rightarrow$
ACTIONS
   signal   ==>
            $x' = 1$;
   release   ==>
            $x' = 0$
HISTORY
   $(x = 0) \odot \clubsuit (\text{self} \in \overline{\text{Semaphore\_1}} := \text{true}, 1)$ $\wedge$
   mutex({ signal, release }) $\wedge$
   self_mutex({ signal, release }) $\wedge$
   $\square(\overline{\text{signal}} \Rightarrow x = 0)$ $\wedge$
   $\square(\overline{\text{release}} \Rightarrow x = 1)$
END CLASS

The first conjunct of the history constraint asserts that $x = 0$ in the initial state.

Note that here it is not possible to prove the **mutex** assertion from the remainder of the class specification, since the ACTIONS and permission predicates can only control the value of x at initiation and termination times of the methods. However the requirements

   #fin(signal) $\geq$ **#act(release)** $\wedge$

#fin(release) $+ 1 \geq$ **#act(signal)**

can be shown, assuming **mutex** and **self_mutex**, as follows.

Since $x = 1$ is required at each initiation of **release**, and since the methods are executed in a strictly mutex fashion, for each initiation time $\uparrow(\textbf{release}, i)$ there must be a preceding termination time $\downarrow(\textbf{signal}, j)$.

However for each i there is a *unique* j, which is the index of the most recent termination of **signal**, since if two distinct invocations i_1 and i_2 of **release** had the same most recent termination of **signal**, the state at initiation of the later invocation of release would be $x = 0$, a contradiction. Thus at each time point there must be at least as many completed executions of **signal** as initiated executions of **release**, ie:

#fin(signal) $\geq$ **#act(release)**

at each time point. Similar reasoning gives the other inequality.

This reasoning is quite low-level, and it is preferable to use LTL reasoning in this case, since it is clear that **Semaphore_1** is durative in addition to being mutex and self-mutex. We have the properties:

$\square(\underline{\textbf{release}} \Rightarrow \bigcirc(x = 0))$
$\square(\underline{\textbf{signal}} \Rightarrow \bigcirc(x = 1))$

under the constraints of **Semaphore_1**, since an ACTIONS specification

```
m  x  y   ==>
       PRE  Pre
       THEN
              Post
       END
```

implies $\square(\underline{\textbf{m}} \Rightarrow \bigcirc\textbf{Post}[v/v'])$ in a mutex and self-mutex class in which $\square(\underline{\textbf{m}} \Rightarrow \textbf{Pre})$ holds, and where **Post** refers only to post-state variables v'.

Therefore, since

$\square(\underline{\textbf{release}} \vee \underline{\textbf{signal}})$

holds, it is clear that

$\square(\underline{\textbf{release}} \Rightarrow \bigcirc\underline{\textbf{signal}})$ and $\square(\underline{\textbf{signal}} \Rightarrow \bigcirc\underline{\textbf{release}})$

as required.

From these the inequalities on **#act** and **#fin** which define the alternation property can be derived by reasoning by cases.

In contrast, to implement **BasicSemaphore** we need the class **BasicSemaphore_1**:

CLASS **BasicSemaphore_1**
OWNS
  x : $\mathbb{N}$

```
OPERATIONS
  signal : →;
  release : →
ACTIONS
  signal    ==>
             x′ = 1;
  release   ==>
             x′ = 0
HISTORY
  durative(release) ∧
  mutex({ signal, release }) ∧
  self_mutex({ signal, release }) ∧
  □(signal ⇒ x = 0)
END CLASS
```

durative(signal) follows from its permission guard and postcondition.

Notice that **Semaphore** is a subtype of **BasicSemaphore** since its history constraint is stronger. **Semaphore_1** is a subtype of **BasicSemaphore_1** which can be expressed using inheritance:

```
CLASS Semaphore_1 EXTENDS BasicSemaphore_1
HISTORY
  (x = 0)⊙♣(self ∈ Semaphore_1 := true, 1) ∧
  □(release ⇒ x = 1)
END CLASS
```

Therefore, if we needed to implement both **Semaphore** and **BasicSemaphore**, it would be sufficient to implement the latter, and express the implementation of **Semaphore** in terms of that of **BasicSemaphore**.

Thus we have an instance of the situation shown in Figure 5.6.

In general there may be problems in attempting to use refined classes as supertypes, particularly at the code generation stage, since it becomes possible to use attributes and data of the refined class which are not present in its abstract specification and hence cannot be relied upon to be supported by its code implementation. Such cases therefore require a certain amount of manual translation. See the dictionary example in Chapter 8 for a further illustration of the issue.

5.3.2 Preservation of Refinement and Subtyping in Class Composition

Also of significance, particularly at the implementation level, is the degree to which a class using another as a supplier is a monotone context with respect to subtyping or refinement. This situation will explicitly arise for generic classes, when it is desirable that a class **G[C]** is refined by the class **G[D]** if C is refined by **D**.

Alternatively we may be interested in using a specific refinement **D** of a class **C** as a supplier. For instance, **D** might be a particular form of **Table**

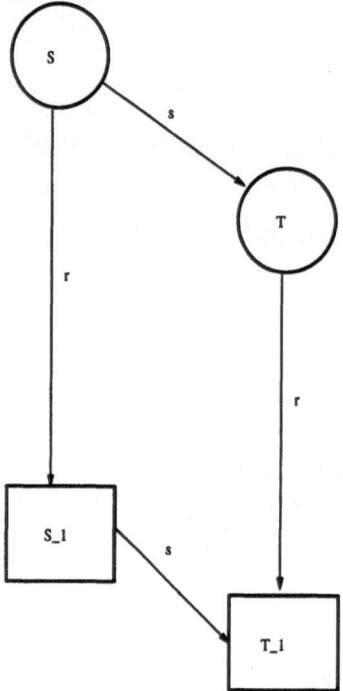

Figure 5.6: Using Subtypes of Implementations

class with a highly optimised set of operations for a specific task. In this case
we could prefer to prove a refinement step from an abstract specification **A**
to **G[C]**, and know the result that **G[C]** is refined by **G[D]** simply from a
previously established refinement **C** $\sqsubseteq$ **ref** **D**.

Let **G[X]** involve references to **X** only as an output type of operations, and
as the type of an attribute of **G[X]**, with all operations of **X** being invoked
in a refinement-preserving context, that is, in a context without a use of the
$\S$ operator or logical operators apart from $\wedge$. Then **G[X]** can be shown to
preserve subtyping and refinement of **X**. The subtyping relation between **G[C]**
and **G[D]** is built from the @**R** map between @**D** and @**C**, where **R** is the
refinement relation from **D** to **C**.

For example, if **G[X]** involves an attribute

$\quad$ **x** : seq(**X**)

and **C** is refined by **D** via **R** (and the identity renaming of methods), then a
refinement between **G[C]** and **G[D]** is constructed by

$$\#\mathbf{x} = \#\mathbf{x1} \; \wedge$$
$$\forall \mathbf{i} : 1 .. \#\mathbf{x1} \bullet \mathbf{x(i)} = @\mathbf{R}(\mathbf{x1(i)})$$

where **x1** is the corresponding variable in **G[D]**.

In VDM++ the additional condition of adequacy would be satisfied by this construction because of the stipulated adequacy of @**R** (see Appendix A).

It is possible however for **G[D]** to be inconsistent even if **D** and **G[C]** are consistent. An example would be where a requirement

$$\forall i : \mathbb{N}_1 \bullet \uparrow((\mathbf{m}, \mathbf{x}), i+1) = \uparrow((\mathbf{m}, \mathbf{x}), i) + \mathbf{td}$$

in **G[X]**, for **x** : **X**, states that **m** periodically executes with a period of **td** time units. **C** may allow such behaviour for **m**, but **D** may have a stronger history constraint which, for instance, states that **m** must execute more frequently than this:

$$\forall i : \mathbb{N}_1 \bullet \uparrow(\mathbf{m}, i+1) - \uparrow(\mathbf{m}, i) < \mathbf{td}$$

resulting in a **false** history constraint in **G[D]**.

5.4 VDM++

The concept of refinement in VDM++ is identical to that in Z++, except that the refinement relation **R** is always a function from the state of the refined class **D** to that of the unrefined class **C**, and there is an additional condition of *adequacy* on **R**. This condition asserts that every abstract state has some concrete state corresponding to it under **R**.

For sequential classes the definition can be simplified as follows. Let **C** be the class:

```
class C
instance variables
   vC : TC;
inv objectstate == InvC;
init objectstate == InitC
methods
   MP(x : X)
      pre PreMP,C(x, vC) ==
      [ext wr vC
       post PostMP,C(x, vC̄, vC)];
   ...
   MF() value y : Y
      pre PreMF,C(vC) ==
      ([ext rd vC
        post PostMF,C(vC, y)];
        return(y));
   ...
end C
```

where **MP** represents a typical update operation, and **MF** a typical enquiry operation.

D is defined analogously. Then it can be shown that the following conditions are sufficient (but not necessary) for **D** to refine **C** via a retrieve function $\mathbf{R} : \mathbf{T_D} \rightarrow \mathbf{T_C}$ and a renaming ϕ of the methods of **C** to those of **D**:

1. *(adequacy)*: $\forall s : \mathbf{T_C} \cdot \mathbf{Inv_C}(s) \Rightarrow \exists t : \mathbf{T_D} \cdot \mathbf{Inv_D}(t) \wedge \mathbf{R}(t) = s$;
2. *(initial)*: $\forall t : \mathbf{T_D} \cdot \mathbf{Init_D}(t) \Rightarrow \mathbf{Init_C}(\mathbf{R}(t))$;
3. *(invariant)*: $\forall t : \mathbf{T_D} \cdot \mathbf{Inv_D}(t) \Rightarrow \mathbf{Inv_C}(\mathbf{R}(t))$;
4. *(domain$_1$)*: $\forall t : \mathbf{T_D} \cdot \mathbf{Inv_D}(t) \wedge \mathbf{Pre_{MP,C}}(x, \mathbf{R}(t)) \Rightarrow \mathbf{Pre_{NP,D}}(x, t)$;
5. *(result$_1$)*: $\forall t, t' : \mathbf{T_D} \cdot \mathbf{Inv_D}(t) \wedge \mathbf{Pre_{MP,C}}(x, \mathbf{R}(t)) \wedge$
   $\mathbf{Post_{NP,D}}(x, t, t') \Rightarrow \mathbf{Post_{MP,C}}(x, \mathbf{R}(t), \mathbf{R}(t'))$;
6. *(domain$_2$)*: $\forall t : \mathbf{T_D} \cdot \mathbf{Inv_D}(t) \wedge \mathbf{Pre_{MF,C}}(\mathbf{R}(t)) \Rightarrow \mathbf{Pre_{NF,D}}(t)$;
7. *(result$_2$)*: $\forall t : \mathbf{T_D} \cdot \mathbf{Inv_D}(t) \wedge \mathbf{Pre_{MF,C}}(\mathbf{R}(t)) \wedge$
   $\mathbf{Post_{NF,D}}(t, y) \Rightarrow \mathbf{Post_{MF,C}}(\mathbf{R}(t), y)$.

where $\phi(\mathbf{MP}) = \mathbf{NP}$, $\phi(\mathbf{MF}) = \mathbf{NF}$, *(domain$_1$)* and *(result$_1$)* hold for each update operation $\mathbf{MP}$, and *(domain$_2$)* and *(result$_2$)* hold for each enquiry operation $\mathbf{MF}$. The initialisation is treated as if it were the postcondition of an update operation. This formulation allows the introduction of new attributes in $\mathbf{D}$, whilst logical equivalence would preclude this.

ϕ maps internal methods to internal methods, and external methods to external methods, and must be surjective on external methods. It may be non-injective on both groups, so that two methods in $\mathbf{C}$ can be implemented by the same method in $\mathbf{D}$, and may be non-surjective on internal methods, allowing new methods to be introduced in $\mathbf{D}$.

Types, functions and constants in $\mathbf{C}$ must have corresponding interpretations in $\mathbf{D}$. These interpretations must satisfy the logical properties asserted about these items in $\mathbf{C}$.

The *domain* and *result* laws are a special case of the requirement that the definitions of the methods of $\mathbf{D}$ satisfy the corresponding specifications of $\mathbf{C}$. Reasoning using weakest preconditions is required in the case that $\mathbf{D}$'s methods involve procedural constructs:

$$\mathbf{Pre_{MF,C}}(\mathbf{R}(t)) \Rightarrow ([\mathbf{Code_{NF,D}}(t, y)]\mathbf{Post_{MF,C}}(\mathbf{R}(t)))[t/\overleftarrow{t}\,]$$

where $\mathbf{Code_{NF,D}}(t, y)$ is the body of $\mathbf{NF}$, with weakest precondition [ ] for the specification statement (**pre**/**post**) defined as in the refinement calculus [285].

The **adequacy** condition is an alternative means of stating that no new requirements are introduced in the refinement class – in particular that no element of the state space of $\mathbf{C}$ is excluded by the specification of $\mathbf{D}$. If the **Elephant** example of Chapter 2 is re-examined, it will be seen that it fails to satisfy this condition[2].

Then many of the approaches described above can also be taken in VDM^{++}. The $\|$ operator of VDM-SL is somewhat different to that of Z^{++} and B AMN: $\| (x := e, y := f)$ in VDM simply abbreviates a bounded choice between $x := e;\ y := f$ and $y := f;\ x := e$, rather than the generalised assignment $x, y := e, f$ [152]. As a result it can always be refined by $x := e;\ y := f$, for example.

---

[2]However there is a generalisation of adequacy which requires that every abstract state is represented in *some* subclass – this condition could be ensured for the **Elephant** example by defining additional subclasses for each choice of colour.

The concurrent elements of a VDM++ class require special treatment. The use of semaphores to implement synchronisation policies can be achieved in VDM++ as for Z++. In general, a specification class defining permission guards P_i for methods m_i can be implemented by a class containing a thread, each of whose **answer m_i** or **self!m_i(args)** statements can only be reached if the condition P_i holds.

A class containing a trace specification can similarly be refined by a class containing a thread specification, using standard techniques for implementing entity life history constraints [58]. Dynamic behaviour expressed in threads can be directly translated into corresponding select statement constructs in procedural languages, such as ALT in OCCAM, and SELECT in Ada [146].

Conclusions

This chapter has introduced some techniques for refinement. Subsequent chapters will give many more examples of this process, and of other techniques suitable for reactive systems.

A choice has been made in defining refinement and subtyping, regarding internal operations. The definition requires that each internal operation **m** of the abstract class **C** has a corresponding internal operation $\phi(\mathbf{m})$ in its refinement or subtype **D**. Thus it is not possible to eliminate such operations, even though they are irrelevant to external users of the class. This (more restrictive than necessary) definition has been chosen in order to simplify the definition of subtyping and refinement in terms of theory extension: for every sentence of the language $\mathcal{L}_\mathbf{C}$ of **C** there is a corresponding sentence of $\mathcal{L}_\mathbf{D}$. This would not be true if we could eliminate method symbols. It also helps to avoid introducing new modal symbols $\square^\mathbf{ext}$, $\diamond^\mathbf{ext}$ and $\bigcirc^\mathbf{ext}$, which quantify over method initiation times of *external* methods only. In practice internal operations are used in much the same way from abstract specifications down to code, so this restriction is not critical.

Chapter 6

Proof Methods and Techniques

This chapter describes strategies for proof during specification (ie, of internal class consistency, or of validation properties) and design (ie, of refinement properties). The implications of the definitions of subtyping and refinement adopted for reasoning about object-oriented systems will be described.

There are several uses of formal proof or rigorous argument within a formal development process:

- validation of a specification against informal requirements by deriving properties which are expected to hold if the specification correctly captures the users intuitions about the domain;
- proof of internal consistency of a specification, ie, that it has an executable implementation;
- proof of refinement or subtyping.

A special case of validation is where specific properties are required for a system in order that the system is *safe* (ie, in a safety critical system, that hazardous situations cannot arise) or *responsive* (ie, in an on-line system, that certain actions are always available).

An example of safety reasoning is given in Section 6.1, and examples of availability or liveness reasoning in Section 6.2. Internal consistency proofs are covered in Section 6.3, and subtyping and refinement proofs in Section 6.4. Issues related to object identity are discussed in Section 6.5. Section 6.6 describes how information about the change in the global state can be derived from changes to the local state of objects. Section 6.7 gives approaches for discharging synchronisation requirements.

6.1 Safety Reasoning – Monitor and Gate

A *safety* property is one which expresses that a certain situation can never arise. Such a property is typically expressed by a formula of the form

$$\Box^\tau \varphi$$

"At all times in the future, φ holds."

The typing constraints of the attributes of a class are such a property. If class **C** (in Z^{++} or VDM^{++}) has an attribute declared as **att** : **T**, then the theory Γ_C of **C** contains the axiom

$$\square^r(\text{att} \in \mathbf{T})$$

An example from the requirements of the traffic light example of Chapter 7 is that at least one of the farm road or main road lights are red at all times.

A weaker class of assertions are those properties which must hold at a distinguished set of times. A class invariant is a simple example, which excludes certain states from arising during execution of the class – it has the logical interpretation $\square \mathbf{Inv_C}$ and $\forall i : \mathbb{N}_1 \bullet \mathbf{Inv_C} \circledcirc \downarrow (\mathbf{m}, \mathbf{i})$ for each method **m** of **C** – "$\mathbf{Inv_C}$ holds at each initiation and termination time of a method of **C**". Class invariants may legitimately fail to hold during execution of a method[1].

For the traffic light system, a desirable (but not always true) property would be that the main road lights should be green if there is no traffic on the farm road.

For systems formalised from statecharts, reasoning about which sequences of actions are forbidden, and how state residence of different objects connected by clientship relations are related, are typical activities. The extended RTL language of Chapter 4 can be used to reason about both Z^{++} and VDM^{++} formalisations of statecharts.

In the case of the monitor and gate system described in Chapter 3, a safety constraint could be that at each time point that the monitor **m** is in the state **Crossing**, the associated gate **m.g** is in the state **Down**. Formally, this is:

$$\forall i : \mathbb{N}_1 \bullet \exists j : \mathbb{N}_1 \bullet$$
$$\clubsuit((\text{mstate} = \text{crossing}) := \text{true}, i) \geq$$
$$\clubsuit((\text{g.gstate} = \text{down}) := \text{true}, j) \wedge$$
$$\clubsuit((\text{mstate} = \text{crossing}) := \text{false}, i) \leq$$
$$\clubsuit((\text{g.gstate} = \text{down}) := \text{false}, j)$$

A more concise expression of this assertion as

$$(\text{g.gstate} = \text{down}) \; covers \; (\text{mstate} = \text{crossing})$$

can be given using interval relations: Appendix A gives further details.

More realistically a "safe period" of at least 100 seconds between the closing of the gate and the passing of the train may be required:

$$\clubsuit((\text{mstate} = \text{crossing}) := \text{true}, i) \geq$$
$$\clubsuit((\text{g.gstate} = \text{down}) := \text{true}, j) + 100$$

---

[1] The requirement that the invariant holds at each method initiation and termination implies that external users cannot however observe an object whilst it is in an "inconsistent" state.

We can prove this in the theory of the monitor class, as follows. From the formalisation of the statechart we know that:

$$\clubsuit((\mathbf{mstate = crossing}) := \mathbf{true, i}) \;=\; \downarrow(\tau_1, \mathbf{i})$$

Call this time t1. Then:

$$\rightarrow(\tau_1, \mathbf{i}) + 300 \;\leq\; \mathbf{t1} \;\leq\; \rightarrow(\tau_1, \mathbf{i}) + 350$$

and we also (presume) that

$$
\begin{aligned}
\rightarrow(\tau_1, \mathbf{i}) \;&=\; \downarrow(\mathbf{at\_half\_mile}, \mathbf{i}) \\
&=\; \uparrow(\mathbf{at\_half\_mile}, \mathbf{i}) + \mathbf{d_1} \\
&=\; \uparrow((\mathbf{lower}, \mathbf{g}), \mathbf{j}) + \mathbf{d_1}
\end{aligned}
$$

for some $\mathbf{j} : \mathbb{N}_1$.

But also

$$\clubsuit((\mathbf{g.gstate = down}) := \mathbf{true}, \mathbf{j}) \;=\; \downarrow((\tau_2, \mathbf{g}), \mathbf{j})$$

Call this time t2. Then:

$$
\begin{aligned}
\clubsuit(\mathbf{enabled}(\tau_2, \mathbf{g}) := \mathbf{true}, \mathbf{j}) + 20 \;&\leq\; \mathbf{t2} \\
&\leq\; \clubsuit(\mathbf{enabled}(\tau_2, \mathbf{g}) := \mathbf{true}, \mathbf{j}) + 50
\end{aligned}
$$

and

$$\clubsuit(\mathbf{enabled}(\tau_2, \mathbf{g}) := \mathbf{true}, \mathbf{j}) = \downarrow((\mathbf{lower}, \mathbf{g}), \mathbf{j}) = \uparrow((\mathbf{lower}, \mathbf{g}), \mathbf{j}) + \mathbf{d_2}$$

Thus

$$
\begin{aligned}
\mathbf{t1} \geq \uparrow(\tau_1, \mathbf{i}) + 300 \;&=\; \uparrow((\mathbf{lower}, \mathbf{g}), \mathbf{j}) + 300 + \mathbf{d_2} \\
&\geq\; \mathbf{t2} + 250
\end{aligned}
$$

as required, where $0 < \mathbf{d_1}, \mathbf{d_2} < 1^2$.

If it had only been assumed that:

$$\uparrow(\mathbf{at\_half\_mile}, \mathbf{i}) \;=\; \leftarrow((\mathbf{lower}, \mathbf{g}), \mathbf{i}) \;\leq\; \uparrow((\mathbf{lower}, \mathbf{g}), \mathbf{j})$$

then $\mathbf{t1} \geq \mathbf{t2}$ could still be proved, provided that the delay in initiating execution of **lower** was not more than 250 seconds.

In particular, if several monitors can own the same gate controller, then the gate may not be in a state where **lower** can immediately be executed. It can however be seen from the statechart (and formally proved using its formalisation) that the maximum time taken to arrive in a state from which **lower** can be executed from one in which it cannot is 70, which is less than the bound of 250 seconds given above.

---

[2] When reasoning about a statechart, we usually assume that transitions take some non-zero but "negligible" time compared to the other time intervals contained in a specification.

This reasoning is an example of a characteristic form of reasoning used with timed statecharts, which compares the cumulative time bounds of corresponding paths through related statecharts. In order to prove an inequality between two events on distinct charts C and D, this process involves identifying time points α at which C and D are synchronised (here, it is the time point $\uparrow(\text{at\_half\_mile}, i)$), and then reasoning forward or backward from these time points to the points β for which the inequality is required. All possible paths from α to β will need to be considered, and the time bounds for the paths constructed as sums of the corresponding transition bounds.

In this case the path from $\uparrow(\text{at\_half\_mile}, i)$ to

$$\downarrow(\tau_1, i) = \clubsuit((\text{mstate} = \text{crossing}) := \text{true}, i)$$

consists of the following events and time intervals between them:

$$
\begin{array}{ccccc}
\uparrow(\text{at\_half\_mile}, i) & \text{------} & d_1 & \text{------} & \downarrow(\text{at\_half\_mile}, i) = \\
\rightarrow(\tau_1, i) & \text{------} & l_1 & \text{------} & \downarrow(\tau_1, i)
\end{array}
$$

in the chart for the monitor, where

$$0 < d_1 < 1$$
$$300 \le l_1 \le 350$$

and

$$
\begin{array}{ccccc}
\rightarrow((\text{lower}, g), j) = \uparrow((\text{lower}, g), j) & \text{------} & d_2 & \text{------} & \\
\downarrow((\text{lower}, g), j) = \rightarrow((\tau_2, g), j) & \text{------} & l_2 & \text{------} & \downarrow((\tau_2, g), j)
\end{array}
$$

where

$$0 < d_2 < 1$$
$$20 \le l_2 \le 50$$

for the gate.

It is therefore clear that

$$l_1 + d_1 \ge l_2 + d_2 + 100$$

which is the required inequality.

A similar argument provides the second conjunct of the requirement. It is possible to automate reasoning in RTL, provided that a suitable sublanguage is chosen, which avoids use of the $\circledast$ and $\odot$ constructs, and which uses a finite axiomatisation of a system. The Bledsoe–Shostak semi-decision procedure for Presburger arithmetic [272] could then be used, and would provide explicit counter-examples for assertions which do not follow from a given RTL specification.

6.2   Liveness Reasoning – Dining Philosophers

A liveness property is one which asserts that a system is always able to make progress or respond to particular requests. A special case is the assertion of the absence of *deadlock* [146]. Such properties are typically formalised by formulae with the structure $\diamond\varphi$, $\diamond^\tau\varphi$ or $\square\diamond\varphi$. Such properties are shown by contradiction, by building suitable "timeouts" into a system, or by finding a quantity **v** in the attributes of the class which is a positive integer, is strictly decreased by all the methods except the method **m** which is required to eventually execute, and for which the property

$$\square(\mathbf{v} = 0 \Rightarrow \underline{\mathbf{m}})$$

holds – ie, **m** is forced to execute when $\mathbf{v} = 0$.

As an example consider the dining philosophers case study of Chapter 4. A liveness constraint is that, at any time that the system is inspected, for every philosopher at the table there will eventually be a future time at which either that philosopher has left the table, or at which that philosopher is eating. This constraint is stated in the history of **Table** via the formula

$$\square(\forall\,\mathbf{p} : \mathbf{Philosopher} \mid \mathbf{p} \in \mathbf{philosophers} \bullet$$
$$\diamond(\mathbf{p} \notin \mathbf{philosophers} \vee \mathbf{p.pstate} = \mathbf{eating}))$$

This cannot be proved from the remainder of the class specification. A counter-example can be constructed as follows. Let **p**, **p1**, **p2**, **f1** and **f2** be in the configuration shown in Figure 6.1.

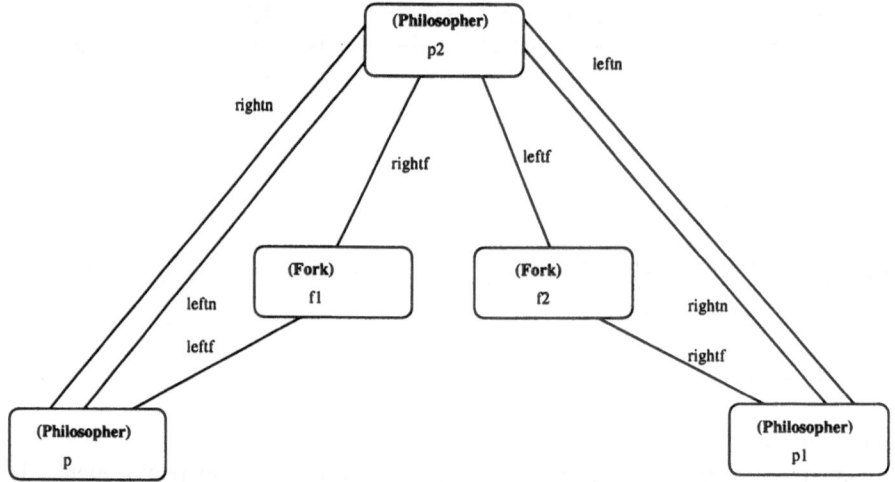

Figure 6.1: Example of Table Configuration

Then the following behaviour might occur (Table 6.1), where all philosophers begin in the **Thinking** state at time 0, and where a number beneath a state denotes the time at which this state is exited. In other words, **p** and

Philosopher	Thinking	Hungry	Eating	Thinking	Hungry	Eating
p	120	120	300	420	420	600
p1	300	300	420	540	600	
p2	120	?				

Table 6.1: Exclusion of Philosopher by Neighbours

p2 might reach the **Hungry** state together, but only one is chosen to enter the **Eating** state. Whichever is chosen (say **p**) can then conspire with **p1** to prevent **forks free** ever holding for **p2**, by strictly alternating membership of the **Eating** state between them. **p** spends 180 seconds on each 300 second cycle within the **Eating** state, and 120 seconds outside this state, whilst **p1** spends 180 seconds outside this state and 120 seconds within it.

The approach taken to solving this problem is to carry out a refinement. Since the notion of refinement is based on theory extension, a refinement of **Table** will have a stronger RTL theory as its history constraint, and hence will establish the liveness requirement. In its turn, this history constraint must be shown to hold in a further refinement, until eventually the level of source code is reached. We do not wish to place the appropriate condition directly in the **Philosopher** class, because this could limit the reuse possibilities for this class. Alternative refinement paths could be constructed for the class in the case that liveness is not a concern.

In this case the refinement simply involves placing a stronger constraint on the transition **forks_up**. This constraint is:

$$\textbf{residence(hungry)} \geq \textbf{residence(leftn, hungry)} \ \wedge$$
$$\textbf{leftf.fstate} = \textbf{down} \ \wedge$$
$$\textbf{residence(hungry)} \geq \textbf{residence(rightn, hungry)} \ \wedge$$
$$\textbf{rightf.fstate} = \textbf{down}$$

where (for a general statechart formalisation)

$$\exists\, i : \mathbb{N}_1 \mid t \in \overleftarrow{\textbf{p.state} = \textbf{S}, i} \bullet$$
$$\textbf{residence(p, S)} \circledast t \; = \; t - \inf(\overleftarrow{\textbf{p.state} = \textbf{S}, i}) \ \vee$$
$$(\neg \ \exists\, i : \mathbb{N}_1 \mid t \in \overrightarrow{\textbf{p.state} = \textbf{S}, i}) \ \wedge$$
$$\textbf{residence(p, S)} \circledast t \; = \; 0$$

Where $\overleftrightarrow{\varphi, i}$ is the i-th interval in which φ is true (the definition of this is given in Appendix A), and $\inf(\mathbf{X})$ gives the infimum of a set $\mathbf{X}$ of real numbers.

residence(p, S) therefore denotes the length of time that **p** has spent in the state **S**, from the last time that it entered **S** to the present (this interval is 0 if **p** is not currently in **S**). **residence(S)** is defined similarly, but without the qualification of **state** by **p**.

The new constraint therefore allows the current philosopher to move to the **Eating** state only if it has been waiting in the **Hungry** state at least as long as its immediate neighbours. Clearly this specification is a refinement of the previous case (apart from the liveness constraint).

It also ensures the liveness requirement, as follows. Let $p \in$ **philosophers** at the event time $\clubsuit(E, i)$.

Assume **p.pstate** = **thinking** for generality, and that $p \in$ **philosophers** at each further event time that we consider. Since **p.pstate** = **hungry** must become true within 300 seconds of $\clubsuit(E, i)$, it is sufficient to show that eventually **p** will be the only element of **philosophers** for which the **forks_up** transition is enabled. Such a **p** will perform a transition to the **Eating** state as soon as it becomes enabled because no other **q** can overtake it: such **q** will be blocked while **p** remains in the **Hungry** state. This can be shown by induction on the number **n** of $q \in$ **philosophers** such that

$$\text{residence}(q, \text{hungry}) \geq \text{residence}(p, \text{hungry})$$

A further form of liveness property which it might be required to express are bounds on the relative residence times of the Thinking versus Eating states.

To express these, define a term **time_in(S, t)** which gives the total residence time in the state **S** up to and including the time denoted by the time-valued term **t**. This is:

$$
\begin{aligned}
\textbf{time\_in(S, t)} =\ & \\
\Sigma\{i : \mathbb{N}_1 \mid\ & \clubsuit((\text{state} = S) := \text{false}, i) \leq t\ \bullet \\
& \clubsuit((\text{state} = S) := \text{false}, i) - \clubsuit((\text{state} = S) := \text{true}, i)\} + \\
\Sigma\{i : \mathbb{N}_1 \mid\ & \clubsuit((\text{state} = S) := \text{true}, i) \leq t\ \wedge \\
& \clubsuit((\text{state} = S) := \text{false}, i) > t\ \bullet \\
& t - \clubsuit((\text{state} = S) := \text{true}, i)\}
\end{aligned}
$$

for an initial state **S**. For a non-initial state it is defined as:

$$
\begin{aligned}
\textbf{time\_in(S, t)} =\ & \\
\Sigma\{i : \mathbb{N}_1 \mid\ & \clubsuit((\text{state} = S) := \text{false}, i + 1) \leq t\ \bullet \\
& \clubsuit((\text{state} = S) := \text{false}, i + 1) - \\
& \quad \clubsuit((\text{state} = S) := \text{true}, i)\} + \\
\Sigma\{i : \mathbb{N}_1 \mid\ & \clubsuit((\text{state} = S) := \text{true}, i) \leq t\ \wedge \\
& \clubsuit((\text{state} = S) := \text{false}, i + 1) > t\ \bullet \\
& t - \clubsuit((\text{state} = S) := \text{true}, i)\}
\end{aligned}
$$

In this problem it can be shown that

$$
\forall i : \mathbb{N}_1 \mid i > 1 \bullet \\
\tfrac{1}{5} \leq \textbf{time\_in(eating, t)}/\textbf{time\_in(thinking, t)} \leq 6
$$

The duration in each state is assessed at the endpoints $t = \clubsuit((\text{pstate} = \text{thinking}) := \text{true}, i)$ of the life cycles of the philosophers.

6.3 Internal Consistency Proofs

Internal consistency proofs are frequently quite mechanical and direct to resolve. In addition it is possible to reuse proof techniques and theories when performing these proofs, because classes derived from OMT models often have close structural similarities to each other, even if the names of attributes and the domain meaning of these classes differ.

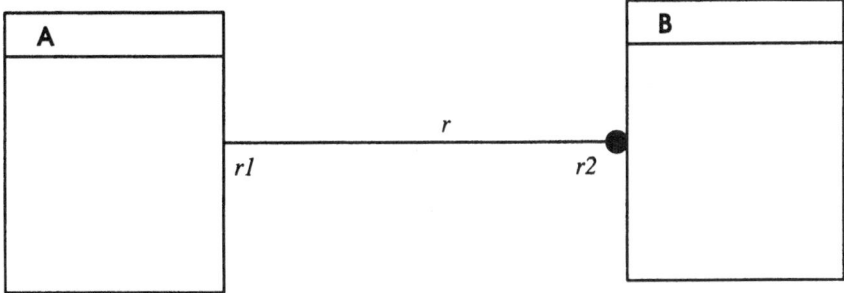

Figure 6.2: Typical Association in Object Model

A frequently occurring case concerns the standard operations generated from object model descriptions to manipulate associations. A typical operation, formalised from Figure 6.2, has the form:

```
add_r2(b: @B) ==
    [ext wr r2
    post  r2 = r2˜ union { b }]
```

As a result there is the internal consistency proof obligation

$$b \in @\mathbf{B} \wedge r2 \in \mathbb{F}(@\mathbf{B}) \Rightarrow r2 \cup \{b\} \in \mathbb{F}(@\mathbf{B})$$

which is directly shown from set theory and predicate logic. This proof is independent of the meaning of the association $\mathbf{r}$, and of any other additional properties of this association, so can be reused for similar classes.

6.4   Refinement and Subtyping Proofs

This section will discuss a variety of issues concerning refinement and proofs of refinement and subtyping. Section 6.4.1 provides an illustration of "annealing" or the "independent structuring" approach to refinement. Section 6.4.2 provides an illustration of the 'continuity of structure' approach. Section 6.4.3 demonstrates reasoning about method polymorphism. Section 6.4.4 considers how the locality constraints present in refinement proofs can be verified. Section 6.4.5 gives an example of the introduction of auxilliary operations.

The core element of proving that class $\mathbf{D}$ refines class $\mathbf{C}$ via a translation of methods ϕ and state $\mathbf{R}$ is showing that the theory $\Gamma_{\mathbf{D}}$ of $\mathbf{D}$ proves each translated axiom $\phi(\varphi[\mathbf{R}(\mathbf{v})/\mathbf{u}])$ of $\Gamma_{\mathbf{C}}$. It is usual to decompose this proof by only making use of the corresponding axiom $\varphi_{\mathbf{D}}$ of $\mathbf{D}$ to establish $\phi(\varphi[\mathbf{R}(\mathbf{v})/\mathbf{u}])$. Thus, for example, the (translation of the) fact that $\mathbf{Inv_C}$ holds at each method initiation and termination time of a method of **C** should be provable from the corresponding fact for **Inv_D** in **D**:

$$\Box_{\mathbf{D}}\mathbf{Inv_D} \wedge \forall i : \mathbb{N}_1 \bullet \mathbf{Inv_D} \!\odot\! \downarrow (n, i) \vdash$$
$$\phi(\Box_{\mathbf{C}}\mathbf{Inv_C}) \wedge \forall i : \mathbb{N}_1 \bullet \phi(\mathbf{Inv_C} \!\odot\! \downarrow (m, i))$$

assuming an identity data refinement, and that $n = \phi(m)$.

A sufficient, but not necessary condition to establish this is that

$$\Box^\tau (\mathbf{Inv_D} \Rightarrow \mathbf{Inv_C}) \!\odot\! 0$$

A proof tool can therefore present the developer with this more general proof obligation, and only consider the more complex but logically weaker obligation if this cannot be established. A similar choice arises for obligations for methods and for particular forms of history constraint such as permission requirements.

6.4.1 Hamming Sequences

This refinement example illustrates the case where the structure of a specification and implementation are entirely different, with the specification consisting of a single highly abstract class, and the implementation being constructed from a number of special purpose classes. It shows how a standard object-oriented design approach (replacing complex algorithms by complex object structuring) can be imitated in the formal development context.

Consider the following abstract specification of the "hamming sequence" [146].

CLASS **Hamming** EXTENDS **Sorter_Definitions**
FUNCTIONS

---
hamming_sequence : $\mathbb{N}_1 \to \mathbb{N}_1$

$\forall i : \mathbb{N}_1 \bullet$
$\quad \forall p : \mathbf{Primes} \mid$
$\quad\quad$ p divides **hamming_sequence**(i) $\Rightarrow$ p $\in \{2, 3, 5\}$ $\wedge$
$\quad$ **sorted**$(1 .. i \lhd$ **hamming_sequence**) $\wedge$
$\quad \forall n : \mathbb{N}_1 \mid$
$\quad\quad (\forall p : \mathbf{Primes} \bullet$
$\quad\quad\quad$ p divides n $\Rightarrow$ p $\in \{2, 3, 5\}) \bullet$
$\quad\quad\quad$ n $\in$ **ran**(**hamming_sequence**))

[hamming_sequence consists exactly of those positive natural numbers whose prime divisors are 2, 3 or 5, and it is ordered]

OPERATIONS
  init : $\to$;
  hamming : $\mathbb{N}_1 \to \mathbb{N}_1$
ACTIONS
  hamming k? out! ==>
      out! = hamming_sequence(k?)
END CLASS

Note that the operation **init** must be listed since it will be expected to be part of the interface of the subsystem specified by **Hamming**, even if it cannot be given a non-trivial definition in this specification.

Primes denotes the usual set of prime numbers, whilst **divides** denotes arithmetic integer divisibility.

This class is an abstract declarative specification, suitable for use as a complete specification of these particular requirements in a formal development.

It will be refined using a "dataflow architecture" [10] in which separate objects have the tasks of generating all multiples $p * i$ where $i \in \text{ran}(\textbf{hamming\_sequence})$, for $p \in \{2, 3, 5\}$. A further object will sort the resulting numbers, and the feedback from the output of this sorter to the multiplier objects will be coordinated by a manager object.

A basic multiplier is as follows:

```
CLASS Mult
FUNCTIONS
   | scale : N
OWNS
   output : Pushable[N]
OPERATIONS
   compute : N  →;
   set_output : Pushable[N]  →
ACTIONS
   compute n?   ==>
         output.push(n? * scale);

   set_output p?  ==>
         output' = p?
END CLASS
```

where:

```
CLASS Pushable[X]
OPERATIONS
   push : X  →
END CLASS
```

These classes are then specialised as follows:

```
CLASS Sorter EXTENDS Pushable[N], Sorter_definitions
OWNS
   sort_queue : seq(N)
INVARIANT
   sorted(sort_queue)
OPERATIONS
   *init : →;
   access : N₁ → N
ACTIONS
   *init ==>   sort_queue' = ⟨ ⟩;

   push n? ==>
```

ran(sort_queue$'$) = ran(sort_queue) $\cup$ { n? } $\wedge$
sorted(sort_queue$'$);

access i? n! ==>
    PRE i? $\leq$ #sort_queue
    THEN
        n! = sort_queue(i?)
    END
HISTORY
  Mutex$_C$ $\wedge$ SelfMutex$_C$ $\wedge$
  $\forall$ i? : $\mathbb{N}_1$ $\bullet$ $\Box$($\underline{\text{access(i?)}}$ $\Rightarrow$ i? $\leq$ #sort_queue)
END CLASS

As a result of the permission guard on **access**, execution of this operation will be blocked (the invocation will be in a **waiting** state) until sufficient elements of the queue have been accumulated for the access to succeed.

    Sorter_definitions is the class:

CLASS **Sorter_definitions**
FUNCTIONS

$$
\begin{array}{l}
\text{sorted } \_ : \mathbb{P}(\text{seq}(\mathbb{N})) \\
\hline
\forall\, sq : \text{seq}(\mathbb{N}) \bullet \\
\quad \text{sorted}(sq) \ \equiv \\
\qquad \forall\, i, j : \text{dom}(sq) \mid i < j \bullet sq(i) < sq(j)
\end{array}
$$

END CLASS

    Multipliers for particular constants are created by inheritance:

CLASS **Mult2** EXTENDS **Mult**
FUNCTIONS
  scale = 2
END CLASS

Classes **Mult3** and **Mult5** are defined similarly. (An alternative, and perhaps preferable approach, would be to use a single **Mult** class and to provide an operation to initialise **scale**.)

    The following class refines **Hamming**, via the identity renaming of methods. Note that it does not need to provide an interpretation of the **hamming_sequence** function since all references to this function have been replaced by procedural code.

CLASS **Hamming_1** EXTENDS **Sorter_definitions**
OWNS
  mult2 : **Mult2**;
  mult3 : **Mult3**;
  mult5 : **Mult5**;

```
    sorter :  Sorter
OPERATIONS
   init :  → ;
   hamming :  N₁  →  N₁
ACTIONS
   init  ==>
        New_Mult2[mult2/mult2!]  ∧
        New_Mult3[mult3/mult3!]  ∧
        New_Mult5[mult5/mult5!]  ∧
        New_Sorter[sorter/sorter!]  ∧
        mult2'.output  =  sorter  ∧
        mult3'.output  =  sorter  ∧
        mult5'.output  =  sorter;

   hamming k? out!   ==>
        VAR i :  N;   y :  N
        IN
            i  :=  1;
            sorter.push(1);
            WHILE i  ≤  k?
            DO
                 y  ⟵  sorter.access(i);
                 mult2.compute(y);
                 mult3.compute(y);
                 mult5.compute(y);
                 i  :=  i + 1
            END;
                 out!  ⟵  sorter.access(k?)
        END
END CLASS
```

In this class there is a mixture of quite abstract method definitions (**init**) and procedural definitions (**hamming**). A further refinement step would be needed before procedural code can be automatically generated.

The structure of the development is shown in Figure 6.3. Note that the structure of the first stage of refinement is almost entirely different to the structure of the abstract specification, which only contains the **Hamming** and **Sorter_definitions** classes. In contrast the first refinement stage has necessitated the definition of an additional six classes and subtyping relationships between them. At this level of the development there are therefore five subsystems which will need to be refined to code: **Hamming**, **Mult2**, **Mult3**, **Mult5** and **Sorter**. **Sorter_definitions** may also need to be implemented.

How can this refinement be proved correct? A first requirement is to show that $\#sorter.sort\_queue \geq k?$ is ensured by the loop when the request out! $\longleftarrow$ sorter.access(k?) is made, so that the access does take place without blocking.

This is shown by proving that the following two predicates are invariant

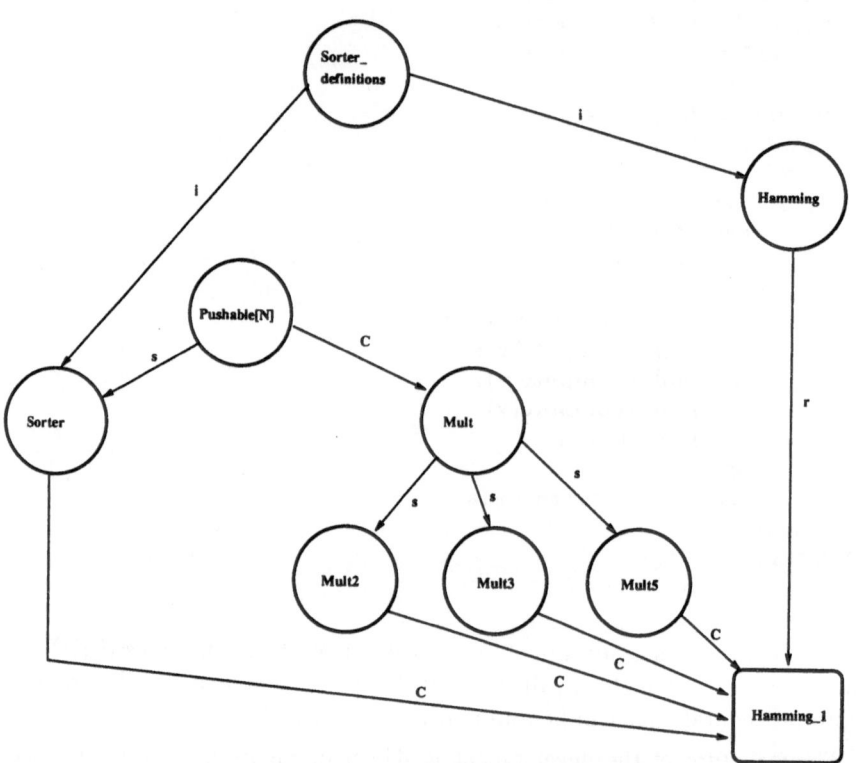

Figure 6.3: Structure of **Hamming** Development

over the loop:

(I$_1$) : $\forall i : 1 .. \#$**sorter.sort_queue** •
$$\textbf{sorter.sort\_queue}(i) \geq i$$

(I$_2$) : $i \leq \#$**sorter.sort_queue**

The first also requires the easily proved assertion that ran(**sorter.sort_queue**) $\subseteq$ $\mathbb{N}_1$.

(**I$_1$**) follows since it is clear that a **sorter.access** operation preserves this property, and a **sorter.push(x)** operation also does since either

1. **x** is already in the sequence, and the result is trivial;
2. **x** is smaller than every element of **sorter.sort_queue** and **sorter'.sort_queue** = $\langle x \rangle \frown$ **sorter.sort_queue** – in which case, since $x \geq 1$, and $x <$ **sorter.sort_queue**(1), **sorter.sort_queue**(1) ≥ 2, etc, and **sorter.sort_queue**(j) $\geq$ j for each j : $\mathbb{N}_1$, we have **sorter'.sort_queue**(j + 1) = **sorter.sort_queue**(j) $\geq$ j + 1 as required;
3. **x** is greater than every element of **sorter.sort_queue** so that **sorter'.sort_queue** = **sorter.sort_queue** $\frown \langle x \rangle$, and since

$$x > \textbf{sorter.sort\_queue}(\#\textbf{sorter.sort\_queue}) \geq$$
$$\#\textbf{sorter.sort\_queue}$$

we know that $x \geq \#$**sorter.sort_queue** + 1 as required;

4. **x** is inserted into the body of **sort_queue**, ie: **sorter'.sort_queue** = $s1\frown$ $\langle x \rangle \frown s2$ where **sorter.sort_queue** = $s1 \frown s2$ – this case is a combination of the previous two.

(**I$_2$**) follows from this since it is true at the first iteration of the loop, and assuming it holds at the beginning of the loop, then, after execution of **y** ⟵ **sorter.access(i)**, **y** will hold the value of **sorter.sort_queue(i)** at this point, and the three elements generated from the multipliers will be $5 * \textbf{y}$, $3 * \textbf{y}$ and $2 * \textbf{y}$ which are all strictly greater than **y**, and hence **i**. Thus they are added to the part of **sorter.sort_queue** strictly after **i**:

$$(1 .. i) \lhd \textbf{sorter'.sort\_queue} = (1 .. i) \lhd \textbf{sorter.sort\_queue}$$

and $i + 1 \leq \#$**sorter'.sort_queue** as required.

Thus all accesses to **sorter.sort_queue** are valid. A similar argument proves that **out!** is in fact **hamming_sequence(k?)** as required for the refinement.

Testing of the resulting system is however the most immediately convincing validation of its correctness, and should be performed, if possible, before any detailed proofs are entered into, in order to avoid wasted effort.

A further refinement would involve a tabulation of the already computed values, so that these values can immediately be returned when requested:

```
CLASS Hamming_2 EXTENDS Sorter_definitions
OWNS
    mult2 :  Mult2;
    mult3 :  Mult3;
    mult5 :  Mult5;
    sorter :  Sorter;
    table :  Table[ℕ,ℕ]
OPERATIONS
    init :  → ;
    hamming :  ℕ₁  →  ℕ₁
ACTIONS
    init  ==>
        BEGIN
            mult2  ⟵  New_Mult2;
            mult3  ⟵  New_Mult3;
            mult5  ⟵  New_Mult5;
            sorter  ⟵  New_Sorter;
            table  ⟵  New_Table[ℕ,ℕ] ;
            mult2.set_output(sorter);
            mult3.set_output(sorter);
            mult5.set_output(sorter)
        END;

    hamming k? out!  ==>
            IF  table.defined(k?)
            THEN
                out!  ⟵  table.access(k?)
            ELSE
                    VAR i :  ℕ;  y :  ℕ
                    IN
                        i  :=  1;
                        sorter.push(1);
                        WHILE i  ≤  k?
                        DO
                                y  ⟵  sorter.access(i);
                                mult2.compute(y);
                                mult3.compute(y);
                                mult5.compute(y);
                                i  :=  i + 1
                        END;
                        out!  ⟵  sorter.access(k?)
                    END;
                    table.enter(k?, out!)
            END
END CLASS
```

where **Table** is a generic class with the outline definition:

```
CLASS Table[X, Y]
OWNS
    contents :  X  ⇸  Y
```

```
RETURNS
   defined : X  →;
   access : X  →  Y
OPERATIONS
 *init : →;
   enter : X Y  →
ACTIONS
   defined x?  ==>
            x? ∈ dom  contents;

   access x? y!  ==>
            PRE x? ∈ dom  contents
            THEN
                y!  =  contents(x?)
            END;

 *init  ==>  table'  =  ∅;

   enter x? y?  ==>
            contents'  =  contents ⊕ { x? ↦ y? }
END CLASS
```

Exercise: why would it be wrong to use a call to the previous definition of the **hamming** operation:

$$\text{out!} \longleftarrow \text{Hamming\_1.hamming(k?);}$$

in place of its expansion in the definition of **hamming** in **Hamming_2**?

Solution: there are two reasons. The first is that to satisfy scope requirements (cf: the law of Demeter), **Hamming_1** must be an ancestor (or supplier) of **Hamming_2**, which it is not. Secondly, and more significantly, **Hamming_2.hamming** is the implementation of **Hamming_1.hamming**, so that this nested call is actually a self-recursion. Self-recursion is allowed (although discouraged) in Z^{++} and VDM^{++}, but in this case it will lead to an infinite sequence of calls to **table.defined(k?)** since the *same* argument k? is passed down from one invocation of **hamming** to the next.

In contrast, a use of self recursion such as

```
class Selfref
methods
   m(x: nat) value y: nat ==
               (if x < 2
                then y := 1
                else
                  (y := self!m(x - 1);
                   y := y*x);
                return y)


end Selfref
```

is legitimate, but baroque.

6.4.2   Refinement of Person Specification

This development continues the specification and refinement of the system introduced in Chapter 3. It is an example of a case where a recursive function is implemented as a loop, and is also an example of a system development which maintains a similar structure from the abstract specification to the first level of refinement.

Completing the specification of **WorkingPerson**, we can abstractly state its formal requirements as:

```
class WorkingPerson is subclass of Person
instance variables
  employments: seq of @Employment;
init objectstate == employments = []
methods
  total_salary() value r: nat ==
    (topology [ext rd employments
               post r = Sigma([employments(i).salary |
                             i in set inds(employments)])];
     return r);

  underage() value b: bool ==
    ([ext rd age
     post b = (age < 16)];
     return b)

end WorkingPerson
```

Sigma is defined in:

```
class PersonDefs
types
  Age = nat
  inv age == age <= 200;
  String = seq of char
functions
  Sigma: (seq of nat) -> nat
  Sigma(s) == if (s = [])
              then 0
              else hd(s) + Sigma(tl(s))
end PersonDefs
```

The specification of **total_salary** involves a sequence comprehension and direct access to the instance variable **salary** of **Employment**. This provides a clear expression of the desired functionality, without the procedural aspects which a formalisation involving method application would require. An alternative VDM++ formulation is:

```
total_salary() value r: nat ==
  (dcl tot: nat := 0;
   for all ee in set elems(employments)
   do
     def vv = ee!salary_value()
     in
       tot := tot + vv;
   return tot);
```

The **def** construct acts like a **let** definition, but allows method applications to be used to assign values to local identifiers.

The refinement of the classes of this specification is a direct process, at least for the initial refinement step, which we will concentrate on. The refinement of **Person** is:

```
class Person_1 is subclass of PersonDefs
-- refines Person;
-- retrieve function: identity;
-- method renaming: identity;
instance variables
  age: Age;
  address: String;
init objectstate ==
  age = 0 and address = []
methods
  change_address(nad: String) ==
    (address := nad);

  birthday() ==
    if age < 200
    then
      age := age + 1;

  current_age() value Age ==
      return age

thread
  periodic(31536000)(birthday)
end Person_1
```

Notice that under the weak interpretation of a periodic thread

```
    periodic(t)(m)
```

as

$$\forall i : \mathbb{N}_1 \bullet t * i \leq \uparrow(m,i) \ \wedge \ \downarrow(m,i) \leq t * (i+1)$$

we could not guarantee that a person's birthday was recorded until a year too late! Instead we should specify that it must occur within a day of each $t * i$:

```
aux reasoning
```

```
history
   forall i: nat1 & \|/(birthday,i) <= 31536000*i + 24*60*60
end Person_1
```

Implementation of the declarative thread specification will be considered in Chapter 8.

Inheritance of **Person** is used to construct the refinement of **WorkingPerson** in order to insulate it from changes to the representation of **Person**.

```
class WorkingPerson_1 is subclass of Person
-- refines WorkingPerson;
-- retrieve function: identity;
-- method renaming: identity;
instance variables
   employments: seq of @Employment;
init objectstate ==  employments = []
methods
   total_salary() value  nat ==
     (dcl i: nat := 1;
      dcl sum: nat := 0;

      while (i <= len(employments))
      do
        (dcl job: @Employment := employments(i);
         dcl sv: nat := 0;

         sv := job!salary_value();
         sum := sum + sv;
         i := i+1);
      return sum);

   underage() value  bool ==
     (dcl a: Age := self!current_age();
      return (a < 16))

end WorkingPerson_1
```

The abstract function **Sigma** has now been eliminated from the specification, and so does not need to be implemented: it has been replaced by code in the refinement of the class in which it is used. The refinement proof uses a loop invariant which relates the code to the **Sigma** function:

$$\text{sum} = \text{Sigma}([\text{employments}(j).\text{salary} \mid j \in \text{inds}(\text{employments}) \wedge$$
$$j < i]) \wedge$$
$$i \leq \text{len}(\text{employments}) + 1$$

Heuristics for the creation of loop invariants are given by [131, 33]. In this case we have used the *replace constant by variable* heuristic, which searches for a way of obtaining a candidate invariant $A(v)$ from the desired postcondition **Post**

$$\text{sum} = \text{Sigma}([\text{employments}(j).\text{salary} \mid j \in \text{inds}(\text{employments})])$$

such that **v** depends on the loop index variables, and such that the negation ¬ **E** of the loop test, together with **A(v)**, implies **Post**. In this case the negation of the loop test will imply $i \geq len(employments) + 1$, so **A(i)** has to express a "partial sum" property as above.

The refinement of the other classes in the system is direct. Thus we have the system architecture shown in Figure 6.4. This describes an initial refinement stage.

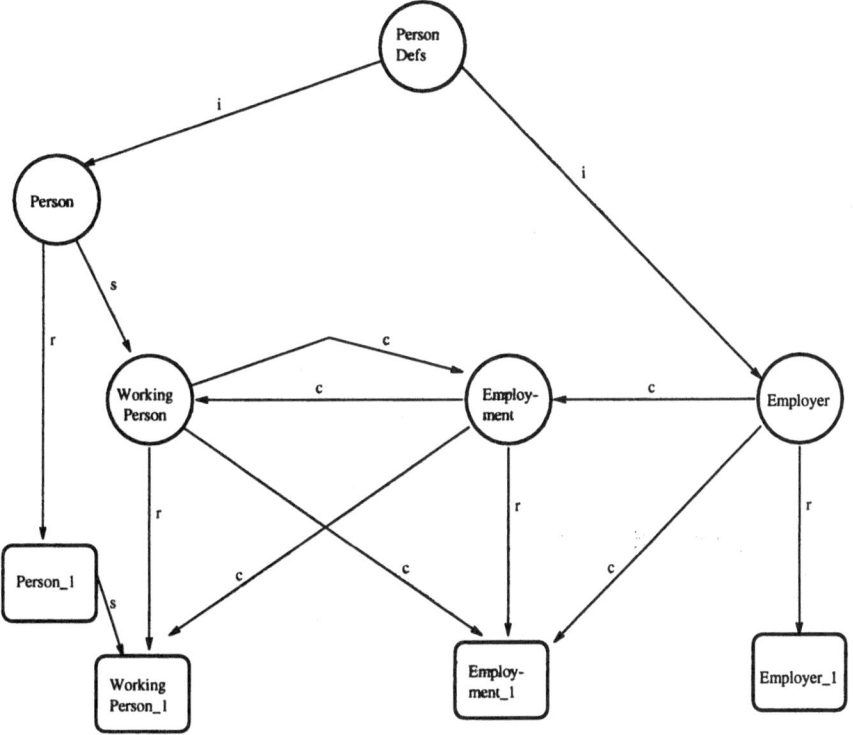

Figure 6.4: Architecture of **Persons** Development

Exercise (6.1): Why is it the case that **C** is refined by **D** where these classes are:

```
CLASS C
OWNS
   x : N
OPERATIONS
   inc : N →
ACTIONS
   inc v?  ==>  x' > x + v?
END CLASS


CLASS D
```

```
OWNS
  x: N
OPERATIONS
  inc: N →
ACTIONS
  inc v? ==> x' > x
HISTORY
  □(inc ⇒ self ∉ D̄)
END CLASS
```

How can such spurious refinements be avoided?

6.4.3   Reasoning About Subtypes and Polymorphism

Consider the situation where a class C is a client of a class S, where S has a non-trivial subtype S_1 via a retrieve function R and renaming ϕ. Specifically, let C have a method

```
call_m(d: @S) ==
                  ( ...
                  d!m();
                  ...)
```

where m is a method of S. Then we can legitimately supply an actual object d to **call_m** where $d \in \overline{S_1}$, and this will be interpreted as an element of $\overline{S}$ via the mapping $@R : @S_1 \to @S$ of object identities.

In C we can however only reason on the basis of the definition of m given in S. This is because the relativised theory of S is included in that of C. For instance, let m in S be defined by

```
m() ==
       [ext wr x
        post x > x~]
```

whilst in S_1 it is defined by

```
m() ==
       [ext wr x
        post x = x~ + 20]
```

where there is an additional (unmodified) state variable y in S_1.

Then an axiom of the theory of S defines how the value of the attribute x changes over time:

$$\forall i : N_1 \bullet x \circledast \downarrow (m, i) > x \circledast \uparrow (m, i)$$

and this axiom, in relativised form, gives us, in C:

$$\forall i : N_1 \bullet d.x \circledast \downarrow ((m, d), i) > d.x \circledast \uparrow ((m, d), i)$$

where **m** denotes **S'm**, the version of **m** defined in **S** (in VDM++).

Even if we assume that $\mathbf{d} \in \overline{\mathbf{S_1}}$, we can only infer the above fact about @R(d), and not the more specific definition of **m** which applies in actual fact.

In order to obtain more information on the execution of **m**, we need to be within another client of (the object attached to) **d**, and in which it is known to be an element of $\mathbf{S_1}$, ie, this class needs to be a client of $\mathbf{S_1}$ – this is reasonable since it is only in such clients that we are actually interested in reasoning about properties of members of $\mathbf{S_1}$.

In such a client, say **D**, we have the relativisation of the axiom defining the semantics of **m** in $\mathbf{S_1}$:

$$\forall \mathbf{i} : \mathbb{N}_1 \bullet \mathbf{d.y}\circledast\downarrow((\mathbf{m}, \mathbf{d}), \mathbf{i}) = \mathbf{d.y}\circledast\uparrow((\mathbf{m}, \mathbf{d}), \mathbf{i}) \; \wedge$$
$$\forall \mathbf{i} : \mathbb{N}_1 \bullet \mathbf{d.x}\circledast\downarrow((\mathbf{m}, \mathbf{d}), \mathbf{i}) = \mathbf{d.x}\circledast\uparrow((\mathbf{m}, \mathbf{d}), \mathbf{i}) + 20$$

In **D** we can observe events which take place on **d**, even if they are initiated from another object, such as an instance of **C**. Since we have the fact that

$$\uparrow((\mathbf{S'm}, @R(\mathbf{d})), \mathbf{i}) = \uparrow((\mathbf{S_1'm}, \mathbf{d}), \mathbf{i})$$

and similarly for other events, we can deduce that the call of **m** on **d** in **C** has the desired effect if **d** is actually in a proper subtype of **S**.

6.4.4 Locality Conditions

The theory of a $\mathbf{Z^{++}/RTL}$ class contains a locality condition [100] in the form of the **frame** axiom (see Appendix A). For a class **C** this axiom is:

(**frame**) :

$$(\mathbf{t1} < \mathbf{t2} \; \wedge$$
$$\forall \mathbf{i} : \mathbb{N}_1 \bullet \neg\, \mathbf{executing}(\mathbf{t1}, \mathbf{t2}, \mathbf{m_1}, \mathbf{i}) \wedge \ldots \wedge$$
$$\neg\, \mathbf{executing}(\mathbf{t1}, \mathbf{t2}, \mathbf{m_n}, \mathbf{i})) \Rightarrow$$
$$\mathbf{c}\circledast\mathbf{t1} \;=\; \mathbf{c}\circledast\mathbf{t2}$$

where **c** is the tuple of attributes of **C**, $\mathbf{m_1}, \ldots, \mathbf{m_n}$ are all the methods of **C** and $\mathbf{executing}(\mathbf{t1}, \mathbf{t2}, \mathbf{m}, \mathbf{i})$ for time-valued terms **t1** and **t2** stands for the predicate:

$$\exists \mathbf{x} : \mathbf{IN_m} \bullet \mathbf{t1} \leq \uparrow(\mathbf{m}(\mathbf{x}), \mathbf{i}) < \mathbf{t2} \; \vee$$
$$\mathbf{t1} < \downarrow(\mathbf{m}(\mathbf{x}), \mathbf{i}) \leq \mathbf{t2} \; \vee$$
$$(\uparrow(\mathbf{m}(\mathbf{x}), \mathbf{i}) < \mathbf{t1} \wedge \mathbf{t2} < \downarrow(\mathbf{m}(\mathbf{x}), \mathbf{i}))$$

That is, **t1** and **t2** are either both strictly within the interval of the **i**-th execution of **m(x)**, or the interval [**t1**, **t2**] intersects (non-trivially) a subrange of this execution.

In the refinement obligation

$$\vdash \mathbf{H_D} \wedge \Box^r \mathbf{R} \Rightarrow \phi(\mathbf{H_C})$$

there is therefore the requirement $\phi(\mathbf{frame_C})$. Ideally this should be provable from the corresponding axiom of $\mathbf{D}$, ie, $\mathbf{frame_D}$, together with the predicate $\Box^r\mathbf{R}$ linking the values of abstract and concrete variables at each time point (in fact, only $\Box\mathbf{R}$ is really relevant here).

That is, the obligation:

$$\vdash \mathbf{frame_D} \wedge \Box\mathbf{R} \;\Rightarrow\; \phi(\mathbf{frame_C})$$

should be provable.

This can be broken into two parts. It will hold if:

$$\vdash \forall\mathbf{i}:\mathbb{N}_1 \bullet \bigwedge_{\mathbf{m}\in\underline{\mathbf{methods}}(\mathbf{C})} \neg\, \mathbf{executing}(\phi(\mathbf{t1}),\phi(\mathbf{t2}),\phi(\mathbf{m}),\mathbf{i}) \Rightarrow$$
$$\forall\mathbf{i}:\mathbb{N}_1 \bullet \bigwedge_{\mathbf{m}\in\underline{\mathbf{methods}}(\mathbf{D})} \neg\, \mathbf{executing}(\phi(\mathbf{t1}),\phi(\mathbf{t2}),\mathbf{m},\mathbf{i})$$

for each $\phi(\mathbf{t1}) < \phi(\mathbf{t2})$, $\mathbf{t1}$ and $\mathbf{t2}$ being time-valued terms of $\mathbf{C}$, and if:

$$\mathbf{d}\circledast\phi(\mathbf{t1}) = \mathbf{d}\circledast\phi(\mathbf{t2}) \wedge \Box\mathbf{R} \;\Rightarrow\; \mathbf{c}\circledast\phi(\mathbf{t1}) = \mathbf{c}\circledast\phi(\mathbf{t2})$$

for $\mathbf{d}$ the tuple of attributes of $\mathbf{D}$, $\mathbf{c}$ of $\mathbf{C}$ and $\mathbf{t1}$ and $\mathbf{t2}$ as in the previous obligation.

The first of these obligations effectively requires any method $\mathbf{m}$ of $\mathbf{D}$ not in the range of ϕ to be defined to invoke at least one method of $\mathbf{C}$ throughout its duration (although in intervals where no state of $\mathbf{C}$ is changed, there does not need to be such an executing method). That is, the theory of $\mathbf{D}$ must establish assertions of the form:

$$\forall\mathbf{i}:\mathbb{N}_1;\; \exists\mathbf{j}:\mathbb{N}_1 \bullet \uparrow(\mathbf{m},\mathbf{i}) = \uparrow(\mathbf{t}_1,\mathbf{j}) \;\;\wedge \ldots \wedge$$
$$\forall\mathbf{i}:\mathbb{N}_1;\; \exists\mathbf{j}:\mathbb{N}_1 \bullet \downarrow(\mathbf{m},\mathbf{i}) = \downarrow(\mathbf{t_n},\mathbf{j})$$

where $\mathbf{t}_1$ and $\mathbf{t_n}$ are in ran ϕ.

A particular example of this situation is given in the following. Let $\mathbf{BBuf}$ be the following class, defining an abstract bounded buffer:

```
CLASS BBuf
TYPES
  Bstate  ::=  empty | partial | full
FUNCTIONS
```

$$\begin{array}{|l}
\text{bsize} : \mathbb{N} \\
\hline
\text{bsize} > 2
\end{array}$$

```
OWNS
  m_in:  N;
  m_out:  N;
  bstate  :  Bstate
INVARIANT
  m_in  ≤  m_out  +  bsize
OPERATIONS
```

```
  init : →;
  put : ℕ →;
  get : → ℕ
ACTIONS
  init  ==>   m_in' = 0 ∧ m_out' = 0 ∧ bstate' = empty;

  put x?  ==>
      m_in' = m_in + 1  ∧
      (m_in' = m_out + bsize   ⇒   bstate' = full)  ∧
      (¬ (m_in' = m_out + bsize)   ⇒   bstate' = partial);

  get y!  ==>
      m_out' = m_out + 1  ∧
      (m_in = m_out'   ⇒   bstate' = empty)  ∧
      (¬ (m_in = m_out')   ⇒   bstate' = partial)
HISTORY
  mutex(methods(BBuf))
  self_mutex(methods(BBuf))
  ∀ i : ℕ₁ •
      (bstate ≠ full)⊙↑(put, i)
      (bstate ≠ empty)⊙↑(get, i)
END CLASS
```

This should be a supertype of:

```
CLASS XBuf
TYPES
  Xstate ::= empty | x_one | x_partial | full
FUNCTIONS
```

$$\begin{array}{|l}
\text{xsize} : \mathbb{N} \\
\hline
\text{xsize} > 2
\end{array}$$

```
OWNS
  x_in, x_out : ℕ;
  xstate : Xstate
INVARIANT
  x_in ≤ x_out + xsize
OPERATIONS
  init : →;
  put : ℕ →;
  get : → ℕ;
  get2 : → ℕ
ACTIONS
  init  ==>   x_in' = 0 ∧ x_out' = 0 ∧ xstate' = empty;

  put x?  ==>
      x_in' = x_in + 1  ∧
      (x_in' = x_out + xsize   ⇒   xstate' = full)  ∧
      (x_in' = x_out + 1   ⇒   xstate' = x_one)  ∧
```

$$(\neg\,(x\_in' = x\_out + xsize \lor x\_in' = x\_out + 1) \Rightarrow$$
$$xstate' = x\_partial);$$

```
get y!  ==>
    x_out' = x_out + 1  ∧
    (x_in = x_out'  ⇒  xstate' = empty) ∧
    (x_in = x_out' + 1  ⇒  xstate' = x_one) ∧
    (¬ (x_in = x_out' ∨ x_in = x_out' + 1)  ⇒
```
$$xstate' = x\_partial)$$

```
get2 y!  ==>
    VAR y1
    IN
      y1  ⟵  get;
      y!  ⟵  get
    END
HISTORY
  mutex({ put, init, get })
  mutex({ put, init, get2 })
  self_mutex(methods(XBuf))
  ∀ i : ℕ₁ •
      (xstate ≠ full)⊙↑(put, i)
      (xstate ≠ empty)⊙↑(get, i)
      (xstate = full ∨ xstate = x_partial)⊙↑(get2, i)
END CLASS
```

An additional constraint is needed, stating that the only executions of **get** which can occur during an execution of **get2** are those that are explicitly described there. This issue is discussed further in Appendix A.

The subtyping relation **R** between these classes can be expressed as a function:

$$\mathbf{R}((\mathbf{xstate}, \mathbf{x\_in}, \mathbf{x\_out}), (\mathbf{bstate}, \mathbf{m\_in}, \mathbf{m\_out})) \equiv$$
$$\mathbf{bstate} =$$
$$\text{if } \mathbf{xstate} \in \{\mathbf{empty}, \mathbf{full}\}$$
$$\text{then } \mathbf{xstate}$$
$$\text{else } \mathbf{partial} \;\land$$
$$\mathbf{m\_in} = \mathbf{x\_in} \;\land$$
$$\mathbf{m\_out} = \mathbf{x\_out}$$

so that the simplified version of the subtyping and refinement obligations given in Chapter 4 could be used.

The type **Bstate** is interpreted by **Xstate** in **XBuf**, and the constant **msize** by **xsize**.

It is direct to verify that the sequential subtyping conditions hold under the above refinement relation. For example, for the **get** operation the execution of the abstract operation produces a poststate $(\mathbf{bstate'}, \mathbf{m\_in'}, \mathbf{m\_out'})$ which is **R**-related to the poststate produced by execution of the concrete operation on a prestate $(\mathbf{xstate}, \mathbf{x\_in}, \mathbf{x\_out})$ **R**-related to $(\mathbf{bstate}, \mathbf{m\_in}, \mathbf{m\_out})$. This is shown by cases on **xstate'**.

It is also clear that the history constraint of **XBuf** implies the explicit history constraint of **BBuf** via the relation **R**, since:

$$\vdash \Box R \wedge (\mathbf{xstate} \neq \mathbf{full}) \odot \uparrow (\mathbf{put}_{\mathbf{XBuf}}, i) \Rightarrow$$
$$(\mathbf{bstate} \neq \mathbf{full}) \odot \uparrow (\phi(\mathbf{put}_{\mathbf{BBuf}}), i)$$

for each $i \in \mathbb{N}_1$, where $\mathbf{put}_{\mathbf{XBuf}} = \phi(\mathbf{put}_{\mathbf{BBuf}})$, the version of **put** in **XBuf**. Similarly for **get**.

The difficulty in establishing the subtyping arises from the need to prove $\phi(\mathbf{frame}_{\mathbf{BBuf}})$, the locality constraint of **BBuf**.

The procedural definition of **get2** can be logically interpreted as the formulae:

$$\forall i : \mathbb{N}_1 \bullet \exists j : \mathbb{N}_1 \bullet$$
$$\uparrow(\mathbf{get2}, i) + \mathbf{td} = \uparrow(\mathbf{get}, j) \wedge$$
$$\downarrow(\mathbf{get}, j) = \uparrow(\mathbf{get}, j + 1) \wedge$$
$$\downarrow(\mathbf{get}, j + 1) = \downarrow(\mathbf{get2}, i) \wedge$$
$$(\mathbf{get}, j + 1).\mathbf{y} = (\mathbf{get2}, i).\mathbf{y}$$

where $\mathbf{td} \in \mathrm{T}(\mathbf{decl}(\mathbb{N}))$ is a possible time taken to allocate storage for the variable **y1**. We have the property that the state of **XBuf** is not changed during this interval, ie:

$$(\mathbf{xstate}, \mathbf{x\_in}, \mathbf{x\_out}) \circledast \uparrow (\mathbf{get2}, i) = (\mathbf{xstate}, \mathbf{x\_in}, \mathbf{x\_out}) \circledast \uparrow (\mathbf{get}, j)$$

for **i** and **j** as above.

Thus $\phi(\mathbf{frame}_{\mathbf{BBuf}})$ will follow from $(\mathbf{frame}_{\mathbf{XBuf}})$ since

$$\vdash \forall i : \mathbb{N}_1 \bullet \bigwedge_{m \in \underline{\mathbf{methods}(\mathbf{BBuf})}} \neg \, \mathbf{executing}(\phi(\mathbf{t1}), \phi(\mathbf{t2}), \phi(\mathbf{m}), i) \Rightarrow$$
$$\forall i : \mathbb{N}_1 \bullet \bigwedge_{m \in \underline{\mathbf{methods}(\mathbf{XBuf})}} \neg \, \mathbf{executing}(\phi(\mathbf{t1}), \phi(\mathbf{t2}), m, i)$$

at every pair $\phi(\mathbf{t1}) < \phi(\mathbf{t2})$, except for the endpoints of the intervals in which the local variables $(\mathbf{get2}, \mathbf{k}).\mathbf{y1}$ are declared. However neither the state of **BBuf** or **XBuf** is modified between such a pair of endpoints, so the inference follows in this case. For other cases, it is clear that

$$\mathbf{d} \circledast \phi(\mathbf{t1}) = \mathbf{d} \circledast \phi(\mathbf{t2}) \wedge \Box R \Rightarrow \mathbf{c} \circledast \phi(\mathbf{t1}) = \mathbf{c} \circledast \phi(\mathbf{t2})$$

for **d** the tuple of attributes of **XBuf**, **c** of **BBuf** and **t1** and **t2** as in the previous obligation.

6.4.5   Auxilliary Operations

Auxilliary operations can be introduced into a class during the refinement process. One reason for doing this is to make explicit which activities of the class can be executed in parallel – auxilliary operations can be defined to represent "critical sections" which must be executed in mutual and self-exclusion, but the methods which call these critical sections can otherwise overlap in their executions.

As an example, consider an abstract queue class:

```
CLASS AbsQueue[X]
FUNCTIONS
  | bound : ℕ₁
OWNS
  queue :  seq(X)
INVARIANT
  #queue  ≤  bound
OPERATIONS
  init : →;
  send :  X  →;
  receive : →  X
ACTIONS
    init  ==>  queue' = ⟨ ⟩;

    send x?  ==>
      PRE #queue  <  bound
      THEN
          queue'  =  ⟨ x? ⟩  ⌢  queue
      END;

    receive y!  ==>
      PRE #queue  >  0
      THEN
          queue  =  queue'  ⌢  ⟨ y! ⟩
      END
HISTORY
  true
END CLASS
```

There are no mutual exclusion constraints placed on the methods, other than those which follow from their state transition specifications. For example, it is impossible for a **receive** and **send** invocation to begin and end simultaneously. It is possible for these operations to overlap however (eg, a **send**(x_2) followed by a **receive** of this element could occur within a **send**(x_1) operation on an empty queue).

It may be refined by a class which implements the queue as an array with pointers. In this class a local operation **Shift_down** is introduced which rearranges the array when the pointers creep over the end of the array.

```
CLASS ConcQueue[X]
FUNCTIONS
  | bound : ℕ₁
OWNS
  head_idx :  1 .. bound;
  tail_idx :  0 .. bound;
  contents :  1 .. bound  →  X
INVARIANT
  head_idx  ≤  tail_idx + 1
OPERATIONS
  init : →;
  *Shift_down : →;
```

```
    send :  X  →;
    receive :  →  X;
 *Send0 :  X  →;
 *Receive0 :  →  X
ACTIONS
     init   ==>
          tail_idx' = 0  ∧  head_idx' = 1;

  *Shift_down   ==>
       PRE tail_idx = bound
       THEN
            (∀ i : 1 .. bound | head_idx ≤ i ≤ tail_idx •
                    contents'(i − head_idx + 1) = contents(i) )   ∧
            tail_idx' = tail_idx − head_idx + 1   ∧
            head_idx' = 1
       END;

    send x?   ==>
       PRE tail_idx − head_idx + 1 < bound
       THEN
            IF tail_idx = bound
            THEN
               Shift_down;
               Send0(x?)
            ELSE
               Send0(x?)
            END
       END;

    receive y!   ==>
       PRE tail_idx − head_idx + 1 > 0
       THEN
            IF tail_idx = bound
            THEN
               Shift_down;
               y! ⟵ Receive0
            ELSE
               y! ⟵ Receive0
            END
       END;

  *Send0 x?   ==>
       tail_idx' = tail_idx + 1   ∧
       contents' = contents ⊕ { tail_idx' ↦ x? };

  *Receive0 y!   ==>
       y! = contents(head_idx) ∧
       head_idx' = head_idx + 1
HISTORY
 self_mutex(methods(ConcQueue))
```

mutex({ send, init }) $\land$ mutex({ receive, init })
mutex({ Shift_down, init }) $\land$ mutex({ Shift_down, Send0 })
mutex({ Shift_down, Recieve0 })

END CLASS

The updates to **tail_idx** and **head_idx** in **Shift_down** can be implemented in parallel, as can the operations **Send0** and **Receive0**.

The refinement relation **R** is

$$\text{queue} = \{i : \text{head\_idx} \mathbin{..} \text{tail\_idx} \bullet \text{tail\_idx} - i + 1 \mapsto \text{contents}(i)\}$$

and it can be seen that

$$\#\text{queue} = \text{tail\_idx} - \text{head\_idx} + 1$$

In order to formally prove that this is a refinement, we need to show that **Shift_down** does not modify the state of **AbsQueue** via **R**. That is, if **queue'** denotes the value

$$\{i : \text{head\_idx}' \mathbin{..} \text{tail\_idx}' \bullet \text{tail\_idx}' - i + 1 \mapsto \text{contents}'(i)\}$$

after application of **Shift_down** within its precondition, then **queue'** = queue, where **queue** is the corresponding retrieved state of **AbsQueue** from the prestate of **Shift_down**. Obviously $\#\text{queue}' = \#\text{queue}$.

Also **queue'** is $\{i : 1 \mathbin{..} \#\text{queue} \bullet \#\text{queue} - i + 1 \mapsto \text{contents}'(i)\}$ where

$$\text{contents}'(i) = \text{contents}(i + \text{head\_idx} - 1)$$

for **i** in this range.

Let **i** be of the form **head_idx** + **j** in the definition of **queue**. Then we obtain

$$\text{queue}(\#\text{queue} - j) = \text{contents}(\text{head\_idx} + j)$$

Similarly, let **i** be of the form **j** + 1 in the definition of **queue'**. Then

$$\begin{aligned}
\text{queue}'(\#\text{queue} - j) &= \text{contents}'(j + 1) \\
&= \text{contents}(\text{head\_idx} + j)
\end{aligned}$$

as required.

It can be similarly shown that **Send0** and **Receive0** refine **send** and **receive** of **AbsQueue** under **R**, and therefore so do **send** and **receive** in **ConcQueue**.

ConcQueue is one step away from an implementation in which all possible concurrency is made explicit. Overlapping executions of **Send0** and **Receive0** must be considered so that the effect specified in the abstract specification is correctly implemented. This is achieved by placing the update to **contents** in **Send0** after the increment of **tail_idx**.

```
CLASS ImpQueue
FUNCTIONS
  | bound: N₁
OWNS
  head_idx: 1 .. bound;
  tail_idx: 0 .. bound;
  contents: 1 .. bound → X
INVARIANT
  head_idx ≤ tail_idx + 1
OPERATIONS
    init: →;
  *Shift_down: →;
   send: X →;
   receive: → X;
  *Send0: X →;
  *Receive0: → X
ACTIONS
    init ==>
          BEGIN
           tail_idx := 0 |||
           head_idx := 1
          END;

  *Shift_down ==>
        PRE tail_idx = bound
        THEN
          IF head_idx ≠ 1
          THEN
              VAR ind: N
              IN
                 ind := head_idx;
              WHILE ind ≤ tail_idx
              DO
                 contents(ind - head_idx + 1) := contents(ind);
                 ind := ind + 1
              END;
              tail_idx := tail_idx - head_idx + 1;
              head_idx := 1
            END
          END
        END;

    send x? ==>
        PRE tail_idx - head_idx + 1 < bound
        THEN
            IF tail_idx = bound
            THEN
                Shift_down;
                Send0(x?)
            ELSE
```

```
            Send0(x?)
              END
        END ;

   receive y!  ==>
        PRE tail_idx  −  head_idx  +  1  >  0
        THEN
            IF tail_idx  =  bound
            THEN
                Shift_down;
                y!  ⟵  Receive0
            ELSE
                y!  ⟵  Receive0
            END
        END ;

   *Send0 x?  ==>
        BEGIN
          tail_idx  :=  tail_idx  +  1;
          contents(tail_idx)  :=  x?
        END ;

   *Receive0 y!  ==>
        BEGIN
          y!  :=  contents(head_idx);
          head_idx  :=  head_idx  +  1
        END
HISTORY
 self_mutex(methods(ImpQueue))
 mutex({ send, init })  ∧  mutex({ receive, init })
 mutex({ Shift_down, init })  ∧  mutex({ Shift_down, Send0 })
 mutex({ Shift_down, Recieve0 })

END CLASS
```

Assignments are assumed to be mutually and self-exclusive, and to only modify the (outer) variable of their left-hand side expression, and any variables aliased with this variable. A final refinement step here would need to eliminate the explicit preconditions (if Eiffel was the destination language they could be retained, however).

Executions of the form shown in Figure 6.5 are acceptable for this class.

At time point 1 (the start of the execution of $Send0(x1)$) there are two elements in the queue, and head_idx $= 3$, tail_idx $= 4$. At time point 2, at the start of the execution of $Receive0$, and within the execution of $Send0(x1)$, the value of head_idx is stable since there is no currently executing instance of $Receive0$, however it is not known whether tail_idx has been modified (or how, within its type) or whether $x1$ has been added to the end of the queue. At time point 3, at a time point where only the $Receive0$ instance is executing, the value of tail_idx is stable, and is 5, and $x1$ has been added to the end of

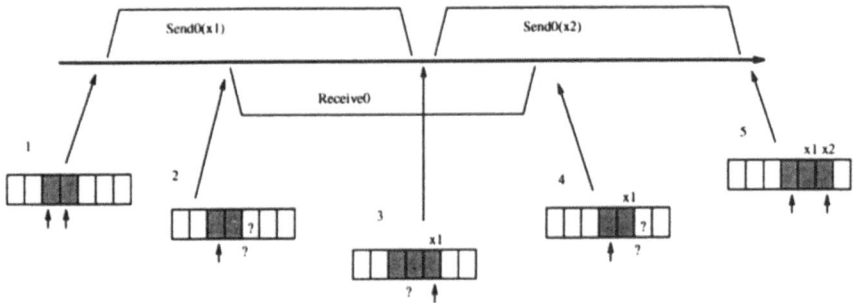

Figure 6.5: Internally Concurrent Execution of **Queue**

the queue. The value of **head_idx** is not known.

At time point 4 the **Receive0** instance has completed, so that **head_idx** is stable, and **tail_idx** is not stable. Finally at time point 5 there is no executing operation, and the expected effect of the three operation invocations has been achieved. Both pairs of invocation instances satisfy the requirements of the history constraint, since for the first **Send0, Receive0** pair the respective values of **tail_idx** and **head_idx** are 4 and 3. For the second pair the values are 5 and 3.

6.5 Object Identity

6.5.1 Object Sharing and Migration

Object identity becomes a significant issue for class correctness when situations arise in which objects may be shared between other objects (including cycles of mutual references). As an example, consider a situation where a mutual exclusion property is being implemented via a semaphore:

```
CLASS C
OWNS
  ...
OPERATIONS
  m : X  →  Y;
  ...
ACTIONS
  m x? y!  ==>  Def_m ;
  ...
HISTORY
  self_mutex({ m })
END CLASS

CLASS C_1
OWNS
  s :  Semaphore;
```

```
   ...
OPERATIONS
   m :  X  →  Y;
   set_semaphore :  Semaphore  →  ;
   ...
ACTIONS
   m  x?  y!   ==>
             BEGIN
                s.signal;
                Code;
                s.release
             END;

   set_semaphore  s?   ==>
                        s'  =  s?;


   ...
END CLASS
```

where **Code** implements the state transitions defined in $\mathbf{Def_m}$.

If it were possible for two objects $\mathbf{a} \neq \mathbf{b}$, $\mathbf{a}, \mathbf{b} : \mathbf{C}$ to have $\mathbf{a.s} = \mathbf{b.s}$, then these objects would exclude each other from executing the body of $\mathbf{m}$ – and this behaviour is clearly not the intention of the specification of $\mathbf{C}$.

Exercise (6.2) (advanced): Does this give a counter-example to Liskov's definition of subtyping in [201]? That is, an example which satisfies the formal conditions of [201] but not the intuitive definition of subtyping given in that paper and in Chapter 1?

Aliasing, the general situation in which there may be more than one way to access a given object reference, is the cause of considerable difficulty in proof, but is also a source of considerable power. For example, if it had been required for a and b to exclude each other on $\mathbf{m}$:

```
CLASS System
OWNS
   a,  b :  C
HISTORY
   #active(m, a)  +  #active(m, b)  ≤  1
END CLASS
```

then the following would be a valid implementation:

```
CLASS System_1
OWNS
   a,  b :  C_1;
   sl :  Semaphore
OPERATIONS
```

```
    init : →
ACTIONS
    init  ==>
          BEGIN
          New_Semaphore[s1/semaphore!];
          a.set_semaphore(s1);
          b.set_semaphore(s1)
          END
```

END CLASS

In this section we will only provide a language for reasoning about such situations, and some general principles.

In the semantics it is considered that each class C defines a type $@C$ of object identities. These types are assumed to be countably infinite, and therefore can be identified with 1-1 renamings of the natural numbers $\mathbb{N}$. In an actual implementation they could be strings or addresses (and the set of existing objects of each class will be finite at all times).

In terms of [291], $@C$ is $\mathbf{ext}(C)$ and the value of $\overline{C}$ at time π is $\mathbf{ext}_\pi(C)$.

Consider a situation in which C is a supertype of D via a renaming ϕ of methods and a data refinement $R: C \sqsubseteq_{\phi,R} D$. Then there is a corresponding map $@R : @D \to @C$ which implements the "is-a" relation, and which has the properties:

$$\Box^r \forall d : \overline{D} \bullet R(*_C(@R(d)), *_D(d))$$
$$\Box^r \forall d : @D \bullet d \in \overline{D} \equiv @R(d) \in \overline{C}$$

The $@R$ are not necessarily injective, because elements d_1 and d_2 of $@D$ may be distinguishable as elements of $@D$, but $@R(d_1)$ and $@R(d_2)$ could be the same element of $@C$ without contradiction. For example, $*_D(d_1).att \neq *_D(d_2).att$ for some attribute att of D which has no corresponding expression in C.

The case considered in [291] is that of $D = \mathbf{PASSENGER}$ and $C = \mathbf{PERSON}$, where indeed distinct journeys undertaken by the same person could be modelled using distinct instances of D.

In an actual implementation $@R$ may be constructed as a concrete mapping from object identifiers of D to those of C. For example, a $\mathbf{PASSENGER}$ identifier could effectively be a pair (person_identifier, journey_identifier) in which case $@R$ is simply projection onto the first element.

The concepts of *subtype migration, dynamic* and *static* subclasses can be defined in this framework. Note that although the semantics of Z^{++} allows objects to migrate between subtypes, it is not committed to this concept, which seems in some ways to be redundant and conceptually confused. Such subtypes could alternatively be represented via states in a dynamic model: the **Mixing Tank** example of [271], for example, could be specified using nested statecharts (Syntropy [64] also takes this approach).

Let D_1 and D_2 be subtypes of C via ϕ_1, R_1 and ϕ_2, R_2 respectively.

These subtypes are a *partition* of C if, at all times

$$\overline{C} = @R_1 (\!|\ \overline{D_1}\ |\!) \cup @R_2 (\!|\ \overline{D_2}\ |\!)$$

and

$$@R_1 (\!|\ \overline{D_1}\ |\!) \cap @R_2 (\!|\ \overline{D_2}\ |\!) = \varnothing$$

Similarly for a set of subtypes. $r (\!|\ S\ |\!)$ denotes the set of elements in the range of r which are related by r to an element of S.

If it is possible for an element of C to migrate from D_1 to D_2 then, necessarily, $@D_1 \cap @D_2 \neq \varnothing$. The elements of this intersection are those objects which may be regarded as elements of either (or both) subtypes at particular moments in time[3].

A pair of subtypes D_1 and D_2 of C are *(exclusive) dynamic* subtypes if

$$\Box^\tau (\overline{D_1} \cap \overline{D_2} = \varnothing)$$
$$(\Diamond^\tau (\exists\, d : @D_1 \cup @D_2 \bullet$$
$$d \in \overline{D_1} \wedge \Diamond^\tau (d \in \overline{D_2})) \ \vee$$
$$\Diamond^\tau (\exists\, d : @D_1 \cup @D_2 \bullet$$
$$d \in \overline{D_2} \wedge \Diamond^\tau (d \in \overline{D_1})))$$

Inclusive dynamic subtypes may not satisfy the first condition. Static subclasses satisfy the negation of the second condition.

As an example, consider a cargo ship, which can contain a set of compartments, divided into two categories: **Cargo** compartments, which can carry ore, food, stores, etc, and **Ballast** compartments, which are used to balance loads along the ship and maintain a correct position for the ship. The latter can only be filled with water.

In principle it is possible for the use of a compartment to be alternated between these categories. However, it is of course the case that at any one time, a compartment fulfils only one of these roles. Thus there is the specification:

$$\Box^\tau (\overline{\text{Cargo\_compartment} \cap \text{Ballast\_compartment}} = \varnothing)$$
$$\Diamond^\tau (\exists\, \text{comp} : @\textbf{Cargo\_compartment} \cup @\textbf{Ballast\_compartment} \bullet$$
$$\text{comp} \in \overline{\text{Cargo\_compartment}} \wedge \Diamond^\tau (\text{comp} \in \overline{\text{Ballast\_compartment}}))$$

and similarly if ballast compartments can become cargo compartments.

Exclusive ownership of an object $a : C$, $a = b.\text{att}$ by an object $b : D$ can be specified by stating that a is not referenced by any other attribute of any other existing object or method instance which involves the type C.

In the case of such D, assuming that **att** is the only C-valued expression involving attributes of D, this can be specified by the formula

$$\forall\, d : \overline{D} \mid d \neq b \bullet d.\text{att} \neq b.\text{att}$$

---

[3] It is sometimes convenient to regard the set of object identities of a subtype as a subset of those of the supertype, this constraint also ensures that $\textbf{New}_C$ is refined as an operation when it is applied to refinements of C. It is an oversimplification if a subtype of C may be a subtype via two distinct relations – an example is given in Appendix A.

One way in which this form of exclusion can be proved is to create **att** within **b**, and to never pass this value out as an output of a method of **D**, use it as a parameter in method calls in **D**, allow reference to this attribute in client classes, or take as input to a method any value of type **C**. Parameter passing conditions are ensured by disallowing use of **C** in the signatures of **D**'s methods.

Assume that such exclusive ownership has been established for every instance of **D**. Then the **frame** axiom of **D** can be extended to assert that

$$(\{\text{att}\} \lhd *_C) \circledast t_1 = (\{\text{att}\} \lhd *_C) \circledast t_2$$

for each pair of terms t_1 and t_2 within an interval in which no method of **D** is executing. In other words, no attribute of **b.att** can be changed, for each instance **b** : **D**, in such intervals.

Similar assertions can be stated if **D** exclusively owns a set **aset** : $\mathbb{P}(\mathbf{C})$:

$$(\text{aset} \lhd *_C) \circledast t_1 = (\text{aset} \lhd *_C) \circledast t_2$$

and so forth.

Thus in the above case of a **Semaphore**, it is sufficient to specify:

```
CLASS C_1
OWNS
  s :  Semaphore;
  ...
OPERATIONS
  init :  →;
  m :  X  →  Y;
  ...
ACTIONS
  init  ==>
          BEGIN
            New_Semaphore[s/semaphore!]
          END;

  m  x?  y!   ==>
          BEGIN
            s.signal;
            Code;
            s.release
          END;
  ...
END CLASS
```

and to observe the constraints set out above (in particular, to not allow the value of **s** to be set using inputs to a method of **C_1**). It may be worth introducing syntax to assert that an object is private to another, this syntax would then automatically generate the enhanced frame axioms for the class, and the constraints could be checked by tools for the language. The notation

att : *private* **C**

is suggested.

6.5.2   Capacity Reasoning

An important type of reasoning which has traditionally been absent from the capabilities of formal methods, is that concerning the space requirements of the specified system.

The use of explicit variables $\overline{C}$ for the sets of *all* existing instances of C within an application enables specification of bounds on the sizes of such sets, and analysis of the required capacity of an application. For example, if we have a class

```
CLASS A
OWNS
  c : C
OPERATIONS
  create : →;
  del : →
ACTIONS
  create ==>
      New_C[c'/c!];

  del ==>
      Unset_C
END CLASS
```

Then we can prove that

$$\#\overline{C} \geq \#\textbf{fin}(\textbf{create})$$

provided that no other part of the system deletes C objects. $\#\textbf{fin}(\textbf{m})$ denotes the number of terminations of $\textbf{m}$ up to the present time.

Thus the more times we execute **create**, the more memory will be taken up and this cannot be reclaimed by using **del**. Instead the user should make use of the operation $\textbf{Forget}_C(c)$ which does:

$$*'_C = \{c\} \vartriangleleft *_C$$

Ie: this removes any link $c \mapsto \textbf{cval}$ between the reference c and an object value. This strictly reduces the size of $\overline{C}$ if $c \in \overline{C}$ (because $\overline{C} = \text{dom}(*_C)$).

6.6   Reasoning About Concurrent Object Execution

The axiomatic system for RTL and Z^{++} or VDM^{++} provides a means of deriving facts about the set of all objects of a particular class from information about the histories of individual objects.

To see this, it is important to note that the semantics of a method execution $\textbf{m}$ on an object $\textbf{a} : \textbf{C}$ only defines the value of $*_C(\textbf{a})$ at times $\downarrow(\textbf{m}, \textbf{i})$ in terms of the value of $*_C(\textbf{a})$ and other supplier object states at times $\uparrow(\textbf{m}, \textbf{i})$. It does not constrain $*_C(\textbf{b})\circledast\downarrow(\textbf{m}, \textbf{i})$ for $\textbf{b} \neq \textbf{a}$.

In order to determine the value of $*_C$ as a whole at some time $\downarrow(\mathbf{m}, \mathbf{i})$, therefore, we have to consider the state of all objects of $\overline{C}$ at this time.

As an example, consider the situation shown in Figure 6.6.

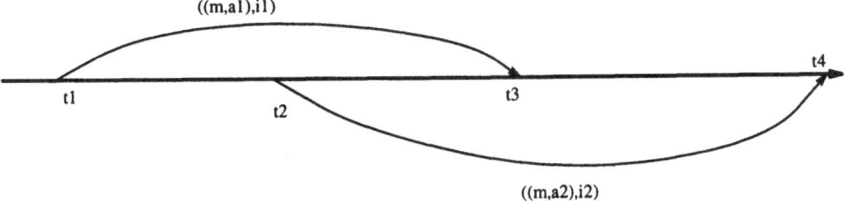

Figure 6.6: Concurrent Object Execution

Assume only $\mathbf{a1}, \mathbf{a2} \in \overline{C}$ throughout this period. Then at $t3$ we know $*_C(\mathbf{a1})$ in terms of $*_C(\mathbf{a1}) \circledast t1$. At $t4$ we know $*_C(\mathbf{a2})$ in terms of $*_C(\mathbf{a2}) \circledast t2$. Additionally $*_C(\mathbf{a2}) \circledast t2 = *_C(\mathbf{a2}) \circledast t1$ by global frame – even if $\mathbf{a2}$ contains a reference to $\mathbf{a1}$. $*_C(\mathbf{a1}) \circledast t4 = *_C(\mathbf{a1}) \circledast t3$ by global frame.

Thus $*_C \circledast t4$ is specified in terms of $*_C \circledast t1$.

A more complex situation arises when two objects $\mathbf{a}$ and $\mathbf{b}$ of C share a common object $\mathbf{c} : S$. For example, we could have the VDM^{++} classes:

```
class S
instance variables
  yy : N;
init objectstate == yy = 0
methods
  n(v : N) ==
     [ext wr yy
        post yy = v]
end S
```

and

```
class C
instance variables
  x : @S
methods
  m(v : N) ==
        x!n(v)
end C
```

Let $\mathbf{a}, \mathbf{b} : C$, $\mathbf{a.x} = \mathbf{b.x} = \mathbf{c}$ where $\mathbf{c} \in \overline{S}$.

Then if two executions $((\mathbf{m}, \mathbf{a}), \mathbf{i})$ and $((\mathbf{m}, \mathbf{b}), \mathbf{j})$ terminate together:

$$\downarrow((\mathbf{m}, \mathbf{a}), \mathbf{i}) = \downarrow((\mathbf{m}, \mathbf{b}), \mathbf{j})$$

then so do the corresponding executions of $\mathbf{n}$ on $\mathbf{c}$:

$$\downarrow((\mathbf{n}, \mathbf{c}), \mathbf{k}) = \downarrow((\mathbf{n}, \mathbf{c}), \mathbf{l})$$

As a result, the value of the **v** argument supplied to both of these calls must be equal:

$$((n, c), k).v =$$
$$(c.yy) \circledast \downarrow ((n, c), k) =$$
$$(c.yy) \circledast \downarrow ((n, c), l) = ((n, c), l).v$$

and hence this must also be the case for the calls to **m**:

$$((m, a), i).v = ((m, b), j).v$$

6.7   Synchronisation Refinement Proofs

Proofs involving the semaphore concept introduced in Chapter 5 typically involve reasoning using equalities and inequalities between event counters #**act**, #**fin** and #**req** (more usually, just the first two). This reasoning is more general than that carried out using linear temporal logic, since object histories can be arbitrary sequences of events, constrained only by the syntax of the class and logical properties of events given in Appendix A.

In a typical situation, a set of semaphores are introduced as suppliers to a refinement C_1 of a class C which specifies some synchronisation constraints on its methods.

For example, to obtain alternation between two methods m_1 and m_2 in C, the following is required in C_1:

```
CLASS C_1
OWNS
  s1, s2 : Semaphore;
  ...
OPERATIONS
  m₁ :  X₁  →  Y₁;
  m₂ :  X₂  →  Y₂
ACTIONS
  m₁ x₁? y₁!  ==>
        BEGIN
          s1.signal;
          Code₁;
          s2.signal
        END;

  m₂ x₂? y₂!  ==>
        BEGIN
          s2.release;
          Code₂;
          s1.release
        END

END CLASS
```

To see this, note that

$$\#act(m_1) = \#act(signal, s1)$$
$$\#fin(m_1) = \#fin(signal, s2)$$
$$\#act(m_2) = \#act(release, s2)$$
$$\#fin(m_2) = \#fin(release, s1)$$

Therefore

$$\#active(m_1) + \#active(m_2) =$$
$$\#act(signal, s1) - \#fin(signal, s2) +$$
$$\#act(release, s2) - \#fin(release, s1) =$$
$$(\#act(signal, s1) - \#fin(release, s1)) +$$
$$(\#act(release, s2) - \#fin(signal, s2))$$
$$\leq 1$$

from the history constraint of **Semaphore**. Similarly

$$\#fin(m_1) = \#fin(signal, s2) \geq \#act(release, s2) = \#act(m_2)$$

and

$$\#fin(m_2) + 1 = \#fin(release, s1) + 1 \geq \#act(signal, s1) = \#act(m_1)$$

as required.

A more complex example is given by the general readers and writers problem. In this case there must be mutual (and self) exclusion between the writers w_1, w_2, w_3 (for example), whilst the readers r_1, r_2 and r_3 must also exclude any of the writers, but not each other. The specification is therefore:

CLASS **ReadersWriters**
OPERATIONS
  $w_1 : X_1 \rightarrow Y_1;$
  ...
  $w_3 : X_3 \rightarrow Y_3$
RETURNS
  $r_1 : X_4 \rightarrow Y_4;$
  ...
  $r_3 : X_6 \rightarrow Y_6$
HISTORY
  $mutex(\{ w_1, w_2, w_3 \}) \wedge$
  $self\_mutex(\{ w_1, w_2, w_3 \}) \wedge$
  $mutex(\{ r_1, w_1, w_2, w_3 \}) \wedge$
  $mutex(\{ r_2, w_1, w_2, w_3 \}) \wedge$
  $mutex(\{ r_3, w_1, w_2, w_3 \})$
END CLASS

An implementation is:

CLASS **ReadersWriters_1**
OWNS

```
    s, s1, s2, s3 : Semaphore
OPERATIONS
    w₁ :  X₁  →  Y₁ ;
    ...
    w₃ :  X₃  →  Y₃
RETURNS
    r₁ :  X₄  →  Y₄ ;
    ...
    r₃ :  X₆  →  Y₆
ACTIONS
    w₁ x₁? y₁!  ==>
            BEGIN
              BEGIN
                s.signal ||| s1.signal |||
                s2.signal ||| s3.signal
              END;
                Code₁ ;
              BEGIN
                s.release ||| s1.release |||
                s2.release ||| s3.release
              END
            END;


    ...  / * Similarly for w₂ and w₃ * /

    r₁ x₄? y₄!  ==>
          BEGIN
            s1.signal;
            Code₄ ;
            s1.release
          END;


    r₂ x₅? y₅!  ==>
          BEGIN
            s2.signal;
            Code₅ ;
            s2.release
          END;


    r₃ x₆? y₆!  ==>
            BEGIN
              s3.signal;
              Code₆ ;
              s3.release
            END


END CLASS
```

Where **Code₁** implements the abstract state-transformation definition of **m₁**, and so forth.

Note that for each **mutex(S)** assertion, a distinct semaphore **s** is used, with s.**signal** being performed at activation of any method of **S**, and s.**release** at each termination of a method of **S**. Such semaphores also ensure **self_mutex(S)**.

Exercise (6.3): Define **m** *covers* **n** by the predicate

$$\#\mathbf{act}(m) \geq \#\mathbf{act}(n) \ \wedge \ \#\mathbf{fin}(n) \geq \#\mathbf{fin}(m)$$

(This means that every execution of **n** is contained within an execution of **m**.) Construct a refinement of the following class using a single semaphore to implement the synchronisation constraint.

```
CLASS C
TYPES
   BoilerState ::= on | off
   ValveState ::= open | closed
OWNS
   bstate : BoilerState;
   vstate : ValveState
OPERATIONS
   activating : →;
   maintain_open : →
ACTIONS
   activating ==> bstate' = on;

   maintain_open ==> vstate' = open
HISTORY
   activating covers maintain_open
END CLASS
```

Prove it correct.

Additionally, consider how **mutex** can be implemented for a class without **self_mutex** also being implemented. [Hint: consider the following generalisation of a semaphore.]

```
CLASS MultiSemaphore
OPERATIONS
   signal : ℕ →;
   release : ℕ →
HISTORY
   ∀ i : ℕ₁; j, k : ℕ | j ≠ k •
               (#fin(release(j)) = #act(signal(j)))⊙↑(signal(k), i)
END CLASS
```

That is, at ↑(**signal(k), i**), no other virtual semaphore in the indexed collection should have any outstanding signals.

6.8   General Refinement Proof Techniques

The following general proof techniques are applicable in the two languages
considered here.

- induction over event times. In particular, the LTL induction principle

$$\phi \odot \mathbf{min}(\{\clubsuit(\uparrow\mathbf{m_1}, 1), \ldots, \clubsuit(\uparrow\mathbf{m_n}, 1)\}) \ \wedge \ \Box(\phi \Rightarrow \bigcirc\phi) \ \Rightarrow \ \Box\phi$$

  holds for each LTL formula ϕ;
- decomposition of refinement proof obligations using the weakest precondition calculus. This works since at the lower levels of design proofs of
  operation refinements often involve establishing that the concrete operation establishes the same result as the abstract, and the former operation
  is defined by a complex piece of code including loops.

Conclusions

This chapter has discussed some reasoning techniques that can be used with the
Z++ and VDM++ languages. At present there are no automated tools which
support this reasoning, however it is possible to use the B-Tool of B Core UK
Ltd to carry out reasoning in the Z mathematical language. Prototype proof
obligation generation and proof facilities have been developed in Prolog for
VDM++ and Z++. Extensions of the VDM-SL proof tool, Mural, for VDM++,
were also considered during the AFRODITE project.

Chapter 7

Concurrent and Real-time Behaviour

This chapter will describe ways in which the Z^{++} and VDM^{++} specification languages can be used to specify real-time behaviour of systems. The two languages address different types of systems, with VDM^{++} focussed on *continuous real-time* systems, and Z^{++} on *discrete event* systems. The facilities of the languages will be illustrated with a number of case studies, and detailed translation procedures from Harel statecharts into the two notations will be given, with examples.

Section 7.1 gives the translation of extended Harel statecharts into Z^{++} and VDM^{++}, including AND composition and nesting of statecharts. Section 7.2 covers the specification of mutual exclusion, fairness properties, priorities and interrupts, and continuous real-time systems.

7.1 Extended Harel Statecharts

In Chapter 3 we gave a translation from a small subset of the timed statechart notation into Z^{++} and VDM^{++}. In this section we will extend this translation to cover activities within states, entry and exit actions, AND composition and nesting of statecharts.

7.1.1 VDM^{++}

An important construction used in statecharts is the nesting of statecharts within states. In general, we will have a superstate s with a finite set s_1, ..., s_n of substates, and with these substates being organised into a statechart internal to s. Any transition t with source s is actually a common transition from each of the s_i. A transition into s is also a transition to the initial state of the enclosed chart. An example is given in Figure 7.1.

Formalisation of this chart involves the maintenance of a separate state variable for each level of statechart contained in a nested statechart system. Thus membership of s would be explicitly recorded, and a transition away from

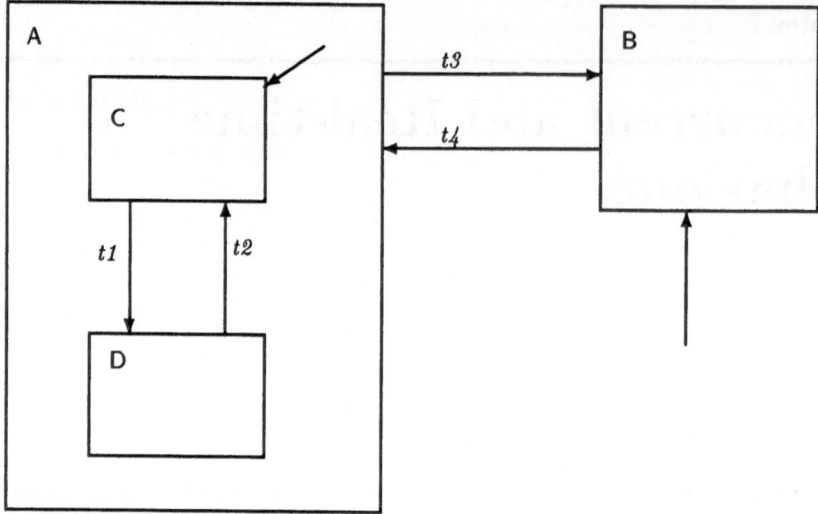

Figure 7.1: Example of Nesting of Statecharts

s would be formalised as in Chapter 3. However, the state representations $< s_1 >, \ldots, < s_n >$ only have meaning at points where the superstate variable has value $< s >$, so any test on these values would need to also include a test on the superstate value. Using this approach, we would obtain a thread of the following form for the statechart in Figure 7.1:

```
while true do
   sel  svar0 = <B>  answer t4 ->
                     while svar0 = <A> do
                        sel
                           answer t3,
                           svar1 = <C>  answer t1,
                           svar1 = <D>  answer t2;
```

The method **t4** sets **svar0** to **<A>** and **svar1** to **<C>**, and **t3** sets **svar0** to **<B>**. **t1** sets **svar1** to **<D>**, and **t2** sets **svar1** to **<C>**.

Notice that this thread is compatible with the thread of the diagram without the nested chart:

```
while true do
   sel  svar0 = <B>  answer t4 ->
                       answer t3
```

because the additional transitions **t1** and **t2** do not affect **svar0**.

More precisely, the retrieve function from the subtype class simply forgets **svar1**, so that the new methods **t1** and **t2** do not affect the state of the abstract class representing the un-nested statechart, when their effects are interpreted via this retrieve function. Moreover, the extended definition of **t4** is identical to its abstract definition on the abstract state. **t3** is unchanged between the

two classes. Thus the body of the thread loop in the subtype is a refinement
of that in the supertype, and thus so is the complete thread.

It is generally the case that adding a nested statechart to a state is a subtyping transformation, provided that history sensitivity or transitions out of
the enclosing state from internal nested states are not used.

Entry and exit actions on states, and internal activities of states can also
be formalised in VDM^{++}. Activities in a state are expressed as methods which
are preconditioned by membership of this state, and do not change the *svar*
variable.

A further construct which occurs in statecharts is AND composition. This
construct builds a chart **X** from two charts **A** and **P**, say, in which the set of
states is the cartesian product of the states of **A** and **P**, and the transitions
are the union of those of the separate charts, except that transitions present in
both charts must occur simultaneously in the resulting chart. An example is
shown in Figure 7.2.

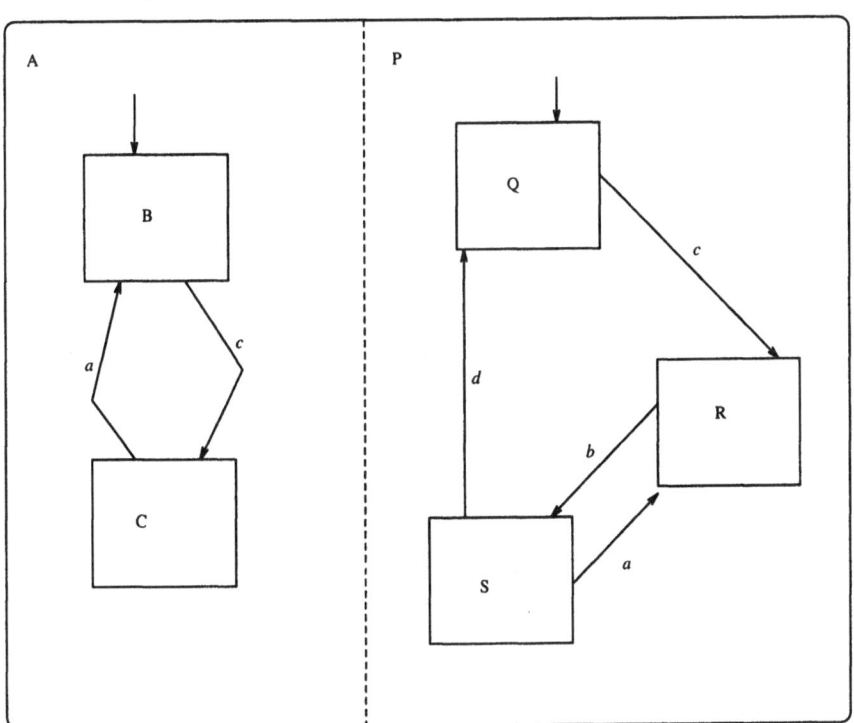

Figure 7.2: Example of AND Composition

In this chart the transitions **d** and **b** can occur from any state of the form
$(\alpha, \mathbf{S})$ or $(\alpha, \mathbf{R})$ respectively, where α is a state of **A**. However the transition
a can only occur from the source state $(\mathbf{C}, \mathbf{S})$. Similarly for **c**.

Assume that the two factors of the composed chart are separately formalised
in classes **A** and **P**. Then the thread specifications of these classes are of the
form:

```
while true do
   sel
      (svarA = <B>) answer c -> ...,
      ...
```

where associated actions and activities are listed in the statement part of each select clause, as previously specified. AND composition of **A** and **P** is the multiple inheritance **X** of these classes into the empty class, with the exception that common methods will be combined: their preconditions and postconditions conjoined in the case of purely abstract specifications, or their statements performed in parallel (an undetermined order), in the case of procedural definitions.

The permission statements for a common method will have permission condition the conjunction of those for the method in the separate machines.

The thread specification of **X** is an infinite loop of a `sel` statement which consists of the select clauses of the threads of **A** and **P**, in the same relative order as in the original classes, except that the clauses for shared methods must have guard conditions the conjunction of those of the original select clauses, and statement part the parallel composition of the statement parts of the original select clauses. Thus for the above chart there is the clause:

```
(svarA = <C> and svarP = <S>) answer a,
```

for the shared transition.

The formalisation procedure can now be extended to the following:

1. for entry actions of a state s, place these as actions to be undertaken after the actions of the transition itself in the statement part of each select clause representing a transition into s;
2. for the activity of the state s create a new method **s_activity** which is preconditioned by membership of s and which does not change the state. The method is invoked: **self!s_activity()** within the statement part of each select clause of each transition into s. This invocation should immediately follow the entry action, if any;
3. for internal events of the state, create new methods which are preconditioned by membership of the state, and which do not change the state. Corresponding select clauses are defined for these events and listed in the `sel` statement within the class thread;
4. exit actions of the state are listed as the first action in the statement part of any transition away from s.

Thus the most general form of a select clause representing a transition from state s_1 to s_2 will be:

```
t_enabled answer t  ->  (s_1_exit; t_action;
                         s_2_entry; s_2_activity),
```

An alternative interpretation, in which the transition action **t_action** is performed *after* the entry action, could also be adopted. This interpretation is used by Syntropy [64].

7.1.2 Case Study: Traffic Control

As an example of this process, consider the following archetypical reactive system, of a traffic controller.

Requirements

The system is a controller for two pairs of traffic lights for a crossing between a busy main road and a small farm road. There is one pair of traffic lights for each road: the lights for the farm road should be green for at most *max farm road green* seconds. If there is still traffic waiting on the farm road after this interval then the main road lights should be green for at most *max main road green* seconds. It is assumed that *max main road green* > *max farm road green*.

Analysis

The following entities can be identified from the requirements:

- TrafficLight with states red, amber and green and operations to turn red and to turn green;
- Monitor with states traffic_absent and traffic_present (both from the viewpoint of the farm road).

In addition, a controller which synchronises the two instances of TrafficLight and the farm road Monitor is needed. The statecharts are given in Figures 7.3, 7.4 and 7.5.

The statecharts are then composed to form the complete system. Common transitions on distinct charts must be performed simultaneously. The events **clear** and **approach** are inputs to the system, but the controller has its own internal behaviour, such as a cycle between the states TrafficMoving and TrafficBlocked if the farm road is continually busy. Note that we include the possibility that the farm road may become clear even if the lights are not green, because of traffic deciding to abandon the wait for the lights to clear and finding an alternative route.

Some advantages of a development approach which combines diagrammatic and formal methods can be identified here. The suitability of statecharts for (semi) formalising requirements for reactive systems implies that it is quite direct to express the requirements in a set of statecharts, once the entities of the system have been identified. Statecharts are more precise and more immediately comprehensible than natural language text. It is also easier to manipulate and transform statecharts (for example, to factor out common actions on all transitions into the TrafficMoving and TrafficBlocked states and make them entry actions of these states) than to perform corresponding transformations on the formal models.

Formalisation

In formalising the traffic lights, we can simplify the corresponding class by conflating the delay of duration **inamber** in the Amber states and the τ transitions, into single (durative) transitions from the Red and Green states to each other:

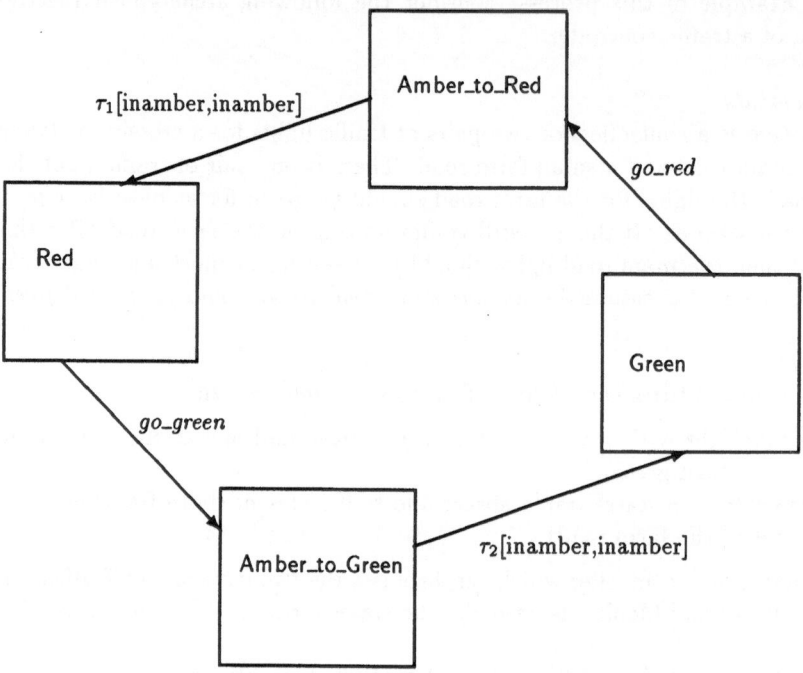

Figure 7.3: Statechart of Traffic Lights

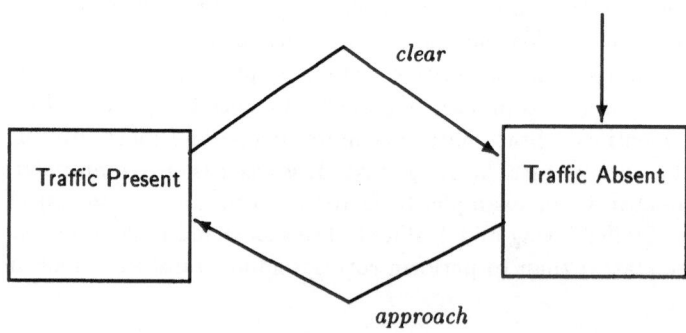

Figure 7.4: Statechart of Monitor

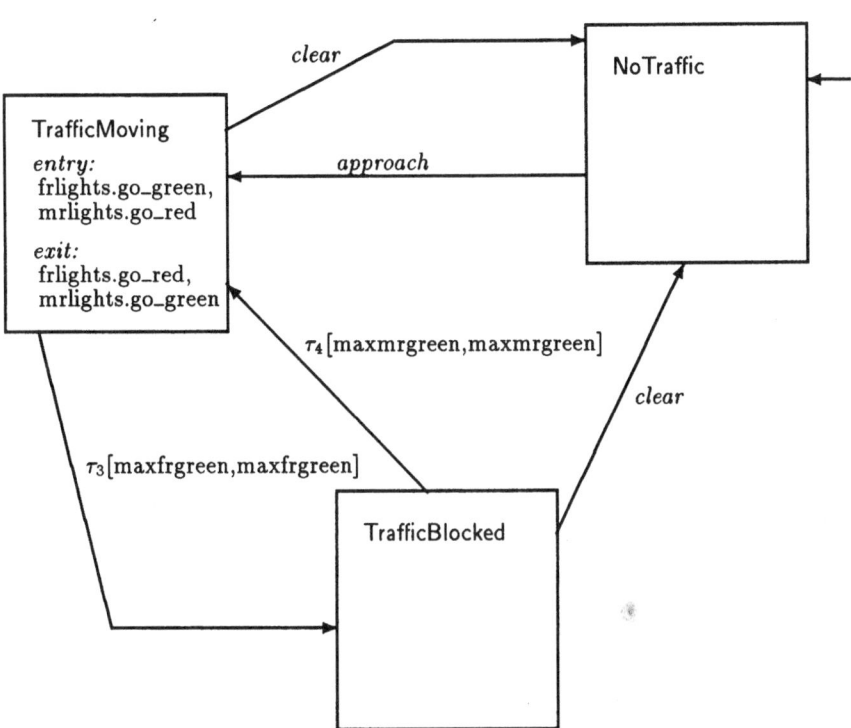

Figure 7.5: Statechart of Controller

```
class TrafficLights
types
  TLState  = < red > | < green >
values
  inamber : ℝ  = undefined
instance variables
  tlstate :  TLState;
init objectstate ==
  tlstate  = < red >  ∨   tlstate  = < green >
methods
  initialise_red()  ==
    [ext wr tlstate
     post  tlstate  = < red >];

  initialise_green()  ==
    [ext wr tlstate
     post  tlstate  = < green >];

  go_red()  ==
    [ext wr now, tlstate
     post  now  =  now̅  +  inamber   ∧
           tlstate  = < red >];

  go_green()  ==
    [ext wr now, tlstate
     post  now  =  now̅  +  inamber  and
           tlstate  = < green >]

sync
  per go_red   ⇒   tlstate  = < green >;
  per go_green  ⇒   tlstate  = < red >

thread
  (sel answer initialise_green,
      answer initialise_red;
   while true do
      sel
        tlstate  = < green >  answer go_red,
        tlstate  = < red >    answer go_green)
end TrafficLights
```

We can separate out the monitor from the controller by expressing the latter as a subtype (extension) of the former.

```
class Monitor
types
  MState  = < traffic_absent > | < traffic_present >
instance variables
  mstate :  MState;
init objectstate ==    mstate  = < traffic_absent >
```

```
methods
  approach()  ==
    [ext wr mstate
     post mstate  =  < traffic_present >];

  clear()  ==
    [ext wr mstate
     post mstate  =  < traffic_absent >]
sync
  per approach      ⇒      mstate  =  < traffic_absent >;
  per clear         ⇒      mstate  =  < traffic_present >
thread
  while true do
    sel   mstate  =  < traffic_absent >   answer approach,
          mstate  =  < traffic_present >  answer  clear
end Monitor
```

The permission statements are redundant here, since they are duplicated in the thread select statement. They are included for the sake of clarity.

The subtyping relation between **Controller** and **Monitor** is:

$$((\text{cstate} = <\text{no\_traffic}>) \equiv (\text{mstate} = <\text{traffic\_absent}>)) \wedge$$
$$((\text{cstate} = <\text{traffic\_moving}> \vee \text{cstate} = <\text{traffic\_blocked}>) \equiv$$
$$(\text{mstate} = <\text{traffic\_present}>))$$

```
class Controller
  is subclass of TimeDefs
types
  CState  =  < no_traffic >  |  < traffic_moving >  |  < traffic_blocked >
values
  maxfrgreen :  ℝ  =  undefined;
  maxmrgreen :  ℝ  =  undefined
instance variables
  frlights, mrlights :  ©TrafficLights;
  cstate :  CState;
  lastentered :  ℝ;
init objectstate ==
  cstate  =  < no_traffic >  ∧   lastentered  =  0
methods
  initialise()  ==
    (frlights  :=  TrafficLights!new;
     mrlights  :=  TrafficLights!new;
     mrlights!start;
     frlights!start;
     frlights!initialise_red();
     mrlights!initialise_green());

  approach()  ==
    [ext wr cstate
```

```
      post lastentered  =  now   ∧
          cstate  =  < traffic_moving >];

  clear()  ==
    [ext wr cstate
     post lastentered  =  now   ∧
         cstate  =  < no_traffic >];

  τ₃()  ==
    [ext wr cstate, lastentered
     post  lastentered  =  now   ∧
          cstate  =  < traffic_blocked >];

  τ₄()  ==
    [ext wr cstate, lastentered
     post  lastentered  =  now   ∧
          cstate  =  < traffic_moving >];

  traffic_moving_entry()
    pre cstate  =  < traffic_moving >   ==
                         (mrlights!go_red();
                          frlights!go_green());

  traffic_moving_exit()
    pre  cstate  =  < traffic_moving >   ==
                         (frlights!go_red();
                          mrlights!go_green())
sync
  per τ₃   ⇒   cstate  =  < traffic_moving >;
  per τ₄   ⇒   cstate  =  < traffic_blocked >
thread
  (self!initialise();
   while true do
     sel
       cstate  =  < no_traffic >  answer  approach  ->
                                   self!traffic_moving_entry(),
       cstate  =  < traffic_moving >  answer  clear ->
                                   self!traffic_moving_exit(),
       cstate  =  < traffic_blocked > answer   clear,

       (cstate  =  < traffic_moving > ∧
         lastentered  +  maxfrgreen  ≤  now)  ->
                                   (self!traffic_moving_exit();
                                    self!τ₃()),

       (cstate  =  < traffic_blocked >   ∧
         lastentered  +  maxmrgreen  ≤  now)  ->
                                   (self!τ₄();
                                    self!traffic_moving_entry())))
end Controller
```

A safety constraint which could be specified in RTL is that at least one set of lights is always red:

$$(\square^r(\mathbf{frlights.tlstate} = \; <\mathbf{red}> \; \vee$$
$$\mathbf{mrlights.tlstate} = \; <\mathbf{red}>))\odot\downarrow(\mathbf{initialise}, 1)$$

This is provable provided the controller has exclusive ownership of the traffic lights.

Exercise (7.1): sketch a proof of this safety constraint.

7.1.3 $\mathbf{Z}^{++}$

The formalisation process described in Chapter 3 is extended as follows. Activities within a state are typically durative and can involve complex data transformations (which are not easily expressed on statecharts). In this case the semantics of such activities will be specified as part of the formalisation process. An activity **act** in state S will become an operation:

$$\mathbf{act} \; \mathbf{x?} \; \mathbf{y!} \quad ==>$$
$$\text{PRE } \mathbf{state} \; = \; \mathbf{s}$$
$$\text{THEN } \mathbf{Definition}$$
$$\text{END}$$

This is preconditioned by membership of S and does not modify **state**.

A required duration on the activity can simply be expressed in the form

$$\forall \mathbf{i} : \mathbb{N}_1 \bullet \mathbf{l} \leq \mathbf{duration}(\mathbf{act}, \mathbf{i}) \leq \mathbf{u}$$

An entry action of a state is a special form of state activity **entry_s** which commences execution as soon as the state is entered:

$$\forall \mathbf{i} : \mathbb{N}_1 \bullet \uparrow(\mathbf{entry\_s}, \mathbf{i}) = \clubsuit((\mathbf{state} = \mathbf{s}) := \mathbf{true}, \mathbf{i})$$

and whose termination coincides with the start of any activity **act** associated with the state:

$$\forall \mathbf{i} : \mathbb{N}_1 \bullet \uparrow(\mathbf{act}, \mathbf{i}) = \downarrow(\mathbf{entry\_s}, \mathbf{i})$$

There may be several actions also specified to take place at state entry. These can be asserted to commence execution at the same time as **entry_s**, or in some suitable sequential order.

If there is an activity but no entry action then the axiom

$$\forall \mathbf{i} : \mathbb{N}_1 \bullet \uparrow(\mathbf{act}, \mathbf{i}) = \clubsuit((\mathbf{state} = \mathbf{s}) := \mathbf{true}, \mathbf{i})$$

holds. Entry actions do not change the **state** attribute.

Exit actions can be expressed as the first action to be performed by each transition which leaves the state. Alternative interpretations, as discussed above for VDM^{++}, can also be expressed.

Nested states are formalised using separate attributes to record the current state for each level of statechart contained in a nested statechart system, as above. In the example of Figure 7.1 the formalisation would include the elements, for each $i \in \mathbb{N}_1$:

$$(\textbf{svar0} = \textbf{a}) \odot \uparrow (\textbf{t1}, \textbf{i})$$
$$(\textbf{svar1} = \textbf{c}) \odot \uparrow (\textbf{t1}, \textbf{i})$$
$$(\textbf{svar0} = \textbf{a}) \odot \uparrow (\textbf{t2}, \textbf{i})$$
$$(\textbf{svar1} = \textbf{d}) \odot \uparrow (\textbf{t2}, \textbf{i})$$

$$(\textbf{svar0} = \textbf{b}) \odot \uparrow (\textbf{t4}, \textbf{i})$$
$$(\textbf{svar0} = \textbf{a}) \odot \uparrow (\textbf{t3}, \textbf{i})$$

$$\exists \textbf{j} : \mathbb{N}_1 \mid \textbf{j} \geq \textbf{i} \bullet \downarrow (\textbf{t1}, \textbf{i}) = \clubsuit((\textbf{svar1} = \textbf{c}) := \textbf{false}, \textbf{j})$$
$$\downarrow (\textbf{t4}, \textbf{i}) = \clubsuit((\textbf{svar0} = \textbf{a}) := \textbf{true}, \textbf{i})$$
$$\exists \textbf{j} : \mathbb{N}_1 \mid \textbf{j} \geq \textbf{i} \bullet \downarrow (\textbf{t4}, \textbf{i}) = \clubsuit((\textbf{svar1} = \textbf{c}) := \textbf{true}, \textbf{j})$$

The final three formulae correspond to the fact that $\textbf{svar1} = \textbf{c}$ can become **false** as a result of the transitions **t1** or **t3**, and can become **true** as a result of the transitions **t2** or **t4**.

The effects of methods are given by:

t4   ==>   svar0$'$ = a $\wedge$ svar1$'$ = c;

t1   ==>   svar1$'$ = d

and so forth.

It can be seen that enhancing an existing state by adding an internal statechart of this state will lead to a subtype of the resulting formalised class. In particular, all axioms of the original chart will be true for the new chart.

Formalisation of AND composition is achieved using the $\wedge$ operator on classes, discussed in Section 7.1.4 below. For example, consider the chart shown in Figure 7.2.

Assume that the two factors of the composed chart are separately formalised in classes **A** and **P**. Then the specification of $\textbf{A} \wedge \textbf{P}$ includes the following elements:

a   ==>   state_P$'$ = r $\wedge$ state_A$'$ = b;

HISTORY
   $\forall$ i : $\mathbb{N}_1$ $\bullet$
       (state_P = s) $\odot \uparrow$ (a, i)
       (state_A = c) $\odot \uparrow$ (a, i)
       . . .
END CLASS

The states of $C \wedge D$ are the elements of the cartesian product of the sets of states of C and D. Activities in states of C and D are effectively performed in parallel in the product states of the class $C \wedge D$. The delay interval $[l, u]$ of a transition common to C and D is the intersection of the delay intervals of the transition on the separate charts. The resulting class is a subtype of the individual classes.

A subtle distinction in dynamic behaviour which can be expressed in statecharts is the difference between an automatic (unlabelled) transition away from a state with an activity and an event-triggered transition away from this state. In the latter case it can be interpreted that the transition may interrupt the activity and lead to an exit of the state before the activity is completed.

Since we do not distinguish between termination of a method and (abnormal) halting or failure of the method, this distinction cannot be completely formally represented. However, each method which can fail should provide a means to signal that it has failed. At the abstract level, the definition of such a method would be of the form:

$$\textbf{m } \textbf{x? } \textbf{y! } \textbf{m\_ok! } ==>$$
$$(\textbf{m\_ok! } = \textbf{ yes } \wedge \textbf{ Post}_m) \vee$$
$$(\textbf{m\_ok! } = \textbf{ no } \wedge \textbf{ Inv}'_C \wedge \textbf{ y! } \in \textbf{Y})$$

where $\textbf{m\_ok!}$ is a result variable of $\textbf{m}$ which records if a failure has occurred or not in the most recently terminating instance of $\textbf{m}$. If it has, then only the state invariant can be guaranteed for the post-state of the method (and any outputs can only be assumed to be within their declared types).

It is usually the case that

$$\uparrow(\textbf{act}, \textbf{i}) = \clubsuit((\textbf{state} = \textbf{s}) := \textbf{true}, \textbf{i})$$
$$\downarrow(\textbf{act}, \textbf{i}) \leq \clubsuit((\textbf{state} = \textbf{s}) := \textbf{false}, \textbf{i})$$

for an activity $\textbf{act}$ of state S without entry actions. If S is not an initial state, then $\textbf{i} + 1$ is used in the second formula: $\downarrow(\textbf{act}, \textbf{i}) \leq \clubsuit((\textbf{state} = \textbf{s}) := \textbf{false}, \textbf{i} + 1)$.

If the completion of the activity coincides with the exit from the state, then the second formula becomes an equality.

This formalisation could also be adapted to represent the dynamic models of OOA [271], since OOA specifies that:

- only one activity of an object can be in execution at any point in time;
- activities are durative;
- activities of distinct objects can take place simultaneously;
- an activity of an object must complete before another event can be accepted by the object.

OOA takes a queueing interpretation of events: events are never lost. It also assumes that there is no delay between generation of events and arrival at the target object, ie, for each time $\leftarrow((\textbf{event}(\textbf{p}), \textbf{target}, \textbf{source}), \textbf{i})$ there is a corresponding (equal) event time $\rightarrow((\textbf{event}(\textbf{p}), \textbf{target}), \textbf{j})$.

Events generated from an object **source** are received by the **target** in the order in which they are sent:

$$\forall\, i, j, k : \mathbb{N}_1 \,|$$
$$\clubsuit(\leftarrow(\text{event}(p), \text{target}, \text{source}), i) = \rightarrow((\text{event}(p), \text{target}), j) \;\wedge$$
$$\clubsuit(\leftarrow(\text{event}(p), \text{target}, \text{source}), i+1) \;=$$
$$\rightarrow((\text{event}(p), \text{target}), k) \bullet$$
$$j < k$$

However it is not specified in which order events are received if they are sent by different sources.

7.1.4   Example of AND Composition

The following example is taken from the paper [101]. It involves the description of a simple communication channel with re-transmission facilities, and is defined using AND composition of two statecharts (Figures 7.6 and 7.7).

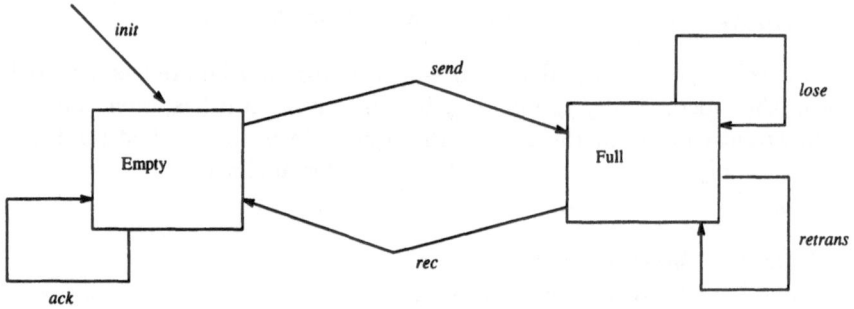

Figure 7.6: Statechart of Channel

The classes corresponding to these statecharts are:

```
CLASS Channel
TYPES
  CState  ::=  empty | full
OWNS
  cstate : CState
OPERATIONS
  init : →;
  send : →;
 *lose : →;
  retrans : →;
  rec : →;
  ack : →
ACTIONS
  init ==>  cstate′ = empty;
```

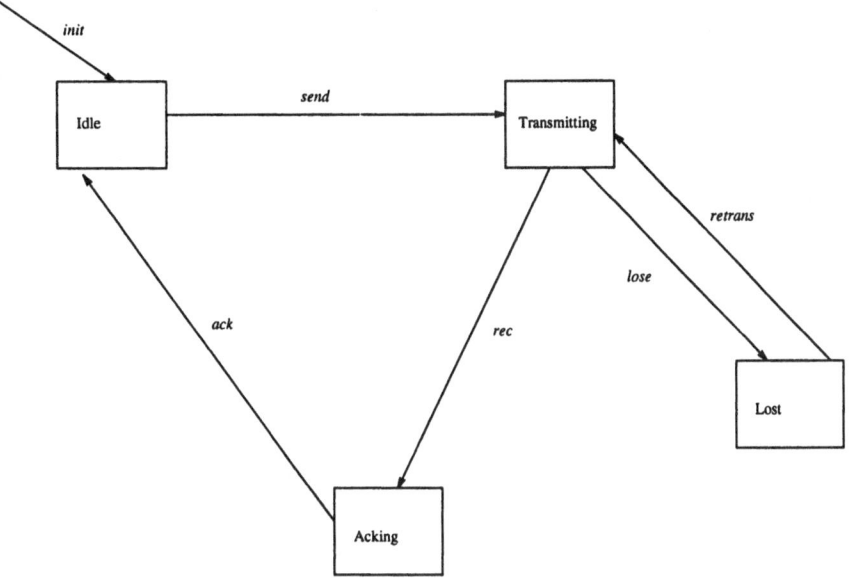

Figure 7.7: Statechart of Link

```
  ...
HISTORY
  Mutex_Channel ∧ SelfMutex_Channel ∧
  □(send ⇒ cstate = empty) ∧
  /* other permission predicates */
END CLASS

CLASS Link
TYPES
  LState ::= idle | transmitting | lost | acking
OWNS
  lstate : LState
OPERATIONS
  init : →;
  send : →;
 *lose : →;
  retrans : →;
  rec : →;
  ack : →
ACTIONS
  init  ==>   lstate' = idle;

  send  ==>   lstate' = transmitting;

 *lose ==>   lstate' = lost;

  retrans ==>   lstate' = transmitting;
```

$$\text{rec} \implies \text{lstate}' = \text{acking};$$

$$\text{ack} \implies \text{lstate}' = \text{idle}$$

HISTORY
  Mutex$_{\text{Link}}$ $\wedge$ SelfMutex$_{\text{Link}}$ $\wedge$
  $\Box(\underline{\text{send}} \Rightarrow \text{lstate} = \text{idle})$ $\wedge$
  $\Box(\underline{\text{rec}} \Rightarrow \text{lstate} = \text{transmitting})$ $\wedge$

  /* other permission predicates */
END CLASS

Note that we have formalised **lose** as internal, since it is not performed by an external user, but non-deterministically by the **Link** and **Channel** objects concerned. **retrans** could also be marked as internal if it was required that the system detect the loss of a message and perform recovery action autonomously.

In the latter case we would expect to specify properties such as:

$$\forall i : \mathbb{N}_1 \bullet \uparrow(\textbf{retrans}, i) = \downarrow(\textbf{lose}, i)$$

ie: recovery action takes place as soon as a **lose** event is detected.

Then the conjunction of these two classes, written as:

$$\textbf{System} \mathrel{\widehat{=}} \textbf{Channel} \wedge \textbf{Link}$$

has set of method identifiers, the union of those of **Channel** and **Link** (methods with the same identifier must have identical signatures in the two classes), attributes, the union of those of the two classes, and invariant, the conjunction of the two invariants.

Each method **m** occurring in both **Channel** and **Link** has definition **Channel.m** $\wedge$ **Link.m** in **System**, whilst the history constraint H$_{\text{System}}$ of **System** is the conjunction of H$_{\text{Channel}}$ and H$_{\text{Link}}$. Methods with procedural definitions are combined using the $\|$ operator of B AMN.

As a result, **System** can be expanded out into:

CLASS System
TYPES
  CState ::= empty | full
  LState ::= idle | transmitting | lost | acking
OWNS
  cstate : CState;
  lstate : LState
OPERATIONS
  init : $\rightarrow$;
  send : $\rightarrow$;
  *lose : $\rightarrow$;
  retrans : $\rightarrow$;
  rec : $\rightarrow$;
  ack : $\rightarrow$
ACTIONS

init ==>   cstate$'$ = empty $\wedge$ lstate$'$ = idle;

send ==>   cstate$'$ = full $\wedge$ lstate$'$ = transmitting;

*lose ==>   lstate$'$ = lost;

retrans ==>   lstate$'$ = transmitting;

rec ==>   cstate$'$ = empty $\wedge$ lstate$'$ = acking;

ack ==>   lstate$'$ = idle
HISTORY
  Mutex$_{\mathrm{System}}$ $\wedge$ SelfMutex$_{\mathrm{System}}$ $\wedge$
  $\Box$(send $\Rightarrow$ cstate = empty $\wedge$ lstate = idle) $\wedge$
  $\Box$(rec $\Rightarrow$ cstate = full $\wedge$ lstate = transmitting) $\wedge$

  /* other permission predicates */
END CLASS

The history constraint has this form since we have **durative(m)** for each method of **System** from the specification of **Link** (because every transition always changes the state of the **System**). In addition

$$\Box(A \Rightarrow B) \wedge \Box(A \Rightarrow C) \equiv \Box(A \Rightarrow B \wedge C)$$

A similar technique may be used with significantly more complex systems, and assists in decomposing the specification into meaningful components.

If a subtype of **Link** is required, for example, to define a class **QualityLink** which contains an extra history constraint which prevents two or more successive **lose** occurrences:

$$\Box\neg (\text{lose} \wedge \bigcirc \bigcirc \text{lose})$$

then **Channel** $\wedge$ **QualityLink** will be a subtype of **System**. In general, $\wedge$ is monotone with respect to subtyping.

Exercise (7.2): Produce the object and dynamic models for the following set of requirements, and formalise these models in a suitable set of object classes:

- the system is to model a set of ships and ship compartments, each compartment may be a member of at most one ship, and can be either a ballast compartment for storing water ballast, or a cargo compartment for storing various forms of cargo;
- operations of loading and unloading a ship are to be modelled. A ship loading operation can be decomposed into a sequence of compartment loading operations – however it must be the case that when one compartment is being loaded, another (ballast) compartment must be being deballasted, in order to preserve buoyancy. Similarly an unloading operation can be decomposed into a sequence of compartment unloading operations;

- each compartment has a maximum allowed load mass which it can hold. Loading operations specify the total mass to be transfered as a parameter: when a pair of a ballast and cargo compartment are being deballasted and loaded, respectively, the total mass transferred by these two sub-operations must be equal.

The dynamic model and formal specification of a ship only need to specify the **load** operation, not the **unload** operation.

7.2 Specifying Reactive System Properties

This section considers some additional issues in the expression of requirements of mutual exclusion, fairness, priorities and synchronisation.

7.2.1 Permission Guards for Mutual Exclusion

It is sufficient to place guards on the initiation of executions of methods of a class in order to ensure mutual and self exclusion properties.

For mutual exclusion of a set $\{\mathbf{m_1}, \ldots, \mathbf{m_n}\}$ of methods the permission guard

$$\bigwedge\nolimits_{\mathbf{j}:1..\mathbf{n} \wedge \mathbf{j} \neq \mathbf{i}} \#\mathbf{active}(\mathbf{m_j}) = 0$$

must be placed on each method $\mathbf{m_i}$.

For self-exclusion of $\mathbf{m_i}$ the guard $\#\mathbf{active}(\mathbf{m_i}) = 1$ must be placed on $\mathbf{m_i}$.

That these are sufficient can be shown as follows. For mutual exclusion the required result is

$$\Box^{\tau}(\underline{\mathbf{m_i}} \Rightarrow \bigwedge\nolimits_{\mathbf{j}:1..\mathbf{n} \wedge \mathbf{j} \neq \mathbf{i}} \#\mathbf{active}(\mathbf{m_j}) = 0)$$

for each $\mathbf{i}:1..\mathbf{n}$ and we actually have, as a result of the permission guard:

$$\Box(\underline{\mathbf{m_i}} \Rightarrow \bigwedge\nolimits_{\mathbf{j}:1..\mathbf{n} \wedge \mathbf{j} \neq \mathbf{i}} \#\mathbf{active}(\mathbf{m_j}) = 0)$$

for each $\mathbf{i}:1..\mathbf{n}$. The latter formula could also be expressed as

$$\Box(\underline{\mathbf{m_i}} \Rightarrow \bigwedge\nolimits_{\mathbf{j}:1..\mathbf{n} \wedge \mathbf{j} \neq \mathbf{i}} \neg \, \underline{\mathbf{m_j}})$$

Let $\mathbf{t}$ be any time at which $\#\mathbf{active}(\mathbf{m_i}) > 0 \wedge \#\mathbf{active}(\mathbf{m_j}) > 0$ where $\mathbf{j} \neq \mathbf{i}$. Then there are instances $(\mathbf{m_i}, \mathbf{k})$, $(\mathbf{m_j}, \mathbf{l})$ of the methods for which

$$\uparrow(\mathbf{m_i}, \mathbf{k}) < \mathbf{t} \leq \downarrow(\mathbf{m_i}, \mathbf{k})$$
$$\uparrow(\mathbf{m_j}, \mathbf{l}) < \mathbf{t} \leq \downarrow(\mathbf{m_j}, \mathbf{l})$$

Without loss of generality assume that $\uparrow(\mathbf{m_j}, \mathbf{l}) \leq \uparrow(\mathbf{m_i}, \mathbf{k})$ so that at $\uparrow(\mathbf{m_i}, \mathbf{k})$ we have $\#\mathbf{active}(\mathbf{m_i}) > 0 \wedge \#\mathbf{active}(\mathbf{m_j}) > 0$ which is a contradiction. Thus, since (in VDM^{++})

$$(\forall \mathbf{v} : \mathbf{TIME} \bullet \psi \circledcirc \mathbf{v}) \Rightarrow \Box^{\tau} \psi$$

the result follows.

Similarly for self-exclusion. If we have

$$\square(\underline{m_i} \Rightarrow \#\mathbf{active}(m_i) = 1)$$

then let t be any time at which $\#\mathbf{active}(m_i) \geq 2$. Then there are distinct k, l such that

$$\uparrow(m_i, k) < t \leq \downarrow(m_i, k)$$
$$\uparrow(m_i, l) < t \leq \downarrow(m_i, l)$$

Assume $\uparrow(m_i, l) \leq \uparrow(m_i, k)$. Then $\#\mathbf{active}(m_i) \geq 2$ also holds at $\uparrow(m_i, k)$, a contradiction.

It should also be realised that if a method execution (m, i) is instantaneous, so that $\#\mathbf{active}(m) = 0$ is possible at $\uparrow(m, i)$, then the execution cannot change the state, so that although mutual or self-exclusion cannot be guaranteed in a true sense by the above formulae for such executions, nevertheless these executions cannot interfere with other method executions.

Exercise (7.3): Prove that instantaneous methods cannot change the state of the object they execute on. [Hint: use the axiom (**xi**) defining the semantics of methods and reason by contradiction].

7.2.2 Separating Synchronisation from Functional Specification

In some situations it may be useful to be able to specify the functionality of a class independently of any particular synchronisation policy which may be required for its use. Inheritance can be used to combine this functional specification with a variety of synchronisation policies. For example, consider an abstract specification of the functionality of a buffer:

```
class Buffer
   is subclass of Elem
instance variables
   contents :  seq(ITEM);
init objectstate ==  contents  = ⟨ ⟩
methods
   put(x :  ITEM)  ==
      [ext wr contents
       post contents  =  ‾‾‾‾‾‾‾‾‾‾‾
                         contents  ⌢ ⟨ x ⟩];

   get() value x :  ITEM
         pre len(contents)  >  0   ==
         ([ext wr contents
          post ‾‾‾‾‾‾‾‾
               contents  =  ⟨ x ⟩  ⌢  contents];
          return x);
```

```
  size() value n :  ℕ  ==
    (n  :=  len(contents);
       return n)
end Buffer
```

where **Elem** just contains the type declaration `ITEM = token`. By default we have $\mathbf{mutex}(\{put, get, size\})$ and $\mathbf{self\_mutex}(\{put, get, size\})$ for this class. However, this is more restrictive than necessary, since in an environment where many objects will be clients of a particular buffer, it is quite reasonable for more than one of these clients to enquire about the size of the buffer simultaneously (provided that no client is executing a **put** or **get**). Thus a more liberal "readers-writers" protocol could be instead used:

```
class RWBuffer
  is subclass of Buffer
sync
  per put  ⇒  #active(put)  +  #active(get)  +  #active(size)  ≤  1;
  per get  ⇒  #active(put)  +  #active(get)  +  #active(size)  ≤  1;
  per size ⇒  #active(put)  +  #active(get)  =  0
end RWBuffer
```

In words: a **put** invocation can only begin to execute if there are no other **put**, **get** or **size** invocations executing. Similarly for **get**. **size** however is not excluded from executing with other invocations of itself, but only with invocations of **put** and **get**.

  get and **put** are classified as "writers" in this protocol, because they change the state of the buffer, whilst **size** is a "reader".

  Notice that although **RWBuffer** inherits from **Buffer**, it is not a subtype of **Buffer**, because its synchronisation constraints are strictly weaker.

  An alternative synchronisation constraint could also be built on the basic **Buffer** functionality, this time to specify bounded buffer behaviour:

```
class BoundedBuffer
  is subclass of Buffer
sync
  per put  ⇒  len(contents)  <  1000;

  mutex({ put, get, size });

  self_mutex({ put, get, size })
end BoundedBuffer
```

In this class $\mathbf{len}(contents) \leq 1000$ can be proved to hold at all method termination times, and could be asserted as an invariant.

  BoundedBuffer is a subtype of **Buffer**, since the synchronisation constraints of **Buffer** are written explicitly in **BoundedBuffer**. The mutex constraints are necessary because otherwise the reference to **contents** in the permission guard of **put** would not be secure: **contents** could be in an undefined state (being written to) by another method at the initiation time of a **put** invocation.

The mutex constraints need to be explicitly written in this class since the use of **per** statements in a **sync** clause breaks the default mutual exclusion assumptions made for VDM^{++} classes.

Inheritance can thus be used to separate out functional specification from synchronisation specification, which enhances the degree of reuse in system specifications.

7.2.3 Subtyping and Synchronisation

As indicated in the previous section, inheritance in VDM^{++} does not necessarily preserve the synchronisation or concurrency properties of a class. The precise rules for VDM^{++} are as follows. Recall that the dynamic behaviour of a VDM^{++} class is given by:

- *traces* – which allow declarative specification of the allowed sequences of method executions that an object should support;
- *permission constraints* – which specify under what conditions methods of the class should not execute;
- *periodic threads* – which specify periodic behaviour of the objects of the class;
- *procedural threads* – which give an explicit code definition for the ongoing activity of objects of the class.

It is not possible to specify both a trace and permission constraints, or to specify both a periodic and a procedural thread. All other combinations are allowed. In particular, there may be more than one periodic thread in a class (but only at most one procedural thread).

As a result all the ancestors of a class must have the same form of synchronisation constraint (trace or permission constraints) as the class itself. If the ancestors use traces, then the trace specification of the descendent is the *weave* of all the separate traces – that is, the interleaving of the traces, with common methods identified. If the ancestors use permission constraints, then the descendent has permission constraints which conjoin all the separate constraints given for each method.

These definitions are the correct ones with regard to subtyping: an instance of the descendent will satisfy all the behaviour constraints of each of its ancestors.

The situation for threads is considerably more complex [92]. If the ancestors and the current class only have periodic threads, then inheritance is allowed, and the set of threads of the resulting class is simply the union of those of the individual classes. The resulting class may be inconsistent however, if for example the threads imply that two methods specified as mutually exclusive must in fact overlap in their executions.

It is not permitted to mix periodic and procedural threads, so if any ancestor (or the descendent) has a periodic thread, no other ancestor can use a procedural thread. If some of the classes have threads of the form

```
while  true do
  sel
    c1,1 answer m1,1 -> s1,1 ,
    ...
    cn1,1 answer mn1,1 -> sn1,1
```

then the resulting thread is the "union" of these threads, provided that no links
between the variables of the separate classes are made in the invariant of the
descendent. That is, the result is a thread

```
while  true do
  sel
    c1,1 answer m1,1 -> s1,1 ,
    ...
    cn1,1 answer mn1,1 -> sn1,1 ,
    ...
    cnm,m answer mnm,m -> snm,m
```

where there are m classes with procedural threads involved in the inheritance,
and they have n_1, ..., n_m clauses in their threads, respectively. This combination is not "fair", because sel is sensitive to textual order – the resulting
thread therefore favours actions of the first ancestor class over the second, and
so forth.

In the case of traces a very natural specification style is to define an abstract
supertype with a wide range of possible traces, and to then define subtypes on
the same alphabet which specialise the sets of traces to particular subsets of
the general case. A useful feature is the ability to define identifiers to represent
parts of traces (ie, subprocesses in the life of an entity) in the supertype, and
to then use these identifiers to help define the subtype trace.

As an example, consider the specification of a general flight booking process:

```
class Flight
types
  Date = nat*nat
methods
  book_flight(d: Date)
    is not yet specified;

  change_date(d: Date)
    is not yet specified;

  pay(m: nat)
    is not yet specified;

  confirm()
    is not yet specified;

  cancel()
    is not yet specified;

  collect_ticket()
```

```
        is not yet specified;

    embark()
        is not yet specified;

    arrive()
        is not yet specified
sync
    subtrace PaySequence = < (book_flight; pay),
                                    {pay, book_flight} >;
    subtrace Change = < change_date*, {change_date} >;
    subtrace BookSequence = <(PaySequence; Change),
                                    {pay, book_flight,
                                     change_date}>;
    general Flight = <{book_flight, change_date, pay, cancel,
                    confirm, collect_ticket, embark, arrive }*,
                  {book_flight, change_date, pay, cancel,
                    confirm, collect_ticket, embark, arrive }>

end Flight
```

Recall that sequencing of actions is denoted by ; and iteration (zero or more) by *. Thus **BookSequence** specifies all traces of the forms

$$\langle \text{book\_flight}, \text{pay}\rangle$$
$$\langle \text{book\_flight}, \text{pay}, \text{change\_date}\rangle$$
$$\langle \text{book\_flight}, \text{pay}, \text{change\_date}, \text{change\_date}\rangle$$

and so forth.

If **A** is a set of method names, then $\mathbf{A}^*$ denotes the set of arbitrary sequences of elements of **A**. Thus here a lifetime of an instance of **Flight** can be any arbitrary sequence of invocations of its methods. This is acceptable since **Flight** is a virtual class, and will not have direct instances. The logical interpretation of this trace specification is simply

$$\textbf{mutex}(\underline{\text{methods}}(\textbf{Flight})) \wedge \textbf{self\_mutex}(\underline{\text{methods}}(\textbf{Flight}))$$

so that subclasses of **Flight** will automatically be subtypes in addition, provided that they use traces to specify their behaviour as a subset of the general **Flight** behaviour.

The subclasses give alternative life histories for **Flight** objects – each instance of **Flight** will satisfy only one of these trace specifications. The following class describes a "normal" flight booking and travel process:

```
class NormalFlight
    is subclass of Flight
sync
    general Flight = <(BookSequence; confirm;
                    collect_ticket; embark;
```

```
                         arrive),
                 { book_flight, change_date, pay,
                    confirm, collect_ticket, embark, arrive }>
```

end NormalFlight

Alternatively, we can cancel our flight provided we have not confirmed it:

```
class AbortedFlight
  is subclass of Flight
sync
  general Flight = <(BookSequence; cancel),
                   { book_flight, change_date, pay,
                                             cancel }>
```

end AbortedFlight

Finally, a flight may be "lost" (a euphemism for any non-standard arrival or failure to arrive):

```
class LostFlight
  is subclass of Flight
sync
  general Flight = <(BookSequence; confirm;
                     collect_ticket; embark),
                   { book_flight, change_date, pay,
                     confirm, collect_ticket, embark }>
```

end LostFlight

7.2.4 Fairness Properties

Using the translation of statecharts into formal classes, it is possible to assert a number of fairness properties. Consider a situation where a state **A** has two outgoing transitions s1, a self transition, and s2 to a state **B** (Figure 7.8). In this case it is possible for s2 to be continuously enabled but never activated.

A temporal constraint preventing such a situation is:

$$\Box^\tau((\text{state} = \mathbf{A}) \;\Rightarrow\; \Diamond^\tau(\text{state} \neq \mathbf{A} \;\vee\; \underline{\text{s}_2}))$$

This asserts that eventually s_2 will occur, unless (in some other way) the state **A** is exited. This general form of constraint serves as a fairness obligation for any transition with source state **A**.

enabled(m) for a transition **m** is a condition which must hold at its initiation:

$$\forall \mathbf{i} : \mathbb{N}_1; \; \mathbf{e} : \mathbf{IN} \bullet \mathbf{enabled}(\mathbf{m}(\mathbf{e}))\mathord{\uparrow}(\mathbf{m}(\mathbf{e}), \mathbf{i})$$

It is therefore a permission guard, and is implied by any obligation requirement for **m(e)**.

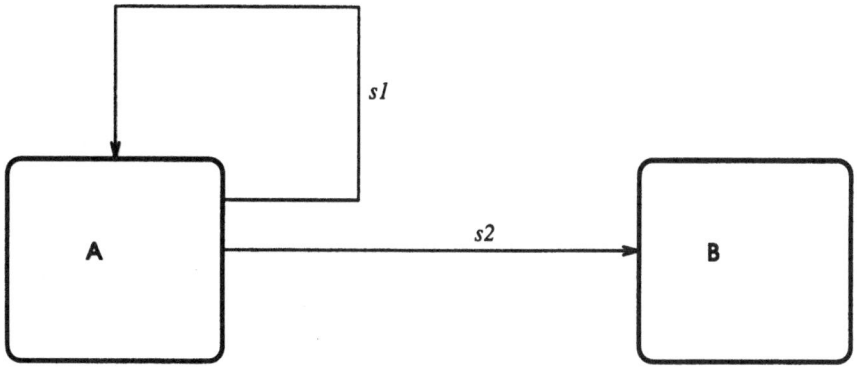

Figure 7.8: Possible Starvation at a State

In VDM^{++} we require that **enabled(m)** is also the *strongest* permission guard for **m**: Statements

per Method ⇒ Cond

are interpreted as **enabled(Method) ⇒ Cond** – that is, if **Cond** does not hold, **Method** is not enabled. Thus **enabled(Method)** places an upper bound on the strength of the restrictions on the initiation of **Method** which can be defined using **per**.

The weak form of fairness that if **m** is continuously enabled then it must be taken infinitely often, is expressed by the formula

□**enabled(m) ⇒ □◇m**

(if we interpret "continuous" in the rather weak sense of "at each method initiation time").

The strong form, that if **m** is enabled infinitely often then it must eventually be taken, is expressed by:

□◇**enabled(m) ⇒ ◇m**

More general versions of these formulae, involving event times and the □$^\tau$ and ◇$^\tau$ quantifiers, can also be used.

Exercise (7.4): Prove that the strong form of fairness implies the weak form.

7.2.5   Required Non-determinism

In some cases it may be necessary for an implementation of a system to allow clients to either perform one or another of two methods m_1 or m_2. Thus it would be an error to refine a specification **C** of such a system to a class which did not permit $\mathbf{m_2}$ to execute:

$$\Box\neg\,\underline{\mathbf{m_2}}$$

or

$$\forall\,\mathbf{i}:\mathbb{N}_1\bullet(\mathbf{self}\notin\overline{\mathbf{C}})\circledcirc\!\uparrow\!(\mathbf{m_2},\mathbf{i})$$

Required non-determinism can be asserted by means of the predicate **enabled(m)**. For example, for the **Buffer** specification above, we could require that **put** is *always* available for use if there are no more than 1000 elements in the buffer, and if there are no executing invocations of the other methods:

```
aux reasoning
history
  enabled(put)  ≡
      len(contents)  <  1000  ∧  #active(put)  ≤  1  ∧
      #active(get)  =  0  ∧  #active(size)  =  0
```

With this specification **BoundedBuffer** would still be a subtype of **Buffer**, however if a stronger permission constraint **G** was specified (eg, to include a constraint **len(contents)** < 500), the formula

$$\mathbf{enabled(put)}\Rightarrow\mathbf{G}$$

would be false, resulting in an inconsistent subclass.

7.2.6   Priorities and Interrupts

There are a number of ways in which it can be asserted that one operation has priority over another. If $\mathbf{m_1}$ and $\mathbf{m_2}$ are two operations in a mutex class $\mathbf{C}$, then the permission guard

$$\Box(\underline{\mathbf{m_2}}\Rightarrow\#\mathbf{waiting}(\mathbf{m_1})=0)$$

states that $\mathbf{m_2}$ can only start to execute if there is no waiting invocation of $\mathbf{m_1}$. In VDM^{++} this is

$$\mathbf{per\ m_2}\quad\Rightarrow\quad\#\mathbf{waiting}(\mathbf{m_1})\ =\ 0$$

Another case of prioritisation involves operations which are designed to handle emergency situations, or which for other reasons must be executed within a certain maximum time bound of their request time. If $\mathbf{m}$ is such an operation, with a time bound $\mathbf{k}$, possibly depending on input parameter values $\mathbf{e}:\mathbf{IN}$ of the request, then the constraint

$$\forall\,\mathbf{i}:\mathbb{N}_1;\ \mathbf{e}:\mathbf{IN}\bullet\mathbf{delay}(\mathbf{m(e)},\mathbf{i})\le\mathbf{k(e)}$$

is asserted. Such an interrupt may force other operations to terminate immediately it starts executing, if the class is mutex, or it could be specified that it leads to termination of a particular operation within a certain time delay.

These interrupts can in turn be generated by a critical condition arising in a monitored system:

$$\forall \mathbf{i} : \mathbb{N}_1 \bullet$$
$$\rightarrow(\mathbf{interrupt}, \mathbf{i}) \;=\; \clubsuit(\varphi := \mathbf{true}, \mathbf{i})$$

In VDM^{++} a proposed syntax for such event-triggered actions is:

on event do action

in the **sync** clause. This asserts that as soon as **event** is detected, the code in **action** is executed atomically, interrupting any on-going activity. Possible events are **req(m)**, **act(m)** and **fin(m)**, representing the events of request arrival, activation and termination of method **m**, or $\varphi := \mathbf{true}$, $\varphi := \mathbf{false}$ for a predicate φ over the attributes of the class.

7.2.7 Removing Callbacks via Threads

A common mechanism in object-oriented design is the *callback*, whereby two objects can access each other, and where a method of one object may invoke a method on the other even if it was originally itself invoked by that object. Whilst overlapping execution of methods of the same object is allowed in VDM^{++} and Z^{++}, it should be avoided unless it is essential for improved responsiveness to external events.

There are a number of ways of avoiding this problem, here we will describe an approach using the **thread** of a VDM^{++} class.

Consider the following two classes, which represent a highly simplified communication system:

```
class A
instance variables
  x : N;
  b : ◆B;
init objectstate == x = 0
methods
  make_call() ==
      (x := x + 1;
        b!answer_call(x));

  confirm_call() ==
      x := 0
end A

class B
instance variables
  y : N;
  a : ◆A;
init objectstate == y = 0
methods
```

```
  answer_call(x :  ℕ)  ==
      (y  :=  x;
        a!confirm_call())
end B
```

Assume that we have two objects **a** of **A** and **b** of **B** with **a.b = b** and **b.a = a**.

Then an invocation of **make_call** on **a** leads to the three overlapping method calls shown on Figure 7.9. It is possible to reason about the overall

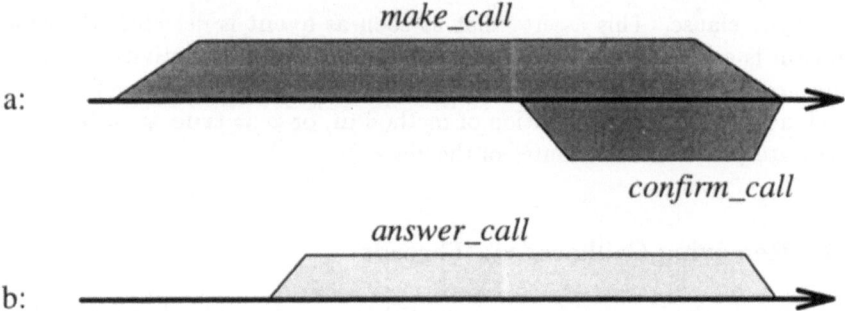

Figure 7.9: Callback Between Two Objects

effect of the methods of **a** because the execution of **make_call** can be decomposed into two parts, the first (assignment) sets **x** to $\overleftarrow{x} + 1$ where $\overleftarrow{x}$ is the value of **x** at initiation of the method, and the second part sets **x** to 0. Nevertheless this is unnecessarily complex, and can be improved by removing all method calls in **A** and **B** into the threads of these classes:

```
class A'
instance variables
  x :  ℕ;
  b :  @B';
init objectstate == x = 0
methods
  make_call()  ==
      x  :=  x + 1;

  confirm_call()  ==
      x  :=  0
thread
  while true do
    sel
      answer make_call ->
                    b!answer_call(x),
      answer confirm_call
end A'

class B'
instance variables
  y :  ℕ;
```

```
   a :  @A';
init objectstate == y = 0
methods
  answer_call(x : N) ==
                       y := x
thread
  while true do
     sel
        answer answer_call ->
                      a!confirm_call()
end B'
```

The pattern of interaction between these objects is now purely sequential, as
shown in Figure 7.10. At any point in time there is now only one active object.

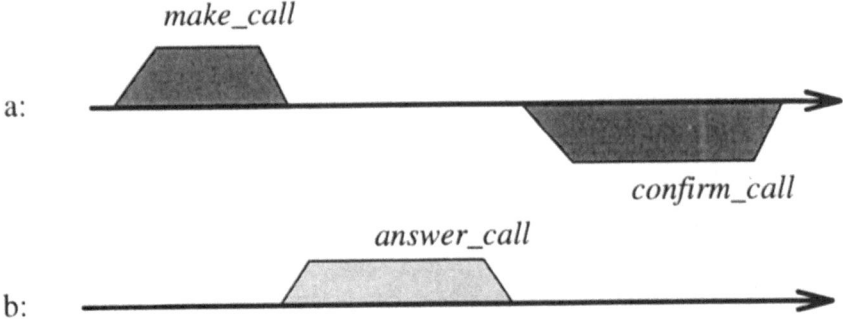

make_call

a:

confirm_call

answer_call

b:

Figure 7.10: Revised Callback System Using Threads

Notice that such a transformation may also be an optimisation for a system,
in that it reduces the time that a caller of a method such as **answer_call** needs
to wait for it to complete. This optimisation is akin to the moving of return
statements up through a method definition in the formalism of [160].

7.2.8 Proving Equivalences Between Programs

This section illustrates how equivalences between alternative ways of specifying
class behaviour can be proven. Consider a specification that three methods aa,
bb and cc should be executed in self and mutual exclusion, and that they are
executed in a cyclic manner:

```
class Cyclic
methods
  aa()
       is not yet specified;

  bb()
       is not yet specified;
```

```
cc()
      is not yet specified
sync
    general Cyclic =
                < (aa; bb; cc)*, { aa, bb, cc } >
end Cyclic
```

According to the semantics [169] this is the same as writing:

```
class Cyclic₂
methods
  aa()
      is not yet specified;

  bb()
      is not yet specified;

  cc()
      is not yet specified

aux reasoning
history
```

$$\forall\ i:\ \mathbb{N}_1\ \bullet$$
$$\uparrow(bb, i)\ \geq\ \downarrow(aa, i)\ \ \wedge$$
$$\uparrow(aa, i+1)\ \geq\ \downarrow(cc, i)\ \ \wedge$$
$$\uparrow(cc, i)\ \geq\ \downarrow(bb, i)$$

```
end Cyclic₂
```

But this can also be rephrased in terms of event counts. That is, the definition of **Cyclic$_2$** asserts that the predicate (1):

$$\#act(bb) \leq \#fin(aa)\ \wedge$$
$$\#act(aa) \leq \#fin(cc) + 1\ \wedge$$
$$\#act(cc) \leq \#fin(bb)$$

is always true.

This property is provable in the following class:

```
class Cyclic₃
methods
  aa()
      is not yet specified;

  bb()
      is not yet specified;

  cc()
      is not yet specified
```

```
sync
   per aa   ⇒   #act(aa) ≤ #fin(cc) + 1;
   per bb   ⇒   #act(bb) ≤ #fin(aa);
   per cc   ⇒   #act(cc) ≤ #fin(bb)
```

end **Cyclic₃**

This holds because initially (1) is true for this class, since it is true if all event counts are zero. In addition, all events must preserve the invariant:

- no request event can affect the invariant;
- an activation of **aa** can only invalidate the invariant if it results in $\#act(aa) > \#fin(cc) + 1$. But the permission guard prevents such an activation. Similarly for activations of **bb** and **cc**;
- a termination of **aa** cannot invalidate the invariant. Similarly for terminations of **bb** and **cc**.

Thus (1) holds at all times. Formally this shows that **Cyclic₃** is a subtype of **Cyclic₂** (and, since there is no state in either class, and both have the same set of methods, it is also a refinement of it).

Finally, an entirely procedural version of the class is:

```
class Cyclic₄
methods
   aa()
       is not yet specified;

   bb()
       is not yet specified;

   cc()
       is not yet specified

thread
   while true
   do
     (sel answer aa;
      sel answer bb;
      sel answer cc)
```

end **Cyclic₄**

The semantics of **answer** is quite complicated [169], but in order to show that **Cyclic₄** refines **Cyclic₃** it is sufficient to ensure that the appropriate permission guards hold at each method activation. If an **answer m** statement occurs in a class thread, where **m** is a method of the class, then this implies that the *only* invocations of **m** are those which occur when the control flow of the thread has reached such an **answer** statement:

$$\forall j : N_1 \bullet \exists i : N_1 \bullet$$
$$\uparrow(m, j) = \uparrow(answer\ m, i)$$

As a result, a conventional weakest-precondition style reasoning applied to the loop code will establish that the permission guards for **aa**, **bb** and **cc** hold at the relevant code locations, and therefore for all activations of these methods allowed by the class.

7.2.9   Continuous Real-time Systems

An important feature of VDM^{++} is a notation which supports the specification of idealised physical systems such as electronic components or hydraulic systems [90].

Such systems are modelled by *continuous classes*, which in addition to instance variables include attributes which can vary continuously over time, and are used to represent inputs or outputs to the system. The system maintains a relationship between these attributes, with an **assumption** clause recording what is known about the input attributes, and an **effect** clause recording how the system constrains its outputs.

For example, a general electronic component is:

```
class Component is subclass of SysTypes
time variables
   input i_in :  current;
         i_out :  current;
         v :  voltage;

   effect i_out  ==   i_out(t)  =  i_in(t)

instance variables
   name :  char*;
   val :  ℝ
end Component
```

i_out and **v** have output modality. The types **current** and **voltage** are defined in **SysTypes**.

i_out, i_in and **v** are implicitly analytic functions or time series of type **TIME** $\rightarrowtail$ **current** and **TIME** $\rightarrowtail$ **voltage** respectively, where **TIME** is the set of non-negative real numbers with the usual ordering and operations. Their domains are the closed intervals $[0, \textbf{now}]$ at each time point **now**.

The **effect** clause for i_out here states that the input and output currents are the same at all times. That is, formally, it denotes

$$\Box^\tau(\text{i\_out}(\textbf{now}) = \text{i\_in}(\textbf{now}))$$

or (equivalently)

$$\forall t : \textbf{TIME} \bullet \text{i\_out}(t) = \text{i\_in}(t)$$

val will denote the value of the resistance, inductance, or capacitance of the component. In contrast to Z^{++}, and to instance variables in VDM^{++}, the values of time variables can change over intervals at which no method of the class is executing.

Particular forms of component are expressed as subtypes of this class:

class Resistor is subclass of Component
time variables
   assumption i_in == i_in(t)^2 * val ≤ **maxdiss**;

   effect v == v(t) = i_in(t) * val

instance variables
  maxdiss : $\mathbb{R}$
end Resistor

maxdiss gives the maximum heat which the resistor can dissipate. Similarly:

class Inductor is subclass of Component
time variables
   assumption i_in == $\frac{d\ i\_in(t)}{dt}$ ≤ **maxRate**;

   effect v == v(t) = val * $\frac{d\ i\_in(t)}{dt}$

instance variables
  maxRate : $\mathbb{R}$
end Inductor

class Capacitor is subclass of Component
time variables
   assumption i_in == $\frac{1}{val}\int_0^t$ i_in(t) dt ≤ **maxVoltage**;

   effect v == v(t) = $\frac{1}{val}\int_0^t$ i_in(t) dt

instance variables
  maxVoltage : $\mathbb{R}$
end Capacitor

A component representing the source voltage has

    effect v == v(t) = $v_0 * \sin(\omega * t + \phi)$

where v_0, ω and ϕ are constants defined in this class.

Instances **r, i, c** and **s** of these components can then be linked together by a topology statement:

topology [**post** s.i_out = l.i_in ∧
                  l.i_out = r.i_in ∧
                  r.i_out = c.i_in ∧
                  c.i_out = s.i_in]

This is interpreted as (i): $\Box^\tau(\mathbf{s.i\_out(now)} = \mathbf{l.i\_in(now)})$ and so forth[1]. In the (workspace) class where this topology statement occurs, we also constrain the models by *Kirchoff's Law* (ii):

$$\Box^\tau(-\mathbf{s.v(now)} = \mathbf{r.v(now)} + \mathbf{i.v(now)} + \mathbf{c.v(now)})$$

Using the definitions of these output variables given in the classes, this can be rewritten in terms of a single current value $\mathbf{i(t)} = \mathbf{s.i\_out(t)}$ and $\mathbf{s.v(t)}$.

Thus, this specification describes an idealised system in which there are no time delays across components. Its solutions are effectively all pairs $\mathbf{i}$ and $\mathbf{v}$ of real-valued functions where $\mathbf{i}$ is analytic, and which satisfy the constraints (i) and (ii).

As a more elementary example, consider the continuous classes

```
class Differentiator
time variables
  input x :  ℝ;
        y :  ℝ;
```
$$\text{effect } \mathbf{y} \;==\; \mathbf{y(t)} \;=\; \frac{\mathrm{d}\ \mathbf{x(t)}}{\mathrm{dt}}$$
```
end Differentiator
```

and

```
class Copy
time variables
  input a :  ℝ;
        b :  ℝ;
        c :  ℝ;

  effect b  ==    b(t)  =  a(t);
  effect c  ==    c(t)  =  a(t)
end Copy
```

If these are linked together in a loop:

```
class Workspace
instance variables
  dd :  @Differentiator;
  cc :  @Copy
methods
  initialise()  ==
        ( dd  :=  Differentiator!new ;
          cc  :=  Copy!new ;
            topology [
                        post dd.y  =  cc.a  ∧
                             dd.x  =  cc.b] )
end Workspace
```

---

[1] This is a special case which applies only to time variables. It is preferable to just write formulae such as (i) rather than these topology statements.

Then the models of the system are essentially all analytic functions which are equal to their own differential at all times. That is, all functions $\mathbf{f}$ of the form

$$\mathbf{f(t)} = \mathbf{k} * \mathbf{e^t}$$

for some constant $\mathbf{k}$.

The trivial solution with $\mathbf{k} = 0$ can be excluded by requiring

$$\diamond^\tau(\mathbf{y(now)} \neq 0)$$

in the **history** of **Differentiator**.

The effect of time variables can be achieved in Z^{++} by defining a method which is continuously active throughout the life of the class. Effect and assumption clauses are then expressed in the HISTORY clause by formulae of the form $\Box^\tau \varphi$.

Further examples of continuous real-time systems are given in Chapter 9.

Exercise (7.5): Why is there no "previous execution initiation" operator ● corresponding to ○? [Hint: consider the following class:]

```
class Oscillator
time variables
        displacement :  ℝ;
  effect displacement  ==
            (0 ≤ t ∧ t ≤ 5) ⇒
                displacement(t)  =  (5 − t) * sin(π/(5 − t))
methods
  activate()  ==  skip
history
   ∀ i :  ℕ₁ · ↑(activate, i)  =  5 − 1/(2*i)
end Oscillator
```

Exercise (7.6): Consider the radar track-former exercise of Chapters 3 and 4. Specify the additional properties that **confirm_tracks** and **delete_tracks** are performed periodically (but mutually exclusively) every time that 20 new plots have been added since the last time they executed. Consider how **Track** can be modified so that plots can be simultaneously added to a track, and how **System** could be similarly modified to support the addition of plots which arrive at the same time (ie, multiple **add_plot** invocations start simultaneously).

Exercise (7.7): Give the dynamic model for the following system, and give an outline class in VDM^{++}:

- the system is an automated telephone response service which users can connect to and carry out one of three operations: *record message* in which they dictate a message for other users to access; *listen to own message* in which they can playback the message they have just recorded, and *access messages* in which they can playback all messages left for themselves. In the latter case however they must supply a password (number) which is verified by the system;

- after completion of any of these operations the user can disconnect from the system.

Implicitly each number that may be dialled by a user corresponds to the identity of an object which manages the message-leaving and accessing for that number. The system maintains this set of objects, and a password/verification system associated with it.

Is there anything which seems likely to have been omitted from the above requirements?

7.2.10   Sampling and Discretisation

Consider the patient data monitoring case study of Chapter 4. How can the invariant

$$\forall \ i, j : \ 1..\#\text{reading\_sequence} \mid i < j \ \bullet$$
$$\text{reading\_sequence}(i).\text{timestamp} \ <$$
$$\text{reading\_sequence}(j).\text{timestamp}$$

of the **Patient** class be guaranteed?

We could define a method **take_reading**:

```
take_reading read?  ==>
        reading_sequence'  =  reading_sequence ⌢ ⟨ read? ⟩;
```

HISTORY
$$\forall \ i : \ \mathbb{N}_1 \ \bullet$$
$$(\text{reading\_sequence}(\#\text{reading\_sequence}).\text{timestamp}) \circledast$$
$$\downarrow(\text{take\_reading}, i) \ =$$
$$\uparrow(\text{take\_reading}, i)$$

END CLASS

In other words, the time stamp reflects the time at which this method was initiated. Thus, because **take_reading** is durative, the invariant can be proved.

It could also be specified that the **take_reading** method executes at regular intervals:

$$\forall \ i : \ \mathbb{N}_1 \ \bullet$$
$$\uparrow(\text{take\_reading}, i+1) \ = \ \uparrow(\text{take\_reading}, i) \ + \ \mathbf{k}$$

where **k** is a constant.

A discrete version of a continuous VDM^{++} class would serve as a specification of a software *simulator* of the idealised physical or analogue situation described by the continuous class. That is, it provides the starting point for development of a computable approximation of the properties of such a system.

In the case of the electronic components described in the previous section, we could write:

```
class DiscreteComponent is subclass of Component
instance variables
   id_in :  ℝ*;
   id_out :  ℝ*;
   vd :  ℝ*;
   currvalue :  ℝ
methods
   getCurrent() value idiscrete :  ℝ  ==
       ([ext rd i_in
             wr idiscrete
          post ∃ t ∈ { ‾now‾, …, now } · i_in(t)  =  idiscrete ];
          return idiscrete);

   take_sample()  ==
       (dcl currvalue :  ℝ  :=  self!getCurrent();
          [ ext wr id_in
             post id_in  =  ‾id_in‾ ⁀ ⟨ currvalue ⟩ ])
thread
   periodic(δ)(take_sample)
end DiscreteComponent
```

The sequences **id_in**, **id_out**, etc replace the partial time series **i_out**, **i_in**, etc in the abstract class.

   In subtypes of this class corresponding to **Inductor**, **Resistor**, etc, the sequence of **id_out** and **vd** values would be defined in terms of the sequence of **id_in** values, using approximations to differentials and integrals where necessary. δ is a constant describing the sampling interval, and would be defined in a superclass.

   Either all the components in the circuit simulator have to be synchronised on the same interval, and pass the values of **id_out** instantaneously to one another, or they need to be able to access the most recently computed value of the outputs of their predecessor component in the circuit.

Exercise (7.8): Does the following class represent a good approach to the definition of a system clock? How could it be guaranteed that errors could not occur?[2]

```
class Clock
instance variables
   seconds, minutes: nat;
init objectstate ==   seconds = 0 and minutes = 0
methods
   set_sec() ==
       seconds := (seconds + 1) mod 60;
```

---

[2] This exercise is based on an actual example of PC clock software in which the date and time were updated by separate interrupts, with the time update having the higher priority: resulting in times being inaccurate by a day for several seconds after midnight if the processor was busy then – the vendor shall remain nameless . . ..

```
set_min() ==
    minutes := (minutes + 1) mod 60;

get_time() value nat*nat ==
    return mk_(minutes,seconds)
thread
  periodic(1)(set_sec);
  periodic(60)(set_min)

end Clock
```

Conclusions

This chapter has addressed some of the issues which arise in stating and establishing concurrent and real-time properties of systems.

Temporal logic has been a widely used formalism for the specification of the properties of reactive systems, although in some cases it is too abstract to effectively specify real-time requirements. The book [242] uses a real-time temporal logic formalism, RTTL, to express safety and liveness properties of reactive systems. A general framework for the use of temporal logic in object-oriented system specification is given in [268]. An alternative approach, based on algebraic specification and process algebra, is used in the TROLL language [137] and in the RAISE specification language [111]. Proposals for adding RTL to RAISE to handle real-time properties were made in the MORSE DTI project [53].

A quite different approach to concurrent system specification is given by the process algebras CSP, CCS, the π-calculus and other variants of these languages [146, 232]. These languages are less declarative and more procedural than temporal logics, and are less directly related to logical formulae and proof.

VDM^{++} appears to be the first formal object-oriented specification language to include a notion of continuous time variable. This concept was based on the approach of Hayes and Mahoney [141, 205, 206] in Z. Other formalisation approaches for real-time systems are given in [73].

Chapter 8

Implementation and Code Generation

In this Chapter the process of translation of implementation-oriented formal classes into executable code in Eiffel, Ada and C++ will be described.

Section 8.1 covers the translation steps for Z^{++} and VDM^{++} specifications into procedural languages. Sections 8.2 and 8.3 give case studies in implementation. Finally, Section 8.4 considers the role of testing in formal object-oriented development.

8.1 Translation into Procedural Languages

8.1.1 Eiffel

A translation from implementation classes in VDM^{++} and Z^{++} into Eiffel classes is possible, however the parts of these languages concerned with the specification of concurrent and real-time behaviour cannot be translated.

In outline, the translation for VDM^{++} is as follows, where we assume that the only types remaining in the implementation classes are basic types and multi-dimensional arrays of basic types.

- declarations using one-dimensional array types $v : a..b \rightarrow T$ are replaced by $v : \mathbf{ARRAY}[T']$ with the operation $v.\mathbf{Create}(a, b)$ being specified in the interpretation of the initialisation operation. T' is the translation of T;

- the **String** type must be interpreted as the **STRING** class type, with specific size bounds being defined in the initialisation of elements of this type;

- declarations involving class types can only otherwise be of the form $v : @S$ in the implementation sublanguage of VDM^{++}, and these simply become $v : S$ in Eiffel (if we adopted the convention that $@S$ only denotes non-void object references, then the type $[@S]$ in VDM^{++} would correspond to S in Eiffel);

- the initialisation predicate in VDM^{++} becomes the explicit code of the **Create** procedure in the Eiffel class, which has no input parameters. This predicate must therefore consist of a set of equalities defining specific values for the attributes, using expressions which are directly translatable into Eiffel;
- the invariant predicate must consist of expressions which can be immediately expressed in Eiffel, and it then becomes the invariant of the Eiffel class;
- a subclass clause in VDM^{++} becomes an **inherit** clause in Eiffel. Methods which are implicitly redefined in the descendent (because they are listed there in addition to in the ancestor) must be listed in a **redefines** clause in Eiffel;
- controlled inheritance in VDM^{++} cannot be directly expressed in Eiffel: if **D** inherits **C** and hides methods $m_1, \ldots, m_n$ of **C**, then the corresponding Eiffel class **D'** must inherit **C**, and not list any of $m_1, \ldots, m_n$ in its export clause. Renaming in Z^{++} can be expressed as renaming in Eiffel;
- local functions and constants will be translated into Eiffel functions and constants – the latter must however be simple scalar values. The translation of class-valued constants uses the concept of a *once* function [225] defined in the class that is the type of the constant and invoked in the **Create** method of the client class;
- attributes of a class become Eiffel attribute features.

The name of the Eiffel class is that of the initial abstract specification of the implementation class being translated.

The translation of code constructs and method definitions is as follows:

- assignments to array elements: $a = \overleftarrow{a} \oplus \{i \mapsto e\}$ become calls a.**enter**(i, e);
- accesses to array elements a(i) become a.**entry**(i);
- sequential composition is translated to sequential composition;
- local declarations dcl v: T := e; S become local variable declarations local v: T' do (v := e)'; S' where T' etc are the Eiffel translations of these elements – local declarations can only occur at the outermost level of a method definition in Eiffel;
- conditionals if E then C1 else C2 become if E' then C1' else C2' end in Eiffel;
- loops while E do S become from until not(E)' loop S' end – invariants and variants can be explicitly recorded in Eiffel, as can initialisation statements, and a manual transformation should make use of these facilities;
- method calls a!m(e) become a.m(e) in Eiffel (after translation of a and e into Eiffel);
- method preconditions can be expressed in the **requires** clause of the corresponding Eiffel method;
- named result attributes in VDM^{++} methods are replaced by the **Result** expression throughout the text of the translated method. The method header is translated directly into a corresponding Eiffel method header.

This implies that topology statements should be replaced in implementations by invocations of methods which explicitly set the appropriate attributes.

As an example, consider the **Person_2** class given in Section 8.3. This can be translated as:

```
class Person export
  change_address, birthday, current_age
feature
  age: Age;
  address: STRING;

  Create is
     do
        address.Create(50)
     end;

  change_address(nad: STRING) is
     do
        address := nad
     end;

  birthday is
     do
        if age.value < 200
        then
          age.set_value(age.value + 1)
        end
     end;

  current_age: Age is
     do
        Result := age.value
     end

end -- class Person
```

Where **Age** has been formalised as a class type:

```
class Age export
          value, set_value
feature
  value: INTEGER;

  set_value(v: INTEGER) is
     require 0 <= v; v <= 200
     do
        value := v
     end

invariant
   0 <= value; value <= 200
end -- class Age
```

It may also be useful to include a translation from abstract VDM^{++} classes into abstract Eiffel classes (ie, classes whose methods only have **ensure** and **require** clauses). This translation must necessarily be partial however, as the mathematical language of VDM^{++} is strictly more expressive than that of Eiffel.

The structural correspondence between a VDM^{++} development architecture and the resulting inheritance structure of the Eiffel system is as follows:

- if **A** and **B** are classes both of which are "concrete" in the sense that they will have instances in the executable system, and **B** is a subtype of **A**, then the subtyping relationship should also be asserted in the resulting Eiffel system – in order for this to work, **B** and its refinements must use **A** by means of *strict* inheritance: all updates to attributes inherited from **A** must be achieved by calls **self!MP(e)** to methods of **A**, whilst accesses to attributes of **A** must, at the implementation level, be achieved by calls to enquiry operations **val := self!MF(e)**. This situation is shown in Figure 8.1. The advantage of this approach is that the common parts of the two lines of development are only developed once (in the path for **A**). However the two developments must be coordinated to the extent that asserting the subtype relation at the implementation level is valid in Eiffel.

As an example, consider the skeleton classes

```
class Dictionary_as_set
instance variables
  dict: F(WORD);
init objectstate == dict = {}
methods
  / * Operations to add, delete and find words * /
end Dictionary_as_set

class Dictionary_with_definitions
  is subclass of Dictionary_as_set
instance variables
  defs: WORD ⟶ᵐ F(WORD);
inv objectstate ==
  dom(defs) = dict;
init objectstate == defs = { ↦ }
methods
  add_defn(wd: WORD, def: WORD) ==
       if wd ∈ dict
       then
         ...;

end Dictionary_with_definitions
```

We would like to be able to separately refine these classes to code. If we choose the refinement:

```
class Dictionary_as_seq
-- refines Dictionary_as_set
-- retrieve function: dict = elems(sq)
instance variables
  sq : seq(WORD);
init objectstate == sq = ⟨ ⟩
methods

  ...

end Dictionary_as_seq
```

then any refinement of **Dictionary_with_definitions** should not depend upon this choice. Indeed, for the subtype, we may want to make a different choice of representation for the dictionary word set. Thus it would seem that we should still use **dict** as a set in refinements of **Dictionary_with_definitions**. However, at the level just before code, such direct use must be replaced with mechanisms which can be directly translated into code. Thus the test **wd** ∈ **dict** for example should be replaced by the result of a method call **isin := self!in_dictionary(wd)**;

- if **A** is a virtual class with subtypes A_1, ..., A_n, then **A** is implemented by an Eiffel class in which all methods are supplied only with **requires** and **ensures** clauses, and the appropriate subtype relations are asserted between this implementation and the implementations of the A_i (Figure 8.2). For simplicity, method renaming should be avoided.

It is however possible to share some refinement steps between the supertype and the subtype. For example, consider the case where we define a subclass **StandardWorkingPerson** of **WorkingPerson** which has the additional invariant **len(employments)** ≤ 1. The operations of this class are, for simplicity, identical to those of its supertype, except that an operation **add_employment** must now have the additional precondition **len(employments)** = 0.

This new version of the operation cannot be defined by:

```
add_employment(e: @Employment)
    pre len(employments) = 0   ==
            self!add_employment(e);
```

because this would introduce self-recursion. Instead, we must use the qualified supertype operation[1]:

```
add_employment(e: @Employment)
    pre len(employments) = 0   ==
            self!WorkingPerson'add_employment(e);
```

Only the aspects of the new class relating to this new invariant and precondition need to be additionally developed to code in the refinement path of **StandardWorkingPerson**. This could also be achieved by renaming **add_employment** to **wp_add_employment** and then using the latter method.

---

[1] This is akin to the use of the super object in Smalltalk.

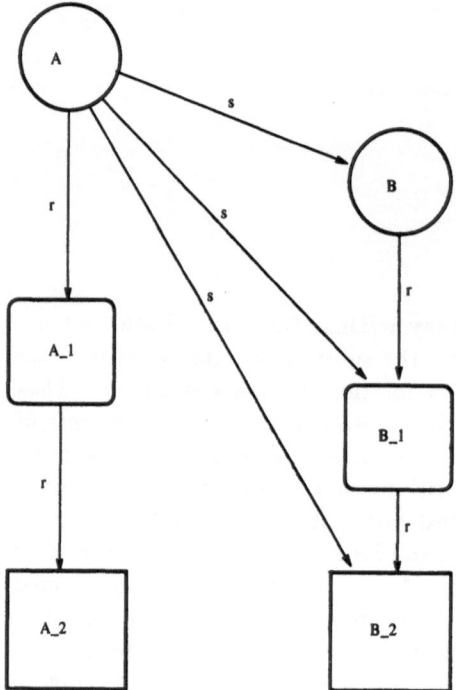

Figure 8.1: Strict Subtyping and Refinement

There is not a **renames** mechanism in basic VDM^{++}. It can however be simulated by using class composition.

Similarly, if we wish to provide an alternative implementation in the subtype of an operation **m** inherited from a supertype, and so perform a redefinition, then in the Eiffel translation this redefinition must be made explicit via a **redefines** clause.

A partial translation of the concurrent parts of VDM^{++} into the proposed concurrent extension [228] of Eiffel is possible. This translation would use some of the following correspondences:

- forking a method call: !a.m(e) corresponds to an Eiffel method call on a **separate** object **a**, provided that **m** is a pure updater (with no return values);
- private objects: suppliers declared without a **separate** qualification;
- permission guards: preconditions (on methods invoked from separate clients);
- threads: instantiation of the **live** method of the **PROCESS** class.

For Z^{++}, internal actions can be translated into internal (non-exported) features in Eiffel.

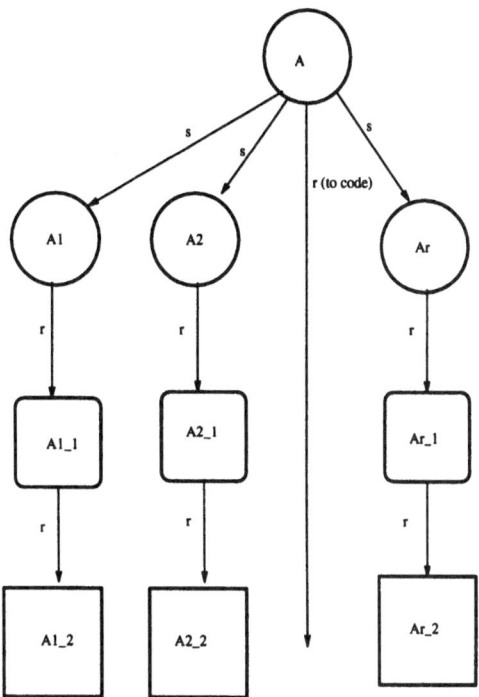

Figure 8.2: Abstract Supertypes and Refinement

8.1.2 Ada

Ada is not an object-oriented language, although some object-oriented aspects have been introduced in Ada95 [155]. In many respects the language feature of Ada which has the closest affinity with the concept of an object in Z^{++} or VDM^{++} is the *task* [30]. However tasks, whilst they support object creation and concurrent object execution and communication, do not support subtyping. This implies that implementation-level formal classes which are constructed using inheritance or subtyping must be fully expanded out into classes which are not descendants of other classes before translation into Ada code – this is however a mechanical process. More significantly it implies that runtime polymorphism cannot be achieved. An alternative is to use the *tagged types* of Ada95, which provide operation polymorphism. Thus if a class **C** has instance variable declaration $v_1 : T_1; \ldots; v_n : T_n$, the corresponding Ada95 tagged record declaration is:

```
type C_T is   tagged
  record
    v₁ :  T1;
      ...
    vₙ :  Tn;
  end record;
```

where $\mathbf{Ti}$ is the Ada type representing $\mathbf{T_i}$.

The correspondences between VDM^{++} and Ada are as follows; similar correspondences apply for Z^{++}.

- class declaration – package containing state data type and task type declaration (specification and body);
- class reference type – access type to state record and to task type;
- object – state record and task;
- method – subprogram and task entry;
- instance variables – local variables of package and task body;
- method call – subprogram and entry invocation(s);
- method code – subprogram and accept statement code;
- select statements – select statements;
- answer statements – accept statements;
- permission guards – select guards;
- types, functions and constants – corresponding items defined in a package enclosing the task type definition.

The translation of implementation-level types (integer subranges, enumerated types, records, etc) is immediate. Recursively specified methods cannot however be implemented in this way unless they involve no synchronisation constraints (as task entries are non-reentrant).

Thus, if we have a class representing passive objects:

```
class C
instance variables
  v :  T
methods
  m(w :  S) value u :  P  ==
                       Code_m
sync
  per m  ⇒  Cond
end C
```

we would have the corresponding Ada declarations

```
package C is
-- type and constant definitions
  type C_T is private

  procedure m(C_object: in out C_T; w: in S; u: out P);

  task type C_task is
    entry m;
  end C_task;

  type C_task_ref is access C_task;

  type C_ref is access C_T;
```

```
private
  type C_T is tagged
    record
      v: T;
      C_sync_task: C_task_ref
    end record;

end C;

package body C is

  procedure m(C_object: in out C_T; w: in S; u: out P) is
  begin
    C_object.C_sync_task.m(w,u); -- concurrency control
    Proc_Code;
  end m;

  task body C_task is
    -- synchronisation variables, if any
  begin
    loop
      select
        when Cond =>
          accept m(w: in S; u: out P) do Sync_Code end m;
        or
          -- accept statements for other methods, if any
      end select;
    end loop;
  end C_task;

end C;
```

The code of C has been separated into conventional procedural elements, implemented in the **Proc_Code** of C.m, and code which exists only to maintain synchronisation properties such as mutual exclusion, which is implemented in the body of the **C_task** instance associated with each object instance. Similarly the instance variables of the class would be (disjointly) partitioned between the two Ada items (although, in the current VDM^{++} language, there is not a syntactically distinct category of synchronisation variable, such an extension would be coherent and useful).

Notice that the abstract types **S** and **P** may become implemented by types **S′** and **P′** in the Ada code: for simplicity we have written them using different fonts.

Objects **Object** of type @C are declared by

```
Object: C.C_ref
```

and created by

```
Object := new C.C_T;
```

```
Object.C_sync_task := new C.C_task;
```

Invocations **Object!m(e)** of **m** become

```
C.m(Object.all,e)
```

Event counters can also be implemented in Ada tasks, invoked at the beginning and end of procedure bodies. For example, we could implement a class in which methods **m** and **n** are mutex, and in which **n** has priority over **m**, as follows:

```
package C is
  -- definitions of Data
  procedure m(C_object: in out C_T; ...);

  procedure n(C_object: in out C_T; ...);

  task type C_task is
    entry start_m;
    entry start_n;
    entry end_m;
    entry end_n;
  end C_task;

  type C_task_ref is access C_task;

  type C_ref is access C_T;

private
  type C_T is tagged
    record
      v: T;
      C_sync_task: C_task_ref
    end record;

end C

package body C is

  procedure m(C_object: in out C_T; ...) is
  begin
    C_object.C_sync_task.start_m;
    -- procedural code
    C_object.C_sync_task.end_m;
  end m;

  procedure n(...) is
  begin
    C_object.C_sync_task.start_n;
    -- procedural code
    C_object.C_sync_task.end_n;
```

```
end n;

task body C_task is
  active_m, active_n: natural := 0;
begin
  loop
    select
      when active_m = 0  =>
        accept start_n
        do
          active_n := active_n + 1;
        end start_n;
      or
      when (active_n = 0 and start_n'count = 0) =>
        accept start_m
        do
          active_m := active_m + 1;
        end start_m;
      or
        accept end_n
        do
          active_n := active_n - 1;
        end end_n;
      or
        accept end_m
        do
          active_m := active_m - 1;
        end end_m;
    end select;
  end loop;
end C_task;

end C;
```

The value of **start_n'count** is assumed to implement **#waiting(start_n)** (and therefore **#waiting(n)**).

In contrast active objects will have a task body closely related to the (procedural) thread specification. In particular, threads formalised from statecharts have a particularly direct interpretation – in place of the condition

$$\mathbf{lastentered} + l \leq \mathbf{now} \leq \mathbf{lastentered} + u$$

guarding a transition $\mathbf{t[l, u]}$ in the thread of a VDM^{++} class, we can simply write

```
select
   ...
or
   when t_enabled  =>
     delay l;
     select
```

```
        accept t() ...
      or
        delay u;
        t_enabled := False;
      end select;
            -- remain in current state, but inhibit  t
  end select;
```

That is, other transitions from the current state will be performed if possible until l seconds have elapsed from the beginning of this cycle of the select statement (ie, from completion of the previous state transition), and then requests for the transition t will be accepted until the timeout bound u has elapsed, after which the transition will be inhibited (an alternative interpretation would be that t is then forced to occur at this point, ie, we would have a select alternative **delay u; Code** where **Code** is the code definition of t).

Since Ada select statements do not use a fixed priority ordering to select one open and executable guard from a set of such guards, the priority mechanism of VDM^{++} select statements cannot be directly implemented.

Obligation specifications

$$\Box(\chi \Rightarrow \underline{m})$$

are implemented by placing χ as a guard in a select statement executed within a loop:

```
loop
  select
    when χ => accept m() ...
```

where all other guards are logically inconsistent with χ.

Strictly, such a statement can only guarantee that **m** is executed after a certain delay from the point where χ becomes true. This is because the body of some other select choice may be in execution at this point, and must terminate before execution of **m** becomes possible. Indeed the statement may fail to detect some intervals in which χ holds, for the same reason. Thus it can only be proved correct if we have additional knowledge. For example, that the minimum time that χ remains true is greater than the maximum duration of any other select body, plus the time taken to cycle around the loop to the beginning of the select statement:

$$\forall i, j : \mathbb{N}_1 \bullet \mathbf{duration}(s_k, j) + t < \clubsuit(\chi := \mathbf{false}, i+1) - \clubsuit(\chi := \mathbf{true}, i)$$

for each **k**, and $t \in \mathbf{T}(\mathbf{brfloop}) \dotplus \mathbf{T}(\mathbf{eval}(\mathbf{true}))$, in the case that χ is false initially. **i** would be used in place of $i+1$ if χ were true initially (see Appendix B for a definition of $\mathbf{T}$ and $\dotplus$).

Subtypes of a class, and subtype operations, are all declared and defined in the same package as the ancestor type, each subtype has its own (additional) sync task to perform concurrency control (as the nature of this control may become more restrictive in subtypes).

An Ada translator is being developed within the AFRODITE consortium. It will make use of guidance from the user in order to simplify the translation process for VDM^{++} classes which do not make use of the full concurrency or polymorphism capabilities of the language.

8.1.3 Increasing Parallelisation During Refinement

If the target execution environment supports concurrent execution of processes, then it is useful to be able to refine a system which has initially been specified in a purely sequential manner into implementations which utilise concurrency.

An example of increasing the parallelisation in an implementation could be in a class which manages a complex data structure, with operations which both return values describing properties of parts of this structure and which transform the structure. If invocations of a method on distinct parts of the structure are non-interfering, then the transformation parts of the method can be conducted in parallel, whilst the value returned by the method can be passed back before it terminates.

As an example, consider a distributed tree data structure:

CLASS **Tree[X]**

$$\text{eventual\_descendents} : \text{seq}(\overline{\text{Tree[X]}}) \rightarrow \mathbb{F}(\overline{\text{Tree[X]}})$$

$$\text{eventual\_descendents}(\langle\rangle) = \varnothing \ \wedge$$
$$\forall \, \text{ts} : \text{seq}(\overline{\text{Tree[X]}}); \ \text{t} : \overline{\text{Tree[X]}} \ \bullet$$
$$\quad \text{eventual\_descendents}(\langle \text{t} \rangle \frown \text{ts}) =$$
$$\quad\quad \{\text{t}\} \cup \text{eventual\_descendents}(\text{t.immediate\_descendents}) \ \cup$$
$$\quad\quad\quad \text{eventual\_descendents}(\text{ts})$$

OWNS
  immediate_descendents : seq($\overline{\text{Tree[X]}}$);
  node_value : **X**
INVARIANT
  #immediate_descendents $=$ #ran(immediate_descendents)

  $\forall \, \text{t, s} : \text{ran}(\text{immediate\_descendents}) \mid \text{t} \neq \text{s} \ \bullet$
      eventual_descendents($\langle \text{t} \rangle$) $\cap$ eventual_descendents($\langle \text{s} \rangle$) $= \varnothing$
OPERATIONS
  slim : $\rightarrow \ \mathbb{N}$;
  ...
ACTIONS
  slim bf! ==>
        VAR i : $\mathbb{N}$
        IN
          bf! := #immediate_descendents;
          i := bf!;
          WHILE i > 0

```
              DO
                immediate_descendents(i).slim;
                i := i - 1
              END
              /* plus actions to create new nodes if necessary to reduce
              branching factor of this node to 2 */
          END
END CLASS
```

In a global class which manages all existing tree instances, two invocations n_1.slim and n_2.slim can be executed in parallel if $n_1 \neq n_2$, because the sub-trees starting from these two nodes have no nodes in common. In particular, the nested invocation of **slim** within itself is legitimate.

In OCCAM a particular instantiation of this class could be implemented as follows:

```
WHILE TRUE
  ALT
    slim[self]?ANY
      VAR i:
        slim_result_bf[self]!tail_ptr[self]
        i := tail_ptr[self]
        WHILE (i > 0)
          slim[immediate_descendents[self][i]]!ANY
          i := i - 1
        ...
```

where an array of channels

```
CHAN slim[m], slim_result_bf[m]
```

is defined, representing the method **slim** of the tree objects 0 .. m. **immediate_descendents** is an integer array which identifies the immediate descendents of each tree object.

tail_ptr is an integer-valued array which identifies the subpart of the **immediate_descendents** array which is meaningful.

A client object of elements of this class would use code of the form

```
slim[obj]!ANY
slim_result_bf[obj]?len
```

to implement an invocation **obj.slim[len/bf!]** in its specification. When the output value is not required (as in the nested calls in the definition of **slim**) it is not necessary to include the receive statement on **slim_result_bf**.

8.1.4   C++

Refinement Using Synchronisation Code
A refinement route for concurrent classes, which allows synchronisation and fairness requirements expressed in a Z^{++} or VDM^{++} specification to be dis-

charged, makes use of the concept of *synchronisation code* [215].

This is a general concept, which involves the definition of actions (state transformations on *synchronisation variables*) which are performed immediately after events. An event is either the creation of an object, a reception of a request for a method execution, the start of an execution of a method, or the termination of execution of a method. Thus the approach is consistent with the extended RTL formalism, and with statecharts.

Synchronisation variables and functions over these are then used to control the permission to execute methods via permission guards.

The refinement of a class (at the end of a data and procedural refinement process) into a C++ class with synchronisation code can be formally checked by an induction over events. This induction will be that the abstract declarative history constraint of the Z^{++} or VDM^{++} class is always true at each event time, with respect to the translation between specification and C++ variables.

As an example, consider the specification that requests of **m** are served in a first-come, first-served manner (FCFS):

```
CLASS C
OPERATIONS
  m : →
HISTORY
  ∀ i, j: N₁ | →(m,i) < →(m,j) • ↑(m,i) ≤ ↑(m,j)
END CLASS
```

An appropriate C++ class is (following [215]):

```
class C{
  m() {}
synchronisation
  int clk;
  int arr_time local to m;

  start(C) --> clk = 0;
  arrival(m) --> this_inv.arr_time = clk++;

  m: there_is_no(p in waiting(m): p.arr_time < this_inv.arr_time);
}
```

We can relate these two versions of C as follows. The concrete expression this_inv.arr_time refers to a local (synchronisation) variable of a specific instance (m, i) of an invocation of **m**. This can be formalised as (m, i).arr_time. From the code it follows that: (m, i).arr_time = $clk \circledast \rightarrow(m, i)$.

By induction on events it can be shown that this value is also

$$\text{previous\_requests}(m, \rightarrow(m, i)) = \#\{j : N_1 \mid \rightarrow(m, j) < \rightarrow(m, i)\}$$

(The only relevant events are those listed in the concrete class, and it is assumed that object creation occurs before any (m, i) invocation.)

The set **waiting(m)** of outstanding invocation instances of **m** has the formal counterpart **waiting_instances(m, t)** = $\{i : N_1 \mid \rightarrow(m, i) \leq t \wedge \neg (\uparrow(m, i) \leq t)\}$ for each time-valued term **t**.

Therefore the concrete guard has corresponding formal permission requirement

$$\forall i : \mathbb{N}_1 \bullet$$
$$(\neg \ \exists \, \textbf{pind} : \mathbb{N}_1 \mid \textbf{pind} \in \textbf{waiting\_instances}(\textbf{m}, \uparrow(\textbf{m}, i)) \bullet$$
$$\textbf{previous\_requests}(\textbf{m}, \rightarrow(\textbf{m}, \textbf{pind})) \ <$$
$$\textbf{previous\_requests}(\textbf{m}, \rightarrow(\textbf{m}, i))) \circledast \uparrow(\textbf{m}, i)$$

Given this, it is impossible for there to be **pind** $<$ **i** with $\rightarrow(\textbf{m}, \textbf{pind}) <$ $\rightarrow(\textbf{m}, \textbf{i})$ but $\uparrow(\textbf{m}, \textbf{i}) < \uparrow(\textbf{m}, \textbf{pind})$.

Assume otherwise. Then **pind** $\in$ **waiting_instances**$(\textbf{m}, \uparrow(\textbf{m}, \textbf{i}))$. But

$$\textbf{previous\_requests}(\textbf{m}, \rightarrow(\textbf{m}, \textbf{pind})) < \textbf{previous\_requests}(\textbf{m}, \rightarrow(\textbf{m}, \textbf{i}))$$

since **pind** is a member of the second set and not the first (and **previous_requests**$(\textbf{m}, \textbf{t})$ is monotonically increasing with $\textbf{t}$), contradicting the guard for **m**.

Translation Steps for Sequential Classes

A translator from low-level Z^{++} classes without history constraints has been implemented in Prolog. This translator transliterates the B AMN procedural constructs into corresponding C++ constructs, and maps inheritance in Z^{++} into public inheritance in C++. Arrays of basic types can be translated. Internal methods are translated as protected functions in C++.

As a simple example, consider the low-level classes

```
CLASS name0
OWNS
  xx :  ℤ;
  yy :  BOOL;
  ff :  0 .. 12  →  ℕ
OPERATIONS
  init :  →;
  inc :  ℕ  →
ACTIONS
  init  ==>
      xx' = 5 ∧ yy' = TRUE;

  inc vv ==>
      BEGIN
        ff := ff ⊕ { xx ↦ 5 * ((3 * xx) + vv) };
        yy := yy ∧ (xx = 10)
      END
END CLASS

CLASS name
EXTENDS name0
OWNS
  aa :  name0
OPERATIONS
```

```
    use :  →
ACTIONS
  use  ==>
            IF true
            THEN
                    aa.inc(5)
            ELSE
                    aa.inc(10)
            END
END CLASS
```

These translate into the following C++ class declarations:

```
#include <stdio.h>
#include "zpp.h"

class name0{
  int xx;
  int yy;
  int ff[13];

public:
  name0(){
    xx = 5;
    yy = TRUE;};

  void inc(int vv){
    ff[xx] = 5 * (3 * xx + vv);
    yy = yy && (xx == 10);
    };

};

class name: public name0{
  name0 aa;

public:
  void use(){
    if (TRUE)
      aa.inc(5);
    else {
      aa.inc(10);
    };
    };

};
```

zpp.h defines **TRUE**, **FALSE** and other common macros used in the translation.

In general, the interface declaration of a class **C** will be generated in a file **C.h** whilst the definitions of its methods will be listed in a file **C.cc**, in accordance with standard industry practice.

This translation is similar to that given for Object-Z in [255], with the difference that we do not distinguish between constants of a class and instance variables, and that we explicitly represent internal methods as protected parts of a C++ class (that is, visible within the class and its descendents, but not to clients).

A code translator into GNU C++ has been implemented for VDM++. This translator makes extensive use of a purpose-built library of classes for mathematical data structures (sets, sequences, maps, etc). In principle it is possible to generate code from specification classes which contain no specification statements or concurrent specification facilities (traces, sync clauses or threads), but which may contain abstract mathematical data structures and operations on these. Thus a form of animation via rapid prototyping can be supported relatively early in the development process. However for efficient implementation, code generation should be carried out after further stages of reification and optimisation of data structures and algorithms.

As an example, consider the **Person_2** class given in Section 8.3. The generated code for this looks as follows:

```
/* Person__2.h: */

#ifndef _Person__2_h
#define _Person__2_h

#include <math.h>
#include "metaiv.h"
#include "cg.h"
#include "cg_aux.h"
#include "Employment.h"
#include "Persons.h"
#include "Sequence__manager.h"

#define VDM_Person__2 3

class vdm_Person__2 : public virtual vdm_Persons {
protected:
  Class vdm_eseq;
public:
  virtual Int vdm_total__salary();
  virtual Bool vdm_underage();

  vdm_Person__2() { class_s.Insert((Int) VDM_Person__2); }

  virtual ~vdm_Person__2() {}
};

#endif


/* Person__2.cc: */
```

```
#include "Person__2.h"

Int vdm_Person__2::vdm_total__salary() {
  Int vdm_r;
  {
    Int vdm_i;
    vdm_i = (Int) 1;
    Int vdm_sum;
    vdm_sum = (Int) 0;
    Class vdm_local(VDM_Employment);
    Bool vdm_fin;
    {
      Class rhs_26(VDM_Employment);
      rhs_26 = ((vdm_Sequence__manager *) (vdm_eseq.GetRef()))
                          -> vdm_Sequence__manager::vdm_first();
      vdm_local = rhs_26;
    }
    {
      Bool rhs_28;
      rhs_28 = ((vdm_Sequence__manager *) (vdm_eseq.GetRef()))
                          -> vdm_Sequence__manager::vdm_finished();
      vdm_fin = rhs_28;
    }
    {
      Bool whCrtl_30;
      while ( TRUE){
        Bool unArg_31;
        unArg_31 = vdm_fin;
        whCrtl_30 = (Bool) (!unArg_31.GetValue());
        if (whCrtl_30.GetValue()) {
          Int vdm_sv;
          vdm_sv = (Int) 0;
          {
            Int rhs_32;
            rhs_32 = ((vdm_Employment *) (vdm_local.GetRef()))
                            -> vdm_Employment::vdm_salary__value();
            vdm_sv = rhs_32;
          }
          {
            Class rhs_34(VDM_Employment);
            rhs_34 = ((vdm_Sequence__manager *) (vdm_eseq.GetRef()))
                            -> vdm_Sequence__manager::vdm_next();
            vdm_local = rhs_34;
          }
          {
            Bool rhs_36;
            ....
        }
        else
```

```
          break;
        }
      }
      {
        Int rexpr_44;
        rexpr_44 = vdm_sum;
        return rexpr_44;
      }
    }
    return vdm_r;
  }

Bool vdm_Person__2::vdm_underage() {
  Bool vdm_b;
  {
    Int vdm_a;
    vdm_a = vdm_Persons::vdm_current__age();
    {
      Bool rexpr_46;
      {
        Int var1_47;
        var1_47 = vdm_a;
        Int var2_48;
        var2_48 = (Int) 16;
        rexpr_46 = (Bool) ((var1_47.GetValue()) < (var2_48.GetValue()));
      }
      return rexpr_46;
    }
  }
  return vdm_b;
}
```

Although this code is somewhat unreadable, it will not be directly maintained
itself. Rather, the specification it is derived from will be maintained.

8.2   Introducing Concurrency in Implementations

For a specification to be abstract and easily understood it is sometimes necessary to write it as a sequential system. However, it would then be useful to
be able to transform it via refinement into an efficient implementation which
utilises concurrency. The following example shows how such a transformation
can be achieved, using new internal actions.

Consider an abstract specification of a generic queue:

```
CLASS Abs[X]
OWNS
  contents :  seq(X);
  size :  N
INVARIANT
```

```
    size = #contents
OPERATIONS
  enter :  X  →;
 *remove_empty :  →  X;
  remove :  →  X
ACTIONS
  enter x?   ==>
      contents' =  contents ⌢ ⟨ x? ⟩ ∧
      size' = size + 1;

 *remove_empty y! ==>
      y! ∈ X;

  remove y! ==>
      (contents = ⟨ ⟩ ⇒
              remove_empty) ∧
      (contents ≠ ⟨ ⟩ ⇒
              ran(contents') = ran(contents) \ { y! } ∧
              size' = #contents')
HISTORY
  mutex({ enter, remove }) ∧ self_mutex({ enter, remove })
END CLASS
```

Since the updates to **size** and **contents** in **enter** are independent, they can be carried out in parallel:

```
CLASS Abs_1[X]
OWNS
  contents :  seq(X);
  size :  ℕ
INVARIANT
  size = #contents
OPERATIONS
  enter :  X  →;
 *remove_empty :  →  X;
  remove :  →  X;
 *append :  X  →;
 *set_size :  ℕ  →
ACTIONS
   enter x?   ==>
          append(x?) ||
          set_size(size + 1);

   . . .

   remove y! ==>
      IF contents = ⟨ ⟩
      THEN
              remove_empty
      ELSE
              ran(contents') = ran(contents) \ { y! } ∧
```

     set_size(#contents′)
  END;

 *append x? ==>
  contents′ = contents ⌢ ⟨ x? ⟩;

 *set_size n? ==>
  size′ = n?

HISTORY
 mutex({ enter, remove }) ∧ self_mutex({ enter, remove })
END CLASS

A use of a method invocation within a logical operator *does not* imply that an actual invocation occurs (ie, that the request, initiation and termination events associated with such an invocation occur). Such an inference can only be made when the method invocation is in a procedural context.

  Mutual exclusion properties for the internal operations here nevertheless follow from those of the external operations, since they can only be executed via these operations (in this class, although in subtypes additional operations may invoke them). Thus **set_size** is self mutex since it is only executed via the operations **enter** and **remove**, which are mutually exclusive and self mutex. Similarly **append** and **remove_empty** are self mutex, although **append** and **set_size** are not mutex. **remove_empty** is mutex with **append** and **set_size**.

  When **enter** is implemented via ||| in the final refinement step, it can be proved that it establishes the required state transition by using the laws given about the ||| operator in Appendix B.

  That is:

$$\textbf{size}\circledast\!\downarrow(\textbf{enter}(e), i) =$$
$$\textbf{size}\circledast\!\downarrow(\textbf{set\_size}(\textbf{size}\circledast\!\uparrow(\textbf{enter}(e), i) + 1), j) =$$
$$\textbf{size}\circledast\!\uparrow(\textbf{enter}(e), i) + 1$$

for some $j : \mathbb{N}_1$, and similarly for **contents** because

$$\textbf{size}\circledast\!\uparrow(\textbf{enter}(e), i) = \textbf{size}\circledast\!\uparrow(\textbf{set\_size}(\textbf{size}\circledast\!\uparrow(\textbf{enter}(e), i) + 1), j)$$

as $\uparrow(\textbf{enter}(e), i) = \uparrow(\textbf{set\_size}(\textbf{size}\circledast\!\uparrow(\textbf{enter}(e), i)), j)$. In addition the value of size cannot be changed in any interval between $\downarrow(\textbf{enter}(e), i)$ and $\downarrow(\textbf{set\_size}(\textbf{size}\circledast\!\uparrow(\textbf{enter}(e), i)), j)$ because of the information we have about non-interference (the write frame of the method – **append** – which can co-execute with **enter** does not include **size**).

8.3 Implementation Case Study: Personnel System

This example continues the personnel system development from Chapters 3, 4 and 6.

  The **Person_1** class can be implemented as follows.

```
class Person_2
-- refines Person_1;
-- retrieve function: identity;
-- method renaming: identity;
instance variables
  age: Age;
  address: String;
init objectstate ==
  age = 0 and address = []
methods
  change_address(nad: String) ==
    (address := nad);

  birthday() ==
    if age < 200
    then
      age := age + 1;

  current_age() value Age ==
      return age;

  delay(d: nat) ==
    [ext wr now
    post now~ + d = now]

thread
  while true
  do
    self!birthday();
    self!delay(31536000)
end Person_2
```

This makes clear that **birthday** and **delay** are purely internal, whilst **change_address** and **current_age** are external, following the discipline advised in Appendix B. The class is now in a form that can be directly translated into Ada.

The **WorkingPerson_1** class is refined by replacing the sequence of employments by a supplier object which encapsulates such a sequence. We assume the existence of a library component

```
class Sequence_manager
functions
  seq_remove: (seq of @X)*@X -> (seq of @X)
  seq_remove(s,x) ==
                    if s = []
                    then s
                    else
                      if hd(s) = x
                      then seq_remove(tl(s),x)
                      else [hd(s)]^seq_remove(tl(s),x)
instance variables
```

```
   contents: seq of @X;
   counter: nat;
init objectstate == contents = []
                  and counter = 0;
inv objectstate ==
                  counter <= len(contents)
methods
  add_element(ee: @X) ==
       [ext wr contents
        post contents = contents~ ^ [ee]];

  remove_element(ee: @X) ==
       [ext wr contents, counter
        post
          if (ee in set elems(contents))
          then
            contents = seq_remove(contents~,ee) and
            counter <= len(contents)
          else
            contents = contents~ and counter = counter~];

  first() value ee: @X
     pre len(contents) > 0   ==
     ([ext rd contents
          wr counter
       post ee = contents(1) and
            counter = 1];
      return ee);

  next() value ee: @X   ==
     ([ext rd contents
          wr counter
       post (if counter~ < len(contents)
             then
               counter = counter~ + 1
             else
               counter = 1) and
            ee = contents(counter)];
      return ee);

  finished() value bb: bool ==
     ([ext rd  contents, counter
       post  bb = (counter = len(contents))];
      return bb)

end Sequence_manager
```

This is instantiated for particular classes, such as **Employment**, by textually
replacing **X** by **Employment** in the class declaration.

```
class WorkingPerson_2 is subclass of Person
```

```
-- refines WorkingPerson_1;
-- retrieve function: employments = eseq.contents;
-- method renaming: identity;
instance variables
   eseq: Sequence_manager  -- of @Employment objects
methods
  total_salary() value nat ==
    (dcl i: nat := 1;
     dcl sum: nat := 0;
     dcl local: @Employment;
     dcl fin: bool;

     local := eseq!first();
     fin := eseq!finished();

     while not(fin)
     do
       (dcl sv: nat := 0;

        sv := local!salary_value();
        local := eseq!next();
        fin := eseq!finished();

        sum := sum + sv;
        i := i + 1);

     return sum);

  underage() value bool ==
    (dcl a: Age := self!current_age();
     return (a < 16))

end WorkingPerson_2
```

The retrieve function from **WorkingPerson_2** to **WorkingPerson_1** is then **employments = eseq.contents** so that the revised loop invariant is simply the composition of this function with the previous invariant:

$$\textbf{sum} = \textbf{Sigma}([\text{eseq.contents(j).salary} \mid$$
$$j \in \text{inds(eseq.contents)} \wedge j < i]) \wedge$$
$$i \leq \text{len(eseq.contents)} + 1$$

8.4 Testing

8.4.1 Testing and Refinement

It has been argued by some proponents of formal methods that the use of formal methods removes the need for unit testing of formally developed modules, and for integration testing between such modules. However, it is never the case that a formal development is absolutely reliable, because even if detailed formal proofs of every refinement step are carried out, errors may exist in these proofs whether they were performed manually (so introducing the possibility of human error and wishful thinking) or by tools (which may have bugs in them). Thus unit and integration testing should be used to complement and to provide a check on the formal development.

In particular, if a proof step during internal consistency proof or refinement was of significant complexity and difficulty, then a corresponding test case should be devised to check the formal specification element concerned. Methods for systematically achieving this are beyond the scope of this book, however the following guidelines may be of use in identifying suitable test cases.

In general a refinement proof obligation between code-like method definitions will involve consideration of all control flow paths of both definitions. It will actually have the form:

$$\forall\, \mathbf{path} : \mathbf{cfp}(\phi(\mathbf{m}), \mathbf{Implementation}) \bullet$$
$$\exists\, \mathbf{path'} : \mathbf{cfp}(\mathbf{m}, \mathbf{Abstraction}) \bullet$$
$$\mathbf{path'} \sim \mathbf{path}$$

where $\sim$ denotes that the two paths have the same result values and the same effect on the internal states of the abstraction and implementation, relative to the refinement relation. $\mathbf{cfp}(\mathbf{m}, \mathbf{C})$ denotes the set of control flow paths of $\mathbf{m}$ in $\mathbf{C}$ – effectively linear program fragments. As a result it can be difficult to gain an intuition into the meaning of particular proof obligations without the help of a tool which identifies the source of the obligation as a comparison between two execution paths.

Thus in refining a conditional IF $\mathbf{E}$ THEN $\mathbf{C}_1$ ELSE $\mathbf{C}_2$ END to another conditional IF $\mathbf{E'}$ THEN $\mathbf{S}_1$ ELSE $\mathbf{S}_2$ END there will be four separate proof obligations corresponding to distinct pairs of paths through the refinement and abstraction. If a particular proof obligation is very difficult to prove, then a test case should be created for the implementation path involved to identify whether or not it follows the state transformation specified in the abstraction path involved.

The complexity of such proofs is one reason for deferring the introduction of code-like constructs until the last one or two refinement steps. However, data structure complexity also has an effect on proof complexity.

In the B AMN development environment, it is possible to automatically generate interfaces for subsystems within a development, and so to incrementally unit test a development, layer by layer [147].

Functional tests, which check the compliance of the developed software with user requirements, are performed as for conventionally developed software.

8.4.2   Testing and Animation

Scenarios used during animation should generally be used as the basis of test cases. There should be agreement between the results of the animation and testing – this agreement validates the formal verification step or rigorous reasoning used to verify the translation from the specification to the code. Testing may uncover inconsistencies between the specification and the user expectations which were concealed at the specification level by the presence of non-determinism.

Indeed it is possible for animation scenarios to consider system behaviour which is allowed by the specification, but which can never occur in the eventual implementation, as a result of the particular refinement path chosen. This does not mean that the animations were valueless – they may have significance if alternative implementations became necessary. For *virtual* classes in particular, the non-determinism present in the specification of the abstract superclass may be essential in capturing the common aspects of the behaviour of all of its subclasses.

In some respects it is easier to "test" a specification than an implementation, because mathematical rather than programming data structures are used, and because implementation details are absent. On the other hand, it is more difficult because the presence of non-determinism makes complete test coverage harder to achieve or to measure. Some results for test coverage of algebraic specifications are given in [110].

8.4.3 Equivalence Partitioning

A standard approach to testing of a module is to partition the state of that module into equivalence classes. All the members of a given class are then assumed to be equivalent in respect of their utility as test cases (the system fails on one member iff it fails on all the others). It is useful to notice that the VDM^{++} concept of refinement implies that a specification-level partition yields an implementation-level partition. More precisely, if we have a class $\mathbf{C}$, refined by a class $\mathbf{D}$ via a retrieve function $\mathbf{R}$, then a partitioning relation $\sim_{\mathbf{C}}$ on the state of $\mathbf{C}$ can be used to generate a partitioning relation $\sim_{\mathbf{D}}$ on the state of $\mathbf{D}$, defined by:

$$\mathbf{v} \sim_{\mathbf{D}} \mathbf{v}' \equiv \mathbf{R}(\mathbf{v}) \sim_{\mathbf{C}} \mathbf{R}(\mathbf{v}')$$

It is direct to check that if $\sim_{\mathbf{C}}$ is an equivalence relation, so is $\sim_{\mathbf{D}}$. Moreover, the equivalence classes for $\sim_{\mathbf{D}}$ are generated from those of $\sim_{\mathbf{C}}$:

$$[\mathbf{v}]_{\mathbf{D}} = \mathbf{R}^{-1}(\!| \, [\mathbf{R}(\mathbf{v})]_{\mathbf{C}} \, |\!)$$

Indeed, the number of partitions under $\sim_{\mathbf{D}}$ is the same as that under $\sim_{\mathbf{C}}$. This result depends on the property of *adequacy* of $\mathbf{R}$: it can also be shown for any adequate refinement in Z^{++}.

As an example, consider the concurrent queue development given in Chapter 6. A partition of the abstract state **queue** : seq($\mathbf{X}$) of **AbsQueue** into five equivalence classes could be:

> $\#$queue $= 0$
> $\#$queue $= 1$
> $\#$queue $=$ **bound**
> $\#$queue $=$ **bound** $- 1$
> $1 < \#$queue $<$ **bound** $- 1$

Assuming that **bound** > 2.

The corresponding classes in the refinement **ConcQueue**, whose state is:

> head_idx : 1 .. **bound**;
> tail_idx : 0 .. **bound**;
> contents : 1 .. **bound** $\rightarrow$ **X**

would be defined using **tail_idx** $-$ **head_idx** $+ 1$ in place of $\#$**queue**.

However, there may be finer equivalence relations (with more partitions) which can be defined only at the refinement level. Here, for instance, we might consider that **head_idx** $= 1$, **head_idx** $=$ **bound** and

$$1 < \textbf{head\_idx} < \textbf{bound}$$

are significant distinctions in the state of **ConcQueue**. These additional partitions are a sub-equivalence of that obtained from **AbsQueue**. As a result, for each partition of $\sim_{\textbf{AbsQueue}}$ we will already have one test case for the new sub-partitions of $\sim_{\textbf{ConcQueue}}$, and only two new cases need to be generated.

If class **D** has been shown to be a refinement of **C** via **S**, then the test cases **v** and **S(v)** should have the same result. Formally, let the correctness of a test be determined by the abstract specification **Spec** which **C** (and **D**) refines: a method **m** of **Spec** (and of **C** and **D**) passes a test given by a pair $(\textbf{w}, \textbf{w}') \in \textbf{State}_{\textbf{D}} \times \textbf{State}_{\textbf{D}}$ if:

1. $\textbf{R}(\textbf{S}(\textbf{w})) \in \textbf{Pre}_{\textbf{m},\textbf{Spec}} \Rightarrow \textbf{w} \in \textbf{Pre}_{\textbf{m},\textbf{D}}$ "if **m** should be defined on **w** according to the abstract specification, then **m** in **D** is defined on **w**";
2. $\textbf{R}(\textbf{S}(\textbf{w})) \in \textbf{Pre}_{\textbf{m},\textbf{Spec}}$ and $(\textbf{w}, \textbf{w}') \in \textbf{Def}_{\textbf{m},\textbf{D}}$ implies $(\textbf{R}(\textbf{S}(\textbf{w})), \textbf{R}(\textbf{S}(\textbf{w}'))) \in \textbf{Def}_{\textbf{m},\textbf{Spec}}$ "if **w**' is a possible result of executing **m** in **D** on **w**, then this pair must obey the abstract specification of **m** in **Spec**".

S is the retrieve function from **State**$_\textbf{D}$ to **State**$_\textbf{C}$, and **R** the retrieve function from **State**$_\textbf{C}$ to **State**$_\textbf{Spec}$.

Thus it is clear that **m** passes the test $(\textbf{w}, \textbf{w}')$ in **D** iff **m** passes the test $(\textbf{S}(\textbf{w}), \textbf{S}(\textbf{w}'))$ in **C**.

Testing of **D** on the corresponding test cases to those of **C** can therefore be used to check the correctness of the refinement proof, or can be avoided if the confidence in the proof is very high.

Conclusions

This chapter has identified some techniques for the implementation of Z^{++} and VDM^{++} in programming languages. Within the AFRODITE ESPRIT project a C++ translator has been developed, which can produce executable code for a large subset of the language. However code generation from highly abstract specifications is not intended for production use, but for animation purposes. Code translation from low-level specifications, in which efficient algorithms have been used, should be of production quality. For Z^{++}, tools for the generation of procedural pseudocode, to be used in manual implementation, have been developed, in addition to a C++ translator [163].

The code generation techniques described here are not directly applicable to hardware compilation. This is being addressed within the AFRODITE project by a translation of VDM^{++} into the hardware description languages VHDL and ELLA.

Perhaps the most effective code-generation tools which currently exist for a formal method are those for the B Abstract Machine Notation, within the B Toolkit of B Core UK Ltd [16]. This utilises a form of "forced reuse" – a developer must eventually specify their implementations using only library components as suppliers. Since these library components are provided with pre-developed executable C code, and since B AMN implementations can only use directly translatable code-like constructs, the code generation step is direct. The RAISE toolkit also provides C++ and Ada translators for the RSL notation [111].

The B Toolkit approach to code generation might be termed "pragmatic" in contrast to the "idealistic" approach of tools such as the C++ code generator for VDM^{++}. The latter are based on the assumption that no maintenance or reading of the generated code is ever necessary, and that any such modification should be carried out using the formal notations (the style of code generation adopted certainly discourages manual modification of the code). In contrast the B code generator produces code that is in close correspondence with the formal specification and that is in a small subset of C.

The integration of testing and formal methods is an under-researched area. However work has been carried out in the generation of test cases from specifications (eg. [66, 76, 110]). In addition, animation tools such as the B Toolkit animator, or the IFAD VDM-SL toolset animator, can be used to "test" specifications. Both of these tools have batch-mode capabilities, enabling the use of standard test suites. The IFAD tool also possesses a test coverage analysis capability.

Chapter 9

Case Studies

This Chapter presents a range of case studies in VDM^{++} and Z^{++}, illustrating the techniques described in the remainder of the book, and expanding on some issues particularly concerning reactive and real-time systems.

9.1 Invoice System

This specification is a well-known example of a B specification [168]. Instead of using inverse functions and direct product of relations as in [3], we adopt a more systematic approach to the construction of VDM^{++} classes from analysis of the data model and enquiry access paths of the system. The benefit of this approach is that it is applicable to many different software systems. It also produces a clearer and more easily verified specification.

Section 9.1.1 summarises the problem statement. In section 9.1.2 we perform domain and requirements analysis for the case study. In section 9.1.3 we identify the specification structure needed to support the problem requirements and detail the formal specification of the elements of the problem.

9.1.1 Problem Statement

Data Requirements
The system to be constructed is intended to support the following data:

1. sets of *clients*, *products*, and *invoices*;
2. for *clients*, attributes of *category* (whether a client is to be considered *normal*, *dubious* or a *friend*), and of *allowance* (maximum amount of currency allowed to the client);
3. for *invoices*, there are attributes of the *customer* client to whom the invoice is issued, the *discount* percentage associated with the invoice and the set of *lines* of the invoice (one for each product being invoiced for);

4. for a *line*, there are attributes of the *unit price* of the product associated with the line, the *product*, and the *number of units* of that product included in the line;

5. for *products*, attributes of *price, status*, and a set of possible *substitute* products. Each product status can be either *available, soldout* or *deleted.*

Process Requirements
The following operations are required (adopting the somewhat informal specification of [3]):

1. to create, modify and query a client;
2. to create, modify and query a product;
3. to create, modify and query an invoice.

Consistency Requirements
Various consistency constraints must also be satisfied (and will therefore lead to preconditions for the above operations):

1. a sold out product cannot be added to an invoice;
2. any available substitute for a sold out product should be used on an invoice;
3. no two lines of the same invoice should correspond to the same product;
4. no invoice should be made for clients in the *dubious* category;
5. the total sum of items on an invoice should not be greater than the allowance of the corresponding client;
6. clients in the *friend* category get a 20% discount.

9.1.2 Domain and Requirements Analysis

Static Data Modelling
There are three necessary entity types which we need to represent in our analysis model: *product, client* and *invoice.* The entity type *line* is identified as an additional entity suggested by the problem definition. Most of the attributes of the entities are mandated in the requirements, as are the enumerated domains of product status and client category.

The static data model of the system is therefore as shown in Figure 9.1, using OMT Object Model notation. At this stage, we do not represent operations.

That an association is considered to be directed in a particular way is indicated by placing the name of the function which is represented by the association at the range end of this function. Thus **lines_of** represents a function from an invoice to a set of lines. **article** represents a function from a line to a single product.

Redundancy of representation can be identified at this stage: the attributes **allow** of an invoice and **cost** of a line are (apparently) redundant. They represent the values of the **allowance** of the customer assigned to the invoice and

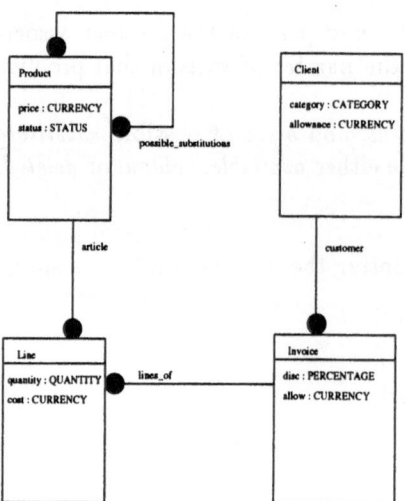

Figure 9.1: Static Data Model for Invoice System

the values of the **price** of the article assigned to the line, at the time of creation of the invoice or line, respectively. However, under this interpretation of the domain, they are not redundant if changes to the allowance of a customer and price of an article cannot have a retrospective impact on previously issued invoices.

Process Modelling

The required *enquiry access paths* which will be needed by the above operations of the system are as follows:

1. access to each attribute of an entity for update and read;
2. access from an invoice to its set of lines (in order to return the total price associated with an invoice);
3. access from a product to its set of possible substitutions;
4. access from an invoice to its associated customer;
5. access from a line to its associated article.

By examination of the diagram (or, possibly, by the use of a suitable simple CASE tool) we can check that these paths are actually supported by the data model. Graphical representation of the required functions and their inputs could be performed, using OMT or Booch operation models.

9.1.3   From Analysis to Outline Specification

The following attributes are added as a result of analysis: **total** to **Invoice**, and the new values **deleted** to customer status, and **inactive** to client categories.

Both the attributes of an entity (including the associations with their source at the entity) and the operations that are required upon an entity must be considered in decomposing the static data model of a system into a set of classes linked by suitable mechanisms: composition, inheritance or subtyping.

If we restrict consideration to the following operations:

Client :
  createclient : **CURRENCY** → clients
  modifycategory : clients **CATEGORY** →
  modifyallowance : clients **CURRENCY** →
  deleteclient : clients →

Product :
  createproduct : **CURRENCY** → products
  modifyprice : products **CURRENCY** →
  modifystatus : products **STATUS** →
  addsubstitute : products products →
  deleteproduct : products →

Line :
  createline : products **QUANTITY** → lines
  incline : lines products **QUANTITY** →

Invoice :
  createinvoice : clients lines → invoices
  addline : invoices lines →
  modifyline : invoices lines products **QUANTITY** →

we can derive the following outline hierarchical decomposition of the set of entities:

Product ⟶ **Line**

Line ⟶ **Invoice**

Product ⟶ **Invoice**

Client ⟶ **Invoice**

That is, there is a dependency of **Line** on **Product**, etc. We do not want to use inheritance in any of these cases however, but rather clientship, since we expect that there will be several lines (eg, of different invoices) with the same associated product, and several lines for each invoice, etc. In addition, subtyping is not the correct construction mechanism either, since a line is not a product, and similarly for the other pairs of entities here.

Thus we can formulate the following outline usage diagram:

Product $\longrightarrow$ c $\longrightarrow$ **Line**

Line $\longrightarrow$ c $\longrightarrow$ **Invoice**

Product $\longrightarrow$ c $\longrightarrow$ **Invoice**

Client $\longrightarrow$ c $\longrightarrow$ **Invoice**

The third relationship here will be seen to be redundant and can be deleted.

Formal specifications of the components can now be given, based on the analysis models.

InvoiceDefs
This class contains global parameters for the invoice system.

```
class InvoiceDefs
types
  CURRENCY = nat;
  STATUS = <available> | <soldout> | <deleted>;
  QUANTITY = nat;
  CATEGORY = <friend> | <dubious> | <normal> | <inactive>
end InvoiceDefs
```

Product
The specification of this class follows directly from the data model of the corresponding entity type.

```
class Product is subclass of InvoiceDefs
instance variables
  price: CURRENCY;
  status: STATUS;
  possible_substitutions: set of @Product;
init objectstate ==
  price = 0 and status = <available> and possible_substitutions = {};
methods
  createproduct(pcost: CURRENCY)   ==
    [ext wr price
     post price = pcost];

  addsubstitute(subst: @Product)
    pre not(status = <deleted>) ==
    [ext wr possible_substitutions
     post possible_substitutions =
                   possible_substitutions~ union {subst}];

  modifyprice(pcost: CURRENCY)
```

```
     pre not(status = <deleted>) ==
     [ext wr price
      post price = pcost];

   modifystatus(stat: STATUS)
     pre not(status = <deleted>) ==
     [ext wr status
      post status = stat]

 end Product
```

The form of a creation operation is, for the most part, forced by the data definitions. In general to create an instance of "Entity", we need to supply values for each attribute of Entity. Default values for attributes may be used instead of supplied values. It would be useful in this respect for initialisations in VDM^{++} to be parameterised operations, as in Eiffel or Z^{++}, rather than predicates.

Enquiry operations returning attributes of this class are also needed.

The following requirements are expressed in the above specification:

- data 1, in part, by the type @**Product**;
- data 5, by the attributes of **Product**;
- process 2, by the respective operations of **Product**.

Client
This follows a similar pattern to **Product**. The class **Client** is:

```
class Client is subclass of InvoiceDefs
instance variables
  category: CATEGORY;
  allowance: CURRENCY;
init objectstate ==
  category = <normal> and allowance = 0
methods
  createclient(aa: CURRENCY) ==    -- needed since no parameters in init
    [ext wr allowance
     post  allowance = aa];

  modifycategory(cat: CATEGORY)
    pre not(category = <inactive>) ==
    [ext wr category
     post category = cat];

  modifyallowance(allow: CURRENCY)
    pre not(category = <inactive>) ==
    [ext wr allowance
     post allowance = allow];

  deleteclient() ==
    [ext wr category
```

```
      post category = <inactive>]
```

end Client

The following requirements are met:

- data 1, in part;
- data 2;
- process 1.

Again, enquiry operations are added as necessary.

Line

This is a more complex specification. We must be clear about the location of operations upon lines. Even though every line is subordinate to a particular invoice, with modifications to a line having potential impact on the consistency of its invoice (eg, one cannot arbitrarily increase the quantity of a product on an invoice line if this would cause the invoice to exceed the limit for that customer), we still consider that operations to modify and access a line belong in the **Line** class: it is the responsibility of **Invoice** operations to apply operations upon **lines** in a way which preserves the invariant of the **Invoice** class.

The class is then:

```
class Line is subclass of InvoiceDefs
instance variables
  article: @Product;
  quantity: QUANTITY;
  cost: CURRENCY;
init quantity, cost ==   quantity = 0 and cost = 0
methods
  createline(prod: @Product, quan: QUANTITY)
    pre prod.status = <available>  ==
    [ext wr  article, quantity, cost
     post  article = prod and
           quantity = quan and
           cost = prod.price];

  incline(prod: @Product, quan: QUANTITY)
    pre prod = article  ==
    [ext wr quantity
     post  quantity = quantity~ + quan]
```

end Line

The cost of an article recorded in a line is its price at the time the line was formed: there is no obligation to update this cost in line with new prices. Clearly a more sophisticated system would need to model dates in addition!

Direct access to the supplier attributes can only be avoided in **createline** by replacing the **pre** construct with an if, and making an appropriate enquiry on the supplier state:

```
createline(prod: @Product, quan: QUANTITY) ==
  (def ps = prod!statusvalue()
   in
     if ps = <available>
     then
       ([ext wr  article, quantity
         post article = prod and
              quantity = quan];
         cost := prod!pricevalue()));
```

The following requirements are expressed in this specification:

- domain 4.

Invoice

For this machine we need to make a decision about the specification and design of the **total** constant or attribute of an invoice. In the original specification of [3], **total** is considered as a macro or as a constant. This leads to complex proof obligations and an unclear specification. Instead, we can transform the specification via *finite differencing* to become a specification in which **total** is a (derived) attribute of an invoice, and is re-computed incrementally when an operation is performed which can change it.

The class is:

```
class Invoice is subclass of InvoiceDefs
types
  PERCENTAGE = nat
functions
  discount: CATEGORY -> PERCENTAGE
  discount(<friend>) == 80
instance variables
  customer: @Client;
  disc: PERCENTAGE;
  allow: CURRENCY;
  lines_of: set of @Line;
  total: CURRENCY;
inv objectstate  ==
  total <= allow;
init disc, allow, total, lines_of ==
                                disc = 0 and
                                allow = 0 and
                                lines_of = {} and
                                total = 0
methods
  createinvoice(cli: @Client)
    pre not(cli.category = <dubious>) ==
    [ext wr customer, disc, allow
     post
       customer = cli and
       disc = discount(cli.category) and
```

```
        allow = cli.allowance];

  addline(line: @Line)
    pre line  not in set  lines_of  and
        line.article  not in set
                                  { ll.article | ll in set lines_of }  and
        total + (line.quantity * line.cost * disc)/100  <=  allow  and
        line.article.status = <available>   ==
    [ext wr  lines_of, total
         rd  disc
      post  lines_of = lines_of~ union { line }  and
            total = total~ + (line.quantity * line.cost * disc)/100]

aux reasoning
  card({ ll.article | ll in set lines_of }) = card(lines_of) and
  not(customer.category = <dubious>)
end Invoice
```

The invariant is split into those parts which refer to supplier state (and which therefore must be placed in the **auxilliary reasoning** clause) and those which only refer to local state.

The first line of the invariant expresses constraint 5, the second line expresses constraint 3, and the third expresses constraint 4. It is not possible for the **Invoice** class to ensure the second and third invariant conjuncts, unless it has exclusive access to the items concerned.

Note that information about discounts is only given for the **friend** category in the requirements – other discounts are therefore not determined in the abstract **Invoice** class.

The architecture of the specification is as given in Figure 9.2.

9.1.4   Implementation

The implementation of **Product** and **Client** are direct (**Product** must use the **Set_manager** library component to support the **possible_substitutions** attribute).

The implementation of **Line** is as follows:

```
class Line_1 is subclass of InvoiceDefs
-- refines Line
-- retrieve function: identity
-- method renaming: identity
instance variables
  article: @Product;
  quantity: QUANTITY;
  cost: CURRENCY
init quantity, cost == quantity = 0 and cost = 0
methods
  createline(prod: @Product, quan: QUANTITY) ==
```

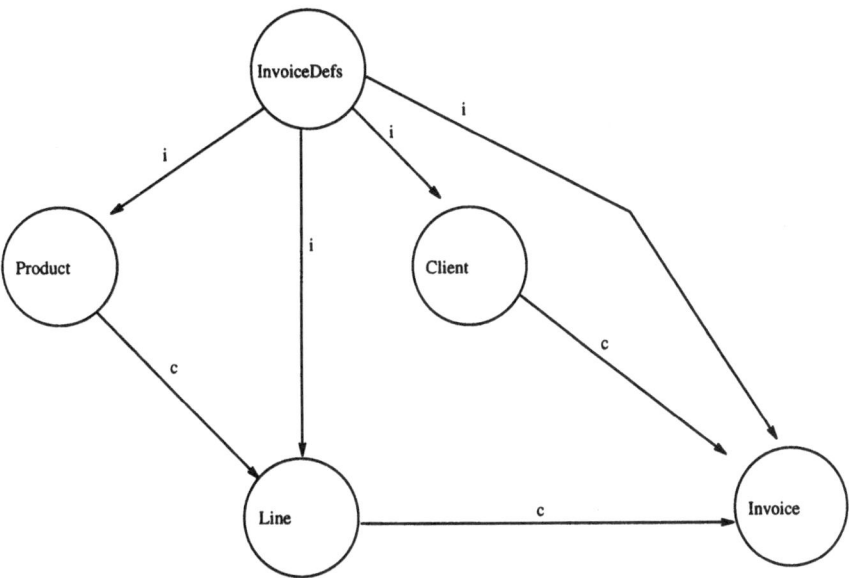

Figure 9.2: Architecture of Invoice System Specification

```
(dcl prodstat: STATUS := prod!statusvalue();
   if prodstat = <available>
   then
     article := prod;
     quantity := quan;
     cost := prod!pricevalue());

incline(prod: @Product, quan: QUANTITY) ==
   if (prod = article)
   then
     quantity := quantity + quan

end Line_1
```

where we assume the additional operations:

```
statusvalue() value ps: STATUS  ==
   ([ext rd status
     post ps = status];
    return ps);

pricevalue() value pr: CURRENCY ==
   ([ext rd price
     post pr = price];
    return pr);
```

of **Product**.

Similarly a partial refinement of **Invoice** is:

```
class Invoice_1 is subclass of InvoiceDefs
-- refines Invoice
-- retrieve function: projection, forgets articles
-- method renaming: identity
types
  PERCENTAGE = nat
functions
  discount: CATEGORY -> PERCENTAGE
  discount(v) == if (v = <friend>) then 80 else 100
instance variables
  customer: @Client;
  disc: PERCENTAGE;
  allow: CURRENCY;
  lines_of: set of @Line;
  total: CURRENCY;
  articles: set of @Product;
inv objectstate ==  total <= allow  and
                    card(articles) = card(lines_of);
init disc, allow, total, lines_of, articles ==
                                    disc = 0 and
                                    allow = 0 and
                                    lines_of = {} and
                                    total = 0 and
                                    articles = {}
methods
  createinvoice(cli: @Client) ==
    (dcl clicategory: CATEGORY := cli!categoryvalue();
      if not(clicategory = <dubious>)
      then
        customer := cli;
        disc := discount(clicategory);
        allow := cli!allowancevalue());

  addline(line: @Line) ==
    (dcl linearticle: @Product := line!articlevalue();
     dcl linequantity: QUANTITY := line!quantityvalue();
     dcl linecost: CURRENCY := line!costvalue();
      if not(line in set lines_of) and
        not(linearticle in set articles)
      then
        (dcl ppstat: STATUS := linearticle!statusvalue();
          if (total + (linequantity*linecost*disc)/100 <= allow) and
            ppstat = <available>
          then
            lines_of := lines_of union { line };
            articles := articles union { linearticle };
            total := total + (linequantity*linecost*disc)/100))

aux reasoning
  articles = { ll.article | ll in set lines_of } and
```

```
not(customer.category = <dubious>)
end Invoice_1
```

where the enquiry operations **categoryvalue** and **allowancevalue** are defined in **Client**, and **articlevalue**, **quantityvalue** and **costvalue** in **Line**.

Further refinement of this class would introduce **Set_manager** objects to manage the sets of lines and articles, and replace applications of set union by calls to methods of these objects.

9.2 Expedited Data Queue

This is a problem which has been studied using a number of concurrent formalisms. It provides a further example of replacing a complex algorithm by complex object structure.

The requirements are:

1. a queue of message items of two different levels of priority is to be maintained, with operations to add an item to a queue and to remove an item from a queue;
2. messages of the higher priority type are to be removed in preference to lower priority items: that is, if a high priority item is added to the queue then it will be removed before any low priority item which is in the queue at the time when the high-priority item is added;
3. within each priority level, first in first out behaviour is to be followed.

We can formalise these requirements at a very abstract level by defining an outline class of expedited data queues:

```
class EDQueue
methods
  add(x :  ●Item)
    is not yet specified;
  remove() value x :  ●Item
    is not yet specified
aux reasoning
history
/*  FIFO condition for elements of Item :  */
```

$$\forall \ i, \ j: \ \mathbb{N}_1; \ x, \ y: \ \bullet \text{Item} \ \bullet$$
$$\downarrow(\text{add}(x), i) \ < \ \downarrow(\text{add}(y), j) \ \Rightarrow$$
$$\downarrow(\text{remove}(x), i) \ < \ \downarrow(\text{remove}(y), j)$$

```
/*  FIFO condition for elements of Item2 :  */
```

$$\forall \ i, \ j: \ \mathbb{N}_1; \ x, \ y: \ \bullet \text{Item2} \ \bullet$$
$$\downarrow(\text{add}(x), i) \ < \ \downarrow(\text{add}(y), j) \ \Rightarrow$$
$$\downarrow(\text{remove}(x), i) \ < \ \downarrow(\text{remove}(y), j)$$

/ *   *Preferential treatment of elements of* **Item2** : */

$\forall$ i, j : N_1; x : **@Item**; y : **@Item2** •
  $\downarrow$(add(x), i) < $\downarrow$(add(y), j) < $\uparrow$(remove(x), i) $\Rightarrow$
                    $\downarrow$(remove(y), j) < $\downarrow$(remove(x), i)

end EDQueue

We make the simplifying assumption that **Item** and **Item2** are class types, and that **Item2** is a subtype of **Item** (at a cost of some additional complexity it would suffice to assume that they had a mutual supertype).

Implementing these requirements is however more complex. Notice that **add** takes as input an element **x** of **@Item** – **x** could be in fact an element of **@Item2** but there is no way to test for this within **EDQueue** (at least, not without violating object-oriented principles, and hard-coding knowledge about the subtype hierarchy into method definitions). Instead we must exploit polymorphism to obtain different behaviours for the different priority messages. We choose to maintain two distinct queues:

```
class EDQueue_1
instance variables
  q1 : @ItemQueue;
  q2 : @Item2Queue
methods
  add(x : @Item)  ==
          x!add_to_queue(q1, q2);

  remove() value x : @Item  ==
          (dcl emp : bool := q2!isempty();
             if emp
             then  (dcl res : @Item := q1!top();
                         q1!pop();
                         return res)
             else  (dcl res : @Item2 := q2!top();
                         q2!pop();
                         return res) )
```

end EDQueue_1

where **ItemQueue** is an instantiation of the generic **Queue** class with **@Item** as its type of elements, and **Item2Queue** an instantiation of **Queue** with **@Item2**.

In VDM^{++}, a **return** statement acts like a C++ return statement, and terminates the block in which it appears. Thus return statements should always appear at the end of the control flow of a particular statement branch.

This specification relies upon a standard (generic) queue component, presumed to already have been specified and implemented and contained in a library, and upon the following method definitions in **Item** and **Item2**:

```
class Item
   ...
```

methods
   add_to_queue(q1 : **@ItemQueue**, q2 : **@Item2Queue**) ==
       q1!add(self);
   . . .
end Item

class Item2 is subclass of Item
   . . .
methods
   add_to_queue(q1 : **@ItemQueue**, q2 : **@Item2Queue**) ==
       q2!add(self);
   . . .
end Item2

It can be proved that this design meets the previous specification as follows:

- requirement 3 follows because if **x** and **y** are both elements of **Item** (and not elements of **Item2**) then they are added and removed using q1 and are removed from q1 in the order in which they were added – this is a requirement upon the subordinate subsystem **Queue** which should directly follow from its specification. Similarly for elements of **Item2**;
- requirement 2 follows because if **x** is in **Item**, **y** is in **Item2**, and **y** is added to the system while **x** is in the system, then **x** is in q1 and **y** is added to q2 – thus q2 is non-empty until **y** is removed, and thus until this occurs **x** cannot be removed from q1, as required.

This informal reasoning can be formalised using the expanded definitions of the methods concerned.

9.3   Fire Control

This example illustrates alternative approaches to concurrency in VDM^{++}, and the necessity of internal object concurrency in particular cases.

Consider an automatic gun control, which contains operations to fire and reload its gun,[1] where we expect that reloading only occurs relatively occasionally (there will be at least one **fire** invocation between successive **reloads**):

class Gun
instance variables
   clip : **@Clip**;
init objectstate ==   not(void(clip))
methods
   reload() ==
       clip := **Clip!new**;

---

[1] Apologies for the militaristic nature of this example. The reader is invited to substitute a more socially acceptable interpretation of the specifications.

```
fire()
    pre not(clip.rounds = 0)   ==
                    clip!get_round()
```

```
sync
  general Gun =
      < fire*; (reload; fire+)*, { reload, fire } >
end Gun
```

The not(void(clip)) constraint ensures that access to the clip by **fire** does not produce an error. It could be omitted if the interpretation of @S as meaning "the type of references to existing instances of S" was used (see Appendix B).

Clip is defined by:

```
class Clip
instance variables
  rounds : ℕ;
init objectstate ==   rounds > 0
methods
  get_round()
      pre rounds > 0 ==
        [ext wr rounds
        post  rounds = rounds‾ − 1];

  roundsleft() value rl : ℕ ==
        ([ext rd rounds
          post  rl = rounds];
         return rl)

end Clip
```

Gun can be refined by using a declarative thread:

```
class Gun_1
instance variables
  clip : @Clip;
init objectstate ==  not(void(clip))
methods
  reload() ==
      clip := Clip!new;

  fire() ==
      def cliprounds = clip!roundsleft()
      in
        if cliprounds > 0
        then clip!get_round();

  fire_action() ==
      (dcl fr : ℕ := clip!roundsleft();
         if fr = 0
         then self!reload()
```

```
          else self!fire())
```

thread
 periodic(10)(fire_action)

end Gun_1

This specification makes no assumptions about the number of rounds in each clip, thus it is more flexible than a version that (for instance) assumes there are always 20 rounds in a clip. Since **reload** and **fire** are called from the thread of the class, they are *internal* methods of the class – that is, they are events that the gun controller object generates, rather than services provided to an external user.

It satisfies the axioms of the abstract version of the class as follows. The trace specification of **Gun** asserts that **fire** and **reload** are mutex and self-mutex. In addition it asserts that if **reload** is executing, either it is the first invocation instance of either **reload** or **fire** to execute, or the immediately preceding execution (out of these two) is one of **fire**.

This axiom is valid in **Gun_1** since

$$(\textbf{clip.rounds} > 0)\circledast\downarrow(\textbf{reload}, \textbf{i})$$

from the theory of **Clip**:

$$\textbf{Init}_{C}\circledast\clubsuit(\textbf{self} \in \overline{C} := \textbf{true}, \textbf{i})$$

holds for any VDM^{++} class **C**, where **Init$_C$** is the initialisation predicate of **C**.

Thus the next time that **fire_action** is executed after an execution of **reload**, the **fire** method will be invoked. That is:

$$\Box_{\textbf{Gun}}(\underline{\textbf{reload}} \Rightarrow \bigcirc\textbf{fire})$$

which implies the trace specification.

In order for **reload** and **fire** to be mutex and self-mutex in **Gun_1**, the period 10 in the periodic thread must be longer than the maximum possible durations of **reload** and **fire**. This may be undesirable if **reload** takes much longer to complete than **fire**, since a requirement of the system is to maximise the firing rate.

An alternative approach which avoids this problem is to use a procedural thread to handle reloading:

```
class Gun_2
instance variables
  clip : @Clip;
init objectstate == not(void(clip))
methods
  reload() ==
      clip := Clip!new;
```

```
fire()  ==
    def cliprounds  =  clip!roundsleft()
    in
      if cliprounds  >  0
      then clip!get_round()
```

```
thread
  while true
  do
    (dcl rl:  ℕ  :=  clip!roundsleft();
       if rl  =  0
       then self!reload(),
       else self!fire())
```

end **Gun_2**

Again the trace specification of **Gun** is satisfied because the condition
clip.rounds = 0 cannot be true on successive iterations of the thread loop.
Thus if **reload** is selected for execution on iteration **i**, say, then on iteration
i + 1, **fire** will be selected. A thread specification implies mutual exclusion
between the statements executed on distinct branches, and self-exclusion for
individual branches.

Now however there is no specified regularity in the events associated with
the gun controller.

An example where internal concurrency within a conceptual object is necessary is the following aggregate of two guns (using Z^{++} notation):

CLASS Emplacement
OWNS
  gun1, gun2 : **Gun**
HISTORY
  #active(gun1.reload) + #active(gun2.reload) ≤ 1
END CLASS

The history constraint may be alternatively stated as

$$\Box^r \neg \; (\textbf{gun1.reload} \land \textbf{gun2.reload})$$

since **reload** is durative.

An **Emplacement** is a pair of guns, one of which must always be firing
(alternatively, at most one of which is being reloaded at any time). The contained objects are therefore executing concurrently, with no constraints other
than this availability requirement. Ensuring the requirement may be quite difficult however, unless there is a means to check how many rounds there are in
a clip before loading it, and a means of selecting an appropriate clip to load in
order that the next pair of reloadings do not overlap.

Exercise (9.1): Consider the following class:

class Concurr

```
methods
  m()
      is not yet specified;
  n()
      is not yet specified
thread
  periodic(5)(m);
  periodic(3)(n)
end Concurr
```

Taking the weak interpretation of periodic threads, what are the implications for the possible durations of the methods? Define a suitable scheduling strategy in the case that both methods always take 1 time unit each, and where **m** has priority.

9.4 Specification of Reactive Systems

The next case study concerns a particular set of techniques for the synthesis of controllers for reactive systems (more precisely, "discrete event systems"). This section describes the general approach, which may be applied to either Z^{++} or VDM^{++}, although only VDM^{++} will be used as a source of examples.

The techniques have some similarities to *deductive synthesis* of discrete event system controllers [42], in that our process aims to derive the minimal properties of a controller necessary to ensure the requirements. The derivation corresponds to the construction of a proof that these requirements are met, together with the executable code of the controller. The key element is the linking of requirements expressed in a temporal logic formalism to procedural elements in VDM^{++}. Examples of such connections are those between temporal invariants and permission statements and select statements, and between method invocation times and explicit queues of invocation data.

The following steps are taken to synthesise a software controller for a reactive system:

1. *Elicitation of requirements*, identification of controlled system components, states and transitions, and the roles of the controller and operator. The results of this stage can be expressed using:

    (a) natural language statements of requirements, both of invariant properties, desired properties, timing constraints and of required procedures (sequences of transitions or events);

    (b) a control and data flow diagram identifying the flows of information between components, and the degree to which the controller and user can influence the system – this is expressed in Ward/Mellor RTSA notation [222];

    (c) a statechart for each component, with the AND composition of these forming the statechart of the entire system. Constraints on transitions which follow from the physical laws of the domain, or of the components themselves (eg, because of inbuilt hardware interlocks) can be expressed on this statechart in order to reduce the number of states to be considered by the synthesis process.

2. *Priority ordering of the requirements*, and formalisation of these in terms of the states of the system components. Validation of the formalisation would check that these constraints are not contradictory. Resolution of any contradictions would be achieved by making use of priorities where possible. The results of this stage are:

   (a) formal expression of invariant, desired and procedural requirements, in simple (propositional) logical notation. Formal expression of timing constraints using RTL;

   (b) a simplified system statechart with states and transitions forbidden by the requirements eliminated. This statechart describes the desired controlled system, and can be formalised in an outline VDM^{++} class.

3. *Interpretation of the invariant and desired constraints* as permission guards on methods corresponding to events: either events which are inputs to the controller, and which the controller must therefore respond to in order to maintain the required properties, or events which are outputs from the controller. In the latter case the controller must invoke the methods only if the permission conditions hold.

   The duality between these two cases is similar to that between the permissions and obligations of deontic logic [207].

   The permission guards for output events are added to the specification, and controller responses become definitions of transitions on the controlled system statechart, and methods of the VDM^{++} class describing the controller;

4. *Definition of the dynamic behaviour of the controller* via a **thread** or event-triggered actions, and verification that this definition ensures the permission constraints, and the formalised dynamic and timing requirements;

5. code generation in Ada or other suitable language.

There are other aspects to be considered, in particular how system components should be modelled by classes, and the ways in which these classes should be inter-related. In the simple case there is one-way information transfer (via events or discrete data flows) between a component and the controller, and the relationship can be modelled by the target of the information flow being a supplier to the source. However if there is two-way information flow (eg, if the controller can access the state of a component which it controls) then there are two alternatives: modelling via clientship as in the previous case, or via aggregation (inheritance of the system components into a single class representing the uncontrolled system).

9.5 Mine Pump Control

This case study is a classic example of a reactive system problem [141]. We will focus on the safety properties here, and not consider in detail the issues of conversion between continuous and discrete data.

9.5.1 Requirements Identification

The components of this system are:

- a pump, which receives commands to switch on and off from the controller;
- a methane sensor, which sends signals to the controller when the methane level becomes safe or unsafe;
- a water sensor, which sends signals to the controller when the water level passes a particular point;
- the operator, which sends commands to enable and disable the controller.

Thus the data and control flow diagram of the system is as shown in Figure 9.3 (using the notation of Ward/Mellors RTSA). Continuously varying data flows

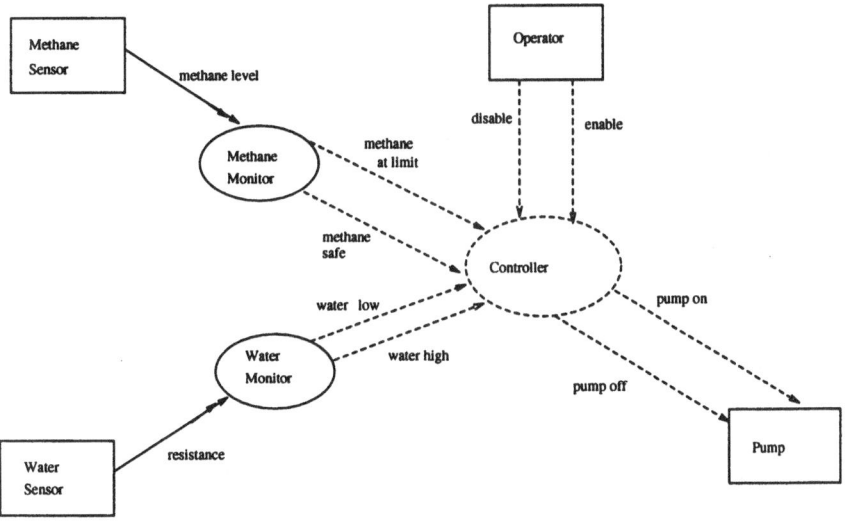

Figure 9.3: Data and Control Flow for Mine System

such as the level of resistance between two contacts (used to sense the presence of water at a certain location) or in a semiconductor sensor for methane are marked as solid lines. These flows are converted into discrete events by the appropriate monitors (probably implemented in hardware, but this is not a concern of the specification as yet). The main operation of the system is to transform flows of events from the two sensors, and from the user of the system, into a suitable flow of events to the pump.

Dashed ovals indicate processes which transform event streams into event streams, whilst solid ovals indicate data transformation processes. We will show that a VDM^{++} specification of the system can be given which is closely related to the analysis models in RTSA/statechart notation.

There are 2 possible states for each monitor, and 2 primary states for the controller (enabled versus disabled) and for the pump. Thus there are 16 states in the system. We will only consider the 8 states corresponding to the **enabled** controller state initially.

The process description for the **WaterMonitor** process is:

- a **water_high** event is triggered exactly when the monitored resistance value passes the lower limit **wllimit** on its way down (water between the contacts will decrease the resistance), and a **water_low** event is triggered when the resistance value passes the upper limit **wulimit** on its way up.
- **wllimit** < **wulimit** in order to obtain clean switching.

Thus we can define the class:

```
class WaterMonitor
values
   wllimit:  N  =  undefined;
   wulimit:  N  =  undefined
time variables
   input resistance:  R
instance variables
   controller:  @Controller;
inv objectstate ==  wulimit  >  wllimit
sync
  on resistance  <  llimit  :=  true
        do controller!water_high();

  on resistance  >  wulimit  :=  true
        do controller!water_low()

end WaterMonitor
```

using the extension of event-triggered actions to VDM^{++}. The monitors are formalised as clients of the controller, since there is unidirectional communication from the monitors to the controller.

The methane monitor has a very similar specification:

```
class MethaneMonitor
values
   mllimit:  N  =  undefined;
   mulimit:  N  =  undefined
time variables
   input methane_level:  R
instance variables
```

```
    controller :  ●Controller;
inv objectstate == mulimit > mllimit
sync
  on methane_level ≥ mulimit := true
          do controller!methane_at_limit();

  on methane_level ≤ mllimit := true
          do controller!methane_safe()
```

end MethaneMonitor

The state of the water and methane monitors are denoted by **wstate** and **mstate** respectively. These will actually be maintained in the controller for the particular system design described here.

An alternative way of specifying these monitors, avoiding the use of interrupts, would be:

```
class MethaneMonitor1
values
    mllimit :  N  =  undefined;
    mulimit :  N  =  undefined
time variables
    input methane_level :  R
instance variables
    controller :  ●Controller;
    old_state :  R;
inv objectstate == mulimit > mllimit;
init objectstate == old_state = 0
methods
  sample()  ==
      (if methane_level ≥ mulimit ∧
        old_state < mulimit
       then controller!methane_at_limit()
       else
         if methane_level ≤ mllimit ∧
           old_state > mllimit
         then controller!methane_safe();
         old_state := methane_level)
thread
  periodic(1)(sample)
end MethaneMonitor1
```

This is however less abstract, in specifying a particular sampling interval, and in making assumptions about the duration of the **sample** method.

The textual requirements are:

1. "whenever the methane level is unsafe, the pump must be off" (invariant);
2. "whenever the water level is high and the methane level is safe, the pump should be on" (invariant);
3. "if the water level is low then the pump should be off" (our interpretation of "the pump should not be on unnecessarily") (a desirable condition).

These requirements are prioritised in this order – that is, it is more important that safety requirements (1 and 2) are met than that the time that the pump is on should be minimised.

9.5.2   Formalisation of Requirements

As initially presented, the requirements were ambiguous and unclear. Formalising such requirements should be an interactive process in general, whereby the specifier defines particular precise interpretations of the requirements, and confirms these with the person or organisation that initiated the requirements.

In this case the requirements are formalised as the following invariants of the controlled system (where we refer to state variables as if they were globally accessible, ie, without making any assumptions about the actual design of the system or interconnections of software components):

mstate = < **mnotok** > ⇒ **pstate** = < **off** >

wstate = < **whigh** > ∧ **mstate** = < **mok** > ⇒ **pstate** = < **on** >

wstate = < **wlow** > ⇒ **pstate** = < **off** >

pstate records the state of the pump (which is either on or off). These properties reduce the 8 states of the uncontrolled system to 4 states:

1. methane ok, water high, pump on;
2. methane ok, water low, pump off;
3. methane not ok, water low, pump off;
4. methane not ok, water high, pump off.

As far as the controller is concerned the final two states are largely equivalent, and they will be considered together in the following. Technically this is a result of a transformation on a statechart which is an "equivalence" in a certain sense. Such equivalences can be shown because of the formal interpretation of statecharts in RTL given in [176].

The fact that each of these states satisfies the requirements shows that these requirements are mutually consistent.

9.5.3   Specification

In general, safety requirements for a reactive system are not simply invariants of a class which specifies that system. Instead, they are "always true" assertions of the form $\Box^\tau \varphi$. In contrast, a class invariant is not necessarily true during the execution of a method.

By standard reasoning however, properties of the form $\Box^\tau \varphi$ hold for a class if they are true in the initial state, and if no event of the class can change their truth value. In practice this means that the only events which can lead to their violation must be guarded in such a way that they cannot lead to a breaking of the property.

Thus, for the first requirement we have that the **pump_on** and **methane_at_limit** events can violate the property, so they must be guarded:

$$\text{per } \textbf{pump\_on} \quad \Rightarrow \quad \text{mstate} \ = \ < \text{mok} >$$

$$\text{per } \textbf{methane\_at\_limit} \quad \Rightarrow \quad \text{pstate} \ = \ < \text{off} >$$

The first guard is a constraint on how the controller can invoke the **pump_on** operation, and is in principle satisfiable by a suitable coding of the controller. The second concerns an input event to the controller, so that the controller can only react to **methane_at_limit** by a suitable transition that should (apart from within a negligible time interval) maintain the invariant. Clearly this is a transition from state 1 or 2 to state 3/4, which invokes **pump!pump_off** in the first case.

For the second requirement we have

$$\text{per } \textbf{pump\_off} \quad \Rightarrow \quad \text{wstate} \ = \ < \text{wlow} > \ \lor \ \text{mstate} \ = \ < \text{mnotok} >$$

$$\text{per } \textbf{water\_high} \quad \Rightarrow \quad (\text{mstate} \ = \ < \text{mok} > \ \Rightarrow \ \text{pstate} \ = \ < \text{on} >)$$

$$\text{per } \textbf{methane\_safe} \quad \Rightarrow \quad (\text{wstate} \ = \ < \text{whigh} > \ \Rightarrow \ \text{pstate} \ = \ < \text{on} >)$$

Again the first constrains when the controller can invoke **pump_off**. The second and third indicate how the controller should react to the events **water_high** and **methane_safe**: by transitions from state 2 to state 1 in the second case if **mstate** $= <$ **mok** $>$ when **water_high** occurs, or from state 3 to itself in the second case if **mstate** $= <$ **mnotok** $>$ at this time point. To implement the third permission statement we need to transition from state 3 to state 1 if **wstate** $= <$ **whigh** $>$ when **methane_safe** occurs, and from state 3 to state 2 if **wstate** $= <$ **wlow** $>$ when this event occurs.

For the third requirement we have

$$\text{per } \textbf{water\_low} \quad \Rightarrow \quad \text{pstate} \ = \ < \text{off} >$$

$$\text{per } \textbf{pump\_on} \quad \Rightarrow \quad \text{wstate} \ = \ < \text{whigh} >$$

As a result we give the controller a transition from state 1 to state 2, and from state 3 to itself, on the **water_low** event. The second is an additional constraint on when the controller can invoke **pump_on**.

As a result of this analysis we can give the statechart of the controller, as shown in Figure 9.4. Here we have also included the effect of the operator actions.

Therefore we have the following description (where the initial state has been chosen to ensure that each invariant holds):

```
class Controller
types
   CState  = < disabled > | < running > | < ready > | < methane_high >;
```

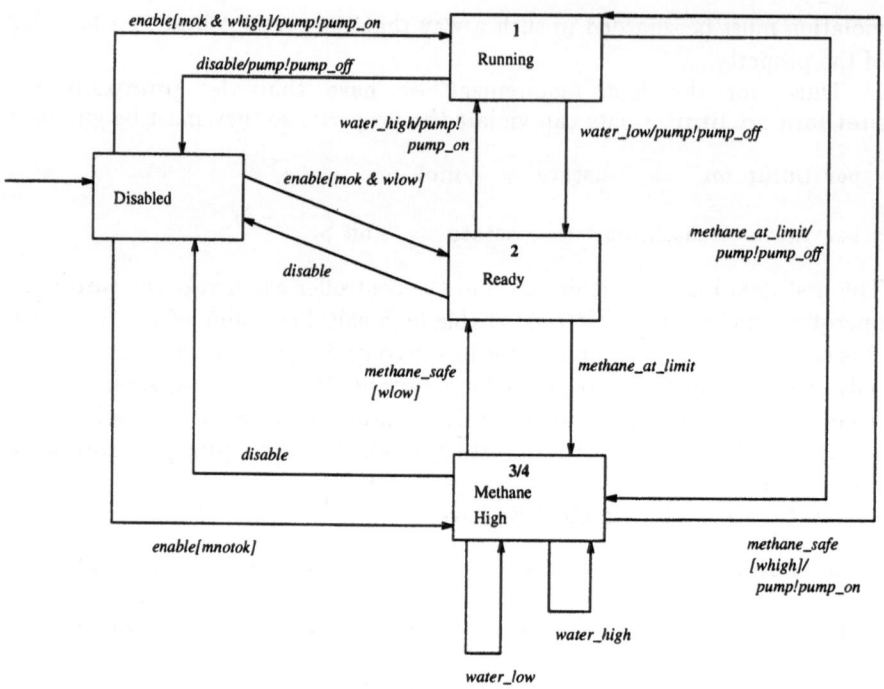

Figure 9.4: Statechart of Controller

WState = < whigh > | < wlow >;
MState = < mok > | < mnotok >;
instance variables
  cstate : CState;
  wstate : WState;
  mstate : MState;

  pump : @Pump;
init objectstate == cstate = < disabled > ∧
                     wstate = < wlow > ∧
                     mstate = < mok >
methods
  water_high() ==
          (wstate := < whigh >;
           if cstate = < ready >
           then cstate := < running >);

  water_low() ==
          (wstate := < wlow >;
            if cstate = < running >
            then cstate := < ready >);

methane_at_limit() ==

```
             (mstate := < mnotok >;
                if cstate  ≠ < disabled >
                then cstate := < methane_high >);

   methane_safe() ==
             (mstate := < mok >;
                if cstate  ≠ < disabled >
                then
                   if wstate = < whigh >
                   then cstate := < running >
                   else
                        cstate := < ready >);

   enable() ==
             if wstate = < whigh > ∧ mstate = < mok >
             then cstate := < running >
             else
                if mstate = < mnotok >
                then cstate := < methane_high >
                else cstate := < ready >;

   disable() ==
             cstate := < disabled >
 sync
   per enable ⇒ cstate = < disabled >;
   per disable ⇒ cstate ≠ < disabled >
 thread
   while true
   do
      sel
        cstate = < running > answer methane_at_limit ->
                                            pump!pump_off(),
        cstate = < ready > answer water_high ->
                                            pump!pump_on(),
        cstate = < running > answer water_low ->
                                            pump!pump_off(),
        cstate ≠ < running > answer methane_at_limit,
        cstate ≠ < ready > answer water_high,
        cstate ≠ < running > answer water_low,
        wstate = < whigh > answer methane_safe ->
                                            pump!pump_on(),
        wstate = < wlow > answer methane_safe,
        cstate = < disabled > ∧ wstate = < whigh > ∧
                   mstate = < mok > answer enable ->
                                            pump!pump_on(),
        cstate = < disabled > answer enable,
        cstate = < running > answer disable ->
                                            pump!pump_off(),
        cstate ≠ < disabled > answer disable
```

end Controller

In the thread we have again ordered the select clauses depending on the priority order of urgency to which the controller should respond to the events. As described in Chapter 7, actions associated with a transition (here, **pump_on** and **pump_off**) take place in the target state of the transition.

Notice that the controller keeps track of the states of the controlled system components within itself, rather than directly accessing their states. This raises problems of the accuracy of this representation, ie, how delays in updating this internal representation may affect controller actions.

If the above approach did not guarantee a fast enough response to the **methane_at_limit** event, then it could instead be treated as an interrupt of the thread:

sync
  on req(methane_at_limit) **do** pump!pump_off()

and similarly for other critical events. This **sync** specification states that as soon as a request for **methane_at_limit** arrives at the controlled system object, it must interrupt any ongoing action and atomically perform the associated action. This action should not affect the result of any other processing which may be in progress at the point of the interrupt.

9.5.4   Verification

We must show that the permission guards identified for the **pump** transitions are ensured by the code of the controlled system thread and methods. In addition, we must ensure that the permission guards in **Controlled_system** are actually obeyed by its thread (so that the **sync** clause is redundant).

For the **pump_on** action we have the permission guards

$$\text{mstate} = <\text{mok}> \wedge \text{ wstate} = <\text{whigh}>$$

These are ensured since **pump_on** can only be invoked in the **ready** state as a result of the **water_high** event, or in the **methane_high** state as a result of the **methane_safe** event, with wstate $= <$ whigh $>$, or by **enable**, with both properties holding. In each case the required conditions hold.

For **pump_off**, this has the permission guard

$$\text{wstate} = <\text{wlow}> \vee \text{ mstate} = <\text{mnotok}>$$

which is satisfied by the calls resulting from **methane_at_limit** and **water_low** events, from the **running** state, but not by the **disabled** event transition. This is acceptable if we allow the user to override the behaviour of the controller in this respect.

It is clear that the thread establishes the other permission guards.

The specification of **Pump** is direct. The workspace for the system only contains three external methods: **initialise** to set up the system, **enable** to switch on the controller, and **disable** to switch it off. This emphasises that the **water_high**, etc, methods of **Controller** are purely internal to the controlled system and are meant to be invoked only by the active monitor objects.

```
class Workspace
instance variables
   controller :  ¢Controller;
   methane_monitor :  ¢MethaneMonitor;
   water_monitor :  ¢WaterMonitor;
   pump :  ¢Pump
methods
   initialise()  ==
              (controller  :=  Controller!new;
               methane_monitor  :=  MethaneMonitor!new;
               water_monitor  :=  WaterMonitor!new;
               pump  :=  Pump!new;

               topology [
                         post controller.pump  =  pump  ∧
                              methane_monitor.controller  =  controller  ∧
                              water_monitor.controller  =  controller];
               methane_monitor!start;
               water_monitor!start;
               controller!start);

   enable()  ==
               controller!enable();


   disable()  ==
               controller!disable()


end Workspace
```

The **new** statements create new objects of the appropriate classes. The topology statement is used to establish connections between the software modules representing the controlled components. **start** statements initiate the threads or internal activities of active objects.

Glossary

Abstract specification class: a class which is not the product of a refinement step, ie, which represents the complete specification of a particular subsystem. It may be constructed using inheritance, subtyping or composition, and does not necessarily correspond to a *virtual* class in the usual sense of object-orientation.

Active object: an object which has an ongoing internal behaviour independent of external clients. In VDM^{++} an active object is one which has a thread, and it is *purely* active if it does not contain answer statements.

Aggregation: describes a situation in which the existence of an entity requires the existence of certain subcomponents or parts. The entity is then termed an aggregate of these parts. An example would be a lift system, involving one or more lifts, each with an associated cable. There is sometimes only a subtle distinction between modelling a situation via aggregation or via associations.

As we suggest in Chapter 3, rather than having a single concept of aggregation, it would be more accurate to have a variety of graduations of containment, such as:

- components have lifetimes that coincide with their containers, and which cannot be shared (eg: cylinders of an engine);
- a component cannot exist except as part of a container (eg: a division of a company);
- as in the previous case, and without sharing being possible;
- no sharing, but with the possibility of components being replaced in the lifetime of the container (eg, wheels of a car);
- possible sharing and separate existence, but with the set of components being constant over the lifetime of each container.

All of these definitions can be formalised.

Analysis: the process of specifying the visible and expected behaviour of a system in terms of the domain of operation of the system.

Association: an association between two entities or classes is a relation, possibly with cardinality constraints and attributes intrinsic to the relation. An example of the latter would be an association **employed_by** between employees and employers, where each element of the association can have attributes such as **salary**. An instance of an association is termed a *link*.

Attribute: a feature of a class or association which consists of a single named variable of a specified type. Attributes may include variables of a class type or of a type derived from a class (such as a sequence of elements of a class). Attributes which are of a class type correspond to links or associations.

Class: a template for objects which share common attributes, invariant predicates on these attributes, and operations. A class is usually regarded as a type, of which objects of the class are elements, termed *instances*. Objects can be declared to be of a class type (usually by the notation **object : Class**). The interpretation of this declaration varies, however, depending on the underlying semantics for objects assumed. A class may also be regarded as a theory in a formal language, whose instances are models of its axioms.

Client class: a class which uses an instance of another class via composition.

Compositionality of classes: the use of objects of one class (the **supplier**) within another (the **client**), with this use being restricted to access to the *interface* of the supplier – that is, the operations of the supplier with their signatures and most abstract specification can be assumed in the client, but internal data representations cannot be accessed. Composition or clientship relationships partition a development into a set of "layers", whereby the specification or implementation of one layer makes use of the specification of another via composition.

Demeter's Law: the principle that objects may only make references to data and operations of objects which are "local" to the referencing object [38, p 219]. It therefore aims to decrease the coupling of a set of classes, and increase their modularity and maintainability.

In its weak form it permits a method of class **C** to make reference to methods of suppliers to **C** and of locally declared supplier objects to the method (including formal input and output parameters) and permits reference to the data of the class and its supertypes. The *strong form* of the law requires additionally that all accesses to data of supertypes is achieved via operations of these supertypes. This amounts to *strict inheritance* in the sense of [182], and insulates the subtype development from changes in the data representation of its supertypes.

Design: the definition of the architecture, decomposition and components of a system. This development stage can be separated into *logical* and *physical* design steps, with the logical step being concerned with design independent of a particular implementation environment (hardware and software), and with physical design being concerned with specialisation of the logical design to the particular environment.

Dynamic binding: an implementation mechanism which allows the choice of a method definition to be applied to a given object to be made at runtime, based on the class to which the object belongs.

Encapsulation: selective hiding of the local environment (attributes and operations) of a software module (such as an object) from a global environment. This is a key aspect of object-oriented software development, allowing control over the accesses allowed to the private state of modules, and hence allowing changes to a supplier subsystem to be made with reduced impact on its clients.

Feature: any named item declared within a class, such as constant data, attributes or methods.

Genericity: the property of a specification component which enables it to be instantiated by different types in order to specify data and behaviour properties in a consistent manner over these different types. In this respect the specification component can also be said to be *polymorphic*.

Inheritance: the inclusion of the features of one class (the inherited class) in another (the inheriting). Inheritance may (but need not) correspond to an "is-a" relationship between the respective classes: every instance of the inheriting class may be considered to be an instance of the inherited. This form of inheritance is termed *conformant inheritance* or subtyping. Other forms of inheritance allow, for example, methods of the inherited class to be deleted or hidden in the inheriting, such as *controlled inheritance* in VDM^{++}.

Object: an entity encapsulating state and operations upon that state. An object has a persistent state (that is, the values of variables or attributes of that object persist from the last application of an operation upon that object, rather than being re-initialised at each operation invocation). For each object there is a single class of which it is an identified instance, although, depending on the type system adopted, there may be other classes (e.g. supertypes of the identified class) of which it can also be regarded as an instance. The effect of operations applied to the object is defined in this identified class (often called the "owning" class).

Object identity: an intrinsic property of an object, which is preserved over all applications of operations upon the object, and which is not dependent on the values of the attributes of the object (i.e. two different objects can have identical values for all attributes). According to the OMG Object Model:

> *Each object has a unique identity that is distinct from and independent of any of its characteristics. Characteristics can vary over time whereas identity is constant.*

OMG: Object Management Group – a group of some 250 users and developers of object technology, aiming to develop specifications for the portability, re-usability and interoperability of software.

Passive object: an object whose behaviour is determined by the external calls it receives from clients.

Polymorphism: the ability of a specification or software component to deal with objects or values from a range of types. Both genericity and dynamic binding are examples of polymorphic behaviour which are supported by some object-oriented languages.

Promotion: in Z and Z-related languages, the specification construct which takes an operation **OpL** on a local state **L**, together with a *framing* schema **F** on a global state **G**, and creates a new operation **OpG** on **G** which applies **OpL** to an element or elements of **L** selected via **F**.

Refinement: the process of moving from an abstract specification of a data type or operation to a more concrete specification of the component. Several precise definitions exist, such as that used by Abrial for the B Abstract Machine Notation, and that which is used in Z. There are two main forms of refinement: *data refinement*, in which a relation or function linking the states of the abstract and concrete versions of a class is asserted, and *procedural refinement*, in which the state space of the class remains the same, but operations may be replaced by more deterministic or more robust definitions in the refining class. Usually, procedural refinement is a special case of data-refinement in which the data-refinement relation is the identity map.

Specialisation: the process of restricting the sets of instances of a class by strengthening its invariant, strengthening the pre-conditions of its operations, or by enriching its state, typically to make the class fit more closely to the real-world situation to which it corresponds. An example would be restricting the pre-condition of a *marry* operation to *living* rather than possibly *dead* people.

Subtyping: the standard definition of subtyping is given in [200]:

> *"A type hierarchy is composed of subtypes and supertypes. The intuitive idea of a subtype is one whose objects provide all the behaviour of another type (the supertype) plus something extra. What is wanted here is something like the following substitution property: If for every object o1: S there is o2: T such that for all programs P defined in terms of T, the behaviour of P is unchanged when o1 is substituted for o2, then S is a subtype of T."*

Supplier: a class **C** is a *supplier* to another (say, **D**) if instances of **C** are used by composition within **D**.

Validation: comparison of a specification against its requirements, by means such as animation, or manual emulation of particular scenarios. The aim is to ensure the correctness of the specification as a formalised expression of the user requirements.

Verification: comparison of implementation against specification, to ensure that all properties of the required system given in the specification are satisfied by the implementation. Techniques may include static and semantic analysis, or a step-by-step verification by proof of refinement obligations.

Virtual class: a class which cannot be instantiated directly, but only by instantiating some proper subtype of it. It satisfies an equivalence of the form:

$$\forall a : @C \bullet a \in \overline{C} \equiv$$
$$\exists a_1 : @C_1 \bullet a_1 \in \overline{C_1} \wedge a = @R_1(a_1) \ \vee \ldots$$
$$\exists a_n : @C_n \bullet a_n \in \overline{C_n} \wedge a = @R_n(a_n)$$

where C_i is a subtype of **C** via R_i, for $i : 1 .. n$.

Bibliography

[1] M Abadi and L Cardelli. An imperative object calulus. In P D Mosses, M Nielsen, and M I Schwartzbach, editors, *TAPSOFT '95*, volume 915 of *Lecture Notes in Computer Science*. Springer-Verlag, May 1995.

[2] J R Abrial. A refinement case study (using the Abstract Machine Notation). In *4th Refinement Workshop*, Workshops in Computing. Springer-Verlag, 1991.

[3] J R Abrial. *Assigning Programs to Meaning*. Prentice Hall International, 1995 (to appear).

[4] A V Aho, R Sethi, and J D Ullman. *Compilers – Principles, Techniques and Tools*. Addison-Wesley, 1986.

[5] A J Alencar and J A Goguen. OOZE: An object-oriented Z environment. In P America, editor, *ECOOP '91 Proceedings*, volume 512 of *Lecture Notes in Computer Science*, pages 180–199. Springer-Verlag, July 1991.

[6] G Alkhatib. The maintenance problem of application software: An empirical analysis. *Software Maintenance: Research and Practice*, 4:83–104, 1992.

[7] J F Allen. Maintaining knowledge about temporal intervals. *CACM*, 26(11):832–843, November 1983.

[8] P America. Issues in the design of a parallel object-oriented language. *Formal Aspects of Computing*, 1(4):366–411, 1989.

[9] P America. Designing an object-oriented programming language with behavioural subtyping. In *Foundations of Object-oriented Languages*, volume 489 of *LNCS*. Springer-Verlag, 1990.

[10] E A Ashcroft. Dataflow and eduction: Data-driven and demand-driven distributed computation. In J W de Bakker, W P de Roever, and G Rozenberg, editors, *Current Trends in Concurrency*, volume 224 of *Lecture Notes in Computer Science*, pages 1–50. Springer-Verlag, 1986.

[11] W D Atkinson, J P Booth, and W J Quirk. Modal action logic for the specification and validation of safety. In *Mathematical Structures for Software Engineering*. The Institute of Mathematics and its Applications Conference Series 27, Clarendon Press, 1991.

[12] S Aujla, T Bryant, and L Semmens. A rigorous review technique: Using formal notations with conventional development methods. In *Software Engineering Standards Symposium*. IEEE Computer Society Press, 1993.

[13] S Austin and G I Parkin. Formal Methods: A Survey. Technical report, National Physical Laboratory, Queens Road, Teddington, Middlesex, TW11 0LW, March 1993.

[14] Australian Ordnance Council. *Assessment of munition related safety critical computing systems*, Aug 1993. Pillar Proceeding 223.93.

[15] B Core UK Ltd, Oxford Science Park, Oxford. *B-tool Reference Manual*, 1994.

[16] B Core UK Ltd, Oxford Science Park, Oxford. *B Toolkit Reference Manual*, 1994.

[17] T Bar-David. Specification and program refinement: The minimal program satisfying a specification. Technical report, Deerworks and Monmouth College, April 1992.

[18] R Barden, S Stepney, and D Cooper. *Z in Practice*. Prentice Hall, 1994.

[19] N S Baron. *Computer Languages: A Guide for the Perplexed*. Penguin, 1988.

[20] L M Barroca, J S Fitzgerald, and L Spencer. The architectural specification of an avionic subsystem. In *IEEE Workshop on Industrial-strength Formal Specification Techniques*, pages 17–29. IEEE Press, 1995.

[21] R S M Barros and D J Harper. Formal development of relational database applications. In *International Workshop on Specifications of Database Systems*. Springer-Verlag, 1991.

[22] V Basili, S K Abd-El-Hafiz, and G Caldiera. Towards automated support for extraction of reusable components. In *Proceedings of IEEE Conference on Software Maintenance*, pages 212–219, 1991.

[23] S Bear. An overview of HP-SL. In *VDM '91, Formal Software Development Methods*, volume 551 of *Lecture Notes in Computer Science*, pages 571–587. Springer-Verlag, 1991.

[24] I Benbasat and J S Dhaliwal. A framework for the validation of knowledge acquisition. *Knowledge Acquisition*, 1:215–233, 1989.

[25] D Bobrow and M Stefik. Perspectives on artificial intelligence programming. In *Artificial Intelligence and Software Engineering*. Morgan Kaufmann, 1986.

[26] B W Boehm. The economics of software maintenance. In R S Arnold, editor, *Software Maintenance Workshop*. IEEE Computer Society Press, December 1983.

[27] B W Boehm. A spiral model of software development and enhancement. *IEEE Computer*, 21, No 5, May 1988.

[28] G Booch. *Software Engineering in Ada*. Addison-Wesley, 1988.

[29] G Booch. *Object-oriented Design with Applications*. Benjamin Cummings, 1994.

[30] G Booch and D Bryan. *Software Engineering in Ada (4th Edition)*. Benjamin/Cummings, 1994.

[31] Paulo Borba and Silvio Meira. From VDM specifications to functional prototypes. *Journal of Systems and Software*, 21(3):267–78, June 1993.

[32] J Bowen and V Stavridou. Safety-critical systems, formal methods and standards. *Software Engineering Journal*, 8(4):189–209, July 1993.

[33] P Breuer and K Lano. From code to Z specifications. In *Z User Meeting 1989*, Workshops in Computing. Springer-Verlag, 1990.

[34] British Railway Board. *Safety related software for railway signaling*, 1991. BRB/LU LTD/RIA Technical Specification no. 23.

[35] F P Brookes. *The Mythical Man-Month*. Addison-Wesley, 1974.

[36] F P Brookes. No silver bullet: Essence and accidents of software engineering. In H-J Kluger, editor, *Information Processing '86*. Elsevier Science Publishers B.V., 1986.

[37] D Brownbridge. Using Z to develop a CASE toolset. In J Nicholls, editor, *4th Annual Z User Meeting*, Workshops in Computing, pages 142 – 149. Springer-Verlag, 1990.

[38] T Budd. *An Introduction to Object Oriented Programming*. Addison-Wesley, 1991.

[39] R Buhr. *Practical Visual Techniques in System Design: With Applications to Ada*. Prentice Hall International, 1991.

[40] T Bull. An introduction to the WSL program transformer. In *Proceedings of IEEE Conference on Software Maintenance*, pages 242–250. IEEE Press, 1990.

[41] L Burd. The spiral model and object-orientation: A path towards successful reuse. In *Workshop on Object-Oriented Methodologies*. KBSL, 1992.

[42] J Burghardt. Deductive synthesis applied to the production cell case study. In *Case Study "Production Cell": A comparative study in formal software development*, chapter XI. FZI Publication 1/94, University of Karlsruhe, 1994.

[43] R M Burstall and J A Goguen. The semantics of Clear, a specification language. In *Lecture Notes in Computer Science 86*, pages 292–332. Springer-Verlag, 1980.

[44] P Byers. The role of formal methods in the engineering of safety critical systems. In F Redmill and T Anderson, editors, *2nd Safety-Critical Systems Symp, Technology and Assessment of Safety-Critical Systems*, pages 247–257. Springer-Verlag, 1994.

[45] R Cam and S Vuong. A formal specification, in LOTOS, of a simplified cellular mobile communication system. In S Vuong, editor, *Formal Description Techniques, II (FORTE'89)*, pages 485–499. North-Holland, 1990.

[46] L Cardelli. A semantics of multiple inheritance. *Information and Computation*, 76:138–164, 1988.

[47] D Carrington, D Duke, R Duke, P King, G A Rose, and G Smith. Object-Z: An object-oriented extension to Z. In *Formal Description Techniques, II (FORTE'89)*, pages 281–296. North-Holland, 1990.

[48] C Carter. Object-oriented analysis and recursive development in safety-critical system development. In *Proceedings of Object Technology '93*, 1993.

[49] E Casais. An incremental class reorganisation approach. In *ECOOP '92 Proceedings*, volume 615 of *Lecture Notes in Computer Science*, pages 114–132. Springer-Verlag, 1992.

[50] CESG. CESG computer security manual 'F': A formal development methodology for high confidence systems, Issue 1.0, CESG, GCHQ, 1991.

[51] K Chadha, C Hunnicutt, S Peck, and J Tebes. Mobile telephone switching office. *Bell Sys. Tech. J.*, 58(1):71–95, 1979.

[52] P Chapront. Vital coded processor and safety related software design. In H H Frey, editor, *Safety of Computer Control Systems 1992 (SAFECOMP '92), Computer Systems in Safety Critical Applications, Proc IFAC Symp.*, pages 141 – 145. Pergamon Press, 1992.

[53] M Christian. Timing and RSL. Technical Report MORSE/LLOYD's/MMC/22/V1, Lloyd's Register, July 1992.

[54] P Coad, D North, and M Mayfield. *Object Models: Strategies, Patterns and Applications*. Prentice Hall, 1995.

[55] P Coad and E Yourdon. *Object-oriented Analysis*. Yourdon Press Computing Series, 1990.

[56] E F Codd. A relational model of data for large shared data banks. *CACM 13, No.6*, June 1970.

[57] E F Codd. Extending the database relational model to capture more meaning. *ACM Transactions on Database Systems*, 4(4):397–434, December 1979.

[58] D Coleman, P Arnold, S Bodoff, C Dollin, H Gilchrist, F Hayes, and P Jeremaes. *Object-oriented Development: The FUSION Method*. Prentice Hall Object-oriented Series, 1994.

[59] D Coleman, P Arnold, S Bodoff, H Gilchrist, and F Hayes. An evaluation of five object-oriented development methods. *Hewlett-Packard Technical Report*, May 1991.

[60] D Coleman, F Hayes, and S Bear. Introducing objectcharts or how to use statecharts in object-oriented design. *IEEE Transactions on Software Engineering*, 18(1), January 1992.

[61] B P Collins, J E Nicholls, and I H Sørensen. Introducing formal methods: The CICS experience with Z. Technical report, Programming Research Group, Oxford University, 1988.

[62] Commission of the European Communities. *Information Technology Security Evaluation Criteria (ITSEC)*, June 1991. Provisional Harmonised Criteria.

[63] S Cook. Interpreting object oriented models. In *Proceedings of Object Technology '93*, 1993.

[64] S Cook and J Daniels. *Designing Object Systems: Object-Oriented Modelling with Syntropy*. Prentice Hall, Sept 1994.

[65] E Cusack. Object-oriented modelling in Z. In P America, editor, *ECOOP '91 Proceedings*, Lecture Notes in Computer Science. Springer-Verlag, 1991.

[66] E Cusack and C Wezeman. Deriving tests for objects specified in Z. In J Nicholls, editor, *Z User Meeting 1992*, Workshops in Computing. Springer-Verlag, 1993.

[67] O Dahl. Object orientation and formal techniques. In *VDM'90, VDM and Z - formal methods in software development*, volume 428 of *Lecture Notes in Computer Science*. Springer-Verlag, 1990.

[68] O J Dahl. *Object-Oriented Specifications*. Research Directions in Object-Oriented Programming. MIT Press, 1987.

[69] C DaSilva, B Dehbonei, and F Mejia. Formal specification in the development of industrial applications: The subway speed control mechanism. In *FORTE '91*, pages 207 – 221. North-Holland, 1991.

[70] C Date. The relational model ... is alive and well! Technical report, Codd and Date Co., 1992.

[71] A M Davis. *Software Requirements: Analysis and Specification*. Prentice Hall, 1990.

[72] J Dawes. *The VDM-SL Reference Guide*. Pitman, 1991.

[73] J W de Bakker, C Huizing, W P de Roever, and G Rozenburg, editors. *Real Time: Theory in Practice*, volume 600 of *Lecture Notes in Computer Science*. Springer Verlag, 1991.

[74] B Dehbonei and F Mejia. Formal development of safety-critical software systems in railway signalling. In J Bowen and M Hinchey, editors, *Applications of Formal Methods*. Prentice Hall, 1995.

[75] J Dick. Using Prolog to animate Z specifications. In *Z User Meeting 1989*, Workshops in Computing. Springer-Verlag, 1990.

[76] J Dick and A Faivre. Automating the generation and sequencing of test cases from model-based specifications. In *FME '93*, volume 670 of *Lecture Notes in Computer Science*, pages 268–284. Springer-Verlag, 1993.

[77] A Diller. *Z, An Introduction To Formal Methods*. John Wiley, 1990.

[78] C Dollin and D Coleman. The FUSION Method. In *Proceedings of BCS Christmas Meeting on Object-orientation and Formal Methods*. Springer-Verlag, 1995. to appear.

[79] C Draper. Practical Experiences of Z and SSADM. In J Bowen, editor, *Proceedings of 1992 Z User Meeting*, Workshops in Computing. Springer-Verlag, 1993.

[80] D D'Souza. Teacher! Teacher! *Journal of Object-Oriented Programming*, 5(2), May 1986.

[81] D Duke and R Duke. Towards a semantics for Object-Z. In *VDM'90: VDM and Z!*, volume 428 of *Lecture Notes in Computer Science*. Springer-Verlag, 1990.

[82] R Duke, P King, G Rose, and G Smith. The Object-Z Specification Language. Technical Report 91-1 (Version 1), University of Queensland, Department of Computer Science, Software Verification Research Centre, May 1991.

[83] R Duke, P King, and G Smith. Formalising behavioural compatibility for reactive object-oriented systems. In *Proc 14th Australian Compt. Sci. Conf. (ACSC-14)*, 1991.

[84] R Duke and G Rose. Modelling object identity. Technical report, University of Queensland, Department of Computer Science, Software Verification Research Centre, 1993.

[85] R Duke, G Rose, and A Lee. Object-oriented protocol specification. In L Logrippo, R L Probert, and H Ural, editors, *Protocol Specification, Testing, and Verification, X*, pages 325–338. 1990.

[86] E Durr. Afrodite Esprit III Project Technical Annex, 1992. CAP Gemini Innovation.

[87] E Durr. Syntactic description of the VDM^{++} language, Version 2.0.1, Afrodite Report FI 92-6, September 1992.

[88] E Durr. VDM^{++}: A formal specification language for object-oriented designs. In P Dewilde and J Vandewalle, editors, *IEEE CompEuro 92 Proceedings*, pages 214 – 219. IEEE Press, 1992.

[89] E Durr. Description of the VDM^{++} language. Technical Report AFRO / CG / ED / SYNTAX / V5.2, CAP Gemini Innovation, March 1993.

[90] E Durr. The Use of Object Oriented Specifications in Physics (PhD Thesis, Utrecht University), September 1994.

[91] E Durr and E Dusink. The role of VDM^{++} in the development of a real-time tracking and tracing system. In J Woodcock and P Larsen, editors, FME '93, Lecture Notes in Computer Science. Springer-Verlag, 1993.

[92] E Durr, A Duursma, and N Plat. VDM^{++} language reference manual. Technical Report AFRO / CG / ED / LRM / V9.1, CAP Gemini Innovation, May 1994.

[93] E Durr, S Goldsack, and N Plat. Rigorous development of concurrent and real-time object-oriented systems. Technical report, TOOLS 94 Tutorial, March 1994.

[94] R Elmasri and S B Navethe. *Fundamentals of Database Systems*. Benjamin Cummings, 1989.

[95] H B Enderton. *Elements of Set Theory*. Academic Press, 1977.

[96] E Foster *et al.* PoeT: Object engineering in public transport. In *Proceedings Object Technology '93*, 1993.

[97] M Eva. *SSADM Version 4: A User's Guide*. International Series in Software Engineering. McGraw-Hill, 1992.

[98] A Evans. Position paper, Workshop on Formal Specification and Object Orientation, Logica, 1992.

[99] M E Fagan. Advances in software inspections. *IEEE Transactions on Software Engineering*, 12(7), 1986.

[100] J Fiadiero and T Maibaum. Sometimes "Tomorrow" is "Sometime". In *Temporal Logic*, volume 827 of *Lecture Notes in Artificial Intelligence*, pages 48–66. Springer-Verlag, 1994.

[101] C Fidge. Specification and verification of real-time behaviour using Z and RTL. In J Vytopil, editor, *Proceedings of Second International Symposium on Formal Techniques in Real-Time and Fault-Tolerant Systems*, volume 571 of *Lecture Notes in Computer Science*, pages 393–409. Springer-Verlag, 1992.

[102] C Fidge. Proof obligations for real-time refinement. In *Proceedings of 6th Refinement Workshop*, Workshops in Computing. Springer-Verlag, 1994.

[103] A Fitzsimmons and T Love. A review and evaluation of software science. *ACM Computing Surveys*, 10(1):3–18, 1977.

[104] C Floyd. Theory and practice of software development: Stages in a debate. In *TAPSOFT '95*, volume 915 of *Lecture Notes in Computer Science*. Springer-Verlag, May 1995.

[105] Z Fluhr and P Porter. Control architecture. *Bell Sys. Tech. J.*, 58(1):43–69, 1979.

[106] R France. Semantically extended data flow diagrams: A formal specification tool. *IEEE Transactions on Software Engineering*, 18(4), April 1992.

[107] R France. From structured analysis to formal specifications: State of the theory. In *1994 ACM Computer Science Conference*. ACM Press, 1994.

[108] M D Fraser, K Kumar, and V Vaishnavi. Informal and formal requirements specification languages: Bridging the gap. *IEEE Transactions on Software Engineering*, 17(5), May 1992.

[109] E Gamma, R Helm, R Johnson, and J Vlissides. *Design Patterns: Elements of Reusable Object-Oriented Software*. Addison Wesley, October 1994.

[110] M-C Gaudel. Testing can be formal too. In *TAPSOFT '95*, volume 915 of *Lecture Notes in Computer Science*. Springer-Verlag, 1995.

[111] C George, P Haff, K Havelund, A E Haxthausen, R Milne, C B Nielsen, S Prehn, and K R Wagner. *The RAISE Specification Language*. Prentice Hall, 1992.

[112] C George and S Prehn. *The Raise Justification Handbook*. Technical Report LA-COS/CRI/DOC/7/V4, Computer Resources International, October 1992.

[113] S Gerhart, D Craigen, and D Ralston. Experience with formal methods in critical systems. *IEEE Software*, Jan 1994.

[114] S Gerhart, D Craigen, and D Ralston. Regulatory case studies. *IEEE Software*, Jan 1994.

[115] J Goguen and T Winkler. Introducing OBJ3. Technical Report SRI-CSL-88-9, SRI projects 1243, 2316 and 4415, Computer Science Laboratory, SRI International, August 1988.

[116] J A Goguen. How to prove algebraic induction without induction: With applications to the correctness of data type representations. In Wolfgang Bibel and Robert Kowalski, editors, *Lecture Notes in Computer Science*, volume 87, pages 356–373. Springer-Verlag, 1980.

[117] J A Goguen. Parameterized programming. *IEEE Transactions on Software Engineering*, SE-10(5), September 1984.

[118] J A Goguen. An algebraic approach to refinement. In *Proceedings, VDM'90: VDM and Z – Formal Methods in Software Development*, volume 428 of *Lecture Notes in Computer Science*, pages 12–28. Springer-Verlag, 1990.

[119] J A Goguen. Types as theories. In George Michael Reed, Andrew William Roscoe, and Ralph F. Wachter, editors, *Topology and Category Theory in Computer Science*, pages 357–390. Oxford, 1991. Proceeding of a Conference held at Oxford, June 1989.

[120] J A Goguen and J Meseguer. Unifying functional, object-oriented and relational programming, with logical semantics. In Bruce Shriver and Peter Wegner, editors, *Research Directions in Object-Oriented Programming*, pages 417–477. MIT, 1987. Preliminary version in *SIGPLAN Notices*, Volume 21, Number 10, pages 153-162, October 1986.

[121] J A Goguen and J Meseguer. Order-sorted algebra I: Equational deduction for multiple inheritance, overloading, exceptions and partial operations. Technical Report SRI-CSL-89-10, SRI International, Computer Science Lab, July 1989.

[122] J A Goguen, A Stevens, H Hilberdink, and K Hobley. 2OBJ, a metalogical framework based on equational logic. *Transactions of the Royal Society, Series A*, 1992.

[123] J A Goguen, J Thatcher, and E Wagner. An initial algebra approach to the specification, correctness and implementation of abstract data types. In Raymond Yeh, editor, *Trends in Programming Methodology IV*, pages 80–149. Prentice Hall, 1978.

[124] J A Goguen and D Wolfram. On types and FOOPS. In *Proceedings of Working Conference on Database Semantics*, Windermere, Lake District, United Kingdom, July 1990.

[125] A Goldberg and D Robson. *Smalltalk-80: The Language and its Implementation*. Addison-Wesley, 1983.

[126] R Goldblatt. *Topoi: The Categorial Approach to Logic*. North-Holland, 1982.

[127] S Goldsack, E Durr, and N Plat. Reification classes. Technical report, Dept. of Computing, Imperial College, 1994.

[128] S Goldsack, E Durr, and N Plat. Rigorous Development of Concurrent and Real-time Object-oriented Systems (TOOLS '94 Tutorial). Technical report, Dept. of Computing, Imperial College, 1994.

[129] A Gravell. What is a good formal specification? In J E Nicholls, editor, *Proceedings of Fifth Annual Z User Meeting*, Workshops in Computing, pages 137–150. Springer-Verlag, 1990.

[130] C Green, D Luckham, and R Balzer. Report on a knowledge-based software assistant. In *Artificial Intelligence and Software Engineering*. Morgan Kaufmann, 1986.

[131] D Gries. *The Science of Programming*. Prentice Hall, 1986.

[132] A Hall. Specifying and Interpreting Class Hierarchies in Z. In *8th Z User Meeting*, Workshops in Computing. Springer-Verlag, 1994.

[133] V Hamilton. Experience of combining Yourdon and VDM. In *Methods Integration Conference*, Workshops in Computing. Springer-Verlag, 1991.

[134] D Harel. Statecharts: A visual formalism for complex systems. *Science of Computer Programming*, (8):231–274, 1987.

[135] J S Hares. *SSADM for the Advanced Practitioner*. Wiley Series in Software Engineering Practice, 1990.

[136] T Hartmann, R Jungclaus, and G Saake. Aggregation in a behaviour oriented object model. In *ECOOP '92 Proceedings*, volume 615 of *Lecture Notes in Computer Science*, pages 57–77. Springer-Verlag, 1992.

[137] T Hartmann, J Kusch, G Saake, and P Hartel. Revised version of the conceptual modelling and design language TROLL. In *Proceedings of IS-CORE '94*, pages 89–103. Faculteit der Wiskunde en Informatica, Free University, Amsterdam, 1994.

[138] H Haughton and K Lano. *B Abstract Machine Notation: A Reference Manual*. McGraw-Hill, 1995.

[139] I Hayes, editor. *Specification Case Studies*. International Series in Computer Science. Prentice Hall, 1987.

[140] I J Hayes and C B Jones. Specifications are not (necessarily) executable. *Software Engineering Journal*, 4(6):320 – 338, November 1989.

[141] I J Hayes and B Mahony. A case study in timed refinement: A mine pump. *IEEE Software*, 18(9), September 1992.

[142] R Helm, I M Holland, and D Gangopadhyay. Contracts: Specifying behavioural compositions in object-oriented systems. In *ECOOP/OOPSLA '90 Proceedings*. Springer-Verlag, 1990.

[143] J V Hill. Software development methods in practice. In *Proceedings 6th Annual Conference on Computer Assurance (COMPASS)*, 1991.

[144] M Hinchey and J Bowen. Ten commandments of formal methods. Technical report, Cambridge University Department of Computing, 1994.

[145] C A R Hoare. Programming: Sorcery or science. *IEEE Software*, April 1984.

[146] C A R Hoare. *Communicating Sequential Processes*. Prentice Hall, 1985.

[147] J Hoare. The use of B in CICS. In J Bowen and M Hinchey, editors, *Applications of Formal Methods*. Prentice Hall, 1995.

[148] J Hogg. Islands: Aliasing protection in object-oriented languages. In *OOPSLA '91 Proceedings*. Springer-Verlag, 1991.

[149] I Houston. Formal Specification of the OMG Core Object Model. Technical report, IBM UK, Hursely Park, 1994.

[150] P L Iachini and R Di Giovanni. HOOD and Z for the development of complex software systems. In *VDM and Z, VDM 90*, volume 428 of *Lecture Notes in Computer Science*, pages 262–289. Springer-Verlag, 1990.

[151] IEC. *Software for Computers in the Application of Industrial Safety-Related Systems*. IEC 65A (Secretariat) 122.

[152] IFAD. *The IFAD VDM-SL Language*, February 1994.

[153] D Ince. *Object-Oriented Software Engineering with C++*. McGraw-Hill, 1992.

[154] CISI Ingenierie and MATRA Espace. *HOOD Reference Manual*. HOOD Technical Group, 1990.

[155] Intermetrics, Inc, 733 Concord Ave., Cambridge, Massachusetts 02138, USA. *Ada 95 Reference Manual (International Standard ANSI/ISO/IEC-8652:1995)*, 1995.

[156] IPSYS Limited. *TBK Version 2.5.2 Manual (3 Volumes)*, 1992.

[157] P Johnson. *Human Computer Interaction*. McGraw-Hill, 1992.

[158] R E Johnson and B Foote. Designing re-usable classes. *JOOP*, 1(2):22–35, June/July 1988.

[159] C B Jones. *Systematic Software Construction using VDM*. Prentice Hall, 1990.

[160] C B Jones. An object-based design method for concurrent programs. Technical Report UMCS-92-12-1, Manchester University, 1993.

[161] T Korson and J D McGregor. Understanding object-orientation: A unifying paradigm. *Communications of the ACM*, September 1990.

[162] B R Ladeau and C Freeman. Using formal specification for product development. *Hewlett-Packard Journal*, (6):62–66, 1991.

[163] K Lano. Validation through refinement and execution of specifications: REDO project document 2487-TN-PRG-1041. Programming Research Group, Oxford University.

[164] K Lano. Z^{++}, an object-oriented extension to Z. In J Nicholls, editor, *Z User Meeting, Oxford, UK*, Workshops in Computing. Springer-Verlag, 1991.

[165] K Lano. Combining object-oriented representations of knowledge with proximity to conceptual prototypes. In *IEEE CompEuro '92 Proceedings*. IEEE Press, 1992.

[166] K Lano. Functional specification of mapping of MVS and DOS JCL into the JCL Schema. Technical report, Applied Information Engineering, Lloyd's Register, February 1993.

[167] K Lano. The mapping of OS/VS COBOL into the COBOL schema. Technical report, Applied Information Engineering, Lloyd's Register, March 1993.

[168] K Lano. Method case study: An invoice system. Technical Report BUT-TN-LR-1030, Lloyd's Register, 1993.

[169] K Lano. Expressing the semantics of VDM^{++} in RTL. Technical Report AFRO/IC/KL/SEM2/V2, Imperial College, 1994.

[170] K Lano. Formal object-oriented specification of real-time systems. Technical report, Dept. of Computing, Imperial College, 1994.

[171] K Lano. Formalisation of Statecharts in VDM^{++}. Technical report, Dept. of Computing, Imperial College, 1994.

[172] K Lano. Integrating Formal and Structured Object-oriented Methods in VDM^{++}. Technical report, Dept. of Computing, Imperial College, 1994.

[173] K Lano. Reactive system specification and refinement. Technical report, Dept. of Computing, Imperial College, 1994.

[174] K Lano. Reasoning techniques in VDM^{++}. Technical Report AFRO/IC/KL/RT/V1, Imperial College, 1994.

[175] K Lano. Refinement in object-oriented specification languages. In D Till, editor, *6th Refinement Workshop*. Springer-Verlag, 1994.

[176] K Lano. Reactive system specification and refinement. In *TAPSOFT '95*, volume 915 of *Lecture Notes in Computer Science*. Springer-Verlag, 1995.

[177] K Lano. Specification and Development in Z^{++}. In J Bowen and M Hinchey, editors, *The Z Handbook*. Prentice Hall, 1995.

[178] K Lano and S Goldsack. Should refinement equal subtyping?: Alternative development paradigms. Technical Report AFRODITE project document AFRO/IC/KL/RS/V1, Dept. of Computing, Imperial College, 1994. Also presented at ISCORE '94 and TFM '94.

[179] K Lano and H Haughton. A specification-based approach to maintenance. *Journal of Software Maintenance*, December 1991.

[180] K Lano and H Haughton. An algebraic semantics for the object-oriented specification language Z^{++}. In *AMAST '91 Conference Proceedings*, Workshops in Computing. Springer-Verlag, 1992.

[181] K Lano and H Haughton. Extracting design and functionality from code. In *CASE '92 Conference Proceedings*. IEEE Press, 1992.

[182] K Lano and H Haughton. Reasoning and refinement in object-oriented specification languages. In *ECOOP '92 Conference Proceedings*. Springer-Verlag, 1992.

[183] K Lano and H Haughton. Representation of concurrent systems in object-oriented specification languages, 1992. Lloyd's Register.

[184] K Lano and H Haughton. Reuse and adaptation of Z specifications. In *Proceedings of Z User Meeting 1992*, Workshops in Computing. Springer-Verlag, 1992.

[185] K Lano and H Haughton. *The Z^{++} Manual*, October 1992. A User-Guide and Reference Manual for the Z^{++} Toolset.

[186] K Lano and H Haughton. Approaches to object identity. In *EROS II Workshop*. LBMS London, 1993.

[187] K Lano and H Haughton. Integrating formal and structured methods in reverse engineering. In *Working Conference on Reverse-Engineering*. IEEE Press, 1993.

[188] K Lano and H Haughton. *Object-Oriented Specification Case Studies (First Edition)*. Prentice Hall, 1993.

[189] K Lano and H Haughton. *Reverse-Engineering and Software Maintenance: A Practical Approach*. McGraw-Hill, 1993.

[190] K Lano and H Haughton. Improving the process of system specification and refinement in B AMN. In D Till, editor, *6th Refinement Workshop*. Springer-Verlag, 1994.

[191] P LeBlanc. VENUS User Manual; Combined Use of OMT and VDM^{++}. Technical Report afro/verilog/plb/um/v2.3, Verilog, 1995.

[192] M K O Lee, P N Scharbach, and I H Sørensen. Engineering real software using formal methods. In *4th Refinement Workshop*, Workshops in Computing. Springer-Verlag, 1991.

[193] M Lehman. Programs, life cycles, and laws of software evolution. *Proceedings IEEE*, 68(9):1060–1076, 1980.

[194] M Lehman, M Meir, L A Belady, and A Laszlo. *Program Evolution – Processes of Software Change*. Academic Press, 1985.

[195] A W Leigh. *Real Time Software for Small Systems*. Halstead Press, 1988.

[196] S Leonard, J Pardoe, and S Wade. Software maintenance – Cinderella is still not getting to the ball. In *BSC/IEE Conference on Software Engineering*, pages 104–106, Liverpool Polytechnic, 1988.

[197] H Lin. Complete inference systems for weak bisimulation equivalences in the π-calculus. In *TAPSOFT '95*, volume 915 of *Lecture Notes in Computer Science*. Springer-Verlag, May 1995.

[198] T Lin. A Formal Semantics for MooZ, PhD Thesis. Technical report, DI/UFPE, Recife/PE, Brazil, 1994.

[199] R C Linger, P A Hausler, M G Pleszlioch, and A R Heruer. Using function abstraction to understand program behaviour. *IEEE Software*, January 1990.

[200] B Liskov. Data abstraction and hierarchy. In *OOPSLA '87 Conference Proceedings*, 1987.

[201] B Liskov and J Wing. Family values: A behavioral notion of subtyping. Technical Report CMU-CS-93-187, School of Computer Science, Carnegie Mellon University, 1993.

[202] C Loosley. CASE tools and repositories: The challenge of integration. In *Nord-DATA '92*. DataBase Associates, 1992.

[203] P Lupton. Promoting forward simulation. In *Z User Meeting 1990*, Workshops in Computing. Springer-Verlag, 1991.

[204] V MacDonald. The cellular concept. *Bell Sys. Tech. J.*, 58(1):15–41, 1979.

[205] B Mahony and I J Hayes. A case study in timed refinement: A central heater. In *Proceedings of 4th BCS/FACS Refinement Workshop*. Springer Verlag, January 1991.

[206] B Mahony and I J Hayes. Using continuous real functions to model timed histories. In P A Bailes, editor, *Proceedings of 6th Australian Software Engineering Conference*. Australian Computer Society, July 1991.

[207] T Maibaum and D Gabbay. *Handbook of Logic in Computer Science*. Oxford University Press, 1994.

[208] R Martil. Task analysis results. Technical Report 2487-TN-LR-1039, Lloyd's Register, 1990.

[209] I Maung. Simulation, subtyping and substitutability, September 1993. Accepted for publication in FACS journal.

[210] I Maung and J R Howse. Introducing Hyper-Z: A new approach to object orientation in Z. In *Z User Meeting 1992*, Workshops in Computing. Springer-Verlag, 1993.

[211] D May. Use of formal methods by a silicon manufacturer. In C A R Hoare, editor, *Developments in Concurrency and Communication*, chapter 4, pages 107–129. Addison-Wesley, 1990.

[212] T McCabe. A Complexity Measure. *IEEE Transactions on Software Engineering*, SE-2, Number 4:308–320, December 1976.

[213] D D McCraken and M A Jackson. Life cycle concept considered harmful. *ACM Software Engineering Notes*, pages 29–32, April 1982.

[214] J McDermid. An approach to the specification of real-time systems, York University, 1992.

[215] C McHale, S Baker, B Walsh, and A Donnelly. Synchronisation variables. Technical Report Amadeus Project report TCD-CS-94-01, University of Dublin, 1994.

[216] C B Medeiros and P Pfeffer. Object integrity using rules. In P America, editor, *ECOOP '91 Proceedings*. Springer-Verlag, 1991.

[217] S R L Meira and A L C Cavalcanti. Modular object-oriented Z specifications. In *Z User Meeting 1990*, Workshops in Computing, pages 173–192. Springer-Verlag, 1991.

[218] S R L Meira and A L C Cavalcanti. The MooZ specification language. Technical report, Universidade Federal de Pernambuco, Departamento de Informática, Recife - PE, 1992.

[219] S R L Meira, A L C Cavalcanti, J C Fernandes, and S M Holanda. An object-oriented formal specification of a distributed object-oriented programming language. Technical report, Universidade Federal de Pernambuco, Departamento de Informática, Recife - PE, 1991.

[220] S R L Meira, A L C Cavalcanti, and C S Santos. ForMooZ: An environment for formal object-oriented specification and prototyping. Technical report, Universidade Federal de Pernambuco, Departamento de Informática, Recife - PE, 1991.

[221] S R L Meira, R Motz, and J F Tepedino. A formal semantics for SQL. *Intern. J. Computer Math.*, 34:43–63, 1990.

[222] S Mellor and P Ward. *Structured Development for Real-time Systems (3 Volumes)*. Yourdon Press, 1985.

[223] E Merlo, K Kontogiannis, and J F Girard. Structural and Behavioral Code Representation for Program Understanding. In *CASE '92 Proceedings*, pages 106–108. IEEE Press, 1992.

[224] B Meyer. Genericity versus inheritance. In *OOPSLA '86 Proceedings*. ACM Press, September 1986.

[225] B Meyer. *Object-Oriented Software Construction*. Prentice Hall, 1988.

[226] B Meyer. Tools for the new culture: Lessons from the design of the Eiffel libraries. *Communications of the ACM*, 33(9), September 1990.

[227] B Meyer. *Eiffel: The Language*. Prentice Hall, 1992.

[228] B Meyer. Systematic concurrent object-oriented programming. *Communications of the ACM*, 36(9):56–80, 1993.

[229] C A Middelburg. Syntax and semantics of VVSL. Technical Report Ph.D. Thesis, University of Amsterdam, September 1990.

[230] R Milne. Transforming axioms for data types into sequential programs. Technical Report 221, University of Cambridge Computer Laboratory, May 1991.

[231] R Milner. A theory of type polymorphism in programming. *Journal of Computer and System Sciences*, 17(3):348–375, 1978.

[232] R Milner. *Communication and Concurrency*. Prentice Hall, 1991.

[233] R Milner. The polyadic π-calculus: A tutorial. In M Broy, editor, *Logic and Algebra of Specification*. Springer-Verlag, 1992.

[234] Ministry of Defence. *Draft Interim Defence Standards 00-55 and 00-56*, April 1991.

[235] E F Moore. *Gedanken-experiments on Sequential Machines*. Princeton University Press, 1956.

[236] C Morgan. *Programming From Specifications*. Prentice Hall, 1990.

[237] M Moriconi. A practical approach to semantic configuration management. In *Proceedings of ACM Sigsoft 89 Conference on Software Testing, Analysis and Verification*, December 1989.

[238] B Moszkowski. *Executing Temporal Logic Programs*. Cambridge University Press, 1986.

[239] R Motz. Formal analysis of an object-oriented data model. Technical Report Master's Thesis (In Portuguese), Departamento de Informática – UFPE, 1990.

[240] M R Moulding and L E Smith. Formalising a CORE requirements model in the air traffic control domain. In *IEE Colloquium on Software in Air Traffic Control Systems – The Future*, June 1992.

[241] G J Myers. *Reliable Software Through Composite Design*. Van Nostrand Reinhold, 1975.

[242] J S Ostroff. *Temporal Logic for Real-Time Systems*. John Wiley, 1989.

[243] S Owre, J Rushby, and N Shankar. Formal verification for fault-tolerant architectures. *IEEE Transactions on Software Engineering*, To appear, 1995.

[244] D Parnas and P Clements. A rational design process: How and why to fake it. *IEEE Transactions on Software Engineering*, SE-12(2), 1986.

[245] L J Pinson and R S Wiener. *An Introduction to Object-Oriented Programming and Smalltalk.* Addison-Wesley, 1988.

[246] D Pitt and P Byers. The rest stays unchanged (concurrency and state based specification). *Formal Aspects of Computing,* to appear, 1994.

[247] A Pnueli. Applications of temporal logic to the specification and verification of reactive systems: A survey of current trends. In J de Bakker, W P de Roever, and G Rozenberg, editors, *Current Trends in Concurrency,* volume 224 of *Lecture Notes in Computer Science.* Springer-Verlag, 1986.

[248] F Polack and M Whiston. Formal methods and system analysis. In *Methods Integration Conference,* Workshops in Computing. Springer-Verlag, 1991.

[249] C Ponder and B Bush. Polymorphism considered harmful. *ACM Sigplan Notices,* 27(6), June 1992.

[250] L H Putman. A general empirical solution to the macro software sizing and estimation problem. *IEEE Transactions of Software Engineering,* SE-4 No.4:335–361, July 1987.

[251] D R Pyle. Specifying object semantics. In *Workshop on Object-Oriented Methodologies.* KBSL, 1992.

[252] D R Pyle and M Josephs. Enriching a structured method with Z. In *Methods Integration Conference,* Workshops in Computing. Springer-Verlag, 1991.

[253] D R Pyle and M Josephs. Entity-relationship models expressed in Z: A synthesis of structured and formal methods, 1991. Programming Research Group, Oxford University.

[254] Quintus Corporation, 2100 Geng Road, Palo Alto, California, 94303. *Quintus Prolog III: Interfaces and Delivery Tools, Release 3.1,* February 1991.

[255] G-H B Rafsanjani and S J Colwill. From Object-Z to C++: A structural mapping. In *Z User Meeting 1992.* Springer-Verlag, 1993.

[256] C A Richter. An assessment of structured analysis and structured design. *Software Engineering Notes,* 11(4):75–83, August 1986.

[257] B Ritchie. Proof with Mural, 1993. Rutherford Appleton Laboratory, Informatics Department, Chilton, Didcot, Oxon OX11 0QX, UK.

[258] J Robinson. The need for methods in an object-oriented environment. In *Workshop on Object-oriented Methodologies.* KBSL, 1992.

[259] W W Royce. Managing the development of large software systems: Concepts and techniques. In *Proceedings of Wescon,* August 1970.

[260] S Rudkin. Modelling Information Objects in Z. In J de Meer, editor, *International Workshop on ODP.* North Holland, 1992.

[261] J Rumbaugh, M Blaha, W Premerlani, F Eddy, and W Lorensen. *Object-Oriented Modelling and Design.* Prentice Hall, 1991.

[262] A Sampaio and S Meria. Modular extensions to Z. In *VDM and Z,* volume 428 of *Lecture Notes in Computer Science.* Springer-Verlag, 1990.

[263] C S Santos. ForMooZ: Um Ambiente Multi-usuário Baseado em Hipertexto de Suporte à Construcao de Especificacões Formais Orientadas a Objeto, 1992. Master's thesis, Universidade Federal de Pernambuco, Departamento de Informática, Recife - PE.

[264] S A Schuman and D H Pitt. Object-oriented subsystem specification. In L G Meertens, editor, *Program Specification and Transformation,* pages 313–341. North Holland, 1987.

[265] S A Schuman, D H Pitt, and P Byers. Object-oriented process specification. In *Specification and Verification of Concurrent Systems,* Workshops in Computing, pages 21–70. Springer-Verlag, 1990.

[266] S A Schuman, D H Pitt, and S G Ley. Object-oriented formal specification and behavioural refinement. Invited talk, 6th Refinement Workshop, London, 1993.

[267] L Semmens, R France, and T Docker. Integrated structured analysis and formal specification techniques. *The Computer Journal*, 35(6), 1992.

[268] A Sernadas and C Sernadas. Object certification. In *Proceedings of IS-CORE '94*, pages 198–215. Faculteit der Wiskunde en Informatica, Free University, Amsterdam, 1994.

[269] B Sheil. Power tools for programmers. In *Artificial Intelligence and Software Engineering*. Morgan Kaufmann, 1986.

[270] S Shlaer and S Mellor. *Object-Oriented Systems Analysis: Modelling the World in Data*. Yourdon Press Computing Series, 1988.

[271] S Shlaer and S Mellor. *Object Lifecycles: Modeling the World in States*. Yourdon Press Computing Series, 1992.

[272] R Shostak. The Sup-Inf method for proving Presburger formulae. *J ACM*, 24(4):529–543, 1977.

[273] G Smith. A logic for Object-Z. In *Z User Meeting '95*, Lecture Notes in Computer Science. Springer Verlag, 1995.

[274] M D Smith and D J Robson. Object oriented programming – the problems of validation. In *Proceedings of IEEE Conference on Software Maintenance*, pages 272–281, 1990.

[275] J M Spivey. *Understanding Z: A Specification Language and its Formal Semantics*. Cambridge Tracts in Theoretical Computer Science. Cambridge University Press, 1988.

[276] M Spivey. *The Z Notation: A Reference Manual*. Prentice Hall, 2nd edition, 1992.

[277] S Stepney, R Barden, and D Cooper, editors. *Object Orientation in Z*. Workshops in Computing. Springer-Verlag, 1992.

[278] P A Swatman. Using formal specification in the acquisition of information systems: Educating information systems professionals. In *Z User Meeting 1992*, Workshops in Computing. Springer-Verlag, 1993.

[279] C A Szyperski. Import is not inheritance - why we need both: Modules and classes. In *ECOOP '92 Proceedings*, volume 615 of *Lecture Notes in Computer Science*, pages 19–32. Springer-Verlag, 1992.

[280] A S Tannenbaum. *Operating Systems: Design and Implementation*. Prentice Hall, 1987.

[281] J F Tepedino, R Motz, and S R L Meira. From model-based specifications to object-oriented prototypes - a method. Technical report, X Congresso da SBC, Vitria, Brazil, July 1990.

[282] M Thomas and C Kirkwood. Experiences with specification and verification in LOTOS. In *Industrial-Strength Formal Specification Techniques*. IEEE Press, 1995.

[283] B Todd and R Stamper. The formal specification of diagnostic systems. Technical report, Programming Research Group, Oxford University, 1991.

[284] T H Tse and J Goguen. Functional object-oriented design. Technical report, Programming Research Group, Oxford University, 1990.

[285] M Utting and K Robinson. Towards an object-oriented refinement calculus. Technical report, University of New South Wales, 1991.

[286] P Ward. How to integrate object orientation with structured analysis and design. *IEEE Software*, pages 74–82, March 1989.

[287] R Waters. Program translation via abstraction and re-implementation. *IEEE Transactions on Software Engineering*, 14(8), August 1988.

[288] B Wegner. The object-oriented classification paradigm. In *Research Directions in Object-Oriented Programming*, pages 479–560. MIT Press, 1987.

[289] B Wegner. Concepts and paradigms of object-oriented programming. *OOPS Messenger*, 1(1):7–78, August 1990.

[290] P Whysall and J McDermid. An approach to object-oriented specification using Z. In *Z User Meeting 1990*, Workshops in Computing. Springer-Verlag, 1991.

[291] R Wieringa, W de Jonge, and P Spruit. Roles and dynamic subclasses: A model logic approach. Technical Report IS-CORE report, Faculty of Mathematics and Computer Science, Vrije Universiteit Amsterdam, 1993.

[292] N Wilde and R Huitt. Maintenance support for object-oriented programs. In *Proceedings of Conference on Software Maintenance*. IEEE Computer Society Press, 1991.

[293] A Wills. Capsules and types in Fresco: Program verification in Smalltalk. In P America, editor, *ECOOP '91 Proceedings*, volume 512 of *Lecture Notes in Computer Science*, pages 59–76. Springer-Verlag, 1991.

[294] A Wills. Formal specification of object-oriented programs, 1992. Ph.D. Thesis, University of Manchester, UK.

[295] A Wills. Specification in Fresco. In S Stepney, R Barden, and D Cooper, editors, *Object Orientation in Z*. Springer-Verlag, 1992.

[296] J Wing. A study of 12 specifications of the library problem. *IEEE Software*, pages 66–76, July 1988.

[297] R J Wirfs-Brock and R E Johnson. Surveying current research in object-oriented design. *Communications of the ACM*, September 1990.

[298] K Won. On unifying relational and object-oriented database systems. In *ECOOP '92 Proceedings*, volume 615 of *Lecture Notes in Computer Science*, pages 1–18. Springer-Verlag, 1992.

[299] J Woodcock. Mathematics as a management tool: Proof rules for promotion. In *Procs. CSR 6th Annual Conference on Large Software Systems*. Elsevier, 1989.

[300] J Woodcock and S Brien. W: A logic for Z. Technical report, Programming Research Group, Oxford University, 1991.

[301] J Woodcock and M Loomes. *Software Engineering Mathematics*. Pitman, 1988.

[302] E Yourdon. *Modern Structured Analysis*. Prentice Hall, 1989.

[303] E Yourdon and L L Constantine. *Structured Design*. Yourdon Press, 1979.

[304] ZIP Consortium. *Z Base Standard, Version 1.0*, 1993.

[305] H V Zuylen. *The REDO Compendium of Reverse-Engineering*. Wiley, 1993.

[306] N Zvegintov. The future of present systems. In *Software Maintenance Workshop, Centre for Software Maintenance, Durham University*, September 1990.

Appendix: Z^{++}

This appendix summarises the Z and Z^{++} notation and logic. Proofs of the results cited here can be found in the papers [170, 173, 185].

A.1 Mathematical Notation

The mathematical notation of Z and Z^{++} is based on classical set theory, and provides a variety of types of sets, sequences and functions, and operations on values of these types.

Sets   A set is the most primitive kind of structured data-type: it simply records the presence $x \in S$ or absence $x \notin S$ of an element x in a collection of elements S of the same type as x. The simplest set is the empty set $\varnothing$ or $\{\}$ which has no members. A finite set S with elements a_1, ..., a_n is written as $\{a_1, \ldots, a_n\}$.

The type of finite subsets of type T is denoted by $\mathbb{F}(T)$. For example, $\varnothing$ and $\{4, 5, 8998\}$ are elements of $\mathbb{F}(\mathbb{N})$. However the set **Primes** of prime numbers is not an element of this type, as it is infinite. The type $\mathbb{P}(T)$ is the type of arbitrary subsets of T, including infinite subsets.

The $\cup$ operation allows elements to be added to a set ($S \cup T$ contains exactly those elements which are either in S or in T or in both), whilst the $\setminus$ operation allows elements to be removed ($S \setminus T$ contains exactly those elements which are in S but not in T). Generalised union is defined as the union of all the elements of the single argument (a set). Thus

$$\bigcup \{\{1, 2, 3\}, \{44, 55, 2\}, \{3\}\} \;\; = \;\; \{1, 2, 3, 44, 55\}$$

for example. Generalised intersection $\bigcap$ is defined analogously.

Of key importance is the ability to define sets of elements which satisfy particular properties. If $\varphi(x)$ is a predicate with free variable x of type T, then the notation

$$\{x : T \mid \varphi\}$$

denotes the set of all $x \in T$ which satisfy φ. A list of variables x may be used here – the resulting set is then a relation.

Thus

$$\{x : \mathbb{N} \mid \exists y \in \mathbb{N} \bullet x = y * y\}$$

denotes the (infinite) set $\{1, 4, 9, 16, 25, \ldots\}$ of natural numbers which are perfect squares.

If we had instead written

$$\{y : \mathbb{N}; \ x : \mathbb{N} \mid x = y * y\}$$

then the result would be the relation

$$\{(1,1), \ (2,4), \ (3,9), \ldots\}$$

which gives for each number its corresponding square (note the order of the identifiers in the set comprehension here).

It is usual to use $\mathbb{F}$ rather than $\mathbb{P}$ to define the types of variables, and most constants, because actually infinite data items will not exist in executable programs.

Relations   A relation $r \in X \leftrightarrow Y$ is a set of pairs (x, y) of elements $x \in X$ and $y \in Y$.

For relations, there is a notion of relational image (this also exists for functions, because functions are a special form of relation). This is denoted by $r(\!| \ |\!)$ and for r as above has the type:

$$r(\!| \ |\!) \in \mathbb{P}(X) \rightarrow Y$$

It is defined by:

$$r(\!| \ S \ |\!) \ = \ \{y : Y \mid \exists x \bullet x \in S \wedge (x, y) \in r\}$$

That is, $r(\!| \ S \ |\!)$ consists of all those elements in Y which are related by r to some element of S. Thus for the perfect square relation, $r(\!| \ \{2, 3\} \ |\!) \ = \ \{4, 9\}$.

The *domain* of a relation r is the set of elements

$$\mathrm{dom}(r) \ = \ \{x : X \mid \exists y \bullet y \in Y \wedge (x, y) \in r\}$$

whilst the *range* is the set

$$\mathrm{ran}(r) \ = \ \{y : Y \mid \exists x \bullet x \in X \wedge (x, y) \in r\}$$

r is then also a relation with the typing

$$r \in \mathrm{dom}(r) \leftrightarrow \mathrm{ran}(r)$$

Relational overriding $\oplus$ is an important operator that will be used in many specifications involving functions. Informally, if

$$f \in X \leftrightarrow Y \ \wedge$$
$$g \in X \leftrightarrow Y$$

then $f \oplus g$ denotes the set of pairs $x \mapsto y$ which are either in g, or which are in f and for which there is no pair of the form $x \mapsto z$ in g.

Thus g "overrides" the relations between elements given by f. Formally, overriding is defined by:

$$f \oplus g = \{x : X; \; y : Y \mid x \in \text{dom}(f) \cup \text{dom}(g) \; \wedge$$
$$(x \in \text{dom}(g) \wedge (x \mapsto y) \in g) \; \vee$$
$$(x \notin \text{dom}(g) \wedge (x \mapsto y) \in f)\}$$

Relational composition is used to describe the effect of performing one operation after another, when both are abstractly described in terms of relationships between pre and post states. If $r : X \leftrightarrow Y$ and $s : Y \leftrightarrow Z$, then $r \, \S \, s$ is of type $X \leftrightarrow Z$ and is defined by:

$$r \, \S \, s = \{x : X; \; y : Y; \; z : Z \mid (x,y) \in r \wedge (y,z) \in s \bullet (x,z)\}$$

Other operators which we have used are range and domain restriction and anti-restriction. Let $r \in X \leftrightarrow Y$ and $S \subseteq X$. Then

$$S \lhd r = \{x : X; \; y : Y \mid (x,y) \in r \wedge x \in S\}$$

produces a "subrelation" of r which only includes those pairs whose source is in S. Similarly:

$$S \lhd\!\!\!- r = \{x : X; \; y : Y \mid (x,y) \in r \wedge x \notin S\}$$

only includes those pairs whose source is *not* in S.

Let $R \subseteq Y$, then we have the corresponding operators on the range of r:

$$r \rhd R = \{x : X; \; y : Y \mid (x,y) \in r \wedge y \in R\}$$
$$r \rhd\!\!\!- R = \{x : X; \; y : Y \mid (x,y) \in r \wedge y \notin R\}$$

Functions A relation $r \in X \leftrightarrow Y$ is a function if for every $x \in X$ there is at most one $y \in Y$ such that $(x,y) \in r$. Formally:

$$\forall x : X \bullet \#r(\!|\{x\}|\!) \leq 1$$

Its typing can then be given as

$$r \in X \nrightarrow Y$$

If in addition we know that

$$\forall x : X \bullet \#r(\!|\{x\}|\!) = 1$$

(for every x in X there is a *unique* y in Y such that $x \mapsto y$ is in r) then we can write

$$r \in X \rightarrow Y$$

All set and relation operators apply to functions as special cases. Consider the function

$$\mathbf{f} = \{1 \mapsto 2, 2 \mapsto 3, 3 \mapsto 5\}$$

This could be part of an explicit enumeration of the prime numbers. **f** is a set (of pairs):

$$\mathbf{f} = \{(1, 2), (2, 3), (3, 5)\}$$

and $\#\mathbf{f} = 3$. **f** is also a partial function of the type

$$\mathbb{N} \nrightarrow \mathbb{N}$$

with domain

$$\mathrm{dom}(\mathbf{f}) = \{1, 2, 3\}$$

and range

$$\mathrm{ran}(\mathbf{f}) = \{2, 3, 5\}$$

It is a relation between natural numbers:

$$\mathbf{f} \in \mathbb{N} \leftrightarrow \mathbb{N}$$

f is a total function on its domain:

$$\mathbf{f} \in 1 \mathinner{.\,.} 3 \rightarrow \mathbb{N}$$

where $\mathbf{a} \mathinner{.\,.} \mathbf{b}$ for $\mathbf{a}, \mathbf{b} \in \mathbb{N}$ denotes the contiguous interval of natural numbers $\mathbf{a}, \mathbf{a} + 1, \ldots, \mathbf{b}$ between **a** and **b**.

Specialised types of functions are denoted by variations on the $\rightarrow$ symbol:

$$\mathbf{S} \nrightarrow\!\!\!\!\rightarrow \mathbf{T}$$

denotes the type of *finite* partial functions from **S** to **T**.

$$\mathbf{S} \rightarrowtail \mathbf{T}$$

denotes the set of total *injective* functions from **S** to **T**, where **f** is injective if $\mathbf{x} \neq \mathbf{z} \;\Rightarrow\; \mathbf{f}(\mathbf{x}) \neq \mathbf{f}(\mathbf{z})$ for all $\mathbf{x}, \mathbf{z}$ in $\mathrm{dom}(\mathbf{f})$.

$$\mathbf{S} \rightarrowtail\!\!\!\!\!\!\nrightarrow \mathbf{T}$$

is the set of partial injective functions.

Sequences   In Z, sequences are regarded as finite functions whose domain is of the form $1 \mathrel{..} x$ for some natural number x. Thus:

$$\mathrm{seq}(T) \;=\; \{f : \mathbb{N} \nrightarrow T \mid \exists\, n : \mathbb{N} \bullet \mathrm{dom}(f) = 1 \mathrel{..} n\}$$

A sequence $\{1 \mapsto s_1, 2 \mapsto s_2, \ldots, n \mapsto s_n\}$ is more concisely written as $\langle s_1, s_2, \ldots, s_n \rangle$.

An important operation on sequences is concatenation: $s \frown t$ is the sequence whose first $\#s$ elements are those of s, in the order given in s, and whose last $\#t$ elements are those of t in the order given in t – these are all the elements of $s \frown t$.

Thus $\langle 2, 3 \rangle \frown \langle 4, 6, 0 \rangle$ is $\langle 2, 3, 4, 6, 0 \rangle$, for example.

The first element of a non-empty sequence s is given by $\mathbf{head}(s) = s(1)$. The sequence of all elements except the first is given by $\mathbf{tail}(s)$, whilst the last element $s(\#s)$ is given by $\mathbf{last}(s)$.

Notice that the example function f given above is a sequence:

$$f \in \mathrm{seq}(\mathbb{N})$$

and can be written as

$$\langle 2, 3, 5 \rangle$$

For $ss, tt : \mathrm{seq}(X)$, $ss \ll tt$ denotes that ss is a prefix of tt, ie: tt restricted to the domain $1 \mathrel{..} \#ss$ is just ss. For example, $\langle 3, 5 \rangle \ll \langle 3, 5, 7, 88 \rangle$.

A.2   Z Notation

Only a subset of the Z specification notation is included in Z^{++}. This subset includes all the type and constant definition mechanisms of Z, although use of the schema calculus and schema types is discouraged (schema types may usually be replaced by class types).

The inbuilt Z types are $\mathbb{N}$, natural numbers, $\mathbb{N}_1$, the non-zero natural numbers, and $\mathbb{Z}$ (integers). In this book we will also use the real numbers $\mathbb{R}$.

A type definition

[**TYPE**]

defines **TYPE** as a "given" set, with no inherent structure, except that it is countably infinite.

A "free type" definition provides a general means to define recursive types (which can preferably be defined using recursive classes) or finite "enumerated sets" via the notation

TYPE ::= $\mathrm{elem}_1 \mid \ldots \mid \mathrm{elem}_n$

This defines **TYPE** to have just the listed elements, and these identifiers then denote fixed distinct values in this type.

Abbreviation types are defined via the notation

TYPE == DEF

where **DEF** is a type expression possibly involving previously defined type identifiers, inbuilt types, or applications of type constructors ($\mathbb{P}$, $\mathbb{F}$, $\times$, $\rightarrow$, etc) to such types.

Thus the definition

TYPE $==$ $(\mathbb{N} \rightarrow \textbf{WORD}) \times (\textbf{WORD} \rightarrow \mathbb{F}(\textbf{WORD}))$

defines **TYPE** as the type of pairs $(\mathbf{a}, \mathbf{b})$ where $\mathbf{a}$ is a total function from natural numbers to the type **WORD**, and $\mathbf{b}$ is a total function from **WORD** to finite sets of elements of **WORD**.

Schema types **S** are defined via the notation

$$
\begin{array}{|l}
\underline{\textbf{S}} \\
\textbf{att}_1 : \textbf{T}_1; \\
\dots \\
\textbf{att}_n : \textbf{T}_n \\
\hline
\chi(\textbf{att}_1, \dots, \textbf{att}_n) \\
\end{array}
$$

They provide a static equivalent of a class type

```
CLASS S
OWNS
  att₁ :  T₁;
  ...
  attₙ :  Tₙ
INVARIANT
  χ(att₁,  ...,  attₙ)
END CLASS
```

A.3 Z++ Specification Notation

A.3.1 Z++ Syntax

A Z++ specification consists of a collection of *class* definitions, including generic classes. A schematic Z++ class is of the form:

```
CLASS   C[TypeParameters]
EXTENDS Ancestors
TYPES
   Tdefs
FUNCTIONS
   Axdefs
OWNS
   c
```

```
INVARIANT
  Inv_C
OPERATIONS
  [*] m : IN_m  →  OUT_m;
  ....
RETURNS
  r : IN_r  →  OUT_r;
  ....
ACTIONS
  Pre_{m,C} &
        [*] m x? y!  ==>   Def_{m,C};
  ....
HISTORY  H_C
END CLASS
```

Each of the clauses in the body of a class definition are optional, although an ACTIONS clause requires an OPERATIONS clause. The **TypeParameters** are a list (possibly empty) of *generic* type parameters used in the class definition. A parameter **X** can be required to be a descendent of a class **A** via the notation $A \ll X$ here. The **EXTENDS** list is the set of previously defined classes that are inherited by this class. The **TYPES** clause contains a list of Z style type declarations: classes can be used as types in this clause. c contains attribute declarations, in the style of variable declarations in Z. The **FUNCTIONS** clause contains a list of Z style axiomatic definitions of constants. Again, classes can be used as types in this clause and in the following clauses. The **OPERATIONS** list declares the types of the operations, as functions from a sequence of input domains to an output domain. The **RETURNS** list defines those attributes and functions of the internal state that are externally visible; these are operations with no side-effect on the state. The **INVARIANT** gives a predicate that specifies the properties of the internal state which must hold at any time point where the object is interacting with other objects or external agents. The default invariant (ie, if this clause is omitted) is **true**.

The **ACTIONS** list gives the definitions of the various operations that can be performed on instances of the object. The default action for a method, if no action for it is listed, is the completely non-deterministic operation on the state of the class and its parameter types. Input parameters are listed before the output parameters in the action definitions. Z predicates, method invocations and the B0 procedural code constructs of Abrial's B Notation [3] can be used to define methods. Operations are given explicit preconditions by the notations

$$\text{Pre}_{m,C} \text{ \& } \qquad\qquad\qquad\qquad \text{m x y ==>}$$
$$\quad\text{m x y ==> } \text{Def}_{m,C} \qquad \text{or} \qquad \text{PRE } \text{Pre}_{m,C} \text{ THEN } \text{Def}_{m,C} \text{ END}$$

The default precondition is **true**. Methods with a preceding * are *internal actions* and are discussed further below. The HISTORY of a class is an RTL predicate, the forms of which are given in Section A.4.

The following Z schemas are implicitly defined by this declaration:

$$
\begin{array}{|l}
\underline{\text{State}_C}\\
\quad c\\
\hline
\quad \text{Inv}_C\\
\end{array}
$$

for the state of the class, and for each method m of the class:

$$
\begin{array}{|l}
\underline{\text{In}_m}\\
\quad x : IN_m\\
\end{array}
$$

$$
\begin{array}{|l}
\underline{\text{Out}_m}\\
\quad y : OUT_m\\
\end{array}
$$

In these last two schemas, variables and types are listed in pairs in the conventional Z style.

$\text{Pre}_{m,C}$ is a predicate on the (pre) state of the class and the input parameters only.

$$
\begin{array}{|l}
\underline{\text{SPre}_{m,C}}\\
\quad \text{State}_C;\\
\quad \text{In}_m\\
\hline
\quad \text{Pre}_{m,C}\\
\end{array}
$$

Outside of this precondition, the execution of m may have an arbitrary behaviour within the state and operation typing constraints.

$$
\begin{array}{|l}
\underline{\text{Schema}_{m,C}}\\
\quad \Delta\text{State}_C\\
\quad \Delta\text{SupplierInstances}_{m,C}\\
\quad \Xi\text{NonSupplierInstances}_{m,C}\\
\quad \text{In}_m\\
\quad \text{Out}_m\\
\hline
\quad \text{Def}_{m,C}\\
\end{array}
$$

$\text{SupplierInstances}_{m,C}$ is the collection of all Instances_S schemas (see below) where an instance of S is used in a method invocation in $\text{Def}_{m,C}$. $\text{NonSupplierInstances}_{m,C}$ is the collection of specification class instance schemas for other classes of the specification.

Callbacks are forbidden, that is, a method m cannot be defined in terms of itself, whether directly or via an intermediate chain of methods. $\text{Def}_{m,C}$ is assumed to be expanded with the implicit equalities $v' = v$ for each state variable v such that v' does not occur in the explicit text of $\text{Def}_{m,C}$, and identities $\Xi\text{Instances}_T$ where appropriate.

In the predicate of this schema, method applications are treated as Z schema predicates.

The notation

$$C \sqsubseteq_{\phi,R}^{ref} D$$

denotes that **C** is refined by (is an abstraction of) **D**, via a renaming of methods ϕ and a data refinement relation **R** on the combined state **State$_C$; State$_D$** of the two classes. The notation **C** $\sqsubseteq_{\phi,R}$ **D** indicates that **C** is a supertype of **D** via these items. An inheritance does not automatically produce a subtyping relation: suitable $\sqsubseteq$ assertions must be explicitly included in a specification text if it is desired to exploit operation or attribute polymorphism between two classes. These assertions require proof in general.

In order to represent object identity the sets of potential and existing objects for each class need to be differentiated. For each class **C** is defined, in the semantics of the language, a given set:

[@**C**]

This represents the set of all possible objects of the class. The following schema encapsulates the set $\overline{C}$ of existing objects of **C**, and a dereference map $*_C$ which obtains object values from object identities:

$$
\begin{array}{|l}
\hline
\text{\textbf{Instances}}_C \\\hline
*_C : @\mathbf{C} \nrightarrow \mathbf{State}_C \\
\overline{C} : \mathbb{P}(@\mathbf{C}) \\\hline
\overline{C} = \mathrm{dom}(*_C) \\\hline
\end{array}
$$

A.3.2 Access to Supplier Attributes in a Client Class

In conventional object-oriented development, the attributes of a class are considered to be private to that class, and not available to client classes. The reason for this restriction is that direct reference increases the dependence or coupling between the client and supplier, so that changes to the internal data representation of the supplier will directly impact on the client code.

In a formal specification however such references may be regarded as legitimate, provided the client **C** is only referring to the *abstract specification* **S** of the supplier class, rather than its implementation. **S** represents a particular mathematical model of the subsystem it specifies, and its attributes may be implemented by significantly more complex data structures in further refinement steps. Such implementations may be changed without affecting the text of the abstract specification or the validity of clients **C** of **S**.

The prime advantage of direct reference to supplier attributes is that it allows a more abstract specification style (compare the two versions of the **total_salary** method of **WorkingPerson** given in Chapter 6). This helps to avoid assumptions about the interfaces of classes at a premature stage. In general such access should only be allowed if **S** is an abstract specification class, ie, the starting point of a refinement path to code.

Furthermore, in a situation where different objects need to be synchronised for a system operation to take place, there is sometimes no natural way of avoiding such access. For example, if a system involves control of a set of machine tools, which drill holes in pieces of metal when these are correctly positioned on their corresponding belts, then the drill controller will need access to attributes (sensors) of belts which identify the location of pieces:

```
class Drill
types
  DState  = < drilling >  |  < extended >  |  < retracted >
instance variables
  dstate :  DState;
init objectstate ==    dstate  = < retracted >
methods
  extend()  ==
      [ext wr dstate
       post dstate  = < extended >];

  drill()  ==
      [ext wr dstate
       post dstate  = < drilling >];

  ⋮

sync
  per extend   ⇒   dstate  = < retracted >;
  per drill    ⇒   dstate  = < extended >;

  ⋮

end Drill


class Belt
types
  BState  = < positioned >  |  < unpositioned >
instance variables
  bstate :  BState;
init objectstate ==    bstate  = < unpositioned >
methods
  ⋮

end Belt


class Controller
instance variables
  drills :  seq(@Drill);
  belts :  seq(@Belt);
  i :  ℕ₁;
```

```
inv objectstate ==   i ≤  len(drills) ∧
                     i  =  len(belts)
methods
  drill_piece(ind :  N₁)
      pre ind ≤  len(drills)   ==
          [ext wr i
            post i  =  ind];

  ⋮

sync
  per drill_piece(i)   ⇒
              drills(i).dstate  = < retracted > ∧
              belts(i).bstate  = < positioned >
thread
  while true
  do
    sel
      answer drill_piece ->
                    (belts(i)!halt();
                      drills(i)!extend();
                      drills(i)!drill()),

      ⋮

end Controller
```

(In the current version of VDM++ we cannot refer to parameters of a method in a permission statement or select clause guard condition.)

In VDM++ we can sometimes avoid this problem by using inheritance or indexed inheritance to make the attributes of aggregation components such as drills or belts attributes of the overall aggregation (the controller).

Thus **Controller** could be written as:

```
class Controller
  is subclass of Drill[1, ..., 5],  Belt[1, ..., 5]
instance variables
  i :  N₁;
inv objectstate ==   i ≤  5
methods
  drill_piece(ind :  N₁)
      pre ind ≤  5   ==
          [ext wr i
            post i  =  ind];

  ⋮


sync
  per drill_piece(i)   ⇒
              Drill[i]'dstate  = < retracted > ∧
              Belt[i]'bstate  = < positioned >
thread
```

```
  while true
  do
    sel
      answer drill_piece ->
                (self!Belt[i]'halt();
                 self!Drill[i]'extend();
                 self!Drill[i]'drill()),
      ⋮
end Controller
```

This approach cannot however be used if the components were not part of an aggregation, but could be dynamically added and removed (eg, in a train control system, where part of the synchronisation between the trains and the station is achieved by onboard software, and where trains continually leave and enter the subsystem).

A.3.3   Weakest Precondition Calculus

A predicate **S** over pre and post-state variables of a class can be given a weakest precondition semantics in the usual way. Here we will consider two alternative definitions, [ ], which regards attributes **att** which do not occur in the form **att′** in **S** as being not determined by **S**, and [ ]= which regards such attributes as being left unchanged by **S**.
   We have:

$$[S]\varphi \ \equiv \ \forall\, c' \bullet S \Rightarrow \varphi[v'/v]$$

where it is assumed that φ is a predicate over undecorated versions **v** of the attributes of **C**. $\varphi[e/v]$ denotes substitution of **e** for the identifier **v** in φ.
   In contrast:

$$[S]_=\varphi \ \equiv \ \forall\, b' \bullet S \Rightarrow \varphi[u'/u]$$

where **u** is the sublist of attributes of **C** which occur in post-decorated form in **S**, and **b** is the corresponding sub-declaration of **c**.
   To illustrate the difference, consider the following class:

```
CLASS C
OWNS
  x, y : ℕ
OPERATIONS
  inc : →;
  inc2 : →;
  trans : →
ACTIONS
  inc ==>
        x' = x + 360;
```

```
inc2  ==>
        IF  y  >  x
        THEN
                inc
        ELSE
                x'  =  y
        END;


trans  ==>
        x'  =  y'
```

END CLASS

In a client **D** of an object **a** of this class we might have operations

```
use1  ==>
        a.inc  ∧  z'  =  z + 1;

use2  ==>
        a.inc  ∧  a.trans;

use3  ==>
        BEGIN
                a.inc
        END;

use4  ==>
        IF  z  >  12
        THEN
                a.inc2
        END
```

Where **D** contains the attributes **a** : **C** and **z** : ℕ only.

In **C** the use of **inc** in **inc2** is in a procedural context so $[\ ]_=$ is used to evaluate its semantics. In other words the interpretation $x' = x + 360 \wedge y' = y$ of **inc** is taken, and the meaning of **inc2** as a predicate is

$$(y > x \Rightarrow x' = x + 360 \wedge y' = y) \wedge$$
$$(y \leq x \Rightarrow x' = y \wedge y' = y)$$

which is also its meaning in a procedural context.

Formally

$$[\text{IF } \mathbf{E} \text{ THEN } \mathbf{C}_1 \text{ ELSE } \mathbf{C}_2 \text{ END}]\varphi \equiv$$
$$(\mathbf{E} \Rightarrow [\mathbf{C}_1]_=\varphi) \wedge (\neg\, \mathbf{E} \Rightarrow [\mathbf{C}_2]_=\varphi)$$

and similarly for all other code-like operation constructors.

$[\ ]_=$ for such constructors has the same definition.

Method applications in a client class are given a procedural and declarative weakest precondition interpretation as follows.

$$[\mathbf{a.m(e)}]\varphi \equiv$$
$$\forall \mathbf{Instances'_C};\ \mathbf{State'_C};\ z' : \mathbf{Z}\ |$$
$$*'_C(\mathbf{a}) = \theta\mathbf{State'_C} \wedge \mathbf{Def_{m,C}}[e/x] \bullet \varphi[*'_C/*_C, \overline{C}'/\overline{C}, z'/z]$$

where $\mathbf{a}$ is an identifier, $\mathbf{a} \in \overline{C}$, $\mathbf{m}$ is a method of $\mathbf{C}$, this invocation occurs in a client $\mathbf{D}$ of $\mathbf{C}$, and z is the tuple of the remaining attributes of $\mathbf{D}$. In other words, the call is effectively an assignment

$$*'_C(\mathbf{a}) = \theta\mathbf{State'_C} \wedge$$
$$z' = z$$

where $\mathbf{State'_C}$ satisfies the properties of $\mathbf{Def_{m,C}}[e/x]$.

$[\mathbf{a.m(e)}]_=$ is defined similarly, but with implicit equalities on attributes $\mathbf{att}$ of $\mathbf{C}$ not referred to in the form $\mathbf{att'}$ in $\mathbf{Def_{m,C}}$ added.

Notice that no constraints are specified on the value of $*_C(\mathbf{b})$ for $\mathbf{b} \neq \mathbf{a}$. Reasoning about changes in $*_C$ must make use of the global frame axiom in general, which states that in an interval over which methods of $\mathbf{C}$ are executing on objects in a set $\mathbf{aset}$ only, the value of $*_C$ on $\overline{C} \setminus \mathbf{aset}$ does not change.

We can now analyse the semantics of the use3 method in $\mathbf{D}$, with the quantifiers used in $[\ ]_=$ also ranging over $z : \mathbb{N}$ in $\mathbf{D}$. Thus it has the denotation

$$\mathbf{a'.x} = \mathbf{a.x} + 360 \wedge z' = z \wedge \mathbf{a'.y} = \mathbf{a.y}$$

In contrast the use of **inc** in use1 and use2 is in a declarative context, so that

$$[\mathbf{use1}]\varphi \equiv$$
$$\forall \mathbf{Instances'_C};\ \mathbf{State'_C};\ z' : \mathbb{N}\ |$$
$$z' = z + 1 \wedge x' = x + 360 \wedge *'_C(\mathbf{a}) = \theta\mathbf{State'_C} \bullet$$
$$\varphi[*'_C/*_C, \overline{C}'/\overline{C}, z'/z]$$

which does not constrain $\mathbf{a'.y}$ except by typing.

An example of the utility of such an interpretation is given in use2, where changes to disjoint parts of the state of $\mathbf{a}$ are performed in two separate operations and then combined to form an operation on the complete state of $\mathbf{a}$. (Note that **trans** itself is a non-deterministic re-assignment of both x and y, constrained only by typing and the equality of the two attributes at termination of the operation.)

The interpretation of **use1** in a procedural context would adjoin the additional constraint $\mathbf{a'.y} = \mathbf{a.y}$.

In a refinement of $\mathbf{C}$ we could have:

```
CLASS C_1
OWNS
  x, y : N
OPERATIONS
```

```
    inc : →;
    inc2 : →;
    trans : →
ACTIONS
  inc ==>
        BEGIN
                x := x + 360
        END;

  inc2 ==>
        IF y > x
        THEN
                inc
        ELSE
                x := y
        END;

  trans ==>
        BEGIN
                y := x
        END

END CLASS
```

These operations can now no longer be used as predicates, but only in a procedural context. It is clear that they do procedurally refine the corresponding specification operations, and are strictly more deterministic than these operations. Note that refinement proofs use $[\mathbf{Def_m}]_=$ for methods **m**.

Similarly for **D**:

```
  use1 ==>
        BEGIN
            a.inc;
            z := z + 1
        END;

  use2 ==>
        BEGIN
            a.inc;  a.trans
        END;

  use3 ==>
        BEGIN
                a.inc
        END;

  use4 ==>
        IF z > 12
        THEN
                a.inc2
        END
```

In **use1** we could also have used the $\|$ operator to combine two operations on disjoint sets of attributes.

For predicates **A** and **B**, $\mathbf{A} \wedge \mathbf{B}$ is procedurally refined by $\mathbf{A} \ \| \ \mathbf{B}$, provided they modify distinct sets of data, because:

$$\neg \, [\mathbf{A} \ \| \ \mathbf{B}]_= \neg \, (\mathbf{x}' = \mathbf{x} \wedge \mathbf{y}' = \mathbf{y} \wedge \mathbf{z}' = \mathbf{z}) \ \equiv$$
$$\neg \, [\mathbf{A}]_= \neg \, (\mathbf{x}' = \mathbf{x} \wedge \mathbf{z}' = \mathbf{z}) \ \wedge$$
$$\neg \, [\mathbf{B}]_= \neg \, (\mathbf{y}' = \mathbf{y} \wedge \mathbf{z}' = \mathbf{z})$$

where **x** is the tuple of variables explicitly modified by **A**, **y** those variables explicitly modified by **B**, and **z** the remaining set of variables in scope in either predicate. This is then

$$(\exists \mathbf{x}'' : \mathbf{X} \bullet \mathbf{A}[\mathbf{x}''/\mathbf{x}'] \wedge \mathbf{x}' = \mathbf{x}'' \wedge \mathbf{z}' = \mathbf{z}) \ \wedge$$
$$(\exists \mathbf{y}'' : \mathbf{Y} \bullet \mathbf{B}[\mathbf{y}''/\mathbf{y}'] \wedge \mathbf{y}' = \mathbf{y}'' \wedge \mathbf{z}' = \mathbf{z})$$

However the definition of $[\mathbf{A} \wedge \mathbf{B}]_=$ means that

$$\neg \, [\mathbf{A} \wedge \mathbf{B}]_= \neg \, (\mathbf{x}' = \mathbf{x} \wedge \mathbf{y}' = \mathbf{y} \wedge \mathbf{z}' = \mathbf{z})$$

is

$$\exists \mathbf{x}'' : \mathbf{X}; \ \mathbf{y}'' : \mathbf{Y} \bullet (\mathbf{A} \wedge \mathbf{B})[\mathbf{x}''/\mathbf{x}', \mathbf{y}''/\mathbf{y}'] \wedge \mathbf{x}' = \mathbf{x}'' \wedge \mathbf{y}' = \mathbf{y}'' \wedge \mathbf{z}' = \mathbf{z}$$

which is weaker than the definition of $\neg \, [\mathbf{A} \ \| \ \mathbf{B}]_= \neg \, (\mathbf{x}' = \mathbf{x} \wedge \mathbf{y}' = \mathbf{y} \wedge \mathbf{z}' = \mathbf{z})$ as required.

For code constructs, we have the usual recursive definitions

$$[\text{IF } \mathbf{E} \text{ THEN } \mathbf{C}_1 \text{ ELSE } \mathbf{C}_2 \text{ END}]_= \varphi \ \equiv$$
$$(\mathbf{E} \Rightarrow [\mathbf{C}_1]_= \varphi) \wedge (\neg \, \mathbf{E} \Rightarrow [\mathbf{C}_2]_= \varphi)$$

$$[\text{PRE } \mathbf{E} \text{ THEN } \mathbf{C}_1 \text{ END}]_= \varphi \ \equiv$$
$$(\mathbf{E} \wedge [\mathbf{C}_1]_= \varphi)$$

$$[\text{ANY } \mathbf{v} \text{ WHERE } \mathbf{E} \text{ THEN } \mathbf{C}_1 \text{ END}]_= \varphi \ \equiv$$
$$\forall \mathbf{v} \mid \mathbf{E} \bullet [\mathbf{C}_1]_= \varphi$$

$$[\text{VAR } \mathbf{v} \text{ IN } \mathbf{C}_1 \text{ END}]_= \varphi \ \equiv$$
$$\forall \mathbf{v} \bullet [\mathbf{C}_1]_= \varphi$$

$$[\mathbf{C}_1; \ \mathbf{C}_2]_= \varphi \ \equiv \ [\mathbf{C}_1]_= [\mathbf{C}_2]_= \varphi$$

$$[\text{CHOICE } \mathbf{C}_1 \text{ OR } \mathbf{C}_2 \text{ END}]_= \varphi \ \equiv \ ([\mathbf{C}_1]_= \varphi \wedge [\mathbf{C}_2]_= \varphi)$$

$$[\text{SKIP}]_= \varphi \ \equiv \ \varphi$$

$$[\mathbf{x} := \mathbf{e}]_= \varphi \ \equiv \ \varphi[\mathbf{e}/\mathbf{v}]$$

$[\ ]$ has an identical definition except on predicates.

A.4 Z++/RTL Logic

In the following sections a description of the logic of Z++/RTL will be given. Class names will be denoted by **C**, **D**, $\mathbf{C}_1$, $\mathbf{C}_2$, etc, events by **E**, $\mathbf{E}'$, $\mathbf{E}_1$, $\mathbf{E}_2$, etc, objects by **a, b, c**, etc, general terms by e, e_1, etc, methods by **m, n, m_1, m_2**, etc, indices of events by **i, j, k**, etc, and time valued terms by **t, t_1, t_2**, etc.

A definition of the semantics of the logic, and a proof of soundness, are given in [170].

A.4.1 Logic

For each class **C** a logical RTL language $\mathcal{L}_{\mathbf{C}}$ is defined, and a theory $\Gamma_{\mathbf{C}}$ expressing the semantics of **C** in this language can be given.

Events
For each method **m** of **C** there is an associated set of events:

- $\uparrow$**m**(e), $\downarrow$**m**(e), $\rightarrow$**m**(e) for e $\in$ **IN_m**, denoting the initiation, termination and the arrival of a request at the object class of an invocation instance of **m**(e) respectively.

In addition, there are events of the form:

- φ := **true**, φ := **false** for a predicate φ without modal operators or occurrences of **now**, which denote the events of this predicate becoming true or false, respectively.

These events, together with events of the form $\leftarrow$(**n**(x1), **a**) for **a** : **S** a supplier object to **C**, and **n** a method of **S** (the sending of a request for **a** to execute **n**(x1)), are collectively referred to as **BasicEvent$_{\mathbf{C}}$**. The complete set of events of **C** also include the following:

- $\uparrow$(**n**(x1), **a**), $\downarrow$(**n**(x1), **a**), $\rightarrow$(**n**(x1), **a**) where **a** and **n** are as above;
- $\leftarrow$(**n**(x1), **a**, **b**) where both **a** and **b** are supplier objects to **C**, **a** : **S**, and **n** is a method of **S**.

The first set of events is denoted by **BasicEvent$_{\mathbf{S}}$(a)**. The complete collection of events of **C** is denoted by **Event$_{\mathbf{C}}$**.

Terms
For a given class **C**, the following terms can occur in the formulae of its RTL language:

1. variables $\mathbf{v_i}$: **i** $\in$ $\mathbb{N}$ – only variables can be quantified over;
2. attributes of the class, its ancestors and supertypes;
3. **f**($e_1, \ldots, e_n$) for an **n**-ary function symbol **f** and terms $e_1, \ldots, e_n$, and other Z expressions in terms and schema texts;
4. ♣e where e is an *event occurrence* (**E, i**), where **E** is in **Event$_{\mathbf{C}}$**;

5. **Op**(**m**(e), **i**) where **m** ∈ **methods**(C), e in the input type of **m**, **i** : $\mathbb{N}_1$ and **Op** ∈ {↑, ↓, →}, and ←((**m**(e), **a**), **i**) for a supplier object **a** : **D** and method **m** of **D**;

6. e⊛t and ◯e where e is a term, t a time-valued term – the value of e at t and at the next method execution initiation, respectively;

7. #act(**m**(e)), #fin(**m**(e)), #req(**m**(e)), #req(**m**), #fin(**m**), #act(**m**) for **m** ∈ **methods**(C);

8. **self**, **now**.

Time-valued terms are arithmetic combinations of terms of the form 4 or 5 and elements of $\mathbb{N}$. The domain **TIME** of time-valued terms is required to be a total order, that is, satisfying the axioms of a partial order together with a designated element 0 with 0 ≤ t for each element t of **TIME**, and with t < t′ ∨ t = t′ ∨ t > t′ for every pair of elements t, t′ of **TIME**. The time domain satisfies the axioms of the set of non-negative elements of a totally ordered topological ring, with addition operation + and unit 0, and multiplication operation ∗ with unit 1. $\mathbb{N} \subseteq$ **TIME** can be assumed.

Relativised versions #act(**m**(e), **a**), etc of event counters for suppliers **a** : **D** of **C** are also included, as are attributes **a**.att of such suppliers.

In addition, method names **m** from supertypes **D** of **C** can be used in its events. They will be interpreted (if unambiguous) as $\phi(\mathbf{m})$ in the semantics of the language, where **D** ⊑ $_{\phi,R}$ **C** or **D** ⊑ $_{\phi,R}^{\text{ref}}$ **C** is asserted in the specification.

Ā and ∗$_\mathbf{A}$ can be referred to, for any class **A** in the specification. This enables control over object sharing and aliasing.

void(**obj**) abbreviates ¬ (**obj** ∈ **C̄**), where **obj** :@**C**.

⊛ binds more closely than any other binary operator on terms (although the name constructor . binds more closely), but less than any unary term operator. Thus **v** ≥ #act(**m**)⊛**v** denotes **v** ≥ (#act(**m**)⊛**v**).

Formulae

For any class **C** the following are the formulae in its RTL language.

1. **P**(e$_1$, . . . , e$_\mathbf{n}$) for an **n**-ary predicate symbol **P** and terms e$_1$, . . ., e$_\mathbf{n}$;

2. $\phi \wedge \psi$, $\phi \vee \psi$, $\phi \Rightarrow \psi$, ¬ ϕ for formulae ϕ and ψ;

3. ϕ⊙t for formulae ϕ and time-valued terms t – "ϕ holds at time t";

4. ∀**SD** • ϕ, ∃**SD** • ϕ for declarations **SD** and formulae ϕ;

5. □$^r\theta$, □θ and ◯θ for formulae θ;

6. ◇$^r\theta$, ◇θ for formulae θ;

7. **enabled**(**m**) and **enabled**(**m**(e)) for methods **m**, e in the input type of **m**.

Relativised forms of the latter predicates may also be used, ie, **enabled**(**m**, **a**) for suppliers **a** of **C**.

□ϕ denotes that ϕ holds at each initiation time of a method from the class. As in the formalism of [100] it is possible to relate the different interpretations of this operator in each class, in the case of subtypes or refinements. □$^r\phi$

denotes that ϕ holds at all future times – it is not relative to **C**. $\diamond$ and $\diamond^\tau$ are the corresponding "eventually" operators.

⊚ binds more closely than $\square$, $\diamond$, $\bigcirc$, $\square^\tau$ and $\diamond^\tau$. These latter operators bind as for $\neg$.

Axioms

In addition to the axioms of classical propositional logic in this language, and the axioms of the Z mathematical toolkit, the axioms used in this book are:

(i) : $\forall i : \mathbb{N}_1 \bullet \exists j : \mathbb{N}_1 \bullet \clubsuit(\leftarrow(\mathbf{m(x)}, a, b), i) \leq \clubsuit(\rightarrow(\mathbf{m(x)}, a), j)$
(ii) : $\forall i : \mathbb{N}_1 \bullet \clubsuit(\rightarrow\mathbf{m(x)}, i) \leq \clubsuit(\uparrow\mathbf{m(x)}, i)$
(iii) : $\forall i : \mathbb{N}_1 \bullet \clubsuit(\downarrow\mathbf{m(x)}, i) \geq \clubsuit(\uparrow\mathbf{m(x)}, i)$

The first axiom states that every request for execution of $\mathbf{m(x)}$ on a originating from an object **b** eventually arrives at **a**. The second states that there cannot be more activations of $\mathbf{m(x)}$ than requests for it, at any time. Similarly the third states that there cannot be more terminations of $\mathbf{m(x)}$ than activations.

(frame) :

$$(t1 < t2 \ \wedge$$
$$\forall i : \mathbb{N}_1 \bullet \neg \, \mathbf{executing}(t1, t2, \mathbf{m}_1, i) \wedge \ldots \wedge$$
$$\neg \, \mathbf{executing}(t1, t2, \mathbf{m}_n, i)) \ \Rightarrow \ c \circledast t1 \ = \ c \circledast t2$$

where **c** is the tuple of attributes of **C**, and $\mathbf{executing}(t1, t2, \mathbf{m}, i)$ for time-valued terms $t1$ and $t2$ is the predicate:

$$\exists x : \mathbb{IN}_m \bullet t1 \leq \uparrow(\mathbf{m(x)}, i) < t2 \ \vee \ t1 < \downarrow(\mathbf{m(x)}, i) \leq t2 \ \vee$$
$$(\uparrow(\mathbf{m(x)}, i) < t1 \wedge t2 < \downarrow(\mathbf{m(x)}, i))$$

That is, $t1$ and $t2$ are either both strictly within the interval of the i-th execution of $\mathbf{m(x)}$, or the interval $[t1, t2]$ intersects a subrange of this execution. $\mathbf{m}_1, \ldots, \mathbf{m}_n$ are all the methods of **C**. This axiom expresses that attributes of **C** can only change in value if a method of **C** is currently executing – it is a form of *locality* property in the sense of [100].

It can be expressed in a more concise form closer to that of [100] by writing

$$c \circledast t1 = c \circledast t2 \ \vee \ \mathbf{cov}(\underline{\mathbf{m}_1}) \cap [t1, t2] \neq \varnothing \ \vee$$
$$\ldots \vee \ \mathbf{cov}(\underline{\mathbf{m}_n}) \cap [t1, t2] \neq \varnothing$$

where

$$\mathbf{cov}(\psi) \ = \ \bigcup \{ i : \mathbb{N}_1 \mid \overleftrightarrow{\psi, i} \}$$

the set of all times at which ψ holds, and $[t1, t2]$ is the closed interval from $t1$ to $t2$.

There is a version of this axiom which asserts that no object is modified during an interval apart from those on which methods are executing during this interval:

> **(global frame)** :
> $(t1 < t2 \wedge \text{aset} \subseteq \overline{\mathbf{A}} \wedge$
> $\qquad \neg \, \exists\, \mathbf{a} : \mathbf{A};\; \mathbf{i} : \mathbb{N}_1 \bullet \mathbf{a} \notin \text{aset} \wedge$
> $\qquad\quad \text{executing}(t1, t2, m_1, \mathbf{a}, \mathbf{i}) \wedge \ldots \wedge$
> $\qquad\qquad \text{executing}(t1, t2, m_n, \mathbf{a}, \mathbf{i})) \; \Rightarrow$
> $\qquad\qquad\qquad (\text{aset} \vartriangleleft *_{\mathbf{A}}) \circledast t2 = (\text{aset} \vartriangleleft *_{\mathbf{A}}) \circledast t1$

where $\text{executing}(t1, t2, m, \mathbf{a}, \mathbf{i})$ is $\text{executing}(t1, t2, m, \mathbf{i})$ relativised to a.

The local frame axiom restricts the subtyping relation in a way similar to that of Liskov's definition of subtyping. If it is accepted as a part of the theory $\Gamma_{\mathbf{C}}$ of a class, then we cannot prove that a class

```
class C
instance variables x : Z
methods
  inc() == x := x + 1;

  val() value Z ==
      return x
end C
```

is a supertype of

```
class D is subclass of C
methods
  dec() == x := x - 1
end D
```

because there are state changes possible for $\mathbf{d} : @\mathbf{D}$ which are not possible for any instances of $\mathbf{C}$. It may be useful instead to consider **frame** as a desirable internal consistency constraint which should be provable about a class, but which is not included in the theory of the class. It can also be weakened to consider only *observable* changes in the state attributes.

> $\textbf{(iv)}: \quad \forall\, \mathbf{i}, \mathbf{j} : \mathbb{N}_1 \bullet \mathbf{i} \le \mathbf{j} \Rightarrow \clubsuit(\mathbf{E}, \mathbf{i}) \le \clubsuit(\mathbf{E}, \mathbf{j})$
> $\textbf{(v)}: \quad \forall\, t_1, t_2 : \textbf{TIME} \mid$
> $\qquad\quad (\text{self} \in \overline{\mathbf{C}}) \circledast t_1 \wedge (\text{self} \in \overline{\mathbf{C}}) \circledast t_2 \bullet$
> $\qquad\qquad \neg\, \exists\, t_3 : \textbf{TIME} \mid t_1 < t_3 < t_2 \bullet (\text{self} \notin \overline{\mathbf{C}}) \circledast t_3$

for $\mathbf{E} \in \textbf{BasicEvent}_{\mathbf{C}}$. (v) states that "objects have continuous lives"

> $\textbf{(vi)}: \qquad \square^\tau (\#\textbf{fin}(m) \le \#\textbf{act}(m) \le \#\textbf{req}(m))$
> $\qquad\quad \forall\, \mathbf{i} : \mathbb{N}_1 \bullet (\#\textbf{req}(m)) \circledast \clubsuit(\rightarrow m, \mathbf{i}) \ge \mathbf{i}$
> $\qquad\qquad (\#\textbf{act}(m)) \circledast \clubsuit(\uparrow m, \mathbf{i}) \ge \mathbf{i}$
> $\qquad\qquad (\#\textbf{fin}(m)) \circledast \clubsuit(\downarrow m, \mathbf{i}) \ge \mathbf{i}$

Axiom **(iv)** asserts that event occurrences are indexed in order of their time of occurrence. Axiom **(v)** asserts that either an object never exists, or that it does exist for a contiguous interval (having once been destroyed, it can never come back into existence). Axiom (**vi**) relates the event counters and times of event occurrences.

Similarly for the **m(e)** history counters and relativised event counters. These are related to the **#act(m)** counters by axioms of the form **#act(m)** = $\sum_{e:IN_m}$ **#act(m(e))**, etc.

$$(\textbf{vii}): \quad \forall j : \mathbb{N}_1 \bullet (\textbf{m}(e),j).\textbf{x}_i \circledast \uparrow (\textbf{m}(e),j) = e_i \circledast \uparrow (\textbf{m}(e),j)$$

where e is a tuple of length $\textbf{n} \geq \textbf{i}$, **m** a method with formal input parameters $\textbf{x}_1, \ldots, \textbf{x}_n$.

$$(\textbf{viii}): \quad \forall i : \mathbb{N}_1 \bullet \phi \circledcirc \clubsuit (\phi := \textbf{true}, i) \wedge$$
$$(\neg \phi) \circledcirc \clubsuit (\phi := \textbf{false}, i)$$

There are also axiom schemas expressing the fact that there cannot be more than **i** changes in the truth value of ϕ before $\clubsuit(\phi := \textbf{false}, \textbf{i})$. In addition:

$$(\Box^\tau (\varphi \equiv \psi)) \circledcirc 0 \Rightarrow$$
$$\forall i : \mathbb{N}_1 \bullet \clubsuit(\varphi := \textbf{true}, i) = \clubsuit(\psi := \textbf{true}, i)$$

and similarly for the := **false** times.

$$(\textbf{ix}): \quad \forall i, j, k : \mathbb{N}_1 \mid j = k \circledast \clubsuit(\textbf{E}', i) \bullet$$
$$(\theta \circledcirc \clubsuit(\textbf{E}, k)) \circledcirc \clubsuit(\textbf{E}', i) \equiv \theta \circledcirc \clubsuit(\textbf{E}, j)$$

for any events **E**, **E**$'$.

$$(\textbf{x}):$$
$$\forall i : \mathbb{N}_1; \ e : \textbf{IN}_m \bullet \clubsuit(\twoheadrightarrow \textbf{m}(e), i) = \twoheadrightarrow (\textbf{m}(e), i)$$
$$\forall i : \mathbb{N}_1; \ e : \textbf{IN}_m \bullet \exists j : \mathbb{N}_1 \bullet \uparrow (\textbf{m}(e), i) = \clubsuit(\uparrow \textbf{m}(e), j)$$
$$\forall i : \mathbb{N}_1; \ e : \textbf{IN}_m \bullet \exists j : \mathbb{N}_1 \bullet \downarrow (\textbf{m}(e), i) = \clubsuit(\downarrow \textbf{m}(e), j)$$
$$\forall i : \mathbb{N}_1; \ e : \textbf{IN}_m; \ a : \textbf{X} \bullet \exists j : \mathbb{N}_1 \mid j \geq i \bullet \leftarrow ((\textbf{m}(e), a), j) =$$
$$\clubsuit(\leftarrow (\textbf{m}(e), a), i)$$

for each supplier object **a** : **X** in **C**. The duals of the last three formulae here are also needed:

$$\forall i : \mathbb{N}_1; \ e : \textbf{IN}_m \bullet \exists j : \mathbb{N}_1 \bullet \uparrow (\textbf{m}(e), j) = \clubsuit(\uparrow \textbf{m}(e), i)$$
$$\forall i : \mathbb{N}_1; \ e : \textbf{IN}_m \bullet \exists j : \mathbb{N}_1 \bullet \downarrow (\textbf{m}(e), j) = \clubsuit(\downarrow \textbf{m}(e), i)$$
$$\forall i : \mathbb{N}_1; \ e : \textbf{IN}_m; \ a : \textbf{X} \bullet \exists j : \mathbb{N}_1 \mid j \leq i \bullet \leftarrow ((\textbf{m}(e), a), i) =$$
$$\clubsuit(\leftarrow (\textbf{m}(e), a), j)$$

In the last axiom $\leftarrow((\textbf{m}(e), a), \textbf{i})$ denotes the time at which the **i**-th request for **m(e)** on **a** is sent (counting over all potential senders of such requests) and $\clubsuit(\leftarrow (\textbf{m}(e), a), \textbf{i})$ denotes the time that the **i**-th request from the *current* object is sent. Thus $\forall i : \mathbb{N}_1 \bullet \leftarrow((\textbf{m}(e), a, b), i) = \leftarrow((\textbf{m}(e), a, c), i)$ for any clients $b \neq c$ of **a**.

(**xi**) : $\forall e : \mathbf{IN_m};\ i : \mathbb{N}_1 \bullet$

$$(\mathbf{self} \in \overline{\mathbf{C}} \wedge \mathbf{Pre_{m,C}}) \odot \uparrow(\mathbf{m(e)},\mathbf{i}) \ \Rightarrow$$
$$\mathbf{Def_{m,C}}[\mathbf{v} \circledast \downarrow(\mathbf{m(e)},\mathbf{i})/\mathbf{v'}] \odot \uparrow(\mathbf{m(e)},\mathbf{i})$$

for each method **m** of **C**, defined by a predicate $\mathbf{Def_{m,C}}$, with input type $\mathbf{IN_m}$, where the appropriate versions $(\mathbf{m(e)},\mathbf{i}).\mathbf{x_j}$ of formal input or output parameters are used in $\mathbf{Pre_{m,C}}$, $\mathbf{Def_{m,C}}$. If **m** is defined using procedural code, the $[\ ]_=$ predicate transformer is used to obtain an equivalent representation as a predicate on **v** and **v'**.

(**xii**) : $\downarrow(\text{INIT},1) = \clubsuit((\mathbf{self} \in \overline{\mathbf{C}}) := \mathbf{true},1) \ \wedge$

$$\#\mathbf{act}(\text{INIT}) \leq 1$$
$$\square^\tau(\forall \mathbf{x} : \mathbf{T} \bullet \mathbf{g(x)} = (\mathbf{g(x)} \circledast \clubsuit((\mathbf{self} \in \overline{\mathbf{C}}) := \mathbf{true},1)))$$

for each constant **g** with arguments **x** of type **T**, and initialisation operation INIT. The first axiom can be weakened to $(\mathbf{xii})'$: $\clubsuit((\mathbf{self} \in \overline{\mathbf{C}}) := \mathbf{true},1) \leq \uparrow(\text{INIT},1)$ if INIT is not an internal action. In VDM++ the corresponding axiom is simply that the initial state predicate holds at object creation:

$$\mathbf{Init_C} \odot \clubsuit((\mathbf{self} \in \overline{\mathbf{C}}) := \mathbf{true},1)$$

Axioms of linear temporal logic (LTL) [247]:

(**xiii**) :

$\square\psi \Rightarrow \bigcirc\psi$	$\square(\square\psi \Rightarrow \psi)$
$\neg \bigcirc \varphi \Rightarrow \bigcirc\neg \varphi$	$\bigcirc(\varphi \Rightarrow \psi) \Rightarrow (\bigcirc\varphi \Rightarrow \bigcirc\psi)$
$\square\psi \Rightarrow \bigcirc\square\psi$	$\neg \bigcirc \mathbf{false} \Rightarrow (\bigcirc P(e) \equiv P(\bigcirc e))$
	for predicate symbols **P**.

$$\forall \mathbf{v} : \mathbf{T} \bullet \bigcirc\psi \equiv \bigcirc\forall \mathbf{v} : \mathbf{T} \bullet \psi \qquad \square(\underline{\mathbf{m}_1} \vee \ldots \vee \underline{\mathbf{m}_n})$$

where $\underline{\mathbf{methods}}(\mathbf{C}) = \{\mathbf{m}_1, \ldots, \mathbf{m}_n\}$ in the last formula. Also:

$$\square^\tau\psi \Rightarrow \square\psi \qquad \square^\tau\psi \Rightarrow \diamond^\tau\psi \qquad \diamond\psi \Rightarrow \diamond^\tau\psi$$

Note that the axiom $\square\psi \Rightarrow \diamond\psi$ need not be valid since there may not be any method activations at or after the current time. In addition, $\square\varphi$ is not equivalent to $\neg \diamond \neg \varphi$, and similarly for $\square^\tau\varphi$, because of the potential non-existence of objects at future times.

The induction scheme:

$$\phi \odot \min(\{\clubsuit(\uparrow\mathbf{m}_1,1), \ldots, \clubsuit(\uparrow\mathbf{m}_n,1)\}) \ \wedge \ \square(\phi \Rightarrow \bigcirc\phi) \ \Rightarrow \ \square\phi$$

holds for each LTL formula ϕ.

(**xiv**) :

$(\square^\tau\psi) \odot 0 \Rightarrow (\psi \odot t)$	$\neg (\psi \odot t) \equiv (\neg \psi) \odot t$
$(\psi \wedge \varphi) \odot t \equiv \psi \odot t \wedge \varphi \odot t$	$(\psi \vee \varphi) \odot t \equiv \psi \odot t \vee \varphi \odot t$
$(\psi \Rightarrow \varphi) \odot t \equiv \psi \odot t \Rightarrow \varphi \odot t$	
$(\exists \mathbf{v} : \mathbf{T} \bullet \varphi) \odot t \equiv \exists \mathbf{v} : \mathbf{T} \bullet \varphi \odot t$	
$(\forall \mathbf{v} : \mathbf{T} \bullet \varphi) \odot t \equiv \forall \mathbf{v} : \mathbf{T} \bullet \varphi \odot t$	

for any time-valued term **t** and formulae ψ and φ. In the last two formulae, **t** has no free variables.

The general inference for quantification is:

$$(\forall \mathbf{v} : \mathbf{T} \bullet \varphi) \Rightarrow \varphi[e/\mathbf{v}]$$

where e is free for the variable $\mathbf{v}$ in φ (that is, no variable free in e is bound at the locations of the substituted occurrences of $\mathbf{v}$ in φ), and such that the substitution does not introduce occurrences of attributes within modal operators in φ. Axioms of equality are:

$$e = e$$
$$e_1 = e_2 \;\Rightarrow\; (\varphi[e_1/\mathbf{v}] \equiv \varphi[e_2/\mathbf{v}])$$

where e is any term, and e_1 and e_2 are terms free for $\mathbf{v}$ in φ, which must not contain any modal operators.

$$(\Box^r(e_1 = e_2))\circledcirc 0 \;\Rightarrow\; (\varphi[e_1/\mathbf{v}] \equiv \varphi[e_2/\mathbf{v}])$$

for any formula φ, where e_1 and e_2 are terms free for $\mathbf{v}$ in φ.

$$(\mathbf{xv}): \qquad \clubsuit(\mathbf{enabled}(\mathbf{m}(e)) := \mathbf{true}, i) = \rightarrow(\mathbf{m}(e), i)$$

for internal actions, and

$$\forall i : \mathbb{N}_1; \; e : \mathbf{IN_m} \bullet \mathbf{enabled}(\mathbf{m}(e))\circledcirc\uparrow(\mathbf{m}(e), i)$$

for all methods $\mathbf{m}$ of $\mathbf{C}$.

Additional properties of terms include $(\mathbf{a}+\mathbf{b})\circledast\mathbf{t} = \mathbf{a}\circledast\mathbf{t}+\mathbf{b}\circledast\mathbf{t}$ and similarly for other arithmetic operators, for numeric terms. Obviously $\mathbf{n}\circledast t_1 = \mathbf{n}\circledast t_2$ for $\mathbf{n} \in \mathbb{Z}$ and t_1 and t_2 time-valued terms. Other Z operators also commute with $\circledast$.

Other useful properties of $\circledast$ are:

$$e\circledast t = (e\circledast \mathbf{now})\circledast t$$
$$(e\circledast t_1)\circledast t_2 = e\circledast(t_1\circledast t_2)$$

The invariant of a class is true at every method initiation and termination time:

$$(\mathbf{xvi}): \quad \Box\mathbf{Inv_C} \wedge \forall i : \mathbb{N}_1 \bullet \mathbf{Inv_C}\circledcirc\downarrow(\mathbf{m_j}, i)$$

for each method $\mathbf{m_j}$ of $\mathbf{C}$. However, the typing constraints for attributes are *always* true:

$$\Box^r(\mathbf{att} \in \mathbf{T})$$

for each attribute declaration $\mathbf{att} : \mathbf{T}$ of $\mathbf{C}$.

Axioms of the modal logic $\mathbf{S_5}$ hold:

$(\mathbf{xvii}):$

$$\Box(\Box\varphi \Rightarrow \varphi) \qquad\qquad \Box\varphi \vee \neg\,\Box\varphi$$
$$\Box(\varphi \Rightarrow \psi) \Rightarrow (\Box\varphi \Rightarrow \Box\psi) \qquad\qquad \Box\varphi \Rightarrow \Box\Box\varphi$$

The same axioms hold for $\Box^\tau$ in place of $\Box$.

$$\Box^\tau(\theta \odot t) \equiv \theta \odot t \qquad\qquad \theta \odot t \Rightarrow \Box(\theta \odot t)$$
$$\diamond^\tau(\theta \odot t) \equiv \theta \odot t \qquad\qquad \diamond(\theta \odot t) \Rightarrow \theta \odot t$$

where in the last four formulae, t is a time-valued term without free variables.

(xviii) : $\qquad \theta \odot t \equiv \theta^{*t}$

for θ without modal operators, and where θ^{*t} is θ with each (outermost) term e occurring in a subformula of θ replaced by $e \circledast t$, and t is a time-valued term without free variables. Similarly

$$g(e_1 \circledast t, \ldots, e_n \circledast t) = g(e_1, \ldots, e_n) \circledast t$$

and

$$\neg\,(\bigcirc\mathbf{false}) \;\Rightarrow\; g(\bigcirc e_1, \ldots, \bigcirc e_n) = \bigcirc g(e_1, \ldots, e_n)$$

for each constant **g**.

Additional axioms assert that @C is countably infinite for each **C**, and that $\Box^\tau(@\mathbf{C} \neq \overline{\mathbf{C}})$.

If there is a refinement or subtyping **R** asserted from **D** to **C**, then the existence of a function $@\mathbf{R} : @\mathbf{D} \rightarrow @\mathbf{C}$ can be assumed, with the properties:

$$\Box^\tau(\forall d : \overline{\mathbf{D}} \bullet \mathbf{R}(*_\mathbf{C}(@\mathbf{R}(d)), *_\mathbf{D}(d)))$$
$$\Box^\tau(\forall d : @\mathbf{D} \bullet d \in \overline{\mathbf{D}} \equiv @\mathbf{R}(d) \in \overline{\mathbf{C}})$$

In VDM^{++}, the condition of adequacy has a counterpart for @R when **R** is a refinement: we expect that

$$\forall c : \overline{\mathbf{C}} \bullet \exists d : \overline{\mathbf{D}} \bullet @\mathbf{R}(d) = c$$

holds at all times.

Inference Rules
The usual inference rules of classical logic are taken. In addition the following rule is assumed:

$$\frac{\vdash \theta}{\vdash \Box^\tau \theta}$$

Derivability in the logic is denoted by $\vdash$ as usual.

Abbreviations
$\varphi \equiv \phi$ abbreviates $(\varphi \Rightarrow \phi) \wedge (\phi \Rightarrow \varphi)$ as usual.
methods(C) abbreviates the set of methods of a class **C**, including inherited and internal methods.
$\underline{\varnothing}$ is the class

CLASS $\varnothing$
INVARIANT true
END CLASS

which is a supertype of any other class.
false$_S$ is the class

CLASS **false$_S$**
INVARIANT false
OPERATIONS
   S
HISTORY
   $\Box^r$ **false**
END CLASS

where **S** is a set of method signatures. This class is a subtype of any class with operations **S**.
classes_of(S) denotes the set of classes in a specification **S**.
#active(m) abbreviates **#act(m) − #fin(m)**, the number of currently active instances of **m**.
#waiting(m) abbreviates **#req(m) − #act(m)**, the number of instances of **m** awaiting execution.
delay(m, i) abbreviates $\uparrow(m, i)-\!\!\rightarrow(m, i)$. **duration(m, i)** abbreviates $\downarrow(m, i)-\uparrow(m, i)$.
mutex({m$_1$, ..., m$_n$}) abbreviates the assertion

$$\textbf{\#active(m}_1) \; = \; \sum_{i=1}^{n} \textbf{\#active(m}_i) \quad \vee \; ... \; \vee$$
$$\textbf{\#active(m}_n) \; = \; \sum_{i=1}^{n} \textbf{\#active(m}_i)$$

self_mutex({m$_1$, ..., m$_n$}) abbreviates the assertion

$$\textbf{\#active(m}_1) \leq 1 \; \wedge \; ... \; \wedge \; \textbf{\#active(m}_n) \leq 1$$

The conjunction of both formulae is equivalent to $\sum_{i=1}^{n} \textbf{\#active(m}_i) \leq 1$.
responsive(S) abbreviates $\forall i : \mathbb{N}_1 \bullet \textbf{delay(m}_1, i) = 0 \wedge ... \wedge \textbf{delay(m}_r, i) = 0$, where $\textbf{S} = \{\textbf{m}_1, ..., \textbf{m}_r\}$.
m abbreviates **#active(m)** > 0.

A *durative method* **m** is a method which satisfies **durative(m)**: $\forall i : \mathbb{N}_1 \bullet \downarrow(m, i) > \uparrow(m, i)$. A *durative class* is a class all of whose methods are durative. For such a class, the property $\forall i : \mathbb{N}_1 \bullet \underline{\textbf{m}} \odot \uparrow(m, i)$ holds for each method **m**.

The LTL connectives can also considered to be abbreviations, via the equivalences:

$$(\Box\phi)\odot t \; \equiv$$
$$\forall i : \mathbb{N}_1 \mid \uparrow(m_1, i) \geq t \bullet \phi \odot \uparrow(m_1, i) \; \wedge ... \wedge$$
$$\forall i : \mathbb{N}_1 \mid \uparrow(m_n, i) \geq t \bullet \phi \odot \uparrow(m_n, i)$$

where $\underline{\text{methods}}(\mathbf{C}) = \{\mathbf{m_1}, \ldots, \mathbf{m_n}\}$.

$$(\bigcirc\phi)\circledcirc\mathbf{t} \equiv$$
$$\forall \mathbf{i} : \mathbb{N}_1 \mid \uparrow(\mathbf{m_1}, \mathbf{i}) > \mathbf{t} \wedge$$
$$\text{minimal}(\mathbf{i}, \mathbf{m_1}, \{\mathbf{m_1}, \mathbf{m_2}, \ldots, \mathbf{m_n}\}, \mathbf{t}) \bullet \phi\circledcirc\uparrow(\mathbf{m_1}, \mathbf{i}) \wedge \ldots \wedge$$
$$\forall \mathbf{i} : \mathbb{N}_1 \mid \uparrow(\mathbf{m_n}, \mathbf{i}) > \mathbf{t} \wedge$$
$$\text{minimal}(\mathbf{i}, \mathbf{m_n}, \{\mathbf{m_1}, \mathbf{m_2}, \ldots, \mathbf{m_n}\}, \mathbf{t}) \bullet \phi\circledcirc\uparrow(\mathbf{m_n}, \mathbf{i})$$

Where $\text{minimal}(\mathbf{i}, \mathbf{m_n}, \{\mathbf{m_1}, \mathbf{m_2}, \ldots, \mathbf{m_n}\}, \mathbf{t})$ asserts that there is no $\mathbf{j} : \mathbb{N}_1$, $\mathbf{k} : 1 \ldots \mathbf{n}$ with $\mathbf{t} < \uparrow(\mathbf{m_k}, \mathbf{j}) < \uparrow(\mathbf{m_n}, \mathbf{i})$.

$$(\diamond\phi)\circledcirc\mathbf{t} \equiv$$
$$\exists \mathbf{i} : \mathbb{N}_1 \mid \uparrow(\mathbf{m_1}, \mathbf{i}) \geq \mathbf{t} \bullet \phi\circledcirc\uparrow(\mathbf{m_1}, \mathbf{i}) \vee \ldots \vee$$
$$\exists \mathbf{i} : \mathbb{N}_1 \mid \uparrow(\mathbf{m_n}, \mathbf{i}) \geq \mathbf{t} \bullet \phi\circledcirc\uparrow(\mathbf{m_n}, \mathbf{i})$$

It is the case that $\mathbf{S} \subseteq \mathbf{T}$ implies $\text{mutex}(\mathbf{T}) \Rightarrow \text{mutex}(\mathbf{S})$ and $\text{self\_mutex}(\mathbf{T}) \Rightarrow \text{self\_mutex}(\mathbf{S})$.

Each method definition using B AMN B0 code (together with parallel composition $|||$, object creation $\mathbf{New_C}$ and embedded method invocations) can also be interpreted as a set of RTL formulae constraining the durations, request, activation and termination times of statements. The rules of [102] are used to compute the times of basic operations. Details are in [170]. This interpretation allows code-level verification (ie, proofs of refinement) to be undertaken.

The operation construct $\bigwedge_{\mathbf{a} \in \mathbf{a\_set}} \mathbf{a}.\mathbf{m}(\mathbf{e})$ where $\mathbf{a\_set} \in \mathbb{P}(@\mathbf{C})$ for a class type $\mathbf{C}$, and $\mathbf{m}$ is a method of $\mathbf{C}$ with inputs $\mathbf{x_1}, \ldots, \mathbf{x_n}$, denotes:

$$*'_\mathbf{C} = *_\mathbf{C} \oplus \{\mathbf{a} : @\mathbf{C}; \text{Schema}_{\mathbf{m},\mathbf{C}} \mid \mathbf{x_1} = \mathbf{e_1} \wedge \ldots \wedge \mathbf{x_n} = \mathbf{e_n} \wedge$$
$$\mathbf{a} \in \mathbf{a\_set} \wedge *_\mathbf{C}(\mathbf{a}) = \theta\text{State}_\mathbf{C} \bullet \mathbf{a} \mapsto \theta\text{State}'_\mathbf{C}\}$$

In other words, the simultaneous application of $\mathbf{m}$ to every instance of $\mathbf{C}$ in a_set.

It can be shown that a version of the LTL system of Manna-Pnueli logic given in [242] is derivable from $\mathbf{Z^{++}}$/RTL logic. In addition, $\mathbf{Z^{++}}$/RTL is conservative with respect to Manna-Pnueli logic in the sense that each LTL formula derivable from $\mathbf{Z^{++}}$/RTL is valid in the semantics of Manna-Pnueli logic. An interpretation of the traces/failures model of CSP [146] can also be given in this formalism. Details are in [170].

A.4.2 Refinement and Subtyping

This section covers some more advanced issues concerning subtyping and refinement.

Decomposing Data Refinements
When we define a functional data refinement $\mathbf{R}$ between classes $\mathbf{D}$ and $\mathbf{C}$, we actually consider that for each attribute $\mathbf{att_{C,i}} : \mathbf{T_{C,i}}$ of the abstract class $\mathbf{C}$,

there is a mapping $\mathbf{R_i} : \mathbf{State_D} \to \mathbf{T_{C,i}}$ which gives the interpretation of $\mathbf{att_{C,i}}$ in terms of the attributes of $\mathbf{D}$.

Thus the notation $\varphi[\mathbf{R(v)/u}]$ which we have used to define refinement and subtyping actually denotes

$$\varphi[\mathbf{R_1(v)/att_{C,1}, R_2(v)/att_{C,2}, \ldots, R_n(v)/att_{C,n}}]$$

where $\mathbf{att_{C,1}}, \ldots, \mathbf{att_{C,n}}$ are all the attributes of $\mathbf{C}$.

As an example, consider class $\mathbf{D}$ with attributes

$$\mathbf{x, y, z} : \mathbb{N}$$

and $\mathbf{C}$ with attributes

$$\mathbf{v} : \mathbb{Z};$$
$$\mathbf{u} : \mathbb{N}$$

and relation $\mathbf{R}$ defined by:

$$\begin{array}{|l} \mathbf{R} : \mathbb{N} \times \mathbb{N} \times \mathbb{N} \to \mathbb{Z} \times \mathbb{N} \\ \hline \forall\, \mathbf{a, b, c} : \mathbb{N} \bullet \\ \qquad \mathbf{R(a, b, c)} = \mathbf{(a - c, a + b)} \end{array}$$

Then $\mathbf{R}$ can also be expressed as $\mathbf{R(a, b, c)} = \mathbf{(R_v(a, b, c), R_u(a, b, c))}$ where $\mathbf{R_v}$ and $\mathbf{R_u}$ have the obvious definitions.

If $\mathbf{C}$ then had an invariant $\mathbf{Inv_C}$ such as

$$\mathbf{u} = \mathbf{v}^2$$

we would therefore need $\mathbf{D}$ to establish the proposition

$$\mathbf{Inv_C[R_v(x, y, z)/v, R_u(x, y, z)/u]}$$

which is

$$\mathbf{(x + y)} = \mathbf{(x - z)^2}$$

Repeated Subtyping

The problem of repeated subtyping (where class $\mathbf{D}$ is a subtype of another class $\mathbf{C}$ "more than once") occurs in a specification language in a somewhat more sophisticated way than in a programming language.

It is possible for there to be two subtyping (or refinement) relationships $\mathbf{C} \sqsubseteq_{\mathbf{R_1}, \phi_1} \mathbf{D}$ and $\mathbf{C} \sqsubseteq_{\mathbf{R_2}, \phi_2} \mathbf{D}$ between the same classes, in which there is no simple relation between $\mathbf{R_1}$ and $\mathbf{R_2}$ or between ϕ_1 or ϕ_2. A very "mathematical" example could be as follows. Let $\mathbf{Monoid}$ be a class that defines the data components of a mathematical structure known as a *monoid* (a group without an identity operation):

```
CLASS Monoid
TYPES
    [MONOID]
FUNCTIONS
```

$$
\begin{array}{|l}
\mathbf{e} : \text{MONOID} \\
\mathbf{star} : \text{MONOID} \times \text{MONOID} \to \text{MONOID} \\
\hline
\forall \mathbf{x}, \mathbf{y}, \mathbf{z} : \text{MONOID} \bullet \\
\quad \mathbf{star}(\mathbf{e}, \mathbf{x}) = \mathbf{x} \ \wedge \\
\quad \mathbf{star}(\mathbf{x}, \mathbf{e}) = \mathbf{x} \ \wedge \\
\quad \mathbf{star}(\mathbf{x}, \mathbf{star}(\mathbf{y}, \mathbf{z})) = \mathbf{star}(\mathbf{star}(\mathbf{x}, \mathbf{y}), \mathbf{z})
\end{array}
$$

END CLASS

This defines an associative operator **star** which has e as its left and right identity.

As is known from elementary discrete mathematics, there are two main ways in which the set of natural numbers can be seen as such a structure: by interpreting **star** by addition, and e by 0, or by interpreting **star** by multiplication, and e by 1.

Thus if we define a class:

CLASS **Nat**
FUNCTIONS

$$
\begin{array}{|l}
\mathbf{one} : \mathbb{N} \\
\mathbf{zero} : \mathbb{N} \\
\mathbf{mult} : \mathbb{N} \times \mathbb{N} \to \mathbb{N} \\
\mathbf{add} : \mathbb{N} \times \mathbb{N} \to \mathbb{N} \\
\hline
\mathbf{one} = 1 \ \wedge \ \mathbf{zero} = 0 \\
\forall \mathbf{x}, \mathbf{y} : \mathbb{N} \bullet \\
\quad\quad\quad \mathbf{mult}(\mathbf{x}, \mathbf{y}) = \mathbf{x} * \mathbf{y} \\
\quad\quad\quad \mathbf{add}(\mathbf{x}, \mathbf{y}) = \mathbf{x} + \mathbf{y}
\end{array}
$$

END CLASS

We have two refinement relations (where **MONOID** is interpreted by $\mathbb{N}$ in both cases):

1. $\mathbf{R_1}$: **one** = e $\wedge$ **mult** = **star**;
2. $\mathbf{R_2}$: **zero** = e $\wedge$ **add** = **star**.

It is therefore not possible to consider that both $@\mathbf{R_1}$ and $@\mathbf{R_2}$ are the identity (or inclusion) mappings from $@\mathbf{Nat}$ to $@\mathbf{Monoid}$.

This subtyping also provides an example of the connection between the concept that instances are *models* (in a mathematical logic sense) of their classes (ie, of the theories of their classes), and that subtypes of a class are stronger theories which can provide an abstract interpretation of the supertype theory. Here the subtype theory **Nat** is completely determined: all models of **Nat** have identical data values, and only differ in their object identities. In contrast instances of the supertype theory **Monoid** can be wildly different, and can range in cardinality upwards from singleton groups {e} to infinite groups of arbitrary cardinality.

Properties of Statements

An important point is that the theory extension requirement for VDM^{++} and Z^{++} refinement or subtyping does not apply to predicates concerning statements used to define methods. Such statements are purely internal to a given version of a class, and only properties concerning the method duration or functionality are required to be established in further refinements.

Thus for example, we can change the way that a method is defined between two refinements or subtypes:

CLASS C
⋮
ACTIONS
  m x? y! ==>
       BEGIN
         s1; s2
       END

can be refined by

CLASS D
⋮
ACTIONS
  m x? y! ==>
       BEGIN
         s3; s4; s5
       END

provided that the functional and timing properties of **m** which follow from its definition in **C** are satisfied by its definition in **D**.

In particular, any relationships between event times derivable from **m**'s definition in **C** must be established in **D**. Thus if s1 commenced with a call **a.n** to a supplier object **a**, so must s3, if **a** is interpreted by itself in **D**.

A.4.3 Temporal Logic for Operation Specifications

It is possible to use temporal logic in place of the Z notation to specify the state transition semantics of operations, at least for mutex and durative classes. The operation specification

  m x? y! ==>
       PRE **Pre$_m$**
       THEN
            Def$_m$
       END

is interpreted as the formula **Ax$_m$**

$$\Box(\underline{m} \wedge \mathbf{Pre_m} \Rightarrow \mathbf{Def_m^{\bigcirc}})$$

where χ^O replaces each data reference of the form $\textbf{att}'$ or $\textbf{att}'.\textbf{satt}$ by $\bigcirc\textbf{att}$ and $\bigcirc\textbf{att}.\textbf{satt}$ respectively. Output attributes $\textbf{y}$ are also replaced by $\bigcirc\textbf{y}$.

This formula does not constrain the values of attributes which do not appear in the form $\textbf{att}'$ in the poststate predicate $\textbf{Def}_\textbf{m}$.

Notice that the formula $\square(\underline{\textbf{m}} \Rightarrow \textbf{Def}_\textbf{m}^O)$ where $\textbf{Def}_\textbf{m}$ involves no occurrence of an undecorated variable actually proves

$$\square^\tau(\underline{\textbf{m}} \Rightarrow \textbf{Def}_\textbf{m}^O)$$

since, if $\textbf{t}$ is any time at which $\underline{\textbf{m}}$ holds then there must be a unique most recent method initiation time $\uparrow(\textbf{m}, \textbf{i})$ of $\textbf{m}$: this holds since $\textbf{m}$ is mutex and durative because then

$$(\#\textbf{active}(\textbf{m}) = 1)\circledcirc\textbf{t}$$

and this activation of $\textbf{m}$ must be the most recent to initiate execution since otherwise there would be a time point at which $\#\textbf{active}(\textbf{m}) > 1$, a contradiction.

At $\uparrow(\textbf{m}, \textbf{i})$ the time of the next method initiation is the same as it is at $\textbf{t}$, so the result follows.

In a refinement or subtyping proof theory extension then requires that

$$\Gamma_\textbf{D} \vdash \phi(\textbf{Ax}_\textbf{m}[\textbf{R}(\textbf{v})/\textbf{u}])$$

where $C \sqsubseteq_{\phi,\textbf{R}} D$ and $\textbf{v}$ is the tuple of attributes of $\textbf{D}$, $\textbf{u}$ of $\textbf{C}$.

Ideally the corresponding axiom of $\phi(\textbf{m})$ in $\textbf{D}$ would be sufficient to establish this result:

$$\vdash \textbf{Ax}_{\phi\textbf{m}} \Rightarrow \phi(\textbf{Ax}_\textbf{m}[\textbf{R}(\textbf{v})/\textbf{u}])$$

As an example, consider the standard refinement of a set by a sequence (Figure A.1).

Then $\textbf{add\_element}$ in $\textbf{Seq}_1[\textbf{X}]$ refines $\textbf{add\_element}$ in $\textbf{Set}[\textbf{X}]$ because:

$$\square(\underline{\textbf{add\_element}} \wedge \textbf{x} \in \textbf{X} \Rightarrow \bigcirc\textbf{sq} = \textbf{sq} \frown \langle\textbf{x}\rangle) \Rightarrow$$
$$\square(\underline{\textbf{add\_element}} \wedge \textbf{x} \in \textbf{X} \Rightarrow \bigcirc\textbf{ran}(\textbf{sq}) = \textbf{ran}(\textbf{sq}) \cup \{\textbf{x}\})$$

as required. Similarly for the other operations.

A sufficient, but not necessary condition for the refinement of each operation is then

$$\square(\underline{\textbf{m}} \wedge \textbf{Pre}_{\textbf{m},\textbf{C}}[\textbf{R}(\textbf{v})/\textbf{u}] \Rightarrow \textbf{Pre}_{\textbf{D},\phi(\textbf{m})}) \wedge$$
$$\square(\underline{\textbf{m}} \wedge \textbf{Pre}_{\textbf{m},\textbf{C}}[\textbf{R}(\textbf{v})/\textbf{u}] \wedge \textbf{Def}_{\textbf{D},\phi(\textbf{m})}^O \Rightarrow \textbf{Def}_{\textbf{m},\textbf{C}}[\textbf{R}(\textbf{v})/\textbf{u}]^O)$$

In general proof tools would work with the sufficient conditions where possible, only presenting the weaker exact conditions where necessary.

```
CLASS Set[X]                        CLASS Seq₁[X]
OWNS                                OWNS
  s : 𝔽(X)                            sq : seq(X)
OPERATIONS                          OPERATIONS
  add_element : X  →;                 add_element : X  →;
  init : →;                           init : →;
  del : X →                          del : X →
RETURNS                             RETURNS
  is_in : X →                         is_in : X →
ACTIONS                             ACTIONS
  add_element x?  ==>                 add_element x?  ==>
    s' = s ∪ { x? };                   sq' = sq ⌢ ⟨ x? ⟩;
  init ==>                            init ==>
    s' = ∅;                            sq' = ⟨ ⟩;
  del x? ==>                          del x? ==>
    s' = s \ { x? };                   sq' = squash(sq ⩥ { x? });
  is_in x?  ==>                       is_in x?  ==>
    x? ∈ s                             x? ∈ ran(sq)
END CLASS                           END CLASS
```

Figure A.1: Refinement of Set by Sequence

A.4.4 Specification of Interval Relations

There are 13 basic relations between pairs of intervals on the real line [7]. These are:

1. **i before j** – interval **i** is strictly to the left of interval **j**;
2. **i meets j** – the right-hand end of interval **i** is the left-hand end of interval **j**;
3. **i overlaps j** – **i** is to the left of **j**, but the right-hand end of **i** is strictly to the right of the left-hand end of **j**;
4. **i starts j** – **i** is strictly contained in **j**, and the left-hand ends of the two intervals are the same;
5. **i finishes j** – **i** is strictly contained in **j**, and the right-hand ends of the two intervals are the same;
6. **i during j** – **i** is strictly contained in **j**, and does not start or finish **j**;
7. **i equal j** – **i** and **j** coincide.

together with the converses of 1–6.

Each of these can be formalised in RTL, in a variety of ways. Of particular interest is a means to specify the relationships between the execution intervals of two methods **m** and **n**.

If the i-th execution interval $[\uparrow(\mathbf{m}, \mathbf{i}), \downarrow(\mathbf{m}, \mathbf{i})]$ of **m** always follows the i-th execution interval of **n**, then we write **n before m** and define this by

$$\forall \mathbf{i} : \mathbb{N}_1 \bullet \downarrow(\mathbf{n}, \mathbf{i}) < \uparrow(\mathbf{m}, \mathbf{i})$$

Clearly it is transitive in the sense that

$$\text{m before n} \wedge \text{n before r} \Rightarrow \text{m before r}$$

The non-strict interval relations between method executions can be specified by a formula of the form $\Box^r \chi$, where χ only involves terms #act and #fin. The other relations can be given by:

- n meets m – $\#\text{fin}(n) = \#\text{act}(m)$;
- n overlaps m – $\forall i : \mathbb{N}_1 \bullet \uparrow(m, i) < \downarrow(n, i) \wedge \downarrow(m, i) > \downarrow(n, i) \wedge \uparrow(m, i) > \uparrow(n, i)$;
- n starts m – $\#\text{act}(n) = \#\text{act}(m) \wedge \forall i : \mathbb{N}_1 \bullet \downarrow(n, i) < \downarrow(m, i)$;
- n finishes m – $\#\text{fin}(n) = \#\text{fin}(m) \wedge \forall i : \mathbb{N}_1 \bullet \uparrow(n, i) > \uparrow(m, i)$;
- n during m – $\forall i : \mathbb{N}_1 \bullet \uparrow(n, i) > \uparrow(m, i) \wedge \downarrow(n, i) < \downarrow(m, i)$;
- n equal m – $\#\text{act}(m) = \#\text{act}(n) \wedge \#\text{fin}(m) = \#\text{fin}(n)$.

Similar types of interval relations can be specified for the intervals in which predicates are true. Thus φ before ψ means that

$$\forall i : \mathbb{N}_1 \bullet \overleftrightarrow{\varphi, i} \text{ before } \overleftrightarrow{\psi, i}$$

where $\overleftrightarrow{\phi, i}$ is the i-th interval in which a predicate ϕ is true. This interval is defined as $[\clubsuit(\phi := \text{true}, i), \clubsuit(\phi := \text{false}, i)]$ if $\phi \odot 0$, and as $[\clubsuit(\phi := \text{true}, i), \clubsuit(\phi := \text{false}, i + 1)]$ if $\neg (\phi \odot 0)$.

Thus to say that a gate is always down when a train is crossing, we could write

$$(\text{gstate} = \text{down}) \text{ covers } (\text{mstate} = \text{crossing})$$

Where **covers** is a non-strict version of **during**:

- i intersects j – i and j overlap, with i starting and finishing first;
- i covers j – the endpoints of i are contained in j.

The corresponding relations for method executions can be characterised by the formulae

$$\Box(\#\text{act}(m) \geq \#\text{fin}(n) \wedge \#\text{fin}(n) \geq \#\text{fin}(m) \wedge \#\text{act}(n) \geq \#\text{act}(m))$$

for **n intersects m**, and

$$\Box(\#\text{act}(n) \geq \#\text{act}(m) \wedge \#\text{fin}(n) \leq \#\text{fin}(m))$$

for **n covers m** respectively. In both cases these are direct reformulations of the corresponding inequalities between event times. Eg, compare with

$$\forall i : \mathbb{N}_1 \bullet \uparrow(n, i) \leq \uparrow(m, i) \wedge \downarrow(n, i) \geq \downarrow(m, i)$$

in the second case.

We have:

n intersects m $\wedge$ m intersects n $\Rightarrow$ n equals m

n covers m $\wedge$ m covers n $\Rightarrow$ n equals m

n meets m $\wedge$ m meets n $\Rightarrow$ n equals m

although in the latter case the antecedent implies that **n** and **m** are always instantaneous.

Notice also that if non-strict versions of **start** and **finish** are used:

- a begins b – #act(a) = #act(b) $\wedge$ #fin(a) $\geq$ #fin(b);
- a ends b – #fin(a) = #fin(b) $\wedge$ #act(b) $\geq$ #act(a).

then #active(a) $\leq$ #active(b) so that

self_mutex($\{b\}$) $\wedge$ a begins b $\Rightarrow$ self_mutex($\{a\}$)

and

self_mutex($\{b\}$) $\wedge$ a ends b $\Rightarrow$ self_mutex($\{a\}$)

In addition

$\underline{a}$ $\wedge$ a begins b $\Rightarrow$ $\underline{b}$

$\underline{a}$ $\wedge$ a ends b $\Rightarrow$ $\underline{b}$

Notice that for intervals we would have

i begins j $\equiv$ i equal j $\vee$ i starts j

i intersects j $\equiv$ i meets j $\vee$ i overlaps j

For predicates, φ **covers** ψ is equivalent to $\mathbf{cov}(\psi) \subseteq \mathbf{cov}(\varphi)$. Thus assertions of the form **m covers n** are useful for establishing that the frame axiom of a supertype **C** is provable from the frame axiom of a subtype **D** in which **n** is introduced as a new internal method.

Appendix: VDM++

B.1 VDM++ Mathematical Notation

The VDM++ notation for sequences, sets and functions is very similar to that of Z, and the concepts are also similar. For a more detailed explanation of the underlying VDM-SL notation used in VDM++, see [152]. Some differences from Z notation are:

- notation for sets – set comprehensions are denoted by

  {expression | binding & predicate}

  to describe the set of values of **expression** generated by the data given in **binding** that satisfies the **predicate**. As an example,

  { x | x: nat & 1 <= x and x <= 5 }

  defines the interval $1..5$. This can also be written as an interval $\{1, \ldots, 5\}$;
- notation for sequences – sequences are not considered to be special kinds of functions in VDM++, but a distinct type with their own operators. A literal sequence of elements a_1 to a_n is written in square brackets: $[a_1, \ldots, a_n]$. There is a "sequence comprehension" constructor, which has the form

  [expression | ind in set s & predicate(ind)]

  and creates a sequence **sq** of values of **expression** defined using an indexing variable **ind**. The first element of **sq** is the value **expression(i1)** where **i1** is the first value of the index set (a subset of $\mathbb{Z}$) satisfying **predicate**, etc. An example is

  [x*2 | x in set { 3, 5, 6 } & 1 <= x and x <= 5]

  which has the value $\langle 6, 10 \rangle$ (in Z notation).

The length of a sequence **sq** is denoted by **len(sq)**, its first element by **hd sq**, and the subsequence of its remaining elements by **tl sq**.

The set of elements of a sequence **sq** is denoted by **elems(sq)**, and the set of its indices by **inds(sq)**.

The notation $\mathbf{X}^*$ may be used instead of seq($\mathbf{X}$) to denote the type of sequences of $\mathbf{X}$;

- notation for pairs – instead of $(\mathbf{a}, \mathbf{b})$, $(\mathbf{a}, \mathbf{b}, \mathbf{c})$, etc, the notation $\mathbf{mk\_(a, b)}$, $\mathbf{mk\_(a, b, c)}$, etc is used;

- notation for maps – the type of (finite) partial functions from **S** to **T** is denoted by $\mathbf{S} \xrightarrow{m} \mathbf{T}$. The range of a map is denoted by **rng(m)**, although in this book we often use ran(**m**) as in Z. Map override is alternatively denoted by † instead of ⊕. The ascii notation for this operator is ++. The empty map is denoted $\{\mapsto\}$ to distinguish it from the empty set;

- in defining a type **T** with an attached predicate φ, instead of specifying a schema type:

$$\underline{\quad\mathbf{TS}\quad\rule{8cm}{0pt}}$$
$$\begin{array}{|l|}\hline \mathbf{x} : \mathbf{T} \\ \hline \varphi(\mathbf{x}) \\ \hline \end{array}$$

or abbreviation definition:

$$\mathbf{TS} \;\; == \;\; \{\; \mathbf{x} : \; \mathbf{T} \;\mid\; \varphi(\mathbf{x}) \;\}$$

we write instead

$$\mathbf{TS} \;=\; \mathbf{T}$$
$$\text{inv } \mathbf{x} \;==\; \varphi(\mathbf{x})$$

in the **types** clause of a VDM++ class.

- elements of an enumerated type are written between angle brackets (they are called quotation literals): < **item**1 >, < **item**2 >, etc.

- given sets in VDM++ are instead specified as **token** types via the declarations

types
  GG = **token**

As in Z, they are then assumed to be countably infinite.

The VDM-SL statement

let **v**: T be st P in S

corresponds to ANY **v** : **T** WHERE **P** THEN **S** END in Z++.

dcl **v**: T := e in S

corresponds to VAR **v** : **T** IN **v** := e; **S** END in Z++.

Further examples of the correspondences between the different notations used in the book are given in Table B.1.

Meaning	*VDM++ ASCII*	*VDM++ LaTeX*	*Z++*
Literal sequence	[s1, s2, s3]	$[s1, s2, s3]$	$\langle s1, s2, s3 \rangle$
Concatenation	s1^s2	$s1 \frown s2$	$s1 \frown s2$
Elements of sequence	elems(sq)	$elems(sq)$	$ran(sq)$
Indices of sequence	inds(sq)	$inds(sq)$	$dom(sq)$
Sequence length	len(sq)	$len(sq)$	$\#sq$
Sequence tail	tl(sq)	$tl(sq)$	$tail(sq)$
Sequence head	hd(sq)	$hd(sq)$	$sq(1)$
Range of a function	rng(f)	$rng(f)$	$ran(f)$
Map override	f ++ g	$f \dagger g$	$f \oplus g$
Domain restriction	s <: f	$s \lhd f$	$s \lhd f$
Domain anti-restriction	s <-: f	$s \ntriangleleft f$	$s \ntriangleleft f$
Range restriction	f :> s	$f \rhd s$	$f \rhd s$
Range anti-restriction	f :-> s	$f \ntriangleright s$	$f \ntriangleright s$
Set union	s1 union s2	$s1 \cup s2$	$s1 \cup s2$
Set membership	x in set s	$x \in s$	$x \in s$
Set size	card(s)	$card(s)$	$\#s$
Numeric range	a,...,b	$a,...,b$	$a..b$
Set type	set of T	$T\text{-set}$	$\mathbb{F}(T)$
Sequence type	seq of T	T^*	$seq(T)$
Map type	map T to S	$T \xrightarrow{m} S$	$T \nrightarrow S$
Quantification	forall i:T & E	$\forall i \in T \cdot E$	$\forall i : T \bullet E$
Method application	obj!m(e)	$obj!m(e)$	$obj.m(e)$
Method results	v := obj!m(e)	$v := obj!m(e)$	$v \longleftarrow obj.m(e)$
Request	->>(m,i)	$\rightarrow(m,i)$	$\rightarrow(m,i)$
Activation	/|\(m,i)	$\uparrow(m,i)$	$\uparrow(m,i)$
Termination	|/(m,i)	$\downarrow(m,i)$	$\downarrow(m,i)$

Table B.1: Comparison of Z++ and VDM++

B.2   VDM++ Specification Notation

A VDM++ specification consists of a set of class definitions, where a class definition contains the sections:

1. a *class header* containing the class name and an (optional) representation inheritance clause:

   class C is subclass of C1, ..., Cn

   This clause allows polymorphic application of methods between C and each of the Ci. It is up to the user to prove subtyping relationships which establish that such polymorphism is semantically valid rather than just a programming convenience;

2. a state internal to the object, also referred to as *instance variables*. Invariant expressions and initialisation expressions can be formulated for these instance variables (encouraged but not mandatory);

3. a *collection of methods* (the *protocol* of the object) which can be used to update the instance variables of the objects. A method can be used by the object itself or by clients of the object. Methods can be defined in an *implicit* manner (by means of pre- and post conditions), in an *explicit* manner (through imperative statements), or be *declared but not (yet) specified*. The latter can be useful when the environment of an object demands the existence of a method, but at the same time – at that stage of development – it is not considered necessary or possible to present its exact definition;

4. a *behaviour inheritance declaration* identifying which methods are inherited from which superclasses;

5. a specification of the *synchronisation constraints* on the use of an object's methods, either using permission guards on the initiation of methods, or by using *traces*;

6. a specification of the *internal process of the object* (relevant for active objects only), by using threads. Threads can be specified in a *declarative* manner, using periodic obligations or in a *procedural* manner, using code constructs including a select statement form. A thread takes precedence over the sync clause, and implies mutex for all methods;

7. a place holder for *auxilliary reasoning* about the behaviour of a class, its objects, or – in case of a workspace – the properties of the (sub)system;

8. a *class tail*, which is just a syntactic construct indicating the end of a class description.

Each section of a class description is optional, with the exception of the class header and the class tail. The sections are listed in a class description usually in the order below:

```
class C is subclass of C₁, ...
inherit -- classes extended by controlled inheritance
types
```

```
  T  =  TDef
values
  const :  T  =  val
functions
  f :  A  →  B
  f(a)  ==  Defn_f(a)
instance variables
  v_C :  T_C;
inv objectstate == Inv_C;
init objectstate == Init_C
methods
  MP(x :  X)
    pre Pre_{MP,C}(x, v_C) ==
    [ext wr v_C
      post Post_{MP,C}(x, \overline{v_C}, v_C)];
  ...
  MF()  value y :  Y
    pre Pre_{MF,C}(v_C) ==
    ([ext rd v_C
      post Post_{MF,C}(v_C, y)];
      return y);
  ...
sync
  ...
thread
  ...
aux reasoning
  ...
end  C
```

As with Z^{++}, the extended RTL language given in Appendix A can be used to provide a semantics for such classes. Methods may not be "pure" enquiry or update operations as suggested here, but can combine output parameters with updates to the local state. In addition, if the output parameter name **y** is not used in the definition of **MF** (since we can write **return** e for an expression e of type **Y**), then it can be omitted from the operation header.

Methods can be defined in an abstract declarative way, using *specification statements*, or by using a hybrid of specification statements, method calls and procedural code. Input parameters are indicated within the brackets of the method header, and results after a **value** keyword. Preconditions of a method are given in the **pre** clause. The form of a specification statement is:

```
[ext wr write frame
     rd read frame
 pre precondition
 post postcondition]
```

In the **postcondition** the value of an attribute **att** at initiation of execution of the specification statement is denoted by $\overline{\text{att}}$. An additional **timed post** clause may be given after the postcondition.

Other statements which may be used in specifications are method invocations **obj!MP**(e) in the case of an updating operation **MP**, and **v** := **obj!MF**() for a value-returning operation **MF**, where **obj** : @S is declared, and **MP** and **MF** are methods of **S**. Statements can be combined via sequential composition, conditionals, loops and other procedural constructs.

Other clauses of a class definition control how **C** inherits from other classes: the **is subclass of** clause in the class header lists classes which are being extended by the present class – that is, all their methods become exportable facilities of **C**. An **inherits** clause in **C** lists classes which are being included via *controlled inheritance*: whereby some inherited methods are made internal to **C**. For example, if we specified a tree in terms of a list of subtrees, we could write:

```
class TreeList
-- instantiation of a generic List class for @Tree
end TreeList

class Tree
is subclass of TreeList
inherit from TreeList :: go
instance variables

   ...
end Tree
```

where **go**(n : N) is a method that specifies movement to the **n**-th element of the list. Other methods of **TreeList**, such as **update** or **remove** are hidden from clients of **Tree** by the **inherit** clause, but are internally available (via calls **self!update**(**val**), etc) within method definitions of **Tree**.

Dynamic behaviour of objects of **C** is specified in the **sync** and **thread** clauses, which must not conflict. In the **sync** clause, which describes the behaviour of *passive* objects, either an explicit history of an object can be given, as a *trace* expression involving regular expressions in terms of method names, or as a set of *permission* statements of the form:

> **per Method** ⇒ **Cond**

restricting the conditions under which methods can initiate execution. **Cond** may involve attributes of the class or the event counters #**act**(**m**), #**fin**(**m**) and #**req**(**m**) for methods **m** of the class, and the derived counters #**active**(**m**) and #**waiting**(**m**).

An extension of this notation, based on the *synchronisation variable* concept of [215], allows the definition of local variables in the **sync** clause, and event-triggered action statements of the form:

> **on event do statement**

where **event** is **req**(**m**), **act**(**m**) or **fin**(**m**) for a method **m** of the class, or φ := **true**, φ := **false** as described in Appendix A. Such statements act like interrupts in that **statement** executes atomically, interrupting any other ongoing activity of the object.

Threads describe the behaviour of active objects. A declarative procedural thread

    `periodic(`δ`)(m)`

can be given two interpretations. A strong interpretation requires that **m** be initiated exactly at each time $i * \delta + t_0$ for $i : \mathbb{N}_1$:

$$\forall i : \mathbb{N}_1 \bullet \uparrow(m, i) = i * \delta + t_0$$

where t_0 is the time that the object was started. A weaker interpretation is that the i-th execution of **m** must occur sometime within the interval from $i * \delta + t_0$ to $(i + 1) * \delta + t_0$:

$$\forall i : \mathbb{N}_1 \bullet$$
$$i * \delta + t_0 \leq \uparrow(m, i) \ \wedge$$
$$\downarrow(m, i) \leq (i + 1) * \delta + t_0$$

A procedural thread can involve general statements, including a **select** statement construct allowing execution paths to be chosen on the basis of which messages are received first by the object, similar to the **select** of Ada or **ALT** of OCCAM. A set of internal consistency requirements are associated with a class, which assert that its state space is non-empty, and that the definition of a method maintains the invariant of the class, and that the initialisation predicate implies the invariant. The syntax of traces and threads is given in [92]. A trace definition in the simplest case has the form

sync
    general ClassName =
        < trace_expression, trace_set >

where **trace_expression** is built from method names of the class, together with operators ; , * and +. **trace_set** is the set of method names used in **trace_expression**. Formally for trace expressions **e** and **f**:

1. **e*** is the trace expression meaning "any number of iterations of **e**";
2. **e; f** is the trace expression meaning "**e** followed by **f**";
3. **e**+ is the trace expression meaning "any number (at least one) of iterations of **e**".

Thus if a class **C** has methods m_1, m_2 and m_3, a valid trace specification would be:

sync
    general C =
        < (m_1; m_2)*; m_3, { m_1, m_2, m_3 } >

indicating that objects of **C** can only have histories which consist of a sequence of executions of m_1; m_2, followed by a single execution of m_3. The specification of a trace implies that all the methods mentioned are mutex and self-mutex.

Entity life histories and sequences of steps which correspond to significant processes which an object may execute may also be specified using the **subtrace** facility. For example, we could write:

```
sync
  subtrace PaySequence = < (book_flight; pay),
                                        pay, book_flight >;
  subtrace Change = < change_date*, change_date >;
  subtrace BookSequence = <(PaySequence; Change),
                                      pay, book_flight,
                                              change_date>;
```

as part of a specification of the process of buying an airline ticket and travelling. There are operations to combine trace specifications, such as the **w_** (weave) operator which interleaves two trace sets, synchronising on the common methods. For example, the trace **LiberalBooking** defined by

```
subtrace LiberalBooking = PaySequence w_ Change
```

is equivalent to an explicit definition

```
subtrace LiberalBooking =
          < (change_date*;book_flight;change_date*;pay;change_date*),
            {pay, book_flight, change_date} >
```

As discussed in Chapter 7, the use of subtyping provides a means to supply the (presently) missing choice operator | between trace sets.

Excluded from VDM-SL are the trap, recursive trap and always statements, and the exit, error and non-deterministic statements. Omitted expressions are the iota and lambda expressions, and function types and type variables. In particular polymorphic and higher-order functions are not available in VDM++ [92].

It is proposed that the existence of object references without corresponding object values are handled by defining object variables **att** by:

```
att: [@S]
```

This denotes an "optional type", whose values are either elements of @**S** or the special "undefined" value **nil**. @**S** by itself as a type would then represent $\overline{S}$ in terms of Z^{++}. Given this convention, **void(att)** can be defined as **att = nil**. We will not adopt this approach in this book, however.

B.3   The VDM++ Model of Concurrency

VDM++ makes a distinction between *active* and *passive* objects. Active objects initiate events within a system of objects, via the use of a thread which contains calls to methods of objects which are suppliers to the object executing the thread. Passive objects in contrast do not initiate events, but simply respond to external calls or internal events. It is possible for an executing system to consist of a set of concurrently executing active and passive objects. Concurrency within an object is also allowed. Specifically, it is possible, within a single object, for two or more invocations of the same method to be concurrently executing, and for two or more invocations of different methods to be executing.

If the first type of concurrency is not allowed for objects of a class C, we say that C is *self-mutex*. If the second is not allowed we say that C is *mutex*. By default a class is mutex and self-mutex, with this default being overridden if a `sync` clause with permission statements or event-driven action statements is given (a trace implies mutex and self-mutex for methods listed in the trace set).

A trace and a thread can be specified in the same class: the trace specification must then be consistent with the thread. Similarly a set of permission statements and a thread can be given in the same class, with the same internal consistency constraint. It is not possible to have both a trace and permission statements, or to have more than one thread.

The Ada *rendezvous* semantics is taken as the standard interpretation of method calls between objects: that is, the caller which initiated the call must wait for the called object to complete execution of the invoked method before the calling thread can progress. Within a thread definition an Ada-style `select` statement can be written, with the general syntax:

```
sel
    cond₁ answer m₁ -> s₁ ,
    ...
    condₙ answer mₙ -> sₙ ,
    condₙ₊₁   ->  sₙ₊₁ ,
    ...
    condᵣ  ->  sᵣ  ;
```

where the s_i are statements, the m_i method names and the $cond_i$ expressions.

Execution of this is similar to that of the corresponding Ada construct, except that the clauses are prioritised in order of textual appearance. That is, the textually first clause whose condition is true and for which there is a pending method request is executed, or, if none of the clauses with **answer** statements have pending requests, then the first of the clauses $s_{n+1} \ldots s_r$ which has a true condition is executed.

The calling thread and the invoked method execute synchronously, however once the method m_i has completed its execution, the caller may execute concurrently with the corresponding select clause statement s_i in the called object.

In general it is assumed that there can be time delays between the issuing of a request for execution of a method and the arrival of this request at the target object, and that there can also be delays in the response of an object to a request for one of its methods.

Various levels of complexity can be defined for the interaction between the methods specification, thread specification and sync parts of a class. In the simplest case a class may represent a purely passive component, which has no internal thread, but whose methods may be constrained to execute in mutual exclusion, or in accordance with other synchronisation protocols such as readers-writers or cyclic order. Callers (clients) who attempt to invoke such methods will be blocked unless the method can initiate in a state which satisfies its permission guards and trace constraints. Purely active classes possess a thread, without **answer** statements. Methods may be defined for such a class, however they should normally be purely internal to the class: invoked within its methods and thread but not available to clients. This prevents problems concerning invalid simultaneous accesses to instance variables. The thread should only update variables of the class by calling these internal operations (this restriction allows a simpler proof that the invariant is preserved over the actions of the thread). Internal methods used in this way correspond approximately to procedures in Ada.

In the most complex situation, a thread may have both answer statements and calls to methods of the class. Any method named in an answer statement is an externally available service of the class, and should not be invoked within the thread (ie, by the statement **self!method**(e)), since this would usually create deadlock. A method named in an answer statement can *only* initiate execution when the control flow of the thread reaches this statement. Such methods correspond approximately to task entries in Ada. As in the previous case, methods of the class which are invoked by the thread should be made internal to the class, and state changes to the class achieved by calls to these internal methods.

A thread may also be *deterministic* (if it does not contain select statements), or *non-deterministic* (if it does).

Although these restrictions are assumed, they are not critical to the definition of the semantics, which allows more general forms of interaction between the class elements. However, such restrictions are significant in practical reasoning about the semantics of a class. More critical restrictions are that methods should not be defined in a mutual or self-recursive manner (ie, there are no "callbacks" in the usual terminology of object-oriented programming). In addition, non-deterministic expressions are forbidden (their use can always be replaced by suitable quantified predicates).

B.4   The Semantics of Procedural Statements

Specifications involving timing constraints can only be shown to be satisfied if knowledge is available regarding the timing properties of the ultimate translation form of the implementations of these specifications – that is, the number of clock cycles taken by each assembler op-code to execute on the particular hardware being used.

We will adopt the approach of [102] for the expression of the real-time semantics of a procedural language. For each primitive operation **op**, which is one of: **gaddr** (get an address), **stor** (store a value in an address), **eval**(e) (evaluate expression e), **decl**(**T**) (define storage for a variable of type **T**), **brt**, **brtloop** (branch on true), **brf**, **brfloop** (branch on false), there are corresponding *sets* **T**(**op**) of possible durations for this operation.

T(**op**) should always be a small finite set, thus allowing reasoning by case analysis. The definition of **T** will vary between destination processor architectures. An operation $\dot{+}$ performs addition of such sets, ie:

$$\mathbf{S} \dot{+} \mathbf{T} = \{s + t \mid s \in \mathbf{S} \wedge t \in \mathbf{T}\}$$

Then the duration and delay of each compound statement can be derived from the timing specifications of its components. These constraints can also be used to establish conceptually simpler requirements concerning the equivalence of parallel and sequential versions of an operation. We will use an extension of the language of a class by event times $\uparrow(\mathbf{S}, \mathbf{i})$, $\rightarrow(\mathbf{S}, \mathbf{i})$ and $\downarrow(\mathbf{S}, \mathbf{i})$ for each occurrence $\mathbf{S}$ of a procedural statement in a method of the class. This extension is *not* significant for refinement or subtyping, but is a purely internal language which allows relationships between method and predicate event times of the class to be established, in addition to functional properties of methods.

The semantics will be given for some selected VDM++ statements, a similar analysis holds for the corresponding $\mathbf{Z}^{++}$ constructs.

B.4.1 Assignment

The predicate transformer for assignments not involving method invocations or **new** statements is:

$$[\mathbf{x} := \mathbf{e}]\psi \equiv \psi[\mathbf{e}/\mathbf{x}]$$

Note that, together with the axioms defining the meaning of the **methods** specification of a method, this transformer states that all other variables apart from those in the list $\mathbf{x}$ are left unchanged by this statement. Effectively assignments are performed in mutual exclusion. If it was required to weaken this constraint to allow arbitrary changes to other variables, then a predicate transformer of the form

$$\forall \mathbf{w}' \in \mathbf{T_C} \cdot \psi[\mathbf{w}'/\mathbf{w}, \mathbf{e}/\mathbf{x}]$$

would be required, where $\mathbf{w}$ is the list of attributes in scope apart from $\mathbf{x}$.

For timing properties we have the axioms:

$$\rightarrow(\mathbf{x} := \mathbf{e}, \mathbf{i}) = \uparrow(\mathbf{x} := \mathbf{e}, \mathbf{i})$$
$$\downarrow(\mathbf{x} := \mathbf{e}, \mathbf{i}) - \uparrow(\mathbf{x} := \mathbf{e}, \mathbf{i}) \in \mathbf{T}(\mathbf{gaddr}) \dot{+} \mathbf{T}(\mathbf{stor}) \dot{+} \mathbf{T}(\mathbf{eval}(\mathbf{e}))$$

where the last equation only holds at the implementation level, that is, in the specification which is the last step before code generation.

More concisely:

$$\mathbf{delay}(\mathbf{x} := \mathbf{e}, \mathbf{i}) = 0$$
$$\mathbf{duration}(\mathbf{x} := \mathbf{e}, \mathbf{i}) \in \mathbf{T}(\mathbf{gaddr}) \dot{+} \mathbf{T}(\mathbf{stor}) \dot{+} \mathbf{T}(\mathbf{eval}(\mathbf{e}))$$

There is no delay in executing the assignment after its request, and its duration is a sum of possible durations for its constituent steps.

B.4.2   Sequential Composition

Let S be $S_1; S_2$.

Its predicate transformer is

$$[S]\psi \;\equiv\; [S_1][S_2]\psi$$

In addition:

$$\rightarrow(S, i) = \rightarrow(S_1, i)$$
$$\uparrow(S, i) = \uparrow(S_1, i)$$
$$\downarrow(S_1, i) \leq \uparrow(S_2, i)$$
$$\downarrow(S_2, i) = \downarrow(S, i)$$

The third formula can be strengthened to $\downarrow(S_1, i) = \uparrow(S_2, i)$ assuming that there is no overhead or interruption within the sequential composition.

There are the derived properties:

$$\text{delay}(S, i) = \text{delay}(S_1; i)$$
$$\text{duration}(S, i) \geq \text{duration}(S_1, i) + \text{duration}(S_2, i)$$

B.4.3   Method Invocations

Let S be $a!m(e)$ for some supplier object a. Then $\rightarrow(S, i)$ is $\rightarrow((m, a), j)$ for some $j \geq i$. Similarly for requests on the current object **self**.

S modifies the map $*_D$ where $a : @D$ and m is a method of D according to axiom (**ix**).

$$[S]\psi \;\equiv\; \psi$$

because no values of attributes of C are modified by the call in the absence of callbacks.

For some $k : \mathbb{N}_1$ we also have

$$\uparrow(S, i) = \uparrow((m, a), k)$$
$$\downarrow(S, i) = \downarrow((m, a), k)$$

These equations correspond to the synchronous interpretation of method calls discussed in Section B.3, that is, the delay perceived by the caller in executing the call is the same as the time taken by the called object in responding to this request, and the duration of the call is the same as that of the method execution.

B.4.4   Parallel

Let S be $S_1|||S_2$. Then $[S]$ is defined implicitly by:

$$\neg [S] \neg (\psi_1 \wedge \psi_2) \;\equiv\; \neg [S_1] \neg \psi_1 \wedge \neg [S_2] \neg \psi_2$$

where the set of variables $\mathbf{x}$ updated or accessed in S_1 is disjoint from the set of variables $\mathbf{y}$ updated or accessed in S_2, ψ_1 is $\mathbf{x} = \mathbf{x}'$ and ψ_2 is $\mathbf{y} = \mathbf{y}'$. Thus for example,

$$[\mathbf{x} := \mathbf{e} \, ||| \, \mathbf{y} := \mathbf{f}]\psi \; \equiv \; \psi[\mathbf{e}/\mathbf{x}, \mathbf{f}/\mathbf{y}]$$

where the substitutions are "simultaneous" (occurrences of $\mathbf{x}$ in $\mathbf{f}$ are not replaced by $\mathbf{e}$, etc).

$$\rightarrow(\mathbf{S}, \mathbf{i}) = \rightarrow(\mathbf{S}_1, \mathbf{i}) = \rightarrow(\mathbf{S}_2, \mathbf{i})$$
$$\uparrow(\mathbf{S}, \mathbf{i}) = \uparrow(\mathbf{S}_1, \mathbf{i}) = \uparrow(\mathbf{S}_2, \mathbf{i})$$
$$\downarrow(\mathbf{S}, \mathbf{i}) = \mathbf{max}(\downarrow(\mathbf{S}_1, \mathbf{i}), \downarrow(\mathbf{S}_2, \mathbf{i}))$$

Thus:

$$\mathbf{delay}(\mathbf{S}, \mathbf{i}) = \mathbf{delay}(\mathbf{S}_1, \mathbf{i}) = \mathbf{delay}(\mathbf{S}_2, \mathbf{i})$$
$$\mathbf{duration}(\mathbf{S}, \mathbf{i}) = \mathbf{max}(\mathbf{duration}(\mathbf{S}_1, \mathbf{i}), \mathbf{duration}(\mathbf{S}_2, \mathbf{i}))$$

B.4.5   Select Statements

The semantics of a select statement can be expressed in RTL as follows. Let S be the statement:

```
sel
    cond₁ answer m₁ -> s₁ ,

    ...

    condₙ answer mₙ -> sₙ ,
    condₙ₊₁   ->   sₙ₊₁ ,

    ...

    cond_r  ->  s_r ;
```

For each select clause sc_i: $cond_i$ answer m_i -> s_i we define a conjunct C_i of the weakest precondition

$$[\mathbf{S}]\phi \; = \; \mathbf{C}_1 \wedge \ldots \wedge \mathbf{C}_r$$

as follows:

- if $i \leq n$ and there are no textually preceding select clauses with answer statement for the same method as sc_i, then C_i is

$$cond_i \Rightarrow [s_i]\phi$$

- otherwise, for $i \leq n$, let clauses $sc_{i_1}, \ldots, sc_{i_t}$ be all preceding select clauses in S with m_i as their answered method (ie, $i_1 < i$, $i_2 < i$, etc, and each m_{i_j} is m_i). Then C_i is

$$cond_i \wedge \neg cond_{i_1} \wedge \ldots \wedge \neg cond_{i_t} \Rightarrow [s_i]\phi$$

- for $i : n+1 .. r$, C_i is:

$$\text{cond}_i \wedge \neg \, \text{cond}_{i-1} \wedge \ldots \wedge \neg \, \text{cond}_{n+1} \;\Rightarrow\; [s_i]\phi$$

Note that

```
sel
  s1,
  s2;
```

is therefore equivalent to s1. However

```
sel
  answer m -> s1,
  answer n -> s2
```

(where **m** and **n** are distinct) is equivalent to a non-deterministic choice of s1 or s2, with predicate transformer $[s_1]\psi \wedge [s_2]\psi$.

As a result a class with a thread

```
thread
  while true
  do
    sel
      answer m1 -> s1,
      answer m2 -> s2
```

will be a supertype of the class in which this thread is replaced by

```
thread
  while true
  do
    sel
      answer m1 -> s1
```

because the predicate transformer of the former select statement is $[s1]\phi \wedge [s2]\phi$, which implies $[s1]\phi$ for any ϕ. More intuitively, any execution of the loop body of the second thread is a possible execution of the loop body of the first thread, so it cannot be distinguished by an external observer. Likewise, if a guard condition is strengthened, the result is a subtype; if:

```
thread
  while true
  do
    sel
      G1 answer m -> s
```

is replaced by

```
thread
  while true
  do
    sel
      G2 answer m -> s
```

where $G2 \Rightarrow G1$, the result is a subtype, because again any execution of the select statement with $G2$ will be a possible execution of that with $G1$.

For the dynamic behaviour:

(i) :
$$\forall i : \mathbb{N}_1 \bullet$$
$$(\text{cond}_1 \vee \ldots \vee \text{cond}_r) \odot \rightarrow (S, i)$$

That is: at least one guard condition is true at the point where the target object receives the request to execute S.

In addition, one of the following conditions (ii), (iii) or (iv) holds:

(ii) :
$$\forall j : \mathbb{N}_1 \bullet \exists l, k : \mathbb{N}_1 \mid 1 \leq j \bullet$$
$$\rightarrow (S, j) = \uparrow(S, j) \wedge$$
$$(\text{cond}_i \wedge \#\text{waiting}(m_i) > 0) \odot \rightarrow (S, j) \wedge$$
$$\uparrow(S, j) = \uparrow(m_i, k) \wedge$$
$$\downarrow(m_i, k) = \uparrow(s_i, l) \wedge$$
$$\downarrow(S, j) = \downarrow(s_i, l)$$

where $i : 1 \ldots n$ is least such that the second conjunct holds.

In other words, there is a waiting method with a true guard at the point at which S is invoked, and the textually first clause of this kind is chosen for execution. As in POOL, first the answered method is executed, then the associated sequence s_i of statements are executed – they are not executed in parallel.

(iii) :
$$\forall j : \mathbb{N}_1 \bullet \exists l : \mathbb{N}_1 \mid 1 \leq j \bullet$$
$$\rightarrow (S, j) = \uparrow(S, j) \wedge$$
$$\neg ((\text{cond}_1 \wedge \#\text{waiting}(m_1) > 0) \odot \rightarrow (S, j)) \wedge$$
$$\ldots$$
$$\neg ((\text{cond}_n \wedge \#\text{waiting}(m_n) > 0) \odot \rightarrow (S, j)) \wedge$$
$$\text{cond}_t \odot \rightarrow (S, j) \wedge$$
$$\uparrow(S, j) = \uparrow(s_t, l) \wedge$$
$$\downarrow(S, j) = \downarrow(s_t, l)$$

where $t : n + 1 \ldots r$ is least such that cond_t holds at the request time for S.

In other words, there is no waiting method with a true guard at the invocation of S, but there is a true guard in the set cond_{n+1} to cond_r. The textually first select clause with a true guard is then chosen.

(iv) :

$$\forall j : \mathbb{N}_1 \bullet \exists 1, l' : \mathbb{N}_1 \mid l' \le j \bullet$$
$$\uparrow(S,j) > \to(S,j) \ \wedge$$
$$\uparrow(S,j) = \to(m_i,l) = \uparrow(m_i,l) \ \wedge$$
$$\downarrow(m_i,l) = \uparrow(s_i,l') \ \wedge$$
$$\downarrow(S,j) = \downarrow(s_i,l') \ \wedge$$
$$\neg\, [\exists k : \mathbb{N}_1 \bullet \to(S,j) \le \to(m_1,k) < \to(m_i,l) \ \wedge$$
$$((cond_1 \wedge \#waiting(m_1) > 0) \ \vee$$
$$(cond_{n+1} \vee \dots \vee cond_r))\circledcirc\!\to(m_1,k) \ \vee$$
$$\dots \ \vee$$
$$\to(S,j) \le \to(m_n,k) < \to(m_i,l) \ \wedge$$
$$((cond_n \wedge \#waiting(m_n) > 0) \ \vee$$
$$(cond_{n+1} \vee \dots \vee cond_r))\circledcirc\!\to(m_n,k)] \ \wedge$$
$$\neg\,(cond_{n+1}\circledcirc\uparrow(S,j)) \wedge \dots \wedge \neg\,(cond_r\circledcirc\uparrow(S,j))$$

Where $i : 1 \dots n$ is least such that

$$cond_i \wedge \#waiting(m_i) > 0$$

holds at $\uparrow(S,j)$ but fails at all event times in the interval $[\to(S,j), \uparrow(S,j))$.

In other words, the select statement must wait for the first request of a method m_i such that $cond_i$ is true at the time of this request. The textually first such m_i at this time point is then chosen.

The semantics of other statements can be defined using the same approach. Details are in [169].

B.5   Tool Support

The VDM++ toolkit is called "Venus". It consists of four separate components:

1. The *LOV/OMT* environment supporting the OMT notation, with editors for class diagrams;
2. The *VPP* environment supporting VDM++;
3. A code generator from VDM++ to C++;
4. A *coupling module*, consisting of a transformer from class diagrams to VDM++ specifications, and graphical display facilities for VDM++ specifications. This transformer can be configured to particular desired translation strategies.

There are versions for Sun-4 (Sparc) and HP 9000/700 platforms and the Sun-OS 4.1, Solaris 2.3 and HP-UX version 9 operating systems. Evaluation copies are available, together with introductory packages of training and tutorial material, and academic and research discounts. A 5-day training course covering all aspects of the language is provided by CAP Volmac and Imperial College.

Type-checking and syntax checking facilities of *VPP* can catch many basic errors in specification, whilst the code generation step can produce executable

(iv) :

$$\forall j : \mathbb{N}_1 \bullet \exists l, l' : \mathbb{N}_1 \mid l' \leq j \bullet$$
$$\uparrow(S, j) > \rightarrow(S, j) \ \wedge$$
$$\qquad \uparrow(S, j) = \rightarrow(m_i, l) = \uparrow(m_i, l) \ \wedge$$
$$\qquad \downarrow(m_i, l) = \uparrow(s_i, l') \ \wedge$$
$$\qquad \downarrow(S, j) = \downarrow(s_i, l') \ \wedge$$
$$\qquad \neg\, [\exists k : \mathbb{N}_1 \bullet \rightarrow(S, j) \leq \rightarrow(m_1, k) < \rightarrow(m_i, l) \ \wedge$$
$$\qquad\qquad ((cond_1 \wedge \#\mathbf{waiting}(m_1) > 0) \ \vee$$
$$\qquad\qquad\qquad (cond_{n+1} \vee \ldots \vee cond_r)) \odot \rightarrow(m_1, k) \ \vee$$
$$\qquad\qquad \ldots \vee$$
$$\qquad\qquad \rightarrow(S, j) \leq \rightarrow(m_n, k) < \rightarrow(m_i, l) \ \wedge$$
$$\qquad\qquad ((cond_n \wedge \#\mathbf{waiting}(m_n) > 0) \ \vee$$
$$\qquad\qquad\qquad (cond_{n+1} \vee \ldots \vee cond_r)) \odot \rightarrow(m_n, k)] \ \wedge$$
$$\qquad \neg\, (cond_{n+1} \odot \uparrow(S, j)) \wedge \ldots \wedge \neg\, (cond_r \odot \uparrow(S, j))$$

Where $i : 1 \ldots n$ is least such that

$$cond_i \wedge \#\mathbf{waiting}(m_i) > 0$$

holds at $\uparrow(S, j)$ but fails at all event times in the interval $[\rightarrow(S, j), \uparrow(S, j))$.

In other words, the select statement must wait for the first request of a method m_i such that $cond_i$ is true at the time of this request. The textually first such m_i at this time point is then chosen.

The semantics of other statements can be defined using the same approach. Details are in [169].

B.5   Tool Support

The VDM++ toolkit is called "Venus". It consists of four separate components:

1. The *LOV/OMT* environment supporting the OMT notation, with editors for class diagrams;
2. The *VPP* environment supporting VDM++;
3. A code generator from VDM++ to C++;
4. A *coupling module*, consisting of a transformer from class diagrams to VDM++ specifications, and graphical display facilities for VDM++ specifications. This transformer can be configured to particular desired translation strategies.

There are versions for Sun-4 (Sparc) and HP 9000/700 platforms and the Sun-OS 4.1, Solaris 2.3 and HP-UX version 9 operating systems. Evaluation copies are available, together with introductory packages of training and tutorial material, and academic and research discounts. A 5-day training course covering all aspects of the language is provided by CAP Volmac and Imperial College.

Type-checking and syntax checking facilities of *VPP* can catch many basic errors in specification, whilst the code generation step can produce executable

```
thread
  while true
  do
    sel
      G2 answer m -> s
```

where $\mathbf{G2} \Rightarrow \mathbf{G1}$, the result is a subtype, because again any execution of the select statement with $\mathbf{G2}$ will be a possible execution of that with $\mathbf{G1}$.

For the dynamic behaviour:

(i) :
$$\forall \mathbf{i} : \mathbb{N}_1 \bullet$$
$$(\mathbf{cond}_1 \vee \ldots \vee \mathbf{cond}_r) \circledcirc \rightarrow (\mathbf{S}, \mathbf{i})$$

That is: at least one guard condition is true at the point where the target object receives the request to execute $\mathbf{S}$.

In addition, one of the following conditions **(ii)**, **(iii)** or **(iv)** holds:

(ii) :
$$\forall \mathbf{j} : \mathbb{N}_1 \bullet \exists \mathbf{l}, \mathbf{k} : \mathbb{N}_1 \mid 1 \leq \mathbf{j} \bullet$$
$$\rightarrow (\mathbf{S}, \mathbf{j}) = \uparrow (\mathbf{S}, \mathbf{j}) \wedge$$
$$(\mathbf{cond}_i \wedge \#\mathbf{waiting}(\mathbf{m}_i) > 0) \circledcirc \rightarrow (\mathbf{S}, \mathbf{j}) \wedge$$
$$\uparrow (\mathbf{S}, \mathbf{j}) = \uparrow (\mathbf{m}_i, \mathbf{k}) \wedge$$
$$\downarrow (\mathbf{m}_i, \mathbf{k}) = \uparrow (\mathbf{s}_i, \mathbf{l}) \wedge$$
$$\downarrow (\mathbf{S}, \mathbf{j}) = \downarrow (\mathbf{s}_i, \mathbf{l})$$

where $\mathbf{i} : 1 .. \mathbf{n}$ is least such that the second conjunct holds.

In other words, there is a waiting method with a true guard at the point at which $\mathbf{S}$ is invoked, and the textually first clause of this kind is chosen for execution. As in POOL, first the answered method is executed, then the associated sequence $\mathbf{s}_i$ of statements are executed – they are not executed in parallel.

(iii) :
$$\forall \mathbf{j} : \mathbb{N}_1 \bullet \exists \mathbf{l} : \mathbb{N}_1 \mid 1 \leq \mathbf{j} \bullet$$
$$\rightarrow (\mathbf{S}, \mathbf{j}) = \uparrow (\mathbf{S}, \mathbf{j}) \wedge$$
$$\neg ((\mathbf{cond}_1 \wedge \#\mathbf{waiting}(\mathbf{m}_1) > 0) \circledcirc \rightarrow (\mathbf{S}, \mathbf{j})) \wedge$$
$$\ldots$$
$$\neg ((\mathbf{cond}_n \wedge \#\mathbf{waiting}(\mathbf{m}_n) > 0) \circledcirc \rightarrow (\mathbf{S}, \mathbf{j})) \wedge$$
$$\mathbf{cond}_t \circledcirc \rightarrow (\mathbf{S}, \mathbf{j}) \wedge$$
$$\uparrow (\mathbf{S}, \mathbf{j}) = \uparrow (\mathbf{s}_t, \mathbf{l}) \wedge$$
$$\downarrow (\mathbf{S}, \mathbf{j}) = \downarrow (\mathbf{s}_t, \mathbf{l})$$

where $\mathbf{t} : \mathbf{n} + 1 .. \mathbf{r}$ is least such that $\mathbf{cond}_t$ holds at the request time for $\mathbf{S}$.

In other words, there is no waiting method with a true guard at the invocation of $\mathbf{S}$, but there is a true guard in the set $\mathbf{cond}_{n+1}$ to $\mathbf{cond}_r$. The textually first select clause with a true guard is then chosen.

prototypes at early specification stages, and hence support animation and validation.

Type checking can be either set to "Definite" (errors are reported if there are values which can make the specification incorrect) or "Possible" (errors are only reported if there are *no* possible values which can make the specification correct).

For example, in an abstract binary tree specification we would get the following error messages from definite type checking:

```
class BinTree
types
  TreeId = token
instance variables
  left_subtree: map TreeId to [TreeId];
  right_subtree: map TreeId to [TreeId];
  node_value: map TreeId to nat;
  current: [TreeId];
inv objectstate ==
  dom(left_subtree) = dom(right_subtree) and
  dom(right_subtree) = dom(node_value) and
  (current = nil or
  current in set dom(node_value));
init objectstate ==
  left_subtree = { |-> } and
  right_subtree = { |-> } and
  node_value = { |-> } and
  current = nil
methods
  insert(node: TreeId, x: nat)
    pre node in set dom(node_value)  ==
    if x > node_value(node)
                    ^ERROR(22,22): Error : Given domain element
                    may not exist in Map-Apply-Expr
                    ^ERROR(22,22): Error : Map may be empty
    then
      self!check_insert(right_subtree(node),x)
                              ^ERROR(26,38): Error : Given domain
                              element may not exist in
                              Map-Apply-Expr
                              ^ERROR(26,38): Error :
                              Map may be empty
    else
      if x < node_value(node)
                    ^ERROR(30,24): Error : Given domain element
                    may not exist in Map-Apply-Expr
                    ^ERROR(30,24): Error : Map may be empty
      then
        self!check_insert(left_subtree(node),x);

  check_insert(t: [TreeId], x: nat) ==
```

```
      if t = nil
      then
        let nn: TreeId be st not(nn in set dom(node_value))
        in
          [ext wr node_value, left_subtree, right_subtree
          post node_value = node_value~ ++ { nn |-> x } and
               left_subtree = left_subtree~ ++ { nn |-> nil } and
               right_subtree = right_subtree~ ++ { nn |-> nil }]
      else
        self!insert(t,x);
              ~ERROR(48,12): Error : Method is
              not applied with parameters of the correct type
              ~ERROR(48,12): Error : Error in Invoke-Stmt

    set_value(node: TreeId, x: nat) ==
      node_value := node_value ++ { node |-> x }


  end BinTree
```

We can reason that **node** ∈ dom(**node_value**) in **insert** on the basis of the precondition of the method, and that **node** ∈ dom(**right_subtree**) because of this precondition and the class invariant, so that **insert** is actually type-correct. The error in **check_insert** arises because the type-checker cannot infer that $t \neq$ **nil** in the call **self!insert**(t, x), although this must be the case because of the control flow of the method definition. No errors arise under "possible" type-checking.

More information on Venus can be obtained from:

- Mr. Philippe Leblanc (Verilog S.A., 150 rue Nicolas Vauquelin, B.P. 1310, 31106 Toulouse Cedex, France). Phone: +33-61-192939. Fax: +33-61-408452. E-mail: leblanc@verilog.fr.

or from:

- Mr. Henrik Voss (IFAD, Foskerparken 10, 5230 Odense M, Denmark). Phone: +45-63-157131. Fax: +45-65-932999. E-mail: henrik@ifad.dk.

A www page for the AFRODITE project is at:

`http://www.ifad.dk./projects/afrodite.html`

This has links to pages for VDM++ and Venus. The language reference manual and example training material is available from the VDM++ web page.

The development of Venus has been partially funded by the Commission of the European Communities (CEC) under the ESPRIT-III programme in the area of Information Processing Systems, project no. 6500: "Applying Formal Methods to Real-sized Object Oriented Designs in Technical Environments" (*AFRODITE*).

B.6   Syntax Summary of VDM++

The following BNF description gives the syntax of VDM++ according to the
latest version of the language reference manual (Version 10). Each syntactic
component is expanded out successively until identifiers or VDM-SL items (in
italic) are reached. The former are defined at the end of the list, and all
statements are also grouped together. Items in typewriter font enclosed in ⌜ ⌝
brackets are concrete parts of the ASCII syntax. Sequencing of syntactic items
is indicated by juxtaposition, whilst alternatives are indicated by |. Optional
items are enclosed by [ ]. Items within { } may occur zero or more times.

```
system_specification  =  class_description { class_description }
class_description  =  class_header [ class_body ] class_tail


class_header  =  ⌜class⌝ class_id [ inheritance_clause ]
class_body  =  spec_part { spec_part }
class_tail  =  ⌜end⌝ class_id
```

The **class_id** in the tail of a class must be the same as that in its header.

```
inheritance_clause  =  ⌜is subclass of⌝ inherit_class_list
spec_part  =  definition_part  |
              controlled_inheritance_part  |
              instance_variable_part  |
              time_variables_part  |
              method_part  |
              synchronisation_part  |
              thread_part  |
              aux_reasoning_part
```

At most one **sync**, **methods**, **aux_reasoning** or **thread** clause can be listed in
a class, although all four could be included.

```
inherit_class_list  =  inherit_class { inherit_class }
definition_part  =  type_definitions   |
                    value_definitions  |
                    function_definitions
controlled_inheritance_part  =  ⌜inherit⌝ (inheritance_list  |
                                          ⌜allsuper⌝)
instance_variable_part  =  ⌜instance variables⌝ [instance_vars_decls]
                           [⌜;⌝ invariants] [⌜;⌝ initialisations]
time_variables_part  =  ⌜time variables⌝ time_spec {⌜;⌝ time_spec }
method_part  =  ⌜methods⌝ method_definition {⌜;⌝ method_definition }
synchronisation_part  =  ⌜sync⌝ synchronisation_condition
thread_part  =  ⌜thread⌝ thread_specification
aux_reasoning_part  =  ⌜aux reasoning⌝ expression


inherit_class  =  class_id [ legacy_list ]
inheritance_list  =  inheritance_spec {⌜;⌝ inheritance_spec }
instance_vars_decls  =  instance_vars_decl {⌜;⌝ instance_vars_decl}
```

```
invariants = invariant {⌜;⌝ invariant }
initialisations = initialisation {⌜;⌝ initialisation }
time_spec = time_var_decls | assumption | effect
method_definition = prel_method_definition |
                        full_method_definition
synchronisation_condition = declarative_synchronisation |
                              trace_synchronisation
thread_specification = declarative_thread_spec |
                          procedural_thread_spec


legacy_list = ⌜[⌝ range_list ⌜]⌝
inheritance_spec = ⌜from⌝ class_name ⌜::⌝ ( method_name_list |
                      ⌜all⌝ )
instance_vars_decl = instance_vars ⌜:⌝ type_indication
invariant = ⌜inv⌝ instance_var_names ⌜==⌝ expression |
              ⌜inv objectstate ==⌝ expression
initialisation = ⌜init⌝ instance_var_names ⌜==⌝ expression |
                  ⌜init objectstate ==⌝ expression
time_var_decls = time_var_decl {⌜;⌝ time_var_decl}
assumption = ⌜assumption⌝ instance_var_names ⌜==⌝ formula
effect = ⌜effect⌝ instance_var_names ⌜==⌝ formula
prel_method_definition = method_header prel_method_body
full_method_definition = method_header method_body
declarative_synchronisation = permission_statement
                                {⌜;⌝ permission_statement}
trace_synchronisation = [ subtracestr { subtracestr } ]
                                generaltracestr
declarative_thread_spec = periodic_obligation
                                {⌜;⌝ periodic_obligation}
procedural_thread_spec = statement


range_list = range {⌜,⌝ range }
method_name_list = method_name {⌜,⌝ method_name }
instance_vars = instance_var_id {⌜,⌝ instance_var_id }
type_indication = object_reference_type | bracketed_type |
                    basic_type | quote_type |
                    composite_type | union_type |
                    product_type | optional_type |
                    set_type | seq_type | map_type |
                    type_name
instance_var_names = instance_var_name {⌜,⌝ instance_var_name }
expression = vdmsl_expression | vdmpp_expression
time_var_decl = [⌜input⌝] instance_var_names ⌜:⌝ type_indication
method_header = [ class_id legacy_index ⌜'⌝] method_id
                  ⌜(⌝ [par_typelist]
                  ⌜)⌝ [ value_part ]
prel_method_body = ⌜is not yet specified⌝ |
                      ⌜is subclass responsibility⌝
```

```
method_body  =  [ pre_condition ] ⌜==⌝ statement [time_post]
permission_statement  =  ⌜per⌝ method_name ⌜=>⌝ guard_condition
subtracestr  =  ⌜subtrace⌝ trace_id ⌜=⌝ trace_structure ⌜;⌝
generaltracestr  =  ⌜general⌝ trace_id ⌜=⌝ trace_structure
periodic_obligation  =  ⌜periodic (⌝ expression ⌜)(⌝ method_name ⌜)⌝
```

Event counters may be used in guard conditions, in addition to VDM-SL or
VDM++ expressions as defined above. A **formula** will include continuous time
formulae involving integral calculus operators, in addition to expressions.

```
range  =  label | number_range
method_name  =  [ class_name ⌜'⌝] method_id
object_reference_type  =  ⌜@⌝ class_id
instance_var_name  =  [ class_name ⌜'⌝] instance_var_id
type_name  =  [ class_name ⌜'⌝] type_id
vdmpp_expression  =  isofbaseclass_expression | isofclass_expression |
                     sameclass_expression | samebaseclass_expression
legacy_index  =  ⌜[⌝ expression ⌜]⌝
par_typelist  =  par_type {⌜,⌝ par_type }
value_part  =  ⌜value⌝ id_type_pair
pre_condition  =  ⌜pre⌝ expression
time_post  =  ⌜time post⌝ time_expression
trace_structure  =  identifier |
                    ⌜<⌝ trace_set ⌜,⌝ alphabet ⌜>⌝ |
                    ⌜pref (⌝ trace_structure ⌜)⌝ |
                    ⌜del  (⌝ method_name ⌜,⌝ method_name ⌜)⌝ |
                    trace_structure ⌜w_⌝ trace_structure |
                    ⌜(⌝ number ⌜,⌝ number ⌜) sync (⌝
                    method_name ⌜,⌝ method_name ⌜)⌝ |
                    ⌜(⌝ number ⌜,⌝ number ⌜) qsync (⌝
                    method_name ⌜,⌝ method_name ⌜,⌝
                    method_name ⌜,⌝ method_name ⌜)⌝ |
                    trace_structure ⌜**⌝ alphabet

label  =  quote_type | number | boolean_literal
number_range  =  number ⌜,...,⌝ number
class_name  =  class_id [ legacy_index ]
isofbaseclass_expression  =  ⌜isofbaseclass (⌝ class_id ⌜,⌝ identifier ⌜)⌝
isofclass_expression  =  ⌜isofclass (⌝ class_id ⌜,⌝ identifier ⌜)⌝
sameclass_expression  =  ⌜sameclass (⌝ identifer ⌜,⌝ identifier ⌜)⌝
samebaseclass_expression  =  ⌜samebaseclass (⌝ identifer ⌜,⌝ identifier ⌜'⌝
par_type  =  par_name_list ⌜:⌝ type_indication
id_type_pair  =  [ identifier ⌜:⌝ ] type_indication
time_expression  =  expression | duration_expression |
                   approx_expression
trace_set  =  trace_expression | alphabet ⌜*⌝ | ⌜t_⌝ trace_structure
alphabet  =  ⌜{⌝ method_name {⌜,⌝ method_name } ⌜}⌝ |
                    ⌜a_⌝ trace_structure

par_name_list  =  identifier { ⌜,⌝ identifier }
duration_expression  =  ⌜duration(⌝ method_name ⌜)⌝
```

```
                    rel_operator expression
approx_expression  =  ⌜=~⌝ expression


statement  =  vdmsl_statement  |  vdmpp_statement
rel_operator  =  ⌜<⌝  |  ⌜=⌝  |  ⌜>⌝  |  ⌜<=⌝  |  ⌜>=⌝


vdmsl_statement  =  block_statement   |   def_statement   |
                    let_statement   |   let_be_statement   |
                    assign_statement   |   sequence_for_loop   |
                    set_for_loop   |   index_for_loop   |
                    while_loop   |   if_statement   |
                    cases_statement   |   return_statement   |
                    identity_statement
vdmpp_statement  =  new_statement  |  topology_statement  |
                    start_statement  |  startlist_statement  |
                    invoke_statement  |  specification_statement  |
                    delay_statement  |  select_statement


new_statement  =  class_id ⌜!new⌝
topology_statement  =  ⌜topology⌝ specification_statement
start_statement  =  object_reference ⌜!start⌝
startlist_statement  =  ⌜startlist(⌝ expression ⌜)⌝
invoke_statement  =  object_reference ⌜!⌝ method_invocation
specification_statement  =  ⌜[⌝ implicit_body ⌜]⌝
delay_statement  =  ⌜delay(⌝ expression ⌜)⌝
select_statement  =  ⌜sel⌝ select_clause {⌜,⌝ select_clause }
```

In the **topology** statement the postcondition may refer to attributes of supplier objects via the notation **object.attribute**. The same applies to the expression in the **aux reasoning** clause. VDM++ statements may be used within the corresponding VDM-SL statement forms of the language. It is conventional to only use topology statements in a **Workspace** class.

```
object_reference  =  instance_var_name  |  ⌜self⌝  |  invoke_statement  |
                     new_statement
method_invocation  =  method_name ⌜(⌝ [ expression_list ] ⌜)⌝
implicit_body  =  [ externals ] [ pre_condition ] post_condition
                  [ time_post ] [ error_predicates ]
select_clause  =  [ expression ] [ answer_statement ] [ ⌜->⌝ statement ]
```

Each select clause must contain at least one of the three optional subclauses (condition, answer statement or action statement).

```
externals  =  ⌜ext⌝ var_info { var_info }
post_condition  =  ⌜post⌝ expression
error_predicates  =  ⌜errs⌝ error { error }
answer_statement  =  ⌜answer⌝ ( method_name | ⌜all⌝ )


var_info  =   mode  instance_var_names [⌜:⌝ type_indication ]
error  =  identifier ⌜:⌝ expression ⌜->⌝ expression


mode  =  ⌜rd⌝  |  ⌜wr⌝
```

A postcondition can contain hooked variables $\overleftarrow{\mathbf{v}}$ for any **v** listed in the **wr** clause.

method_id = identifier
instance_var_id = identifier
type_id = identifier

identifier = lowercase_letter { letter | digit | $\ulcorner\_\urcorner$ | $\ulcorner{}^{\backprime}\urcorner$ }
class_id = uppercase_letter { letter | digit | $\ulcorner\_\urcorner$ | $\ulcorner{}^{\backprime}\urcorner$ }

letter = lowercase_letter | uppercase_letter

A lowercase letter is one of **a** upto **z** and an uppercase letter is one of **A** upto **Z** as usual. A digit is **0** upto **9**. A number is a sequence of digits, either being just **0** or starting with a non-zero digit.

Appendix C

Exercise Answers

Exercise (3.1): We have to show that the equivalence

$$\forall \, \mathbf{wp} : \overline{\mathbf{WorkingPerson}}' \, ; \, \mathbf{emp} : \overline{\mathbf{Employment}}' \, \bullet$$
$$\mathbf{emp} \in \mathrm{ran}(\mathbf{employments}'(\mathbf{wp})) \equiv$$
$$\mathbf{wp} = \mathbf{employee}'(\mathbf{emp})$$

for the modified values $\overline{\mathbf{WorkingPerson}}'$ etc of these sets and relations at termination of the operation.

If $\mathbf{emp} \in \overline{\mathbf{Employment}}'$ then either $\mathbf{emp} = \mathbf{emp}?$, or $\mathbf{emp} \neq \mathbf{emp}?$, and $\mathbf{emp} \in \overline{\mathbf{Employment}}$. Thus if

$$\mathbf{wp} = \mathbf{employee}'(\mathbf{emp})$$

in the first case we have $\mathbf{wp} = \mathbf{wp}?$ and

$$\mathbf{emp} \in \mathrm{ran}(\mathbf{employments}'(\mathbf{wp}))$$

as required. In the second case

$$\mathbf{wp} = \mathbf{employee}(\mathbf{emp})$$

since $\mathbf{employee}'$ only differs from $\mathbf{employee}$ on $\mathbf{emp}?$, so

$$\mathbf{emp} \in \mathrm{ran}(\mathbf{employments}(\mathbf{wp})) \subseteq \mathrm{ran}(\mathbf{employments}'(\mathbf{wp}))$$

as required.

In the converse direction, in the first case if

$$\mathbf{emp}? \in \mathrm{ran}(\mathbf{employments}'(\mathbf{wp}))$$

then $\mathbf{emp}? \notin \mathrm{ran}(\mathbf{employments}(\mathbf{w}))$ for any $\mathbf{w}$, since $\mathbf{emp}? \notin \mathrm{dom}(\mathbf{employee})$ from the precondition. As a result, $\mathbf{wp}$ can only be $\mathbf{wp}?$, and then

$$\mathbf{wp} = \mathbf{employee}'(\mathbf{emp})$$

as required. In the second case, if **emp** ∈ ran(**employments′(wp)**) then
emp ∈ ran(**employments(wp)**) because the only new element in

$$\bigcup\{\mathbf{wp} : \overline{\mathbf{WorkingPerson}'} \bullet \mathrm{ran}(\mathbf{employments'(wp)})\}$$

is **emp**? (since **wp**? is already in dom(**employments**)). As a result

wp = employee(emp)

and so **wp** = employee′(emp) as required, because again **employee** is only
modified on **emp**? ≠ emp.

The first precondition is needed in the above argument, whilst the second
is needed in order to make the reference to **employments(wp?)** well-formed
in the definition of the operation.

Exercise (3.2): The entities are Track and Plot, with object model given in
Figure C.1. Notice that the stated operations are all operations at the system

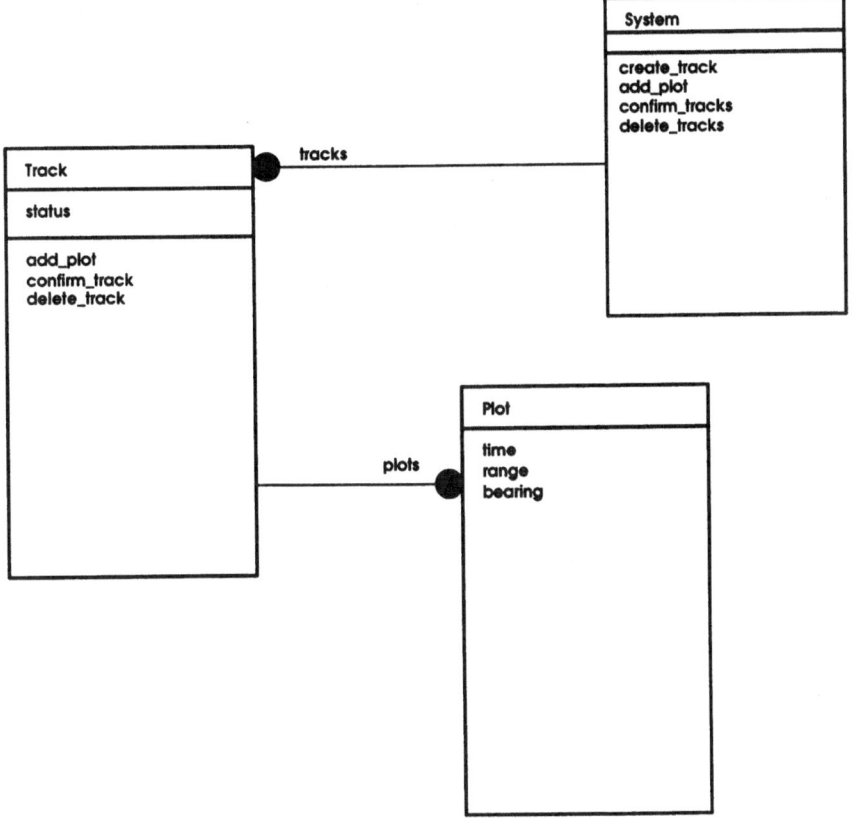

Figure C.1: Object Model of Track-former System

level, because the requirements imply that they are all facilities which are available to the user. However it is clear that to add a plot to the system, we will need to select suitable track(s) and add the plot to these – so an **add_plot** operation is needed on tracks as well. Similarly for **confirm_track** and **delete_track**, since these modify the **status** attribute of a track so must be located in this class. Each class has in addition an implicit **init** operation, which in the case of tracks, serves to implement **create_track** at the track level.

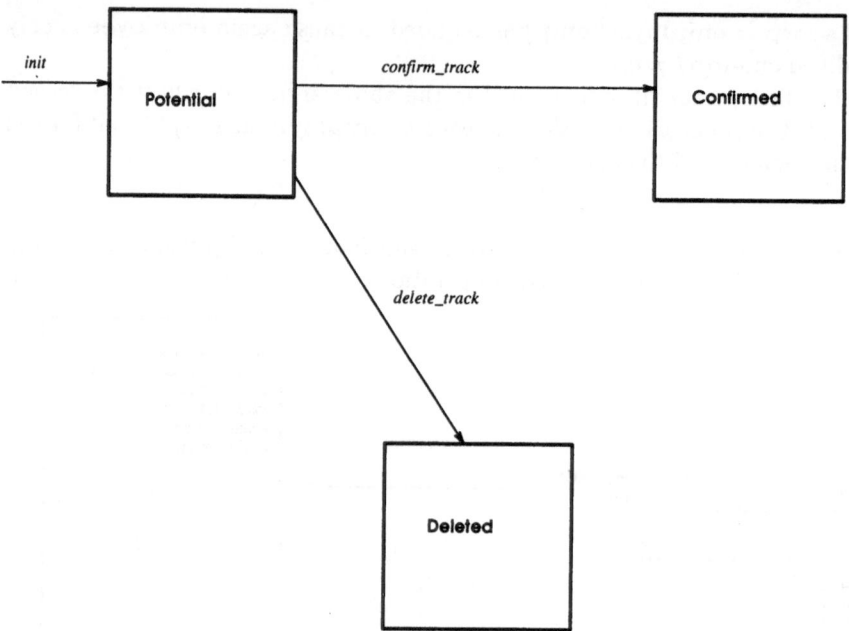

Figure C.2: Dynamic Model of Track

Figure C.2 gives the dynamic model of the only dynamically interesting entity in the application. Note that we had to assume (using "common sense") that tracks start out in the **potential** state, and cannot leave the **deleted** or confirmed states – this is an incompleteness in the requirements.

The outline classes are therefore:

```
CLASS Plot
OWNS
   time : N;
   range : N;
   bearing : N
OPERATIONS
   init : →
END CLASS
```

We have made the assumption that the data types can be represented by natural numbers – in a real set of requirements these data types would (presumably) be precisely described.

```
CLASS Track
TYPES
   STATUS ::= potential | confirmed | deleted
OWNS
   status : STATUS;
   plots : seq(Plot)
OPERATIONS
   init : →;
   add_plot : Plot →;
   confirm_track : →;
   delete_track : →
END CLASS

CLASS System
OWNS
   tracks : F(Track)
OPERATIONS
   init : →;
   create_track : → Track;
   add_plot : Plot →;
   confirm_tracks : →;
   delete_tracks : →
END CLASS
```

Notice that we use seq in the declaration of **Track** because the requirements told us that plots are stored in a particular order. On the other hand, only the F constructor is used in **System** since no ordering is specified for tracks. F is used rather than $\mathbb{P}$, since in a physically based situation such as this there will only ever be finitely many instances of each entity type being present in the system at any point of time. In contrast the countably infinite sets @**Plot** and @**Track** provide sufficiently many potential "object identities" or labels for entity instances that we know that creation of such instances cannot fail for reasons of insufficient labels.

The invariant of the **Track** class specifies the ordering constraint given in the requirements:

$$\forall i, j : \text{dom}(\text{plots}) \mid i < j \bullet \text{plots}(i).\text{time} \le \text{plots}(j).\text{time}$$

(we use $\le$ rather than $<$ in the consequent here in order to accommodate the possibility that several plots may arrive at the same time).

The **add_plot** operation should probably check that the new plot is not already an element of the plot sequence of the track – any necessary quality check would have been done in the **System** class when a decision on which track to assign a new plot to was made.

The **confirm_track** operation should check that the **status** is **potential**, as should the **delete_track** operation.

The **System** class does not have an invariant, and the **add_plot** operation should have a precondition that the new plot has not already been added to the system (for this check it may be useful to explicitly represent all existing plots in the system as a set-valued attribute in **System** – in this case there would then be an invariant in **System**). **confirm_tracks** and **delete_tracks** do not have preconditions.

Exercise (3.3): $\mathbf{mutex}(\{\mathbf{m_1}, \mathbf{m_2}\})$ indicates that $\#\mathbf{active}(\mathbf{m_1}) = 0$ or $\#\mathbf{active}(\mathbf{m_2}) = 0$. Since $\#\mathbf{active}(\mathbf{m}) = \#\mathbf{act}(\mathbf{m}) - \#\mathbf{fin}(\mathbf{m})$, it is possible for $\#\mathbf{active}(\mathbf{m})$ to be 0 at the time point $\downarrow(\mathbf{m}, \mathbf{i})$ of termination of $\mathbf{m}$ (provided there is no other ongoing execution of $\mathbf{m}$ at this time). Intuitively $\#\mathbf{act}(\mathbf{m})$ is incremented (instantaneously) at the activation times $\uparrow(\mathbf{m}, \mathbf{i})$ of $\mathbf{m}$, whilst $\#\mathbf{fin}(\mathbf{m})$ is incremented instantaneously at the times $\downarrow(\mathbf{m}, \mathbf{i})$.

Therefore, in the absence of other method executions, at a time point $\downarrow(\mathbf{m_1}, \mathbf{i}) = \uparrow(\mathbf{m_2}, \mathbf{j})$, $\#\mathbf{active}(\mathbf{m_1}) = 0$ and $\#\mathbf{active}(\mathbf{m_2}) = 1$, which satisfies the mutex requirement.

Exercise (4.1):

1. OPERATIONS
     inc : $\mathbb{Z}$ →;

   ACTIONS
     inc vv? ==>
             $\mathbf{xx}' = \mathbf{vv}? + \mathbf{xx}$;

   If this method was used as a predicate, the value of $\mathbf{yy}'$ would not be constrained, however $\mathbf{yy}' = \mathbf{yy}$ is implicit if it is used as an operation;

2. OPERATIONS
     inc : $\mathbb{Z}$ →;

   ACTIONS
     inc vv? ==>
             PRE $\mathbf{vv}? + \mathbf{xx} \geq 0$
             THEN
               $\mathbf{xx}' = \mathbf{vv}? + \mathbf{xx}$
             END;

   The precondition is needed for reasons of internal consistency and type correctness: $\mathbf{xx}'$ must be given a value in $\mathbb{N}$ by each operation that modifies it;

3. OPERATIONS
     add : $\mathbb{N}$ →;

   ACTIONS
     add vv? ==>
             IF $\mathbf{vv}? \notin \mathrm{ran}(\mathbf{ss})$
             THEN
               $\mathbf{ss}' = \mathbf{ss} \frown \langle\, \mathbf{vv}? \,\rangle$
             END;

A less determined version of this operation would simply use the implicit assignment $\text{ran}(\text{ss}') = \text{ran}(\text{ss}) \cup \{\textbf{vv}?\}$;

4. OPERATIONS
   len : → ℕ;

ACTIONS
   len yy! ==>
         yy! = #ss;

The typing **yy!** : ℕ can be given since we know that the length of a sequence cannot be negative. If **yy!** can be bounded above because of other contextual knowledge, then a more restricted type should be given, to avoid difficulties in later refinement steps arising from the finiteness of implementation data types.

Exercise (4.2):

1. the methods are:

OPERATIONS
   *inc_overflow : ℤ → **REPORT**;
   *inc_underflow : ℤ → **REPORT**;
   *inc_normal : ℤ → **REPORT**;
   inc : ℤ → **REPORT**;

ACTIONS
   *inc_overflow vv? yy! ==>
         vv? + xx > 20 ∧
         xx' = xx ∧ yy! = overflow;

   *inc_underflow vv? yy! ==>
         vv? + xx < 1 ∧
         xx' = xx ∧ yy! = underflow;

   *inc_normal vv? yy! ==>
         1 ≤ vv? + xx ≤ 20 ∧
         xx' = xx + vv? ∧ yy! = ok;

   inc vv? yy! ==>
         inc_overflow ∨ inc_underflow ∨ inc_normal;

This specification makes clear the fact that **inc_overflow, inc_underflow** and **inc_normal** are intended purely for internal use within the class, in order to clarify the specification of **inc** by decomposing it into cases. They are not externally available services of the class. This is in contrast to a Z specification, where each of these methods would be (globally available) operation schemas.

If the CHOICE construct was used instead of $\vee$ then it would not be necessary to include the $\mathbf{xx'} = \mathbf{xx}$ specification in the two error cases, however the above is slightly more abstract and hence is preferred. In VDM^{++} we can use a conditional

> if NormalCondition
> then NormalCase
> else AbnormalCase

to achieve similar effects.

Exercise (4.3):

1. These obligations are:

$$\exists\, \mathbf{sq} : \mathrm{seq}(\mathbf{X}) \bullet \mathbf{true}$$

$$\mathbf{x} \in \mathbf{X} \wedge \mathbf{sq} \in \mathrm{seq}(\mathbf{X}) \;\Rightarrow\; \mathbf{sq} \frown \langle \mathbf{x} \rangle \in \mathrm{seq}(\mathbf{X})$$

$$\mathbf{x} \in \mathbf{X} \wedge \mathbf{sq} \in \mathrm{seq}(\mathbf{X}) \;\Rightarrow\; \exists\, \mathbf{sq'} : \mathrm{seq}(\mathbf{X}) \bullet \mathbf{sq'} = \mathbf{sq} \frown \langle \mathbf{x} \rangle$$

$$\langle \rangle \in \mathrm{seq}(\mathbf{X})$$

$$\mathbf{x} \in \mathbf{X} \wedge \mathbf{sq} \in \mathrm{seq}(\mathbf{X}) \;\Rightarrow\; \mathbf{squash}(\mathbf{sq} \rhd \{\mathbf{x}\}) \in \mathrm{seq}(\mathbf{X})$$

$$\mathbf{x} \in \mathbf{X} \wedge \mathbf{sq} \in \mathrm{seq}(\mathbf{X}) \;\Rightarrow\; \exists\, \mathbf{sq'} : \mathrm{seq}(\mathbf{X}) \bullet \mathbf{sq'} = \mathbf{squash}(\mathbf{sq} \rhd \{\mathbf{x}\})$$

ignoring tests of well-formedness of expressions (eg, that ran(sq) is meaningful in the is_in operation because sq is a relation). Each of these obligations is direct to discharge by the properties of the types and operators concerned, and would not normally be explicitly written down by a developer;

2. the obligations are:

$$\exists\, \mathbf{d1}, \mathbf{d2} : @\mathbf{S} \bullet \mathbf{true}$$

$$\mathbf{xx} \in \mathbb{N} \wedge \mathbf{d1} \in \overline{\mathbf{S}} \wedge \mathbf{d2} \in \overline{\mathbf{S}} \;\Rightarrow\;$$
$$\mathbf{d1} \in @\mathbf{S} \wedge \mathbf{d2} \in @\mathbf{S}$$

$$\mathbf{xx} \in \mathbb{N} \wedge \mathbf{d1} \in \overline{\mathbf{S}} \wedge \mathbf{d2} \in \overline{\mathbf{S}} \;\Rightarrow\;$$
$$\#\mathbf{d1.ss} < \mathbf{d1.maxlen} \wedge \#\mathbf{d2.ss} < \mathbf{d2.maxlen} \;\wedge$$
$$\exists\, \mathbf{ss1'}, \mathbf{ss2'} : \mathrm{seq}(\mathbb{N}) \bullet \mathbf{ss1'} = \mathbf{d1.ss} \frown \langle \mathbf{xx} \rangle \;\wedge$$
$$\mathbf{ss2'} = \mathbf{d2.ss} \frown \langle \mathbf{xx} \rangle$$

The unprovable obligation here is the conjunction $\#\mathbf{d1.ss} < \mathbf{d1.maxlen} \wedge$ $\#\mathbf{d2.ss} < \mathbf{d2.maxlen}$ in the third formula. This asserts that the actual precondition of push_2 is implied by its explicit precondition (in this case just the typing constraint). The problem is that the preconditions of the nested calls of push are not ensured by the explicit precondition of push_2. A way of correcting this would be to change push_2 to:

```
push_2 xx?  ==>
    PRE #d1.ss  <  d1.maxlen  ∧  #d2.ss  <  d2.maxlen
    THEN
            d1.push(xx?)  ∧  d2.push(xx?)
    END
```

But a simpler approach would be to define an enquiry operation of **S** which provides information on whether the precondition of **push** holds:

```
RETURNS
  push_pre :  →
```

```
ACTIONS
  push_pre  ==>
        #ss  <  maxlen
```

This would then be used as follows:

```
push_2 xx?  ==>
    PRE d1.push_pre  ∧  d2.push_pre
    THEN
            d1.push(xx?)  ∧  d2.push(xx?)
    END
```

This is a general approach which is reasonable to use except in concurrent execution environments where execution of **push_2** may be interrupted between the test and the assignment by operations on **d1** and **d2** which invalidate the precondition. In these cases a "try it and see if it works" approach is needed instead, where each operation has an additional output parameter that signals if it has been executed successfully. An operation such as **push_2** would then gather the individual success reports from **d1.push** and **d2.push** and only signal success if both of these invocations succeeded.

Exercise (4.4): A possible class would be:

```
CLASS GenQueue
FUNCTIONS
  | bound :  N₁
OWNS
  eseq :  seq(N)
INVARIANT
  #eseq  ≤  bound
OPERATIONS
  add_e x?  ==>
      PRE #eseq  <  bound
      THEN
          eseq'  =  eseq  ⌢  ⟨ x? ⟩
      END
```

```
END CLASS
```

Subtypes with particular bounds would then inherit this class and provide additional constraints on the **bound** value:

```
CLASS Queue10 EXTENDS GenQueue
FUNCTIONS
   bound = 10
END CLASS
```

and so forth.

Exercise (4.5): This class can be completed as follows:

```
CLASS DG[X]
OWNS
   successors :  seq($\overline{DG[X]}$);
   node :  X
OPERATIONS
   add_successor :  DG[X]  →;
   remove_successor :  DG[X]  →
RETURNS
   access :  ℕ  →  DG[X]
ACTIONS
   add_successor dg?   ==>
        successors′  =  successors  ⌢  ⟨ dg? ⟩;

   remove_successor dg?   ==>
        ran(successors′)  =  ran(successors) \ { dg? } ∧
        successors′  ∈  seq($\overline{DG[X]}$);

   access i? dg!   ==>
        PRE i?  ∈  dom(successors)
        THEN
               dg!  =  successors(i?)
        END
END CLASS
```

Exercise (4.6): For the **Track** class we simply have:

```
CLASS Track
TYPES
   STATUS  ::=  potential | confirmed | deleted
OWNS
   status :  STATUS;
   plots :  seq(Plot)
INVARIANT
   ∀ i, j:  dom(plots) | i < j • plots(i).time ≤ plots(j).time
OPERATIONS
   init :  →;
   add_plot :  Plot  →;
   confirm_track :  →;
```

```
    delete_track : →
ACTIONS
    init  ==>    status'  =  potential  ∧
                 plots'  =  ⟨ ⟩;

    add_plot p?   ==>
          PRE p?  ∉  ran(plots)
          THEN
                  plots'  =  plots  ⌢  ⟨ p? ⟩
          END;

    confirm_track  ==>
          PRE status  =  potential
          THEN
                  status'  =  confirmed
          END;

    delete_track  ==>
          PRE status  =  potential
          THEN
                  status'  =  deleted
          END

END CLASS
```

The **System** class is more complex, and involves the definition of a new function
get_best_tracks which returns the set of known tracks which meet the quality
criterion for addition of a new plot. Similar new functions need to be written
to identify sets of tracks to be confirmed or deleted in each step:

```
CLASS System
FUNCTIONS
```

$$\text{qual\_fit} : \text{Plot} \times \text{Track} \to \mathbb{N}$$
$$\text{add\_tolerance} : \mathbb{N}$$

$$\text{qual\_confirm} : \text{Track} \times \mathbb{F}(\text{Track}) \to \mathbb{N}$$
$$\text{confirm\_tolerance} : \mathbb{N}$$

$$\text{get\_best\_tracks} : \text{Plot} \times \mathbb{F}(\text{Track}) \to \mathbb{F}(\text{Track})$$

$$\text{get\_confirmed\_tracks} : \mathbb{F}(\text{Track}) \to \mathbb{F}(\text{Track})$$

$\forall p : \text{Plot}; \ ts : \mathbb{F}(\text{Track}) \bullet$
  $\forall t : \text{Track} \bullet$
    $t \in \text{get\_best\_tracks}(p, ts) \equiv$
      $\text{qual\_fit}(p, t) \geq \text{add\_tolerance} \ \wedge$
      $t \in ts \wedge t.\text{status} = \text{potential}$

$\forall ts : \mathbb{F}(\text{Track}) \bullet$
  $\forall t : \text{Track} \bullet$
    $t \in \text{get\_confirmed\_tracks}(ts) \equiv$
      $\text{qual\_confirm}(t, ts) \geq \text{confirm\_tolerance} \ \wedge$
      $t \in ts \wedge t.\text{status} = \text{potential}$

OWNS
  tracks : $\mathbb{F}(\text{Track})$
OPERATIONS
  init : $\to$;
  create_track : $\to$ Track;
  add_plot : Plot $\to$;
  confirm_tracks : $\to$;
  delete_tracks : $\to$
ACTIONS
  init ==> $\text{tracks}' = \varnothing$;

  create_track t! ==>
    BEGIN
      New$_{\text{Track}}$[t!/track!]$_9^o$
      t!.init
    END;

  add_plot p? ==>
    ANY ts : $\mathbb{F}(\text{Track})$
    WHERE
      ts = get_best_tracks(p?, tracks)
    THEN
      IF ts = $\varnothing$
      THEN
        VAR t : Track
        IN
          t $\longleftarrow$ create_track $_9^o$
          $\text{tracks}' = \text{tracks} \cup \{\ t\ \} \ _9^o$
          t.add_plot(p?)
        END

```
            ELSE
                    ⋀t ∈ ts  t.add_plot(p?)
            END
        END;

  confirm_tracks  ==>
        ANY ts :  𝔽(Track)
        WHERE
            ts  =  get_confirmed_tracks(tracks)
        THEN
            ⋀t ∈ ts  t.confirm_track
        END;

  delete_tracks  ==>
        ANY ts :  𝔽(Track)
        WHERE
            ts  =  tracks \ get_confirmed_tracks(tracks)
        THEN
            ⋀t ∈ ts  t.delete_track
        END
```

END CLASS

We could have chosen to make the functions **get_best_tracks** etc internal operations of the class, especially since they make use of the entire state. In an implementation they may be replaced by suitable loops.

Exercise (5.1): The following is a suitable refinement (and indeed, an implementation).

```
CLASS Factorial_1
OPERATIONS
  factorial :  ℕ  →  ℕ
ACTIONS
  factorial i? f!  ==>
        VAR j :  ℕ
        IN
            j  :=  i?;
            f!  :=  1;
            WHILE j > 1
            DO
                f!  :=  f! * j;
                j  :=  j − 1
            END
        END
```

END CLASS

Exercise (5.2): Since there is no history constraint in either class, the refinement proof obligations are simply those of conventional data refinement. We obviously have that the (functional) data refinement $\mathbf{R}$ is well-typed, ie:

$$sq \in seq(\mathbf{X}) \Rightarrow \mathbf{R}(sq) \in \mathbb{F}(\mathbf{X})$$

All operation preconditions in $\mathbf{Set[X]}$ are simply typing constraints, and therefore it is clear that these preconditions become weaker (or remain equivalent) in $\mathbf{Seq[X]}$.

The key part of the refinement obligations are therefore the postcondition parts of operation refinement. For **add_element** we require:

$$\forall sq, sq' : seq(\mathbf{X}); \ s : \mathbb{F}(\mathbf{X}); \ x : \mathbf{X} \bullet$$
$$s = ran(sq) \wedge sq' = sq \cap \langle x \rangle \Rightarrow$$
$$\exists s' : \mathbb{F}(\mathbf{X}) \mid s' = ran(sq') \bullet s' = s \cup \{x\}$$

which is clearly true. Because $\mathbf{R}$ is functional we can simplify the proof obligations to

$$\forall \mathbf{State_D}; \ d' \bullet$$
$$\mathbf{Pre_{m,C}}[\mathbf{R}(v)/u] \wedge \mathbf{Def_{D,\phi(m)}} \Rightarrow \mathbf{Def_{m,C}}[\mathbf{R}(v)/u, \mathbf{R}(v')/u']$$

in each case.

Thus for **init** we require

$$\forall sq, sq' : seq(\mathbf{X}) \bullet sq' = \langle \rangle \ \Rightarrow \ ran(sq') = \varnothing$$

For **del** we require:

$$\forall sq, sq' : seq(\mathbf{X}); \ x : \mathbf{X} \bullet sq' = squash(sq \rhd \{x\}) \ \Rightarrow$$
$$ran(sq') = ran(sq) \setminus \{x\}$$

For **is_in** we require:

$$\forall sq : seq(\mathbf{X}); \ x : \mathbf{X} \bullet x \in ran(sq) \Rightarrow x \in ran(sq)$$

All of these obligations are directly provable.

Exercise (6.1): The key aspect is that, although the postcondition of $\mathbf{C.inc}$ is stronger than that of $\mathbf{D.inc}$, it is actually impossible for $\mathbf{D.inc}$ to ever execute in the lifetime of an instance of $\mathbf{D}$. Thus, considering the translation of the axiom defining the semantics of $\mathbf{C.m}$, it has the form $\forall i : \mathbb{N}_1 \bullet (\mathbf{self} \in \overline{\mathbf{D}} \Rightarrow \chi) \odot \uparrow(\mathbf{inc}, i)$. But $\mathbf{self} \notin \overline{\mathbf{D}}$ holds at each $\uparrow(\mathbf{inc}, i)$ from the theory of $\mathbf{D}$. Thus this axiom is provable in the theory of $\mathbf{D}$. It is obvious that other requirements from $\mathbf{C}$ are met by $\mathbf{D}$.

This is a valid but somewhat useless refinement step. Instead we should explicitly require in $\mathbf{C}$ that **inc** should be available at various times, ie: via an axiom such as

$$\forall i : \mathbb{N}_1 \mid i \leq 1000 \bullet \mathbf{fires}(\mathbf{inc}, i)$$

or by

$$\text{enabled(inc)} \equiv (\lfloor \text{now} \rfloor \bmod 2) = 0$$

"inc is enabled in all integer intervals beginning with an even number".

Exercise (6.2): The class **C_1** does not introduce new operations which affect the state of **C** (the only new operation, **set_semaphore**, affects only the new state components of **C_1**). It is also assumed to meet the specification of **C** in all other respects as well. However it is possible for a pair of objects **a, b** : **C_1** to exhibit behaviour which could not be observed for a corresponding pair of objects of **C** – that is, they may block each other on execution of the method **m**. Thus it is a counter-example if pairs of objects are considered, rather than just single objects.

Exercise (6.3): The proposed refinement is

```
CLASS C_1
TYPES
  BoilerState ::= on | off
  ValveState ::= open | closed
OWNS
  bstate : BoilerState;
  vstate : ValveState;
  s : Semaphore
OPERATIONS
  activating : →;
  maintain_open : →
ACTIONS
  activating ==>
        BEGIN
            s.signal;
            bstate := on;
            s.release
        END;

  maintain_open ==>
        BEGIN
            s.release;
            vstate := open;
            s.signal
        END
END CLASS
```

This can be proved correct as follows.

$$\#\text{act(activating)} = \#\text{act(signal, s)} \geq$$
$$\#\text{fin(signal, s)} \geq \#\text{act(release, s)} = \#\text{act(maintain\_open)}$$

by virtue of a general property of event counters (2nd comparative) and the definition of **Semaphore** (3rd comparative). Similarly

$$\#\mathbf{fin}(\mathbf{maintain\_open}) = \#\mathbf{fin}(\mathbf{signal}, \mathbf{s}) \geq$$
$$\#\mathbf{act}(\mathbf{release}, \mathbf{s}) \geq \#\mathbf{fin}(\mathbf{release}, \mathbf{s}) = \#\mathbf{fin}(\mathbf{activating})$$

Notice that only the first conjunct in the history constraint of the **Semaphore** is needed for this proof, and hence a weaker semaphore variant could be used to achieve the synchronisation.

To implement **mutex(methods(C))** for a class **C** without **self_mutex(methods(C))** use the generalised semaphore as follows:

```
CLASS C_1
OWNS
   ...
   s :  MultiSemaphore
OPERATIONS
   m₁ :  X₁  →  Y₁;
   ...
   mₙ :  Xₙ  →  Yₙ
ACTIONS
   m₁ x₁? y₁!  ==>
         BEGIN
               s.signal(1);
               Code₁ ;
               s.release(1)
         END;


   ...


   mₙ xₙ? yₙ!  ==>
         BEGIN
               s.signal(n);
               Codeₙ ;
               s.release(n)
         END

END CLASS
```

This works because at $\uparrow(\mathbf{m_i}, \mathbf{k}) = \uparrow((\mathbf{signal(i)}, \mathbf{s}), \mathbf{k})$ we have:

$$\#\mathbf{fin}(\mathbf{release(j)}, \mathbf{s}) = \#\mathbf{act}(\mathbf{signal(j)}, \mathbf{s})$$

for $\mathbf{j} \neq \mathbf{i}$. But this implies that

$$\#\mathbf{fin}(\mathbf{m_j}) = \#\mathbf{act}(\mathbf{m_j})$$

or that $\#\mathbf{active}(\mathbf{m_j}) = 0$, as desired.

Exercise (6.4): The translation of the axiom asserts that for the methods **push** and **pop**, the value of **stack** always changes between successive execution initiation times of these methods. This is not true in the extended class however. A counter-example would start with **stack** = ⟨a, a⟩ for some element a of **X**, at the time ↑(**push, i**), and a is the element being pushed, so that **stack** = ⟨a, a, a⟩ at ↓(**push, i**). The next method to execute is an invocation of **remove**, which results in the state **stack** = ⟨a, a⟩ once more. Thus if the next method to execute is a **push** or **pop**, the translated axiom is false.

The way this situation can be avoided is to make **remove** and **top** purely internal to the operation **pop** of **Strict_Stack**. That is, to assert **pop** *covers* **remove** in this class. (Notice that it is not sufficient simply to make **remove** and **top** internal actions of **Strict_Stack**, because they might then be used in new methods in subtypes of **Strict_Stack**.)

Exercise (7.1): In order to prove an assertion of the form $\Box^{\tau}\varphi$ where φ depends on object attributes or event times, it is often useful to segment the time line into intervals over which the truth or falsity of φ does not change, and where it can be determined.

In this case we start from the time ↓(**initialise, 1**). At this point we know that **frlights.tlstate** = < **red** > because of the postcondition of **initialise_red**, and (provided the traffic lights are exclusively owned by this controller) it remains in this state until an execution of **traffic_moving_entry**. However, it can be seen from the definition of **traffic_moving_entry** that **mrlights.tlstate** = < **red** > is set before the **go_green** method is executed on **frlights**, and therefore the invariant does not become false at any point.

Similarly, if **mrlights.tlstate** = < **red** > then this state can only be changed by an execution of **traffic_moving_exit**, and again, the definition of this method ensures that **frlights.tlstate** = < **red** > is established before execution of **go_green** on **mrlights**, as required.

No other method or thread action of **Controller** can change the states of the traffic lights, so the result follows.

Exercise (7.2):
The object model of the system is shown in Figure C.3. Notice that we want to identify the general **fill** operation of a compartment with the **ballast** and **loadc** operations of the subtypes respectively, and the **empty** operation with the **deballast** and **unloadc** operations. The subtyping relationship is marked as being *exclusive* – this only means that no compartment can simultaneously be in both subtypes, but does not exclude the possibility that a cargo compartment might become (be used as) a ballast compartment on occasion.

The dynamic model of a compartment is very simple (Figure C.4), however the dynamic model of a ship (Figure C.5) requires quite detailed analysis. We must identity various intermediate stages during the loading process:

- initiation of a loading stage, provided that there is at least one unloaded

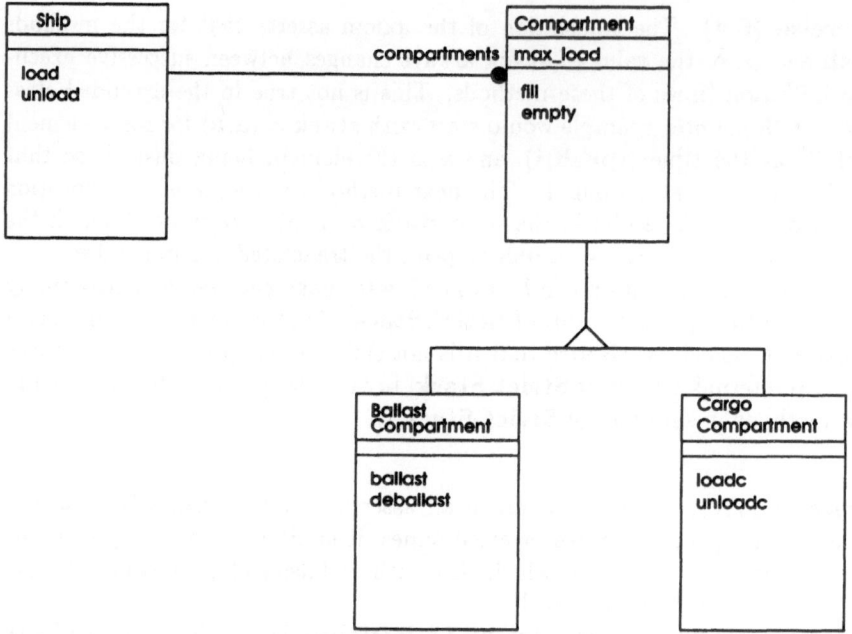

Figure C.3: Object Model of Ship-loading System

cargo compartment and ballasted ballast compartment in the ship;
- completion of a stage of loading, when either all required load has been transferred, or the cargo compartment is full;
- completion of loading, when either all required load has been transferred, or there are no further pairs of unloaded cargo compartments and ballasted ballast compartments in the ship.

The enabling conditions on transitions are generally too complex to easily represent on the statecharts, and have to be described separately. **fill** in Fig-

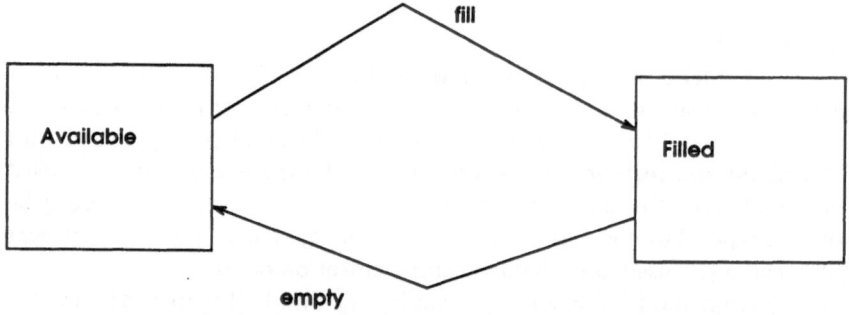

Figure C.4: Statechart of Compartment

ure C.4 corresponds to the event of termination of the **fill** method in the

Compartment class, whilst **empty** corresponds to the event of termination of the **empty** method. We have omitted the enabling (permission) conditions on the transitions in Figures C.4 and C.5 – instead these are presented in the formal classes in order to simplify the diagrams.

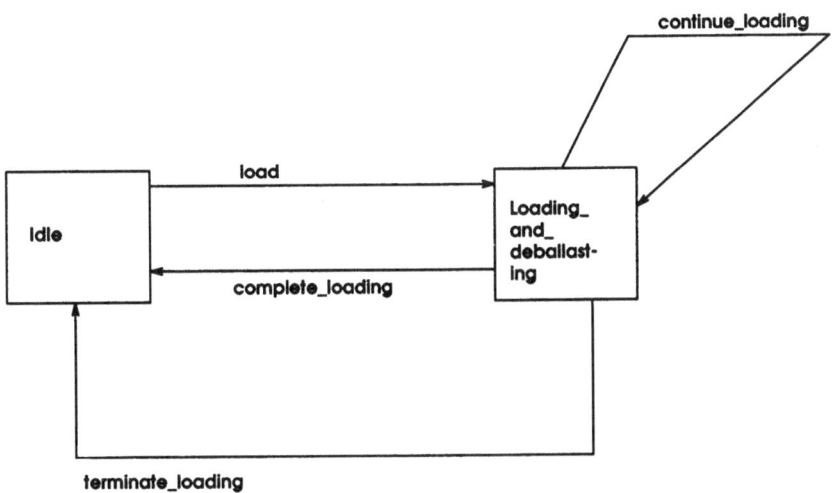

Figure C.5: Statechart of Ship

The formal specifications are then:

```
CLASS Compartment
TYPES
    CState ::= available | filled
FUNCTIONS
    | max_load : ℕ
OWNS
    cstate : CState
OPERATIONS
    fill : ℕ →;
    empty : ℕ →
ACTIONS
    fill ld? ==>
        PRE ld? ≤ max_load ∧ cstate = available
        THEN
                cstate' = filled
        END;

    empty ld? ==>
        PRE cstate = filled
        THEN
                cstate' = available
        END

HISTORY
```

Mutex$_{\text{Compartment}}$ $\wedge$ SelfMutex$_{\text{Compartment}}$

$\forall$ ld: $\mathbb{N}$ • $\square(\overline{\text{fill(ld)}} \Rightarrow$ ld $\leq$ max_load $\wedge$ cstate = available)

$\square(\overline{\text{empty}} \Rightarrow$ cstate = filled)

END CLASS

The history constraint of this class expresses the permission guards. It is clear that each operation is durative (cf. Exercise 7.3), so the temporal logic style specification can be used.

A more refined model would introduce states **filling, emptying** and **partially_filled** to represent the process of filling and emptying more accurately. In addition timing constraints such as

$$\forall i : \mathbb{N}_1; \text{ ld} : \mathbb{N} \bullet \text{duration}(\text{fill}(\text{ld}), i) \leq 10 * \text{ld}$$

could be specified and would allow some inference to be made about the duration of ship-loading operations.

The subtypes are specified simply by renaming, as there are no additional attributes or operations:

CLASS **Cargo_compartment**
        EXTENDS **Compartment[loadc/fill, unloadc/empty]**
END CLASS

CLASS **Ballast_compartment**
        EXTENDS **Compartment[ballast/fill, deballast/empty]**
END CLASS

Where **Class[Substitutions]** denotes renaming of features of **Class** via the replacements **Substitutions**.

CLASS **Ship**
TYPES
   SState ::= idle | loading_and_deballasting
OWNS
   compartments : $\mathbb{F}(\overline{\text{Compartment}})$;
   sstate : SState;
   remaining_load : $\mathbb{N}$
OPERATIONS
   load : $\mathbb{N}$ $\rightarrow$;
   continue_loading : $\rightarrow$
ACTIONS
   init ==>
      compartments$'$ = $\varnothing$ $\wedge$
      sstate$'$ = idle $\wedge$
      remaining_load$'$ = 0;

   load ld? ==>
      PRE sstate = idle $\wedge$

$$\exists\ c1,\ c2\ \in\ \text{compartments}\ |$$
$$c1\ \in\ \overline{\text{Cargo\_compartment}}\ \wedge$$
$$c2\ \in\ \overline{\text{Ballast\_compartment}}\ \bullet$$
$$c1.\text{cstate}\ =\ \text{available}\ \wedge\ c2.\text{cstate}\ =\ \text{filled}$$

THEN

    ANY c1, c2 : Compartment

    WHERE

$$c1\ \in\ \text{compartments}\ \wedge\ c2\ \in\ \text{compartments}\ \wedge$$
$$c1\ \in\ \overline{\text{Cargo\_compartment}}\ \wedge$$
$$c2\ \in\ \overline{\text{Ballast\_compartment}}\ \wedge$$
$$c1.\text{cstate}\ =\ \text{available}\ \wedge\ c2.\text{cstate}\ =\ \text{filled}$$

    THEN

$$c1.\text{fill}(\min(c1.\text{max\_load}, \text{ld}?))\ \wedge$$
$$c2.\text{empty}(\min(c1.\text{max\_load}, \text{ld}?))\ \wedge$$
$$\text{remaining\_load}'\ =\ \text{ld}?\ -\ \min(c1.\text{max\_load}, \text{ld}?)\ \wedge$$
$$\text{sstate}'\ =\ \text{loading\_and\_deballasting}$$

    END

END;

continue_loading ==>

    PRE sstate = loading_and_deballasting $\wedge$

$$\text{remaining\_load}\ >\ 0\ \ \wedge$$
$$\exists\ c1,\ c2\ \in\ \text{compartments}\ |$$
$$c1\ \in\ \overline{\text{Cargo\_compartment}}\ \wedge$$
$$c2\ \in\ \overline{\text{Ballast\_compartment}}\ \bullet$$
$$c1.\text{cstate}\ =\ \text{available}\ \wedge\ c2.\text{cstate}\ =\ \text{filled}$$

THEN

    ANY c1, c2 : Compartment

    WHERE

$$c1\ \in\ \text{compartments}\ \wedge\ c2\ \in\ \text{compartments}\ \wedge$$
$$c1\ \in\ \overline{\text{Cargo\_compartment}}\ \wedge$$
$$c2\ \in\ \overline{\text{Ballast\_compartment}}\ \wedge$$
$$c1.\text{cstate}\ =\ \text{available}\ \wedge\ c2.\text{cstate}\ =\ \text{filled}$$

    THEN

$$c1.\text{fill}(\min(c1.\text{max\_load}, \text{remaining\_load}))\ \wedge$$
$$c2.\text{empty}(\min(c1.\text{max\_load}, \text{remaining\_load}))\ \wedge$$
$$\text{remaining\_load}'\ =\ \text{remaining\_load}\ -$$
$$\min(c1.\text{max\_load}, \text{remaining\_load})$$

    END

END;

complete_loading ==>

    PRE remaining_load = 0 $\wedge$ sstate = loading_and_deballasting

    THEN

$$\text{sstate}'\ =\ \text{idle}$$

END;

terminate_loading ==>

    PRE remaining_load $>$ 0 $\wedge$

$$\text{sstate}\ =\ \text{loading\_and\_deballasting}\ \wedge$$

$$\neg \; \exists \; c1, \; c2 \; \in \; \text{compartments} \; |$$
$$c1 \; \in \; \overline{\text{Cargo\_compartment}} \; \wedge$$
$$c2 \; \in \; \overline{\text{Ballast\_compartment}} \; \bullet$$
$$c1.\text{cstate} \; = \; \text{available} \; \wedge \; c2.\text{cstate} \; = \; \text{filled}$$

THEN
$$\text{sstate}' \; = \; \text{idle}$$
END

END CLASS

The history constraint of this class would simply assert that the preconditions are also permission predicates by using temporal logic. **Ship** is also specified to be mutex and self-mutex.

In an enhancement it would also be useful to distinguish between the final states after successful or unsuccessful loading operations.

Finally, the requirement that compartments must be uniquely owned by a given ship would be specified by an invariant

$$\forall \quad c: \; \textbf{compartment\_set} \; \bullet \; \exists_1 \; s: \; \textbf{ships} \; \bullet$$
$$c \; \in \; s.\textbf{compartments}$$

in a system which manages the creation and deletion of ships and compartments, where $\exists_1$ is the "exists exactly one" quantifier. **compartment_set** holds the set of currently existing compartments.

Exercise (7.3):

Assume otherwise, and let **m** be an instantaneous method, modifying $\mathbf{v} : \mathbf{T}$. Then from (**xi**) we have:

$$(\mathbf{xi}): \; \forall e: \mathbf{IN}; \; i: \mathbb{N}_1 \bullet$$
$$(\text{self} \in \overline{\mathbf{C}} \wedge \mathbf{Pre}_{\mathbf{m,C}}) \odot \uparrow(\mathbf{m}(e), \mathbf{i}) \; \Rightarrow$$
$$\mathbf{Def}_{\mathbf{m,C}}[\mathbf{v} \circledast \downarrow(\mathbf{m}(e), \mathbf{i})/\mathbf{v}'] \odot \uparrow(\mathbf{m}(e), \mathbf{i})$$

and $\uparrow(\mathbf{m}(e), \mathbf{i}) = \downarrow(\mathbf{m}(e), \mathbf{i})$ but $\mathbf{Def}_{\mathbf{m,C}} \Rightarrow \mathbf{v} \neq \mathbf{v}'$. That is, if the object exists at $\uparrow(\mathbf{m}(e), \mathbf{i})$, and satisfies the precondition, then:

$$\forall e: \mathbf{IN}; \; i: \mathbb{N}_1 \bullet$$
$$\mathbf{v} \circledast \uparrow(\mathbf{m}(e), \mathbf{i}) \neq \mathbf{v} \circledast \downarrow(\mathbf{m}(e), \mathbf{i})$$

a contradiction.

Exercise (7.4): Assume that we have

$$\vdash \Box \diamond \mathbf{enabled}(\mathbf{m}) \; \Rightarrow \; \diamond \underline{\mathbf{m}}$$

Then also by a standard inference

$$\vdash \Box(\Box \diamond \mathbf{enabled}(\mathbf{m}) \; \Rightarrow \; \diamond \underline{\mathbf{m}})$$

and hence

$$\vdash \Box\Box \Diamond \,\text{enabled}(\mathbf{m}) \;\Rightarrow\; \Box \Diamond \,\underline{\mathbf{m}}$$

But $\Box\Box\varphi \equiv \Box\varphi$ for any φ, and

$$\vdash \Box\,\text{enabled}(\mathbf{m}) \;\Rightarrow\; \Box \Diamond \,\text{enabled}(\mathbf{m})$$

so

$$\vdash \Box\,\text{enabled}(\mathbf{m}) \;\Rightarrow\; \Box \Diamond \,\underline{\mathbf{m}}$$

as required.

Exercise (7.5): The class **Oscillator** describes a fictional physical process which oscillates more and more rapidly as **t** approaches 5 seconds (and the size of these oscillations tends towards zero). **activate** is triggered at the start of each period of the oscillation:

$$\mathbf{t} = \uparrow(\textbf{activate}, \mathbf{i}) = 5 - \tfrac{1}{2 * \mathbf{i}}$$

implies that $\frac{\pi}{5-\mathbf{t}} = 2 * \mathbf{i} * \pi$, and there is therefore no $\mathbf{i}$ such that $\uparrow(\textbf{activate}, \mathbf{i})$ is the most recent such event time before $\mathbf{t} = 5$. Thus ● is not well defined for this class.

Such situations are somewhat pathological, and cannot occur in a purely discrete computational context. Suitable axioms could be used to state that ● is well-defined, ie, that such situations are disallowed.

Exercise (7.6): Periodic execution of **confirm_tracks** and **delete_tracks** could be specified by:

HISTORY
    #act(**confirm_tracks**) = #fin(add_plot) *div* 20

         / * **confirm_tracks** starts each time a multiple of 20
            add_track operations have completed. * /

    #act(**delete_tracks**) = (#fin(add_plot) + 10) *div* 20

We also need the predicate **mutex**({add_plot, **confirm_tracks**, **delete_tracks**}).

Assume that multiple **add_plot** operations can be called on a single track at the same time. This might arise because there could be multiple radars all sending target information to the same track-former system; it could be important that all of these multiple signals be processed as quickly as possible, and in a consistent manner. One possible approach would be to specify the resulting semantics of the **add_plot** operation in the history of the **Track** class:

HISTORY
$\quad$ ∀ i: $\mathbb{N}_1$ •
$\qquad$ ∃ t: seq(**Plot**) |
$\qquad\qquad$ ran(t) = { j: $\mathbb{N}_1$ | ↑(add_plot, i) < ↓(add_plot, j) ≤
$\qquad\qquad\qquad\qquad\qquad\qquad$ ↓(add_plot, i) •
$\qquad\qquad\qquad\qquad\qquad\qquad\qquad$ (add_plot, j).p? } •
$\qquad\qquad\qquad$ **tracks**⊛↓(add_plot, i) =
$\qquad\qquad\qquad\qquad$ **tracks**⊛↑(add_plot, i) ⌢ t

In words "the value of **tracks** at termination of (**add_plot**, **i**) is the value at initiation of this operation, concatenated with the sequence **t** of all plots which have arrived in this interval." An additional constraint could order these plots in terms of arrival times (notice that multiple arrivals of the same plot do not count). The ACTIONS specification of **add_plot** must be changed to:

ACTIONS
$\quad$ add_plot p? ==>
$\qquad$ PRE p? ∉ ran(**plots**)
$\qquad$ THEN
$\qquad\qquad$ p? ∈ ran(**plots′**) ∧
$\qquad\qquad$ **plots** ≪ **plots′**
$\qquad$ END

where ≪ is the relation of prefixing between sequences.

At the **System** class level, the **add_plot** operation should be divided into three parts – the determination of the set of best fitting tracks for the new plot; creation of a new track if necessary, and addition of the plot to the tracks. If several different plots arrive at the same time, then all of the **get_best_tracks** invocations for these plots can proceed together (as these are read-only), but should all terminate before the start of any **create_track** or **Track.add_plot** operation. Similarly, all necessary **create_track** operations should terminate before any **Track.add_plot** operation. The invocations of the latter operations can proceed together, since **Track** has been modified to allow multiple input plots at any point in time.

Exercise (7.7): The dynamic model is shown in Figure C.6. Thus the outline **PhoneService** class is:

class **PhoneService**
types
$\quad$ PState = < unconnected > | < connected >;
$\quad$ CState = < idle > | < recording_message > |
$\qquad\qquad$ < listening_to_own_message > | < listening >
instance variables
$\quad$ pstate: **PState**;
$\quad$ cstate: **CState**;
$\quad$ password: $\mathbb{N}$;
$\quad$ last_code: $\mathbb{N}$;
init objectstate == $\quad$ pstate = < unconnected > ∧
$\qquad\qquad\qquad$ cstate = < idle > ∧
$\qquad\qquad\qquad$ last_code = 0

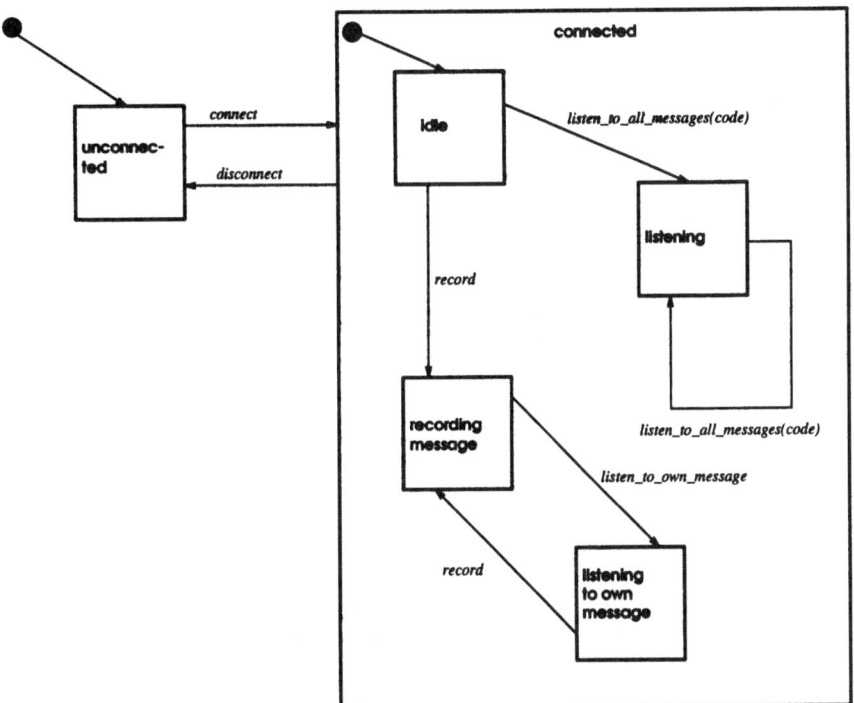

Figure C.6: Dynamic Model of Phone Service

```
methods
  connect() ==
      [ext wr pstate, cstate
       post pstate = < connected > ∧ cstate = < idle >];

  record() ==
      [ext wr cstate
       post cstate = < recording_message >];

  listen_to_own_message() ==
      [ext wr cstate
       post cstate = < listening_to_own_message >];

  enter_password(code : N) ==
      [ext wr last_code
       post last_code = code];

  listen_to_all_messages() ==
      [ext wr cstate
       post cstate = < listening >];

  disconnect() ==
      [ext wr pstate, last_code
       post pstate = < unconnected > ∧
            last_code = 0]

sync
  per listen_to_all_messages  ⇒   last_code = password
thread
  while true
  do
    sel
      pstate = < unconnected >  answer connect ->
                    while pstate = < connected >
                    do
                      sel
                        cstate = < idle > answer record,
                        cstate = < recording_message > answer
                                          listen_to_own_message,
                        cstate = < listening_to_own_message >
                                          answer record,
                      ((cstate = < idle > ∨
                        cstate = < listening >) ∧
                        last_code = password) answer
                                          listen_to_all_messages,
                    answer disconnect
end PhoneService
```

This class is mutex and self-mutex because a thread has been given. Method parameters cannot be used in a permission guard or in select clause guards, so we must separate the **enter_password** method from **listen_to_all_messages**. It is assumed that no valid password has the value 0. The permission statement is redundant with the thread, but has been added to emphasise this guard condition.

The omission in the requirements is that a means of setting the password should also be provided – only a "superuser" (service management) should be able to apply this operation.

Exercise (7.8): The problem is that there may be gaps between the setting of the seconds and the setting of the minutes of the clock. Thus for example, if we had

> **seconds** = 59
> **minutes** = 0

at time t0, and both **set_sec** and **set_min** commenced at this time, but **set_min** terminated at time t1, strictly before the time t2 at which **set_sec** terminated, then we could have:

> **seconds** = 59
> **minutes** = 1

at t1, but

> **seconds** = 0
> **minutes** = 1

at t2, so "time runs backwards" between these points. In particular, an external object could get inaccurate time readings (nearly a minute in error) if it accessed the clock between t1 and t2. The design itself is suspect, and it would be better to carry out the updating of the minute and second values as a *single atomic action*. The present class would only be adequate if **get_time** was mutex with **set_sec** and **set_min**, and if the latter two methods had exactly the same durations.

Exercise (9.1): The duration of **n** must be at most 3, and that of **m** at most 5 in order that executions of **n** do not overlap, and likewise for **m**. This can be specified in VDM^{++} via the syntax:

```
class Concurr
methods
  n()  ==
     [
        post true
        time post duration(n) <= 3 ];

  m()  ==
     [
```

```
          post true
          time post duration(m) <= 5]
thread
  periodic(5)(m);
  periodic(3)(n)
end Concurr
```

However there are additional constraints which arise from the mutual exclusion of n and m. Fully written out these are:

$$\forall i, j : \mathbb{N}_1 \bullet$$
$$5 * i \leq \uparrow(m, i) \ \wedge \ \downarrow(m, i) \leq 5 * (i + 1)$$
$$3 * j \leq \uparrow(n, j) \ \wedge \ \downarrow(n, j) \leq 3 * (j + 1)$$

together with **mutex**($\{m, n\}$). From this it is clear that when $5 * i = 3 * j$ then the sum of the durations **duration**(m, i) and **duration**(n, j) must be at most 3.

A suitable scheduling policy to prioritise **m**, assuming that both methods always take 1 time unit to execute, is defined by:

$$\uparrow(m, i) = 5 * i$$
$$3 * j \bmod 5 = 0 \ \Rightarrow \ \uparrow(n, j) = 3 * j + 1$$
$$3 * j \bmod 5 \neq 0 \ \Rightarrow \ \uparrow(n, j) = 3 * j$$

This schedules **m** at the beginning of each interval of length 5, and **n** at the beginning of each interval of length 3, except at those points where $3 * j = 5 * i$ for some i, when **m** has priority.

Task Analysis

Task analysis is a means of identifying the steps, goals, knowledge and strategies which human beings use in solving complex problems [157]. It is relevant to software engineering because it can help to identify the key concepts of a particular domain; in particular, to identify the "objects" of the domain, and events which affect these objects, in the sense of object-oriented analysis.

Task analysis is performed by obtaining a variety of information about particular tasks from a number of sources using some of the techniques listed below. It, like analysis in general, is an iterative process that involves the analyst interacting with the information sources to confirm partial analyses and expand on understanding gained. Some suitable techniques are:

1. *structured interviews and questionnaires* – the analyst asks prepared questions of the subject, but is flexible in allowing other issues to be addressed. Alternatively a fixed questionnaire is used.

   This technique is considered to be more useful in providing outlines and an overview of tasks and background information than in giving details of how tasks are performed [157, p 167];

2. *observational techniques* – observing the actions of someone performing the task, identifying changes of state and steps undertaken;

3. *concurrent and retrospective protocols* – verbal reports by the task performer, either concurrent with the task, or after its performance;

4. *repertory grid, card scoring*, etc – techniques by which an initial collection of concepts can be grouped and categorised. Other techniques are useful in identifying representativeness and centrality of examples or concepts in a task.

These techniques are significantly more rigorous and user-oriented than techniques which are usually used in requirements elicitation. They not only give the user's view of what they want, but additionally attempt to uncover *what the user really expects* – which may be different from what they know or can communicate about their needs.

An object-oriented view of tasks is as activities undertaken by one or more agents to bring about some change of state in a system. A task is therefore akin to a (system wide) operation in Fusion, which may involve a number of linked and co-operating objects (agents). In Chapter 3 we discussed how drawing a series of instance diagrams showing how the state of a system changes over an operation can be a useful means of simulating a scenario or task. This is a form of observational technique (if the simulation is performed with a user) in which direct observation is replaced by examination of a corresponding process on a more convenient model.

Whilst identification of the key concepts and activities involved in a task may provide guidance on the structure and operations of software intended to support or automate the task, there is not usually a direct translation from the manual to the automated implementation. This is because the manual procedures themselves may be based on inefficient and ineffective approaches that have been used for reasons of tradition. Automation of these procedures should therefore involve a selective use of task knowledge, with more use being made of knowledge about the data concepts of the domain than operational knowledge, as the former is generally more stable and less amenable to revision. Guidelines for ways to utilise task analysis within software specification and design are given in [157, Chapter 13].

A trivial application of task analysis could be the automated gun control system of Chapter 9. In this case the two fundamental actions of **reload** and **fire** could be directly identified from existing manual practices. More usefully, procedures presently used to ensure that at least one gun in an emplacement is always ready to fire could be adopted or used to inspire corresponding auto-mated procedures for software emplacement controllers.

Index

$*_C$ 22

; 151

BasicEvent$_C$ 127

BasicEvent$_S$(**a**) 128

C $\sqsubseteq^{\text{ref}}_{\phi,R}$ **D** 26, 146

C $\sqsubseteq_{\phi,R}$ **D** 113

Event$_C$ 128

Forget$_C$ 123

Instances$_C$ 22

New$_C$ 91

S'm 197

Sequence_manager 152

State$_C$ 22

System *class* 79

T(op) 374

TIME 128

Unset$_C$ 27, 123

[**@S**] 372

[$\mathbf{a_1}, \ldots, \mathbf{a_n}$] 365

#**act(m(e))** 128

#**active(m)** 129

#**fin(m(e))** 128

#**req(m(e))** 128

#**waiting(m)** 129

$\Box\theta$ 129

$\Box^\tau\theta$ 129

Δ 94

Γ_C 114, 348

$\odot$ 95

♣ 128

♣($\uparrow\mathbf{m(x)}, \mathbf{i}$) 127

⊛ 128

Ξ 94

$\bigcap$ 332

$\bigcirc\theta$ 129

$\bigcirc$e 128

$\bigcup$ 332

$\bigwedge$ 24, 94

$\cup$ 332

$\diamond\theta$ 129

$\diamond^\tau\theta$ 129

dom 333

$\dotplus$ 375

$\lhd$ 334

$\varnothing$ 332

$\exists_1$ 408

$\twoheadrightarrow$ 132, 335

$\mathbb{F}$ 24, 333

$\overline{\text{now}}$ 68

$\overleftarrow{\mathbf{v}}$ 36

$\in$ 332

$\wedge$ *composition of classes* 234

$(\!|\ |\!)$ 333

$\ll$ 336, 410

@C 22

$\vartriangleleft$ 334

$\notin$ 332

$\vartriangleright$ 334

$\oplus$ 333

$\overrightarrow{\psi,\mathbf{i}}$ 363

$\overline{\mathbf{C}}$ 22, 91

$\phi(\varphi)$ 114

$\phi\odot$t 129

$\rightarrowtail$ 335

$\mathbb{P}$ 24
ran 333
$\leftrightarrow$ 333
$\triangleright$ 334
$\mathbf{;}$ 97, 334
$\backslash$ 332
$\theta :=$ **false** 127, 348
$\theta :=$ **true** 127, 348
<u>false</u> 117
$\varphi[\mathbf{R}(\mathbf{v})/\mathbf{u}]$ 358
$\varphi[\mathbf{e}/\mathbf{v}]$ 343
cov 350, 364
delay 59
delay(m, i) 129
duration(m, i) 129
enabled(m(e)) 129
enabled(m) 129, 242
e⊛t 128
fires 59
first 156
inf(X) 181
init *operations* 91
inj 335
mutex(S) 129
nil$_C$ 22
now 67
out ⟵ a.m(in) 97
residence 181
second 156
self 123
self_mutex(S) 129
squash 64, 110
time_in 182
void *in VDM^{++}* 372
♣(E, i) 127
$\mathbb{R}$ 336
$\mathcal{L}_C$ 348
↓m(e) 127, 348
→m(e) 127, 348
↑(m(x), i) 127
↑m(e) 127, 348
|| *in VDM^{++}* 174
|| 150
||| 150
AND composition of statecharts 221
Abstract specification classes 145

Active object 314
Ada95 263
Adequacy, of @R 173
Adequacy 38, 173, 174
Aggregation 88, 314
Aliasing 14, 122
Ancestor, immediate 111
Animation 79
Annealing maps 133
Annealing 137
Associations 20, 314
Automatic transitions 231
Auxilliary reasoning 134
B AMN ii, 2
B Toolkit 26, 285
Balking 75
Basic types 93
Booch class diagrams 73
Booch object diagrams 75
Bottom-up design 144
Boundary of system 17
C++ 43, 272
Callbacks 74, 245
Capacity reasoning 212
Class attributes 315
Class auxilliary reasoning part 368
Class behaviour part 368
Class composition 120
Class feature renaming 406
Class features in subtypes 111
Class header 368
Class instance variables 368
Class internal state 368
Class methods part 368
Class name 368
Class synchronisation part 368
Class tail 368
Class, VDM^{++} 368
Class, Z^{++} 21, 337
Classes 7
Class 21, 32, 315
Client 7, 23, 120, 315
Complete specification 110
Compositional implementation 34
Composition 7
Concurrent specification elements 130

Continuity of structure 139
Continuous classes 250
Continuous real-time systems 250
Data components of classes 85
Data refinement techniques 147
Data specification style, Z^{++} 85
Deadlock avoidance 180
Decomposing operations into objects 153
Decomposition of operations 145
Deferred method definitions 93
Delegation 33, 120
Demeters Law 315
Design 137, 315
Developing subtyping hierarchies 116
Development architecture notation 32
Discretisation 254
Durative class 129
Durative method 129
Dynamic binding 315
Dynamic reconfiguration 104
Dynamic subclass 209
ELLA 285
Eiffel 41, 257
Encapsulation 7, 316
Enumerated types, Z 336
Event counters, Ada 266
Example, Ship loading 235
Examples, Abstract lift 131
Examples, Dictionary 260
Examples, Dining philosophers 97, 122, 148, 181
Examples, Directed graphs 124
Examples, Distributed tree 269
Examples, Drill control 342
Examples, Electronic components 250
Examples, Elephant 32
Examples, Expedited data queue 297
Examples, FCFS 271
Examples, Files and directories 35
Examples, Fire control 301
Examples, Flights 155
Examples, Hamming sequences 143
Examples, Intensive care unit 133
Examples, Intensive care unit 86
Examples, Invoice system 286
Examples, Link/channel 232

Examples, Mine Pump Control 305
Examples, Monitor/gate 177
Examples, Monoid 358
Examples, Personnel system 48, 110, 118, 143, 259, 278
Examples, Shapes and points 19
Examples, Sum of squares 153
Examples, Synchronised Buffers 238
Examples, Track sections 45, 60, 88, 165
Examples, Traffic Lights 177, 223
Examples, Unreliable queue 276
Examples, Windows 120
Exclusive ownership 30
Explanatory text 84
FUNCTIONS clause, Z^{++} 88
Fairness properties 242
Features 112
Financially-critical systems 2
Finite differencing 160
Formal development ii
Formal methods, benefits of 2
Formal object-oriented development 16
Functional tests 282
Fusion 43
Generalisation, for reuse 144
Generic classes, Z^{++} 92
Genericity 316
Given set types 336
Given sets 132
Given types 86
Global/local views of data 133
Good specification 84
Hackers 44
Hazard analysis 80
History constraints, standard form 62
Implementation bias 87
Implementation class 138
Implementation sublanguage 34
Implementation 19, 137
Implementing interval relations 164
Implementing mutex 164
Implementing obligation specifications 268
Implementing self-mutex 162
Increasing parallelism 269

Indexed inheritance 343
Information hiding 33
Inheritance, direct 111
Inheritance, indirect 111
Inheritance, problems of 13
Inheritance 316
Initialisation 368
Instances as models 359
Integration testing 281
Internal actions, Z^{++} 94
Internal consistency obligations 108
Internal consistency proofs 182
Internal consistency 104, 176
Internal operations, in design 145
Invariant convention 95
Invariants over supplier objects 120
Invariant 368
Layered development 30, 139
Liveness properties 180
Load management 64
Localising invariants 122
Maintenance 19
Method calls 97
Method composition 97
Method definition constructs 94
Method parameter types 93
Methods as operations 97
Methods as predicates 96
Methods integration, advantages 223
Methods integration 4, 12, 44
Modular decomposability 139
Modular understandability 139
Module importation 111
Monolithic design 139
Monotonicity 35
Mutual exclusion and permission guards 236
Mutual exclusion 46
Nesting of statecharts 219
OMG 316
OMT object model 20, 45
OMT dynamic model 58
OMT 1
OOA 231
Object identity 122, 316
Object-Z 7

Object 316
Once function 258
Open-closed principle 116
Operation preconditions 94
Operation refinement techniques 150
Output parameters, VDM^{++} 369
PVS ii
Passive object 316
Periodic obligations 126
Periodic threads 65, 255, 301
Permission predicates 94
Permission statements, VDM^{++} 65
Permission statements 370
Polymorphism, problems of 13
Polymorphism 7, 113, 316
Priorities and interrupts 244
Private ownership 124
Private references 123
Procedural statements 360
Promotion 316
Proof obligations in design 139
Qualification of identifiers 112
Qualified type names 85
RAISE Toolkit 285
RAISE ii
RTL 58, 347
RTTL 256
Read frame 36
Readers/writers protocol 238
Recursive clientship 124
Redefines 258
Reference to supplier object attributes 37
Refinement and design 18, 137
Refinement classes as suppliers 169
Refinement class 138
Refinement in analysis models 44
Refinement preservation 34
Refinement, VDM^{++} 173
Refinement, definition of 146
Refinement 26, 317
Reification, VDM^{++} 38
Reification 30, 137
Representation inheritance 368
Required non-determinism 243
Requirements analysis 17

Requirements formalisation 17
Responsiveness 176
Retrieve function 38
Reuse-driven design 26
Reuse 15
Safety properties 176
Safety-critical systems 1
Scalar class parameters 90
Scenario 80
Select statements 65, 373
Semaphores, in design 161
Separate decomposition 138
Separate 262
Sequence comprehension, VDM^{++} 192
Set comprehension 332
Shared definitions 145
Shortest job first 127
Specialisation 118, 317
Specification clarity, predicates 90
Specification enhancement 18, 23, 48
Specification of error cases 107
Specification statements, VDM^{++} 36
Starvation 242
Statecharts 58
Static subclass 209
Strong composition 120
Strong fairness 243
Subclasses 7
Subsystem development 34
Subsystem 33
Subtype migration 209
Subtyping in VDM^{++} 118
Subtyping of statecharts 221
Subtyping proof obligations 114
Subtyping versus refinement 115
Subtyping, Liskov definition 114
Subtyping, definition 113
Subtyping 32, 317
Superclass 368
Supplier class 317
Supplier 7, 120, 315
Sync clause, VDM^{++} 65
Synchronisation code 271
Synchronisation variables 271
Syntropy 43
TYPES clause, Z^{++} 85

Tasks 263
Test case generation 285
Testing and animation 282
Testing and proof 282
Threads, VDM^{++} 65
Threads 134
Timed postcondition 369
Token types 132
Top-down design 144
Topology statements 134
Traces, VDM^{++} 65
Traces 299, 368
Unit testing 281
VDM^{++}, background 11
VDM 2
VHDL 285
Validation 44, 79, 176
Virtual classes, implementation 145
Virtual classes 115
Weak composition 120
Weak fairness 243
Weave operator 372
Well-definedness of **a.m**(e) 22
Workspace 72, 368
Write frame 36, 95
Z^{++}, Class description 22
Z^{++}, Method frames 23
Z^{++}, Methods 22
Z^{++}, background 8
"No new operations" rule 112
thread 368
covers 403
ANY 94
CHOICE 94
IF 94
PRE 94
SKIP 94
++ 160
ACTIONS *clause, Z^{++}* 93
HISTORY *clause, Z^{++}* 126
INVARIANT *clause, Z^{++}* 90
OPERATIONS *clause, Z^{++}* 92
OWNS *clause, Z^{++}* 90
RETURNS *clause, Z^{++}* 93
answer m 70
assumption *clause* 250

def 192
effect *clause* 250
init *clause, VDM*$^{++}$ 36
is not yet specified *clause* 38
start *statement* 72, 134
topology *statement* 72